CLARENDON LAW SERIES

Edited by

PETER CANE, TONY HONORÉ, AND JANE STAPLETON

CLARENDON LAW SERIES

Some Recent Titles in this Series

An Introduction to Administrative Law (2nd edition)
By PETER CANE

An Introduction to the Law of Contract (4th edition)
By P. S. ATIYAH

The Principles of Criminal Evidence
By A. A. S. ZUCKERMAN

An Introduction to the Law of Trusts
By SIMON GARDNER

Public Law and Democracy in the United
Kingdom and the United States of America
By P. P. CRAIG

Precedent in English Law (4th edition)
By SIR RUPERT CROSS and J. W. HARRIS

The Philosophical Origins of Modern Contract Doctrine
By JAMES GORDLEY

Principles of Criminal Law
By ANDREW ASHWORTH

Playing by the Rules
By FREDERICK SCHAUER

Norm and Nature
By ROGER A. SHINER

Regulation: Legal Form and Economic Theory
By ANTHONY I. OGUS

PRINCIPLES OF CRIMINAL LAW

ANDREW ASHWORTH

SECOND EDITION

CLARENDON PRESS · OXFORD

1995

Oxford University Press, Walton Street, Oxford OX2 6DP
Oxford New York
Athens Auckland Bangkok Bombay
Calcutta Cape Town Dar es Salaam Delhi
Florence Hong Kong Istanbul Karachi
Kuala Lumpur Madras Madrid Melbourne
Mexico City Nairobi Paris Singapore
Taipei Tokyo Toronto
and associated companies in
Berlin Ibadan

Oxford is a trade mark of Oxford University Press

Published in the United States
by Oxford University Press Inc., New York

British Library Cataloguing in Publication Data
Data available

Library of Congress Cataloging in Publication Data
Data available
ISBN 0–19–876367–0
ISBN 0–19–876368–9 (Pbk.)

1 3 5 7 9 10 8 6 4 2

Typeset by Cambrian Typesetters, Frimley, Surrey
Printed in Great Britain on acid-free paper by
Bookcraft Ltd., Midsomer Norton, Avon

Preface

In the preparation of the second edition, the aims of the work have undergone a slight alteration. One of its chief aims is still the identification and discussion of issues of principle and policy involved in the shaping of the criminal law by the legislature, the courts, the law reform bodies, and academic commentators. However, this edition contains somewhat more citation and discussion of statutes and case law, in the hope that it will be suitable for use by teachers and students as a companion to a collection of cases and materials.

In addition to this modest expansion, the primary task has been to take account of developments in the last four years. This has not simply been a matter of incorporating new statutory provisions and recent cases. There has been a significant increase in the output of the Law Commission in the field of criminal law, with a spate of reports and consultation papers in the last two years which raise wide-ranging questions about the proper outer limits and inner distinctions of criminal law. And, most strikingly, there has been a resurgence in academic writing on criminal law in the form of journal articles, essays, and monographs. Within the confines of this edition it has not been possible to discuss all the important contributions, but an effort has been made to include sufficient references for readers to explore further this revival of criminal law scholarship.

This book does not argue that English criminal law is grounded in a stable set of established doctrines. A more realistic view is that the arguments and assumptions which influence the development of the criminal law form a disparate group, sometimes conflicting and sometimes invoked selectively.

The first step is to identify the principles and policies which appear to play a significant part, sometimes a part not openly avowed in the reasoning of the courts or the commentators. Then questions are raised about each of these doctrines. Are they soundly based, in moral or social terms? How are they related to the proper aims, forms, and limits of the criminal sanction in modern Western societies? Are there other principles and policies which would be more appropriate? In order to produce satisfactory answers to questions of this kind or, in some instances, to demonstrate that no 'answer' can be expected, it would be necessary to travel much further into the realms of moral and political philosophy and into criminology than is possible within the confines of this book. Similarly, comparative law might be used to cast light on some of the issues and on alternative strategies, but this approach has generally been eschewed for space reasons, although there are frequent references to the American Law Institute's Model Penal Code.

Once the context and functions of the criminal law have been outlined in Chapter 1, the foundations for the remainder of the book are laid in Chapter 2, which discusses decisions to criminalize, and in Chapter 3, which identifies a number of key principles and policies. Then, in Chapters 4, 5, and 6, the basic elements of culpability, excuse and justification are examined. Three areas of substantive criminal law are selected for discussion in the chapters which follow: Chapter 7 deals with homicide, Chapter 8 with non-fatal physical violations, and Chapter 9 with offences of dishonesty. The book concludes with Chapter 10 on complicity, and Chapter 11 on inchoate offences.

In the course of preparing this edition I have again incurred many debts of gratitude to friends and colleagues. I am particularly grateful to those who have read and commented on drafts of one or more chapters— Kenneth Campbell, Nicola Lacey, Aileen McColgan, Ronnie Mackay, Ken Oliphant, Stephen Shute, Andrew von Hirsch and Celia Wells. I also derived considerable intellectual benefit, at just the right time, from attending a weekend seminar on criminal law theory organized in Cambridge by Andrew Simester and Tony Smith. At Oxford University Press, John Whelan has gone to considerable trouble to smooth the path of this second edition. I have retained the gender-specific 'he' in most parts of the book, as in the first edition. The vast majority of those tried and convicted are male, and so this concession to elegance has a greater air of social reality in this field than in many others.

I hope that statements about the law were accurate on 1 January 1995; a few subsequent developments have been noted in the appropriate places.

A.J.A.

Contents

Table of Cases

ENGLAND AND WALES

AUSTRALIA

CANADA

Table of Conventions

Table of Legislation

ENGLAND AND WALES

AUSTRALIA

CANADA

FRANCE

US

I

Criminal Justice and the Criminal Law

The operation of the criminal law requires little explanation in clear cases. Someone who deliberately kills or rapes another is liable to be prosecuted, convicted, and sentenced. Criminal liability is the strongest formal condemnation that society can inflict, and it may also result in a sentence which amounts to a severe deprivation of the ordinary liberties of the offender. Of course, there are other official deprivations of our liberties: taxation is one, depriving citizens of a proportion of their income, or adding a compulsory levy to commercial transactions (for example, Value Added Tax). And taxation, no less than the criminal law, may be seen as justified by the mutual obligations necessary for worthwhile community living. But most cases of taxation do not carry any implication of 'ought not to do', whereas criminal liability carries the strong implication of 'ought not to do'. It is the censure conveyed by criminal liability which marks out its special social significance, and it is this censure (as well as the liability to state punishment) which requires a clear social justification.

The chief concern of the criminal law is seriously antisocial behaviour. But the notion that English criminal law is only concerned with serious antisocial acts must be abandoned as one considers the broader canvas of criminal liability. There are many offences for which any element of stigma is diluted almost to vanishing point, as with speeding on the roads, illegal parking, riding a bicycle without lights, or dropping litter. This is not to suggest that all these offences are equally unimportant; it can be argued, by reference to the danger to others, that exceeding the speed limit ought to be regarded in a more serious light than commonly appears to be the case. Yet it remains true that there are many offences for which criminal liability is merely imposed by Parliament as a practical means of controlling an activity, without implying the element of social condemnation character-istic of the major or traditional crimes. An alternative approach might be to create a new regulatory agency and to invoke some kind of civil process, but this is generally regarded as too complex or too expensive, given that the police force (and some existing regulatory agencies) may be adapted to deal with the problem. Thus, the only feature which distinguishes some of these minor offences from civil wrongs, like breach of contract and liability in tort, is the decision by Parliament that they shall be criminal offences, attended by criminal procedures and triable in criminal courts. Therefore, although some offences in the criminal law are aimed at the highest social wrongs, there is no general dividing line between criminal and non-criminal conduct corresponding to a distinction between immoral and moral conduct, or between seriously antisocial and other conduct. The boundaries of the criminal law are explicable largely as the result of exercises of political power at particular points in history. In Chapter 2 we consider whether it is possible to develop some principles on what those boundaries ought to be.

The purpose of this chapter is to convey the 'feel' of the criminal law in outline, so that it may be developed in the succeeding chapters. It begins with a description of the contours of criminal liability, and follows this with a sketch of the reality of the criminal law. After considering the different viewpoints from which the criminal law may be studied, there is a preliminary examination of its aims and functions.

1.1 THE CONTOURS OF CRIMINAL LIABILITY

When we refer to criminal liability, what sort of conduct are we talking about? The answer may differ not only from one country to another, but also from one era to another in the same country. Some acts of homosexuality and abortion which were criminal in England before 1967 are not criminal now, whereas some forms of insider trading on the stock market and the possession of indecent photographs are criminal now, although they were not until a few years ago. There are certain seriously antisocial forms of conduct which are criminal in most jurisdictions but, in general, there is no straightforward moral or social test of whether conduct is criminal. The only reliable test is the formal one: is the conduct prohibited, on pain of conviction and sentence?

The contours of criminal liability may be considered under three headings: the range of offences; the scope of criminal liability; and the conditions of criminal liability. The *range* of criminal offences in England and Wales is enormous. There are violations in respect of:

1. the person, including offences of causing death and wounding, sexual offences, certain public order offences, offences relating to safety standards at work and in sports stadiums, offences relating to firearms and other weapons, and serious road traffic offences;
2. general public interests, including offences against state security, offences against public decency, crimes of breach of trust, offences against the administration of justice, and various offences connected with public obligations such as the payment of taxes;
3. the environment and the conditions of life, including the various

pollution offences, offences connected with health and purity standards, and minor offences of public order and public nuisance; and

4. property interests, from crimes of damage and offences of theft and deception, to offences of harassment of tenants and crimes of entering residential premises.

These are four major spheres of criminal liability, about which more will be said in Chapter 2. As in many other legal systems, there is a whole host of miscellaneous criminal prohibitions as well.

When we turn to the *scope* of criminal liability, we raise the question of the circumstances in which a person who does not cause one of the above harms may, nevertheless, be held criminally liable. In legal terms, the question has two dimensions: inchoate liability and criminal complicity. A crime is described as inchoate when the prohibited harm has not yet occurred. Several of the offences mentioned in the last paragraph are defined in terms of 'doing an act with intent to cause X', and they do not therefore require proof that the prohibited harm actually occurred. More generally, there are the inchoate offences of attempting to commit a crime (e.g. attempted murder), conspiring with one or more other people to commit a crime (e.g. conspiracy to rob), and inciting another to commit a crime. These offences broaden the scope of criminal liability considerably by providing for the conviction of persons who merely tried or planned to cause harm. Turning to criminal complicity, this doctrine is designed to ensure the conviction of a person who, without actually committing the full offence himself, plays a significant part in an offence committed by another. Thus a person may be convicted of aiding and abetting another to commit a crime, or counselling or procuring the commission of a crime by another.

The *conditions* to be fulfilled before an individual is convicted of an offence vary from one crime to another. There are many crimes which require only minimal fault or no personal fault at all. These are usually termed offences of 'strict liability': some of them are aimed at companies, but others (including many road traffic offences) are aimed at individuals. More of the traditional offences, which have been penalized by the common law of England for centuries, are said to require *mens rea*. This Latin term indicates, generally, that a person should not be convicted unless it can be proved that he intended to cause the harm, or that he knowingly risked the occurrence of the harm. The emphasis of these requirements has been upon the defendant's personal awareness of what was being done or omitted, although some judicial decisions have created exceptions to this. Beyond the *mens rea* requirement, which may differ in its precise form from crime to crime, there is a range of possible defences to criminal liability, so that even people who intentionally inflict harms may be acquitted if they acted in self defence, while insane, while under duress, and so on.

The contours of the criminal law are thus determined by the interplay between the range of offences, the scope of liability, and the conditions of liability. Inevitably there are times when the discussion focusses on one of the elements only, but the relevance of the other two must always be kept in view if the discussion is not to lose perspective.

1.2 THE MACHINERY OF ENGLISH CRIMINAL LAW

The criminal courts in England and Wales are the magistrates' courts and the Crown Court. Those offences considered least serious are summary offences, triable only in the magistrates' courts. Those offences considered most serious are triable only on indictment, in the Crown Court. A large number of offences, such as theft and most burglaries, are 'triable either way', in a magistrates' court or the Crown Court. Proceedings to determine the mode of trial are held before magistrates. The magistrates may decide (having heard representations from the prosecutor) that the case is so serious that it should be committed to the Crown Court for trial. If they decide not to commit it to the Crown Court, the defendant still has an absolute right to elect trial by jury. In practice a majority of 'either way' offences are dealt with in magistrates' courts, since neither the defendant nor the magistrates think Crown Court trial necessary. However, the question of a defendant's 'right' to trial by jury is a perennial subject of debate, as we will see in 1.4 below. Finally, it should be added that virtually all prosecutions of persons under 18 are brought in Youth Courts, where hearings are less formal and take place before specially trained magistrates.

1.3 THE SOURCES OF ENGLISH CRIMINAL LAW

The main source of English criminal law has been the common law, as developed through decisions of the courts and the works of such institutional writers as Coke and Hale in the seventeenth century, and Hawkins, Foster, and Blackstone in the eighteenth century. The bulk of English criminal law is now to be found in scattered statutes. There was a major consolidation of criminal legislation in 1861, and the Offences against the Person Act of that year remains the principal statute on that subject. Some offences are still governed by the common law and lack a statutory definition—most notably, murder, manslaughter, assault, and conspiracy to defraud. Many of the doctrines that determine the conditions of criminal liability are also still governed by the common law—not merely defences such as duress, intoxication, insanity, and automatism, but also basic concepts such as intention and recklessness. The judges therefore retain a central place in the development of the criminal law.

Over some three decades the Law Commission has embarked on a project of codifying English criminal law which thus far has resulted in several law reform statutes, such as the Criminal Damage Act 1971, the Criminal Law Act 1977, and the Forgery and Counterfeiting Act 1981. The Law Commission invited a team of academic lawyers to prepare a Draft Criminal Code which, using a uniform terminology, would bring together the principal crimes and general culpability requirements in one place. A draft was submitted to the Law Commission in 1985.[1] There were then consultations with members of the legal profession, and the Law Commission published its Criminal Code for England and Wales in 1989.[2] It now seems to be accepted that the enactment of a 220-section code would be too immense a task for Parliament to accomplish in a single Bill, and so the Law Commission has begun to formulate and promote shorter Bills in the hope that the codification project will make progress. The first such Bill deals with certain non-fatal offences against the person and a few general defences,[3] but the prospects for its enactment depend on the willingness of the Home Office to find time in its legislative programme.

Codification promises improvements in the clarity of the criminal law, in its accessibility and in consistency of terminology. There is also a constitutional dimension to the codification project. If criminal law and punishment are society's most powerful form of censure, is it not proper that decisions on its scope should be taken by the elected Parliament, after published reports and public discussion, rather than by the judges of the past and present?[4] The argument is a strong one, especially since most common law offences lack authoritative definitions. Yet it remains true that any laws created by Parliament fall to be interpreted by the courts, and this inevitably shifts some power back to the judiciary.[5] How do the courts approach the task of interpretation? Practice, as will become apparent, is characterized by variable policies and principles invoked by different courts. How the courts should approach the task is considered further in Chapter 3: the task of interpretation requires both a consciousness of the power which the court is exercising, and attention to the principles and

---

[1] *Codification of the Criminal Law: A Report to the Law Commission*, Law Com No. 143 (1985).

[2] *A Criminal Code for England and Wales*, Law Com No. 177 (two vols, 1989); throughout this book the draft Code and its commentary will be referred to merely as Law Com No. 177.

[3] *Legislating the Criminal Code: Offences against the Person and General Principles*, Law Com No. 218 (1993).

[4] A. T. H. Smith, 'The Case for a Code' [1986] Crim LR 285; and the Law Commission, in Law Com No. 177, i. 2.2.

[5] A. T. H. Smith, 'Judicial Lawmaking in the Criminal Law' (1984) 100 LQR 46.

policies to ensure that the power is exercised in a constitutionally appropriate manner.

The formal virtues claimed for codification should not, however, distract attention away from the important issues of *what* is being codified and *why* some parts of the criminal law have been included in the code rather than others. The draft Criminal Code of 1989 incorporates proposed reforms of the criminal law (on such matters as non-fatal violence, sexual offences, and mental disorder) which have never been placed before Parliament. Thus, it is not simply an exercise in codifying what exists; it is also an exercise in law reform, 'catching up' on recommendations from the Law Commission and other official bodies in the last 20 years which (for a variety of reasons) have not been acted upon. This raises the question of how the subjects to be covered by the code have been selected. Most of the general rules on the scope and the conditions of liability are covered, but the range of offences in the code keeps close to the traditional concept of crime (e.g. 'offences against the person' as conventionally defined, sexual offences, property offences, and public order offences). The Law Commission cites 'the principle of convenience' (*sic*) as a reason for excluding serious road traffic offences, drugs offences, companies offences, and others that are closely linked with complex statutory powers and with clusters of less serious offences. No doubt it is arguable that offences affecting specific fields of activity can be communicated more successfully to those engaging in such activity if they are found in a statute directly concerning such matters, e.g. the Merchant Shipping Acts in relation to maritime safety. Yet it can be argued no less strongly that a criminal code designed to draw together and declare either the most serious criminal offences, or even most of the serious offences, might indeed lead to a re-appraisal of some longstanding assumptions about the relative seriousness of offences,and even to a socially fairer approach to law enforcement.[6]

1.4 THE CRIMINAL LAW IN ACTION

It would be foolish to think that the criminal law as stated in the statutes and the textbooks reflects the way in which it is enforced in actual social situations. The key to answering the question of how the criminal law is likely to impinge on a person's activities lies in the discretion of the police and other law enforcement agents: they are not obliged to go out and look for offenders wherever they suspect that crimes are being committed; they are not obliged to prosecute every person against whom they have

---

[6] Cf. Law Com No. 177, paras 3.3–3.6 and Appendix C, with Celia Wells, 'Restatement or Reform?' [1986] Crim LR 314. See further Ch. 3.2 below.

sufficient evidence. On the other hand, they cannot prosecute unless the offence charged is actually laid down by statute or at common law. So we must consider the interaction between the law itself and discretion in the criminal process if we are to understand the social reality of the criminal law.

Even before the discretion of law enforcement officers comes into play, there is often a decision to be taken by a member of the public as to whether to report a suspected offence. The British Crime Survey suggests that at least a half of all offences are not reported to the police, often because they are thought to be too trivial, or because it is thought that the police would be unable to do anything constructive, or because it is thought that the police 'would not be interested'.[7] Even where an assault results in hospital treatment, a significant proportion of victims fail to report the offence or at least to make a formal complaint.[8] Thus, if an offence is to have any chance of being recorded, either the victim or a witness must take the decision to report the offence to the authorities. About 80 per cent of the offences which come to police attention are reported by the public. This means that people's (sometimes stereotyped) views on what forms of behaviour amount to criminal offences, and also on whether the police should be called, exert considerable influence on the cases entering the criminal justice system. Many offences committed at work or in the home remain concealed from official eyes. As for the 20 per cent of offences which come to light in other ways, most are observed or discovered by the police themselves. There are some crimes, such as drug-dealing and other so-called 'crimes without victims', which are unlikely to be reported and for which the police have to go looking. And there are other crimes, such as obstructing a police officer, and some of the public order offences, which the police may use as a means of controlling situations—charging the offences against people who disobey police instructions about moving on, keeping quiet, etc.[9] In these contexts the police use the criminal law as a resource to reinforce their authority.

It will thus be seen that most police investigations of offences are 'reactive', that is, reacting to information from the public about possible offences. Only in a minority of cases do the police operate 'proactively'. Other law enforcement officials may have a larger proactive role. Various inspectorates are required to oversee the observance of legal standards in industry and commerce—the Health and Safety Executive (which includes

[7] Home Office Research Study No. 132, *The 1992 British Crime Survey* (1993), 26.
[8] See the research reported by C. Clarkson, A. Cretney, G. Davis and J. Shepherd, 'Assaults: the Relationship between Seriousness, Criminalisation and Punishment' [1994] Crim LR 4.
[9] See the research reported by D. Brown and T. Ellis, *Policing low-level disorder: Police use of Section 5 of the Public Order Act 1986* (Home Office Research Study No. 135).

seven inspectorates: Factory, Agriculture, Nuclear, Offshore, Mines, Railway, and Quarries), the Alkali Inspectorate, the Industrial Air Pollution Inspectorate, the Environmental Health Departments of local authorities, and so on. Although these inspectorates often react to specific complaints or accidents—and there is evidence that some two-thirds of reportable workplace accidents are not reported by employers[10]—much of their work involves visits to premises or building sites to check on compliance with the law. It is therefore proactive work, and the number of offences which come to the inspectorate's attention is largely a reflection of the number of visits and inspections carried out. At a time when the staffing of the inspectorates is being tightly controlled, the number of offences which can be discovered is clearly limited.

What happens when an offence has been reported to the police? In most cases the offence is recorded and the police may investigate it. However, the British Crime Survey suggests that around one-third of all incidents reported to the police as crimes are not recorded as such: sometimes the evidence is thought unconvincing, or the offence too minor, or the incident redefined as lost property rather than stolen property.[11] Of those which are recorded as crimes, the police trace about one-quarter to an offender or suspected offender. The proportion of offences thus 'cleared up' is much higher for offences of violence (about 80 per cent)—where the victim often sees and knows the offender—than for the less serious kinds of property offence (under 20 per cent), where the offender's identity will probably be unknown and the offence may be thought not to justify a great investment of police time and resources.

When the police find a suspect, they will invariably question this person. The Police and Criminal Evidence Act 1984 and its Codes of Practice require investigators to follow certain procedures before and during any interrogation, including notifying suspects of the right to a free and private consultation with a lawyer. The tape recording of suspects' statements is now a routine feature at police stations, although statements (allegedly) made elsewhere remain admissible in evidence. Many of the miscarriages of justice uncovered in the late 1980s and early 1990s, after the wrongly convicted people had spent many years in prison, stemmed from misconduct by the police at this stage of the investigation, including the falsification of notes of interviews.[12] Following the quashing of convictions in the cases of the Guildford Four and the Birmingham Six, the Royal Commission on Criminal Justice was appointed in 1991 to examine the

---

[10] National Audit Office, *Enforcing Health and Safety Legislation in the Workplace* (1994), 10.   [11] Ibid., 16.

[12] For fuller discussion of this and the other issues discussed in the next few pages, see A. Ashworth, *The Criminal Process: an Evaluative Study* (1994), esp. Chs 1, 3, and 4; A. Sanders and R. Young, *Criminal Justice* (1994), Chs 1 and 4.

effectiveness of the criminal justice system. It has been claimed that many of those miscarriages of justice could not have happened if the 1984 Act had been enacted ten years earlier, yet recent cases show that the 1984 Act cannot assure proper standards. It is evident from the case of the Cardiff Three that many suspects remain at a significant psychological disadvantage in the police station, despite the tape recorder and the presence of a solicitor or 'legal representative'. In that case Lord Taylor CJ said that the appeal judges had been 'horrified' when listening to the tapes:

Miller was bullied and hectored. The officers . . . were not questioning him so much as shouting at him . . . Short of physical violence, it is hard to conceive of a more hostile and intimidating approach by officers to a suspect. It is impossible to convey on the printed page the pace, force and menace of the officer's delivery.[13]

Research carried out for the Royal Commission on Criminal Justice shows that there remains a need for considerable improvement in the approach of the police to the questioning of suspects.[14] The Royal Commission itself did recognize that 'confessions which are later found to be false have led or contributed to serious miscarriages of justice',[15] but it placed its faith largely in voluntary changes of approach by the police rather than in further regulation.[16] An essential part of the Royal Commission's approach was that suspects should retain their right of silence under police questioning, but the Government rejected this recommendation and the Criminal Justice and Public Order Act 1994, ss 34–37, provide that courts may draw inferences from a defendant's failure to mention certain points when questioned by the police.[17] One result of these provisions, which have been the law in relation to serious fraud and generally in Northern Ireland for some years,[18] may be to weaken still further the position of many suspects in police stations. The right to legal advice cannot be relied upon to rectify the balance, since many of the 'legal advisers' attending police stations are not legally qualified, and even some of those who are seem unwilling or too afraid to insist that the police abide by the rules.[19]

---

[13] *Paris, Abdullahi and Miller* (1983) 97 Cr App R 99, at 103.

[14] E.g. M. McConville and J. Hodgson, *Custodial Legal Advice and the Right to Silence*, RCCJ Research Study No. 16 (1993), S. Moston and G. Stephenson, *The questioning and interviewing of suspects outside the police station*, RCCJ Research Study No. 22 (1993).

[15] Royal Commission on Criminal Justice, *Report* (1993, Cm 2263), 57.

[16] For critical analysis, see R. Reiner, 'Investigative Powers and Safeguards for Suspects' [1993] Crim LR 808, and J. Jackson, 'The Evidence Recommendations' [1993] Crim LR 817.

[17] I. Dennis, 'The Criminal Justice and Public Order Act 1994: the Evidence Provisions' [1995] Crim LR 4.

[18] See J. Jackson, 'The Right of Silence: Judicial Responses to Parliamentary Encroachment' (1994) 57 MLR 270.

[19] J. Baldwin, *The Role of Legal Representatives at Police Stations*, RCCJ Research Study No. 3 (1992); M. McConville, L. Bridges, J. Hodgson and A. Pavlovic (eds) *Standing Accused* (1994).

When the police have completed their questioning, they may release the suspect if they have insufficient evidence. If they believe they have sufficient evidence, or if the suspect has admitted guilt, there are choices to be made. The police have three alternatives: to prosecute, to administer a formal police caution, or to take no further action. The cautioning rate for adults has increased in recent years to almost 20 per cent: the police have been encouraged to prefer a formal caution to prosecution where the offence is relatively minor, where the offender is old, infirm, or suffering from mental disturbance, and in other situations where there is little blame. But by far the highest cautioning rate is for juvenile offenders. Some 80 per cent of offenders under the age of 17 are cautioned, and only 20 per cent are prosecuted; for first offenders and for girls, the proportion cautioned is over 90 per cent. The policy is to delay the entry of young people into the formal criminal justice system, in the belief that a caution is no less likely to be effective in preventing further offences, and that labelling a youth as a delinquent can reinforce that person's tendency to behave like a one. The prosecution of someone under 17 is therefore relatively unusual, and has tended to be confined to those who are believed to have committed especially serious offences or who are persistent in their lawbreaking. The Government has now revised the cautioning guidelines with a view to reducing the use of cautions for repeat offenders and for serious offenders.[20] Although this change is likely to have some impact on practice, it remains true that a large part of the criminal law in action is to provide the background for the administration of formal cautions by the police to young people.

The use of alternatives to prosecution is also favoured for offences which are 'policed' by the various inspectorates and by such other public authorities as the Inland Revenue, HM Customs and Excise, and so forth. Many of these agencies adopt the approach that their main aim is to secure compliance rather than convictions. They therefore tend to rely on informal and formal warnings as a means of putting pressure on companies, employers, taxpayers and the like. The criminal law remains behind them, as the source of the pressure towards compliance which they are able to exert, but most of these agencies regard prosecution as a last resort. Thus, for example, the Inland Revenue brings only a few hundred prosecutions each year, relying chiefly on warnings and on its power to enforce penalties through further taxation as ways of dealing with tax evaders.[21] Similarly in 1992–3 inspectors working for the Health and

---

[20] Home Office Circular 18/94, discussed by R Evans, 'Cautioning: Counting the Cost of Retrenchment' [1994] Crim LR 566.

[21] An approach commended by the Keith Committee on the Enforcement of Revenue Legislation (1983, Cmnd 8822); for discussion, see Andrew Sanders, 'Class Bias in Prosecutions' (1985) 24 Howard JCJ 176.

Safety Executive issued 11,000 enforcement notices and began 2,000 prosecutions.[22] In these spheres of behaviour, then, the criminal law is very much in the background, and the criminal process is experienced by relatively few of those caught breaking the law.[23]

Where the police are involved, however, prosecution remains the normal response for persons aged 18 and over.[24] When the police decide to bring a prosecution, they will charge the suspect and then pass the papers on to the Crown Prosecution Service (CPS). The police and the CPS are in the process of agreeing on sets of 'Charging Standards' which provide guidance on the appropriate charges in given factual situations.[25] The CPS then has the function of reviewing the case file to determine whether the prosecution should be carried forward or discontinued. One of the aspects to be considered is evidential sufficiency: is there enough evidence on each of the elements required to prove the offence, so that it can be said that there is a realistic prospect of conviction? This is not simply a matter of the amount of evidence available. The evidence must also be legally admissible in a criminal case, having regard to the rules and discretions that may lead courts to exclude evidence—such as that obtained by a breach of the Police and Criminal Evidence Act and its codes of practice, or unduly prejudicial evidence.[26] The second, related, factor is whether a prosecution would be in the public interest. There is a Code for Crown Prosecutors which provides guidance on this and other decisions which prosecutors must take. The latest (1994) version adopts a more restrictive stance on use of the CPS power to discontinue prosecutions in the public interest, but also preserves considerable discretion and removes the guidance on certain issues from this public document.[27]

It will be apparent from the preceding paragraphs that the defendants and offences brought to court form a highly selective sample of all detected crimes. Those convicted in court are certainly a small sample of the whole: the Home Office has estimated that if one takes account of those offences not reported, not recorded, not cleared up, and cautioned rather than prosecuted, only 2 per cent of crimes result in a conviction.[28] Although the

---

[22] National Audit Office, *Enforcing Health and Safety Legislation*, 24.

[23] See further Ashworth, *The Criminal Process*, Chs 5, 6, and 10.

[24] The Criminal Justice Act 1991 replaced juvenile courts with Youth Courts and raised the age limit from 17 to 18: the figures in the previous paragraphs refer to the time when the term juvenile applied only to those under 17.

[25] For a summary of the Charging Standards on offences against the person, see [1994] Crim LR 777.

[26] See generally A. A. S. Zuckerman, *The Principles of Criminal Evidence* (1989).

[27] A. Ashworth and J. Fionda, 'The New Code for Crown Prosecutors: (1) Prosecution, Accountability and the Public Interest' [1994] Crim LR 894, and R. K. Daw, '(2) A Response' [1994] Crim LR 904.

[28] Home Office, *Digest 2: Information on the Criminal Justice System in England and Wales* (1993), 29.

percentage rises to 10 for crimes of wounding, it would not be accurate to say that the cases brought to court involve the most serious offences and offenders, because:

1. there are crimes for which a person of 18 or over would be prosecuted whereas a person under 18 would not be;
2. fairly serious crimes committed in the home may not be prosecuted,[29] whereas prosecution is often the normal response to less serious offences in the street; and
3. some of the crimes of petty theft which are prosecuted are, by almost any measure, less serious than many crimes which the Inland Revenue or other regulatory agencies deal with by warnings, civil penalties, or other alternative methods.

What emerges from this is that adults suspected of committing 'traditional' offences outside their own home are much more likely to appear in court than adults known to have committed 'modern' offences such as tax-evasion, pollution, having an unsafe workplace, and so on. Even leaving aside young people, court proceedings are a poor representation of the reality of crime in our society.

It will be evident, too, that it is not rules but discretion which characterizes these early stages in the criminal process. Police decision-making is largely discretionary, structured only by the cautioning guide-lines, local arrangements for dealing with young defendants, police force orders, and internal police supervision. If the police decide to prosecute, the CPS can review the decision, alter the charge, or discontinue the prosecution. If the police decide not to prosecute or not even to record an offence, there is little recourse. The same is largely true of the regulatory and other agencies which have the power to prosecute. Moreover, the elements of discretion do not stop with the decision whether or not to prosecute. A question of particular importance for our present purposes is that of determining what offence to prosecute. In some cases there is little choice, but there are other cases where the prosecutor can choose between a more serious and a less serious offence. If there is a prosecution for the higher offence, it is usually possible for a court to convict of a lesser offence if it does not find the higher offence proved. But this does not mean that prosecutors routinely try for the higher offence. If, for example, the lower offence is triable only summarily (i.e. in a magistrates' court) whereas the higher offence is 'triable either way' (i.e. in a magistrates' court or at the Crown Court), the prosecutor may prefer the lesser charge so as to keep the case in a magistrates' court—for various reasons, one of which may be

---

[29] See L. J. F. Smith, *Domestic Violence* (Home Office Research Study No. 107, 1989), esp. Chs 7 and 8, although there have been changes in practice since then.

the belief that a conviction is more likely if the case is tried by magistrates rather than by a jury.[30] If the prosecution bring an 'either way' charge, the defendant has an absolute right to elect trial by jury in the Crown Court. The Royal Commission, much impressed by the finding that a majority of those who exercise their right of election subsequently change their plea to guilty and then receive a higher sentence than they would have received in a magistrates' court,[31] recommended that the defendant's so-called right to jury trial be abolished. This, however, takes no account of widely-felt reservations about the quality of justice in magistrates' courts.[32]

Whether the case is set down for trial in a magistrates' court or the Crown Court, the prosecution may reach an agreement with the defence (often at the last minute) to accept a plea of not guilty to the offence charged but guilty to a lesser offence. This may appear advantageous to the prosecutor, in the sense that a conviction is assured and the hazards of a trial (with the possibility that a key witness will not give evidence convincingly) are avoided. It may also appear advantageous to the defendant, since the conviction is for a lesser offence and the sentence may be lower, too. However, it will probably come to the defendant's attention that a guilty plea is seen as a significant mitigating factor in sentencing: this could place considerable pressure on a defendant to plead guilty even where innocence is maintained, if defence lawyers emphasize the strength of the evidence for the prosecution, etc., and there are clearly some cases in which innocent persons feel driven to plead guilty.[33] The Royal Commission's recommendations would institutionalize a sentence discount of one-third for an early plea of guilty and would allow defendants to ask the judge for a 'sentence canvass', thereby increasing the pressure on all defendants (guilty or innocent) to plead guilty.[34]

Not only, then, are the cases prosecuted a selective sample of all crimes committed, but the offences for which convictions are recorded may sometimes underestimate the true seriousness of the crimes brought to court. It may be in the apparent best interests of both prosecution and defence to settle for conviction of a less serious offence. The way in which offences are defined may facilitate or constrain many of these decisions,

[30] The acquittal rate in the Crown Court is thought to be almost twice that in magistrates' courts: J. Vennard, 'The Outcome of Contested Trials', in D. Moxon (ed), *Managing Criminal Justice* (1985), 131.
[31] C. Hedderman and D. Moxon, *Magistrates' Court or Crown Court? Mode of Trial Decisions and Sentencing*, HORS 125 (1992).
[32] For elaboration, see Ashworth, *The Criminal Process*, Ch 8.
[33] Cf. D. Riley and J. Vennard, *Triable Either Way Cases: Crown Court or Magistrates' Court?*, HORS 98 (1988), 20, with M. Zander and P. Henderson, *Crown Court Study*, RCCJ Research Study No. 19 (1993), 138–142.
[34] For further discussion, see Ashworth, *The Criminal Process*, Ch 9, Sanders and Young, *Criminal Justice*, Ch 7.

and so the structure of the criminal law may have a greater direct influence at this point than at some earlier stages in the criminal process. However, the predominance of official discretion opens the way for other motivations, including bias and prejudice, to enter in. Although the ratio of male to female known offenders is around 5:1, there is evidence of harsher responses to certain females who do not conform to stereotypes of the good woman or good mother.[35] There is also evidence of racial prejudice in the pre-trial system,[36] although some of this is a form of structural bias stemming from the way in which the system imposes disincentives on those who elect Crown Court trial and who persist in a plea of not guilty.

This brief outline has, it is hoped, demonstrated some of the ways in which the criminal law in action differs from the law as declared in the statutes and in legal decisions. Little has been said about the ways in which defence lawyers may construct their defences around the legal requirements and around the defendant's narrative,[37] but that, too, is a factor in the presentation and the outcome of cases. So far as official agencies are concerned, each case brought to court is the product of a system which is heavily reliant on victims and other members of the public for the detection of offenders and the provision of evidence,[38] and which leaves considerable discretion in the hands of the police, other law-enforcement agencies, and the Crown Prosecution Service. We have seen that that discretion is exercised unevenly: some 60 per cent of all defendants in criminal courts are unemployed, whereas some groups of offenders are rarely brought to court. These are all issues that call for critical scrutiny of the range, the scope, and the conditions of criminal liability, together with a constant awareness that the law in action is far more selective than the law as it appears in the books.

1.5 OUTLINE OF THE AIMS AND FUNCTIONS
OF THE CRIMINAL LAW

Is the criminal law necessary at all? It has been suggested from time to time that law in general, and criminal laws in particular, are needed only in conflict-ridden societies, and that the establishment of a political system based on consensus would remove the sources of crime and, therefore, the

---

[35] M. Eaton, *Justice for Women?* (1987), A. Morris, 'Sex and Sentencing' [1988] Crim LR 163.
[36] M. FitzGerald, *Ethnic Minorities and the Criminal Justice System*, RCCJ Research Study No. 20 (1993); see also R. Hood, *Race and Sentencing* (1992), 146–150, on unexplained differences in remands in custody.
[37] See generally M. McConville *et al.*, *Standing Accused*.
[38] See the fascinating study by Paul Rock, *The Social World of an English Crown Court* (1993).

phenomenon itself.[39] This view may be attacked for its simplistic assessment of the causes of crime, but it is sufficient for present purposes to state that no modern industrially developed country seems able to dispense with criminal law and, indeed, that occasional instances of the breakdown of policing have led to increases in certain forms of criminal behaviour.[40] This suggests that one fundamental reason for having a criminal law backed by sanctions is a deterrent or preventive: so long as its provisions are enforced with some regularity, it constitutes a standing disincentive to crime and reinforces those social conventions and other inhibitions which are already in place. Fundamental though this proposition is, it should not obscure the importance of two related propositions. One is that the criminal law should not be regarded as a primary means of protecting individual and social interests. In terms of prevention, more can probably be achieved through various techniques of situational crime prevention,[41] social crime prevention, and general social and educational policies.[42] The other proposition is that the criminal law and sentencing are largely conservative forces, in that they use coercion to enforce conformity with the norms of those with dominant interest in a given society. Criminal laws give greater protection to property than to changing the conditions of life for many people; they are enforced selectively, and the result (as already mentioned) is that large numbers of disadvantaged people are to be found among convicted offenders.

The underlying deterrent rationale is not the only justification for criminal law and sentencing. Another is that offenders deserve punishment for their offences, and that it is therefore right (and not just expedient) to provide that serious harms culpably caused should lead to punishment. Immediately this raises questions about the people who tend to be convicted and sentenced—the unemployed and the otherwise disadvantaged. This is often seen as a particular drawback of sentencing systems that aspire to proportionality or 'just deserts'. Since 'proportionate' sentences are merely reinforcing existing social inequalities, this does not achieve justice so much as confirm injustice. The point is an important one, but it is an argument against most other aims of sentencing, too. A deterrent

[39] Anarchist theorists such as Godwin held a version of this view (see George Woodcock, *Anarchism* (1962)), and according to Marxist theory, the law would wither away on the attainment of perfect communism (see Hugh Collins, *Marxism and Law* (1982)).

[40] Usually cited in this connection are the police strikes in Liverpool in 1919, and in Melbourne in 1918, and the incarceration of the Danish police force by the Nazis in 1944. Broadly speaking, property crimes increased whilst crimes of violence and sexual crimes did not.

[41] See Ronald V. Clarke, 'Situational Crime Prevention: Its Theoretical Basis and Practical Scope' (1983) 4 *Crime and Justice: An Annual Review*, 225.

[42] See generally K. Pease, 'Crime Prevention', in M. Maguire, R. Morgan, and R. Reiner (eds), *The Oxford Handbook of Criminology* (1994), Ch 14.

theory seeks to reinforce the value structure inherent in the criminal law. A rehabilitative theory would attempt to mould offenders' behaviour towards compliance with the norms of the criminal law. A restorative theory might be chiefly concerned to achieve compensation that restores the status quo ante. Moreover, a system based on desert and proportionality can be operated humanely, without escalation of penalties.[43]

Although it might be widely agreed that general prevention is the underlying reason for having criminal laws, this is not sufficient to justify all the criminal laws of any particular country. Other principles come into play, and one is that the criminal law, being society's strongest form of official censure and punishment, should be concerned only with the central values and significant harms. We have already noted that this is not the case in practice: the criminal law is sometimes used against relatively minor kinds of harm, often because the police are available as a convenient means of enforcement. The reach of the criminal sanction is determined by a number of conflicting social, political, and historical factors. This applies chiefly to the *range* of offences, enlarged on occasion in response to a wave of political concern and without overall consideration of the proper limits of the criminal sanction: a recent example, the Criminal Justice and Public Order Act 1994, is considered in Chapter 2.1. In addition, the *scope* of criminal liability bears witness to similar conflicts (e.g. over the extent of the offence of conspiracy). Finally, the *conditions* of criminal liability barely conceal the conflicts of principle and policy which have shaped them throughout their years of development, with recurrent debate over the merits of fault requirements, necessitating subjective awareness by the defendant, as against the merits of objective standards of liability, based on what the reasonable person would have appreciated in the defendant's position.

In Chapter 2 there will be discussion of some of the values which should underlie the criminal law.[44] One is individual liberty (liberty in the negative sense of freedom from coercion, deception, fear, and so on), and also liberty in the positive sense of freedom to join a public demonstration (within limits), express one's sexuality (within limits), and so on. Even a casual acquaintance with modern systems of criminal law is enough to sustain the point that not only are there conflicts between the two senses of liberty, but there are also other values which are influential here. There are the collective interests, such as national security, preservation of the environment, the safety of public amenities, and so forth. These collective interests inevitably conflict with individual interests at various points, and one can also discern paternalistic principles at work in penalizing failures to

[43] See further A. von Hirsch, *Censure and Sanctions*, Chs 9 and 10.
[44] See also N. Lacey, *State Punishment*, Ch 5.

adopt measures for one's own protection in certain circumstances (e.g. when driving a car, riding a motorcycle, etc.). These factors will be explored in Chapter 2. For the present it is enough to make the point that one cannot simply list the values which the criminal law can justifiably be used to protect, as if they are either self-evident or free from conflict and controversy. They are neither.

1.6 THE CRIMINAL LAW AND SENTENCING

A person who has been found guilty of a criminal offence is liable to be sentenced by the court. A conviction may be bad enough in itself: it is a form of public censure, and many convictions (at least for non-motoring offences) make it difficult or impossible to obtain certain jobs or enter a profession. For most of the offences covered in this book, the sentence is likely to involve considerable deprivation, either of money or of liberty or both. The criminal law may therefore be said to open the way for official acts of coercion against an offender. Indeed, we will see below that sentencing has considerable significance for the contours of criminal liability: when Parliament creates a crime it authorizes not merely the affixing of a label of censure on the perpetrator, but also the imposition of certain deprivations by means of sentence.

The range of sentences available to English courts, and the actual exercise of judicial discretion in imposing sentences, can only be outlined briefly here.[45] The leading recent statutes are the Criminal Justice Acts 1991–93, which establish proportionality of sentence to the seriousness of the crime as the leading principle. For the least serious forms of crime, an absolute or conditional discharge may be thought sufficient. For many offences a fine will be the normal punishment: the size of the fine should reflect the seriousness of the offence, adjusted in accordance with the means of the offender.[46] If the offence is serious enough to warrant it, the court may consider imposing a community sentence. For adult offenders this means: a community service order; a probation order; a curfew order; or a combination order (containing elements of probation and community service).[47] A custodial sentence is only lawful on one of three grounds:

1. where the offender has refused consent to a community sentence;
2. if the offence is a sexual or violent offence, and a custodial sentence is necessary to protect the public from serious harm from him or her; and

---

[45] See A. Ashworth, *Sentencing and Criminal Justice* (2nd edn, 1995); M. Wasik, *Emmins on Sentencing* (2nd edn, 1993).

[46] CJA 1991, s 18, as substituted by the CJA 1993.

[47] Governed by s 6 CJA 1991.

3. most frequently, if the offence or offences are so serious that only a
   custodial sentence can be justified.[48]

The length of any custodial sentence should in most cases be 'commensurate
with the seriousness of the offence': in practice, the courts have continued
to apply a kind of sentencing 'tariff' that evolved at common law and has
been developed more recently through guideline judgments from the Lord
Chief Justice.[49] In deciding on the sentence in a particular case, the court
should take account of any factors that aggravate or mitigate the offence,
and also any other extenuating circumstances relevant to the case.

   How necessary is an understanding of sentencing law and practice to a
study of the criminal law? Ideally the criminal law would be studied in
conjunction with the other elements of criminal justice with which it is so
intimately linked in practice and in theory—prosecution policy and other
aspects of pre-trial criminal process, the laws of evidence, and then
sentencing.[50] This makes the case for two years of teaching in this field, or for
four one-semester modules, to cover the ground. Given that this would be
difficult to achieve in many institutions, many criminal law teachers are left
with a decision about the amount of sentencing or other matters to put into
criminal law modules. At a minimum, the interactions between sentencing
and criminal law must be kept in view. It was argued above that it is
sentencing, largely, that gives the criminal law its bite. It is therefore
important to view decisions on criminal liability as decisions about the
application of censure and coercion. But in some ways the criminal law also
influences sentencing: in the last 20 or 30 years the tendency in statutes
such as the Theft Act 1968 and the Criminal Damage Act 1971 has been to
move away from a multiplicity of narrowly defined offences towards a
smaller number of 'broad band' offences. In sentencing terms one
consequence of this is that there are more broad offences with high
maximum sentences, giving more discretion to the courts at the sentencing
stage.[51] An example of the impact of sentencing on the criminal law is that,
as we shall see in Chapter 7, the shape of the law on murder and
manslaughter has been influenced by the existence of the mandatory
penalty for murder. Another area of interaction between criminal law and
sentencing is where the courts or Parliament have taken a restrictive
approach in defining defences to criminal liability, in the belief that
circumstances which 'almost' amount to a defence might result in

[48] CJA 1991, s 1, as amended by the CJA 1993.
[49] For some details, see Ashworth, *Sentencing and Criminal Justice*, Ch 4, and M. Wasik,
Emmins on Sentencing, Ch 12.
[50] Cf. P. Alldridge, 'What's wrong with the traditional Criminal Law course?' (1990) 10
Legal Studies 38.
[51] D. A. Thomas, 'Form and Function in Criminal Law', in P. R. Glazebrook (ed),
Reshaping the Criminal Law (1978).

significant mitigation of sentence (e.g. some cases of duress and entrapment). On the other hand, courts have tended to adopt a much looser
notion of responsibility at the sentencing stage than at the liability stage:
for example, courts which refuse to accept social or childhood deprivation
as the basis for a defence to criminal liability may be quite willing to accept
it in mitigation of sentence.[52] Thus the criminal law itself proclaims
individual responsibility for actions, maintaining strict standards of
conduct and setting its face publicly against the idea that social or other
circumstances can excuse behaviour, while at the sentencing stage courts
do recognize from time to time the exculpatory force of preceding or
surrounding circumstances.[53]

It was stated earlier that, under the Criminal Justice Act 1991, the
principal rationale for sentencing is proportionality: offenders should
receive the punishment they deserve for the offence(s) for which they are
being sentenced. Alongside it, and surviving from the Criminal Justice
Acts of 1982 and 1988, there is the restorative rationale, which manifests
itself in the courts' duty to consider making a compensation order in favour
of the victim in every case involving death or injury, loss or damage.
However, even the 1991 Act recognizes other rationales for sentencing in
certain types of case—incapacitative or 'public protection' sentences may
be imposed on violent or sexual offenders thought to present a risk of
serious harm to others, and rehabilitative forms of sentence may be
selected for those with identified needs whose offence warrants a
community sentence. The Act did not mention deterrence as the aim of
particular sentences (although, as stated above, general deterrence is an
underlying reason for having a system of criminal law), but the judges lost
little time in reaffirming that it remains one of the principles to which they
have regard when calculating the length of a custodial sentence.[54]

While the notion of general deterrence is crucial as an underlying
justification for the punishment system, the idea of proportionality is of
central importance to the choice and quantum of sanction in a particular
case. Proportionality also has a role, as we will see, in the grading of
offences in the criminal law. Within 'desert' theory there is a distinction
between two kinds of proportionality.[55] One is cardinal proportionality:
this requires that the severity of the punishment be in proportion to the
seriousness of the offence. Exactly what that level of sentences should be in
a particular country is a matter for debate, based on criminological

---

[52] See below, Ch 6.9.
[53] See A. Norrie, *Crime, Reason and History* (1993), Ch 10.
[54] *Cunningham* (1993) 14 Cr App R (S) 444, criticized by Ashworth, *Sentencing and Criminal Justice*, Ch 3.
[55] See von Hirsch, *Censure and Sanctions*, esp. Chs 4 and 5.

research and, inevitably, restricted by social conventions.[56] The second kind of proportionality, more important for our present purposes, is ordinal proportionality. This requires an assessment of the seriousness of the crime in relation to other forms of offending, so as to establish acceptable relativities. The precise meaning of 'seriousness' here will be explored in Chapters 2 and 5, for it represents a combination of the harm done or risked and of the culpability of the offender.

Other approaches to punishment do not necessarily neglect proportionality. Jeremy Bentham's preventive theory of punishment has general deterrence as its main principle for the distribution and amount of punishments.[57] Would punishment of this class of persons deter others from committing crimes? How much punishment is necessary to achieve this deterrent effect? Even so, Bentham expressed his theory as subject to the parameters of proportionality, since he urged that a greater punishment might be ventured against a greater harm. Modern economic theorists, who propose that punishments should be ranged as a kind of scale of costs for law breaking, do not insist on proportionality but probably believe that their approach would reflect and even establish proportionality, by showing how much of their liberty or money citizens are prepared to forfeit in order to commit various offences.[58]

The aims of sentencing are not simply part of the background of the criminal law: they have implications for the shape of the criminal law itself. Thus proportionality should be a key element in the structure of the criminal law. It is a major function of the criminal law not only to divide the criminal from the non-criminal, but also to grade offences and to label them proportionately. As Nils Jareborg expresses it, 'the threat of punishment is not only a conditional threat of a painful sanction. It is also an official expression of how negatively different kinds of action or omission are judged.'[59] On the other hand, there is a divergence between desert theories and deterrence theories on the question of culpability and excuses for causing harm. The answer to the question, 'does this person deserve punishment?', sometimes differs from the answer to the question, 'would the punishment of this person deter others in similar situations?'.

This book is intended as an exploration of principles of the criminal law. It does not purport to be a textbook, and does not treat all the parts of the criminal law. It does, however, attempt to convey a general picture of the

---

[56] A. Ashworth, 'Criminal Justice and Deserved Sentences' [1989] Crim LR 340, at 344–5.

[57] J. Bentham, *Introduction to the Principles of Morals and Legislation* (1789), excerpted in A. von Hirsch and A. Ashworth, *Principled Sentencing* (1993), Ch 2.

[58] R. Posner, *Economic Theory of Law* (2nd edn., 1977), Ch 7, excerpted in von Hirsch and Ashworth, *Principled Sentencing*, Ch 2.

[59] N. Jareborg, 'The Coherence of the Penal System', in his *Criminal Law in Action* (1988).

criminal law in action by including some reference to the myriad laws not usually discussed even in works which are regarded as textbooks. The traditional textbook treatment focusses on the details of certain established crimes, with a few recent arrivals of a similar kind. In this book it is the principles that provide the vehicle of study: once the process and the principles of criminalization have been examined in Chapter 2, many of the principles which do or should inform the criminal law are drawn together for discussion in Chapter 3. These principles are then related to others which have a particular bearing on culpability and the conditions of liability in Chapters 4 to 6. They are kept in mind when analysing three different groups of offences in Chapters 7 to 9. They are also related to questions about the scope of criminal liability in Chapters 10 and 11.

There are also frequent references to research that has a bearing on criminal justice, to give some indication of the social context in which the criminal law operates. Much more coverage could be given to these contextual issues, such as enforcement policy, police powers, the pre-trial construction of cases, and sentencing, but within the confines of this work these issues have been treated as less important that the consideration of doctrine. This means that our discussion of the criminal law is largely centred on appellate courts, as opposed to concentrating on the law as it is enforced by the police and others. We endeavour to recognize the constitutional responsibilities of the courts in developing the law and interpreting legislation, and try to remain alert to the implications for law enforcement of leaving areas of discretion when formulating laws: we saw in Chapter 1.4 how wide this discretion often is, and how the selective policies of various enforcement agencies lead to a rather skewed sample of defendants appearing before the courts. But the centrepiece of this book is the doctrine of the criminal law, by which is meant the policies and social values which underlie the decision to increase or decrease the *range* of the criminal law, the principles and values which bear upon decision about the *scope* of criminal liability, and the principles, policies, and values which relate to the *conditions* of criminal liability.

2

Criminalization

In Chapter 1 it was suggested that the reach of the criminal law depends on the *range* of offences, the *scope* of criminal liability, and the *conditions* of criminal liability. Writings on English criminal law have focussed largely on the conditions of liability (see Chapters 4 to 6) and on the scope of liability (see Chapters 10 and 11), and there has been a tendency to devote little attention to the rightness or wrongness of criminalizing certain conduct. Apart from discussions of the relationship between sexual 'morality' and the criminal sanction, the boundaries of the criminal law have usually been treated as 'given'. This, in turn, may foster the assumption that those boundaries represent some kind of objective dividing line between the criminal and the non-criminal, whereas the actual range of offences is best explained historically as the product of various political and other forces in particular social contexts.

We have seen in Chapter 1 that a system of criminal law may be justified as a mechanism for the preservation of social order. As a type of law, its technique is condemnatory and it authorizes the infliction of state punishment. To criminalize a certain kind of conduct is to declare that it should not be done, to institute a threat of punishment in order to supply a pragmatic reason for not doing it, and to censure those who nevertheless do it. This use of state power calls for justification—justification by reference to democratic principles, and justification in terms of sufficient reasons for invoking this coercive and censuring machinery against individual subjects. Reasons of the second type usually relate to concepts such as harm and culpability. Harm-related questions will be the primary focus of this chapter, although 2.2 will also introduce some of the issues underlying the element of culpability.

The purpose of this chapter is not to search for some objective benchmark of criminality, or for some general theory which will enable us to tell whether or not certain conduct should be criminalized. The range of actual and potential crimes is so wide and variegated that this seems unattainable. In respect of most kinds of conduct, the issues arising are complex and far-reaching. The purpose is rather to identify some principles that may tell for or against making conduct criminal, and to point out some good or bad reasons. Although it is true, as already argued, that the frontiers of criminal liability are not given but are historically contingent, it remains important to strive to identify those interests that warrant the use of the criminal law and to refine notions such as harm which play so prominent a part even in political discussions of these questions.[1]

The concern of this chapter will chiefly be legislative decisions to extend or curtail the criminal law, and the reasons which have been significant or which should have been significant in those decisions. Yet we must recall, as argued in Chapter 1, that the impact of the criminal law on citizens is determined not so much by the legislature as by the practices of the various law enforcement agents—chiefly police officers, but also officials from HM Customs and Excise, the various statutory inspectorates, and so on. Thus the legislature may be said to provide the tools, resources, or authority for law enforcement agents when it creates a criminal offence, but decisions about when to invoke and when not to invoke the available powers are taken by enforcement officers. The exercise of discretionary power therefore provides the key to practical instances of criminalization. Examples of these two pragmatic points—the political nature of many legislative decisions, and the power of law enforcement agents—are discussed in 2.1, before we move on to explore the theoretical justifications for criminalization.

2.1 THE POLITICS OF LAWMAKING

Creating a new criminal offence may often be regarded as an instantly satisfying political response to public worries about a form of conduct that has been given publicity by the newspapers and television. The pressure on politicians to be seen to be doing something may be great, and considered responses such as consultation and commissioning research may invite criticisms of indecision and procrastination. Thus, in many countries, the growth of the criminal law may reflect particular phases in contemporary social history, as written by the mass media and politicians.

We may consider two examples of recent legislative extension of the range of the criminal law: the offences in Part V of the Criminal Justice and Public Order Act 1994 and, first, the offence of causing harassment, alarm or distress in the Public Order Act 1986. In its reform of public order law in the 1980s, the government added to the offences recommended by the Law Commission a further offence, consisting of disorderly behaviour or threatening, abusive or insulting behaviour, likely to cause 'harassment, alarm or distress': Public Order Act 1986, section 5. The reason for adding this offence was to give the police the power to intervene at the early stages of disorder, and also to deal with minor acts of hooliganism.

---

[1] N. Lacey, 'Contingency and Criminalisation', in I. Loveland (ed), *The Frontiers of Criminalisation* (1995).

Much could be said about the origins and import of this provision.[2] For present purposes, it is sufficient to note that the new offence is additional to that created by section 4 of the Act, of using threatening, abusive or insulting words or behaviour with intent to cause others to fear violence or with intent to provoke others to use violence. This raises the question whether there was a satisfactory justification for the further police powers and wider offence in section 5: the requirements of section 5 are so modest and broadly-stated that it could be used to cast the net of criminality very wide. Research into the use of section 5 shows just this: although the reliance of the police on section 5 varies considerably from area to area, one feature is that it has been much used to criminalize people who swear at police officers.[3] This demonstrates at once the use by the police of public order offences as 'resources' to use when people show disrespect,[4] and also the way in which criminalization ostensibly aimed at one set of situations (e.g. disturbing residents by kicking over dustbins) can then be adapted to deal with situations for which its use was not envisaged (i.e. swearing at the police).

The Criminal Justice and Public Order Act 1994 contains various new crimes aimed at penalizing trespassers on land. For many years the general principle has been that trespass to land is not appropriate for criminalization—there are civil remedies, disputes are better decided in the civil courts, and accelerated orders for possession are available to landowners. A few exceptional offences did exist before, but the 1994 Act goes much further by criminalizing aggravated trespass on land with intent to disrupt lawful activities thereon (section 68), by extending the police power to order trespassers off land, with associated offences for non-compliance (section 61), by permitting house owners to take stronger action against squatters (section 72), and by creating a new offence of unauthorized camping (section 77). There may be more political symbolism in these new offences than a real prospect of large-scale police action, but the offences are now on the statute book and several questions arise. Is such conduct so serious that the criminal law ought to be invoked rather than the civil process? Is there not a danger that, as with the Public Order Act 1986, section 5, the wide drafting of these offences will permit their use by the police against other forms of conduct? Aggravated trespass is an offence supposedly aimed at hunt saboteurs, but its wording could encompass many other forms of protest.[5] Unauthorized camping is an

---

[2] Compare A. T. H. Smith, *Offences against Public Order* (1987) with N. Lacey, C. Wells, and D. Meure, *Reconstructing Criminal Law* (1990), 106–27.

[3] D. Brown and T. Ellis, *Policing low-level disorder: Police use of Section 5 of the Public Order Act 1986* (1994).

[4] See the classic article by E. Bittner, 'The Police on Skid Row: a Study in Peacekeeping' (1967) 32 Amer Soc Rev, 699.

[5] A. T. H. Smith, 'The Public Order Offences' [1995] Crim LR, 19.

offence supposedly aimed at New Age travellers, but its wording is clearly apt to criminalize gypsies for following their long-established way of life.[6] Much will therefore turn on patterns of enforcement. If the experience of the 1986 Act, section 5, is a fair indicator, there will be local variations, with some police forces using the powers fully and others declining to do so, and with much depending on the dynamics of particular situations. Senior police officers have already expressed discomfort about enforcing the new offence of unauthorized camping against gypsies,[7] but perhaps the politicians are content that an offence has been created and thus 'something has been done about it'.

These two examples serve to illustrate the complexity of the issues that arise in the criminalization debate. Even on a theoretical plane, fixing the proper boundaries of the criminal law is likely to involve not sharp distinctions and clearly defined categories, but rather judgments of degree relating to such matters as how proximate the harm should be to justify criminalization, and how relevant the availability of alternative mechanisms for enforcement should be. Although in practice examples of political pressures overcoming principled arguments are abundant, they do not account for all instances of criminalization. In some spheres such as financial regulation there is constant debate about the proper boundaries of criminal and regulatory or civil controls.[8] In others, such as bail offences, law enforcement agents themselves may be the main force behind criminalization. In others it may be a report of the Law Commission or other committee, after due consultation, that results in new criminal laws. And in still others, the political argument may be won by a pressure group which has campaigned for expanding the criminal law in areas such as domestic violence, drinking and driving, and so forth. Sheer vote winning, or preserving the position of the powerful over the powerless, accounts for some, but certainly not all, decisions to create new crimes. There is therefore good reason to embark on an exploration of the issues of principle which ought to have a bearing on decisions to criminalize.

2.2 THE PRINCIPLE OF INDIVIDUAL AUTONOMY

At the foundation of criminal liability lies the principle of individual autonomy—that each individual should be treated as responsible for his or her own behaviour. This principle has factual and normative elements that must be explored, briefly, in turn.

---

[6] S. Campbell, 'Gypsies: Criminalising a Way of Life?' [1995] Crim LR, 28.
[7] E.g. Police *Police Review*, Nov. 1994.
[8] E.g. *Serious Fraud Office, Annual Report 1993–94* (1994), 20, on discussions between the Securities and Investment Board and the Serious Fraud Office on these matters.

The factual element in autonomy is that individuals in general have the capacity and sufficient free will to make meaningful choices. Whether this is true cannot be demonstrated conclusively. Over the centuries the 'free will' argument has been contradicted by the 'determinist' claim that all human behaviour is determined by causes that ultimately each individual cannot control. There is an immense literature on these issues, which cannot be examined here.[9] Most philosophers arrive at compromise positions which enable them to accept the fundamental proposition that behaviour is not so determined that blame is generally unfair and inappropriate, and yet to accept that, in certain circumstances, behaviour may be so strongly determined (e.g. by threats from another) that the normal presumption of free will may be displaced. Similar in many ways is the 'principle of alternative possibilities', according to which an individual may properly be held responsible for conduct only if he or she could have done otherwise.[10] In support of these approaches is the fact that most of everyday life is conducted on the basis of such beliefs in individual responsibility, and that in the absence of proof of determinism we should not abandon those assumptions of free will that pervade so many of our social practices.

The factual element in autonomy is rarely stated without qualification. It depends on a general assumption, and the capacities it assumes may not be present in those who are too young or who are mentally disordered. These types of case are discussed later,[11] and for the moment the discussion should be confined to those whom we may call sane adults. In principle, they may properly be held liable for their conduct and for matters within their control, except in so far as they can point to some excuse for their conduct (such as insanity, duress, mistake, and other matters discussed in Chapter 6).

No less important a part of the principle of autonomy are its normative elements: that individuals should be respected and treated as agents capable of choosing their acts and omissions, and that without allowing independence of action to individuals they could hardly be regarded as moral persons.[12] Some such principles lie at the centre of most liberal political theory, and can be found, for example, in Ronald Dworkin's principle that each individual is entitled to equal concern and respect.[13] The principle of autonomy assigns great importance to liberty and individual rights in any discussion of what the state ought to do in a given situation. Indeed, a major part of its thrust is that individuals should be

[9] For an accessible discussion, see A. Kenny, *Freewill and Responsibility* (1978).
[10] For critical discussion, see e.g. J. Fischer, 'Responsibility and Control' (1982) 79 Journal of Philosophy, 24.   [11] See Ch 6.2.
[12] See D. N. MacCormick, *Legal Right and Social Democracy* (1982), 23–4.
[13] R. Dworkin, *Taking Rights Seriously* (1977), 180.

protected from official censure, through the criminal law, unless they can be shown to have chosen the conduct for which they are being held liable. This, as we shall see in 2.4 below, is a central element in the 'defensive' approach to criminalization advanced by Nils Jareborg and others, insisting on the importance of protecting individuals from undue state power.[14] We will see later that H. L. A. Hart's famous principle, that an individual should not be held criminally liable unless he had the capacity and a fair opportunity to do otherwise, is also grounded in the primary importance of individual autonomy.[15] On the other hand, returning to the scope of criminalization, this emphasis on individual choice militates against creating offences based on paternalistic grounds, as we shall see in 2.6 below. If the autonomy of individuals is to be respected, the state should not take decisions 'in their own best interests' but should leave the individuals to decide for themselves.

In liberal theory, the principle of autonomy goes much further than this. Thus Joel Feinberg, towards the end of his discussion of autonomy, states that:

the most basic autonomy-right is the right to decide how one is to live one's life, in particular how to make the critical life-decisions—what courses of study to take, what skills and virtues to cultivate, what career to enter, whom or whether to marry, which church if any to join, whether to have children, and so on.[16]

The difficulty is to decide how far this is to be taken. While the principle of autonomy gives welcome strength to the protection of individual interests against collective and state interests, it seems less convincing in other spheres. In some of its formulations it pays little or no attention to the social context in which all of us are brought up, which both restricts and facilitates the pursuit of certain desired ends. The idea that individuals should be free to choose what to do is quite unsustainable without wide-ranging qualifications. This has led several modern liberals to develop autonomy-based theories which find a central place for certain collective goals, seen as creating the necessary conditions for maximum autonomy. Thus Joseph Raz argues that:

Three main features characterize the autonomy-based doctrine of freedom. First, its primary concern is the promotion and protection of positive freedom which is understood as the capacity for autonomy, consisting of the availability of an adequate range of options, and of the mental abilities necessary for an autonomous life. Secondly, the state has the duty not merely to prevent the denial of freedom,

[14] See Ch 2.
[15] H. L. A. Hart, *Punishment and Responsibility* (1968), discussed in Ch 6.9.
[16] J. Feinberg, *Harm to Self* (1986), 54; cf. his extensive discussion of autonomy in Chs 17, 18, and 19 of that work.

but also to promote it by creating the conditions of autonomy. Thirdly, one may not pursue any goal by means which infringe people's autonomy unless such action is justified by the need to protect or promote the autonomy of those people or of others.[17]

This third feature proposes a minimalist approach to the use of the criminal law, and all three features reappear when we come to consider the principle of welfare.

2.3 THE PRINCIPLE OF WELFARE

The individualist principle of autonomy outlined earlier is not a coherent, or at least not a complete, normative theory. This is why Raz and others have developed an approach which emphasizes the state's obligation to create the social conditions necessary for the exercise of full autonomy by individual citizens.[18] Modern communitarian theorists have gone further, often emphasizing the centrality of collective goals. Thus Nicola Lacey describes the principle of welfare as including 'the fulfilment of certain basic interests such as maintaining one's personal safety, health and capacity to pursue one's chosen life plan'.[19] The specification of the interests to be thus protected should be a matter for democratic (participatory) decision-making: this means both that the interests will be objectively determined, not just according to the preference of each individual, and also that individuals whose preferences are at odds with those of the majority would lose out. Both of these are familiar features of social life. The individualistic principle of autonomy seems to suggest that citizens should be free to determine these matters for themselves, individually, whereas the principle of welfare recognizes the social context of the law.[20] It is more realistic, however, to recognize that the principles of autonomy and welfare do not always or necessarily conflict: if the principle of autonomy is taken to require a form of positive liberty rather than merely negative liberty, then the principle of welfare may work towards the same end by ensuring that citizens benefit from the existence of facilities and structures which are protected, albeit in the last resort, by the criminal law. Some criminalization may therefore be accepted as the only justifiable means of upholding certain social practices as 'necessary for the general good'. Matters such as the obligation to state one's income accurately for the purpose of taxation or the receipt of benefits can hardly be analysed convincingly in terms of individual autonomy: once a public

---

[17] Raz, *The Morality of Freedom* (1986), 425.
[18] Ibid., passim.
[19] Lacey, *State Punishment* (1988), 104.
[20] See Feinberg, *Harm to Self*, 37–47 for discussion.

decision has been made about the system to be adopted, it may be justifiable for at least egregious departures from these rules to be criminalized. The same may be said of laws relating to industrial safety, food safety, environmental protection, and so on. Although it remains to be decided whether violations of these norms should be criminalized or dealt with in some other way, the legitimacy of some criminalization on the basis of welfare as well as on the basis of autonomy cannot be put in doubt.[21] Those versions of the principle of autonomy which suggest that individuals should remain free to decide these matters according to their own preferences are not sustainable.

Yet the value of autonomy as a counterpoint to collective and state action should not be overlooked. In so far as the principle of welfare refers to collective decisions taken in the general interest, it may sometimes go too far. There should be certain aspects of individual autonomy that are assigned a special status, perhaps by calling them individual rights. The core of the principle of autonomy is therefore to be found in the insistence that certain rights of individuals should be granted protected status, even against majority interests. This is one of the principles underlying the European Convention on Human Rights (to be discussed further in Chapter 3), which protects such rights as the right to life, freedom from torture, the right to privacy, the right not to be discriminated against, and so forth. If some such rights are accepted, then this points to the position that 'the criminal law can be conceived as a set of norms backed up by the threat and imposition of sanctions, the function of which is to protect the autonomy and welfare of individuals and groups in society with respect to a set of basic goods, both individual and collective'.[22] This should not be taken, however, to deny the possibility of conflict or to deny the need to take further important decisions. It remains to be decided which individual interests should be regarded as sufficiently fundamental to 'trump' other considerations in most instances. It is argued below and in Chapter 3 that at least those rights declared in the European Convention on Human Rights should be protected from 'balancing' against collective interests. Thus even if it is accepted that the promotion of welfare involves 'the satisfaction of the conditions of *effective* autonomy', since the concept of the common good includes proper respect for 'equal effective autonomy of all',[23] respect for certain individual rights must be maintained while other conflicts relevant to criminalization are resolved.

---

[21] Alan Brudner, 'Agency and Welfare in the Penal Law', in S. Shute, J. Gardner and J. Horder (eds), *Action and Value in Criminal Law* (1993).

[22] Lacey, *State Punishment*, 104–5.

[23] Brudner, 'Agency and Welfare', 44.

2.4 HARM AND MINIMALISM

(a) General Principles

The obvious starting point of any discussion of criminalization is the 'harm principle'. It takes several different forms, but the essence is that the state is justified in criminalizing any conduct that causes harm to others or creates an unacceptable risk of harm to others. John Stuart Mill's statement of the principle is:

the only purpose for which power can be rightfully exercised over any member of a civilized community, against his will, is to prevent harm to others.[24]

This has been developed by Joel Feinberg, who adds arguments in favour of a further reason for criminalization: that it is necessary to prevent hurt or offence to citizens (his 'offence principle').[25] Two later volumes by Feinberg reject 'legal paternalism' and 'legal moralism' as sufficient reasons for criminalization.[26] One cannot proceed far without adopting a definition of harm: can one draw a satisfactory line through such things as physical harm, harm to property, harm to feelings, and indirect harm? The question is both fundamental and somewhat intractable. As Neil MacCormick argues:

'harm' is itself a morally loaded (and essentially contested) concept . . . Nothing . . . could be more obviously a moral question than the question whether individual interests in private property are always, sometimes, or never legitimate. The issue of the justice of systems of private property is a central one in the great clash of ideologies in the contemporary world.[27]

Thus if we wish to define harm in terms of violations of people's legitimate interests, we must remain conscious of the moral, cultural, and political nature of the interests recognized in a particular system. Feinberg's definition of harm as 'those states of set-back interest that are the consequence of wrongful acts or omissions of others'[28] bypasses these wider issues, but itself depends on the concept of 'interest' as matters in which a person has a legitimate stake.[29]

The larger part of Feinberg's work on *Harm to Others* is devoted to a question that becomes crucial for harm theorists: since it is unlikely to be acceptable that a censuring and punitive institution such as the criminal law should be invoked wherever there is any harm to another, how should the

---

[24] J. S. Mill, *On Liberty*, Ch 1, para 9.

[25] J. Feinberg, *Offense to Others* (1986), finding some support in Mill, *On Liberty*, Ch 5, para 7. For discussion, see 2.6 below.

[26] J. Feinberg, *Harm to Self*, and J. Feinberg, *Harmless Wrongdoing* (1988).

[27] MacCormick, *Legal Right and Social Democracy*, 29.

[28] Feinberg, *Harm to Others*, 215.   [29] Ibid., 31–6.

principle be formulated and what limitations on it should be recognized? Feinberg proposes the following definition of the harm principle:

It is always a good reason in support of penal legislation that it would probably be effective in preventing (eliminating, reducing) harm to persons other than the actor *and* there is probably no other means that is equally effective at no greater cost to other values.[30]

One limitation is what the drafters of the Model Penal Code call the '*de minimis* principle'—that the law should not criminalize trifling wrongs.[31] In discussing other possible limitations, Feinberg concludes that the answer often turns on a conscientious balancing of the risk to rights or interests compared with the social value of the conduct. Thus he draws attention to the gravity of the possible harm, its degree of probability, the value of the (otherwise dangerous) conduct.[32]

   In this form the harm principle seems to state a sensible, even inevitable, approach to delineating the boundaries of the criminal law. Yet it lacks a clear focus on the distinctiveness of the criminal sanction, and on the need for special justifications for invoking penal rather than civil or regulatory controls. This focus is supplied by the minimalist approach. Minimalism accepts the need for criminal law in order to safeguard the interests of individuals, the state and collectivities, but it emphasizes the protection of individuals from the abuse of power—whether by state officials or by groups or other individuals. Among other things, the minimalist approach emphasizes respect for the rights of individuals as suspects and defendants (requiring criminal laws to punish only the culpable, and to conform with, for example, the European Convention on Human Rights), and it insists that the criminal law 'should be used only as a last resort or for the most reprehensible types of wrongdoing'.[33] Thus minimalism has no difficulty in accepting the criminalization of direct, victimizing wrongs that harm individuals; but as one moves away from those clear cases, it demands stronger justifications for criminalizing rather than dealing with the problem in another way. The liberal principle of individual autonomy is respected by preserving as wide an area for individuals to make their choices as is compatible with a like freedom for others.
   What kinds of justification for extending the criminal law beyond direct victimizing harms might be accepted? There are some general obligations of citizens that are so important that the criminal sanction might be

---

[30] Feinberg, *Harm to Others*, 26.
[31] American Law Institute, Model Penal Code, s 2.12.
[32] Ibid., Ch 5.
[33] Nils Jareborg, 'What Kind of Criminal Law do we want?', in *Scandinavian Studies in Criminology* (forthcoming, 1995), where he develops a model of 'defensive criminal law policy' that is similar to the minimalist approach.

justified to reinforce them. A core of offences against state security may be justified on these grounds, as may offences against the taxation and benefits system, so long as the thrust of the minimalist principle (last resort, significantly reprehensible conduct) is kept in view. Some would place road traffic offences under this justification, although certain motoring offences involve fairly direct victimization. The difficult issue is whether there are acceptable justifications for going further, and a number of questions may be raised. Is it justifiable to create criminal offences in order to prevent adults from harming themselves? The issue of paternalistic legislation is considered in 2.6 below. Is it acceptable to penalize a person for conduct that may eventually lead to harm being caused either by that person or by another? The problem of remote harms is discussed in 2.7. Is it right to criminalize people who help and advise others to cause harm? This is examined in Chapter 10. Is it right to criminalize, not just direct victimizing harms but also attempts, incitement and conspiracies to cause such harms? These questions are considered in Chapter 11.

The answers to these questions will be affected by the degree of one's commitment to either the principle of autonomy or the principle of welfare on a given issue. We saw in 2.3 that the principle of welfare is likely to favour the use of criminal law to reinforce collective interests rather than private interests and private property, and strong communitarians might be expected to favour a root-and-branch revision of the criminal law in order to achieve that. Yet adherents to the principle of welfare might also be minimalists, that is, they might insist that the criminal sanction should be used as a last resort and only for significantly reprehensible conduct. Someone whose concept of autonomy recognizes the importance of positive liberty may be fairly close to the welfare minimalist, since both would recognize the position of individuals in their social context and thus the need in some circumstances to use the criminal law to prevent incursions on some collective goods as well as on individual rights.

Thus the basic principle is the harm principle: the reduction of harm to others is always a good reason in support of penal legislation. Minimalism draws attention to the criminal law's role as generally the most powerful form of censure, and thus advocates the minimum use of criminalization. In most systems it is hardly practical to restrict the criminal law to direct, victimizing harms. Some obligations of individuals towards the collectivity should be reinforced by the criminal sanction, and we have also mentioned other forms of harm, such as remote harms and harms to self, which will be considered further below. For the remainder of this section, however, we return to the minimalist principle and develop it in the context of some common arguments.

(b) In Favour of Minimalism

The minimalist approach is based on a particular conception of the relationship of the criminal law to other forms of social control. The criminal law is a preventive mechanism, but there are others. Morality, social convention, and peer pressure are three informal sources of control, and in many spheres it seems preferable to leave the regulation of certain behaviour to those forces. Within the law itself there are at least two other major techniques in addition to criminalization: there is civil liability, best exemplified by the laws of tort and contract, and administrative regulation, which includes such measures as licensing and franchizing. What considerations should determine the choice of technique? The obvious answer, particularly for the minimalist, would be that the law's most coercive and condemnatory technique (criminalization) should be reserved for the most serious invasions of interests. Less serious misconduct is more appropriately dealt with by the civil law, by administrative regulation, or even by introducing a new category of non-criminal financial levies.

There are, however, some situations in which it is hardly true that the criminal sanction is the most coercive—for example: the defendant in a defamation action who is ordered to pay a large sum in damages to the plaintiff; the bus company or insurance company whose operating licence is taken away; the council house tenant who is forced to move out of one house or flat to another; even the publican whose licence to run a public house is revoked. All of these might understandably, even justifiably, view a criminal conviction as preferable—even conviction for an offence that is serious enough for minimalists to accept as a proper part of the criminal law (e.g. not strict liability offences). It follows that there are ways of controlling conduct by censure and threats that do not involve criminalization. These are unlikely to apply to many forms of conduct between individuals that the criminal law has traditionally (and rightly) included, but their existence illustrates one of the abiding uncertainties about the proper reach of the criminal law. Indeed, those uncertainties have a further dimension, for one might wish to argue that financial penalties imposed by regulators on those who are regulated ought to be viewed as punishments,[34] raising the question whether regulation does not involve a species of criminalization.

How does minimalism stand in relation to arguments founded on effectiveness?[35] These encompass both the restrictive policy that the

---

[34] In May 1994, the Norwich Union insurance company was fined £300,000 by the Securities Investment Board for breaches of the official code of practice by many of its sales staff.

[35] See now the discussion by J. Schonsheck, *On Criminalization* (1994), Ch 3.

criminal law should not be used if it cannot be effective in controlling conduct, and/or causes consequences at least as bad as non-criminalization, and the expansive policy that the criminal law should be used if it is the most efficient and cost-effective means of controlling conduct. The restrictive policy is a straightforward utilitarian consideration, traceable back to Jeremy Bentham's injunction not to punish 'where it must be inefficacious: where it cannot act so as to prevent the mischief', and 'where the mischief may be prevented . . . without it: that is, at a cheaper rate'.[36] This view may be challenged on the ground that, if conduct is serious or harmful enough to justify criminalization, there is at least an important symbolic reason for declaring it to be criminal. It was suggested in 2.1 above that the purposes of the criminal law are threefold: declaratory, preventive, and censuring. The declaratory purpose may reassure some and deter others. But even if the preventive purpose is largely unfulfilled (as, perhaps, with the 30 m.p.h. speed limit on urban roads), it may achieve some degree of prevention or reduction of the unwanted behaviour. Thus limited efficacy is not necessarily an argument against criminalization, although it provides a good reason to search for supplementary ways of controlling the unwanted conduct. Perhaps the restrictive policy against 'ineffective' laws is a version of the argument that the inclusion of unenforceable offences may bring the criminal law into disrepute: if so, it must be established that the patchy enforcement of speed limits, for example, really does diminish people's respect for other parts of the criminal law.[37] The other thrust of the restrictive policy is more powerful: if the criminalization of certain conduct, such as the possession of soft drugs or various 'vice' offences, gives rise to social consequences that are hardly better than the mischief at which the laws aim, this militates strongly in favour of decriminalization. Thus, drugs and vice laws may:

1. produce active 'black markets';
2. lead the police to adopt intrusive means of enforcement;
3. allow the police to be selective in their enforcement; and
4. lead to a degree of police corruption.[38]

Prohibitions that have these consequences ought to be reconsidered, although in some cases (such as hard drugs) it might be concluded that the case for criminalization outweighs the side effects. This leads on to a more general argument for restraint in criminalization: that, since the enforcement of the criminal law is selective and tends to bear down most heavily on the least advantaged, these injustices should be kept to a minimum.

---

[36] J. Bentham, *Introduction to the Principles of Morals and Legislation* (1789), Ch 13.
[37] Cf. the assertions in S. Kadish, *Blame and Punishment* (1987), 23, 57.
[38] See Kadish, ibid., 22–8, for elaboration of this argument.

Turning to the expansive policy of using the criminal law wherever it is likely to be cost-efficient, this has been an integral element in English criminal legislation for many years. It is rarely spelt out, but underlies the creation and re-enactment every year of scores of offences with low penalties, attached to statutes on sundry matters from the Osteopaths Act 1993 to the Charities Act 1993. There are, however, two arguments of principle against this policy. One is that culpability is central to the notion of wrongdoing, and most of these offences contain little or no culpability requirement. The other is the minimalist principle, also expressed in the *de minimalis* limitation, that the criminal law should not be used for minor wrongs. While some of these 'regulatory' offences are clearly not minor, others are. English law lacks a general sanctioning system which does not involve the censure of the criminal law—a system of civil violations, infractions, or administrative wrongs. This makes it even more unlikely that decisions to criminalize are preceded by a vigorous examination of whether some non-criminal sanction would be sufficient. Small wonder that the expansive policy leads to over-criminalization.

Having identified the harm principle and minimalism, and having considered some other issues relating to criminalization, it is evident that in concrete cases judgments of seriousness are bound to be a critical factor. The possibility of establishing a principled basis for such judgments is explored next.

2.5 ASSESSING THE SERIOUSNESS OF OFFENCES

The practical importance of the enquiry is manifest. The decision to create a criminal offence to cover certain conduct or omissions has obvious consequences for citizens and law-enforcement officers. Where an offence has been created, the maximum penalty assigned to it determines the extent both of the court's powers and of the offender's liability to punishment. The maximum penalties attached to offences may also be taken to convey the relative seriousness of the types of offence: indeed, one of the main functions of criminal law is to express the *degree* of wrongdoing, not simply the fact of wrongdoing. This is integral to determining the proper label for the offence and the appropriate degree of punishment. Moreover, the differing degrees of seriousness have wider practical consequences for the:

- legality of arrest without warrant;
- lawfulness of searches;
- decision to prosecute or to caution;
- decision to try the case in the Crown Court or the magistrates' court;
- sentencing powers of the court;

- decision to release a prisoner on parole; and
- many other considerations at various stages in the criminal process.

We must enquire, therefore, not only whether the behaviour is serious enough to be made into a criminal offence, but also, if it is an offence, how serious it is when compared with other crimes.

It is not difficult to see some toeholds for the assessment of relative seriousness. There is a widely held view that, in general, offences of violence are more serious than property offences. Thus Lord Lane CJ, assessing the relative seriousness of frauds on the social security system, remarked that 'it must be remembered that they are non-violent, non-sexual and non-frightening crimes'.[39] However, the very breadth of modern systems of criminal law means that this point is no more than a toehold. It is not difficult to think of circumstances in which an offence against property (say, stealing £1 million) might be thought more serious than a particular offence of violence (such as one person pushing another while queuing). Thus it is necessary to press the enquiry further by examining those values or interests which are protected by the offence, and those elements which distinguished it from other similar offences. This task soon reveals a bewildering number of separate factors. When passing sentence, the courts have to range the different crimes along a single scale of relative gravity (represented by imprisonment, fines, and other non-custodial sentences). Is it possible to range the various offences along a single scale of social seriousness?

There are some who would argue that, academically interesting though this enquiry might be, it is quite unnecessary in practice, because most people in most countries agree on the relative gravity of harms. Research by the criminologists Sellin and Wolfgang purported to find considerable agreement in ranking criminal offences, whether amongst people from different countries or from different social groups in one country.[40] However, the questions asked in this research were relatively unsophisticated for the purpose of the criminal law,[41] and its findings cannot sustain the argument that it is unnecessary to think further about the grading of crimes as more or less serious. It is true that those American states which have recently introduced sentencing guidelines for their courts had no great difficulty in ranking the offences,[42] but that should not stifle deeper

[39] *Stewart* (1987) 9 Cr App R (S) 135, at 138.
[40] See the Introduction to the revised edition of T. Sellin and M. Wolfgang, *The Measurement of Delinquency* (1978).
[41] Of the many writings on this issue, see P. Rossi, *et al.*, 'Beyond Crime Seriousness: Fitting the Punishment to the Crime' (1985) *Journal of Quantitative Criminology*, 29; and F. T. Cullen *et al.*, 'Consensus in Crime Seriousness: Empirical Reality or Methodological Artefact' (1985) 23 *Criminology*, 99.
[42] See e.g. Ch 5 of A. von Hirsch, K. A. Knapp, and M. Tonry, *The Sentencing Commission and its Guidelines* (1987).

enquiry. After all, the 1980s saw several distinct shifts in the seriousness with which certain forms of offence were viewed—for example, rape, drunken driving, reckless driving, corruption of public officials, and insider dealing on the stock market are all offences which came to be viewed as relatively more serious, as people gained greater awareness of their consequences or their reprehensible unfairness. The arguments for and against changes of this kind are based, surely, on elements of the various crimes and on their value or importance when compared with other crimes. It is arguments of this kind that we are assessing and developing here.

    Another claim is that there is no point in considering offence-seriousness without examining the social structure as a whole, since the criminal law is a reflection of the interests of the powerful in society. This is especially true with enforcement, it is argued, where the often public misbehaviour of the disadvantaged members of society is prosecuted with vigour while the often private crimes of the powerful go unprosecuted: the shoplifter and the late-night brawler go to court, while the tax evader and the industrial polluter go to their club. And, the argument continues, this is also the case with the criminal law itself, since the law provides serious offences with heavy penalties for street violence and public disorder, while providing few offences with relatively low penalties for offences concerned with industrial safety, product safety, and pollution (the social consequences of which can be damaging on a wide-spread scale). An attempt to treat these claims seriously is made below, but their limitations are not difficult to find. It is unlikely to be the case that the whole of the criminal law can be explained purely in terms of conflicts between different social groups, with the powerful imposing their will and their values on the disadvantaged. The possibility of a kind of fundamental 'moral order' should not be ruled out: even a pluralist society with opposing interest groups may share some basic tenets of right and wrong in social behaviour.[43]

    Is it possible to identify any agreed interests that ought to be protected by the criminal law? Some core interests are not difficult to state in general terms (e.g. physical integrity), and there are other widely accepted interests such as personal property. Whether there is a sufficient interest in maintaining a fair financial market (insider trading), or in maintaining the integrity of marriage records (bigamy), for example, is a more difficult issue. In order to take the subject further, the pathbreaking work of Andrew von Hirsch and Nils Jareborg should be introduced.[44] Their essay

---

[43] See Paul Rock, 'The Sociology of Deviancy and Conceptions of Moral Order' (1974) 14 BJ Criminology, 139.
[44] A. von Hirsch and N. Jareborg, 'Gauging Criminal Harms: a Living Standard Analysis' (1991) 11 Oxford JLS, 1, summarized and re-stated in A. von Hirsch, *Censure and Sanctions* (1993), 29–33.

is confined to assessing the seriousness of crimes with individual victims, and their method is to assess the effect of the typical case of particular crimes upon the living standard of typical victims. First, in order to determine what interests are violated or threatened by the standard case of the crime, they identify four generic interests:

1. physical integrity: health, safety, and the avoidance of physical pain;
2. material support and amenity: includes nutrition, shelter, and other basic amenities;
3. freedom from humiliation or degrading treatment; and
4. privacy and autonomy.

The interests affected by the typical case of the crime are then analysed in these terms. Once the nature of the interest(s) violated has been settled, the second step is to estimate the degree to which the living standard of the typical victim would be affected by a typical case of the crime. The idea of 'living standard' refers to the means and capabilities that would ordinarily conduce to the achievement of a good life. Four degrees of effect are set out:

1. subsistence: survival with maintenance of elementary human functions;
2. minimal well-being: maintenance of a minimal level of comfort and dignity;
3. adequate well-being: maintenance of an adequate level of comfort and dignity; and
4. significant enhancement: significant enhancement in quality of life above the merely adequate level.

The question is, therefore, would the typical case affect the typical victim's life at the level of significant enhancement, adequate well-being, minimal well-being, or subsistence? One benefit of this approach is that it moves away from traditional assumptions by rating conduct such as the maintenance of an unsafe workplace or an unsafe transport system at the same level as causing serious injury or death. Of course there are other issues to be discussed, as we shall see in the next two paragraphs. But, in terms of harmfulness, the typical cases are on a par.

   One further dimension of seriousness, though not of harmfulness, is culpability. We will postpone full discussion of that until Chapter 5, but it will be noticed that culpability may create a difference in seriousness between the intentional killer and the negligent operator of a factory whose machines kill, or equally between the negligent killer and the factory owner who knowingly puts employees at risk of serious harm. We have already noted the importance of the culpability requirement in the debate about criminalization, and so the issue will not be taken further here.

Also relevant to seriousness is the question of remoteness. How can one assess the seriousness of offences such as attempts, conspiracies, drunk driving, or possession, which may cause no actual harm? Attempts and conspiracies might be dealt with on the basis of the intended harm, together with the culpability, perhaps making some reduction in the level of seriousness to reflect the fact that no harm was caused and that the danger was more or less remote. However, the scale of the reduction in seriousness would vary according to whether one adopts a harm-based or a fault-based approach—a debate that is outlined later in Chapters 5 and 11. For the present, it is sufficient to note that there are degrees of remoteness: an attempted crime may be very close to being a completed crime, whereas an offence of risk-creation such as drunk driving may be fairly remote, and an offence of possession (e.g. of an offensive weapon) may be very remote from the occurrence of actual harm.

In essence, then, we may distinguish five stages in the calculation of offence-seriousness that von Hirsch and Jareborg propose:

1. the interests violated by the offence are identified;
2. the effect on a typical victim's living standard is quantified on the scale ranging from offences that merely affect significant enhancement to those that affect subsistence;
3. the culpability of the offender is taken into account;
4. the level of seriousness may be reduced to reflect the remoteness of the offence from the actual harm; and
5. transfer this assessment on to a scale that in some way quantifies the degree of seriousness.

It would be possible to devise an elaborate 100-point scale for this, but von Hirsch and Jareborg say that this would give the impression of a 'misleading sense of precision',[45] and their preference is for a scale with five broad bands. This both allows further adjustment within each band and signifies that it remains a rather approximate enterprise.

Inexact it may be, but the enterprise is essential. Judgments of relative seriousness are made frequently in all walks of life—not just by legislators when deciding whether to criminalize and what maximum penalty to assign to an offence, but also by judges and magistrates when sentencing, and also by lay people in commenting on whether the official response is proportionate. The value of the von Hirsch–Jareborg approach is that it identifies the stages of thought through which it is desirable to pass when making these judgments. In practice many of the judgments are made impressionistically, often on the basis of traditional assumptions about the

[45] Ibid., 28.

ranking of offences. The von Hirsch–Jareborg approach urges one to dig deeper, and to look more closely at the interests affected. However, their approach is confined to harms with individual victims. It awaits development to deal with the myriad other forms of conduct that modern systems of criminal law tend to criminalize. For example, what about offences of theft or deception committed against a wealthy company, or against the state? It would hardly make sense to refer to the typical effect on the living standard of the victim here, since many small or even moderate thefts have, at least individually, no significant effect. What about offences against the state and against the administration of justice? It is one thing to argue that offences of espionage may pose a threat to national security; it is quite another thing to transfer this assessment on to a scale of gravity, such as the scale that runs from threats to significant enhancement up to threats to subsistence. Similarly with an offence such as perjury: telling lies in court is a 'serious matter', but how can it be related to a scale of seriousness constructed with reference to harms to individual victims?

The task of assessing the seriousness of offences is therefore as complex and problematic as it is unavoidable and fundamental. The first step in the von Hirsch–Jareborg approach is to consider the generic interests to be protected, and perhaps greater attention should be paid to this. They identify four such interests relevant to harms with individual victims: physical integrity, material support and amenity, freedom from humiliation or degrading treatment, and privacy and autonomy. At least three of these individual rights are recognized explicitly in the European Convention on Human Rights and Fundamental Freedoms. Thus physical integrity is covered by Article 2, which declares that 'everyone's right to life shall be protected by law', and by Article 5: 'everyone has the right to liberty and security of person'. Article 3 declares that 'no one shall be subjected to torture or to inhuman or degrading treatment or punishment'. In part this provision is aimed at governments and at their sentencing systems; but it also yields a more general right not to be subjected to degrading treatment by non-governmental agencies or other individuals. Article 8 formulates a right to privacy. There is one further provision in the European Convention relevant to harms with individual victims, and that is Article 14:

The enjoyment of the rights and freedoms set forth in this Convention shall be secured without discrimination on any ground such as sex, race, colour, language, religion, political or other opinion, national or social origin, association with a national minority, property, birth or other status.

In one sense this might be thought to add nothing of substance. If the generic interests are applied faithfully, there will be no discrimination. However, the actual protection of interests in any particular legal system at a given stage in its history is likely to reflect a number of cultural biasses. Notably, there may well be provisions that result, either directly or indirectly, in the differential treatment of conduct on grounds of class, gender, or race. For example, until 1985 English law provided a maximum punishment of two years' imprisonment for indecent assault on a woman and 10 years' imprisonment for indecent assault on a male;[46] and until 1994 there were separate offences for the conduct of raping a woman and raping a man, with a higher maximum penalty for the former.[47] The Criminal Justice and Public Order Act 1994 might be thought to run counter to Article 14 and its injunction not to discriminate by reference to 'property . . . and other status', in so far as its provisions single out for criminalization those trespassers who are hunt saboteurs or unauthorized campers. The importance of Article 14, then, is that it performs the functions of reasserting the right to equal treatment and of drawing attention to possible sources of discrimination in the criminal law.

The European Convention supplies further candidates for an authoritative list of individual rights—at least, if one casts the net wider than von Hirsch and Jareborg, who limit themselves to harms with individual victims. Thus Article 9 proclaims the right to 'freedom of thought, conscience and religion'; Article 10 establishes a 'right to freedom of expression'; and Article 11 declares the 'right to freedom of peaceful assembly and to freedom of association with others'. Rights of this kind will be of particular importance to the minimalist, since they place limitations on the kinds of laws that may be created under the umbrella of 'crimes against public order'. None of this suggests that the European Convention is beyond criticism or improvement, and there are some obvious candidates for addition to the list of legally protected interests. Protection of the vulnerable, such as the young and the mentally handicapped, is surely worthy of recognition. Offences which arise out of paternalism, such as the selling of tobacco to children, and crimes of intercourse with persons who are under 16 or who are mentally handicapped, illustrate how this interest may be protected. To cater for offences against the administration of justice, it might be fair to add the interest in the integrity of the administration of justice. It might seem natural to add a reference to the interest in the security of the state: the obvious difficulty here is that this heading could be so broad as to encompass almost any act of disrespect to the government, but that is no less a difficulty with the other interests declared. Reliance must be placed on the other stages to refine the assessment in terms of culpability and remoteness. Which of the interests, if any, deals adequately with

---

[46] The Sexual Offences (Amendment) Act 1985 raised the former maximum to 10 years.
[47] See now Criminal Justice and Public Order Act, s 142.

environmental harms? They could be regarded as affecting 'material support and amenity', but much would turn on the meaning attributed to amenity. Clearly there is a considerable distance to travel before we can draw up a list of recognized interests that would help in accepting or rejecting proposals for criminalization.

In order to show that some progress can be made, the next five sections of this Chapter will discuss some controversial issues in criminalization: 'moral' harms; omissions; minor harms; conduct that will only result in harm if a further decision is taken; and so-called victimless crimes. This will give the opportunity to explore some issues of principle that arise in practical debates about the ambit of the criminal law.

2.6 MORALLY WRONG BEHAVIOUR

If certain behaviour is regarded as morally wrong, is this sufficient justification for the creation of a criminal offence? Such a principle is unlikely to be taken to the extreme, for example, of creating general offences of telling lies or breaking promises, but there have been vigorous debates about the proper ambit of the criminal law in the realms of sexual morality. In the notable exchanges between Lord Devlin and Professor Hart,[48] Devlin's argument was that a society is entitled to use the criminal law against behaviour which might threaten its existence; that there is a common morality which ensures that cohesion of society; that any deviation from this common morality is capable of affecting society injuriously; and that therefore it may be justifiable and necessary to penalize immoral behaviour.[49] In response, Devlin's opponents have broadly followed the approach of John Stuart Mill[50] in proclaiming that the only acceptable reason for criminalizing behaviour is that it causes harm to others, and that supposed 'immorality' is not a sufficient reason.

Lord Devlin's argument relies on an unacceptably loose concept of morality. He assumes that immorality is to be defined and measured according to the strength of feelings of ordinary people. If certain behaviour evokes feelings of intolerance, indignation, and disgust among ordinary members of society, that is a sufficient indication that the behaviour threatens the common morality and is therefore a proper object of the criminal law. The difficulty is that these feelings of ordinary people may not be moral in nature, but the expression of prejudice. If a person's reaction to certain behaviour is to be termed 'moral', it ought to be

---

[48] The principal essays written by the protagonists are collected in H. L. A. Hart, *Law, Liberty, and Morality* (1963), and P. Devlin, *The Enforcement of Morals* (1965).

[49] See P. Devlin, *The Enforcement of Morals*, Ch 1.

[50] John ˈStuart Mill, *On Liberty* (1859), passim.

grounded in reasons as well as in feelings, and those reasons ought to be consistent with other standards used by that individual to judge personal behaviour. A theory about morality and the criminal law must be based on a secure definition of morality, not one which confuses it with mere feelings of distaste and disgust.[51]

Is there, then, such a thing as a common morality? On core matters such as the use of force, fear, and fraud there may well be widely shared moral views, but on sexual matters the divergences may be great. Whose morals are to be a guide? Although Devlin maintained that morals and religion are inextricably joined, he did not argue that the teachings of the Established Church constitute the common morality. In this he was realistic: British society contains adherents of several religions, with diverse views on abortion, the control of prostitution, euthanasia, and so forth, and there is a large proportion of the population who profess no religion (though their moral codes may bear some traces of religious teachings). Devlin proposed that the common morality could be discovered by assembling a group of ordinary citizens, in the form of a jury, and asking them to reach decisions on certain types of behaviour. However, not only would this method confound prejudices with moral judgments, but it might also fail to elicit agreement on some subjects such as homosexual behaviour and abortion.

Devlin's opponents have tended to be in the individualistic liberal tradition, linking Mill's principle with Kantian ethics. According to this view, the law should respect the autonomy of each individual above all; it should treat persons as individuals and allow each to pursue his or her own conception of the good life subject only to the minimum number of constraints necessary to secure the same freedom to other individuals.[52] This is prominent in the minimalist approach to criminalization, and in a 'defensive' criminal law policy that treats the protection of individuals from state power as one of its principal objectives.[53] Its thrust, as generally that of the European Convention on Human Rights, is to argue for constraints on lawmaking so as to preserve individual rights, notably for those whose preferences are out of accord with social convention: democratic rule by majority should not be allowed to trample on the rights of individuals. This view has stronger foundations than Lord Devlin's, since it is distinctly a moral theory.

The same may be said of the harm principle which, in the version advanced by Mill and Feinberg, relies on an individualistic conception of autonomy and is therefore incompatible with Devlin's view. However, the

[51] R. M. Dworkin, *Taking Rights Seriously* (1977), Ch 10.
[52] See D. A. J. Richards, 'Rights, Utility and Crime' (1981) 3 Crime and Justice, 247.
[53] See Jareborg, 'What Kind of Criminal Law do we want?'.

European Convention on Human Rights fails to follow it through, qualifying the right of privacy declared in Article 8 by reference to interference 'necessary in a democratic society . . . for the protection of health or morals'. This seems to support the principle of paternalism, justifying the criminalization of harm and risks despite the individual's consent. Feinberg inveighs strongly against this: 'paternalistic interference is offensive morally because it invades the realm of personal autonomy where each competent, responsible adult should reign supreme'.[54] Some liberals, when discussing whether or not to criminalize the non-wearing of seat belts and crash helmets, for example, by people of all ages, might have recourse to the idea of 'harm to others': they might use Mill's principle to argue that the failure to wear seat belts may result in harm to others, in the sense that the individuals involved might become a burden to others, creating human misery and public expenditure that are easily avoidable. It is doubtful whether this style of argument succeeds. Once the concept of harm is extended to cover the risk of remote harms[55] and indirect hardship to other individuals or to the state, Mill's principle is blunted and the possibilities for criminalization are enormous. Either one must qualify Mill by adopting the strong version of paternalism criticized by Feinberg,[56] or one must recognize frankly that there is a competing principle at work here, such as the welfare principle described earlier. The welfare argument might be that it is strongly in the interests of the community, at a time when resources are limited, to avoid unnecessary expenditure on attending to the injuries of citizens who could protect themselves with little inconvenience.

Raz's approach to these issues interprets the harm principle in a different way. The state cannot and should not attempt to force citizens to be moral, but it should strive to provide the conditions for autonomy. Any use of coercion invades autonomy and thus defeats the purpose of promoting it, unless it is done in order to promote autonomy by preventing harm. This approach recognizes that although it may be right to pursue certain moral ideals so as to provide the condition for the exercise of autonomy, it is rarely justifiable to use coercion (or, for that matter, manipulation) so as to achieve this.[57] But it may be justifiable, and thus occasionally the link between criminalization and moral wrong may be recognized. Similarly, minimalists might favour the proposition that conduct should only be criminalized if it is morally wrong, and not simply when it is cost-effective or politically expedient.[58] Indeed, one might go further and argue that

---

[54] Feinberg, *Harmless Wrongdoing* (1988), xvii, summarizing the argument developed in Feinberg, *Harm to Self* (1986), Chs 18 and 19.
[55] Discussed in 2.9 below.
[56] Ibid.
[57] Raz, *The Morality of Freedom*, 420.
[58] See D. Husak, *Philosophy of Criminal Law* (1987), Ch 8, for a strong expression of this view.

certain morally wrong conduct should be criminalized. Although it was accepted earlier that there is no litmus test of moral wrongness, and that many judgments depend on principled argument within a particular cultural context, we can at least state this: that respect for personal autonomy means protecting individuals from being forced to act or debarred from acting in certain ways by the conduct of others, and that this may mean penalizing those who act towards others in these coercive ways.[59] This is a minimum principle: how much further, if at all, should we go?

Almost all theorists, even the most individualistic and 'neutral' liberals, should recognize an exception so as to ensure the protection of the young and the mentally disordered. The value of autonomy applies primarily to adults, and there are dangers in persons below the designated age of majority participating in heterosexual or homosexual activities, in drinking alcohol in public houses, in betting and gaming, etc. (In Britain this age varies according to the activity, and questions may be raised about the justification for this.) This principle of paternalism towards the vulnerable does not imply that all these activities are 'harmful': rather, it implies that they may have potentially far-reaching consequences for the individual concerned, and that only persons who have sufficient capacity should be allowed to take their own decisions about the potential risks. An example of the adjustment of conflicting policies and principles is provided by the report of the Wolfenden Committee on Homosexual Offences and Prostitution in 1957.[60] The Committee followed Mill's approach in asserting that 'there must remain a realm of private morality and immorality which is, in brief and crude terms, not the law's business', but it maintained also that this principle must interact with the need to protect the vulnerable against exploitation and corruption, and with the policy of protecting the citizen 'from what is offensive and injurious'. The protection of the vulnerable has already been discussed, but what about protecting all citizens (adults and the young) from 'offence'?

This goes beyond protection from harm on Feinberg's definition, since individuals can hardly be said to have a stake in not being shocked or offended.[61] The idea of offensive behaviour draws a public–private distinction in respect of decency and shock to feelings; what adults do in private is not the law's business, so long as harm is not inflicted, but what they do in the public domain may be the law's business if it is likely to give serious offence to the feelings of ordinary members of the public. Feinberg's 'offence principle' is that:

[59] See MacCormick, *Legal Right and Social Democracy*, 35–8.
[60] 1957, Cmnd 257.   [61] See n. 50.

It is always a good reason in support of a proposed criminal prohibition that it is probably necessary to prevent serious offence to persons other than the actor and would probably be an effective means to that end if enacted.[62]

This is not just a traditional utilitarian balancing exercise. Feinberg limits his principle to 'serious offence', and this leads him to argue that the judgment of whether to criminalize particular conduct depends always on a complex balancing process which gives particular weight to freedom of expression, except in a small number of cases of 'profound offence' (e.g. desecration of venerated symbols such as flags and icons, mistreatment of corpses).[63] The question of 'offensiveness' may well be involved in the criminalization of prostitution: the conduct itself ceased to be a crime with the Street Offences Act 1959, which was based on the Wolfenden proposals, but it is a crime for a woman to solicit for prostitution in a street, and (since 1985) for a man to solicit a woman for prostitution from a motor vehicle. These crimes are based on rationales of preserving people from offensive behaviour and preventing public nuisance. Similarly, homosexual acts between adult men in private are no longer criminal since the Sexual Offences Act 1967, but homosexual acts in public places (e.g. public lavatories) remain criminal—the public decency or 'offensiveness' rationale—and homosexual acts involving young people remain criminal on the rationale of protecting the vulnerable.[64] Another example of the public decency and offensiveness rationale may be found in the Indecent Displays (Control) Act 1981, which criminalizes the display of any indecent matter which is visible from a public place.

Is this public–private distinction securely based? The behaviour itself may not be morally wrong: the argument is that the psychological effects on ordinary citizens of witnessing events or advertisements which they regard as disgusting or immoral may be so great as to justify criminalization in the same way that the psychological effects of other crimes (e.g. rape, burglary) are taken to aggravate them. It is one thing to indulge in certain practices in private, but quite another thing to parade them in public. Feinberg, at a loss to drive this point home by abstract argument, invites his readers to imagine a ride on a bus during which they witness a number of things that might be perfectly normal in some settings (e.g. nudity, sexual intercourse) but which might well cause considerable offence if witnessed in a public place.[65] To accept this still leaves the awkward issue of drawing the line between sufficiently offensive and insufficiently

[62] Feinberg, *Offense to Others*, Ch 7.
[63] Feinberg, *Offense to Others*, Chs 8 and 9.
[64] Although there remains controversy about the appropriate age limit for protection: s 145 of the Criminal Justice and Public Order Act 1994 reduces the age from 21 to 18, but that is still higher than the age limit for heterosexual intercourse (16).
[65] Feinberg, *Offense to Others*, 10–24.

offensive conduct, a line which fluctuates not only with time but also from locality to locality. In Feinberg's view, much turns on the degree and generality of the disgust felt at certain conduct when done in public. However, even subject to his limitation to 'serious' offence, this may cast the net rather wide. There is a good case for incorporating some limiting considerations. Thus, enforced mutual proximity rather than mere publicness seems to be the distinguishing factor of Feinberg's example of the ride on the bus, and the fact that conduct is known to be insulting to a particular group (rather than mere offensiveness) is surely a better criterion for criminalization.[66]

2.7 CRIMINALIZING OMISSIONS

The common law has been wary of imposing criminal liability for omissions. While there has been a growing tendency for legislation to create offences of 'failing to do x', most of these have formed part of some elaborate statutory scheme of regulation of industry or commerce (e.g. the offence of failing to comply with a limitation, condition, or notice, contrary to the Radioactive Substances Act 1993, section 32, or the offence of failing to comply with a requirement imposed by the Professional Conduct Committee, contrary to the Osteopaths Act 1993, section 32), or of some other licensed and regulated activity such as driving (e.g. failing to report a road accident). In those contexts, people usually expect to have certain obligations imposed on them. Moreover, the obligations may be regarded as part of the conditions for engaging in certain activities. But what about the duties of the ordinary citizen in daily life? English criminal law has tended to restrict criminal liability for omissions by limiting the range of situations in which a duty can be said to arise. A parent's duty to ensure the health and safety of her or his child has long been recognized by statute;[67] a duty to care for another can be assumed by contract, or by undertaking the care of a relative, or even by undertaking the care of a stranger;[68] the owner of property may have a duty to prevent the commission of offences on or with that property;[69] and a person who creates a dangerous situation, even accidentally, has a duty to take steps to avert or minimize the

[66] The proposals of Andrew von Hirsch, reviewing Feinberg in 'Injury and Exasperation' (1986) 84 Michigan LR, 700.

[67] Children and Young Persons Act 1933, s 1.

[68] *Stone and Dobinson* [1977] QB 354, discussed by A. Ashworth, 'The Scope of Criminal Liability for Omissions' (1989) 105 LQR, 424, at 443–5; cf. the discussion of earlier authorities by P. R. Glazebrook, 'Criminal Omissions: the Duty Requirement in Offences against the Person' (1960) 56 LQR, 386.

[69] E.g. *DuCros* v *Lambourne* [1907] 1 KB 40 and *Tuck* v *Robson* [1970] 1 WLR 741, discussed in Ch 10 below.

danger.[70] Beyond those situations, there appear to be no general duties imposed on citizens.

This may seem anomalous and hard to justify when one considers the interests that the criminal law should protect: the interest of individual citizens in life and physical integrity would surely be close to the top of any rank order. Why, then, should we not criminalize the failure to render assistance to another citizen who is in peril, in cases where assistance can be rendered without danger to oneself? Three objections may be considered. First, it is objected that such an offence cannot be stated in other than vague terms: it is bound to include the term 'reasonable', to describe the steps that a citizen must take in order to avoid criminal liability, and this is unfair because it gives no clear warning to citizens of what they must do and when. That is an important claim and, as we shall see,[71] it arises in many parts of the criminal law. Secondly, it is objected that one consequence of this uncertainty is that much reliance is placed on prosecutorial discretion to define the effective scope of the law. This effect, also seen in some other parts of the criminal law, may be criticized as weakening the rule of law.[72] Thirdly, and perhaps most strikingly, it is objected that the imposition of liability for omissions requires much greater justification than the imposition of liability for acts. One argument is that there is a widely felt moral distinction between acts and omissions: 'we do much more moral wrong when we kill than when we fail to save, even when such failure violates a positive duty to prevent death'.[73] But even if such an intuition is widely felt, it would only establish that omissions are generally viewed less seriously than acts, not that they are unsuitable for criminalization. A stronger argument is that the imposition of a duty to act restricts one's liberty to pursue one's own ends and desires by requiring one to do a particular thing at a particular time (e.g. to call the emergency services, or to throw a lifebelt to a drowning person), whereas the normal prohibitions of the criminal law—do not injure, thieve, deceive, etc—leave one largely free to pursue one's own ends and desires. Thus those who place the principle of autonomy above all would be particularly opposed to omissions liability, even if they could be satisfied that omissions can fairly be regarded as the cause of harms to others in certain circumstances.[74] Those who do not count themselves as individualistic liberals might still balk at wider liability for omissions, pointing out that one key element in the principle of autonomy is that it protects

[70] *Miller* [1983] 2 AC 161, below, p. 109.
[71] The principle of fair warning is discussed in Ch 3 below.
[72] For general discussion, see Ch 3.4(i).
[73] M. Moore, *Act and Crime* (1993), 58.
[74] Feinberg, *Harm to Others*, 159–86.

individuals against unfair claims on their time and energy. Thus Alan Norrie, who makes much of the 'tension' between individualist and communitarian approaches to criminalization, argues that omissions liability is one of those fields in which liberalism provides a strong counterpoint to the more authoritarian tendencies that might result from making it a crime not to assist persons in peril and not to assist the police.[75]

Arguments such as these attribute little or no weight to the harm involved, and to the protection of the fundamental interest in life and physical integrity. Of course there is a 'tension' between omissions liability and the principle of maximum certainty, the principle of fair warning, and a principle of minimum restrictions on individual liberty. But these three principles are often to be found in tension with the protection of interests: referring to 'the problem of drawing a non-arbitrary line between reasonably easy and unreasonably difficult rescues', Feinberg remarks that 'similar line-drawing problems exist throughout the law, and most have been found manageable'.[76] Moreover, it can be maintained that when fundamental interests (life, physical integrity) are involved, we should pause before accepting that individuals are better protected by keeping omissions liability to a minimum. Article 63 of the French Penal Code criminalizes:

(1) a person who voluntarily neglects to prevent a serious crime or offence against the person, if that crime could be prevented without personal risk or risk to others; and

(2) a person who voluntarily neglects to give, to a person in peril, assistance which could be rendered without personal risk or risk to others.

Similar provisions are to be found in many other European criminal codes, which have hardly 'rushed headlong' into this field of criminalization.[77] Article 63(2) is a deliberate attempt to set the protection of one citizen's life or safety above the protection of the maximum liberty of other citizens.[78] To some extent the provision is vague; to some extent it leaves considerable prosecutorial discretion (as do many other offences). But it does not appear to have been thought oppressive since its introduction in 1941. The argument for the provision in Article 63(1), and more especially a general duty to take reasonable steps towards law enforcement, might well be weaker in view of the difficulties and social effects of requiring

[75] A. Norrie, *Crime, Reason and History* (1993), 31–2 and 131–3.
[76] Feinberg, 'Harmless Wrongdoing', xii, summarizing his argument in *Harm to Others*, 150–9.   [77] Cf. Norrie, *Crime, Reason and History*, 133.
[78] For discussion, see A. Ashworth and E. Steiner, 'Criminal Omissions and Public Duties' (1990) 10 Legal Studies, 153.

citizens to assist the police.[79] That, however, leaves the arguments in favour of the 'duty of easy rescue' unimpaired.

2.8 MINOR HARMS

A great deal of modern criminal law consists of relatively minor offences designed as a more or less remote threat to those who might jeopardize the smooth running of road traffic, licensing procedures, urban planning, commercial and financial regulations, and so on. In one form or another, such regulations are essential if the functioning of modern society is to make adequate provision for the realization of social and individual goals. But they are far less central to social order than, for example, the preservation of physical integrity. The question therefore arises: since the criminal law is a condemnatory mechanism which may lead to the infliction of punishment, do not offences of this nature violate the principle that a certain degree of wrongfulness should be required before any conduct or omission is made criminal? The challenge is to identify criteria for the lower threshold of the criminal law.

Let us deal first with the problem of assessing which harms are minor. Feinberg's list of criteria was given above:[80] to some extent these depend on empirical evidence, and to some extent on judgments of degree. In his view, 'legal [sc. criminal law's] interference with trivia is likely to cause more harm than it prevents . . . *De minimis non curat lex*, interpreted in a way that is consistent with the priority of innocent over mischievous interests, is a mediating maxim for the application of the harm principle.'[81] The difficult issue is to apply this to so-called 'regulatory' offences, many of which involve failure to comply with requirements to make returns to official agencies such as HM Customs and Excise, the Department of Trade, and so on. Here the argument for criminalization is, in effect, the reverse of the consequentialist point made by Feinberg: that the criminal law is a relatively cheap, convenient, and swift means of reinforcing a system of regulation. No attempt is made to assert that the conduct or omission reaches a sufficient level of wrongfulness to warrant the intervention of a criminal court and the imposition of a criminal sanction. Instead, economic considerations and reasons of expediency are treated as outweighing any argument that the criminal law should be reserved for the most antisocial forms of behaviour. However, there has never been a thoroughgoing examination in this country of the strength of the economic and expediency arguments, and of whether some form on non-criminal

[79] G. Williams, 'Criminal Omissions' (1990) 107 LQR, 86.
[80] See n. 30 and text.
[81] Feinberg, *Harm to Others*, 216.

enforcement could be devised to deal effectively with such matters.[82] In the United States, for example, the Model Penal Code proposes the creation of a separate category of violations, leading to small or moderate financial penalties but not to criminal conviction.[83] If such a separate category were instituted, then the whole argument would move to a different plane. Those who believe that the criminal law should be reserved for seriously wrongful behaviour would have to find some kind of dividing line between conduct serious enough for criminalization and conduct to which an administrative response is adequate.

But there is another question, no less important, raised by these references to 'regulatory' offences. It is easy to slip into assumptions like 'all regulatory offences are minor' and 'all legislation not concerned with traditional crimes such as theft and violence is regulatory', and thus to conclude that the criminal law should really only be concerned with 'real' or 'traditional' crimes, regulatory offences being admitted merely as a concession to expediency. The assumptions are false, and the conclusion therefore flawed. Statutes such as the Control of Pollution Act 1974, the Health and Safety at Work Act 1974, and the Food Safety Act 1990 create offences which may be much more serious in their consequences than a minor theft or criminal damage. Some already carry substantial maximum sentences, others ought to. The seriousness of the wrongdoing involved in such offences must be assessed according to the same criteria as other offences, that is, by reference to the interests affected, the remoteness of the harm from the conduct, and culpability. In principle, the boundary between criminal offences and non-criminal 'violations' should be set according to consistent criteria, and should not vary with the social context in which the wrongdoing occurs. The term 'regulatory' should never be taken at face value when used to describe an offence.

2.9 REMOTE HARMS

One kind of justification offered for criminalization is that certain conduct might create an opportunity for serious harm to be caused subsequently. The conduct may not be harmful in itself, but it is criminalized because of the consequences that may flow from it. The discussion here goes beyond the traditional 'inchoate offences' of attempt, conspiracy, and incitement (see Chapter 11) to embrace offences of possession and other preliminary crimes. One example of this is a prohibition of conduct based on what the

---

[82] There are many academic studies of the operation of laws of this kind, some of which are discussed in Ch 5.3(a) in connection with offences of strict liability. For general surveys of the issues, see K. Hawkins and J. Thomas (eds), *Enforcing Regulation* (1984), and J. Rowan-Robinson and P. Q. Watchman, *Crime and Regulation* (1990).

[83] American Law Institute, Model Penal Code, s 1.04.

individual might do subsequently, e.g. criminalizing the possession of firearms on the basis that they may be used to kill, injure, or threaten unlawfully. Another example is a prohibition of conduct based on what others might be led to do subsequently, e.g. criminalizing certain processions or public demonstrations because of what others might be tempted to do in response.

Two objections to criminalizing remote harms stand out. One is that normal causal principles appear not to support liability, since mere possession or preparatory conduct is insufficient without a further voluntary act to produce any harm. The other is that conduct that is not harmful in itself should not attract liability, or (to accommodate the existing inchoate offences) at least not unless it is accompanied by an intention to commit a substantive offence. This would rule out most offences of possession, which do not require evidence of any further intent. In particular, cases in which the occurrence of harm depends on a further decision by the actor or by another (e.g. to fire the gun unlawfully) are unsuitable for criminalization. In the context of many modern societies, however, it would seem foolish to have no offences of unregistered possession of a firearm or of explosives. The social context could be used as a basis for arguing that abstaining from possession of certain dangerous articles like guns and explosives ought to be recognized as a duty of citizenship. It is, of course, a curtailment of liberty. So are all other criminal prohibitions. The question is whether it is justified as a curtailment of liberty to have a registration system reinforced by some criminal offences. It can be argued that in respect of especially dangerous articles such as guns, explosives, and motor vehicles, it is entirely proper to expect citizens to restrain themselves in certain ways.

A general argument of this kind provides a *prima facie* justification for criminalizing the possession of dangerous articles. Ordinary life is, however, full of dangerous articles—kitchen knives and garden weedkillers, to mention but two. In order to decide which dangerous articles should be restricted by means of penalizing unlicensed possession, there is a need to conduct a kind of cost–benefit analysis. In the US it is often argued that keeping a gun serves to protect law abiding citizens and to deter assailants. Joel Feinberg replies that:

For every criminal who is deterred or apprehended because of private gun use, there are probably many innocent persons shot accidentally . . . hot-headed bar patrons with sensitive egos killed in escalating quarrels, spouses killed in angry domestic disagreements, and so on.[84]

The equation is probably rather different for kitchen knives, where the frequent opportunities for harmless culinary use probably dwarf the

[84] J. Feinberg, *Harm to Others*, 196.

numbers of injuries or deaths, accidental or otherwise. This kind of balancing, informed by some proper statistical evidence, would be the desirable approach to resolving the question of which dangerous articles should be 'protected' by criminalization. In principle, the offences should require proof of culpability, rather than penalizing mere possession.[85]

Another example of criminalizing remote harms may be found in the offence of 'insider dealing', now contrary to the Criminal Justice Act 1993, section 52. When the offence was first introduced in 1980 one of the justifications was that such dealing distorts the market. This is a remote harm of an accumulative nature, i.e. the distortion would presumably occur only if others did the same thing. Although the criminalization of accumulative harms may be justifiable, this particular one is surrounded by doubts about the effects on the market and arguments that non-criminal means of regulation would be no less effective. These are empirical claims that call for full examination. In the end, the true justification for the offence may lie in the notion of gaining an unfair advantage, together with the enormous profits that may be thus made.[86]

2.10 VICTIMLESS CRIMES

When discussing ways of assessing the seriousness of harms in 2.5, it was observed that von Hirsch and Jareborg limit their analysis to crimes with individual victims. Many existing offences may be described as having the state or corporate entities as their victims, but during the twentieth century there has been a growing class of crimes in which there is no victim—or, perhaps, nobody who regards herself or himself as a victim. Chief among these are the various drugs offences. The justifications usually advanced for criminalizing drug possession, dealing, etc., are a combination of paternalism with remote harm. It is claimed that individuals should be protected from harming themselves through the taking of drugs, especially on the theory that soft drugs may lead to hard drugs. It is also claimed that taking drugs may lead others to do the same, and they may then go on to hard drugs, and may eventually suffer an inability to function effectively and even death. The trade in hard or Class A drugs is often regarded almost as an inchoate offence of homicide, as the following remarks of Lord Lane, CJ illustrate:

the most horrifying aspect [is] the degradation and suffering and not infrequently the death which the drug brings to the addict. It is not difficult to understand why in

---

[85] For further analysis, see A. von Hirsch, 'Remote Harms' in A. Simester and A. T. H. Smith (eds), *Harm and Culpability* (Oxford University Press, forthcoming, 1995).
[86] For discussion, see A. T. H. Smith, *Property Offences* (1994), 725–36.

some parts of the world traffickers in heroin in any substantial quality are sentenced to death and executed.[87]

Yet criminal prohibitions on the so-called dangerous drugs did not become prominent in the UK until the 1960s, the matter being treated largely as a medical problem before then.[88] In the US a vigorous prohibition programme has been pursued since the 1920s, at that time contemporaneously with alcohol prohibition. When the prohibition on alcohol was lifted, to some extent because of the racketeering and other criminal activity it had spawned, the prohibition on drugs remained. It is now widely acknowledged that the drugs legislation leads to some organized crime and to many individual property crimes, as addicts try to obtain the money to pay the inflated prices for drugs. Against this background it is no wonder that even senior police officers have been heard to call for open discussion of whether cannabis should be legalized.[89] There is little evidence that cannabis has worse effects than alcohol or tobacco, and efforts to suppress its consumption appear bound to fail. While it would be naive to suggest that legalisation would immediately lead to the disappearance of all drug-related crime, a circumspect approach to decriminalization might bring some reduction in crime, reductions in police and HM Customs and Excise costs, and reductions in tension between the police and certain groups in society.[90] Moreover, any health problems deriving from the excessive use of alcohol, tobacco and drugs could then be treated primarily as an educational, medical and social problem, with greater resources and without the long shadow cast by the criminal sanction. Once accomplished, such a development could then lead to some reconsideration of the proper approach to hard drugs.

The above argument has been conducted essentially on utilitarian grounds—that the existing criminal prohibitions may be bringing more disadvantages than advantages. A more fundamental argument is that respect for individual autonomy should place a heavy burden of proof on those who would wish to criminalize drug taking. In principle, individuals should be free to use drugs recreationally in the same way that they should be free to indulge in dangerous non-contact sports such as rock climbing, whitewater rafting, and so forth. Moral consistency requires, at the least,

---

[87] *Aramah* (1983) 76, Cr App R 190, at 192.

[88] P. Ward and I. Dobinson, 'Heroin: a Considered Response?', in M. Findlay and R. Hogg (eds), *Understanding Crime and Criminal Justice* (1988), 128, cited by N. Lacey, C. Wells, and D. Meure, *Reconstructing Criminal Law* (1990), 183–88.

[89] K. Hellawell, Chief Constable of West Yorkshire, reported in the newspapers for 23 May 1994.

[90] For two recent British pamphlets, see R. Stevenson, *Winning the War on Drugs: to Legalise or Not?* (Institute of Economic Affairs, 1994); F. Coffield and L. Gofton, *Drugs and Young People* (Institute for Public Policy Research, 1994). For discussion of the American decriminalization movement, see D. Husak, *Drugs and Rights* (1992), 51–70.

that the same arguments as are applied to alcohol and tobacco are applied to drugs. Individuals should have the right to self-determination: there is no criminal sanction for attempting suicide or for injuring oneself and, whatever the arguments for criminalizing others who injure someone with his consent,[91] these should not affect a person's liberty to drink, smoke, or take drugs to excess. To the argument that drugs may be addictive, and that this may deprive individuals of the very autonomy that is being advocated, the reply is that this might provide a reason for paternalistic legal intervention if it were established that the withdrawal symptoms are so unbearable that addicts become powerless to stop using drugs. Empirical findings, of course, have a bearing on this.[92] Even if it were concluded that the principle of autonomy and right of self-determination should not be allowed to protect drug use, and that some paternalistic intervention is justified, it does not follow that criminalization is the proper response. Minimalists would look to medical and social methods of dealing with what has now been defined as a 'problem', and the consequentialist arguments in the previous paragraph would militate strongly against deploying the criminal sanction.

2.11 CONCLUSIONS

The main determinants of criminalization continue to be political opportunism and power, both linked to the prevailing political culture of the country. The contours of the criminal law are not given, but are politically contingent. Seemingly objective criteria such as harm and offence tend to melt into the political ideologies of the time, as MacCormick argues:

resort to the criminal law is always parasitic on or ancillary to an established legal order of rights and duties in the spheres of private law and public law. Such an order of rights and duties (et cetera) has to be founded on some (however muddled and patchwork) conception of a just ordering of society. The interests protected from invasion by criminal laws are interests legitimated by a given conception of a just social order. And the harm principle would be vacuous without some such conception of legitimate interests. Hence, naturally, the laws which are justified by the harm principle on a given interpretation of 'harm' do indeed coincide with widely held precepts against 'harmful' behaviour. But they do not merely coincide; the criminal law in so far as it is concerned with fending off harmful behaviour is necessarily geared to protection of what are legitimate interests according to a certain dominant political morality . . .[93]

---

[91] See Ch. 8.3(f).
[92] See, more fully, Husak, *Drugs and Rights*, Ch 3; Schonsheck, *On Criminalisation*, Ch 6.
[93] MacCormick, *Legal Right and Social Democracy*, 30.

Even granting that some of the recent examples of criminalization—such as the offence of harassment and the new trespass offences discussed in 2.1 above—are based on a 'conception of a just ordering of society', their enactment raises questions of principle of the kind discussed above. In addition to the democratic and political principles concerning the notion of representative democracy, there are questions of the theoretical and practical justifications for invoking the criminal law.

In this chapter we have examined some of the main arguments of principle that can be deployed to persuade or dissuade, and to formulate justifications for extending or narrowing the reach of the criminal law. It has been argued that the principle of autonomy or positive freedom, combined with a minimalist version of the welfare principle, provides the foundation. There are some kinds of conduct that ought to be criminalized in order to ensure that individuals do not have their autonomy infringed by the coercive conduct of others and that the conditions for autonomy are preserved but, in general, the principle of autonomy suggests that the criminal law should be kept to a minimum. Other means of regulation should be adopted wherever possible. This leads, generally speaking, to arguments against:

1. criminalizing offensive behaviour unless certain further criteria are fulfilled;
2. the use of paternalistic reasons to justify criminalization;
3. criminal liability for omissions except in strong cases;
4. extending the criminal sanction to minor harms;
5. the use of the criminal law to deal with minor harms; and
6. the creation of so-called victimless crimes.

On the other hand, the principle of welfare lends support to counter-arguments in cases where the consequences for the individuals involved may be so serious as to threaten their own autonomy, for example in relation to omissions and some victimless crimes.

Fundamental to many arguments about criminalization and decriminalization are evidential issues, some of which are empirical, others predictive. Thus, for example, the principled arguments in the debate about drugs and the criminal sanction must be related to empirical evidence of the effects of drugtaking compared with the effects of similar substances, and empirical evidence about the nature and volume of drug-related crimes; the debate must also be related to properly founded predictions of the effects of changing the law. This is only one example: the evidential foundations of arguments for criminalization and decriminalization should always be addressed.

No less necessary is a properly based prediction of the practical effect of introducing new offences, particularly in terms of selective enforcement and creative adaptation. Selective enforcement may mean that the impact falls disproportionately on certain sections of society: traditional patterns of policing may suggest this, and there is some evidence that the Public Order Act 1986, section 5, has been invoked disproportionately against members of racial minorities.[94] Creative adaptation has also been apparent as the police have reinterpreted section 5 in a way not anticipated by the legislators, using it to penalize those who swear at them, and a similar adaptation may flow from the broadly stated powers and offences in Part V of the Criminal Justice and Public Order Act 1994. It may be replied that these are problems for the control of discretion among police and prosecutors, not for the legislature at the stage of criminalization. Leaving aside the objectionable vagueness of offences such as section 5, the question of enforcement cannot be dismissed too readily. Unless there is a prospect of rapid and significant change in on-the-ground policing, the theoretical possibility of greater control of police discretion cannot be a telling counter-argument.

Lastly, it has been shown that one central issue in debates about criminalization is how to assess the relative seriousness of harms. Some ways of making progress were suggested in 2.5 above. However, the question is not seriousness in the abstract but whether the harm is sufficiently serious to justify criminalization. The other part of this equation is what form of social control is likely to be most appropriate and, perhaps, most effective. Discussions of this in England and Wales are blunted by the absence of any established alternative form of regulating unwanted conduct. Although a few particular agencies have alternative methods at their disposal, English law knows no general category of 'infractions', 'violations', 'civil offences' or 'administrative offences'. There is also no unitary machinery for enforcing or adjudicating upon such a category of wrongs. In theory, the criminal law ought to be divided from civil sanctions and administrative regulation by reference to its censuring function, and by the principle—however uncertain in its application—that the ambit of the criminal law should be kept to a minimum. Thus every argument about criminalization and decriminalization should not only examine the empirical issues discussed above but also the justifications for invoking the criminal sanction rather than lesser forms of regulation. Sadly, the English practice is often to add a criminal offence to a regulatory statute without full and open consideration of the arguments. This is a leading cause of the gulf between criminalization in practice and in principle.

[94] Brown and Ellis, *Policing Low-Level Disorder*, 28–34.

3

Principles and Policies

The criminal law is sometimes presented and discussed as if it were a system of rules. It will already have become apparent from Chapters 1 and 2 that this is not true. Although there are rules, and although Parliament often goes through lengthy debates before enacting rules, there is also a great deal of discretion which often enables the police, prosecutors, magistrates, judges, and juries to adopt approaches that cannot be said to have been 'dictated' by the law. Even if it is pointed out that some 90 per cent of cases in the magistrates' courts and 55 per cent in the Crown Court involve a plea of guilty and therefore no trial, it remains the case that some of those guilty pleas will have involved negotiation between prosecution and defence; and, more especially, it must be recalled that the police exercise considerable discretion in their daily encounters with citizens, as was apparent from the discussion in Chapter 2.1 of the use of the Public Order Act 1986, s.5.

There is another sense in which study of the rules is unsatisfactory as the sole or primary approach to understanding the criminal law. Some of the rules of English criminal law evidently stem from, or at least conform with, certain general doctrines—normative assumptions about how the rules of criminal law should be shaped. It is not suggested that there is a great unity in English criminal law, such that a general theory can be constructed and presented as the key to understanding. But some general principles can be discerned, even if only at the level of the rhetoric of English criminal law (since there are often several exceptions or derogations in practice). Those principles also make fleeting appearances in Appeal Court judgments, as part of the reasoning behind judicial interpretation or development of the law. Thus, the principles may, or should, operate both as reasons for creating certain rules and as reasons for interpreting and applying the law in particular ways. They are termed principles because they amount to strong arguments based on moral or political foundations rather than absolute precepts: a principle can still be treated as such even if on occasion it is outweighed by another principle or countervailing consideration. Reference is also made below to certain policies, founded on arguments about what is expedient rather than what is right in principle.

The purpose of this chapter is to identify some of the leading principles and to discuss their credentials. The chapter flits between the descriptive and the normative: the primary aim is to develop a set of principles which ought to influence the contours of the criminal law. The 'ought' derives from the principle of autonomy outlined in Chapter 2.2, modified by a minimal commitment to the principle of welfare, in order to ensure that the social arrangements necessary to enable citizens to exercise their autonomy are also supported by the criminal law where necessary. But there is also a descriptive side to the chapter, inasmuch as it contains examples not only of rules which conform to given principles but also of rules which derogate from the principles. An attempt is made to assess the reasons for these derogations. Thus the principles and policies are presented below in antithetical pairs. For ease of exposition, the discussion is divided into three parts: 3.3 deals with the range of offences, recalling Chapter 2; 3.4 deals with principles bearing on the conditions of liability, to some extent anticipating Chapters 4, 5 and 6; and 3.5 states some procedural principles. Questions of priority will then be discussed in 3.6.

3.2 CONSTITUTIONALITY AND CODIFICATION

In constitutional theory, decisions about what conduct should be criminal should be taken by the legislature, and these decisions should then be implemented by the executive and applied by the courts. Any system that retains elements of a common law of crime allows the courts to exercise a legislative function. This is the Scots tradition: the theory, variously stated, is that the courts have an inherent power to punish conduct that is grossly immoral or mischievous, or is obviously of a criminal nature.[1] This, as we will see,[2] has led the Scottish courts to create new crimes even in modern times. The justification often advanced is one of keeping the criminal law in touch with the community, but this begs questions about the judges' ability to represent or distil community values. On this view, as Lindsay Farmer argues, 'the community is idealized and free of conflicts and, of course, is not represented by the legislature'.[3] In England the Law Commission has tended to place emphasis on Parliament as the proper forum for determining the boundaries of the criminal law. The Commission gave its general support, when putting forward its draft Criminal Code in 1989, to the following proposition:

. . . because a Criminal Code makes a symbolic statement about the constitutional relationship of Parliament and the courts, it requires a judicial deference to the legislative will greater than that which the courts have often shown to isolated and sporadic pieces of legislation. Far from it being a possible disadvantage of codification that it places limitations upon the ability of the courts to develop the

[1] G. H. Gordon, *The Criminal Law of Scotland* (2nd edn, 1978), 23–43; L. Farmer, ' "The Genius of our Law": Criminal Law and the Scottish Legal Tradition' (1992) 55 MLR, 25.
[2] Chapter 3.4(g).   [3] Farmer, 'The Genius of Our Law', 39.

law in directions which might be considered desirable, we believe that for the criminal law this is one of its greatest merits.[4]

Thus, the enterprise of codifying English criminal law was seen partly as an exercise in constitutional propriety, subjecting the contours of the criminal law to the democratic process of Parliament, rather than leaving them largely to the common law and the judges. One might argue that this change would be more symbolic than practical: the parliamentary process may be democratic merely in theory, since a powerful government may push through measures not directly related to its political mandate, and the judiciary is bound to retain considerable powers through its interpretive role. Indeed, the Law Commission's draft Code deliberately left a number of points open for judicial development (e.g. liability for omissions, the development of defences), although the significance of these areas is small compared with the bulk of the Code.

Constitutional propriety apart, the chief aims of codifying the criminal law would be to improve its accessibility (having a large number of offences 'set out in one well-drafted enactment in place of the present fluctuating mix of statute and case-law'),[5] its comprehensibility (adopting a simpler drafting style), its consistency (in the sense of greater uniformity of reasoning and terminology), and its certainty (settling many issues in advance, rather than leaving judicial decisions to do so after the event).[6] We saw in Chapter 1.3 that the codification project was carried forward and shaped by a small team of academic lawyers who produced a draft Code for the Law Commission in 1985,[7] and that the Commission, after consultation, published its own draft Criminal Code in 1989.[8] Influential opinion suggested that it would not be practical to try to put the whole Code through Parliament as a single Bill, since it was too large for the legislative system to cope with satisfactorily,[9] and so the Commission is now adopting another approach. It is preparing a number of shorter Bills, based on the 1989 Code but with some alterations, in the hope that the government will adopt them for its legislative programme in the coming years and that a Criminal Code can be constructed step by step. The first of these shorter Bills deals with non-fatal offences against the person and a few defences to criminal liability,[10] and the Law Commission has sought to

[4] Law Com No. 177, para 2.2, quoting from the submission of the Society of Public Teachers of Law. See also A. T. H. Smith, 'The Case for a Code' [1986] Crim LR 285.
[5] Law Com No. 177, i, para 2.4.
[6] Ibid., i, paras 2.5 to 2.11 for fuller discussion.
[7] Codification of the Criminal Law: a Report to the Law Commission, Law Com No. 143 (1985), submitted by Professors J. C. Smith, E. Griew and I. Dennis.
[8] Law Com No. 177 in two volumes: i, report and draft Bill, ii, commentary on the draft Bill.   [9] See [1990] Crim LR 141–2.
[10] Legislating the Criminal Code: Offences against the Person and General Principles, Law Com No. 218 (1993).

reinforce the point by publishing a paper on possible parliamentary processes for ensuring the smooth passage of substantial law reform Bills.[11]

Codification of the criminal law has considerable virtues, of the kind outlined in the previous paragraphs, and we will see later in this chapter that many of them accord with deep principles. However, the virtues discussed so far are formal virtues, and we saw in Chapter 1.3 that the contents of the draft Code have a particular slant—towards 'traditional' crimes, with no aspiration to declare the most serious types of offence; strongly towards the subjective principle of criminal liability; and without any statement of general principles or canons for interpretation. The approach to codification has certainly had its critics,[12] although the Law Commission is now beginning to answer a few of those criticisms by re-examining areas of the law that had not previously been re-examined,[13] by tackling points that it had previously decided to leave for judicial development,[14] and by showing greater interest in the arguments for objective standards of criminal liability.[15] The question remains, however, whether governments will begin to take seriously the cause of reforming the criminal law. The Law Commission has tried to appeal directly to the instincts of the present government by emphasizing the savings of resources (police, prosecution service, judges, and courts) likely to result from enactment of a coherent and simplified Criminal Code,[16] but there is little sign yet of success.

If one constitutional principle is that the reach of the criminal law should be declared by the legislature, leaving the courts to apply and to interpret the legislation, another is that the criminal law should respect fundamental rights and freedoms. The absence of any coherent statement of principles in the Code or any of the codification documents suggests that the European Convention on Human Rights has not been regarded as an important source or authority. However, some recent publications from the Law Commission do contain discussion of the particular Articles in the

[11] Law Commission, *Parliamentary Procedures and the Law Commission* (1994); see also the remarks in the Law Commission's Twenty-Ninth Annual Report 1994 (Law Com No. 232.

[12] E.g. C. Wells, 'Restatement or Reform?' [1986] Crim LR 314; G. de Burca and S. Gardner, 'The Codification of the Criminal Law' (1990) 10 Oxford JLS, 559; S. Gardner, 'Reiterating the Criminal Code' (1992) 55 MLR, 893.

[13] E.g. LCCP No. 131, *Assisting and Encouraging Crime* (1993), discussed in Ch 10 below.

[14] LCCP No. 134, *Consent and Offences against the Person* (1994), discussed in Ch 8.3 below.

[15] LCCP No. 135, *Involuntary Manslaughter* (1994), discussed in Ch 7.5 below.

[16] E.g. in the opening sections of Law Com No. 218, recommending the enactment of a Bill to modernize the law of non-fatal offences.

Convention,[17] which may betoken a change of approach. Some aspects of the European Convention have already been discussed in Chapter 2.5. Here, an outline of the structure may be given, before particular Articles are discussed in connection with the principles later in this chapter.

- Article 1 requires states to secure the declared rights and freedoms to everyone within their jurisdiction.
- Article 2 protects the right to life, providing exceptions where 'force which is no more than is absolutely necessary' is used:

    '(a) in defence of any person from unlawful violence;
    (b) in order to effect a lawful arrest or to prevent the escape of a person lawfully detained;
    (c) in action lawfully taken for the purpose of quelling a riot or insurrection'.

- Article 3 prohibits 'torture or inhuman or degrading treatment or punishment'.
- Article 4 prohibits slavery and servitude.
- Articles 5 and 6 set out several procedural rights relating to arrest, and generally in the pre-trial and trial phases.

    Article 5.1(e) concerns the detention of persons of unsound mind, and has been interpreted so as to require due account to be taken of 'objective medical expertise', which casts doubt on some English provisions on the insanity defence.[18]

    Also relevant is Article 6.2, which declares that: 'everyone charged with a criminal offence shall be presumed innocent until proved guilty according to law'.

- Article 7.1 states that 'no one shall be held guilty of any criminal offence on account of any act or omission which did not constitute a criminal offence under national or international law at the time it was committed', a provision which raises questions about the common law approach and supports codification.
- Article 8 sets out the right to privacy, although subject to rather wide exceptions.[19]
- Article 9 sets out the right to freedom of thought, conscience, and religion.
- Article 10 sets out the right to freedom of expression.
- Article 11 sets out the right to freedom of peaceful assembly.
- Article 14 declares that the rights and freedoms 'shall be secured without discrimination on any ground'.

[17] E.g. Articles 5 and 6 of the European Convention are discussed in Law Com No. 222, *Binding Over* (1994), and Article 8 on privacy is discussed in LCCP 134 on *Consent and Offences against the Person* (1994). However, *Conspiracy to Defraud*, Law Com No. 228 (1994), fails to mention, let alone discuss seriously, Article 7.

[18] See Ch 6.2 below.   [19] See Ch 2.6 above.

• Article 15 suggests that there is some hierarchy of rights. It permits limited derogation from the Convention. This may only take place 'in time of war or other public emergency threatening the life of the nation,' and it is not permissible to derogate at all from Articles 2, 3, and 7 as described above.

The rights which the European Convention contains and does not contain are not uncontroversial. For example, as we saw in Chapter 2.6, Article 8 on the right to privacy has some wide and almost self-defeating exceptions. However, the Convention remains an authoritative and yet, in England, a much neglected foundational document.

While English writers on criminal law have not tended to approach the subject by seeking to articulate general principles,[20] this has been more frequent in continental Europe and, to some extent, in the United States. One of the pioneering US attempts was that of Jerome Hall, who argued that 'the principles of criminal law consist of seven ultimate notions':

1. mens rea;
2. act (effort);
3. the 'concurrence' (fusion) of mens rea and act;
4. harm;
5. causation;
6. punishment; and
7. legality.[21]

When it came to drawing up the American Law Institute's Model Penal Code, Hall's seven principles appear to have exerted an influence on the form and content of the general provisions in Part I of the Code. In England, while some such principles have been assumed by much text writing and in some official reports, the tendency has often been to regard analysis of their strengths and weaknesses as optional or somehow external to the study of criminal law. Constitutional principles relating to the rule of law and 'legality' have attracted even less discussion. The remainder of this chapter attempts to demonstrate the worth of such inquiry.

3.3 THE RANGE OF THE CRIMINAL LAW

The preceding chapter illustrated the difficulties involved in deciding which interests the criminal law should protect, and in ranking harms so as to achieve some kind of proportionality. Clearly a primary aim of the criminal

---

[20] But see G. Williams, *Criminal Law: the General Part* (2nd edn., 1961), Ch 12, and N. Lacey, *State Punishment* (1988), Ch 5.
[21] J. Hall, *General Principles of Criminal Law* (2nd edn, 1960), 18.

law is to provide for the conviction of those who cause major harms to other citizens or to the community, but it has already been noted that the criminal law contains a myriad of less serious or more controversial offences. What principles and policies are relevant to the decisions to expand or contract the criminal law in these spheres? The enquiry begins by summarizing four principles and policies already discussed in Chapter 2, and then moves on to consider two other relevant principles.

(a) The Principle of Minimum Criminalization

This principle, which was discussed in Chapter 2.4, is that the ambit of the criminal law should be kept to a minimum. It flows from the principle of autonomy and the minimalist notion of welfare already developed in Chapter 2. As we saw, the point is not so much to reduce criminal law to its absolute minimum, as to ensure that resort is only had to the criminalization in order to protect individual autonomy, or to protect those social arrangements necessary to ensure that individuals have the capacity and facilities to exercise their autonomy. The principle is supported by various evidential and pragmatic conditions so that, even if it appears to be justifiable in theory to criminalize certain conduct, the decision should not be taken without an assessment of the probable impact of criminalization, its efficacy, its side-effects, and the possibility of tackling the problem by other forms of regulation and control.

(b) The Policy of Social Defence

Perhaps the strongest arguments against minimum criminalization are thought to derive from the policy of social defence. According to this view, the criminal law may properly be used against any form of activity which threatens good order or is thought reprehensible. There are, on this view, no limits to the use of the criminal sanction apart from financial ones. It was argued in Chapter 2 that many extensions of the criminal law are examples of political posturing, a government response to a matter of social concern about which 'something must be done'. For this reason a sceptical stance should be adopted towards claims of 'social defence', which are easy to advance but which must always be considered in relation to questions about the groups in society who would be defended by a particular law, and whether a case for the criminal sanction rather than other forms of intervention has been made out.

One difficulty with the principle of minimum criminalization is, however, that it could be taken to freeze the contours of the criminal law. If it were interpreted as a barrier against further extensions of criminal law, this would be unsatisfactory as it would take scant account of the many anomalies accumulated in English law, as in other systems, over the years. Rectification of an anomaly (for example, the ruling that a husband may be convicted of the rape of his wife[22]) may well lead to a new sphere of criminalization; so may the extension of the criminal law to cover a newly arising mischief, such as computer crime.[23] These examples are important as a corrective to extreme libertarian arguments deriving from the policy of minimum criminalization. It might well be agreed that we all prefer our behaviour to be subject to as few constraints as possible, but that preference must be placed in the context of our membership of a community. Certain constraints may be reasonable in the interests of the community at large, even though they restrict particular individuals, as we saw when elaborating the principle of welfare in Chapter 2.3. This does not mean that there should necessarily be more criminal law rather than less: one can perfectly well argue for the creation of new offences so as to deal proportionately with new or neglected social harms, while supporting the policy of minimum criminalization. Thus, the extension of the criminal law into areas such as computer fraud and, especially, marital rape may be as significant for its declaration of the degree of wrongdoing inherent in the conduct as for its production of more convictions. However, the main battlefield between minimum criminalization and social defence is the mass of minor offences which have found their way into the statute book, as we saw in Chapter 2.8. There is no evidence that the principle of minimum criminalization has been taken seriously in this respect: there must be a systematic re-evaluation of the myriad crimes thus created, and thorough consideration of the possibility of creating a non-criminal category of regulation for the offence that are truly non-serious.

(c) The Principle of Liability for Acts not Omissions

This principle has often been cited, in the courts and elsewhere, as a reason for restricting the ambit of the criminal sanction.[24] In fact, Parliament has greatly increased the number of offences which penalize persons for 'failing' to fulfil certain requirements, usually concerned with motoring, business, and finance. But when a statute or a judicial precedent falls to be interpreted by a court, its extension to cover omissions is often regarded as exceptional and in need of special justification. The main reason is that positive duties to act are regarded as an incursion on individual liberty: negative duties, which require citizens to avoid certain behaviour, leave them free to pursue their own desires in other directions, whereas a positive duty to act prevents them from doing anything else at the time. Familial ties and voluntarily assumed obligations are fair enough as bases

---

[22] See *R* v *R* [1992] 1 AC 599 and below, Ch 8.5(b).

[23] See the Computer Misuse Act 1990, and below, Ch 9.9.

[24] See Ch 4.4 below and A. Ashworth, 'The Scope of Criminal Liability for Omissions' (1989) 105 LQR, 424.

for criminal liability, it is argued, but it would be wrong to introduce a general duty to assist strangers or to take steps towards enforcing the law. As we saw in Chapter 2.7, this viewpoint is grounded in an individualistic version of the autonomy principle.

(d) The Principle of Social Responsibility

This countervailing principle adopts the welfare-based proposition that society requires a certain level of co-operation and mutual assistance between citizens. The recognition of some social duties is therefore essential if all individuals are to have a proper capacity for autonomy, and the imposition of duties backed by the criminal sanction may be justifiable to safeguard important values (such as life and physical integrity), if this can be done without risk or hardship to the citizen. This principle of social responsibility would therefore support, for example, an offence of failing to render assistance to a citizen in peril, where that assistance can be accomplished without danger to the rescuer. The critical element here is the danger to human life: it is not a prescription for making all citizens into their fellow citizens' keepers. These arguments on social responsibility and omissions liability are developed further in Chapter 4.4(c).

(e) Social Justification

There may be circumstances in which it is socially justifiable to inflict harm on another person or another person's property, as we have seen from Article 2 of the European Convention on Human Rights. The principle is that, where necessary in the enforcement of the law, apprehension of a suspected offender, prevention of crime, or protection of an individual from attack, it may be justifiable to inflict harm on another. The effect is to place society's interest in the prevention of crime above the interests of an attacker or suspected offender, in conditions of necessity, and to recognize the right to resist any unjust and immediate threat to one's life or physical safety. The ambit of the principle is examined more fully in Chapter 4.7.

(f) The Principle of Proportionate Response

This principle operates so as to place limitations on the degree of harm which may lawfully be inflicted under the principle of social justification. No individual, even an offender, should have his or her interests sacrificed except to the extent that it is both necessary on the grounds of social justification and reasonably proportionate to the harm committed or threatened. This should apply equally to law enforcement officers and to ordinary citizens. A sharper formulation of this principle would be that social justification grants the authority to inflict only the minimum harm necessary—a version of the view that one is only justified in using force if it is a lesser evil than allowing events to take their course.[25] On its face, Article 2 of the European Convention contains no qualification of this kind; but it is argued in Chapter 4.7 that a satisfactory law cannot rest on the concept of necessity alone. Thus a concept such as reasonableness must be imported, in order to impose a sense of proportion. As we will see in Chapter 4.7, there may also be arguments for differentiating between sudden and instinctive responses and those cases where there is ample time for reflection. Further, the assumption that the user of force is innocent and the other party is the wrongdoer does not apply in all cases, as we will see in Chapter 6.6.

3.4 THE RULE OF LAW AND FAIR PROCEDURES

In this section we deal at greater length with those principles and policies relating to the function of the criminal law as a means of guiding the conduct of members of society and the conduct of courts and law enforcement officers. In relation to each pair of contrasting precepts, the first-mentioned principle will have the support of the European Convention of Human Rights whereas the second is usually based on pragmatic and political considerations of the time. Three pairs deal with aspects of the principle of legality, sometimes expressed by the maxim *nullum crimen sine lege*. This fundamental principle is more frequently rendered in England in terms of 'the rule of law'. This is a phrase with a powerfully righteous, and sometimes abused, appeal, which is invoked here in its minimal sense of 'being governed by rules which are fixed, knowable, and certain'.[26] This is a fundamental principle, with both procedural and substantive implications. It expresses an incontrovertible minimum of respect for the principle of autonomy: citizens must be informed of the law before it can be fair to convict them of an offence, and both legislatures and courts must apply the rule of law by not criminalizing conduct that was lawful when done.

(g) The Non-Retroactivity Principle

In many other jurisdictions, especially within Europe, it is usual to begin a discussion of general principles of the criminal law by stating the maxim *nullum crimen sine lege*, sometimes known as the principle of legality. However, the connotations of the principle of legality are so wide-ranging that it is preferable to divide it into three distinct principles—the principle of non-retroactivity, the principle of maximum certainty, and the principle of strict construction of penal statutes.

[25] Discussed further below, Ch 4.7 and 4.8.
[26] J. Raz, *The Authority of Law* (1979), 214–15.

The essence of the non-retroactivity principle is that a person should never be convicted or punished except in accordance with a previously declared offence governing the conduct in question. The principle is to be found in the European Convention on Human Rights, Art 7: 'No one shall be held guilty of any offence on account of any act or omission which did not constitute a criminal offence under national or international law at the time when it was committed.' This principle, also enunciated in Article I of the United States Constitution, forbids a legislature to create a criminal offence which applies to behaviour prior to its enactment. How does it apply to the courts? It may seem obvious to state that they should not invent crimes and then punish people for conduct which falls within the new definition. But how would the common law have developed if such a power had not been exercised? The courts have developed and extended English criminal law over the years, untrammelled by the non-retroactivity principle. To 'adapt' the law is a great temptation for a court confronted with a defendant whose conduct it regards as plainly wicked but for which existing offences do not provide.

The conflict between the non-retroactivity principle and the functioning of the criminal law as a means of social defence reached its modern apotheosis in *Shaw* v *DPP* (1962).[27] The prosecution had indicted Shaw with conspiracy to corrupt public morals, in addition to two charges under the Sexual Offences Act 1956 and the Obscene Publications Act 1959. The House of Lords upheld the validity of the indictment, despite the absence of any clear precedents, on the broad ground that conduct intended and calculated to corrupt public morals is indictable at common law. The decision led to an outcry from lawyers and others. One objection to *Shaw* is that it fails to respect citizens as rational, autonomous individuals: a citizen cannot be sure of avoiding the criminal sanction by refraining from prohibited conduct if it is open to the courts to invent new crimes without warning. What happened in *Shaw* was that a majority of the House of Lords felt a strong pull towards criminalization because they were convinced of the immoral and antisocial nature of the conduct—thus regarding their particular conceptions of social defence[28] as more powerful than the liberty of citizens to plan their lives within the law.

But there are two more, interconnected, objections to this decision. First, the new crime was even less defensible, since it concerned a socially controversial realm of conduct (prostitution) rather than behaviour widely accepted as a social evil: if the courts are to legislate, they should at least confine themselves to relatively uncontroversial cases. Secondly, this realm

---

[27] [1962] AC 220.
[28] For the controversial nature of their approach to the relationship between law and morality, see Ch 2.6 above.

of conduct had only recently been considered by Parliament, which had introduced limited reforms in the Street Offences Act 1959; thus it could be argued that since Parliament did not then extend the law to penalize conduct such as Shaw's, the courts were usurping the legislative function when they did so. This constitutional dimension of the decision should not be underestimated. The proper procedure is for a democratically elected legislature to create new offences. What *Shaw* seems to admit is that the police and prosecution may prefer to press a hitherto unknown charge, and the courts may uphold its validity at common law. This accords great power to the executive and the judiciary, and, since an offence thus created operates retrospectively on the defendant, it fails to respect the citizen's basic right that the law be knowable in advance. The criminal law embodies the height of social condemnation, and its extent should be determined in advance by accountable democratic processes rather than *ex post facto* by judicial pronouncement.[29]

It appears that the English courts no longer claim the power to create new criminal offences,[30] apparently accepting the force of the principle of non-retroactivity. The Scottish judiciary does still claim this power, as part of a dynamic system of common law which must be adapted to deal with changing social circumstances. In 1983 the Scottish courts in effect created a criminal offence of selling glue-sniffing equipment,[31] and in 1989 they reached their famous decision to extend the crime of rape to husbands, overturning a long standing exception.[32] Yet the English courts, which ostensibly adhere to the principle of non-retroactivity, have now taken the same decision in relation to marital rape: in *R* v *R* (1992)[33] the House of Lords abolished the husband's immunity from liability for rape of his wife. There are many convincing reasons why the law should have been thus changed,[34] but the relevant question here is whether it should have been changed by judicial decision rather than by the legislature. The Law Commission had already issued a consultation paper proposing the abolition of the husband's immunity, and it subsequently issued a report that shows the need for parliamentary legislation if the change and its ramifications are to be effected properly.[35] The principal reason given by

---

[29] A. T. H. Smith, 'Judicial Lawmaking in the Criminal Law' (1984) 100 LQR, 46.

[30] *Knuller* v *DPP* [1973] AC 435, a case in which, paradoxically, the court appeared to create the offence of outraging public decency.

[31] *Khaliq* v *HM Advocate* 1983 SCCR 483.

[32] *Stallard* v *HM Advocate* 1989 SCCR 248, discussed by T. H. Jones, 'Common Law and Criminal Law: the Scottish Experience' [1990] Crim LR 292 and by L. Farmer, 'The Genius of our Law'.

[33] [1992] 1 AC 599, on which see M. Giles, 'Judicial Lawmaking in the Criminal Courts: the case of Marital Rape' [1992] Crim LR 407.

[34] Summarized in the first edition of this work, at 301–303.

[35] *Rape within Marriage*, Law Com No. 205 (1992).

the courts for changing the law, both in Scotland and in England, was the change in expectations between husbands and wives—plainly a social reason, and probably more appropriate for assessment by a committee taking wide evidence.[36]

The House of Lords has recently articulated five criteria for judicial lawmaking in *C.* v *D.P.P.* (1995)[37], a case on the presumption that children aged 10 to 14 are incapable of *mens rea*:

 (i) if the solution is doubtful, the judges should beware of imposing their own remedy;
 (ii) caution should prevail if Parliament had rejected opportunities of clearing up a known difficulty, or had legislated leaving the difficulty untouched;
(iii) disputed matters of social policy are less suitable areas for judicial intervention than purely legal problems;
 iv) fundamental legal doctrines should not be lightly set aside;
 v) judges should not make a change unless they can achieve finality and certainty.

Whilst these criteria leave many points for discussion, it is noticeable that they incorporate no reference to the 'rule of law' principles or to Article 7 of the European Convention. It remains unclear how far the courts can go in extending an offence or curtailing a defence without infringing Article 7.[38] Some might take leave to doubt whether any citizen could have acted on the faith of the previously-drawn boundaries of the law, but a well drawn defence of mistake of law could cater for that eventuality.[39] However, there is the separate point about constitutional propriety: it is wrong that courts should exercise the power to create new crimes, and people such as the husband in *R* should not be convicted even if they had not acted in reliance of the pre-existing law.

In modern law this kind of issue arises more frequently in the context of statutory interpretation, since there are few common law crimes remaining. However, even if English law were codified, it seems likely that courts would retain some power to develop defences to liability by creating new rules and extending old ones. Mental states such as insanity and intoxication are inconsistent with the kind of reliance presupposed by the

[36] It had been assessed by the Criminal Law Revision Committee, *Sexual Offences* (1984), which was divided on the question.
[37] *The Times* Law Report, 17 March 1995, per Lord Lowry, following Lord Lloyd in *Clegg* [199] 2 WLR 80.
[38] E.g. *Tan* [1983] QB 1053, *Elbekkay* [1995] Crim. LR. 163.
[39] It is worth noting that the defendant in *Shaw* v *DPP* had taken legal advice, but that did not save him, which makes the decision doubly objectionable.

idea of fair warning. These excusatory elements in the criminal law constitute rules of adjudication for the courts rather than rules of conduct to guide citizens, in contrast to the definitions of offences and of the justificatory defences (e.g. self-defence, prevention of crime), which might be relied on by citizens in planning their behaviour. It therefore follows that the usual 'reliance' arguments against judicial creativity do not apply in the sphere of excusatory defences.[40] It may be thought, too, that the constitutional arguments are less troublesome when the courts are dealing with excusatory defences: even if it is not proper for the courts to pursue their own conception of social defence, it may be proper for them to give effect to considerations of individual culpability.[41] An example of this is the judicial creation of a defence of 'duress of circumstances' in the late 1980s.[42] There remains, however, the question of how far this reasoning can be taken. Should courts be permitted to create and extend excusatory defences, but not to abolish or restrict them at a later stage? This was one of the criticisms of the decision of the House of Lords in *Howe* (1987),[43] which reversed a previous decision and held that duress could not be a defence to murder either as a principal or as a secondary party. It could be maintained that this decision breached Article 7 of the European Convention: what D did was not an offence when he did it, since at that stage duress was a defence and he would have been acquitted. Strictly speaking, therefore, once a court has created a defence it cannot abrogate it without running afoul of the principle of non-retroactivity.[44] The House of Lords did approach the matter more broadly in *C. v D.P.P.* (1995)[45], overturning a decision of the Divisional Court which would have abolished the common law presumption that children under 14 are incapable of *mens rea* unless proved otherwise. Important as that decision is, the judges have not yet explored the connection between the non-retroactivity principle and extending or restricting defences.

(h) The 'Thin Ice' Principle

A counterpoint to the non-retroactivity principle is provided by what may be called the 'thin ice' principle, following Lord Morris's observation in *Knuller* v *DPP* (1973) that 'those who skate on thin ice can hardly expect to

---

[40] See P. H. Robinson, 'Rules of Conduct and Principles of Adjudication' (1990) 57 U Chic LR, 729, and P. Alldridge 'Rules for Courts and Rules for Citizens' (1990) 10 OJLS, 487. Cf. Law Com No. 177, cl 4(4).

[41] See the views of Dworkin and Williams, discussed in 3.4(l) below.

[42] See *Willer* (1987) 83 Cr App R, 225, and subsequent decisions, discussed in Ch 6.4 below.

[43] [1987] AC 417, below, Ch 6.4.

[44] G. Fletcher, *Rethinking Criminal Law* (1978), 574, quoted by Smith, 'Judicial Lawmaking', 64–5.   [45] See n. 37 above and text.

find a sign which will denote the precise spot where he [*sic*] will fall in.'[46] The essence of this principle seems to be that citizens who know that their conduct is on the borderline of illegality take the risk that their behaviour will be held to contravene the law. Another popular phrase for this would be 'sailing close to the wind'. On occasions the courts have applied this principle both to the creation of a new offence and to the extension of an existing offence.[47] The arguments in favour of it seem to combine moral/ social and political elements. The social element might be that the criminal law ought to penalize conduct which is widely regarded as immoral; the political element might be that when citizens indulge in antisocial and immoral conduct, they ought also to know that there is a risk of criminal liability being extended to cover activities on the fringe of illegality. There are obvious counterarguments. The principle appears to assume that 'immorality' is a sufficient reason for criminalizing conduct, whereas that has never been maintained in England (for example, neither adultery nor prostitution is a criminal offence); it also appears to assume a consensus on what is or what is not immoral, whereas this is increasingly less common in a pluralist society (although there might be a consensus against selling glue-sniffing kits to young people). The principle also neglects the constitutional point that only Parliament should legislate, and the fairness principle that a citizen should not be convicted on the basis of law which did not exist when the act was done (although a proper defence of mistake of law might deal with the latter point).

Where the 'thin ice' principle is accorded priority over the non-retroactivity principle, the court is both placing strong emphasis on its own conception of social defence and assuming the function of lawmaker. When this amounts to creating a new offence at common law, as in Shaw's case, this is surely an usurpation of the constitutional function of the legislature. To protest that Parliament is too busy, and therefore too slow, to respond to new social evils is not persuasive, since there have been notable recent examples of swift legislative action.[48] It is surely preferable that lawmaking be publicly debated, non-retroactive, created by a democratically elected body, and publicly announced. The days of new crimes created at common law ought to be long gone. However, the arguments alter somewhat when the issue is the interpretation of statutes rather than the creation of new common law crimes, as we shall see below.

---

[46] [1973] AC 435.

[47] For the former, see *Shaw v DPP* [1962] AC 220; for the latter, see *Tan* [1983] QB 1053.

[48] E.g. The Intoxicating Substances (Supply) Act 1985 (sale of glue-sniffing kits) and the Sexual Offences Act 1985 ('kerb-crawling'); such reforms are often introduced into Parliament as Private Members' Bills, the Government 'handing out' small Bills to members who win a place on the annual ballot.

(i) The Principle of Maximum Certainty

The next principle—maximum certainty in defining offences—embodies
what are termed the 'fair warning' and 'void for vagueness' principles in US
law. All these principles may be seen as constituents of the principle of
legality, and there is a close relationship between the principle of
maximum certainty and non-retroactivity principle. A vague law may in
practice operate retroactively, since no one is quite sure whether given
conduct is within or outside the rule. The US terminology of 'void for
vagueness' cannot be followed here because it refers directly to the power
of United States courts to declare criminal legislation unconstitutional if it
is unduly vague—a power not available in the UK. However, the idea of
'fair warning' directs attention to the defendant's awareness of the
existence and extent of the rule: respect for the citizen as a rational,
autonomous individual and as a person with social and political duties,
requires fair warning of the criminal law's provisions and no undue
difficulty in ascertaining them. The criminal law will achieve this respect
more fully if its provisions keep close to moral distinctions that are both
theoretically defensible and widely felt:[49] this suggests a connection
between fair warning and fair labelling.

Two separate political or constitutional implications flow from the
principle of maximum certainty. The first is that, if rules are vaguely
drafted, they bestow considerable power on the agencies of law enforcement: the police or other law-enforcement agents might use a widely
framed offence to criminalize behaviour not envisaged by the legislature.
The offence takes on the definition of the law-enforcement agents instead
of one provided by the legislators, a process well exemplified by the
metamorphosis of the Public Order Act 1986, s. 5.[50] Thus the principle
should contribute to control of discretion as well as to fair warning for
citizens. The second implication is that the principle tends to favour a
codified criminal law rather than a system based on common law. We have
noted that English criminal law still contains several common law offences
with no authoritative definition and, therefore, much uncertainty, together
with many scattered statutes. One argument for codification of the criminal
law is that this would bring together in one place the definitions of the
major crimes, thereby enhancing accessibility and fair warning to citizens.
Another, already noted, is that it might be expected to curtail the powers
of the courts to create new crimes or to extend existing offences
significantly. However, changes of this kind are not inherent in all
codification exercises. In practice a great deal would depend on the
approach of the judiciary to the Code and, more especially, on the

[49] Gardner, 'Rationality and the Rule of Law'.   [50] See Ch 2.1 above.

principles and priorities with which the Code is drafted. If the Code still contains wide or vaguely-worded crimes, such as some of the 'public order' offences[51] and even theft,[52] that is hardly a great improvement in certainty.

It will be noticed, however, that the principle is stated in a circumscribed form—the principle of *maximum* certainty, not *absolute* certainty—which indicates the compromise already inherent in the principle before it is weighed against other principles and policies. In its pure form, the 'rule of law' insists on complete certainty, but this is rarely possible in view of the varying elements which may bear on the characterization of conduct as criminal. It is occasionally prudent for the criminal law to resort to such open-ended terms as 'reasonable' and 'dishonest' rather than to devise an immensely detailed and lengthy definition which might be extremely complicated to apply and which might still fail to cover the ground. Yet those who adhere to the principle of maximum certainty would insist that such derogations be kept to a minimum and always justified by the absence of feasible alternatives, and that where possible the relevant rule should be accompanied by guidelines or illustrative examples which structure the court's discretion.[53] English law sometimes defines an offence very broadly in order to catch a small group of perpetrators: there is an offence of unlawful sexual intercourse with a girl under 16, but it is widely accepted that no prosecutions should be brought where the girl is 15 and the boy is only slightly older. Proposals to narrow the offence by exempting cases in which the age difference is, say, only two years have been rejected on the grounds of undue technicality, as has the proposal to have a separate, more serious, offence which applies where the man occupies some position of authority over the girl.[54] We, therefore, tolerate an offence which has what the Americans call 'overbreadth', in the belief that prosecutorial discretion is a more reliable means of identifying truly criminal incidents than legal definition. This flies in the face of maximum certainty.

Thus, any claim that a derogation from maximum certainty is necessary for the practical administration of the law must be scrutinized carefully. As the US Supreme Court put it in *Conally* v *General Construction Co* (1926): 'A statute which either forbids or requires the doing of an act in terms so vague that men of common intelligence must necessarily guess at its meaning and differ as to its application, violates the first essential of due process of law.'[55] This applies to legislation, whether part of a codifying exercise or not, and also to common law crimes such as outraging public decency, public nuisance, and perverting the course of justice.

---

[51] E.g. Law Com No. 177, clauses 201 and 202; see below, Ch 8.3.
[52] Law Com No. 177, cl 140; see below, Ch 9.2.
[53] E.g. the problem of defining the conduct element in attempts: see Ch 113 below.
[54] CLRC, 15th Report, part V.   [55] (1926) 269 US 385, at 391.

(j) The Policy of Social Defence

The policy of social defence runs counter to the principle of maximum certainty. It maintains that some vagueness in criminal laws is socially beneficial because it enables the police and the courts to deal flexibly with new variations in misconduct without having to await the lumbering response of the legislature. The policy of social defence thus supports the same aims as the 'thin ice' principle. It also suffers from similar defects, such as differing opinions of the social interests to be defended by means of the criminal law. The interests of the powerful are thus likely to prevail.

The policy of social defence would support the enactment of laws vague enough to leave room for the law enforcement agents to apply them to new forms of antisocial action. The Public Order Act 1986, s.5, has already been discussed in this context, as have some of the new public order provisions in the Criminal Justice and Public Order Act 1994,[56] and the common law offence of conspiracy to defraud is another example. To the objection that such crimes delegate far too much *de facto* power over citizens' lives to law-enforcement agents, proponents of social defence would reply that this should be tackled by means of internal guidelines and police disciplinary procedures, rather than by depriving the police and courts of the means of invoking the criminal sanction against conduct which arouses social concern. The offence itself appears to be objectively stated—if broad—but its use may be selective. This is particularly evident with the new public order offences, aimed at hunt saboteurs and New Age travellers and yet not mentioning them or their activities specifically. The result, as Lacey, Wells, and Meure argue, is that 'political power is exercised with a low profile by means of wide discretionary power at all stages of the criminal process, leaving the law clear of political taint'.[57]

Similar policy arguments are sometimes used to support the argument that ignorance of the criminal law should be no excuse. Thus English law authorizes the conviction of persons who were unaware of the existence of a crime, even in circumstances where it would have been difficult for them to find out that they were committing it.[58] This derogation from the notions of maximum certainty and fair warning is usually justified in terms of social defence by suggesting that, if the defence were allowed, everyone would claim it and there would be large-scale acquittals. Such arguments are not persuasive in theory and in practice.[59]

The policy of social defence may be used to point out a distinct social

---

[56] See Ch 2.1 above.
[57] N. Lacey, C. Wells, and D. Meure, *Reconstructing Criminal Law* (1990), 114.
[58] Discussed below, Ch 6.7.
[59] See *Cambridgeshire and Isle of Ely CC v Rust* [1972] 2 QB 426; cf. *Lim Chin Aik v R* [1963] AC 160, discussed below, Ch. 6.7.

dysfunction of the principle of maximum certainty. If members of society can rely upon criminal laws being drafted precisely, and upon enforcement agents and the courts keeping within those boundaries, it is open to resourceful citizens to devise ways of circumventing those laws—conforming to the letter of the law, while dishonouring its spirit. Where this kind of activity is pursued in a systematic way, with powerful financial support, it may be regarded as a distinct threat to the values that the criminal law seeks to uphold. It is said that there are those in the financial and business worlds who make their living on these fringes of legality, exploiting the principle of maximum certainty as a shield to protect them from conviction.[60] Can these people be distinguished from Shaw, Knuller, Tan,[61] and others? It is doubtful whether a distinction between sexual and financial morality would be sufficient to justify a difference in approach. There seems to be a direct conflict between the principle of maximum certainty and the policy of social defence, rather than a dissonance which can be accommodated by means of an exception or compromise. Should we dispense with the idea of 'fair warning' if most citizens do not trouble to ascertain the precise terms of the law, and most of those who do are bent on exploiting its limitations? If a well-drafted defence of mistake of law would deal appropriately with those who genuinely misunderstand, how would one be able to distinguish those aiming to exploit the principle of maximum certainty for financial gain? The proper response is that the principle of legality, and in particular of maximum certainty, would accept that there is a distinction between avoidance and evasion, and that mere avoidance must be combatted by legislative amendments to the law rather than by *ex post facto* stretching by the courts. In fact the wide common law offence of conspiracy to defraud remains in full vigour, with the result that financial misdealers are not safe from its elastic clutches.[62]

(k) The Principle of Strict Construction

Two of the principles which are often brought under the umbrella of the principle of legality have already been discussed (non-retroactivity, maximum certainty); the principle of strict construction is the third. The difference here is that whereas the non-retroactivity principle applies to the lawmaking activities of Parliament and the courts, this principle relates to the courts' task in interpreting legislation. The formulation of the principle is a matter for debate. In its bald form, it appears to state that any doubt in the meaning of a statutory provision should, by strict construction, be

---

[60] See D. McBarnet and C. Whelan, 'The Elusive Spirit of the Law: Formalism and the Struggle for Legal Control' (1991) 54 MLR, 848.   [61] See 3.4(g) above.

[62] In its report on *Conspiracy to Defraud*, the Law Commission favours the retention of the offence for the time being, and gives a rather unsympathetic account of the 'legality' objections to it.

resolved in favour of the defendant. One justification for this might be fair warning: where a person acts on the apparent meaning of a statute but the court gives it a wider meaning, it is unfair to convict that person because that would amount to retroactive lawmaking. Historically speaking, the principle seems to have originated as a means of softening the effect of statutes requiring capital punishment, through the notion of construction *in favorem vitae*.[63] This carries over into the declaration in *Taylor* (1950) that where the Court of Appeal (Criminal Division) is faced with a conflict of precedents, it should adopt the view which favours the defendant.[64] The foundation of this view probably lies in the inequality of power and resources between the individual defendant and the state, a justification also influential in the presumption of innocence.[65]

The status of the principle of strict construction is unclear. References to it have been fitful both in England and the United States, leading to the claim that it is invoked more to justify decisions reached on other grounds than as a significant principle in its own right.[66] There is certainly no difficulty in assembling a list of cases in which it appears to have been ignored.[67] But it may be that it was not properly understood in its more sophisticated form in England, since it is only recently that a sequence of principles to be applied when interpreting criminal statutes has been established. It now appears that, rather than, for example, being bound by any particular dictionary definition of a crucial word in a statute, the courts should construe a legislative provision in accordance with the perceived purpose of that statute.[68] In order to assist in ascertaining that purpose, a court may consult a Hansard report of proceedings in Parliament, a government White Paper or the report of a law-reform committee so as to ascertain the gap in the law which the legislation was intended to remedy.[69]

Those who disagree with the principle have sought to ridicule it by arguing that no system of criminal law can function adequately if absolutely every ambiguity has to be resolved in favour of the defendant.[70] But this line of attack misunderstands the true role of the principle, which has now been reasserted in the courts. Its proper place is in a sequence of points to be considered by a court when construing a statutory offence, i.e. only if doubt remains after examining the legislative purpose. It will be an

[63] L. Hall, 'Strict or Liberal Construction of Penal Statutes' (1935) 48 Harv LR, 748.
[64] [1950] 2 KB, 368. [65] See below, Ch 3.4(m).
[66] Jeffries, 'Legality, Vagueness and the Construction of Penal Statutes'.
[67] E.g. *Caldwell* [1982] AC 341, and *Ayres* [1984] AC 447 in the House of Lords, and many Court of Appeal decisions.
[68] *Attorney-General's Reference (No 1 of 1988* (1989) 89 Cr App R, 60 affirming the Court of Appeal's decision at (1989) 88 Cr App R 191.
[69] Cf. *Black-Clawson International* v *Papierwerke Waldhof-Aschaffenberg AG* [1975] AC 591 with *Pepper* v *Hart* [1993] AC 593.
[70] Jeffries, 'Legality, Vagueness and the Construction of Penal Statutes', and Law Com No. 177, para 3.17.

important advance in the development of English criminal law if other courts routinely follow the approach now established by the House of Lords, although the evidence suggests that neither courts nor counsel consider statutory interpretation to be a discrete subject with its own approach and its own precedents.[71] However, there are further important questions of interpretation to which no authoritative approach has been established. For example, uncertainty still prevails over the proper approach to interpreting statutory offences which do not include a fault requirement in their definition: the courts are still without a coherent approach to the question of strict liability.[72]

What is the argument in favour of the more sophisticated version of the principle of strict construction? The 'fair warning' argument undoubtedly plays a part, in so far as it respects autonomy of the individual, but the primary argument is constitutional. In terms of interpreting statutes the courts are the constitutionally authoritative agency. Just as the principles of non-retroactivity and maximum certainty ought to be recognized by the legislature, so they should be recognized by the courts when engaging in interpretation. Indeed, the argument is even stronger for the courts, for they are the ultimate agency for determining the practical limits of the law, and yet they are an unelected group. Parliament should retain the main responsibility for the extent of the criminal law and, indeed, it has the right to determine the courts' approach towards the task of interpretation (for example, by including some canons of interpretation in the Criminal Code[73]). The practical implication of this approach is that the courts should exercise restraint in their interpretive role, favouring the defendant where they are left in doubt about the legislative purpose.

(l) A Broader Purposive Approach

Militating against the principle of strict construction is a broader purposive approach which relies on the aims of the criminal law as a whole rather than on a particular legislative purpose. Why should the courts allow those who indulge in obviously antisocial behaviour to escape conviction by reference to a principle which assumes that citizens take care to ascertain the law beforehand (which they usually do not), and which also assumes that the government and Parliament can be left to deal promptly with antisocial behaviour which becomes a problem (which they usually cannot, because of pressures on parliamentary time)? Indeed, the argument goes further. Citizens who do act in reliance on a particular view of the law could be excused via a defence of ignorance or mistake of law.[74] As for the

---

[71] For fuller discussion, see A. Ashworth, 'Interpreting Criminal Statutes: a Crisis of Legality?' (1991) 107 LQR, 419.   [72] See below, Ch 5.3(a).
[73] Cf. Law Com No. 177, para 3.17, criticized by Ashworth, 'Interpreting Criminal Statutes', 425–7.   [74] See below, Ch 6.7.

constitutional argument, the assumption seems to be that the principle of legislative supremacy is all-powerful. Important it may be, but there are other political and fundamental values that also have a claim to be taken into account. If one purpose of the criminal law is the deterrence of significant culpable wrongdoing and the punishment of those who engage in it, does this not supply a reason for courts to interpret criminal laws so as to achieve this end? An argument of this kind leaves a great deal to be debated—in Chapter 2 we saw how controversial the boundaries of criminalization can be[75]—but its kernel is that, as with the 'thin ice' principle, it may not be unfair to penalize someone who has positioned himself on the margins of lawfulness. This may be seen as a rationalization of the appellate courts' tendency to stretch the criminal law so as to criminalize people who, they think, have manifestly committed a serious wrong.[76] As John Bell has argued, 'if the law exists to promote collective goals, as well as to protect individual rights, it cannot be altogether unexpected that both of these aspects should come into the resolution of hard cases'.[77]

Three counter-arguments are often heard, in addition to the principle of legislative supremacy. One is the practical point that courts have only rarely put the legislature to the test by refusing to extend existing offences to new forms of antisocial behaviour and leaving the task to Parliament. There are some isolated examples,[78] but in general the courts have not established a tradition of strict construction. If they had either brought in acquittals or quashed convictions in every case where the application of a statutory provision left some room for doubt, then the government would have been highly likely to set up a regular system for redrafting and amending criminal laws. A typical course of events was that in the case of *Charles* (1976):[79] the Court of Appeal favoured the acquittal of a man who, in spite of his bank's prohibition, had deliberately and substantially overdrawn on his bank account, because the court found it difficult to bring the conduct within the definition of the offence charged. Bridge LJ recognized that social defence might be better served by a conviction, but he did not regard it as the court's function to stretch the words of the statute. The House of Lords had no such compunction: it did stretch the

---

[75] Cf. Smith, 'Judicial Lawmaking', 58: 'it may be doubted whether it is possible to formulate any organizing principles according to which conduct is seen to be deserving of condemnation as criminal'.

[76] J. R. Spencer, 'Criminal Law and Criminal Appeals: the Tail that Wags the Dog' [1982] Crim LR 260. A recent example, which illustrates how some of these cases occur because the prosecutor chose the wrong charge and the Court cannot bring itself to acquit or quash the conviction, is *Gomez* [1993] AC 442, discussed in Ch 9.2 below.

[77] J. Bell, *Policy Arguments in Judicial Decisions* (1983), 222.

[78] E.g. *Oxford v Moss* (1979) 68 Cr App R 183 and *Gold and Shifreen* [1988] AC 1063: the Computer Misuse Act 1990 may be seen as a legislative response, at least to the latter decision.   [79] (1976) 63 Cr App R 252.

statutory wording, and restored the conviction.[80] Had the House of Lords adopted the same approach as the Court of Appeal, then the government and Parliament would have been left to decide on the need for an amendment to the law. In the meantime, Charles and a few others would have gone free. It is this consequence which the courts, regarding themselves as custodians of the public interest, have sought to avoid by adopting broad interpretations of statutes. Doubts have been expressed about whether appellate courts are in a proper position to assess the consequences of thus extending the law,[81] and there are some cases in which the courts decided that it was both too difficult and inappropriate to attempt to repair defective legislation.[82] Moreover, there are several avenues to explore before it can be concluded that social defence supports a conviction in this type of case, as Lord Lane CJ recognized a few years later.[83] A court construing a statute is unlikely to receive evidence on these wider social issues and is hardly the most appropriate body to resolve them anyway.

This leads into the second counter-argument: that Article 7 of the European Convention is breached no less by extending an existing offence by analogy than by creating a new offence. In strict terms Article 7 requires that offences be formulated in clear and certain terms and that courts should apply them restrictively, but in practice the European Court of Human Rights appears to have adopted a fairly broad view of these matters. Its decisions suggest that the test is whether, on the domestic courts' normal approach to interpretation, a particular decision could reasonably have been expected.[84] Nonetheless, this establishes that significant extensions by analogy are contrary to the Convention; and states may not derogate from Article 7.

A third, more theoretical counter-argument is that the judicial function is to uphold individual rights, leaving broader issues of social policy to Parliament. Thus Ronald Dworkin has argued that judges ought to ground their decisions in reasons which uphold individual rights and ought not to take account of policies, goals, or overall social welfare.[85] Glanville Williams has advanced a similar argument specifically in relation to criminal law.[86] It may be argued, however, that this adopts a particularly

---

[80] [1977] AC 177.   [81] See A. T. H. Smith, 'Judicial Lawmaking', 52–4.

[82] *Savage, Parmenter* [1992] 1 AC, 699, discussed in Ch 8.3 below.

[83] *Clarke* (1982) 75 Cr App R, 119; see below, Ch 9.7(c).

[84] P. van Dijk and G. J. H. van Hoof, *Theory and Practice of the European Convention on Human Rights* (2nd edn, 1990), 358–61.

[85] R. M. Dworkin, *A Matter of Principle* (1985), Ch 1.

[86] E.g. G. Williams, 'Statute Interpretation, Prostitution and the Rule of Law', in C. Tapper (ed), *Crime, Proof and Punishment* (1981); 'Criminal Omissions—the Conventional View' (1991) 107 LQR, 86, at 96.

one-sided view of the criminal law. Principles of individual fairness are important, and some of them are absolutely fundamental, but this should not be allowed to obscure the wider sense of autonomy advocated in Chapter 2—one which emphasizes the need to provide social conditions and facilities in which a broader autonomy can be exercised. This is not to suggest that courts should be allowed a free rein to draw on whatever social principles they wish when interpreting statutes. It is to argue that, if it is possible to develop some general principles of criminal law, perhaps based on some of the points developed in this Chapter and Chapter 2, these may be used as an interpretive framework no less legitimately than those existing principles based on individual fairness.[87]

(m) The Presumption of Innocence

The principle that a person should be presumed innocent unless and until proved guilty is a fundamental principle of procedural fairness, although its relation to the law of evidence means that it is not always included in discussions of the criminal law. The justifications for the principle may be found in the social and legal consequences of being convicted of a crime, in which context the principle constitutes a measure of protection against error in the process,[88] and in the immense power and resources of the state compared to the position of the defendant. Thus Article 6(2) of the European Convention on Human Rights declares that 'everyone charged with a criminal offence shall be presumed innocent until proved guilty according to law'. The opposite rule—a presumption of guilt upon all those prosecuted for an offence—would impose an oppressive burden on individual citizens, and would place immense power in the hands of the state officials who decide on prosecution. It is distaste for such a regime which underpins the declaration of Lord Sankey LC in *Woolmington* v *DPP* (1935)[89] that 'throughout the web of the English criminal law one golden thread is always to be seen—that it is the duty of the prosecution to prove the prisoner's guilt'. The European Convention does not state that proof must be beyond reasonable doubt, but the European Court has held that 'the burden of proof is on the prosecution, and any doubt should benefit the accused'.[90] The principled basis for these statements is plain, but do they represent rhetoric or reality so far as English law is concerned?

[87] See, e.g., P. H. Robinson, 'Legality and Discretion in the Distribution of Criminal Sanctions' (1988) 25 Harvard Journal on Legislation, 393; Ashworth, 'Interpreting Criminal Statutes'; Z. Bankowski and D. N. MacCormick, 'Statutory Interpretation in the United Kingdom', in D. N. MacCormick and R. S. Summers (eds), *Interpreting Statutes: a Comparative Study* (1991), 397.

[88] See the judgment of Brennan J in the US Supreme Court in *Re Winship* (1970) 397 US 358. [89] [1935] AC 462.

[90] *Barbera, Messegue and Jabardo* (1989) A 146, 33.

(n) The Policy of Ease of Proof

The presumption of innocence is much neglected nowadays: many offences are defined in such a way that the prosecution has to prove little, and then the defence bears the burden of exculpation. Hundreds and thousands of offences have been lifted out of the presumption's ambit, either by the plain words of certain statutes or by the Magistrates' Courts Act 1980, s.101, which places on the defendant the burden of proving any excuse, exemption, proviso, or qualification in the definition of the offence. Neglect of the presumption has not only been a feature of so-called regulatory offences, but it has also been central to legislation with severe maximum penalties, such as the Public Order Act 1986. There is little evidence that Parliament accords significant weight to the presumption of innocence in most of its legislation. The reason for this neglect is prosecutorial convenience: at a time when there is public concern about crime levels and when law enforcement agents and prosecutors are hard pressed, it is expedient to require defendants to prove element in the crime. Sometimes an attempt is made to justify this transfer of burdens by claiming that it is right to expect the defendant to prove elements relating the defence. One difficulty here is that there is no satisfactory analytical distinction between offence and defence.[91] Legislative draftsmen do not follow a single drafting rule, and it may often be a matter of chance whether a given element is expressed as a defence or is rolled up into the definition of the crime.[92] A more reliable argument is that certain matters are much easier for one party to prove than the other: it is generally far easier for a defendant to prove that he or she had a licence or permit than for the prosecution to prove the absence of one. But even if this is conceded, it cannot justify the almost routine placement of burdens on the defendant by modern legislation, although it may be influential in judicial decisions about this placement in cases where the statute is silent on the matter.[93]

The policy of ease of proof does not merely manifest itself through the imposition of burdens on the defence. Parliament has within its control the definition of offences too. Many offences are defined so as to dispense with the need to prove 'subjective guilt' in relation to one or all of the their elements—for example, the offences in the Public Order Act 1986, ss. 1, 2,

[91] See the discussions by Glanville Williams, 'Offences and Defences' (1982) 2 Legal Studies, 233, Paul Robinson, 'Criminal Law Defenses: A Systematic Analysis' (1982) 82 Columbia LR, 199, and Kenneth Campbell, 'Offence and Defence', in I. Dennis (ed), *Criminal Law and Criminal Justice* (1987).
[92] As demonstrated by A. A. S. Zuckerman, 'The Third Exception to the *Woolmington* Rule' (1976) 92 LQR, 402.
[93] See the House of Lords decision in *Hunt* [1987] AC 352, discussed by J. C. Smith, 'The Presumption of Innocence' (1987) 38 NILQ, 223, and by A. A. S. Zuckerman, *The Principles of Criminal Evidence* (1989), Ch 9.

and 3, which refer to conduct 'such as would cause a person of reasonable firmness present at the scene to fear for his personal safety', and then state that 'no person of reasonable firmness need actually be, or be likely to be, present at the scene'. To legislate in this way is no less effective than to flout the presumption of innocence directly. It is not merely wrong that much recent legislation erodes principles of fairness by favouring ease of proof by the prosecution, social defence, and efficient administration; it is also wrong that this position appears to have been reached without systematic examination of the values involved.[94]

3.5 PRINCIPLES RELATING TO THE CONDITIONS OF LIABILITY

Setting the conditions for criminal liability brings into focus the principle of individual autonomy, outlined in Chapter 2.2. We have already seen how this principle underlies the principle of legality in its three manifestations, the principles of non-retroactivity, maximum certainty, and strict construction. Unless a person can know what the criminal law prohibits, it is unfair to impose a conviction. At the heart of the principle of autonomy lies the idea of respect for individuals as rational, choosing persons. This is often taken to suggest, as we shall see in some of the detailed principles below, that an individual should only be held criminally liable for consequences that were knowingly brought about or knowingly risked. Whatever the merits of civil liability for other consequences, an individual should not be liable to censure and punishment for them. In contrast, the principle of welfare insists that the need for social co-operation and community life may create strong arguments for extending the ambit of the criminal law and the conditions of liability—by, for example, imposing duties to take care in certain types of situation and making the negligent liable to conviction. However, it will be argued below that this does not undermine the principle of autonomy if the appropriate conditions are fulfilled, notably that there is fair warning of the imposition of a duty of care reinforced by the criminal sanction, and that there is an exception for those incapable of attaining the required standard. All these points are taken further in Chapter 5: the purpose here is to express schematically the kinds of argument used.

(o) The Principle of Mens Rea

The essence of the principle of autonomy is that the incidence and degree of criminal liability should respect the choices made by the individual. The principle of *mens rea* expresses this by stating that defendants should only be held criminally liable for events or consequences which they intended or

---

[94] For some elaboration, see [1987] Crim LR 153–5.

knowingly risked. Only if they were aware (or, as it is often expressed, 'subjectively' aware) of the possible consequences of their conduct should they be held liable. The principle of *mens rea* may also be stated so as to include the belief principle, since in some crimes it is not (or not only) the causing of consequences that is criminal but behaving in a certain way with knowledge of certain facts. For example, one element in the serious offence of rape is that the man must know that the victim is not consenting, or be reckless as to whether the victim is consenting. If a case arises in which the man claims that he genuinely believed that the victim was consenting, this raises the issue of mistake as a possible defence.[95] Reflecting the element of choice that flows from the principle of autonomy, the principle of *mens rea* would state that a person's criminal liability should be judged on the facts as he believed them to be. All these aspects of the principle of *mens rea* are discussed further in Chapter 5.2 and 5.3. Although it is closely connected with the principle of autonomy, this does not mean that negligence liability cannot be supported on the same basis: so long as there is an exception for incapacity, as argued below, this may be fair.

(p) The Policy of Objective Liability

In spheres of activity that are perceived to be particularly dangerous, it is often thought that there are sufficient justifications for going beyond subjective liability and imposing liability for lack of care. Perhaps the clearest example of this is the road traffic legislation: longstanding offences such as dangerous driving and careless driving make drivers criminally liable for the degree to which they fall below the standards expected of a competent motorist.[96] Among the justifications for this is the principle of welfare, which, in this respect, favours the imposition of standards of behaviour on citizens because their behaviour as motorists can so easily impinge on others, with disastrous consequences. In industrial contexts there is a whole host of offences based on negligence, particularly where hazardous substances or dangerous conditions are involved. Moreover, in many commercial settings the criminal law imposes strict liability on those who sell defective products or unwholesome footstuffs, convicting them in many situations where the fault is small or non-existent. The case for extending the criminal law to these minor harms is based on expediency, and has already been criticized in Chapter 2.8. Strict liability itself is often supported by reference to considerations of welfare, 'policy considerations', or 'social concern', but it will be argued in Chapter 5.3(a) that the justifications for going beyond negligence liability to strict liability are unpersuasive. Criminal liability for negligence, however, so long as it is

---

[95] See Ch 5.3(d) and Ch 6.6 below.   [96] See Ch 7.6.

founded on clear and well-publicized standards and duties for people performing certain activities, is often easier to support. Indeed, liability for negligence is not properly described as 'objective' if there is an exception to ensure that those who lack the capacity to conform their conduct to the required standard are not convicted. Strict liability is generally objectionable but, as will be argued in Chapter 5.3(f), there may be certain spheres in which criminal liability can properly be based on a form of negligence—taking proper account of the seriousness of the harm, the need to warn citizens of their duties, and the need to exempt the incapable.

(q) The Principle of Correspondence

Another implication of the principle of individual autonomy, and its emphasis on choice and control, is the principle of correspondence. Not only should it be established that the defendant had the required fault, in terms of mens rea or belief; it should also be established that the defendant's intention, knowledge, or recklessness related to the proscribed harm. Thus, if the conduct element of a crime is 'causing serious injury', the principle of correspondence demands that the fault element should be intention or recklessness as to causing serious injury, and not intention or recklessness as to some lesser consequence such as a mere assault. Another example, as we shall see,[97] is the law of murder: in English law a person may be convicted of murder if he either intended to kill or intended to cause grievous bodily harm. However, the latter species of fault breaches the principle of correspondence: the fault element does not correspond with the conduct element (which is, causing death), and so a person is liable to conviction for a higher crime than contemplated.

(r) Constructive Liability

The argument for extending the fault element in murder, as described in the previous paragraph, favours constructive liability. This has a Latin tag, *versari in re illicita*,[98] and in its wider form it argues that anyone who decides to transgress the criminal law should be held liable for all the consequences that ensue, even if they are more serious than expected. Whether this is properly described as a policy or a principle is open to debate. Some of its adherents take no trouble to develop a principled argument, whereas others argue that the decision that is morally most significant is the decision to cause harm intentionally to another: once a person has crossed this moral threshold, there is good reason to impose liability for whatever consequences ensue.[99] However, even those who

---

[97] Below, Ch 7.3.   [98] Hall, *General Principles*, 6.
[99] For a modern re-assertion of this principle, see J. Gardner, 'Rationality and the Rule of Law in Offences against the Person' [1994] Camb LJ 502.

accept this moral foundation appear not to apply it generally throughout the criminal law. It seems to be reserved, presumably for policy reasons, to cases where a person intentionally inflicts physical harm on another.

Probably the most vigorous application of constructive liability in English criminal law is the offence of manslaughter by an unlawful and dangerous act: if a person commits a crime, which a reasonable person would realize presented the risk of some harm to another, and in fact it causes death, that person is liable to conviction for manslaughter.[100] There is no shortage of other, less vigorous, examples of constructive liability. The existing law of offences against the person, stemming from an 1861 statute, is replete with examples; and the offence of murder represents a modified example of constructive liability, since a person is liable to conviction for this offence only if the moral threshold of intending to cause grievous bodily harm is crossed. However, the moral threshold argument does not seem convincing, since it depends on the strength of a particular intuition—that morally the most significant element in given conduct is a decision to use force on another, and that there is insufficient moral weight in the plea, 'I only intended to punch/kick/wound slightly, not to cause injuries of that magnitude.' This is surely to adopt an unduly narrow view of moral responsibility. It attributes too little importance to the full context of the actor's decision, and allows a person's criminal liability to turn partly on luck.[101] This argument is pursued further in the next two sections.

(s) The Principle of Fair Labelling

This principle is chiefly applicable to the legislature. Its concern is to see that widely felt distinctions between kinds of offences and degrees of wrongdoing are respected and signalled by the law, and that offences are sub-divided and labelled so as to represent fairly the nature and magnitude of the law-breaking.[102] One good reason for respecting these distinctions is proportionality: one of the basic aims of the criminal law is to ensure a proportionate response to law-breaking, thereby assisting the law's educative or declaratory function in sustaining and reinforcing social standards. This argument is sometimes grounded exclusively in popular opinion: the law must keep in close touch with the sentiments of ordinary people. This point of view is sometimes advocated as the reason for keeping the two offences of murder and manslaughter rather than having a single offence of culpable homicide—people believe that the most heinous

---

[100] Discussed in Ch 7.5 below.

[101] For fuller discussion and references, see the discussion of manslaughter in Ch 7.5 below.

[102] A. Ashworth, 'The Elasticity of Mens Rea', in C. Tapper (ed), *Crime, Proof and Punishment* (1981); G. Williams, 'Convictions and Fair Labelling' [1983] Camb LJ, 85; J. Horder, 'Rethinking Non-Fatal Offences against the Person' (1994) 14 Oxford JLS, 335.

killings should be labelled separately.[103] However, the argument should be about what it is right to do, not about what it is politically prudent to do. Fairness demands that offenders be labelled and punished in proportion to their wrongdoing; the label is important both in public terms and in the criminal justice system, for deciding on appropriate maximum penalties, for evaluating previous convictions, prison classification, and so on. Consequentialists might add that any blurring of this labelling might encourage offenders to reason that they might as well be hanged for a sheep as for a lamb, inducing them to commit significantly more harm because it might appear to involve no greater condemnation.[104]

A second justification for the principle of fair labelling has a more direct connection with common patterns of thought in society. It is that where people generally regard two types of conduct as different, the law should try to reflect that difference. This argument was raised against the possibility of combining the crimes of theft and obtaining by deception into a single offence: people regard stealing and swindling as distinct forms of wrongdoing, and the law should not obscure this.[105] It is worth noting also that this proposal would have strained the principle of maximum certainty, since one consequence of moving towards broader definitions of offences is that they may give wide discretionary powers to the police in enforcement and to the courts in sentencing. English criminal law contains some extremely wide offences. Theft is a single offence with a maximum of seven years' imprisonment, whereas in many other jurisdictions it is sub-divided into greater and lesser forms. Criminal damage is a single offence with a maximum of ten years' imprisonment, with no sub-divisions to reflect the type of property damaged or the magnitude of the damage inflicted. Perhaps the clearest example is robbery, an offence with a maximum sentence of life imprisonment which conjures up an armed raid by masked men seeking substantial money or property, and yet which in English law is fulfilled by a slight push in order to snatch a purse or handbag. If offences of this kind are to remain for pragmatic reasons, it ought to be ensured that the spirit of the principle of fair labelling is honoured by structuring and controlling the discretionary powers of sentencers.

One controversial issue about labelling concerns offences that result in more serious harm than the perpetrator intended or expected. There are two issues here—whether the label of the offence should refer to the unforeseen harm, and whether the court should reflect the unforeseen

---

[103] See below, Ch 7.3.
[104] Bentham was aware of this: see his *Introduction to the Principles of Morals and Legislation* (1789), Ch XIV, para 8.
[105] Below, Ch 9.2(a).

harm in the sentence imposed.[106] Dealing here with the former issue, the recent tendency has been to create or perpetuate offences that refer to the unforeseen harm. Thus we have not only causing death by dangerous driving but also causing death by careless driving while under the influence of alcohol.[107] The controversy has been rekindled by those who argue that the focus of the offence-labels in the Offences against the Person 1861, several of which make reference to unforeseen but resulting harm, ought to be preserved because the labels reflect elements of thought about moral responsibility that should not be obscured by the modern tendency towards wide, morally sanitized formulae for offences.[108] However, it was argued earlier that this view of responsibility rests on the proposition that the decision to use force against someone is, morally, more significant than the expectation of how much injury is to be caused. This makes the extent of criminal liability turn on chance factors when there is no need to do so. Proper respect for autonomy makes it objectionable to ignore the actor's own choices unless there is good reason to do so.

A further question of fairness in labelling concerns offences that differ according to the sex of the defendant. English law is beginning to move slowly towards the principle that the nature and degree of criminal liability should be the same whether the offence is committed by a woman or by a man, unless there are good reasons for a different approach. It was not until 1985 that the law penalized the client for kerb-crawling, even though for many years it had penalized prostitutes for soliciting in the street.[109] The Criminal Justice and Public Order Act, s.142, unifies the offences of female rape and male rape. Respect for the principle of non-discrimination enshrined in Article 14 of the European Convention requires that the criminal law should not contain indefensible distinctions according to sex.

Fair labelling is a principle, not an absolute injunction. Divisions between offences are not self-evident and immutable. Reforms of the law may properly lead to the eradication of some distinctions, and there are many possible formats (such as a single offence with two or three alternative penalty structures).[110] Full adoption of this principle would not necessarily lead to a massive code of finely graded and differential offences, sometimes derided as 'the law professor's dream', although there are places where it might lead to greater detail and more offences than

[106] See Ashworth, 'Taking the Consequences', in S. Shute, J. Gardner, and J. Horder, *Action and Value in Criminal Law* (1993).

[107] Discussed below in Ch 7.6.

[108] J. Gardner, 'Rationality and the Rule of Law'; J. Horder, 'Rethinking Non-Fatal Offences'.

[109] Sexual Offences (Amendment) Act 1985; the law still does not criminalize the client who goes on foot, although it does penalize the loitering prostitute.

[110] E.g. Misuse of Drugs Act 1971, and s 4 of the Criminal Law Act 1967, both discussed by D. A. Thomas, 'Form and Function in Criminal Law', in P. R. Glazebrook (ed), *Reshaping the Criminal Law* (1978).

modern orthodoxy contemplates.[111] The strength of the principle is to ensure that arguments of proportionality, fairness to individuals, and the proper confinement of executive and judicial discretion are taken seriously when new offences with broad definitions and high maximum penalties are under consideration. Is it fair that sexual assaults should be divided, effectively, into only the two categories of rape (defined narrowly) and indecent assault (with a 10 year maximum), particularly when the offence of common assault is a relatively minor offence with a maximum penalty of only six months' imprisonment?[112] Questions of this kind have too frequently been resolved (usually in favour of 'social defence' or economy) without reference to the principles or to the values they uphold.

(t) Efficiency of Administration

The pull towards fewer and broader categories of offence with high maximum penalties derives from the desire to secure greater efficiency in the administration of criminal justice. To some extent, the reasons are economic: broader offences, with fewer boundaries between them, can be expected to lead to fewer disputes in court and to more guilty pleas. The expectation is a welcome reduction in public expenditure on the court system. The labels given to offences are regarded as less important than the actual assessment of culpability, and this can be done expeditiously at the sentencing stage. A further efficiency argument stems from the limitations of juries and lay magistrates: the criminal law must be kept as simple as possible so as to avoid confusing lay people and producing erroneous verdicts, and this argues against finely graded offences which necessitate complex instructions on the law. The policy of social defence also weighs in favour of fewer and broader offences, since they increase the discretion of police, prosecutors, and courts, and make it more likely that antisocial behaviour will result in conviction. A further policy argument to be borne in mind is that some issues are more appropriate for determination at trial (e.g. yes/no issues) whereas others, particularly questions of degree, are more appropriately dealt with at the sentencing stage.[113] This points away from fair labelling towards a conception of efficient administration.

One example of efficient administration gaining priority over the principles of fair labelling and maximum certainty is the common law offence of conspiracy to defraud, left untouched by the 1977 reforms of conspiracy law and covering a broad expanse of financial dealings, with little indication of its boundaries.[114] Action has been taken to structure the discretion of prosecutors in invoking this charge, but this still leaves the

---

[111] Horder, 'Rethinking Non-Fatal Offences', discussed in Ch 8.3(l) below.
[112] See the discussion below, in Ch 8.6(c).
[113] This is the argument of Thomas, 'Form and Function'.
[114] Conspiracy to defraud is discussed in Ch 9.8.

label vague and the sentence at large. The Law Commission is much impressed by the arguments for efficient administration, most of which happen to favour the prosecution, and has decided that 'practicality' requires the retention of the offence of conspiracy to defraud despite its breach of various principles.[115] Many of the reforms brought about by the Theft Act 1968 and the Criminal Damage Act 1971 favoured efficiency of administration, thereby eroding the principle of fair labelling. However, as already noted, some respect was shown for fair labelling by, for example, retaining the separate offences of theft and deception, when it would have been possible to combine the two.[116] In general, however, derogations from the principle of fair labelling on these grounds seem objectionable. 'Efficiency' and 'practicality' are presented as neutral concepts, when they often favour the convenience of prosecutors. Rarely does one hear reference to the efficiency of a rule in protecting individual rights.

(u) The Principle of Contemporaneity

Part of the basic doctrine of criminal law, as described by Hall among others, is that not only must the defendant cause the prohibited consequence and have the required fault, but that conduct and fault must co-exist at the same time. This is the principle of contemporaneity. We will see in Chapter 5.2(c) that the analysis of cases in the light of this principle can become rather difficult where there is a series of acts or a continuing act and where the fault element is only present for part of the time.

(v) The Doctrine of Prior Fault

Even though the defendant did not have the required fault when performing the prohibited conduct, the doctrine of prior fault may be invoked to hold him liable—by fastening on to the defendant's fault at an earlier stage, which then led to an absence of fault at the time when the prohibited conduct took place. The title of Paul Robinson's seminal article, 'Causing the Conditions of One's Own Defence',[117] explains the rationale of the doctrine. A person should not be allowed to rely on an exculpatory condition (e.g. lack of fault through automatism or intoxication) if he or she had deliberately or even negligently brought about that condition (e.g. by failing to take proper medication or by drinking alcohol to excess). Thus the doctrine operates by way of exception to, some would say conflict with, the principle of contemporaneity. The doctrine, which shares some of the roots of constructive liability, is discussed further in Chapter 5.2(d).

---

[115] *Conspiracy to Defraud*, Law Com No. 228.

[116] Criminal Law Revision Committee, 8th Report, *Theft and Related Offences* (1966, Cmnd 2977), para 38.

[117] (1985) 71 Virginia LR 1.

3.6 CONCLUSIONS

The purpose of this discussion has been to identify some of the general principles bearing on the conditions of criminal liability, to illustrate briefly how they and some conflicting policies have interacted in the development of English criminal law, and to make some suggestions for the resolution of these conflicts. It is quite clear that there has been no systematic legislative or judicial recognition of the principles, but there has been the occasional official reference to most of them. Even the rhetoric of the criminal law has not been consistent, and its practice has been far from that. Just as in Chapter 2 it was concluded that the decision to make certain conduct criminal is often a political gesture rather than an objective judgment based on principled considerations, so it appears in this chapter that many of the fairness principles—even those declared in the European Convention on Human Rights—are liable to be jettisoned if there are other advantages apparently to be gained.

Some paradoxes emerge from the different pairs of principles. For example, the advocates of a degree of constructive liability rely on the occurrence of significant harm, however unexpected, as a reason for increasing the grade of an offence; yet they may not place such importance on resulting harm when accepting criminal liability for attempts, incitement, and other inchoate offences. Indeed, while there has been a revival of support for forms of objective liability in recent years, there has at the same time been a legislative tendency to draft new offences in what might be termed an inchoate mode. In other words, instead of adopting the normal 'culpably causing a particular harm' formula for criminal offences, there is an increasing number of offences in the style 'doing x with intent to cause y', where x is a relatively minor act in itself. Examples of this are burglary contrary to the Theft Act 1968, s. 9(1)(a), which may be committed by entering a building as a trespasser with intent to steal; gaining unauthorized access to computer material with intent to commit or facilitate further offences, contrary to the Computer Misuse Act 1990, s.. 2; and placing or dispatching any article with intent to induce another to believe that an explosion is likely, contrary to the Criminal Law Act 1977, s. 51. It is not being suggested that conduct of these kinds should not be criminal. The point is, rather, that the particular way in which the offences are drafted places the emphasis on intention and dispenses with any need to establish that the key result (respectively: theft, damage, further offences, or causing others to fear an explosion) was caused. When one considers that the way of proving intention may be circumstantial or otherwise by inference, one can see that offences defined in the inchoate mode may have the effect of transforming the principle of *mens rea* into an inculpatory principle, making people punishable for manifesting an intention to cause a prohibited result.

Further examples of the resolution of conflicts between principle and pragmatic policy considerations will appear throughout the book. The main thrust of this chapter has been to argue for the primacy of the principle of autonomy when determining the conditions of criminal liability. Thus the subjective principles, the non-retroactivity principle, the principle of maximum certainty, the principle of strict construction, the principle of fair labelling, and the presumption of innocence—all of them tend to emphasize the value of fair warning and predictability in the law, the importance of respecting choices made by autonomous individuals, and the need to control the exercise of power by state officials. They are at the heart of legality, the rule of law, and what has been termed 'defensive criminal law'.[118] Whereas these autonomy-based principles should be accorded priority in relation to the conditions of liability, welfare-based principles and policies of social defence are more relevant to criminalization decisions, and can only rarely justify a derogation from the subjective principles of criminal liability.

It would certainly be wrong to present the resolution of the conflict between the two sets of principles and policies as a question of balancing. In the first place, some principles are more fundamental than others. The European Convention on Human Rights, as we have seen, allows no derogation from Articles 2 (right to life), 3 (freedom from torture), and 7 (principle of legality), and derogation from other articles (such as Article 6.2 on the presumption of innocence) is permitted only if there is a 'public emergency threatening the life of the nation' and then only 'to the extent strictly required by the exigencies of the situation' (Article 15). In relation to principles not protected by the European Convention the same starting point should be adopted. The principle of autonomy should have priority in relation to the conditions of liability, qualified only by a minimalist welfare principle. In some situations it will be justifiable to impose duties of citizenship reinforced by the criminal law, but in 3.3(c) it was argued that this can be done in certain circumstances without compromising the principle of autonomy. This debate, and others connected with it, is taken forward in the context of criminal conduct in the next chapter.

---

[118] N. Jareborg, 'What kind of Criminal Law do we want?', *Scandinavian Studies in Criminology* (1995), discussed in Ch 2.4(a) above.

4

Criminal Conduct

4.1 THE GENERAL PART OF THE CRIMINAL LAW

This chapter and the following two chapters discuss what is usually known as the general part of the criminal law—that which is common to all, or at least to many, offences. It has been traditional for writers on English criminal law to approach the analysis of offences by means of two concepts with Latin names, *actus reus* and *mens rea*: the *actus reus* consists of the prohibited behaviour or conduct; the *mens rea* is usually described as the mental element—the intention, knowledge, or recklessness of the defendant in relation to the proscribed conduct. A more modern way of conveying the same distinction is to refer to the conduct element and the fault element. Whichever terminology is used, the distinction is nothing more than an analytical tool, and at that a rather 'rough and ready' one. It does have implications—for example, if the absence of lawful justification for conduct is treated as an element of the *actus reus*, this indicates that a defendant who was mistaken about the facts giving rise to the justification should not be criminally liable if the offence requires *mens rea* or fault.[1] It also shows what a departure from basic principles is evident in offences of strict liability, which require conduct but not *mens rea* (fault).[2] However, it has some manifest shortcomings: many of the accepted 'defences' to crime cannot be explained in terms of lack of *mens rea*—such defences as duress and even intoxication require a more complex account.

Recognition of the inadequacy of the traditional distinction has led to a search for more helpful ways of characterizing the basic structure of criminal law.[3] German law has long adopted a threefold distinction between wrongdoing, absence of justification, and culpability,[4] but a more elaborate structure is probably needed if it is to be faithful to the inevitable complexity of modern criminal law.[5] No attempt is made here to examine these issues more extensively, since the classification adopted may be said to be less important than an enquiry into that which it might obscure, i.e. 'what the preconditions to criminal liability really are, and how far they

---

[1] See the further discussions of this principle in Ch 5.3(d) below.
[2] For further discussion, see Ch 5(a) below.
[3] See the critical essay by Paul H. Robinson, 'Should the Criminal Law abandon the Actus Reus/Mens Rea Distinction?', in S. Shute, J. Gardner, and J. Horder (eds), *Action and Value in Criminal Law* (1993).
[4] See G. Fletcher, *Rethinking Criminal Law* (1978).
[5] P. H. Robinson, 'A Functional Analysis of Criminal Law', (1994) 88 *Northwestern U.L.R.* 857.

really reflect the principles they are commonly supposed to encapsulate'.[6] For the purposes of exposition the conditions of criminal liability may be divided into four working groups: (i) act requirements; (ii) absence of justification; (iii) positive fault requirements; and (iv) negative fault requirements. Chapter 5 will deal with what are termed 'positive fault requirements', broadly, those mental elements which the prosecution has to establish in order to construct a case for the defence to answer. Chapter 6 will discuss the 'negative fault requirements', broadly, those fault elements which do not correspond with positive requirements and of which the defendant has to provide some evidence in order to raise them as live issues in a case. Although the positive and negative fault requirements fall into the general part of the criminal law, it should not be assumed that they apply invariably and to all offences. We will see that there are controversial issues about the propriety of strict liability offences, and about the unavailability of some defences to those charged with particular crimes.

This chapter deals with both (i) act requirements and (ii) absence of justification. It is fundamental to the characterization of certain conduct as criminal that it is not justified. Although some offences are drafted so as to exclude justifiable conduct, the most usual approach is to define offences without reference to the possibility that the conduct may be justified under certain circumstances. This leaves the justifications in the general part of the criminal law. Perhaps it is for this reason that they are often classified as 'general defences', since they only arise when the defendant raises them. They may be said to function like defences, but their significance is more fundamental. Conduct which is justified is right, or at least permissible, in the circumstances. This is quite different in theory from the operation of defences which are excuses (e.g. insanity, intoxication, mistake), discussed in Chapter 6. There the act is wrongful, but the defendant is excused on account of his condition at the time. Where the defendant's act is regarded as justifiable, the act is not wrongful—even though in most situations, where no justification applies, it would be. Justifications therefore negate criminal conduct. They also afford some guidance or fair warning to citizens of the circumstances in which they are permitted or right to use force, cause damage, etc.

The act requirements discussed in the first few sections of this chapter form a somewhat diverse group. Matters such as voluntariness, acts, omissions, corporate liability, and causation appear to have little in common. Yet they may be said to constitute fundamental prerequisites for criminal liability, in the sense that it would be wrong to convict a person of any offence without proof that that person's voluntary act caused

[6] A. T. H. Smith, 'On Actus Reus and Mens Rea', in P. R. Glazebrook (ed), *Reshaping the Criminal Law* (1978), 95.

the conduct or consequence. They mostly draw their strength from the principle of autonomy (see Chapter 2.2) and from the principles of legality (see Chapter 3.3g), although the criminal liability of corporations raises questions about what constitutes a person, for the purpose of criminal law, and whether standard doctrine needs to be reconsidered in this respect. So far as human beings are concerned, to proceed to conviction without proof of a voluntary act would be to fail, in the most fundamental way, to show respect for individuals as rational, choosing beings. More generally, if people were liable to conviction despite doing nothing, or if something had been done *to* them, this would fail to respect their autonomy and would certainly not give them fair warning of the incidence of the criminal sanction, unless reasonable duties had been made plain to them.[7] Similarly, where it cannot be established that an act of the defendant caused the conduct or consequence prohibited by the crime, there should be no conviction.

These act requirements are therefore needed to protect individual autonomy by ensuring that both Parliament and the courts preserve fair warning and fair opportunity to choose not to offend. In this chapter we will consider to what extent they are honoured in English law, but it is important to bear in mind that they are in one sense formal requirements. As we saw in Chapter 2, the creation of crimes is often a matter of political initiative rather than the result of objective and principled inquiry. There is great diversity in the conduct elements of the various crimes, and Parliament sometimes defines them in an unusual or unprincipled way. In the search for general preconditions, the notion of involuntary conduct and its limits are examined in 4.2. We then turn in 4.3 to various challenges to the 'voluntary act' requirement—where is the act if the law criminalizes the causing of a state of affairs, or mere possession? In 4.4 we consider how the act requirement deals with crimes of omission. If the basis for these requirements lies in the principle of individual autonomy, that raises questions about the propriety of corporate liability, which is discussed in 4.5. We then turn to causation, and later turn to the circumstances in which conduct may be recognized as justifiable.

4.2 INVOLUNTARY CONDUCT

(a) Automatism and Authorship[8]

Automatism is often regarded as a defence to crime rather than as an essential component of criminal conduct. Certainly the following

---

[7] This caters for criminal liability for omissions, discussed in 4.4 below.

[8] See generally R. D. Mackay, *Mental Conditions Defences to Criminal Liability* (1995), Ch 1; R. F. Schopp, *Automatism, Insanity, and the Psychology of Criminal Reponsibility* (1991).

discussion has more in common with the treatment of various excuses in Chapter 6 than the rest of this chapter, and illustrates the heterogeneity of the concept of *actus reus*. Its appearance here, however, reflects its fundamental nature. Automatism is not merely a denial of fault. It is more of a denial of authorship, a claim that the ordinary link between mind and behaviour was absent; the person could not be said to be acting as a moral agent at the time—what occurred was a set of involuntary movements of the body rather than 'acts' of D. The usual examples of this are behaviour following concussion, being physically overpowered by another person, and being attacked by a swarm of bees while driving.

It has been established doctrinally that automatism prevents liability for all crimes. One way of rationalizing this within the traditional framework of *actus reus* and *mens rea* is to maintain that automatism negatives *actus reus*, since it shows that the conduct or omission was not the result of the defendant *acting* but of something *happening to* the defendant. Since all crimes require *actus reus*, even if some of them do not require *mens rea*, it follows that automatism may lead to acquittal on any and every charge. Many of the early cases concerned motoring offences for which strict liability is imposed, leading the defence to attempt to bring the case within automatism. However, since automatism is such a powerful exculpatory factor, the courts have attempted to circumscribe its use, holding that freedom from liability for causing harm should only be available to those who are free from fault. We shall therefore see that involuntariness has been defined fairly narrowly, and that the courts have evolved three major doctrines of limitation.

It is common to refer to automatism as a 'defence'. In practice voluntary conduct is assumed in all cases, but if the defendant brings credible evidence to raise the possibility of involuntariness, the prosecution must establish beyond reasonable doubt that the accused was not in a state of automatism when the conduct occurred. In some cases, only expert medical evidence will be sufficient to provide a foundation for the judge to leave the issue to the jury, or the magistrates to dismiss the charge.[9] Thus, when it is said that 'voluntary action is a fundamental requirement of criminal liability', it should not be overlooked that it is rare for the issue to arise in court.

(b) The Essence of Automatism

Examples of forms of involuntariness which might amount to automatism have been given—convulsions, muscle spasms, acts following concussion, etc. Criminal lawyers used to express the legal position in terms of a requirement of a voluntary act, going on to say that an act is voluntary if it

---

[9] *Cook v Atchison* [1968] Crim LR 266.

is willed.[10] One criticism of this is that it does not explain how the act of will occurs, and suggests an infinite causal regress;[11] another is that it misrepresents and exaggerates our awareness of the movements involved in our behaviour.[12] These criticisms led Hart to propose a 'negative' definition, describing involuntary actions as 'movements of the body which occurred though the agent had no reason for moving his body in that way'.[13] This switches attention to rare occasions of involuntariness, of which two types might be identified—behaviour which was uncontrollable, and behaviour which proceeds from severely impaired consciousness. Uncontrollable behaviour might be illustrated thus: D is physically overpowered by X and is made to stab V. In these circumstances it is fair to say that this was not D's *act* but something which *happened to* D. Other examples might be conduct during an epileptic fit, and reflex actions. Turning to behaviour proceeding from a lack of consciousness, this can be illustrated by things done during a hypoglycaemic episode (which may be the result of taking insulin to correct diabetes). It should be noted that both types of automatism apply equally to offences of omission, excusing those who fail to fulfil a legal duty through physical incapacity arising from inability to control behaviour or through significantly reduced consciousness.[14]

Those final words bring us to an unresolved question. Must a court be satisfied beyond reasonable doubt that the defendant had total control over his behaviour, or substantial control, or what? The answer to this question is perhaps best approached by recalling that, ultimately, the prosecution bears the burden of proof, and all that the defence need do is to bring credible evidence. In *Broome* v *Perkins* (1987)[15] the Divisional Court held in effect that the defence must adduce credible evidence that the defendant was exercising no control over his bodily movements at the time. This stringent test seems to take no account of earlier cases in which the defendant's consciousness was significantly reduced but not totally absent, and yet where this was sufficient for an acquittal.[16]

What, then, should be the extent of the involuntariness doctrine? Hart's definition depends upon the absence of a reason for the movements of the body ('the mind of a man bent on some conscious action'),[17] whereas

---

[10] The classic statement is that of J. Austin, *Lectures on Jurisprudence* (5th edn, 1885), 411–24.

[11] A. I. Melden, 'Willing', in A. R. White (ed), *The Philosophy of Action* (1968), 77.

[12] H. L. A. Hart, *Punishment and Responsibility* (1968), 103.

[13] Ibid. 255–6, reformulating (in response to criticism) the passage appearing at 105.

[14] See Model Penal Code, Art 2.01(1), draft Criminal Code (Law Com No. 177) clause 33(2), and A. Smart, 'Responsibility for Failing to Do the Impossible' (1987) 103 LQR, 532.

[15] (1987) 85 Cr App R, 321; see also *Isitt* (1978) 67 *Cr App R*, 44.

[16] E.g. *Charlson* [1955] 1 WLR 317; *Quick* [1973] QB 910.

[17] Hart, *Punishment and Responsibility*, 106.

the cases seem to have more to do with an absence of capacity. Glanville Williams, taking this point, argues that movements are involuntary if D is unable to avoid them.[18] Not only does this involve a shift of emphasis to capacity, but it also strikes an unusual note in asking not only whether D did control the movements (were they uncontrolled?), but whether D could have controlled them (were they uncontroll*able*?). Williams's approach is preferable here, as the draft Code recognizes; Hart's test dwells on cognition, whereas the essence of automatism is lack of volition. But there is no concealing the questions of judgment it leaves open. The draft Code includes within automatism any movement which '(i) is a reflex, spasm or convulsion; or (ii) occurs while he is in a condition (whether of sleep, unconsciousness, impaired consciousness or otherwise) depriving him of effective control of the act'.[19] The key here is 'effective control', and this, combined with 'impaired consciousness', shows how difficult it is to eliminate questions of degree even from such a fundamental aspect of criminal liability. The *essence* of automatism lies in D's inability to control the movement (or non-movement) of his body at the relevant time, but it may be thought unduly harsh to restrict the doctrine to cases of apparently total deprivation. The phrase proposed by the Law Commission, 'depriving him of effective control', would expressly empower the courts to evaluate and judge D's worthiness for a complete acquittal, whereas at present the decision in *Broome* v *Perkins* seems (unless declared *per incuriam*) to require a conviction whenever the court believes that there was some degree of control in the defendant's behaviour at the time. The advantage of the Law Commission's formula would be to allow sensitivity to the special facts of unusual cases; its disadvantage would lie in the freedom left to courts to incorporate extraneous considerations into their judgments.

At common law the courts have imposed at least three major limitations on the doctrine of automatism—by excluding cases involving insanity, intoxication, and prior fault—and it is to these developments that we must now turn.

(c) Insane Automatism

Even if D's bodily movements were uncontrollable or proceeded from unconsciousness, the doctrine of automatism will not be available if the cause of D's condition was a mental disorder classified as insanity. The courts originally developed this policy for reasons of social defence, since it ensured that those who fall within the legal definition of insanity were subject to the special verdict and therefore to indefinite detention

[18] G. Williams, *Textbook of Criminal Law* (2nd edn, 1983), Ch 29.
[19] Law Com No. 177, cl 33(1).

rather than being allowed to argue that their condition rendered their acts uncontrollable, and that they should therefore have an unqualified acquittal on the grounds of automatism.

The social policy behind this judicial approach was at its clearest in Lord Denning's speech in *Bratty* v *Attorney-General* for Northern Ireland (1963).[20] D based his defence to a murder charge on psychomotor epilepsy, but the trial judge ruled that automatism was not available, holding that the true nature of the condition was a disease of the mind and that therefore insanity was the only defence. The House of Lords upheld the trial judge's approach, and Lord Denning affirmed that 'it is not every involuntary act which leads to a complete acquittal'. D's behaviour may have been involuntary, 'but it does not give rise to an unqualified acquittal, for that would mean that he would be let at large to do it again'. The proper verdict is one of insanity, 'which ensures that the person who suffers from the disease is kept secure in a hospital so as not be a danger to himself or others'. Moreover, Lord Denning was inclined to give 'mental disease' a broad definition for this purpose, so as to include 'any mental disorder which has manifested itself in violence and is prone to recur'. This decision confirmed the dominance of the policy of social defence over considerations of individual responsibility.

In practice, the effect of this strict approach has not been to direct large numbers of cases towards the insanity defence. Typically, if the defence was based on automatism but the judge ruled that, since the origin of D's condition was a 'disease of the mind', the defence should be treated as one of insanity, defendants would decide to plead guilty to the charge rather than to persist with an insanity defence. However, there is now the potential for a different approach, since the Criminal Procedure (Insanity and Unfitness to Plead) Act 1991 removes the mandatory committal to mental hospital and grants courts a discretion to choose committal to hospital, conditional discharge, a guardianship order, or a supervision order.[21] This still places considerable emphasis on social defence, since the court may well make a hospital order where it believes that detention for treatment is required. Yet the new regime also permits a court to order the conditional discharge of a defendant who is found not guilty by reason of insanity, and some defendants may prefer to plead insanity in the hope of a conditional discharge rather than pleading guilty to a crime.

The attractiveness of that option may be rather low if the defendant's condition bears little relation to the common understanding of insanity. In recent years the courts have tended to bring still more varieties of involuntariness out of automatism and into insanity. The leading case is

---

[20] [1963] AC 386.   [21] For further discussion, see Ch 6.2 below.

Quick (1973),[22] where D's defence against a charge of causing actual bodily harm was that the attack occurred during a hypoglycaemic episode brought on by the use of insulin and his failure to eat an adequate lunch. The defence relied on automatism, whereas the prosecution sought and obtained a ruling that the condition amounted to insanity. The defendant then pleaded guilty and appealed. The Court of Appeal, quashing the conviction, held that a malfunctioning of the mind does not constitute a 'disease of the mind' within the insanity defence if it is 'caused by the application to the body of some external factor such as violence, drugs, including anaesthetics, alcohol, and hypnotic influences'. This 'external factor' doctrine was accepted by the House of Lords in *Sullivan* (1984),[23] where it was also restated that 'diseases of the mind' include both permanent and transitory conditions. Thus, where the malfunctioning of the mind is caused by an external factor, the legal classification is automatism rather than insanity; where it is arises from an internal cause, the classification is insanity. This leads to the apparently strange result that a hypoglycaemic episode (resulting from the taking of insulin to correct diabetes) falls within automatism, whereas a hyperglycaemic episode (resulting from a high blood–sugar level which has not been corrected) falls within insanity, since it is an internal condition rather than a condition caused by an external factor.[24] Epilepsy falls within insanity for the same reason.

The courts have found considerable difficulty in classifying somnambulism or sleepwalking. Over the years there have been several cases in which trial courts have permitted acts done during sleepwalking to be classified as involuntary.[25] But in *Burgess* (1991)[26] the Court of Appeal held that, since there is no external cause of sleepwalking, this condition must be regarded as arising from internal causes and therefore classified as insanity, following *Quick* and *Sullivan*. The defendant in *Burgess* had not changed his plea to guilty but succeeded on a plea of insanity. Since the Criminal Procedure (Insanity and Unfitness to Plead) Act 1991 it would be open to a judge to grant a conditional discharge in these circumstances, but nonetheless the 'insanity' label might not be welcome to many defendants.

One type of condition that has not yet been classified authoritatively in England is 'dissociation', which is often marked by a short period of uncharacteristic behaviour accompanied by some degree of memory loss. In *Rabey* (1978)[27] the Supreme Court of Canada ruled, in the case of a

[22] [1973] QB 910.   [23] [1984] AC 156.
[24] *Hennessy* (1989) 89 Cr App R 10, *Bingham* [1991] Crim LR 433.
[25] Perhaps the most cited is Boshears, *The Times*, 18 Feb 1961.
[26] [1991] 2 QB 92.
[27] (1978) 79 DLR (3d) 414, on which see R. D. Mackay, 'Non Organic Automatism— Some Recent Developments' [1980] Crim LR 350.

defendant who attacked a woman who had rejected his admiration for her, that the dissociative state in which he acted could not be classified as automatism. Although D's rejection by the woman might be regarded as an external factor, 'the ordinary stresses and disappointments of life which are the common lot of mankind do not constitute an external cause constituting an explanation for a malfunctioning of the mind which takes it out of the category of a "disease of the mind" '. Thus the rejection was an external factor but not the primary cause of the dissociative state: the Supreme Court thought that this lay in the defendant's 'psychological or emotional make-up'. That approach left open the possibility that an utterly extraordinary event might suffice as an external cause, and a trial judge so ruled in *T* (1990).[28] Here the defendant had been raped three days before she joined two others in a robbery, during which she said 'I'm ill, I'm ill' and then stabbed a bystander. Her defence was one of automatism arising from post-traumatic stress disorder caused by the rape. The judge held that the rape was a sufficient external cause to place the case within the doctrine of automatism rather than insanity.

(d) Automatism through intoxication

Although the Court of Appeal in *Quick* held that automatism arising from intoxication did not fall within the definition of insanity, this does not mean that a person who causes harm while in such an intoxicated state as to have significantly reduced consciousness or to be unable to control movements of the body should be acquitted. If the cause of the involuntariness is intoxication, then the courts would treat the case as falling within the ambit of the intoxication doctrine. It is rare for the evidence to be able to sustain a reasonable doubt that D was sufficiently intoxicated as to be in a state of automatism, but this seems to have been accepted in *Lipman* (1970),[29] where D had taken drugs and believed that he was fighting off snakes and descending to the centre of the earth, whereas he was actually suffocating his girlfriend. A defence of automatism was refused, and the case was treated as one of intoxication, drawing on the doctrine of prior fault discussed below.[30] However, if D's condition appears to have arisen through intoxication followed by concussion resulting from a bump on the head, the court may have to establish the dominant cause of the condition and subsequent behaviour.[31]

(e) Prior Fault

The aim of the doctrine of prior fault[32] is to prevent D taking advantage of a condition amounting to automatism if it arose through D's own fault. In

---

[28] [1990] Crim LR 256 (Snaresbrook Crown Court).   [29] [1970] 1 QB 152.
[30] On which, see below, Ch 6.3.   [31] *Stripp* (1978) 69 Cr App R 318.
[32] Discussed above, Ch 3.5(v), and below, Ch 5.2(d).

relation to automatism, the point was first made in *Quick* (1973),[33] where Lawton L. J. held that this defence would not be available if the condition 'could have been reasonably foreseen as a result of either doing or omitting to do something, as, for example, taking alcohol against medical advice after using certain prescribed drugs, or failing to take regular meals while taking insulin'. According to this view, the question of prior fault is resolved by applying the test of reasonable foreseeability, the test of the reasonably prudent person in D's position. But in *Bailey* (1983)[34] the Court of Appeal held that a person should not be liable to conviction if the condition of automatism arose through a simple failure to appreciate the consequences of not taking sufficient food after a dose of insulin, even if the reasonably prudent person would have realized it. The defence of automatism should be available unless it can be shown that D knew that his acts or omissions were likely 'to make him aggressive, unpredictable and uncontrolled with the result that he may cause some injury to others'. Prior fault therefore requires awareness of risk, sometimes called subjective recklessness.[35]

The doctrine of prior fault conflicts with the principle of contemporaneity of conduct and fault.[36] In some automatism cases an attempt has been made to avoid this conflict by convicting D in respect of conduct at an earlier point of time, when there was fault. Thus in *Kay* v *Butterworth* (1945)[37] D fell asleep while driving home from nightwork, and his car collided with soldiers marching down the road. It was held that he could be convicted of careless driving—not in respect of the collision (when he was asleep and therefore involuntarily omitting to exercise due care), but in respect of his earlier failure to stop driving when he felt drowsy. This approach is only possible where the offence is of a continuing nature, and even then depends on the charge being appropriately worded. It is therefore a tool of limited utility for managing the conflict between the principles of prior fault and contemporaneity.

(f) Reform

The proposition that people should not be held liable for conduct that is involuntary is fundamental, and the common law on automatism has developed from it. However, even accepting that cases of prior fault should continue to be excluded from automatism and that cases resulting from intoxication should be classified under the intoxication rules, one major unsatisfactory feature of the law on automatism is the line drawn between

---

[33] [1973] QB 910; for discussion of this development, see A. J. Ashworth, 'Reason, Logic and Criminal Liability' (1975) 91 LQR, 102.   [34] (1983) 77 Cr App R 76.
[35] On which, see below, Ch 5.3(c).   [36] See above, Ch 3.5(u), and below, Ch 5.2(d).
[37] (1945) 173 LT 191.

this doctrine and the defence of insanity. Now that indefinite commitment to hospital is no longer the mandatory consequence of an insanity verdict, and courts have flexible powers of disposal under the 1991 Act, it might be argued that judicial persistence with the internal/external distinction has less drastic implications for defendants. Nonetheless, there can be no sense in classifying hypoglycaemic states as automatism and hyperglycaemic states as insanity, when the association of both states with such a common condition as diabetes is close. The proper boundaries of the defence of insanity will be examined further in Chapter 6.2(c), but it is apparent from the discussion here that the present scope of the phrase 'disease of the mind' is too wide. There are many states in which the functioning of the mind is affected but which cannot sensibly be included within the concept of insanity. On the other hand, it is difficult to arrive at a clear definition of automatism: the draft Code refers to 'impaired consciousness . . . depriving him of effective control of the act'.[38] This rightly recognizes that total absence of control should not be required, but it therefore leaves us with a test dependent on a judgment of degree and value ('effective'), and does so without identifying the relevance of the defendant's capacity rather than awareness and 'choice'.[39]

4.3 ACTS, STATES OF AFFAIRS, AND POSSESSION

Accepting that a person should not be held liable for things which occur while he or she is in an involuntary state amounting to automatism, should there be a further requirement that liability should be based on acts? At first blush it seems wrong that people should be held liable for things that happen to them, or for doing nothing. Do legal systems succeed in avoiding the creation of offences that do not require an act? Why should they try to avoid such offences?[40]

Before sketching answers to those two questions, we must make the point that not all criminal offences are formulated so as to require proof of a particular *type* of act. For some offences, such as wounding and rape, the definition specifies an act and it is clearly a wrongful act. For some offences, such as doing an act with intent to impede the apprehension of a person who has committed an arrestable offence,[41] and all crimes of attempt, the definition requires an act but not one that is in itself wrongful: the intention with which the act is done is critical, but the act requirement

---

[38] Ch 5.2(d).
[39] Compare Law Com No. 177, paras 11 3–11 4, with the discussion of the case of *T* by J. Horder, 'Pleading Involuntary Lack of Capacity' [1993] Camb L.J., 298 at 312–15.
[40] For a philosophical examination, see Michael Moore, *Act and Crime: the Philosophy of Action and its Implications for Criminal Law* (1993).
[41] Criminal Law Act 1967, s 4.

still functions so as to exclude involuntary movements. (Whether ordinary acts should be penalized simply because of the actor's intentions is discussed elsewhere.[42]) For other offences, the definition refers only to a result (e.g. causing death), and the act requirement is implicit. Any kind of act suffices. Those offences have a tendency to raise questions of causation (did D's act cause the death?), which draws attention to another feature of the act requirement. What is necessary is not merely an act, but an act that causes the conduct or consequence specified in the definition of the offence. This should rule out cases in which D's act is superseded by the voluntary intervening act of some third party—where it is the intervening act, and not D's original act, that is the cause. The troublesome decisions on voluntary intervening acts are reviewed in 4.6.

There are three types of offence that appear to breach, or at least to challenge, the requirement of an act. First, there are offences relating to states of affairs: is it right that a person should be liable to conviction in respect of a state of affairs that happens to him, and is not his act? Secondly, most criminal codes contain offences of possession, and it is questionable whether these require any act. Thirdly, and most obviously, there are offences of omission. The essence of these offences is that they penalize a person for doing nothing when he or she should have done something. We examine in the next section whether, and to what extent, offences of omission can be justified. In the remainder of this section, states of affairs and offences of possession are considered.

Why is the act requirement thought important, and why should one be worried about possible departures from it? The principal answer is close to the one elaborated in the previous section of this chapter but it is not the same. We saw that the exclusion of involuntary movements from criminal liability shows respect for the autonomy of individuals and for their choices about what to do and what not to do. Even if a person does cause harm, liability should not follow if D was moving involuntarily as a result of some sudden affliction. The justification for the act requirement is that there should be no criminal liability without some directed movement. If there were liability for mere thoughts, not resulting in any act, this would be oppressive because there is an important moral distinction between thinking evil thoughts and beginning to put them into effect. The argument here becomes complex and is developed elsewhere.[43]

(a) Situational Liability

Why is it thought objectionable to convict a person simply because a state of affairs exists and not because that person 'did' anything? The leading case is *Larsonneur* (1933),[44] where D left England because the duration of

---

[42] See Ch 11.3, below.   [43] See Ch 11.3, below.   [44] (1933) 149 LT, 542.

her permitted stay had come to an end. She went to Ireland, from where she was deported back to this country. On her return she was convicted of 'being found in the United Kingdom' contrary to the Aliens Order 1920. Her appeal, based on the argument that her return to England was beyond her control, was dismissed by the Court of Criminal Appeal. The case is widely criticized: her return to this country was not her own act, and was contrary to her will and desire. The Court might have quashed her conviction by insisting on proof that a relevant act of the defendant caused the *actus reus* of the crime, whereas in fact it appears that various officials caused her arrival back in England. Alternatively, the court might have found a defence of compulsion, but it refused to do so. The court appears not to have approached the decision from the point of view of principle,[45] but it may be questioned whether there was or is a principle that would entitle a court thus to interpret an offence of 'being found'. The legislature is open to greater criticism for defining an offence in a way that seems to require no act by the defendant as a basis for liability.

The decision in *Larsonneur* does not stand alone. In *Winzar* v *Chief Constable of Kent* (1983)[46] the Divisional Court confirmed a conviction for being found drunk on a highway, in a case where the defendant had been taken from a hospital on to the highway by the police. Another similarly worded offence is that of being drunk in charge of a motor vehicle, and there are many other offences that impose what Peter Glazebrook has termed 'situational liability'.[47] We will see in 4.5(b) how, in certain situations, the courts have imposed 'vicarious liability' on shop owners and employers by construing statutory words so as to achieve convictions. In effect, these individuals and companies are being held liable simply for states of affairs—for the fact that an employee sold American ham as Scottish ham, for example, even though the shop owner had specifically warned against this.[48] It is not just that this may mean conviction without fault; it may also mean conviction without anything on the part of the shop-owner which constitutes an act that causes the prohibited conduct or result. However, it will be argued in 4.5(b) that it may be quite defensible to impose situational liability if the law is so phrased as to ensure that defendants are in control of their activities and know about their duty to avoid certain situations. So long as fair warning is given of the standards expected of those embarking on certain activities or enterprises, the respect for autonomy is upheld by the principles of legality or 'rule of

---

[45] Cf. the analysis by D. J. Lanham, 'Larsonneur Revisited' [1976] Crim LR 276, suggesting that the decision may have been based on prior fault (see below, Ch 5.2(e)).

[46] *The Times*, 28 Mar. 1983.

[47] P. R. Glazebrook, 'Situational Liability', in Glazebrook (ed), *Reshaping the Criminal Law*, 108.   [48] As in *Coppen* v *Moore* [1898] 2 QB 306.

law'.[49] The objection to the general English approach is that the principled standpoint appears not to have been adopted. The legislature sees no objection to creating state-of-affairs offences such as 'being found . . .' or 'being drunk in charge' without any exceptions to cover the person who has been manhandled into the position in which he or she is found or the person who has been rendered drunk by the strategem of others.[50] The courts have failed to develop the common law so as to provide a defence of compulsion or to insist on proof of a (voluntary) act by the defendant which caused the conduct, result or state of affairs proscribed.

(b) Offences of Possession

English law contains several offences of possession, relating to such items as offensive weapons,[51] any articles for use in a burglary, theft or deception,[52] and controlled drugs.[53] In ordinary language one might agree that it is possible to possess an item without any act on one's part. Do offences of this kind therefore breach the act requirement? Most of the difficulties with the concept of possession have arisen in drugs cases. The leading decision is that of the House of Lords in *Warner* v *Metropolitan Police Commissioner* (1969),[54] but neither the speeches of their Lordships nor subsequent cases have rendered the law clear or principled. The first proposition is that a person is not in possession of an item that has been slipped into her bag or pocket without her knowledge. The second proposition is that if a person knows that an article or container has come under her control, she is deemed to be in possession of it even if mistaken about its contents, unless the thing is of a wholly different nature than was believed.[55] The exception is highly restrictive: Warner believed that certain bags contained scent when in fact they contained cannabis, but that was not a sufficiently fundamental mistake. In *Warner* Lord Pearce stated that the mistake would not be sufficiently fundamental if D thought the containers held sweets or aspirins when in fact they held heroin.[56] The narrowness of any exception to the second proposition throws attention back to the first proposition, but that has also been confined tightly. In *Lewis* (1988)[57] it was held that D was rightly convicted of possessing controlled drugs when they were found in a house of which he was tenant but which he rarely visited. His defence was that he neither knew nor suspected that drugs were on the premises. The Court of Appeal appeared to hold that, since he had the opportunity to search the house, he should be

---

[49] See Ch 3.4(g) above.
[50] Cf. *Kingston* (1994) 99 Cr App R 386, below, Ch 6.3.
[51] Prevention of Crime Act 1953.   [52] Theft Act 1968, s 25.
[53] Misuse of Drugs Act 1971.   [54] [1969] 2 AC 256.
[55] These propositions were re-stated by the Court of Appeal in *McNamara* (1988) 87 Cr App R 246.   [56] [1969] 2 AC at 427.
[57] (1988) 87 Cr App R 270, with commentary by J. C. Smith at [1988] Crim LR 517.

held to possess items that he did not know about but could have found. In effect, this reduces the first proposition almost to vanishing point. Surely it could equally be said, of the person into whose bag drugs are slipped by some third party, that she could have searched her bag and found them? Probably this is another example of the so-called 'war against drugs' resulting in the distortion of proper legal standards.

Do offences of possession depart from the act requirement? Although taking possession of an article will often (but not always) involve some act of the defendant, it is surely wrong to regard it as a voluntary act if D was mistaken as to its contents. Thus, the first proposition in *Warner* is right in suggesting that possession is not purely a physical matter but does have a mental component, at least to the extent of realizing that some item or container has arrived in one's pocket, bag or house. Knowledge of this minimal or outline kind is essential. The American Model Penal Code goes further, stating that 'Possession is an act . . . if the possessor knowingly procured or received the thing possessed or was aware of his control thereof for a sufficient period to have been able to terminate his possession.'[58] This looks back to the act of acquiring possession or the omission to disembarrass himself of possession, requiring a degree of knowledge. Sadly the English courts in *Lewis* appear to have neglected even the first proposition from *Warner*, rendering possession in law equivalent to possession in fact (while preserving some unspecified exception for cases of 'fundamental' mistakes). In doing so they have not merely removed the need for an act but have also ridden roughshod over normal principles of causation, which would operate so as to relieve D from liability when the voluntary act of a third party had brought about the possession.

4.4 OMISSIONS

We have already seen, in 2.6, that there are awkward questions about whether the law should criminalize omissions. In some spheres of activity, such as commerce, finance and motoring, it is to be expected that participants will be placed under duties to do certain things in certain situations. In life in general, however, there are powerful arguments for keeping to a minimum the number of positive obligations on citizens that the criminal law reinforces, many of these arguments stemming from the principle of autonomy and from 'rule of law' principles such as fair warning. On the other hand, it was argued in 2.6 that there are also powerful arguments of welfare which suggest that there are good justifications for imposing some duties to act in dire situations.

[58] American Law Institute, *Model Penal Code*, s 2 01(4).

The reason for returning to omissions here is that they are often said to represent an exception to the 'act requirement'. In earlier sections of this chapter much has been made of the importance of requiring proof that the defendant did a voluntary act that caused the prohibited conduct or consequence. In at least some omissions cases one or more of those elements seems to be missing. Are omissions a true exception to the act requirement? If they are, is this another argument against criminalizing them?

One much-discussed preliminary question is the distinction between acts and omissions. Sometimes it is argued that certain verbs imply action and therefore exclude liability for omissions, and that the criminal law should respect the distinctions flowing from this. English courts have often used this linguistic or interpretive approach. It has led to a variety of decisions on different statutes,[59] without much discussion of the general principles underlying omissions liability. The Law Commission's draft Criminal Code may be said to signal the continuation of this approach, by redefining the homicide offences in terms of 'causing death' rather than 'killing', and redefining the damage offences in terms of 'causing damage', rather than 'damaging', so as 'to leave fully open to the courts the possibility of so construing the relevant (statutory) provisions as to impose liability for omissions'.[60] The draft Code would therefore remove any linguistic awkwardness in saying, for example, that a parent killed a child by failing to feed it; but it does so in this specific instance, and without proclaiming a general principle that the act requirement may be fulfilled by omission if a duty can be established. This attachment to the vagaries of the language is no proper basis for delineating the boundaries of criminal liability. It cannot be claimed to reflect the kinds of moral distinction discussed in Chapter 2.6.

In some situations the courts, following the linguistic approach, have nevertheless found themselves able to impose omissions liability. In *Speck* (1977)[61] the defendant was charged with committing an act of gross indecency with or towards a child. The evidence was that an 8-year-old girl placed her hand on his trousers over his penis. He allowed the hand to remain there for some minutes, causing him to have an erection. The Court of Appeal held that the defendant's failure to remove the hand amounted to an invitation to the child to continue with the act, and that the offence would then be made out. In effect, the Court either held that his inactivity in those circumstances constituted an invitation which amounted to an act, or it created a duty in an adult to put an end to any innocent touching of

---

[59] With different interpretations of words such as 'cause': see G. Williams, 'What should the Code do about Omissions?' (1987) 7 *L.S.* 92.

[60] Law Com No 177, ii para 7 13; see generally paras 7.7–7.13.

[61] (1977) 65 Cr App R 151.

this kind, with omissions liability for not fulfilling the duty. The analysis is similar to that in *Miller* (1983)[62], where D fell asleep while smoking, woke up to find the mattress smouldering, but simply left the room and went to sleep elsewhere. He was convicted of causing criminal damage by fire, on the basis that a person who initiates a sequence of events innocently and then fails to do anything to stop the sequence should be regarded as having caused the whole sequence. On this view the conduct constitutes a single, continuing act; Miller caused the damage because he took no steps to extinguish the fire he had innocently started. It must be doubted whether these efforts to find an act which then coincides in point of time with the defendant's knowledge or intention are convincing.[63] Surely the courts are imposing liability for an omission in these cases, by recognizing that a duty arises. *Speck* is a little different from *Miller* since the original act in *Speck* was that of the girl, and the duty must therefore amount to the recognition of an obligation on an adult to put an end to an innocent and indecent touching by a child. In so far as these decisions appear to extend the statutory wording, are they objectionable on grounds of retroactivity and lack of fair warning, or defensible as applications of existing common law doctrine to new situations?

In other situations it seems possible to offer plausible reasons for regarding the same event as either an act or an omission, and this has helped the courts to deal with some medical cases that might otherwise pose problems for criminal law doctrine.[64] Yet it is one thing to say that a doctor who decides not to replace an empty bag for a dripfeed has made an omission whereas a doctor who switches off a ventilator has done an act; it is another thing to maintain that the act–omission distinction should be crucial to any determination of the criminal liability of the two doctors. In *Airedale NHS Trust* v *Bland* (1993)[65] the House of Lords held that it would be lawful for a doctor to withdraw treatment from a patient in a persistent vegetative state, even though death would inevitably be hastened by that conduct. The House held that the withdrawal of treatment would constitute an omission, and thus regarded the duties of the doctor as the central issue. The decision was that a doctor has no duty to continue life supporting treatment when it is no longer in the best interests of the patient, having regard to responsible medical opinion. It is worth considering whether this approach would have been possible if the discontinuance of life supporting treatment were classified as an act (e.g. by unplugging a machine). On the traditional approach to criminal

---

[62] [1983] 2 AC 161.
[63] See the criticisms by J. C. Smith [1982] Crim LR 527 and 774, and D. Husak, *Philosophy of Criminal Law* (1987), 176–8.
[64] See I. M. Kennedy, *Treat me Right* (1988), 169–74.
[65] [1993] AC 89.

liability, liability for an omission can be avoided if the court finds no duty (as in *Bland*), but liability for an act can only be avoided if the court finds either an excuse or a justification for what was done—an issue taken up in 4.9(b) of this chapter.

In view of this difference, the question may be put again: is there any clear means of distinguishing acts from omissions? It has been argued that conduct should be classified as an omission if it merely returns the victim to his or her 'natural' condition, or the condition in which she would have been but for D's attempt to carry out treatment, or a rescue.[66] Disconnecting a life support machine would, therefore, not be classified as an act because it merely returns the patient to the condition in which he or she would have been without any treatment. This view is open to several objections, notably that of deciding what the 'original condition' is in relation to each actor, and the implication that a person who has saved a non-swimmer from drowning could, on discovering that the non-swimmer is an enemy, push him back into the water.[67] However, one advantage of categorizing the conduct as an omission is that it then makes liability depend on the recognition of a duty—which would be straightforward in the case of the rescued non-swimmer. This approach may therefore offer comfort to those who insist that the act–omission distinction should not be used to avoid or foreclose moral arguments about the proper limits of criminal liability. But it is not a clear distinction, since it remains open to manipulation in different situations. The conclusion must therefore be that, although there are some clear cases of omission and some clear cases of act, there are many ambiguous cases in which the act–omission distinction should not be used as a cloak for avoiding the moral issues.[68]

Thus the fragility of the act–omission distinction and the vagaries of the English language suggest that omissions liability should not be opposed in principle. There are some clear cases of omission in which it is desirable to have criminal liability, such as the parent who neglects to feed her or his child or neglects to protect it from abuse.[69] Omissions can be involuntary or not, in the same way as acts; and, it is submitted, omissions can also be causes.[70] Omissions liability may therefore satisfy the principle that no one should be held liable for bodily movements that he or she did not and could not direct. It may also satisfy the principle that no person should be held liable for conduct or consequences that he or she did not cause. The precise point of the act requirement is to exclude liability for mere thoughts that do

---

[66] J. Rachels, 'Active and Passive Euthanasia' (1975) 292 New England Journal of Medicine, 78, as re-stated by M. Moore, *Act and Crime*, 26.

[67] Moore, ibid., 27.

[68] Cf. N. Lacey, C. Wells, and D. Meure, *Reconstructing Criminal Law* (1990), 229.

[69] E.g. *Emery* (1993) 14 Cr App R (S) 394.

[70] This is discussed in 4.6 below, on Causation.

not result in some bodily movement. Omissions liability does not require any bodily movement; instead, it is premised on failure to fulfil a duty. A parent may realize that it is her or his duty to feed a child, but may take no steps to do so. Omissions liability can only be said to uphold the rationale of the act requirement, while departing from its terms, in so far as the relevant duty is widely publicized and widely known. In those circumstances there can be no fairness objection to holding a person liable, provided that he or she is capable of taking some steps to carry out the duty.

4.5 PERSONALITY

(a) Natural and Corporate Personality

Most discussion of criminal liability is concerned with individual defendants as authors of acts or omissions, raising questions of respect for the autonomy of individuals. We saw in Chapter 2.2 and 2.3 that a developed notion of autonomy is not solely about negative liberty, i.e. protecting individuals from harm, but also involves elements of positive liberty or welfare, i.e. providing facilities and social arrangements whereby individuals can exercise autonomy more fully. By providing a framework for individuals to form companies and corporations, the legal system contributes to this end. Corporate activities now play a major part in social life—through companies as employers, as providers of goods and services, as providers of transport and of recreational facilities, and so forth. The criminal law has made increasing inroads into these spheres in recent years: the courts have developed doctrines of vicarious and corporate liability, and the legislature had introduced new offences directed specifically at corporate activities in the financial and commercial sphere (e.g. Financial Services Act 1986, and the Companies Acts 1985–89). Yet historically the criminal law has developed around the notion of individual human beings as the bearers of rights and duties. It is still somewhat trapped in that framework, even though the idea of companies as separate legal entities from their shareholders and their management was established in the nineteenth century. A limited liability company was even treated as a separate legal entity from the one man who controlled it.[71]

The present theory, then, is that corporate personality attaches to companies just as natural personality attaches to individuals (with certain modifications). But does this theory, which has a firm hold in company law, mean that companies can be convicted of offences? The courts moved slowly in this direction in the mid-nineteenth century. Although still doubtful whether companies could be said to *do* 'acts', the courts overcame

[71] *Salomon* v *Salomon* [1897] AC 22.

any reluctance to hold companies liable for *failing* to act[72] and for committing a public nuisance.[73] The driving force behind these innovative decisions, both concerning railway companies in the early days of rail travel, was not legal theory but pragmatism: 'There can be no effective means of deterring from an oppressive exercise of power, for the purpose of gain, except the remedy by an indictment against those who truly commit it, that is, the corporation acting by its majority.'[74] And from there the law developed towards criminal liability for companies, acting through their controlling officers.[75]

(b) Towards Corporate Criminal Liability

This subject was given a pressing social importance in the late 1980s by the series of disasters connected with corporate activities and involving considerable loss of life—for example, the Piper Alpha oil rig explosion, the Clapham rail disaster, the King's Cross fire, the sinking of *The Marchioness*, and in 1987 the capsize of the ferry *Herald of Free Enterprise*. It is difficult to believe that these disasters can be presented as the responsibility of a few individuals. Indeed, enquiries into the disasters have tended to emphasize the role of deficiencies in the systems of management and accountability. Major disasters apart, the newspapers offer evidence of a constant stream of incidents of industrial pollution, unsafe working conditions, impure foods, and unfair business practices which impinge upon, or threaten to impinge upon, the lives of individual citizens.

Growing recognition of the significance of corporate harm-doing has not, however, been accompanied by substantial alteration of the framework of criminal liability. The trend, as we shall see, has been to attempt to fit corporate liability into the existing structure rather than to consider its implications afresh. And, more important in social terms, there has been little change of approach at the level of enforcement. It is one thing to have a set of laws which penalizes corporate wrongdoing as well as individual wrongdoing. It is quite another thing to have a balanced machinery of enforcement which strives to ensure the proportionate treatment of individuals and companies according to the relative seriousness of their offences: present arrangements seem to draw a strong line between frequent police action against individuals and the relatively infrequent action of the various inspectorates, government departments, etc. against

---

[72] *Birmingham and Gloucester Railway Co* (1842) 3 QB 223.
[73] *Great North of England Railway Co* (1846) 9 QB 315.
[74] Per Denham C. J. at 320.
[75] The landmark case was *Moussell Bros v London and North-Western Railway Co* [1917] 2 KB 836. For discussion of the history, see L. H. Leigh, *The Criminal Liability of Corporations in English Law* (1969), Ch 2, and C. Wells, *Corporations and Criminal Responsibility* (1993), Ch 6.

companies.[76] However, the social calculation cannot be presented simply as an imbalance in treatment between 'crime in the streets' and 'crime in the suites'. We must also take into account the finding of social surveys that street crimes cause real harm and fear to people, not least to those who are already among the most disadvantaged in society.[77] It, therefore, does not follow that large resources should be put into the detection and prosecution of corporate harm-doers: other approaches to the problem must be considered, as we shall see.

One straightforward application of the doctrine that a company is a legal person, separate from the individuals involved in its operations, is that a company can commit many offences of strict liability: it can cause pollution, sell goods, fail to submit annual returns, etc. An offence of strict liability is one which requires no fault for conviction: any person many be found guilty simply through doing or failing to do a certain act.[78] Thus, if a company owns the business or premises concerned, it may be convicted for failing to control emissions of pollutants, etc. Outside the criminal law there have been further developments, and the law of torts has established a doctrine of vicarious liability of employers for the conduct of their employees.[79] There is no such general doctrine in the criminal law, but two exceptions have gained a foothold. One is the 'delegation principle': where a statute imposes liability on the owner, licensee, or keeper of premises or other property, the courts will make that person vicariously liable for the conduct of anyone to whom management of the premises has been delegated.[80] This applies whether the defendant is an individual or a company. Pragmatism would appear to be the underlying reason for this principle: such offences would otherwise be unenforceable, since delegation would remove responsibility from the person in effective control. However, this is surely not the only way of making such offences workable. The second exception revolves around the interpretation of such key words in statutes as 'sell', 'use', and 'possess'. The clearest example is where a statute prohibits the selling of goods in certain circumstances. *Coppen* v *Moore (No. 2)* (1898)[81] held the shop owner liable as the person who sold the goods in law, even though he was away from the shop at the time and an assistant carried out the transaction—in breach of the instructions left

[76] See the discussion by D. Nelken, 'White Collar Crime', in M. Maguire, R. Morgan, and R. Reiner (eds), *Oxford Handbook of Criminology* (1994).
[77] T. Jones, D. Maclean, and J. Young, *The Islington Crime Survey*; M. Gottfredson, *Fear of Crime*, Home Office Research Study No 84 (1985).
[78] See above, *Birmingham and Gloucester Railway Co* and the discussion of strict liability in Ch 5.3(a).
[79] P. S. Atiyah, *Vicarious Liability in the Law of Torts* (1967).
[80] Cf. *Allen* v *Whitehead* [1930] 1 KB 211 with *Vane* v *Yiannopoullos* [1965] AC 486; see P. J. Pace, 'Delegation: A Doctrine in Search of a Definition' [1982] Crim LR 627.
[81] [1898] 2 QB 306.

by the owner. So long as the assistant is acting as an agent rather than as a private individual, 'vicarious' liability is imposed.

These two examples of vicarious liability may appear not to respect the principle of individual autonomy, in so far as they hold people (or a company) liable for something that was not their own voluntary act or omission. However, although founded on the principle of welfare, they could be made to respect 'rule of law' values by ensuring fair warning of the standards expected. A third, direct form of corporate liability has also grown up. For this, it must be established that a person who 'represents the directing mind and will of the company' (sometimes termed a 'controlling officer'[82]) committed the act or omission specified in the offence, and had the required fault element. In *Tesco Supermarkets* v *Nattrass* (1971),[83] it was held that the manager of one of the company's supermarkets was not sufficiently high up in the organization to 'represent the directing mind and will of the company', with the result that the company was not liable for giving a wrongful impression of prices. This is a fairly narrow rule: unless the prosecution can identify someone who both holds a sufficiently influential position to be a 'controlling officer' and who had the required fault element, corporate criminal liability cannot be sustained. However, there are qualifications upon this. First, the House of Lords in *Seaboard Offshore Ltd* v *Secretary of State* (1994)[84] held that a company might be convicted of failing to take reasonable steps to secure that a vessel was operated in a safe manner if it were shown that it had failed to establish a safe system. And secondly, even under the *Nattrass* rule convictions are relatively easy to achieve in respect of the activities of small companies, if not larger ones.[85]

(c) Individualism and Corporatism

The history of legal developments in this sphere suggests a somewhat slow progress towards integrating corporations into a legal framework constructed for individuals, with few gestures towards the differences between corporations and individual human beings.[86] There are those who argue that this is only right: social phenomena can only be interpreted through the actions and motivations of individuals, and abstractions

---

[82] As in the draft Criminal Code (Law Com No. 177), clause 30.

[83] [1972] AC 153 For a discussion of this and subsequent decisions, see C. Wells, 'Corporate Liability and Consumer Protection' (1994) 57 MLR, 817.

[84] [1994] 2 All ER 99.

[85] E.g. the conviction of manslaughter of the managing director of an outdoor pursuit centre in respect of the deaths of young canoeists sent out in poor weather with inadequate training and supervision, *The Times*, 9 December 1994.

[86] From among the plentiful literature on this, see particularly C. D. Stone, 'The Place of Enterprise Liability in the Control of Corporate Conduct' (1980) 90 Yale L.J., 1, and Wells, *Corporations and Criminal Responsibility*, passim.

like corporations constitute barriers to proper understanding.[87] Only individuals can *do* things, and so the law is right to concentrate its attentions upon them. Indeed, any other view might threaten the principle of individual autonomy by holding people liable when they did no voluntary act.

The weakness of this argument is that individual actions can often be explained fully only by reference to the social and structural context in which they were carried out. When a government minister is announcing a new policy, he or she is speaking not merely as an individual but also as a representative of the government; when a managing director is initiating a commercial strategy, he or she is acting not merely as an individual but also as an officer of the company. Without reference to the structure and policies of the company and to that person's role within it, there can be no proper explanation of what was said and done. The argument, therefore, is that the behaviour of individuals is often shaped by their relationship to groups and collectivities—'shaped' in a meaningful sense, not 'determined' in the sense that individual autonomy is lost in the process (since individuals normally have some liberty to disengage themselves from the corporation). The thrust is that companies often acquire a momentum and a dynamic of their own which temporarily transcend the actions of their officers. Perhaps the clearest application of this can be found in offences of omission, particularly those involving strict liability. In a case like *Alphacell Ltd* v *Woodward* (1972),[88] where polluting matter escaped from the company's premises into a river, it seems both fairer and more accurate to convict the company rather than to label one individual as the offender: where the law imposes a duty, the company should be organized so as to ensure that the duty is fulfilled.

None of this is meant to suggest that individuals within a corporation should not bear responsibility for their conduct. In appropriate cases they should do so, provided that they have fair warning of any special duties attached to the activities of the company.[89] The important point is that companies should be open to both criminal and civil liability, since it is they who create the structural context for the individual's conduct qua company officer. The corporation appoints the individual and sustains him in this position—the individual is in that place, doing that thing, because of the corporation—and so it is right that the corporation should bear primary liability, or at least concurrent liability with its officer. This does not mean that legality and 'rule of law' principles should be neglected: companies are run by individuals, and therefore need fair warning of their duties. All these arguments may need adjusting for small, even one-person,

[87] Cf. S. Lukes, *Individualism* (1973), Ch 17.
[88] [1972] AC 824; cf. the early decision in *Birmingham and Gloucester Railway Co*.
[89] Wells, *Corporations and Criminal Responsibility*, 146.

companies and also for non-profit organizations. Moreover, they leave open the question whether the criminal law in its traditional form is the most appropriate means of dealing with corporate harm-doing.

(d) Changing the Basis of Corporate Liability

The theoretical arguments in favour of corporate criminal liability seem strong, but developments at common law have established it only in a limited form, since the 'controlling officer' test in *Tesco Supermarkets* v *Nattrass*[90] has a relatively narrow sphere of operation, and the 'vicarious liability' approach is confined by the already strained judicial interpretations of statutes. An alternative strategy of placing the emphasis on individual liability would be unlikely to work. Any particular individual might be dispensable within a corporation (e.g. the 'Company Vice-President responsible for going to gaol'), allowing the company to continue on its course with minimal disruption; or it might be difficult to identify the individual responsible, not least because the lines of accountability within companies are sometimes unclear. A further alternative strategy would be to rely even more on new offences of strict liability to punish corporate harm-doing, but this might not be a sufficient response to some of the disasters mentioned earlier, or to other harm-doing on a broad scale.

A number of different approaches have been canvassed in recent years. Celia Wells has supported the development of two alternative avenues of corporate criminal responsibility. One is aggregation: a company's culpability should be constructed out of the knowledge and the attitudes of employees as a whole, rather than imputing to the company only the knowledge of any single 'controlling officer'.[91] This has been explicitly rejected by the Divisional Court,[92] and would clearly need a change in the law. A second, complementary approach is to use company policies, or their absence, as the basis for liability. This follows the approach of Brent Fisse and John Braithwaite, and particularly their concept of 'reactive fault'.[93] On their view, rather than expending prosecutorial energy and court time trying to disentangle the often convoluted internal structures and policies of corporations, the law should require a company which has caused or threatened a proscribed harm to take its own disciplinary and rectificatory measures. A court would then assess the adequacy of the measures taken. The concept of faith would thus be a *post hoc*

---

[90] [1972] AC 153.

[91] Wells, *Corporations and Criminal Responsibility*, 110–13, 132–3. For reasons why Wells refers to attitudes as well as knowledge, see below, Ch 5.3(d).

[92] *H. M. Coroner for East Kent, ex p Spooner* (1989) 88 Cr App R 10, at 16.

[93] B. Fisse and J. Braithwaite, 'The Allocation of Responsibility for Corporate Crime: Individualism, Collectivism and Accountability' (1988) 11 Sydney L.R., 468; see also L. H. Leigh, 'The Criminal Liability of Corporations and other groups' (1977) 9 Ottawa L.R., 237.

phenomenon. Rather than struggling to establish some antecedent fault within the corporation, the prosecution would invite the court to infer fault from the nature and effectiveness of the company's remedial measures after it has been established that it was the author of a harm-causing or harm-threatening act or omission. The court would not find fault if it was persuaded that the company had taken realistic measures to prevent a recurrence, had ensured compensation to any victims, and had taken the event seriously in other respects.

The unusual features of 'reactive fault' may make the concept slow to gain acceptance, but an aggregative notion of corporate fault has been put forward by the Law Commission as part of its review of manslaughter.[94] The Commission suggests that the key question should be whether the *company* ought to have been aware of the risk of death or serious injury, and then whether the company's conduct fell seriously and significantly below that which could reasonably have been expected. 'Reference to the company's organization, attitude and concern for safety in general will be relevant.'[95] Further, 'if a corporation has chosen to enter a field of activity, it has a clear duty to those affected by that field of activity to take steps to avoid the creation of serious risks'.[96] This proposal is an important step in recognizing the problems of corporate crime, but it is confined to the law of manslaughter. There are good arguments for reconsidering the general structure of criminal offences, making more use of crimes of risk-creation and endangerment and relying on 'due diligence' defences to require defendant companies to demonstrate their efforts to avoid the creation of risks.[97]

Even if wider corporate liability were possible, is there much point in punishing corporations? A company can hardly be imprisoned, moderate fines can be swallowed up as business overheads, and swingeing fines might have such drastic side effects on the employment and livelihoods of innocent employees as to render them inappropriate. Fisse and Braithwaite propose a range of special penalties, some of which are rehabilitative (putting corporations on probation to supervise their compliance with the law), some of which are deterrent (punitive injunctions to require resources to be devoted to the development of new preventive measures), and others of which have mixed aims (e.g. community service by companies).[98] In their view, the primary search should be for a regime which ensures maximum prevention. This

---

[94] Law Commission Consultation Paper No 135, *Involuntary Manslaughter* (1993), 89–107 and 127–33.   [95] Ibid., para 5.84.

[96] Ibid., para 5.87. Cf. C. Wells, 'Corporations: Culture, Risk and Criminal Liability' [1993] Crim LR 551.

[97] J. Gobert, 'Corporate Criminality: New Crimes for the Times' [1994] Crim LR 722.

[98] Fisse and Braithwaite, 'Allocation of Responsibility for Corporate Crime'.

challenges the approach to liability and punishment based on what is deserved for past wrongdoing:[99] the authors explicitly reject the idea of holding corporations criminally liable according to their culpability in causing the harms, chiefly because they believe that the prevention of future harm is of greater social importance in this sphere than any abstract notion of 'justice' based on past events.[100] Desert theory, on the other hand, would draw a distinction between preventive measures and conviction and sentence. In principle, punishment for corporations, no less than for individuals, should be proportioned to culpability: the principle of fair warning should be respected by ensuring clear duties and opportunities to comply with them. Broader preventive measures, perhaps through regulatory mechanisms, should be put in hand in order to reduce the risk of further harms from similar sources. This leaves a wider problem of social justice to be debated.[101] Should the aim be to ensure that companies receive, so far as possible, commensurate punishment for the harm they cause, just like individuals? Granted that resources for law enforcement are not limited, how should priorities be determined as between the inevitably expensive prosecution of corporate crime and policing and prosecutions for the kind of violence that causes such fear in most ordinary people? To some extent this refers to the paradox of fear of crime, the degree of fear being roughly in inverse proportion to the risk of victimization and thus presenting awkward problems for social policy.[102] Even if fear of crime is tackled through social measures rather than by altering policing and prosecution policy, there remains the temptation to accept that pursuing corporate crime is so expensive that regulatory mechanisms should be preferred, a conclusion which would lead to the poor and disadvantaged being criminalized more than the well-to-do.

4.6 CAUSATION

At the beginning of this chapter it was stated that causation is one of the most basic requirements of criminal liability. Whereas for those offences that merely require conduct the voluntariness requirement (automatism) is crucial, for the many crimes which specify consequences the requirement of causation assumes a central place. Just as it seems wrong to impose criminal liability in the absence of a voluntary act or omission by the defendant, so it seems wrong to convict a person who did not cause

---

[99] On desert theory, see Ch 1.5 above.

[100] See further J. Braithwaite, 'Challenging Just Deserts: Punishing White Collar Criminals' (1982) 73 J Crim Law & Criminology, 723, and the reply by A. von Hirsch, 'Desert and White Collar Criminality: A Reply to Dr Braithwaite' ibid., 1164.

[101] Wells, *Corporations and Criminal Responsibility*, 147–9.

[102] See the works cited in n. 77 above.

the consequence or state of affairs specified in the offence. Of course, as we shall see in Chapter 5, one might wish to go further and insist not only that the defendant voluntarily caused the offence but also that he did so knowingly, intentionally, and so on. Here, however, the concern is to explore the minimum conditions for criminal liability.

The reason for requiring that the defendant should be shown to have causal responsibility for the conduct, consequence, or state of affairs lies in the principle of individual autonomy, discussed in Chapter 2.2. That principle respects individuals as capable of choosing their acts and omissions. It follows from this that they should be regarded as agents responsible, at the very least, for the normal consequences of their behaviour. Respect for individual autonomy and responsibility for conduct and consequences go hand in hand. Thus, the approach of the criminal law is to affix causal responsibility to the last individual whose voluntary behaviour impinged on the situation. To take two simple examples, if A wounds V in a way that will surely cause V's death within minutes, and B (unconnected with A) then comes along and shoots V dead, causal responsibility for the death will be imposed on B: his is the last voluntary act. It supersedes A's or, in other words, breaks the causal chain between A's act and V's subsequent death. A may be liable for attempted murder, but not for a homicide offence. The second example concerns a man of 25 who commits an armed robbery: why should not his grandparents, aged 75, also be held to have caused the offence on the basis that their act of intercourse some 50 years earlier was the original or 'true' causal root of his law-breaking? The conventional answer to this is that a person of 25 is an autonomous individual who should be treated as responsible for his decisions and their consequences. There may be many earlier events that shape his behaviour—his upbringing, his experiences at school, the influence of other young men in his locality, the fact that he was offered £5,000 to commit the robbery—but his decision to commit the offence was sufficiently free to make it fair to ascribe causal responsibility to him. These other matters may perhaps affect the degree of his culpability, but that is a separate issue.

Before looking further into the common law approach, two other possibilities must be mentioned. First, one might wish to develop an approach to caution which places particular emphasis on a person's *wrongful* act. A simple example would be where D stabs V and V then receives the wrong treatment in hospital and dies. A straightforward application of the autonomy principle would make the doctor causally responsible for the death, and would confine D's liability to the wounding. But one might wish to say that D should be held liable for the death because it was his conduct that led to the doctor having to treat the victim: but for D inflicting the wound, the doctor would not have been called upon. One problem with this is that it might seem to produce the kind of infinite regress that would have held the grandparents causally responsible in the earlier example. But that problem can be avoided if one were to specify a wrongful or, better, a criminal act. This would at least allow the courts to convict D and others who inflict life-threatening injuries, despite any medical errors that happen to supervene. A second possibility is to point to the extraordinary narrowness of the approach to causation grounded in autonomy. In the discussion of the principle of welfare in Chapter 2.3, we saw that it would be both artificial and undesirable to think of social life in terms of individuals pursuing their own ends in isolation from one another. On the one hand, many decisions are influenced and constrained by others; on the other hand, it is right that certain restrictions are placed on individual freedom in order to maximize the freedom of others to pursue their preferences. The principle of welfare has a clear impact on decisions to criminalize, and there are some occasions on which it rightly influences judgments of culpability,[103] but it seems to be ignored in the field of causation.[104] The criminal law picks out the individual who performed the last voluntary act and places causal responsibility there, without reference to the antecedents and wider social setting of the event. If it were a question of determining the causal responsibility for an industrial dispute or a particular wave of social unrest, it is unlikely that anyone would consider tracing it to a single individual. The causal strength of various contributing factors would be assessed. The traditional approach in criminal law is to ignore these other factors, except in so far as they are relevant later to the issue of culpability, and to focus on the individual. It is not clear how a system of criminal law could function otherwise, but that does not provide a convincing justification for continuing as we are. Moreover, as we will see below, the traditional approach has to be stretched and distorted in order to deal with some types of case.

(a) The General Principle

The definitions of many crimes require that D caused a result (e.g. murder, grievous bodily harm, criminal damage) or that he caused a result by certain means (e.g. obtaining property be deception). In cases where it is clear that D either intended to cause the result or knowingly risked causing it, the causal enquiry is likely to be brief because no court will see much merit in the argument that the result was highly unlikely in the circumstances and probably a coincidence. Thus the dictum 'intended consequences are never too remote' is one expression of the strong effect

---

[103] See Chs 5 and 6, below.
[104] For a critical argument along these lines, see Norrie, *Crime, Reason and History*, Ch 7.

which culpability has in hastening a finding of causation and over-looking restrictive policies which might otherwise be invoked. Where the culpability element does not overshadow the issue—and particularly in crimes of strict liability, where no culpability may be required—the question arises of what minimum connection must be established between D's conduct and the prohibited result. There is a succession of cases on offences of causing pollution in which judges have maintained that causation is a question of fact for the jury or magistrates.[105] Courts have thus been encouraged to take a 'common sense' view of whether a defendant can be said to have caused the pollution, especially when some other factor or person has intervened. However, this approach is quite unsatisfactory. There is a need for principles, and there are decisions that establish them. How coherent they are is a question for discussion later.

The general principle is that the result would not have occurred *but for* D's conduct. Of course there may be many other 'but for' causes of the result, but an explanation has already been offered for the law's concentration on voluntary human behaviour—the principle of individual autonomy. Yet the 'but for' test does appear to be rather undemanding, and it may be consciousness of this which has led English courts to refer to further (though often uncertain) parameters. In *Cato* (1976),[106] for example, the Court of Appeal expressly stopped short of the 'but for' test. D had been convicted of the manslaughter of V, whom he had injected with a heroin compound at V's request. On the issue of whether D's injection of the heroin could be said to have caused V's death, the court stated that: 'As a matter of law, it was sufficient if the prosecution could establish that it was *a* cause, provided it was a cause outside the de minimis range, and effectively bearing upon the acceleration of the moment of the victim's death.'[107] The court later stated that the cause must be 'a cause of substance', although it recognized that the term 'substantial cause' would be putting the requirements too high.[108] Clearly, the court was reluctant to accept 'but for' causation here, fearing that the link between D's conduct and V's death might be too tenuous. But this was a case of manslaughter, and the court may have been using causal arguments to circumscribe the law of constructive manslaughter (see Chapters 5.2(b) and 7.5). If the offence charged had been a crime of intention in which D's intention had been proved, the court would probably have taken a broader view.

Deception cases provide a good example of the puissance of culpability over causality, for what has to be proved for offences such as obtaining property or services by deception is that the obtaining was *caused* by the

---

[105] E.g. *Alphacell* v *Woodward* [1972] AC 854, *Rothwell* v *Yorkshire Water* [1994] Crim LR 444; *National Rivers Authority* v *Yorkshire Water Services* [1994] Crim LR 451.
[106] (1976) 62 Cr App R 41. [107] Ibid., 45.
[108] Ibid., 46; cf. *Cheshire* [1991] 1 WLR 844, referring to a 'significant contribution'.

deception. A difficulty arises where V's mind plainly did not advert to D's deception. This may occur where D was trading on normal assumptions which were not true in his or her case, and where V acted on these normal assumptions without realizing that they were inapplicable. How does the 'but for' test apply here? According to the House of Lords decisions in *Metropolitan Police Commissioner* v *Charles* (1976)[109] and in *Lambie* (1982)[110], D's conduct in using a cheque card or credit card without mentioning that its use was unauthorized may be said to have caused V to hand over the goods (or obtaining), if V would have acted otherwise, had he or she known that D's use of the card was unauthorized. This type of case is complicated by the fact that the key element in D's conduct is an omission, the failure to alert V to the fact that the normal assumptions were untrue. This is not the place to discuss whether D has a *duty* to alert V to his or her lack of authority.[111] If such a duty is established for the purpose of criminal cases, then the question of causation in crimes of omission arises.[112] Otherwise, these decisions might fairly be regarded as straining causal tests in order to secure the conviction of manifestly dishonest people. Culpability has the upper hand, and these decisions might be evidence that the courts sometimes adopt the 'wrongful act' approach, although without stating it.

A further example of the interaction of causation and culpability is provided by the medical cases. At the celebrated trial of Dr Bodkin Adams (1957), charged with murdering a patient by administering excessive does of morphine, Devlin J. stated that orthodox view that to shorten life by days and weeks is to cause death no less than shortening it by years, but he added that a doctor 'is still entitled to do all that is proper and necessary to relieve pain and suffering even if the measures he takes may incidentally shorten life'.[113] This direction to the jury might well be compatible with the principle subsequently espoused in *Cato*, that a *de minimis* contribution (i.e. a minimal cause which 'people of common sense would overlook'[114]) is not a sufficient cause in law. However, this probably does not capture the precise point of the *Adams* direction, which is rather that a doctor's conduct, founded upon clinical judgment, will not be regarded as criminal so long as it remains within reasonable bounds. Although presented as a causal proposition, its substance lies in the realm of culpability. It looks to the doctor's motive as the crucial feature, and the decision is perhaps best characterized as a covert recognition of some form of defence based on clinical medical necessity.[115]

---

[109] [1977] AC 177.   [110] [1982] AC 449.
[111] See A. T. H. Smith, 'The Idea of Criminal Deception' [1982] Crim LR 721, and below, Ch 9.7.   [112] See below, 4.4(c).   [113] [1957] Crim LR 365.
[114] Hart and Honoré, *Causation in the Law*, 344–5.   [115] See below, 4.9(b).

The principle of causation is that it is sufficient if D's conduct was a 'but for' cause which was more than minimal: it need not be a substantial cause, but it seems that a mere 'but for' cause will rarely be sufficient (the deception cases may be an exception here). The principle has been illustrated here in relation to 'result-crimes' but the same approach should be adopted to crimes that penalize conduct or possession, although for those crimes the difficulties will usually concern the exceptions in (b) below.[116] The draft Criminal Code restates the general principle in terms of 'an act which makes more than a negligible contribution to its occurrence',[117] and the Model Penal Code deals with the issue by excluding causes which are too remote to have a just bearing on responsibility.[118] The requirement of 'but for' causation is sometimes termed 'factual causation', which is then contrasted with legal causation—not only to suggest that the law requires something more than 'but for' causation, but also to indicate that there are other aspects of the doctrine to be considered.

(b) Interventions between Conduct and Result

It is rarely relevant to suggest either that another person played a role, since concurrent causation is possible in law,[119] or that the real cause was some coincidental event unconnected with the defendant. English law has no clear principle to deal with the latter point, but the draft Criminal Code refers to an intervening act 'which could not in the circumstances have been reasonably foreseen.'[120] Apart from those types of case, the principle of individual autonomy presumes that, where an individual who is neither mentally disordered nor an infant has made a sufficient causal contribution to an occurrence, it is inappropriate to trace the causation any further. This is taken to justify not only picking out D's conduct from other possible causes and regarding that conduct as operating on a 'stage already set',[121] but also declining to look behind D's conduct for other persons who might be said to have contributed to D acting as he or she did. The doctrine, then, is that voluntary conduct acts as a barrier in any causal enquiry in criminal law: by and large, D's voluntary conduct will usually be regarded as the cause of an act or an omission if it was the last human conduct before the result.

[116] See the discussion of crimes of possession in Ch 4.3(b) above.
[117] Law Com No. 177, cl 17(1)(a).
[118] American Law Institute, *Model Penal Code*, s 2.03.
[119] E.g. *Attorney-General's Reference (No 4 of 1980)* (1981) 73 Cr App R 40.
[120] Law Com No. 177, cl 17(2)(c); cf. the *Model Penal Code*, s 2.03(2)(b), removing causal responsibility where the result is 'too remote or accidental in its occurrence to have a [just] bearing on the actor's liability'.
[121] See H. L. A. Hart and T. Honoré, *Causation in the Law* (2nd edn, 1985), Ch 1 and passim, and the derivative discussions by S. Kadish, *Blame and Punishment* (1987), Ch 8, and H. Beynon, 'Causation, Omissions and Complicity' [1987] Crim LR 539; cf. also Williams, *Textbook of Criminal Law*, Ch 14.

However, a natural event occurring after D's conduct may be treated as terminating D's causal responsibility if it is a coincidence, but not if it could reasonably be expected.[122] The contrast would be between D, whose assault victim catches scarlet fever in hospital and dies (which should be treated as a 'visitation of Providence' and as negativing any causal connection between D and the death), and E, who leaves the assault victim lying on a tidal beach, where he later drowns (this is within the risk which was reasonably foreseeable, and therefore not a sufficient coincidence to prevent causal responsibility for the death).

What if D's act is followed by another human act, which intervenes before the result occurs? Because traditional causal theory does not review the entire situation but tends to focus on the last human act, one might expect an intervening human act to negative D's causal responsibility. But in at least three sets of situations—(i) the conduct of third parties; (ii) the conduct of doctors; and (iii) the conduct of the victim—this is not so, raising questions about what is the general rule and what the exception.

(i) *Conduct of Third Parties.* An example of the type of case in which a third party's intervention may relieve D of liability is provided by *Impress (Worcester) Ltd* v *Rees* (1971),[123] where pollution resulted because some third party opened the valve on an oil tank at the defendant's factory. The Divisional Court held that this unauthorized and unforeseeable act broke the chain of causation. However, later pollution cases have distinguished the *Impress* decision, and in *National Rivers Authority* v *Wright Engineering Ltd* (1994)[124] the act of vandals in releasing the tap on an oil tank was held not to relieve the defendants from liability for causing polluting matter to enter a brook. This development represents a departure from normal causal principles: the courts could perhaps justify it by imposing special duties on certain industries, but instead they have purported to apply a 'common sense' concept of causation.

In other areas the courts have developed express exceptions to the general principle in cases where the third party's intervention would not be described as voluntary. If the third party is an infant or is mentally disordered, this lack of rational capacity may be regarded as sufficient to discount the third party's act in causal terms. The same applies if D sets out to use a responsible adult as an 'innocent agent', giving false information to that person in the hope that he or she will act upon it. The behaviour of the person who has been tricked is discounted as non-voluntary for these purposes. The case of *Michael* (1840)[125] illustrates the principle. D's child

---

[122] Hart and Honoré, *Causation in the Law*, 342.

[123] [1971] 2 All ER 357.

[124] [1994] Crim LR 453; cf. also *National Rivers Authority* v *Yorkshire Water* [1994] Crim LR 451 (clandestine discharge by customer).

[125] (1840) 9 C&P 356; cf. G. Williams, *'Finis for Novus Actus'* [1989] Camb LJ, 391.

was in the care of a fostermother, and D, wishing her child dead, handed a bottle of poison to the fostermother, saying that it was medicine for the child. The fostermother saw no need for the medicine and placed it on the mantelpiece, from which her own five-year-old child later removed it and administered a fatal dose to D's child. The intended result was therefore achieved through the unexpected act of an infant rather than through the mistakenly 'innocent' act of an adult, but neither of these intervening acts was regarded as sufficient to relieve D of causal responsibility.[126]

A similar approach may be taken where the intervening act is one of compulsion, necessity, or duty. If the third party brings about the prohibited harm while under duress from D, then D may be regarded as the legal cause of the result.[127] The same analysis can be applied where D creates a situation of necessity, or where D's behaviour creates a duty to respond in the third party. These points may be illustrated by reference to *Pagett* (1983).[128] D was being pursued by the police and took his pregnant girlfriend hostage, holding her in front of him as a shield while he fired shots at the police. The police fired back at D, but killed the girlfriend. The Court of Appeal upheld D's conviction for the manslaughter of his girlfriend, even though the fatal shots were fired by the police and not by him. The Court offered two reasons in support of this conclusion: first, the police officer's conduct in shooting back at D was necessary for his self-preservation and therefore was not a voluntary act; and secondly, that the police officer was acting from a duty to prevent crime and to arrest D. Both these reasons seem heavily imbued with formality and objectivity—Did a necessity exist? Was there a duty?—and yet they contain no reference to a duty to avoid harm to the person being held hostage. And, arguably, the liberty to act in self-preservation might also be subject to this qualification. These points ought to have been explored at least. Perhaps the true rationale of this decision may be found in a doctrine of 'alternative danger': where D places a person in the position of having to choose between two drastic courses of action, one threatening self-danger and the other threatening danger to another, any response to such an emergency which is not totally irrational or unjustified ought to be treated as depriving the third party of rational choice about the outcome, and the result may therefore be attributed causally to the creator of the emergency. This leaves open the possibility of finding that a trained police officer ought to have acted with greater circumspection towards the hostage on the facts of *Pagett*, if that is a fair judgment on the facts of that case, since the law

---

[126] Cf. *Cogan and Leak* [1976] 1 QB 217, on 'semi-innocent agency', discussed in Ch 10.6 below.   [127] *Bourne* (1952) 36 Cr App R 125; see also below, Ch 10.6.
[128] (1983) 76 Cr App R 279; see Hart and Honoré, *Causation in the Law*, 330–4.

might justifiably expect more of a trained official than a hapless citizen caught up in extreme events.[129]

(ii) *Conduct of Doctors*. The decision in *Pagett* contains more than a hint that the court was far more concerned about convicting a morally culpable person than about the refinements of causation, and similar leanings may be found in cases involving doctors. In cases where a victim receives medical attention, there is rarely any doubt that it may properly be described as 'voluntary': doctors work under pressure, occasionally having to make rapid decisions, but they are trained and trusted to exercise clinical judgment in these circumstances. Perhaps doctors could be regarded as acting under a duty to treat patients, aligning their role with one of the formal reasons in *Pagett*. But the courts have not approached these cases by way of the concept of voluntariness.

A distinction has been drawn between cases where the wound inflicted by D remains a substantial and operating cause of death despite the subsequent medical treatment, in which case D remains causally responsible, and those where the original wound becomes merely 'the setting in which another cause operates', in which case D's responsibility in negatived.[130] The reference to an 'operating and substantial' cause might be regarded as more favourable to D than the general principle of causation, unless the term 'substantial' is read as meaning 'more than minimal'. This is confirmed by the statement in *Cheshire* (1991)[131] that a significant contribution is all that is required, and that the defendant's act does not need to be the sole or even the main cause:

Even though negligence in the treatment of the victim was the immediate cause of his death, the jury should not regard it as excluding the responsibility of the accused unless the negligent treatment was so independent of his acts, and in itself so potent in causing death, that they regard the contribution made by his acts as insignificant.[132]

No clear reason is offered for discounting the voluntary intervening act of the doctor. If the doctor administers a drug to which the patient is known to be intolerant, or gives some other wrong treatment, should the inappropriateness of the medical treatment affect the causal enquiry? The courts' reluctance to discuss the causal significance of the medical treatment probably stems from a desire to ensure the conviction of a culpable offender, and this suggests a strong attachment to a 'wrongful act' approach to causation, deciding the issue by reference to broader

---

[129] See further Ch 6.6 below; cf. the arguments of P. A. J. Waddington, ' "Overkill" or "Minimum Force"?' [1990] Crim LR 695, and pp. 141–2 below.

[130] *Smith* [1959] 2 QB 35, distinguishing *Jordan* (1956) 40 Cr App R 152; cf. the critical attack of Norrie, *Crime, Reason and History*, 147–8.

[131] [1991] 1 WLR 844.   [132] Ibid., 852.

judgments of innocence and culpability. This appears to overlook the fact that D, who inflicted the original wound which gave rise to the need for medical attention, will still be liable for attempted murder or a serious wounding offence even if the medical treatment is held to negative his causal responsibility for the ensuing death. Perhaps, for adherents of the 'wrongful act' approach, this is insufficient: they want to see responsibility for the ultimate result pinned on the defendant. However, a court which declares that it is not the doctor who is on trial but the original wrongdoer[133] is merely offering an unconvincing rationalization of its failure to apply the ordinary causal principle that a voluntary intervening act which accelerates death should relieve the original wrongdoer of liability for the result. If that causal principle is thought unsuitable for medical cases, should we not be absolutely clear about the reasons, and then look closely at a doctrine of clinical medical necessity?[134]

(iii) *Conduct or Condition of the Victim*. The general principle that the law approaches causation by considering the effect of an autonomous individual's conduct upon a 'stage already set' is usually taken to extend to cases where the victim has some special condition which makes him or her especially vulnerable. This is sometimes known as the 'thin skull' principle, or the principle that defendants must take their victims as they find them. If D commits a minor assault on V, and V, who is a haemophiliac, dies from that assault, the principle applies to render D causally responsible for the death.[135] Now this principle of causation may have little practical effect on its own, since most of the serious criminal offences require proof of *means rea* (proof that D intended or foresaw the risk of causing, say, serious injury), and it will usually be possible to show that the *mens rea* was lacking because D was unaware of V's special condition. However, in those systems of law which contain some offences of constructive liability (such as manslaughter in English and American law),[136] the 'thin skull' principle reinforces the constructive element by ensuring that there is no causal barrier to convicting D of an offence involving more serious harm than was intended or foreseen. The objections to constructive manslaughter are set out in Chapter 7.5. The objection to the 'thin skull' principle is that such physical conditions are abnormal and that much of the standard analysis of causation turns on distinctions between normal and abnormal conditions.[137]

What principles should apply to the causal effect of the victim's conduct after D's original act? Should V's conduct be subject to the normal rules of

---

[133] Per Lord Lane CJ, in *Malcherek* (1981) 73 Cr App R 173.
[134] See 4.9 below.
[135] A clear example, on these facts, is the American case of *State* v *Frazer* (1936) 98 SW (2d) 707.   [136] See below, Chs 5.2(a) and 7 7.
[137] See the criticism of Hart and Honoré by Norrie, *Crime Reason and History*, 149–50.

voluntary intervening acts? *Roberts* (1971)[138] was a case in which D, while driving his car, made suggestions to his passenger, trying to remove her coat, at which point she opened the door and leapt from the moving car, suffering injury. The Court of Appeal upheld D's conviction for assault occasioning actual bodily harm, on the basis that a victim's 'reasonably foreseeable' reaction does not negative causation. Whether 'reasonable foreseeability' is an accurate way of expressing the point in question must be doubted; one might well say that the prospect of the woman jumping from the moving car was relatively unlikely. Surely it would be better to consider the principle of 'alternative danger': D's conduct had placed V in a situation of emergency in which she had to make a rapid choice about how to react. One might then say that any reaction which cannot be regarded as wholly abnormal or 'daft'[139] should remain D's causal responsibility. In this sense, V's reaction is non-voluntary.

What if the victim refuses to accept medical treatment for the injury inflicted by D? The question presented itself starkly in *Blaue* (1975).[140] D stabbed V four times, piercing her lung. V was advised that she would die from the wounds unless she had a blood transfusion, but, adhering to her faith as a Jehovah's Witness, she refused to undergo this treatment. She died. The Court of Appeal held D to be causally responsible for her death. Her intervening decision not to accept the 'normal' treatment did not negative D's causal responsibility, because, the court argued, the situation was analogous to that covered by the 'thin skull' rule. Stating that 'those who use violence on other people must take their victims as they find them', the court added that this 'means the whole man [*sic*], not just the physical man. It does not lie in the mouth of the assailant to say that his victim's religious beliefs which inhibited him [*sic*] from accepting certain kinds of treatment were unreasonable.'[141] Is this another example of a court stretching the principles of causation so as to ensure the conviction of a wrongdoer? The 'thin skull' principle applies only to pre-existing physical conditions of the victim. The principle of individual autonomy suggests that, in general, any subsequent act or omission by V should negative D's causal responsibility. Exceptions to this are where V's subsequent conduct falls within the 'reasonable foreseeability' notion in *Roberts*[142] or, perhaps, within the principle of 'alternative danger'. D's actions in *Blaue* can certainly be said to have caused a situation of alternative danger and emergency, and so then the question would be whether V's reaction should be classified as wholly abnormal. In a statistical sense it surely was: it must be rare to refuse a blood transfusion knowing that death will follow that

---

[138] (1971) 56 Cr App R 95.   [139] (1971) 56 Cr App R 95.
[140] (1975) 61 Cr App R 271.   [141] Per Lawton LJ, ibid., 274.
[142] (1971) 56 Cr App R 95.

refusal. To accept this would be to make no distinction between one who refuses treatment for religious reasons and one who refuses out of spite. It could be argued that the standard of normality should be informed by social values rather than enslaved to statistical frequency, that religious beliefs are a matter of conscience which should be respected, and therefore that acts or omissions based on religious conviction should not be set aside as abnormal.

So while it is possible to construct arguments in favour of D's causal responsibility for the death, this may be more a question of legalistic ingenuity that social appropriateness. It would have been possible to convict Blaue of attempted murder or wounding with intent to cause grievous bodily harm, both offences which carry a maximum sentence of life imprisonment. No doubt there was much sympathy and respect for the victim, courageously adhering to her religious beliefs in the face of death, generating the argument that it would not be appropriate to hold her causally responsible for her own death. Perhaps this is, at root, another example of the 'wrongful act' approach. Lawton LJ in *Blaue*[143] clearly regarded this as the common law approach, and evidently it is closely related to the maxim that anyone who knowingly does a wrongful act should take the consequences, discussed in Chapter 5.2(b) in the context of fault requirements. Certainly it is difficult to give a convincing explanation of the judicial approach, here as in the medical cases, without referring to the 'wrongful act' approach or at least, as tentatively suggested above, to some principle of 'alternative danger'.

(c) Causation and Omissions

One of the difficulties sometimes raised about imposing criminal liability for omissions, in addition to those already discussed in Chapters 2.6 and 4.4 above, is the problem of causation. How can an omission be said to cause harm? Or are these cases exceptions to the causal requirement?[144]

Starting with the most basic question, is it possible to say that, but for an omission, a harm would not have resulted? The existence of a duty justifies calling it an omission, and the non-performance of that duty in a situation where it arises can be said to cause the result. To take an extreme example, a parent who makes no attempt to save her or his child from drowning in shallow water can be said to cause the child's death: but for the parent's inaction, the child would almost certainly have lived. It is no answer to say that the child would have drowned anyway if the parent had not been

---

[143] (1975) 61 Cr App R 274.
[144] For discussions, see Husak, *Philosophy of Criminal Law*, Ch 6; A. Leavens, 'A Causation Approach to Omissions' (1988) 76 Cal LR, 547; H. Beynon, 'Causation, Omissions and Complicity' [1987] Crim LR 539.

there, because in that eventuality there would have been no duty and hence no omission. On the facts as they were, the parent was present and but for non-performance of the duty, the child would not have died. When dealing with causation by acts, we have seen that the courts have used terms such as 'significant' and even 'substantial' in some cases, chiefly to rule out remote or minimal causes, but this should create no special difficulty for omissions. One counterargument is that this approach may sometimes lead to the conclusion that many people caused a result: if, in a jurisdiction which imposes a duty of easy rescue, 20 or more people stand by without offering any help or raising the alarm, the conclusion must be that all these people caused the harm that occurred.[145] This is true, and is hardly an argument against the causation approach. Nor would it be a counterargument to say that but for several omissions in the past many crimes would not have been committed: this is really no different from the argument against tracing causation to grandparents, mentioned earlier.

This is not to suggest that there are no difficulties in applying causal arguments to cases of omission. For example, if A stabs V it is obvious that but for A's act V would not have suffered this wound; but if a parent makes no effort to save a child drowning in a pool, it is possible that the duty might have been fulfilled by summoning help (which might have caused delay, and the child's life might have been lost), or that the parent might not have been able to save the child's life anyway (if it had already been in the pool some time before the parent arrived). The point of these examples is that the 'but for' clause may be less concrete in some omissions cases, and may occasionally require a judgment to be made. However, at the very least there are many clear cases where ordinary causal analysis creates no more problems than it does in relation to acts.

(d) Causing Other Persons to Act

Can it ever be held that one person caused another to act in a certain way? The notion would seem to be inconsistent with the general principle of individual autonomy, emphasized above by reiterating the principle that a voluntary intervening act removes or displaces the previous actor's causal responsibility. Yet we have already noted one case in which a person can be said to cause another to act—the case of innocent agency, where the third party lacks rationality or has been tricked. Further cases arise in the law of complicity, that branch of the criminal law which holds people liable for helping or encouraging others to commit crimes, which will be discussed at length in Chapter 10.

One example of the type of case under discussion is where D goes to P

---

[145] See Ch 2.7 above. The much-discussed Genovese case in New York in 1965 had similar facts.

and offers him money to injure or kill V:[146] the law will hold D liable for counselling and procuring P's subsequent offence, and one might say that D *causes* the offence, in some sense. Clearly, however, D did not cause P to act as an innocent agent: P was not, we assume, lacking in rational capacity, and so on the general principle of individual autonomy P would be regarded as causally responsible for the result. D cannot, therefore, be held to have caused that result in the usual sense, but one might follow Hart and Honoré in suggesting that D may be said to have given P a reason for committing it.[147] This is a dilution of the general approach to causation, aimed specifically at rationalizing the criminal liability of certain accomplices.

But it is not only those who 'counsel or procure' who are brought within the English law of accomplice liability. It is also persons who 'aid and abet' others to commit offences. Advice, information, and other acts of assistance and encouragement may be great or small, and may be readily obtainable from others if this would-be accomplice had declined. So, as an element of causal contribution to P's offence, D's 'aiding' may be insignificant indeed—certainly well below the 'but for' threshold, even in the extended sense adopted by the notion of 'occasioning'. Many writers now acknowledge that the element of causation is absent from some cases of 'aiding and abetting'.[148] This brings us to a reconsideration of the role of causation.

(e) Conclusion

Causation is a complex topic, with which we have been able to deal only briefly here. Proof of causation is often said to be an essential precondition of criminal liability, but there is reason to doubt the generality of that requirement. Should those statutes that impose vicarious liability on employers,[149] for example, be opposed because the employer cannot be said to cause the acts of the employees? Should the liability of accomplices for aiding and abetting, discussed in the preceding paragraph, be opposed for the same reason? Rather than insisting on a universal requirement of causation, it may be preferable to argue that liability should be negatived, in general, by the voluntary intervening act of another. Several criticisms of the judicial approach to these exceptional categories of case have been advanced above. Often the explanations they give for their decisions are unconvincing. While traditional or standard causal theory emphasizes the significance of the last voluntary act, there is no reluctance to look wider or to massage the term 'voluntary' in certain situations, especially where D

---

[146] *Calhaem* [1985] QB 808.

[147] Hart and Honoré, *Causation in the Law*, 51.

[148] J. C. Smith, 'Aid, Abet, Counsel and Procure', in Glazebrook (ed), *Reshaping the Criminal Law*; Kadish, *Blame and Punishment*, Ch 8.   [149] See Ch 4.5(a).

clearly started the sequence of events by doing a wrongful act. The challenge is to re-examine the intuitions that lead judges and others to their conclusions (e.g. the wrongful act theory, the approach to medical mistakes, etc), with a view to constructing a law that ensures that the courts respect the various principles outlined in Chapter 3.

4.7 JUSTIFIABLE CONDUCT

Many offences include a qualification such as 'without lawful excuse', 'without lawful authority or reasonable excuse', and so on. We are not concerned here with the different shades of meaning attached to such phrases,[150] nor with the legislature's frequent use of the word 'excuse' to refer to justifications, but rather with some general doctrines which operate as justifications for conduct which would otherwise be criminal. Self-defence is the best known of these justifications, but there are others concerned with the prevention of crime, the arrest of suspected offenders, the protection of property, and so forth. Lawyers frequently speak of these doctrines as defences, e.g. 'the defence of self-defence', and procedurally that is how they function. If there is evidence, usually raised by the defendant, that the conduct may have been justifiable, the prosecution bears the burden of proving beyond reasonable doubt that the conduct was *not* justifiable or lawful. 'If the prosecution fail to do so, the accused is entitled to be acquitted because the prosecution will have failed to prove an essential element of the crime, namely that the violence used by the accused was unlawful.'[151] The consequences of presenting the justifications as the element of unlawfulness required in all crimes will not be taken further here.[152] Neither this, nor the procedural device of treating them as defences, should deflect attention from the fundamental significance of the doctrine of justification. There are certain situations when individuals have a right, or at least a permission, to do things which would generally be prohibited because they cause harm or damage. The most striking occasions are those on which the law justifies one person in killing another. It is sometimes said that justified conduct is right conduct but, in a penetrating new study, Suzanne Uniacke argues that justified conduct is conduct that one has a right to do—it is permissible in the situation, even if it is not necessarily a matter for congratulation.[153] Two other preliminary points flow from this: first, it is not permissible to resist justified conduct;

---

[150] See R. Card, 'Authority and Excuse as Defences to Crime' [1969] Crim LR 359, 415.

[151] Per Lord Griffiths in *Beckford* v *R* [1988] AC 130, at 144.

[152] Cf. R. H. S. Tur, 'Subjectivism and Objectivism: Towards Synthesis', in S. Shute, J. Gardner and J. Horder (eds), *Action and Value in Criminal Law* (1993).

[153] S. Uniacke, *Permissible Killing: the Self-Defence Justification of Homicide* (1994), 26 and Ch 2 generally.

and secondly, the rules of justification should respect the various principles of legality and 'rule of law' for the same reason that offence definitions should, that is, because they may be relied upon to guide behaviour.

(a) Self-Defence and Individual Autonomy

It is hardly surprising that decisions on self-defence formed an important and frequent element in the development of the English common law in days when there was no organized policing and when the carrying of deadly weapons was common. The issues here concern the basic right to life and physical safety. An individual who is attacked or threatened with a serious physical attack must be accorded the legal liberty to repel that attack, thus preserving a basic right. A well-regulated society will provide a general protection, but it cannot guarantee protection at the very moment when an individual is subjected to sudden attack. The criminal law cannot respect the autonomy of the individual if it does not provide for this dire situation.

(b) Social Justification and Conflicting Rights

In terms of individual autonomy, one difficulty with this analysis is that these situations involve two individuals (at least). If the law gives the subject of the attack the liberty to wound or kill his aggressor, what happens to the aggressor's right to life and physical safety? One answer to this is that the aggressor forfeits those rights when he embarks on the attack, and that it is his misconduct in starting the conflict which justifies the law in giving preference to the liberty of his victim. This is the approach favoured by some legal systems, which maintain that an innocent person's rights are absolute and which recognize few limitations to those rights, even when that person is repelling a minor assault or defending property.[154] The common law accepted this approach at one time, and elements of it still remain, such as the liberty to defend one's home.[155] But it should be carefully circumscribed lest it allows the subject of an attack to stand fast and use whatever force is necessary to protect his rights of ownership and liberties of passage. The idea of forfeiture is not objectionable in itself,[156] and it enables a choice to be made when the right to life of an attacker is, in turn, threatened by a defender protecting his right to life. The forfeiture approach bears some similarity to the 'wrongful act' approach in causation[157] and to the theory of constructive liability,[158] in that it attributes great significance to the wrongfulness of a person's initial act. However, this should only be taken so far as to permit the

---

[154] G. P. Fletcher, *Rethinking Criminal Law* (1978), 862–3.

[155] See below, Ch 4.7(c) (iii).

[156] Uniacke argues that there is no conceptual difficulty with the notion of forfeiture so long as we accept that the right to life, like many other rights, is conditional on our conduct: 'Permissible Killing', 201 and Ch 6 generally.   [157] Above, Ch 4.6.

[158] See Ch 3.5(r).

proportionate use of force. Forfeiture of life to protect a person from some minor hurt, loss or damage would promote honour above the suppression of violence.

Thus, in view of the status of the right to life as the most basic value, and the high importance also placed on physical safety,[159] the general prohibition on the use of force should only be lifted in cases where the state is unable to provide protection (i.e. situations of emergency), and even then only to a limited extent. It is unsatisfactory to argue that the innocent subject of an attack may use whatever force is necessary to vindicate his threatened rights: that analysis assigns no value to the rights of the attacker (since it subscribes to the theory of forfeiture of rights). If the criminal law is committed to ensuring that harms are inflicted as rarely as possible, it cannot accept a vindication approach which seems to allow the infliction of gratuitous, or at least disproportionate, harm. The point is not quite taken in the drafting of the European Convention on Human Rights, Article 2 of which provides that 'everyone's right to life should be protected by law', but goes on to declare that 'deprivation of life shall not be regarded as inflicted in contravention of this Article when it results from the use of force which is no more than absolutely necessary (a) in defence of any person from unlawful violence . . .'. The requirement of absolute necessity seems restrictive, but there might be cases in which a relatively minor attack could only be prevented by the infliction of a major harm: in that case the infliction of the major harm would be absolutely necessary, but should it be regarded as justifiable? A nineteenth-century Royal Commission remarked that a law whose only requirement was necessity 'would justify every weak lad whose hair was about to be pulled by a stronger one, in shooting the bully if he could not otherwise prevent the assault'.[160] The example is an extreme one, but its point is central. Thus it would be wrong to support a law which regarded it as justifiable for a police officer to shoot a person suspected of stealing from a shop, or for a landowner to shoot a walker who was trespassing on his land. So far as possible the rights of both individuals should be protected in accordance with their value, and the value of the right to life is such that it should only be forfeited when another's basic rights are under threat.

(c) The Range of Justifications

The development of the common law has focussed on self-defence, but there is also authority for the justifiable use of force in a range of other

---

[159] See Ch 2.4 above.

[160] Report of the Royal Commission on the Law Relating to Indictable Offences (1879, C 2345), note B, at 44; see p. 11 of the report for an assertion of the principle that 'the mischief done by, or which might reasonably be anticipated from, the force used is not disproportioned to the injury or mischief which it is intended to prevent'.

situations. The draft Criminal Code contains a useful statement of six circumstances in which force might be justified:[161]

1. to prevent or terminate crime, or to effect or assist in the lawful arrest of an offender or suspected offender or of a person unlawfully at large;
2. to prevent or terminate a breach of the peace;
3. to protect himself or another from unlawful force or unlawful personal harm (this is self-defence, broadened to cover defensive force in support of another citizen);[162]
4. to prevent or terminate the unlawful detention of himself or another;
5. to protect property (whether belonging to himself or another) from unlawful appropriate, destruction, or damage; and
6. to prevent or terminate a trespass to his person or property.

It is obvious that the amount of physical force which may justifiably be inflicted on another in pursuit of any one of these purposes may vary considerably; much may turn on the purpose which D was pursuing when the force was used. But that variation of circumstances is not enough to warrant variation in the legal standard of justifiable force. At present, English law maintains two different standards: for the justifiable use of force in the protection of personal safety it requires reasonableness and necessity, whereas for the justifiable damaging of another's property it requires only that D *believed* that 'the means of protection adopted . . . would be reasonable having regard to all the circumstances'.[163] The latter rule is more indulgent to the defendant, and, indeed, it hardly embodies a legal standard at all. One feature of the draft Criminal Code is that it would abolish the special rule for property damage.

(d) The Rules and the Principles

A precise statement of English law on the justifications is difficult to locate. The Criminal Law Act 1967, section 3, states that 'a person may use such force as is reasonable in the circumstances in the prevention of crime . . .'. The section was not intended to supplant the common law rules on self-defence,[164] and the courts have continued to develop those rules. It is true that in most situations of self-defence it could be said that the person was preventing crime (i.e. preventing an attack which constituted a crime), but that would still leave certain cases untouched—notably, attacks by a child under 10, by a mentally disordered person, or by a person labouring under a mistake of fact. Such aggressors would commit

---

[161] Law Com No. 177, clause 44.
[162] See *Duffy* [1967] 1 QB 63, and *Devlin v Armstrong* [1971] NI 13.
[163] Criminal Damage Act 1971, s 5(2); cf. *Scarlett*, below, n. 199.
[164] J. C. Smith, 'Using Force in Self-Defence and Prevention of Crime' (1994) 47 CLP 101.

no offence, and so it is the law of self-defence, not the prevention of crime, which governs.

The law of self-defence, as it is applied by the courts, turns on two requirements: the force must have been necessary, and it must have been reasonable. In dealing with particular cases, however, the courts have, as we shall see, reached decisions which suggest certain sub-rules, but they have generally been reluctant to refer to them as such, preferring to make use of the broad flexibility of the concept of reasonableness. This indicates that the principle of maximum certainty is not followed in the English law on justifiable force.[165]

Both the legislation and judicial decisions prefer to state the law in terms of what is 'reasonable' or 'reasonable and necessary'. It may be argued that this derogation from maximum certainty is not a serious matter: people who are attacked suddenly are unlikely to have time to reflect on the provisions of the criminal law before defending themselves. This argument is correct only on its own terms: people who are attacked suddenly may well respond without reflection,[166] but many cases in which justifiable force is raised concern either an expected attack or action by trained law enforcement officers. Moreover, legal certainty is important from the point of view of producing consistent and principled court decisions, as well as guiding the conduct of citizens. The approach of the draft Criminal Code in seeking to articulate some distinct principles and sub-rules is therefore to be welcomed.[167] The enactment of several sub-rules does not deprive courts of the flexibility to respond to new sets of circumstances, and they cover some recurrent issues which it is right to determine in a principled rather than an *ad hoc* fashion.

(e) The Proportionality Standard

The requirement that the use of force must be necessary should be limited, as it is in English law, by a further requirement that it must be reasonable in the circumstances. This shows respect for the rights of the attacker in self-defence cases, and for the rights of suspected offenders in relation to the other justifications. The standard cannot be a precise one: probably the best way of defining it is in terms of what is reasonably proportionate to the amount of harm likely to be suffered by the defendant, or likely to result if the forcible intervention is not made. What is crucial is that it should rule out the infliction or risk of considerable physical harm merely to apprehend a fleeing thief, to stop minor property loss or damage, etc. For offences against the person, it means that deadly force should only be

---

[165] See above, Ch 3 4(i).   [166] See below, 4.7(g).
[167] Law Com No. 177, clause 44 and ii, paras 12 24–12 37; for detailed argument in favour of this approach, see Ashworth, 'Self-Defence and the Right to Life' [1975] CLJ 272.

justified for a life-threatening attack and, perhaps, for certain crimes of extreme seriousness. The United States Model Penal Code provides that deadly force is not justified 'unless the actor believes that such force is necessary to protect himself against death, serious bodily harm, kidnapping or sexual intercourse compelled by force or threat'.[168] It is debatable whether this goes too far in allowing the lawful sacrifice of a life to prevent certain non-fatal assaults, although in practice cases of this kind may present great problems.[169] The reason for inserting the provision, however, was to try to narrow down the permissible use of force in a country which has often given primary weight to the autonomy of the subject of the attack and has therefore accepted deadly force with few limitations.

One aspect of the proportionality principle might be the limitation of the use of force against police officers. A general provision covering the use of force to prevent false imprisonment might be thought to justify a citizen in using force to prevent the police from making an arrest which he or she knows to be mistaken. In fact, English Law renders an arrest lawful if the police officer has reasonable grounds for suspicion. There are English decisions which draw a distinction between resisting a lawful—but mistaken—arrest (which is not justified), and repelling the unlawful use of violence by police (which is justified),[170] and this principle is to be found both in the Model Penal Code and the draft Criminal Code.[171] If one accepts, for policy reasons, that the police should be empowered to act on 'reasonable suspicion', then that necessarily restricts the use of defensive force either by the suspect or by others acting on his or her behalf. On the other hand, a law which prohibited individuals from defending themselves against excessive force by the police would be unduly narrow. The trust on which most social institutions survive can only be taken so far.

(f) Aspects of the Necessity Requirement

The necessity requirement forms part of most legal regimes on justifiable force. The first question to be asked is: necessary for what? We have seen that force may be justified for any one of several lawful purposes. The necessity must be judged according to the lawful purpose which the defendant was trying to pursue: for self-defence, purely defensive force will often be all that is necessary; in order to apprehend a suspected offender, on the other hand, a police officer or citizen will need to behave proactively. These differences may become particularly important in cases where there is a suspicion or allegation that the force was used by way of

---

[168] Model Penal Code, s 3.04.
[169] J. C. Smith, *Justification and Excuse in the Criminal Law* (1989), 109 and Ch 4, passim.
[170] *Fennell* [1971] 1 QB 428; *Ball* [1989] Crim LR 579.
[171] Model Penal Code, s 3.04(2)(a)(i); Law Com No. 177, cl 44(4).

revenge or retaliation rather than in pursuit of a lawful purpose. What was the defendant's purpose? Could the conduct be said to be necessary for that purpose? Is there a mental element in the justifications, such that a person cannot rely on a particular justification if he or she is ignorant of the basic facts needed to support that justification? In *Dadson* (1850)[172] a constable shot a fleeing thief. Such force was justifiable against 'felons', and a thief was a felon if he had two previous convictions. This thief had previous convictions and so was a felon, but the constable fired at him without knowing this. It was held that the constable could not rely on the justification of using force to apprehend a felon because he was unaware of the basic fact needed to constitute the justification. The Northern Irish case of *Thain* (1985)[173] takes this point further, since D, a soldier on duty, stated from the outset that he did not fire the shot in order to apprehend V (who was running away at the time) and said that he shot in reaction to a sudden movement by V. It seems that D might have succeeded if he had maintained that his intention was to arrest, but the court was unable to accept his proffered reason and he was convicted of murder. This decision holds that there is an element of belief or motive whenever a justification is relied upon, and this is surely right. In many circumstances a greater use of force might be justifiable for law enforcement than merely for defence.[174]

In most cases, where no problem of the mental element arises, the main issue is necessity. The English courts have continued to develop the common law, but without always relating the issues to any general themes. An attempt is made here to organize the decisions around six issues.

(i) *Imminence.* It has been stated that the use of force can only be necessary if the attack is imminent or immediate.[175] Presumably the reasoning is that, if there is time to warn the police, then that is the course which should be taken, in preference to the use of force by a private individual. But this apparently does not mean that it is unlawful to prepare or keep armaments for an anticipated attack. In the *Attorney-General's Reference (No.2 of 1983)*[176] D's shop had been looted during rioting which the police had struggled to control; D made some petrol bombs with which to repel any future attack, and the question was whether these were in his possession 'for a lawful object'. It was held that they were, if the jury accepted that D intended to use them only against an attack on his premises which the police could not control. This is an unusually indulgent approach for the criminal courts—a conviction followed by a discharge

---

[172] (1850) 4 Cox CC 358.　　　　　　　　　　　　　　　[173] [1985] NI 457.
[174] For discussion, see e.g. B. Hogan, 'The Dadson Principle' [1989] Crim LR 679; Husak, *Philosophy of Criminal Law*, 212–15; G. R. Sullivan, 'Bad Thoughts and Bad Acts' [1990] Crim LR 559.
[175] E.g. *Attorney-General for Northern Ireland's Reference* [1977] AC 105; *Chisam* (1963) 47 Cr App R 130.　　　　　　　　　　　　　[176] [1984] QB 456.

would be more normal, since it does not signal that such conduct is permissible and thereby 'encourage' less worthy imitators—but it was a response to the rare situation that arose. If the police are unable to offer protection and attack is imminent, the rationale for justifiable force is made out. However, objects as lethal as firebombs should rarely be approved as lawful means of defending business premises, as opposed to defending a home or human beings. This decision also leaves unresolved a problem about the lawfulness of carrying a gun or an offensive weapon in order to repel an anticipated attack: the authorities would seem to suggest that, although the use of the weapon might be lawful if an attack takes place, its possession beforehand remains an offence.[177]

(ii) *A Duty to Avoid Conflict?* One of the most technical but most significant elements in the common law of self-defence was the duty to retreat. Its technicality lay in its careful wording and its exceptions; its significance was that, from an early stage, the common law recognized limitations on the primacy of individual autonomy in these situations. The duty has now disappeared as such. In *Julien* (1969)[178] it was rephrased as a duty to demonstrate an unwillingness to fight, 'to temporise and disengage and perhaps to make some physical withdrawal'. In *Bird* (1985)[179] the Court of Appeal accepted that the imposition of a 'duty' is too strong. The key question is whether D was acting in self-defence or in revenge or retaliation. Evidence that D tried to retreat or to call off the fight might negative a suggestion of revenge, but it is not the only way of doing so. The modification of the law seems to derive from the suggestion in Smith and Hogan's textbook that the 'duty' as described in *Julien* is inconsistent with the liberty to make a pre-emptive strike.[180] It is not. The liberty to make a pre-emptive strike can easily be cast as an exception to the general duty to avoid conflict and, as such, it is no more inconsistent with the rule than any other exception to a rule. The difficulty in regarding the duty to avoid conflict as merely one consideration to be borne in mind here is that it says nothing about the circumstances which might outweigh it. If the law is seriously to pursue the minimization of physical violation, it should at least state that the avoidance of conflict is in general the primary consideration.

(iii) *Protection of the Home.* One long standing exception to the duty to retreat is that a person attacked at home has no duty to withdraw. This may be regarded as one remaining bastion of the autonomy-based view, regarding the individual's home as sacrosanct. Undoubtedly many citizens feel that way about their homes today, but there are two questions to be

---

[177] See *Evans* v *Hughes* [1972] 3 All ER 412, and Smith, *Justification and Excuse*, 117–23.
[178] [1969] 1 WLR 839.   [179] [1985] 1 WLR 816.
[180] J. C. Smith and B. Hogan, *Criminal Law* (5th edn, 1983), 327, quoted by the Court of Appeal in *Bird* [1985] 1 WLR 816.

resolved. The first is whether an exception to the duty to avoid conflict should be recognized here: *should* there be any obligation to retreat if a person enters one's home unlawfully, manifesting an intent to steal property or to carry out an unlawful eviction? Although these are not cases in which direct injury is threatened, the retention of a home is surely such a fundamental part of life that it is related closely to the value of privacy and to autonomy itself. On the other hand, there are several cases in which a firearm, sword or knife has been used against a burglar, which raise questions about the proportionality of the injury done to the value of the interest protected.[181] In principle, greater force is justifiable if occupation of the home is being threatened unlawfully than if mere personal property is being taken, and cases in which burglars have been killed or injured when they had offered no violence to the householder must be scrutinized with care. A second issue is whether a person threatened with violence in or near home should be obliged to leave the home in the hope of avoiding the violence, or be allowed to stand fast. Traditionally there was no duty to retreat from the home and good reasons of privacy and autonomy can be put in support of this. In cases of domestic violence this may present difficulties, assuming that the abode is home to both parties, and it has been argued strongly that a woman who is suffering violence and abuse from her partner should be able to defend herself without in any way being obliged to leave.[182]

(iv) *Freedom of Movement.* English law also recognizes an exception to the duty to avoid conflict (if such a duty exists) in those cases where D is acting lawfully in remaining at, or going to, a place, realizing that there is a risk that someone will force a violent confrontation there. The authority for this is *Field* (1972),[183] where D was warned that some men were coming to attack him. D stayed where he was, the men came and made their attack, and in the ensuing struggle D stabbed one of them fatally. The Court of Appeal quashed his conviction, holding that he had no duty to avoid conflict until his attackers were present and had started to threaten him. The US case of *State* v *Bristol* (1938)[184] takes the point further, holding that D had no duty to avoid entering a bar where he knew his adversary (who had threatened him with attack) to be drinking. The US court declined to lay down a rule which might 'encourage bullies to stalk about the land and terrorize citizens by their mere threats'. These two decisions, together with the well-known case of *Beatty* v *Gillbanks*,[185] promote the value of freedom of movement above any duty to avoid conflict in advance.

---

[181] D. J. Lanham, 'Defence of Property in the Criminal Law' [1966] Crim LR 368, 426; and Smith, *Justification and Excuse*, 109–12.

[182] A. McColgan, 'In Defence of Battered Women who Kill' (1993) 13 Oxford JLS, 508, at 516 and 525.   [183] [1972] Crim LR 435.   [184] (1938) 53 Wyo 304.

[185] (1882) 9 QBD 308.

There are strong arguments in the opposite direction: should not the minimization of physical violation take precedence over mere freedom of movement? Is there not some analogy with omissions to assist in saving life, where a citizen's general liberty should also be outweighed by a specific social duty?[186] These remarks concern self-defence and the defence of property only; clearly, a person who acts with the purpose of preventing crime or arresting a suspected offender cannot be expected to avoid conflict, and is governed chiefly by the proportionality standard.

(v) *Pre-Emptive Strike.* The use of force in self-defence may be justifiable as a pre-emptive strike, when an unlawful attack is imminent.[187] This is a desirable rule, since the rationale for self-defence involves the protection of an innocent citizen's vital interests (life, physical security), and it would be a nonsense if the citizen was obliged to wait until the first blow was struck. The liberty to make a pre-emptive strike is not inconsistent with a duty to avoid conflict (if it were recognized), but it should be read as being subject to that duty. In other words, it would be possible and desirable to have a law which imposed a general obligation to avoid conflict but, where this was not practical, authorized a pre-emptive strike.[188] A law which allows pre-emptive strikes without any general duty to avoid conflict runs the risk, as Dicey put it, of overstimulating self-assertion.[189]

(vi) *Necessity and Law Enforcement.* The point has already been made that a police officer or citizen whose purpose is to prevent a crime or to apprehend a suspected offender must behave proactively. The primary legal restriction on such conduct is the standard of proportionality, in relation to the purpose that the actor was aiming to achieve.[190] How serious an offence was being or had been committed? Is there a real danger of further offending? If there is to be a social policy of the minimization of force, it would seem to follow that any person pursuing such a purpose should not use force unless necessary, and should then use as little as possible. This is most clearly applicable to the use of force to prevent theft, or to arrest someone for minor criminal damage, where little force is justifiable. In the context of serious violence, however, the policy of minimal force may prove unpractical. Increasingly, the police are issued with firearms; they are instructed to open fire only in conditions which would justify killing. Should they shoot to kill, or try only to wound and disable? The policy of minimal force would suggest the latter, but in practice there are difficulties: (i) if the other person is armed, any failure to

---

[186] See above, 4.4.   [187] E.g. *Beckford* v *R* [1988] AC 130, at 144.
[188] See n. 180 above, and accompanying text.
[189] A. V. Dicey, *Law of the Constitution* (8th edn, 1915), 489.
[190] See the discussion of *Thain* above, n. 173 and text.

incapacitate totally may leave the opportunity for a gun to be fired or explosive to be detonated, resulting in the loss of innocent life; and (ii) it is far more difficult to shoot at and hit legs and arms than to shoot at and hit the torso, again making failure and the loss of innocent life more probable.[191] This argument, if sustained, might lead to the paradox that, in order to achieve minimal injury and loss of life, it would be best to shoot to kill as soon as the danger to life becomes apparent.

(g) Justifiable Force and the Emotions

The six foregoing paragraphs have considered principles which might produce consistent and socially acceptable outcomes in those varied situations in which a claim of justifiable force might arise. Some might regard those principles as too mechanical for the sudden and confused circumstances of many such cases. It is well known that a sudden threat to one's physical safety may lead to strong emotions of fear and panic, producing physiological changes which take the individual out of his or her 'normal self'.[192] According to this view, the most just law is the simplest: was the use of force an innocent and instinctive reaction, or was it the product of revenge or some manifest fault?

This simple approach may have the great advantage of recognizing explicitly the role of the emotions in these cases. It is surely right to exclude revenge attacks from the ambit of justifiable force.[193] It is also consistent with the doctrine of prior fault for the law to construe the standards of reasonableness and necessity strictly against someone whose own fault originally caused the show of violence.[194] The question then is how much indulgence should be granted to the innocent victim of sudden attack who reacts instinctively with strong force. In the leading case of *Palmer* (1971)[195] Lord Morris stated that it is 'most potent evidence' of reasonableness that the defendant only did what he or she 'honestly and instinctively thought necessary'. But it cannot be right for absolutely any reaction 'in a moment of unexpected anguish' to be held to be justifiable,[196] even if it is right for the courts to consider 'how the circumstances in which the accused had time to make his decision whether or not to use force and the shortness of the time available to him for

---

[191] Waddington, ' "Overkill" or "Minimum Force"?'
[192] For summaries of the scientific evidence on this point, see H. Grossman, *Physiological Psychology* (1967), 500–15, and, more descriptively, M. D. Vernon, *Human Motivation* (1969), Ch 4.
[193] Cf. excessive force in manslaughter, discussed in Ch 7.7 below.
[194] See Ashworth, 'Self-Defence and the Right to Life', 300, for references, and the draft Criminal Code (Law Com No. 177), clause 44(6); the doctrine of prior fault is assessed in Ch 5.2(e) below.   [195] [1971] AC 814, at 832.
[196] L. H. Leigh (1971) 34 MLR 685.

reflection, might affect the judgment of a reasonable man'.[197] To the extent that in these cases the law moves away from objective standards towards indulgence to the emotions of innocent citizens, the rationale of justification becomes diluted by elements of excuse.

Uniacke develops the useful distinction between defensive conduct that is 'objectively justified' and conduct which is 'agent-perspectivally justified', using the latter category to deal with cases of emotional (over) reaction and mistakes.[198] As for the latter, when a defendant misunderstands the situation (for example, by erroneously believing that V is about to strike, or by mistakenly believing V to be armed), the law is that D should be judged as if the facts were as he or she believed them to be. These examples are discussed separately, as cases of excuse, in Chapter 6.6. Where D believes that V is armed and uses the degree of force thought necessary to respond to that threat, the amount of force necessary should be judged on the facts as D believed them to be.[199] But where D misjudges the amount of force which is reasonable, e.g. to insist on passing along a path barred by another, or to eject a trespasser, this is a mistake of law rather than of fact. Yet, in contrast to the normally strict approach to mistakes of law,[200] the courts tend to grant the wide indulgence signalled in *Palmer* towards the instincts of the innocent.

The fairness of this concession to what Blackstone termed 'the passions of the human mind'[201] is often supported by reference to the famous dictum of Holmes J., namely, that 'detached reflection cannot be demanded in the presence of an uplifted knife'.[202] This dictum is significant for its limited application: it concerns cases of an 'uplifted knife', i.e. typically, sudden and grave threats or attacks; it has no application to cases where the attack is known to be imminent and the defendant has time to consider his position. Nor should it necessarily be conclusive in relation to those who are trained to deal with extreme situations, such as the police and the army. As the element of sudden and unrehearsed emergency recedes, the social interest in the minimal use of force becomes a firmer precept again. In this type of situation, the law ought to give consideration to the relative importance of the sanctity of life and the physical safety of all persons, including offenders, when compared with such other interests as the free movement of citizens. The aphorism about the 'uplifted knife' should not be used to prevent the principled resolution of cases to which it does not apply.

---

[197] Per Lord Diplock, in *Attorney-General for Northern Ireland's Reference* [1977] AC 105.
[198] Uniacke, 'Permissible Killing', 20–2.
[199] *Scarlett* [1993] 4 All ER 629, below, Ch 7.5.   [200] Ch 6.7 below.
[201] *Commentaries on the Laws of England*, iii 3–4.
[202] *Brown* v *United States* (1921) 256 US 335, at 343.

4.8 CHASTISEMENT OF CHILDREN

For centuries it has been the common law that a parent is justified in using reasonable force to discipline her or his child. In one of the few cases to reach the Court of Appeal in modern times, *Smith* (1985),[203] a mother asked the defendant (her partner) to smack her six-year-old child for disobedience, and he gave the child two strokes with his belt. Although it upheld the man's conviction for assault, the Court recognized the defence of reasonable chastisement and held that the prosecution must prove that D 'did more than inflict moderate and reasonable chastisement on the child'. Newspaper reports of acquittals of parents for disciplining children with belts show that the matter remains one of controversy.[204] In their review of the issue, the Scottish Law Commission recognized that several European countries do not accept this justification for the use of force, that there may be a link with child abuse, and that both the UN Convention on the Rights of the Child (1989) and various European resolutions urge Member States to protect children from violence.[205] Their conclusion was that 'it would be going too far to criminalize ordinary safe smacks of the type occasionally resorted to by many thousands of normally affectionate parents',[206] but that the law should state that it should not be a defence that a parent struck a child with a stick, belt or other object, or in such a way as to cause or risk causing injury or lasting pain or discomfort. It appears from the newspaper cases cited above that, if introduced in England and Wales, such a rule would result in more convictions and might have the desirable result of reducing the overall amount of violence in society.

4.9 JUSTIFICATIONS, NECESSITY, AND THE CHOICE OF EVILS

The discussion so far has focussed on self-defence and the justifications relating to law enforcement and the prevention of crime. Little has been said specifically about the use of force in defence of property,[207] although it might be expected that the proportionality requirements would be more strictly enforced in such cases. In general, the justifications relating to self-defence may be linked directly to the principle of autonomy, in the basic sense of self-preservation, whereas the justifications relating to law enforcement may be linked to the principle of welfare, although that principle should also be interpreted so as to insist on the minimal use of

---

[203] [1985] Crim LR 42.

[204] See, e.g. *Daily Telegraph*, 17 Feb. 1993; *The Times*, 28 Aug. 1993; *The Guardian*, 24 June 1994.

[205] Scottish Law Commission, *Report on Family Law* (Scot Law Com No. 135, 1992), 19–33.   [206] Ibid., para 2.95.

[207] See Lanham, 'Defence of Property'.

force. In some situations, however, the principle of individual autonomy is compromised because it may not be possible to protect the autonomy of all persons involved. These are the 'choice of evils' cases, which must now be discussed.

(a) Necessity as a Justification

English law contains limited defences of duress and necessity, which apply when a person commits an otherwise criminal act under threat or fear of death or serious harm. The law on this point is examined in a later chapter,[208] where it will become apparent that many statements about the ambit of the defences (especially in the courts) are ambivalent or even indiscriminate as to whether their basis lies in justification (it was right to use this force) or excuse (the use of force was unjustifiable, but the defendant was not culpable). One apparently clear statement came when the House of Lords, in rejecting duress as a defence to murder, held in Howe (1987)[209] that, even if D's own life is threatened, it cannot be justifiable to take another innocent life. What this means is that one innocent person who stands in danger of imminent death cannot be justified in killing another innocent person. To kill an aggressor in self-defence is one thing, but to kill an uninvolved third party, even in circumstances of absolute necessity, could not be right—even though it might be excusable, as we shall see elsewhere.[210] But what about the possibility of justifying the killing of an innocent non-aggressor when this will save two or more other lives? One example of this emerged from the inquest into the deaths caused by the sinking of the ferry Herald of Free Enterprise.[211] At one stage of the disaster several passengers were trying to gain access to the ship's deck by ascending a rope ladder. On that ladder there was a young man, petrified, unable to move up or down. People were shouting at him, but he did not move. Eventually it was suggested that he should be pushed off the ladder, and this was done. He fell into the water and was never seen again, but several other passengers escaped up the ladder to safety. No English court has had to consider this situation,[212] and it is clear that only the strongest prohibition on the taking of an innocent life would prevent a finding of justification here: in an urgent situation

---

[208] See below, Ch 6.4.　　　　　　　　　　　　　　　　[209] [1987] AC 417.

[210] See, e.g., J. J. Thomson, 'Self-Defence' (1990) 20 Philosophy and Public Affairs, 283; on necessity as an excuse, see below, Ch 6.4(a).

[211] Smith, Justification and Excuse, 73–9.

[212] Cf. Dudley and Stephens (1884) 14 QBD 273, the case in which two men saved themselves by killing and eating the weakest member of a threesome who had been adrift in a boat for many days; but they were rescued the following day, and some have questioned the necessity of their act. See A. W. B. Simpson, Cannibalism and the Common Law (1984), and below, Ch 6.4(a).

involving a decision between n lives and $n + 1$ lives, is there not a strong social interest in preserving the greater number of lives?

Any residual principle of this kind must be carefully circumscribed; it involves the sanctity of life, and therefore the highest value with which the criminal law is concerned. Although there is a provision in the Model Penal Code allowing for a defence of 'lesser evil',[213] it fails to restrict the application of the defence to cases of imminent threat, opening up the danger of citizens trying to justify all manner of conduct by reference to overall good effects. The moral issues are acute: 'not just anything is permissible on the ground that it would yield a net saving of lives.'[214] Closely connected with this is the moral problem of 'choosing one's victim', a problem which arises when, for example, a lifeboat is in danger of sinking, necessitating the throwing overboard of some passengers,[215] or when two people have to kill and eat another if any of the three is to survive.[216] To countenance a legal justification in such cases would be to regard the victim's rights as morally and politically less worthy than the rights of those protected by the action taken, which represents a clear violation of the principle of individual autonomy. Yet it is surely necessary to make some sacrifice, since the autonomy of everyone simply cannot be protected. A dire choice has to be made, and it must be made on a principle of welfare or community that requires the minimization of overall harm. A fair procedure for resolving the problem—perhaps the drawing of lots—must be found. But here, as with self-defence and the 'uplifted knife' cases,[217] one should not obscure the clearer cases where there is no need to choose a victim: in the case of the young man on the rope ladder, blocking the escape of several others, there was no doubt about the person who must be subjected to force, probably with fatal consequences.

These remarks all concern the problem of justifying the infliction of force in extreme circumstances. Even when it cannot be justified, as being either right or permissible in the circumstances, the defendant may still be relieved from liability by being excused on account of the extreme pressure of circumstances. Such cases might be regarded as raising questions of voluntariness similar to those discussed in 4.2. However, acts done under duress or necessity are not 'involuntary' within the definitions offered in 4.2, and so it is better to postpone these issues to Chapter 6.4.

(b) Medical Necessity

Is it ever justifiable for a doctor to act contrary to the letter of the law for

---

[213] Model Penal Code, s 3 02; cf. G. P. Fletcher, *Rethinking Criminal Law* (1978), 788–98.
[214] Thomson, 'Self-Defense', 309.
[215] *United States* v *Holmes* (1842) 26 Fed Cas 360.
[216] *Dudley and Stephens* (1884) 14 QBD 273.
[217] See *Brown* v *United States* (1921) 256 US 335, and the text accompanying n. 202 above.

clinical reasons? There has been little direct discussion of this by the courts or the legislature. The summing up in *Bourne* (1939)[218] is sometimes cited as authority that a doctor may not be convicted (here, for carrying out an abortion) if it is necessary to save the life of the patient, but that particular area of the law is now subject to express statutory provisions.[219] More common in recent times has been the acceptance of 'concealed defences' of medical necessity, by means of stretching established concepts.[220] For example, we saw how Devlin J. in the *Adams* trial modified the general proposition that any acceleration of death satisfies the conduct element for unlawful homicide.[221] And the next chapter will show how the House of Lords in *Gillick* v *West Norfolk and Wisbech Area Health Authority* (1986)[222] deviated from the general proposition that intention includes foresight of virtual certainty. In both decisions the desired effect was to avoid the conviction of a doctor who acted in the 'best interests' of the patient. The courts lacked the courage to develop a new ground of justification, even though the case of *Bourne* might have provided a starting point, and chose instead to create special exceptions to established principles, for doctors actuated by sound clinical motives. This approach is not only juristically clumsy, in so far as it casts doubt on established doctrines of causation and intention,[223] but it also avoids open discussion about the proper limits of justification based on medical necessity and clinical judgment.

A more focussed approach to medical cases would be to create a special defence, which might follow Paul Robinson's suggested draft, for example, justifying reasonable treatment for the promotion of the patient's health.[224] The definition is quite elaborate, but much would turn on the criteria of reasonableness. One of the first English judges to confront some of the issues is Lord Goff in his speech in *Re F* (1990),[225] where he distinguished three forms of necessity—public necessity, private necessity, and necessity in aid of another. The last category was not merely confined to medical cases (e.g. acting to preserve the life of a person who is in a condition that makes it impossible to give consent) but also extends to other cases of action to protect the safety or property of a person unable to give consent. Not surprisingly, the limits of necessity turned largely on the

[218] [1939] 1 KB 687. [219] Abortion Act 1967.
[220] Smith, *Justification and Excuse*, 64–70.
[221] See above, 4.6 at n. 113; see also the 'medical' exception to the principle that a voluntary intervening human act negatives causal responsibility, in 4.6(b)(ii) above.
[222] [1986] AC 112, discussed in Ch 5 3(b).
[223] A further example is the manipulation of the act–omission distinction by courts and writers in relation to the treatment of dying persons by doctors and nurses: see Ashworth, 'The Scope of Criminal Liability for Omissions', 437, and Kennedy, *Treat me Right*, 167–74.
[224] P. Robinson, *Criminal Law Defences* (1984), vol 2, 173.
[225] [1990] 2 AC 1.

reasonableness of the action taken. In *Airedale NHS Trust* v *Bland* (1993)[226] a majority of the House of Lords held that what is 'in the best interests of the patient' should be determined by reference to whether the doctor's decision was 'in accordance with a practice accepted at the time by a responsible body of medical opinion'.[227] Lord Mustill, dissenting, took the view that medical opinion should not be conclusive and that the ultimate question should be for the court. That is right in principle, but would provide little guidance for doctors. The issue cannot be argued to a conclusion here,[228] but the approach should be on the same basis as the other justifications.

(c) Judicial Development of Justifications

In the past almost all justifications have been developed by the judges. If the criminal law is to be codified, should an exhaustive list of justifications be included? The Law Commission thinks not. Its draft Criminal Code includes provisions on duress and on justifiable force, but clause 45(4) provides that a person does not commit an offence by doing an act that is justified or excused by 'any rule of common law continuing to apply by virtue of section 4(4)'.[229] The intended effect is to preserve the power of the courts to develop defences, including justifications. There is an evident need for flexibility in responding to new sets of circumstances, but on the other hand the courts are not suited to the kind of wide-ranging review that ought to be carried out before a justification is recognized or even taken away.[230] A code should go as far as it can in formulating the justifications for what would otherwise be criminal conduct, even if it must rely on terms such as 'reasonable' at various points. This may mean the open discussion not merely of hitherto concealed defences such as medical necessity but also of the factors that may make risk-taking unjustified for the purposes of the definition of recklessness.[231]

4.10 CONCLUSIONS

This chapter has dealt with a number of somewhat disparate issues relevant to criminal conduct. It began by examining how the law reflects such fundamental notions as that it is wrong to convict someone: without

---

[226] [1993] 1 All ER 821; see also the earlier House of Lords decision in *F* v *West Berkshire Health Authority* [1990] 2 AC 1.

[227] Per Lord Browne-Wilkinson at 882.

[228] See I. M. Kennedy and A. Grubb, *Medical Law: Text and Materials* (2nd edn, 1994); A. Ashworth, 'Criminal Liability in a Medical Context: the Treatment of Good Intentions' in A. Simester and A. T. H. Smith (eds), *Harm and Culpability* (forthcoming, 1995).

[229] For discussion, see Law Com No. 177, vol 2, para 12.41.

[230] Cf. the work of the Scottish Law Commission on the physical disciplining of children, in 4.8 above.   [231] See Ch 5.3(c) below.

proving voluntary conduct; without showing that the person acted; without establishing that the person was responsible for causing any prohibited consequence. The link between these notions and the principle of autonomy was brought out, and there was also discussion of the place of corporate personality in criminal law. The conclusion was that not all the doctrines are as pure and as clear as the language of Parliament and the judges sometimes suggests, and some of the conflicting considerations that give rise to that were identified. Nor, indeed, is the subject-matter so neatly divided as some writers suggest: although the topic of the chapter is criminal conduct (sometimes labelled *actus reus*), mental elements and fault elements have been part of the discussion at several points, e.g. involuntariness, omissions, causation, and purpose in cases of justification. The chapter then turned to the requirement that the conduct be unlawful, in the sense of unjustified, and once again we saw that the boundaries of justification depend on conflicting considerations which are often not openly or fully analysed.

The full significance of the issues discussed in this chapter will not become apparent until Chapters 5 and 6, and some of the issues reappear later in the book, but two points may be signalled at this stage. First, this chapter has provided ample evidence of the importance, in shaping the criminal law, of conflicts between the principle of individual autonomy and principles of welfare. For example, even in relation to the voluntariness requirement—the veritable sanctum of individual autonomy—there are the marks of welfare-based limitations where the rules on insanity, intoxication and prior fault impinge. Similar conflicts are found in the legislative and judicial approaches to liability for omissions, and in the slow development of corporate criminal liability. Even in the justifications for force, the strong individualism which favours the 'innocent' defendant has occasionally come into conflict with the underlying social rationale for minimum force in these situations. A second general point is that most of the doctrines considered yield, at crucial junctures, to malleable terminology which leaves considerable discretion to those who apply the law. This is at its plainest with the ubiquitous term 'reasonable' in the justifications, although there is now some evidence of a more principled approach. Discretion is also conceded by the proposition that the boundaries of omissions liability and of vicarious liability are governed by the interpretation of particular words in statutes, by various concepts in the sphere of causation (e.g. de minimis, 'voluntary'), and by such notions as prior fault and 'external factor' in automatism. The presence of these open-ended terms does not empty the rules of their significance, but it raises doubts about the law's commitment to the values upheld by the principle of maximum certainty outlined in Chapter 3.4(i). It is one thing to leave the rules open-ended when persons are unlikely to rely on them (as with the excusatory defences discussed in Chapter 6), although even there the value of consistent judicial decisions should not be overlooked. It is another thing to leave the rules open-ended when citizens as well as courts may rely on them, and the Law Commission's recognition that the law on self-defence can be structured more explicitly is a welcome step away from universal deliverance to 'reasonableness'.

5

Positive Fault Requirements

5.1 THE ISSUES

Once it has been established that D is causally responsible for the act, omission, or state of affairs specified in the definition of an offence, it must also be shown that he fulfilled the fault requirements for the offence. It should not be assumed that there is a single fault requirement for each offence: the point may be illustrated by referring to the several different elements in the abduction offence contrary to the Sexual Offence Act 1956, section 20, which consists of taking—without lawful authority or excuse—an unmarried girl under 16 out of the possession of her parent or guardian against his or her will. Clarity is assisted by analysing crimes such as these in terms of their separate elements—e.g. conduct, circumstances, result—and then ascertaining what form of fault is required for each of these different elements.[1] Indeed, as we go through the specific offences in Chapters 7, 8, and 9 we will see that the fault requirements are diverse, not just terminologically (many statutes contain words such as 'maliciously' and 'wilfully') but also in substance (e.g. requirements such as 'dishonestly' and 'fraudulently'). The discussion in this chapter is general and confined to positive fault requirements, in other words, the mental attitude specified in (or implied within) the offence and which the prosecution must establish. Selected for analysis below are core fault terms such as intention, recklessness, knowledge, and negligence, together with offences that use other terminology which has been held to impose a form of 'strict' or no-fault liability. One difficulty in focussing on a small range of fault terms is that the existing variety of approaches to fault is not captured, and that generalization on the basis of a few fault terms may lead to inaccurate conclusions.[2] We will return to that difficulty at the end of the chapter, after laying some foundations for wider discussion.

The general approach of modern English text-writers has been to assert that subjective guilt should be proved in each case, and that therefore crimes should require proof of D's intention, knowledge, or recklessness.

---

[1] P. H. Robinson and J. Grall, 'Element Analysis in Defining Criminal Liability: The Model Penal Code and Beyond' (1983) 35 *Stanford LR*, 681.

[2] For debate, see J. Gardner and H. Jung, 'Making Sense of Mens Rea: Antony Duff's Account' (1991) 11 *Oxford JLS*, 559; J. A. Laing, 'The Prospects of a Theory of Criminal Culpability: Mens Rea and Methodological Doubt' (1994) 14 *Oxford JLS*, 57; J. Gardner, 'Criminal Law and the Uses of Theory: a Reply to Laing' (1994) 14 *Oxford JLS*, 217.

The orthodoxy is then to criticize crimes of negligence and, even more powerfully, crimes of strict liability for their departure from these standard requirements. The courts, on the other hand, have tended to pursue more variable approaches, upholding subjective principles on some occasions and giving way to objective or 'public policy' arguments on others. Text-writers have also tended to divide 'actus reus' from 'mens rea' on the basis that fault elements fall into the latter category, but we have already seen that there are fault elements in conduct requirements such as voluntariness, causation, and justifiable force. In Chapter 6 we will deal with a further group of 'negative' fault requirements: these are not fault elements which the prosecution has to prove in every case, but various doctrines which suggest the absence of fault and which the prosecution has to negative (generally speaking) if they are raised by D. We begin this chapter by considering some general principles relevant to fault, and then go on to consider the core fault terms.

5.2 SOME GENERAL PRINCIPLES

(a) Choice and the Subjective Principles

The principle of *mens rea* has already been outlined in Chapter 3.5(o), together with the related principles of correspondence (Chapter 3.5(q)) and of fair labelling (Chapter 3.5(s)). The essence of the principle of *mens rea* is that criminal liability should be imposed only on persons who are sufficiently aware of what they are doing, and of the consequences it might have, that they can fairly be said to have chosen the behaviour and its consequences. This approach is grounded in the principle of autonomy (Chapter 2.2): individuals are regarded as autonomous persons with a general capacity to choose among alternative courses of behaviour, and respect for their autonomy means holding them liable only on the basis of their choices. The principle of *mens rea* may also be claimed to enhance the constitutional values of legality and rule of law, by reassuring citizens that they will only be liable to conviction, and to the exercise of state coercion against them, if they knowingly cause a prohibited harm. If this were achieved, the criminal law would ensure that 'each person is guaranteed a greatest liberty, capacity and opportunity of controlling and predicting the consequences of his or her actions compatible with a like liberty, capacity and opportunity for all'.[3] What this liberal view rejects is an approach which holds people criminally liable solely on the ground that liability and punishment would have a general deterrent effect in

---

[3] D. A. J. Richards, 'Rights, Utility and Crime', in M. Tonry and N. Morris (eds), *Crime and Justice: An Annual Review, iii* (1981), 274.

preventing further harms. That approach, associated with utilitarian theories,[4] looks to the probable social effects of liability and punishment, denying the individual defendant any special status in the matter: if the punishment of people in D's position would have an overall deterrent effect, then D should be punished, even though he or she cannot be said to have *chosen* to cause the harm. Deterrent theories therefore tend to give priority to welfare. Theories of punishment in the liberal tradition may recognize the relevance of welfare, at least at the level of justifying the criminal law itself and justifying certain offences, but at the level of individual liability to conviction and censure they tend to regard respect for the principle of individual autonomy as having superior value to general calculations of social utility.

The principle of *mens rea* also encompasses the belief principle, which holds that criminal liability should be based on what defendants believed they were doing or risking, not on actual facts which were not known to them at the time. Also flowing from this, as we saw in Chapter 3.5(q), is the principle of correspondence which insists that the fault element for a crime should correspond to the conduct element specified for the crime. Thus, if the conduct element is 'causing serious injury', then the fault element ought to be 'intention or recklessness as to causing serious injury'; a lesser fault element, such as 'intention or recklessness as to a mere assault', would breach the principle of correspondence. This makes the point that the notion of choice is not an abstract phenomenon, but should in principle be linked to the circumstances or consequences specified in the definition of each crime.

(b) The Boundaries of Subjectivity

We have already seen, in Chapter 3.5(r), that the high value placed by subjectivists on the principle of correspondence is disputed by those who argue that, once a person has crossed a significant moral threshold, what is deserved should reflect the harm done rather than the harm foreseen. This argument must be taken further in the present context. Constructive criminal liability, whereby liability for a more serious offence is constructed out of a lesser degree of fault, has a long history. Its most powerful manifestation at common law was the felony–murder rule, which rendered anyone who caused death while committing a felony liable for the murder of his victim, even though the death was accidental. The felony–murder rule was abolished in England in 1957, but it remains law in many American states.[5] Its spirit survives in modern English law in the law of

---

[4] Notably those of Bentham: for extracts and discussion, see A. von Hirsch and A. Ashworth, *Principled Sentencing* (1993), Ch 2.

[5] For discussion, see P. Robinson, *Fundamentals of Criminal Law* (1989), Ch 9, and Crump and Crump, 'In Defence of the Felony Murder Doctrine' (1985) 8 Harv JLPP, 359.

manslaughter: if D commits a criminal offence which produces a risk of some harm to another person, and death results from that offence, the crime may be manslaughter. This is so, even though D merely intended to commit a minor assault, and the victim, by chance, fell awkwardly. The law of manslaughter takes the criminal intention or recklessness (as to a minor offence), couples it with the harm caused (which is major), and constructs liability for a serious offence. Even though the sentence is unlikely to reflect the death fully,[6] the label (manslaughter) is serious. The doctrine may be supported by arguing that the death, though accidental, is a direct result of D's fault in committing the minor crime, and so D should bear the legal responsibility for it.

This may be criticized as going too far: if the fault in committing minor crimes is so great, why not regard them all as serious? Why not argue that all minor assaults should be punishable up to a maximum of life imprisonment, because any assault could (albeit in unusual circumstances) cause death? Surely one can separate D's fault in committing the minor crime from the accidental consequence of death?[7] One response to this might be that it is the significance of death which is crucial here: life is valued so highly that a person who destroys it in these circumstances should be labelled accordingly. A similar approach is taken to the offence of causing death by dangerous driving: this offence now has a maximum sentence of 10 years' imprisonment,[8] compared with the maximum of two years for dangerous driving, and yet the difference between the two offences turns on an outcome which may often be a matter of chance. There seems to be considerable public sympathy for the policy of marking death with an extra punishment, even when it is not foreseen or even foreseeable as a result of what D was doing.[9] Perhaps this is rooted in a confusion between the notions of compensation and punishment. Certainly it attributes far greater significance to luck or chance than is proper on the autonomy-based approach of choice and control. Luck may be an unavoidable element in life and in moral judgments, but that does not mean that the criminal law should reflect the vagaries of chance when it has the opportunity to eliminate them as a basis for censure.[10] We will return to the conflict between constructive liability and the principle of correspondence when discussing manslaughter in Chapter 7.5.

---

[6] Some guidance on sentencing in this type of case was given by the Court of Appeal in *Coleman* (1992) 13 Cr App R (S) 508; the relevant law is discussed in Ch 7.5(a).
[7] Cf. L. L. Weinreb, 'Desert, Punishment and Criminal Responsibility' (1986) 49 L&CP (No. 3), 64–7, with the discussion in Ch 3.5(r) above.
[8] Criminal Justice Act 1993, s 67; see the discussion in Ch 7.6 below.
[9] See the research by P. H. Robinson and J. M. Darley, *Justice, Liability and Blame* (1995), Ch 6.
[10] See further A. Ashworth, 'Taking the Consequences', in S. Shute, J. Gardner, and J. Horder (eds), *Action and Value in Criminal Law* (1993).

There are other points at which the subjective principles, grounded in autonomy, come into conflict with welfare-based considerations. The most obvious manifestation of this is the mass of criminal offences of 'strict liability', which require hardly any fault element at all, to be discussed in 5.3(a). Even beyond those offences, however, the effects of arguments based on welfare and social defence have come to be felt. Thus, where the harm to be prevented is a fundamental one (such as death), the tendency is for the criminal law to go beyond the principle of *mens rea* and to introduce liability for negligence. The more serious the social harm, the greater care it is fair to expect citizens to take to avoid it. Another example has been the extension of the concept of 'recklessness', previously confined to an assessment of subjective awareness, to cover situations where D failed to see an obvious risk—an extension which, in part at least, challenges the moral basis of subjective recklessness in the notion of choice. The essence of the argument is that there may be just as much culpability in failing to think about an 'obvious' risk as in being aware of it, since part of living in a society is that citizens ought to be conscious of the potential of harm to others of their activities. These issues will be considered in great detail, in 5.3(c)–(g).

(c) The Principle of Contemporaneity

As we saw in Chapter 3.5(u), the principle of contemporaneity states that the fault element must coincide in point of time with the conduct element in order to amount to an offence. This forms part of the ideology that the function of the criminal law is not to judge a person's general character or behaviour over a period of time; its concern is only with the distinct criminal conduct charged. According to this view, whether or not criminal conviction is deserved depends on D's conduct and mental attitude at the relevant time. But this narrow statement of the principle, if indeed it ever represented a complete statement of the law,[11] was abandoned in the face of intuitions to the contrary exemplified in leading cases. In the famous case of *Fagan* v *Metropolitan Police Commissioner* (1969)[12] D accidentally drove his car on to a policeman's foot, and then deliberately left it there for a minute or so. The defence to a charge of assault was that the conduct element had finished before the fault element began; the act and the intent never coincided. The Divisional Court held that D's conduct in driving the car on to the foot and leaving it there should be viewed as a continuing act, so that the crime was committed when the fault element arose (by D deciding to leave the car there). This is not the only occasion on which the courts have invoked the notion of a 'continuing act' to expand the

---

[11] An early general statement was that of Lord Kenyon CJ in *Fowler* v *Padget* (1798) 7 Term Rep 509.   [12] [1969] 1 QB 439.

time-frame of a crime and thus the application of the principle of contemporaneity.[13] However, a different approach was taken by the House of Lords in *Miller* (1982),[14] the case in which a squatter was smoking in bed, accidentally set the mattress on fire, but simply moved to another room without attempting to remedy the problem. Rather than suggesting that the fire was a continuing act that began accidentally but could then be connected with D's fault when he realized that the mattress was on fire, the court held that the accidental creation of danger creates a duty (a continuing duty) which, in this case, D knowingly failed to discharge.

The continuing act approach seems to exert an influence in another area. In *Thabo Meli* v *R* (1954)[15] the plan was to kill V in a hut and then throw his body over a cliff: this was what D believed he was doing, but in fact V died from the fall down the cliff and not from the beating in the hut. The argument for the appellant was based on the lack of contemporaneity (this time it was intent first, death later), but the Privy Council rejected this, holding that the beating and the disposal over the cliff formed part of a planned series of acts which should be regarded as a single course of conduct. That reasoning was extended in *Church* (1966)[16] to cover a series of acts which had not been planned but which simply followed one after the other. Subsequently, in *Le Brun* (1991),[17] the Court of Appeal had to deal with a case in which D had assaulted his wife, and then when he tried to move her unconscious body out of the street he dropped her, causing her to suffer a fractured skull from which she died. The Court held that the conduct and the fault elements 'need not coincide in point of time' so long as they formed part of a 'sequence of events', particularly in a case such as this where D's later acts were an attempt to conceal his initial offence. All these cases could have resulted in convictions for other offences (attempted murder in *Thabo Meli*, grievous or actual bodily harm in the last two cases), but the courts apparently took the view that since the result—death—was caused by D's original culpable conduct, homicide convictions ought to be registered. A similar analysis would be possible in non-homicide cases. The decisions therefore take a rather elastic view of the contemporaneity principle, and seem to be motivated by considerations akin to constructive liability.[18]

It is convenient to deal here with one more awkward situation relating to the link between conduct and fault. In *Attorney-General's Reference (No. 4*

---

[13] E.g. in rape (*Kaitamaki* v *R* [1985] 1 AC 147) and in theft (on appropriation, *Hale* (1978) 68 Cr App R 415). Cf. the critique by M. Kelman, 'Interpretive Construction in the Substantive Criminal Law' (1981) 33 Stanford LR, 591, and the defence by M. Moore, *Act and Crime* (1993), 35–7.   [14] [1983] 2 AC 161, discussed in Ch 4.4 above.
[15] [1954] 1 WLR 228.   [16] [1966] 1 QB 59.   [17] [1991] 1 WLR.
[18] Cf. the felony–murder rule and constructive manslaughter, 5.2(c) above.

of 1980) (1981),[19] it appeared that D was arguing with his female partner at the top of a flight of stairs, that he pushed her away and she fell backwards down the stairs, that he concluded she was dead and then dragged her back to their flat with a rope around her neck and cut up her body. The Court of Appeal held that there could be a conviction on these facts, even though it was not clear which of D's acts caused death. So long as the jury was satisfied that D had sufficient fault for manslaughter when he pushed her backwards, and sufficient fault for manslaughter when he cut up her body, it was immaterial which act caused death. The facts of this case are somewhat stronger than the facts of *Thabo Meli*, *Church*, and *Le Brun*, since in all of those cases it was clear that it was not D's initial act that caused death. Surely in the *Reference* case it should have been possible to convict D if the court was satisfied that there was a sequence of events and that D had the required fault element at some stage; the actual facts, however, were taken not to raise this point.

(d) The Doctrine of Prior Fault

We saw in Chapter 3.5(v) that the principle of contemporaneity conflicts in certain situations with the doctrine of prior fault—the principle that a person should not be allowed to take advantage of any defence or partial defence to criminal liability if the relevant circumstances or condition were brought about by his or her own fault. While the contemporaneity principle insists that the criminal law is concerned with the prohibited event itself, not with its antecedents or its sequels, the doctrine of prior fault points to circumstances in which the antecedents of the event ought to affect a proper moral evaluation of D's conduct. Two examples of the doctrine's operation may be given. First, a person who deliberately drinks to excess in order to stoke up the courage to do a certain act will not be allowed to rely on that intoxication by way of defence because it arose from prior fault.[20] Secondly, if D taunts another in the hope of inducing the other to attack him, D should not be able to rely on provocation or self-defence as defences to a charge or murder, because the attack on D will be regarded as self-induced.[21] Examples of the doctrine of prior fault in operation were noted in Chapter 4, in relation to automatism and self-defence, and will be seen in abundance in Chapter 6 (on intoxication, duress, necessity, etc.)

One remaining question concerns the amount of 'fault' required for the doctrine to take effect. A study by Paul Robinson has shown considerable diversity of provisions in the Model Penal Code and in American laws

---

[19] [1981] 1 WLR 705

[20] See *Attorney-General for Northern Ireland* v *Gallagher* [1963] AC 349, and below, Ch 6.3.

[21] Cf. *Edwards* v *R* [1973] AC 648, with *Johnson* (1989) 89 Cr App 349, and below, Ch 6.5.

generally,[22] and a similar diversity appears in England.[23] Should *any* causal contribution by D make the defence unavailable, or should it be a lack of proper care (for example, drinking alcohol when its possible effects are widely known,[24] joining a gang which is known to use violence . . .[25]) or should the doctrine require proof that D foresaw the possibility that certain conduct might follow? The differences between these approaches ought not to be regarded as unimportant, since the withdrawal of a *defence* simply on the grounds of some small amount of fault on D's part is equivalent to a principle of constructive liability for *offences*. One way of avoiding this difficulty would be to devise a range of offences to cover 'faulty' acts (e.g. excessive consumption of alcohol), and then convict D of an offence of that kind—while not removing any defence to the substantive crime which might otherwise be open.[26] This would introduce further complexities into the law, but at least it attempts a fair solution of a difficult problem.

5.3 VARIETIES OF FAULT

Having introduced the subjective principles and some problems of contemporaneity of conduct and fault, we now move to the core fault elements. First to be considered is strict liability, for which there may be little or no fault at all. One reason for considering these offences first is that they are the most numerous, a fact that belies the prominence often given to intention and recklessness in the rhetoric of English criminal law. We then turn to intention, recklessness, and knowledge, before exploring the little-used concept of negligence.

(a) Strict Liability

There is no clear convention about when criminal liability should be classified as 'strict'. We will use the term here to indicate those offences for which a person may be convicted without proof of intention, knowledge, recklessness, or negligence. Some of the most powerful writings on the subject seem, at times, to muddy the waters. Baroness Wootton campaigned strongly in favour of the extension of strict liability to the major types of offence, but when one looks carefully at one statement of her argument, it seems to be advocating liability for negligence rather than strict liability:

---

[22] P. H. Robinson, 'Causing the Conditions of One's Own Defense: A Study in the Limits of Theory in Criminal Law Doctrine' (1985) 71 Virginia LR, 1.

[23] Cf. the different wording in the draft Criminal Code (Law Com No. 177) on automatism (clause 33(1)(b) and on duress (cl 42(5)), for example.

[24] See below, Ch 6.3(c).   [25] *Sharp* [1987] QB 853, and below, Ch 6.5(c).

[26] Robinson, 'Causing the Conditions of One's Own Defense'.

in the modern world as much and more damage is done by negligence, or by indifference to the welfare or safety of others, as by deliberate wickedness. . . . The time has come for the concept of legal guilt to be dissolved into a wider concept of responsibility . . . in which there is room for negligence as well as purposeful wrongdoing.[27]

Similarly, among the reasons given in the landmark decision in *Sweet* v *Parsley* (1970)[28] for not imposing strict liability were: that Parliament did not intend to make criminals of persons who were not blameworthy;[29] that Parliament did not agree with the conviction of those who, by all reasonable and sensible standards, were without fault;[30] and that it was wrong to penalize someone who had taken all proper care to inform herself of any facts which would make her conduct lawful.[31] The House of Lords decided that it was beyond its powers to impose liability for negligence in this case, preferring to present the choice as lying between strict liability and a requirement *mens rea* (knowledge or reckless knowledge). The arguments adduced, however, were arguments in favour of negligence liability, not in favour of the mens rea which they decided to require.

Some offences allow the defendant to avoid liability on proof of 'due diligence', and there is dispute about whether offences with such provisos are properly termed 'strict liability' offences.[32] For our present purposes such offences will be included within the concept of strict liability. This corresponds with the Canadian approach, which separates strict liability (where a defendant can avoid liability by establishing that there was no negligence) from absolute liability (where the only defences available are the basic ones of insanity, automatism, or necessity).[33] The term 'absolute liability' has its own difficulties, in fact, since one can argue that liability should only be described as absolute where there is no defence available at all to someone who is proved to have caused the prohibited event. What this shows, above all, is the inadequacy of common terminology to give simple expression to the numerous permutations of conditions for liability. If one takes account of the device shifting the burden of proof on to the defendant, then the permutations range from requiring *mens rea*—with the burden of proof on the prosecution—to defining special defences or provisos with an evidential burden on D, defining special defences or provisos with a legal burden or proof on D, requiring proof of negligence by the prosecution, creating a no-negligence defence to be proved by D,

---

[27] B. Wootton, *Crime and the Criminal Law* (2nd edn, 1981); 50.
[28] [1970] AC 132. [29] Per Lord Reid, at 148.
[30] Per Lord Morris, at 153. [31] Per Lord Diplock, 163.
[32] See the study by L. H. Leigh, *Strict and Vicarious Liability* (1982).
[33] See E. Colvin, *Principles of Criminal Law* (1986), 22.

imposing liability with no due diligence defence at all, and even to a dispensation from proving an element of the offence.[34]

Let us leave aside the complexities introduced by changes in the burden of proof, and formulate a central question: what are the arguments for imposing criminal liability with no due diligence defence available? The main argument is a form of protectionism or 'social defence'. It maintains that one of the primary aims of the criminal law is the protection of fundamental social interests. Why should this function be abandoned when the violation of those interests resulted from some accident or mistake by D? Surely, Wootton argued, 'mens rea has got into the wrong place': it should be relevant not to the actual conviction, but to the appropriate means of dealing with the offender after conviction. 'If the object of the criminal law is to prevent the occurrence of socially damaging actions, it would be absurd to turn a blind eye to those which were due to carelessness, negligence, or even accident. The question of motivation is in the first instance irrelevant.'[35] At a time when victims' interests are receiving greater recognition, arguments of this kind may find considerable support. The infliction of the prohibited harm would become the trigger for state action, aimed at minimizing the risk of the harm being repeated.

The strength of the argument lies in its concern for the welfare of citizens in general. Its weakness is to suggest that this is a justification for using the *criminal law* in this way. There are two major questions to be answered here: Would it be fair? Would it be effective? The fairness issue is one which runs through this chapter and, indeed, through the whole book. The criminal law is society's most condemnatory instrument, and, as argued in Chapter 2.2, Chapter 3.5, and 2(a) above, respect for individual autonomy requires that criminal liability be imposed only where there has been choice by D. A person should not be condemned (as distinct, perhaps, from being held civilly liable) for wrongdoing without proof of choice. This is a fundamental requirement of fairness to defendants. Opponents may dismiss this as a mere matter of convention—and outmoded convention at that. The criminal law could simply be regarded as an efficient social resource for the prevention of harm, with conviction carrying no special moral connotations of 'guilt' or 'blame'. Is there not something incongruous in allowing citizens to die or to be injured while the state meticulously observes the 'intent' and 'belief' principles, the presumption of innocence, and other fairness principles so as to facilitate the acquittal of clumsy, ignorant, but nevertheless dangerous people?[36] One answer to this challenge is to reassert that the prevention of harm is neither the sole nor the overriding aim of the criminal law, and that the criminal law is not the

---

[34] A. Ashworth, 'Towards a Theory of Criminal Legislation' (1989) 1 Criminal Law Forum, 41.   [35] Wootton, *Crime and the Criminal Law*, 47.

[36] J. Braithwaite, *Corporate Crime in the Pharmaceutical Industry* (1984), Ch 9.

only official means of preventing harm. Even Bentham, whose general approach was to transcend individual considerations and to weigh the social benefits against the social disadvantages of criminal liability, argued that criminal punishment is an evil which should be reserved for the worst cases, and that legislators should turn first to education, regulation, and civil liability as means of preventing harms.[37]

The subjective principles reflect the value of individual autonomy, but many of the harms which afflict, or threaten to afflict, citizens today are the result of the acts or omissions of corporations. Pollution, defective products, food and drugs, safety at work, transport systems—all these sources of danger are dominated by corporate undertakings.[38] We saw in Chapter 4.5 that the traditional doctrines of the criminal law are not appropriate when it comes to dealing with corporate decision-making and responsibility. Once a secure basis for corporate liability is found, the next question would concern the appropriate conditions of liability for companies. Some corporations operate in spheres of such potential social danger, and wield such power (in terms of economic resources and influence), that there is no social unfairness in holding them to higher standards than individuals when it comes to criminal liability, so long as fair warning is given. This is particularly so when they engage in commercial activities in spheres where public safety may be at risk. The same cannot generally be said of individuals, save in the exceptional category of road traffic offences, where maximum safety is a central issue. Thus the conflict between social welfare and fairness to defendants should be resolved differently according to whether the defendant is a private individual or a large corporation.

Moving to the second question, whether criminal liability without fault is a particularly efficacious means of preventing harm, it is important to keep in mind the differences between individual behaviour and corporate activity. At least two aspects of efficacy arise: the ease of enforcing no-fault offences; and the preventive effects of liability without fault. Ease of enforcement may be thought to be a simple matter: clearly, it is less trouble to prepare a prosecution in which fault does not have to be proved than to prepare one in which proof of fault is needed. For the more serious offences, however, fault will have to be established for the courts to pass sentence on a proper basis.[39] This means that the prosecution will have to prepare some evidence on the point, which in turn diminishes any procedural benefit of strict liability. But there may still be benefits to the prosecutor in not having to prove fault for minor offences, and there may also be indirect benefits as a result of being able to use the threat of

---

[37] *Introduction to the Principles of Morals and Legislation*, Ch XIII.
[38] See above, Ch 2.4, and Ch 4.5.
[39] See *Lester* (1975) 63 Cr App R 144.

prosecution and conviction in order to secure compliance. Many of the regulatory agencies with the power to invoke 'strict liability' offences adopt what may be termed a 'compliance strategy' towards law enforcement— that is, aiming to secure conformity to the law without the need to process and penalize violators.[40] The activities focus on obtaining compliance, and prosecution is reserved for the few cases where either the violator is recalcitrant or the violation is so large that public concern can only be assuaged by a prosecution. This may also mean that prosecutions tend to be brought only in cases where there is fault: indeed, there are regulatory agencies which pursue such a policy, even though they have no-fault offences at their disposal.[41] There is little evidence among the regulatory agencies of a 'deterrence strategy', using criminal prosecution as a primary means of preventing breaches of the law. This approach to law enforce- ment is more typical of the police, who rarely occupy themselves with the so-called regulatory offences dealing with commercial and industrial safety etc. Part of the explanation for this may be that the number of police officers has steadily increased in recent years, whereas the staffing and funding of regulatory agencies has been tightly controlled.[42] Thus, although it appears from the letter of the law that strict liability bears down more harshly on 'middle class' or 'white-collar' defendants, law enforce- ment practices ensure that the reverse happens in reality.

It is therefore difficult to reach a firm conclusion about the preventive efficacy of strict liability. It is probably an overstatement to regard it as a 'means of prevention', since the no-fault offence usually forms one part of a broad regulatory scheme. Some argue that the availability of a no-fault offence strengthens the regulator's hand in ensuring compliance and, therefore, prevention. It enables regulators to use lesser measures, and then to prosecute when there is real fault.[43] Others argue that no-fault offences which are followed by low penalties on conviction are almost counterproductive, resulting in the imposition of derisory fines on large organizations. Indeed, if regulation in such spheres as industrial safety had been harnessed to relatively serious offences requiring proof of fault, then those offences might now be taken much more seriously, integrated into

---

[40] A. Reiss, 'Selecting Strategies of Social Control over Organizational Life', in K. Hawkins and J. M. Thomas (eds), *Enforcing Regulation* (1984).

[41] See e.g. G. Richardson, A. Ogus, and P. Burrows, *Policing Pollution* (1982), B. Hutter, *The Reasonable Arm of the Law* (1988), and the review by G. Richardson, 'Strict Liability for Regulatory Crime: The Empirical Research' [1987] Crim LR 295; cf. R. Baldwin, 'Why Rules Don't Work' (1990) 53 MLR, 321.

[42] S. Box, *Recession, Crime and Unemployment* (1987), 98–102; National Audit Office, *Enforcing Health and Safety Legislation in the Workplace* (1994), Ch 2.

[43] See B. S. Jackson, '*Storkwain*: a Case Study in Strict Liability and Self-Regulation' [1991] Crim LR 892, discussing the role of the Pharmaceutical Society in regulating pharmacists.

people's thinking about offences against the person rather than being regarded as 'merely regulatory' and 'not real crime'.[44] This is, of course, part of a much wider issue about the conventional concepts of crime (as now embodied, for example, in the draft Criminal Code)[45] and about conventional approaches to enforcement which regard some offences as police matters and some not. Thus the issues here turn on the agency through which enforcement takes place, the style of enforcement adopted, and the elements of discretion in choosing and following a style of enforcement.

As a first step in considering the approach of English criminal law to no fault offences, it is worth giving separate consideration to the recurrent issue of offence-seriousness. Is it an argument in favour of, or against, strict liability that the offence is a minor one or a grave one? The English courts have used both triviality and gravity as arguments in favour of strict liability. Many offences with low penalties are, or have been held to be, offences requiring no proof of fault.[46] This reasoning derives some justification from an economic argument based on ease of prosecution: such trivial offences are not worth the public expenditure of prosecution and court time in proving fault. There is hardly any stigma in being convicted of such offences, and so it is thought to be in the public interest to dispose of them quickly. But none of this can apply to grave offences. Principles of individual fairness, even if overridden by economic considerations in respect of minor offences, should surely be central to the question of conviction for grave offences. One clear benchmark here is the availability of imprisonment as a punishment. The US Model Penal Code proposes that imprisonability should be a conclusive reason against strict liability.[47] In practice, the US Supreme Court has been less principled, imposing strict liability for the offence of possession of an unregistered hand-grenade (maximum penalty, 10 years' imprisonment).[48] No strong presumption against the imposition of no-fault liability for imprisonment offences has been enunciated in this country; indeed, English law contains several examples of courts using the seriousness of the offence as an argument in favour of strict liability—a course of reasoning which inevitably results in no-fault liability for some imprisonable crimes. The nadir of such judicial reasoning was probably reached in *Howells* (1977),[49]

---

[44] Ibid.

[45] Cf. the justifications for confining the English codification initiative to 'traditional' offences by the Code Team (Law Com No. 143, paras 2.10–2.13 and Appendix A) and by the Law Commission (Law Com No. 177, paras 3.3–3.6), with the critical remarks of C. Wells, 'Restatement or Reform' [1986] Crim LR 314.

[46] *Alphacell Ltd* v *Woodward* [1972] AC 824, following the notion of 'quasi-crimes' outlined by Lord Reid in *Sweet* v *Parsley* [1970] AC 132.

[47] *Model Penal Code*, s 6.02(4).

[48] *US* v *Freed* (1971) 401 US 601.

[49] [1977] QB 614. See also *Bradish* [1990] 1 QB 981.

where D was charged with possessing a firearm without a certificate, an offence contrary to the Firearms Act 1968, section 1, with a maximum penalty of 3 years' imprisonment. D sought to rely on section 58 of the Act, which exempted 'an antique firearm which is . . . possessed as a curiosity or ornament'. When evidence was given that the gun was not an antique but a reproduction, the defence then argued that D believed it to be an antique, since it had been sold to him as such. This would only be a defence if some requirement of knowledge or belief could be read into the statute. The Court of Appeal ruled this out and upheld strict liability:

First, the wording would, on the face of it, so indicate. Secondly, the danger to the community resulting from the possession of lethal firearms is so obviously great that an absolute prohibition against their possession without proper authority must have been the intention of Parliament when considered in conjunction with the words of the section. Thirdly, to allow a defence of honest and reasonable belief that the firearm was an antique and therefore excluded would be likely to defeat the clear intentions of the Act.[50]

This is poor reasoning. The powerful expression of the second point, the danger to the community, gives no weight at all to the argument against rendering a person liable to imprisonment without proof of fault; indeed, the argument seems not to have been mentioned. The 'danger to the community' argument is surely questionable in itself. Is it really being contended that, the more serious the offence, the stronger the argument for strict liability? Moreover, it is linked here to an assertion about the original intention of Parliament: and yet there is no reference in the judgment to the history of this part of the Firearms Act. The third point in the quotation merely restates the assertion. Everything depends on whether Parliament, by failing to include any fault terms in the relevant section of the Act, did intend to exclude fault, or whether it was merely leaving the issue to be determined by the courts.[51] This brings us back to the first point, that the wording 'on the face of it' favours strict liability. This is a monumentally unhelpful statement, which calls for some discussion of the respective functions of the legislature and the courts in these matters.

Part of Parliament's function in defining offences should be to state any fault requirement for liability. It discharges this function in many cases, but in many others it remains silent, merely enacting a provision which appears to penalize an act or an omission without any reference to fault. Over the years the courts have had to 'interpret' these provisions on many occasions, deciding whether or not to insert a fault requirement. It has been estimated

---

[50] Per Browne LJ, at 626.
[51] P. Devlin, *Samples of Lawmaking* (1970), esp. 71–3.

that over half of some 8,000 offences in English criminal law require no proof of fault.[52] The courts' approach to interpretation has not been a model of consistency. In some cases they regard it merely as a linguistic matter. In others they make high statements of principle, which may briefly raise hopes that a consistent framework is to be established; but those hopes are usually dashed, as the supposed principle is progressively whittled away or, more damningly, simply ignored. The relevant decisions of the courts are legion, covering an enormous variety of offences (including many in the field of road traffic), and the paragraphs which follow aim merely to give the flavour of the main judicial approaches.

One of the earliest statements of principle was that of Wright J in *Sherras* v *de Rutzen* (1895)[53] who stated that 'There is a presumption that mens rea . . . is an essential ingredient in every offence; but that presumption is liable to be displaced either by the words of the statute creating the offence or by the subject-matter with which it deals, and both must be considered.' Thus, in his view, the reason why both bigamy and the abduction of a girl under 16 are offences of strict liability is to be found in the wording of the statutes. What 'subject-matter' displaces the presumption? One example given by Wright J was 'acts which are not criminal in any real sense', where the criminal penalty is attached to acts which are not regarded as morally wrong. This was a reference to offences involved in regulating the sale of tobacco, food, alcohol, and so forth. There were a number of judicial decisions in the 1960s which held persons liable for quite serious drug offences without proof of any fault, in the belief that public policy demanded this, but this trend was arrested in what is probably the leading case, *Sweet* v *Parsley* (1970).[54] The case involved a schoolteacher who was prosecuted for being concerned in the management of premises used for the purpose of smoking cannabis; she had rented her farmhouse to a group of students who, unbeknown to her, smoked cannabis there. The case went up to the House of Lords on the question of whether any fault had to be proved. If one takes the language 'on its face', to refer back to the quotation from *Howells*,[55] it suggests liability without fault. The premises were used for smoking cannabis, and D was concerned in their management. But their Lordships were unanimous in holding that the statute should be construed in the light of the presumption that *mens rea* is required. They regarded it as improper for the courts to impose negligence liability in such cases: the choice lay between *mens rea* and strict liability, and the presumption should be in favour of the former.

This presumption did not fare well during the next decade. It was soon held to be displaced in another House of Lords case, *Alphacell Ltd* v

[52] JUSTICE, *Breaking the Rules* (1980).
[53] [1895] 1 QB 918.
[54] [1970] AC 132.
[55] See n. 51 above.

Woodward (1972),[56] where a company was convicted of causing polluted matter to enter a stream. One reason was linguistic: the word 'cause' was thought to favour strict liability; the maximum penalty was low, and pollution offences were probably regarded as not being criminal in a real sense. We have already seen that the decision in *Howells* is also hard to reconcile with *Sweet* v *Parsley*, but it is not the only one. In *Pharmaceutical Society of Great Britain* v *Storkwain* Ltd (1986)[57] the House of Lords held that a person may be liable to conviction for selling drugs without a valid prescription, contrary to the Medicines Act 1968, without proof of fault. The decision was reached by analysing the statute, with scant reference to general principle and without giving weight to the fact that the offence carried a maximum sentence of two years' imprisonment.

It is manifest that the courts have not confined strict liability to offences which may be described as 'not criminal in any real sense', since they have extended it to several imprisonable crimes.[58] A final and powerful example of this is *Gammon* v *Attorney-General for Hong Kong* (1985).[59] Following the collapse of a building, the defendants were charged with offences against the construction regulations which carried high fines and a maximum prison sentence of three years. Lord Scarman, giving the opinion of the Privy Council, reaffirmed the presumption of *mens rea* laid down in *Sweet* v *Parsley*, and added that 'the presumption is particularly strong where the offence is 'truly criminal' in character'. He went on:

the only situation is which the presumption can be displaced is where the statute is concerned with an issue of social concern; public safety is such an issue . . . Even where a statute is concerned with such an issue, the presumption of mens rea stands unless it can also be shown that the creation of strict liability will be effective to promote the objects of the statute by encouraging greater vigilance to prevent the commission of the prohibited act.

The last few words make it clear that the courts still abide by the principle that strict liability should not be imposed where there is nothing more a defendant could reasonably be expected to do in order to avoid the harm.[60] This means that liability is tethered, however loosely, to the defendant's control; liability is not completely strict in these cases. However, the earlier part of the quotation demonstrates how muddy the waters still are. The courts say that strict liability is appropriate for minor offences which

---

[56] [1972] AC 824.
[57] (1986) 83 Cr App R 359; cf. Jackson's article, above, n. 43.
[58] See e.g. the decisions in *Storkwain* (above, n. 58), *Gammon* v *Attorney-General for Hong Kong* [1985] AC 1, and *R* v *Wells Street Magistrates' Court and Martin, ex p Westminster City Council* [1986] Crim LR 695; cf. the Canadian decision, under the Charter of Rights and Freedoms (1982), s 7, in *References re Section 94(2) of Motor Vehicles Act, RSBC 1979* (1986), 48 CR (3d) 289.   [59] [1985] AC 1.
[60] See *Lim Chin Aik* v *R* [1963] AC 160.

are not truly criminal. Yet they also seem to hold, as in *Howells*[61] and in *Gammon*, that it is appropriate where offences relate to public safety or social concern—a description which could extend to large areas of the criminal law. On some occasions the courts seem to focus on a linguistic analysis of the statute, without reference to general principle. High-sounding declarations in such cases as *Sweet* v *Parsley* become hollow when strict liability is imposed for imprisonable offences. The courts have not explicitly discussed the idea of adopting different approaches for individual and corporate defendants; indeed, there has been an unwillingness to debate the issues at a general level. It is not that the decisions have lacked principles: it is rather that there are too many principles and policies being used by the courts, with no attempt to draw them together into a single coherent pattern. The subject is more appropriate for legislative resolution than judicial decision making. But parliamentary abstention has left a wide area of judicial discretion as to the approach to be taken, with corresponding diminution of the 'rule of law' value of maximum certainty.

This discussion of strict liability as a basis for criminal conviction has raised questions not only about effectiveness of enforcement, but also about the way in which judges use 'social defence' concepts such as public protection and social concern. It is wrong that powerless individuals should be treated more severely, in law or in practice, than powerful corporations. Negligence liability, qualified so as to exclude those incapable of complying, ought to be sufficient where reasons of social welfare are strong and fair warning has been given. The question of strict liability for companies should be considered afresh: should strict criminal liability be regarded as the proper price for engaging in an activity that may impinge on public safety? And in other forms of activity, for example in financial dealings? Would this be a justifiable exception to the free market, and would it not depend on practical enforcement? Would not negligence liability, coupled with fair warning, be sufficient? Or should the emphasis be placed on regulatory sanctions, raising again the issue of fairness towards individuals who remain subject to the criminal law?[62] For the remainder of this chapter the emphasis is upon the appropriate standards of fault for the criminal liability of individuals. We have seen that strict liability for individuals is difficult to justify, and why that is so. What degree of fault it is fair to require is discussed in the following sections of this chapter.

(b) Intention

As noted above, the term *mens rea* has conventionally been used to connote four fault requirements: intention or recklessness as to the

---

[61] [1977] QB 614.   [62] See the discussion in Ch 4.5, above.

specified consequence, and knowledge of, or recklessness as to, the specified circumstance. In discussing offences of strict liability, we have considered the main arguments in favour of requiring *mens rea* as a condition of criminal liability, chiefly arguments of choice and fair warning. Now we move to the more detailed and specific question of drawing distinctions between the four main forms of fault which generally fall under the umbrella of *mens rea*. The task is important, because this is one way in which the law seeks to differentiate between crimes. Intent alone is sufficient for offences of attempt,[63] offences defined in terms of 'doing *x* with intent to do *y*' (such as burglary: entering as a trespasser with intent to steal),[64] and for the crimes of murder and wounding with intent to do grievous bodily harm. The last two crimes are examples of the law using intention as the main method of grading offences: both the murder–manslaughter distinction and the dividing line between wounding under the Offences against the Person Act 1861, section 18 (maximum penalty of life imprisonment) and wounding under section 20 (maximum penalty of five years' imprisonment) turn on the presence or absence of intention.

(i) *Intention in Principle*: It is quite possible—indeed, quite normal—to do things with more than one intention in mind. I can demolish a fence with the simultaneous intentions of making way for a new fence, providing wood for the fire, pleasing my partner (who has repeatedly asked me to demolish the fence), and so on. The approach of the criminal law, however, is generally not to ask with what intentions D committed the act, but to ask whether one particular intention was present when the act was committed. The law, generally speaking, is interested in the presence or absence of one particular intention—that specified in the definition of the offence charged—and not in conducting a general review of D's reasons for the behaviour in question. Did D intend to kill the crew of the aircraft on which he placed a bomb, as well as intending (as he admits) to claim the insurance money on the cargo? Did D intend to assist the enemy by his actions, as well as intending (as he admits) to save his family from a concentration camp?[65]

The law's approach in selecting one intention, and then abstracting it from D's other reasons and beliefs at the time, calls for careful consideration. It is essential to keep in mind the particular intent required by the definition of the offence. It is quite possible to say 'D pulled the trigger of the gun intentionally', without implying that D intended to kill V

[63] Cf. *Khan* (1990) 91 Cr App R 29, establishing that intention combined with reckless knowledge suffices for attempted rape: see Ch 11.3 below.

[64] Burglary is discussed below, Ch 9.5. For a general discussion of offences defined in an inchoate mode, see A. Ashworth, 'Defining Criminal Offences without Harm', in P. F. Smith (ed), *Criminal Law: Essays in Honour of J. C. Smith* (1987).

[65] See the discussion of *Steane*, n. 83 and accompanying text.

when he pulled the trigger. The offence of murder turns (broadly)[66] on the presence or absence of an intention to kill; whether the trigger was pulled intentionally or accidentally may be an important part of the case, but the legally required intention is that D *intended to kill* V. Loose references to whether D 'acted intentionally' can blur this distinction: it is unhelpful to refer to intention without relating it to a particular object or consequence, which in a legal context means the intent specified in the indictment or information.[67]

This definition of intention may avoid some philosophical errors, but is it sufficient? The proper definition of intention has been the subject of theoretical debate and judicial disagreement for many years. The core of 'intention' is surely aim, objective, or purpose; whatever else 'intention' may mean, a person surely acts with intention to kill if killing is the aim, objective, or purpose of the conduct causing death. In *Mohan* (1976)[68] James LJ defined intention as 'a decision to bring about [the proscribed result], in so far as it lies within the accused's power, no matter whether the accused desired that consequence of his act or not'. This definition has the advantage of stating that desire is not essential to intention (one may act out of feelings of duty, for example, rather than desire); it has the disadvantage of referring to a 'decision', whereas in many offences of violence and other crimes the events happen so suddenly and rapidly that a fleeting realization of what one is doing may be the most that time allows. In law this fleeting realization is enough for intention, rendering the term far less concrete than is sometimes assumed.[69]

The *Mohan* case involved an attempted crime, and intention is thought to be crucial to attempts, because one cannot be said to *attempt* to produce a result unless one *intends* to produce it (see Chapter 11.3(a)). The decision in *Mohan* goes some way towards stating the core of the concept of intention, which is intention as purpose. To put the same point differently, one intends consequences that one chooses to produce. But this must be understood as referring both to ends and means. Thus the death of another person is intended if it is chosen as an end in itself, or as a means to an end.[70] This reference to choosing something as a means to an end is important, because otherwise D could always avoid liability by pointing to some ulterior motive for the action: 'it was not my purpose to kill V, because my real purpose in shooting at V was to inherit V's money

---

[66] See below, Ch 7.3(c).

[67] For further study, see R. A. Duff, *Intention, Agency and Criminal Liability* (1990), Chs 3, 4, and 6, critically discussed on this point by A. P. Simester, 'Paradigm Intention' (1992) 11 Law and Philosophy, 235.   [68] [1976] QB 1.

[69] R. Cross, 'The Mental Element in Crime' (1967) 83 LQR, 215.

[70] For discussion, see J. Finnis, 'Intention and Side-Effects', in R. G. Frey and C. W. Morris, *Liability and Responsibility* (1991), 32.

after V's death'. Such a purported detachment of the means from the end is quite unconvincing. Both are part of the intention or purpose with which D fired the shot. Both form part of the core concept of intention.

Should the concept of intention be more extensive than that in the context of criminal liability? Lawyers have tended to assume that intention includes not only purpose but also foresight of certainty; or, to phrase it properly, that D can be said to have intended a result if he or she realized that the result was certain to follow from the behaviour in question. An early example of this may be found in Bentham's writings, and his distinction between direct and oblique intention is one way of expressing the point.[71] One might say that a consequence is *directly* intended if it is D's purpose or desire to produce it, and that it is *obliquely* intended if it is certain but not desired.[72] To regard both these mental attitudes as forms of intention is to make a moral point. It is not necessarily being claimed that ordinary people in their everyday language use the term 'intention' in this way.[73] The claim is that the person who foresees a consequence as certain should be classified as having intended that result rather than as having been merely reckless towards it—and the claim is being made in the knowledge that some killings would thus be classified as murder rather than manslaughter, some woundings described as 'with intent' rather than merely as unlawful, and so on. As soon as the argument moves from the moral to the legal, such questions of classification arise. What has to be established is not that all cases of foresight of certainty are socially or morally as bad as all cases of purpose, but that it is more appropriate to classify them with 'intention' rather than with 'recklessness'.

If we pursue the moral part of the argument further, we find that the shorthand phrase 'foresight of certainty' is perhaps too brief in this context. Few future events in life are absolutely certain, and a reference to consequences as 'certain to follow' would generally mean 'practically certain to follow' or 'certain, barring some unforeseen intervention'.[74] A familiar example is D, who places a bomb on an aircraft with the aim of blowing it up in mid-flight in order to claim the insurance money on the cargo. D knows that it is practically certain that the crew of the aircraft will be killed as a result of the explosion. One might say that D's *purpose* is to claim the insurance money, but if the charge is murder, that is irrelevant. The key question is whether D intended *to kill*. Let us assume that it was *not* D's purpose to kill, i.e. that he had not chosen the death of the air crew

---

[71] Bentham, *Introduction to the Principles of Morals and Legislation*, Ch VIII, on direct and oblique intent. Bentham's definition of oblique intent was wider than that described here, a point discussed by Glanville Williams, 'Oblique Intent' [1988] CLJ 417.

[72] Ibid.

[73] See the discussion of 'ordinary language', n. 89 and accompanying text.

[74] The phrase of Lord Lane CJ, in *Nedrick* (1986) 83 Cr App R 267.

as the means to his end. Should the law extend the definition beyond purpose to cover D's awareness of the practical certainty that the crew would be killed? The argument in favour of this is that D's behaviour shows no respect for the value of human life at all: D knows that the crew will die, and yet he still pursues the purpose of blowing up the aircraft. There is little social or moral difference between that and planning the explosion in order to kill the crew. It is sometimes thought that the 'test of failure' argues against this:[75] since D would not regard the explosion as a failure if the cargo were destroyed but the crew were not killed, this serves to differentiate him from someone whose purpose is to kill. But to establish that a philosophical distinction exists between D and the purposeful killer is not to conclude the matter: to transfer the argument from morality to law, it has to be decided whether the person who foresees death as virtually certain should be bracketed with the purposeful killer (murder) or treated as merely reckless (manslaughter). Recklessness, as we shall see below, includes the taking of relatively small risks. There is a strong argument that someone who takes a risk of death that amounts to a virtual certainty comes very close to the person who chooses someone's death as the means to an end. They both show no respect at all for human life. The draft Criminal Code has it right, surely, in defining intention so as to cover not only the person who acts in order to bring about the prohibited consequence but also the person who acts 'being aware that it will occur in the ordinary course of events'.[76]

(ii) *Intention in the Courts*: At present there is no legislative definition of intention. How have the courts approached the question? The leading decisions concern the crime of murder, to be discussed in a later chapter,[77] but their effect can be summarized here. The first of the leading cases is *Moloney* (1985),[78] in which the House of Lords held that judges should generally avoid defining the term 'intention', beyond explaining that it differs from 'desire' and 'motive'. Only in exceptional cases should the judge depart from this golden rule, notably, where the essence of the defence is that D's purpose was only to frighten, not to harm, the victim. Here the jury should be instructed to decide whether D foresaw the prohibited consequence as 'a natural consequence' of the behaviour: if the answer was yes, they could infer intention from that. In the course of his speech Lord Bridge gave hints of the sort of cases he meant to include— cases where the consequence was 'little short of overwhelming', or 'virtually certain'—but unfortunately the centrepiece of his speech was the term 'natural consequence'. When this was used by the judge to direct the jury in *Hancock and Shankland* (1986),[79] it was held to be unsatisfactory.

[75] Duff, *Intention, Agency and Criminal Liability*, Ch 3.
[76] Law Com No. 177, clause 18, and J. C. Smith, 'A Note on Intention' [1990] Crim LR 85.
[77] See Ch 7.3(c).   [78] [1985] AC 905.   [79] [1986] AC 455.

The House of Lords overruled its own test of 'natural consequence', and Lord Scarman stated that juries should be told that 'the greater the probability of a consequence the more likely it is that the consequence was foreseen, and that if that consequence was foreseen the greater the probability is that that consequence was also intended'.

These decisions left unclear the precise legal meaning of intention and the proper approach to directing a jury, and Lord Lane CJ attempted to synthesize the House of Lords decisions when presiding in the Court of Appeal in *Nedrick* (1986):[80]

Where the charge is murder and in the rare cases where the simple direction is not enough, the jury should be directed that they are not entitled to infer the necessary intention, unless they feel sure that death or serious bodily harm was a virtual certainty (barring some unforeseen intervention) as a result of the defendant's actions and that the defendant realized that such was the case.

Although in terms of precedent this cannot be as authoritative as the House of Lords decisions, it seems to be treated as such. It holds that the courts are entitled to infer intention from foresight of virtual certainty. But if they are only entitled to *infer* intention in these cases, then that means that, logically, intention does not include foresight of virtual certainty. What, then, is the definition of intention? This question has not received a clear answer in the courts, although, extrajudicially, Lord Lane has given the obvious one[81]—that intention does include foresight of virtual certainty—which suggests that the reference to 'inferring' is either redundant or confused. What the courts probably meant to say is that intention includes both purpose and foresight with regard to a particular consequence occurring in the ordinary course of events. Since most of the latter cases involve defendants who deny that they intended such a result, it is inevitable that the jury will be left to draw inferences from the surrounding circumstances. But the evidential process of drawing inferences—which is basic to every case where D does not confess, since one cannot see into another person's mind—should not be confused with the legal definition of intention.[82]

How convincing is this attempt to reconstruct what the judges 'really mean' when they attempt to define intention? If one looks to other appellate decisions in which 'intention' has come up for discussion, one finds that the judges have frequently diverged from this 'standard definition'. Thus in *Steane* (1947)[83] the Court of Criminal Appeal quashed D's conviction under wartime regulations for the offence of doing acts

---

[80] (1986) 83 Cr App R 267.
[81] In a House of Lords debate on murder: HL Deb. 512, col 480 (Nov. 1989).
[82] See E. Griew, 'States of Mind' Presumptions and Inferences', in Smith (ed), *Criminal Law*, and R. A. Duff and A. Norrie [1990] Crim LR 637–44.   [83] [1947] KB 997.

likely to assist the enemy, with intent to assist the enemy. The Court held that if D's acts were as consistent with an innocent intent (such as saving his family from a concentration camp) as with a criminal intent, the jury should be left to decide the matter. This diverges from the standard definition, since it was never discussed whether D knew that it was virtually certain his acts would assist the enemy. The Court could probably have used the defence of duress to quash the conviction, but it evidently thought that adopting a narrow definition of intention provided a simpler route to the desired result. Similarly, in the civil case of *Gillick* v *West Norfolk and Wisbech Area Health Authority* (1986)[84] the House of Lords held that a doctor who gives contraceptive advice to a girl under 16 for clinical reasons, while realizing that this would facilitate acts of unlawful sexual intercourse, is not guilty of aiding and abetting the offence of unlawful sexual intercourse with a girl under 16. The decision might well have been placed on some such ground as 'clinical necessity',[85] but instead Lord Scarman explained that 'the bona fide exercise by a doctor of his clinical judgment must be a complete negation of the guilty mind'. Thus the court held that the doctor did not have the intention required for aiding and abetting, even though it may be assumed that prescribing the contraceptives was foreseen as virtually certain to assist the commission of the offence.

To set alongside these two decisions which favour a narrow definition of intention it is not difficult to find decisions pointing in a different direction. In *Smith* (1960)[86] D had offered a bribe to an official in order to demonstrate that the official was corrupt. The Court of Criminal Appeal upheld his conviction for corruptly offering an inducement to an official, holding that D had an intention to corrupt so long as he intended the offer to operate on the mind of the offeree. In this case D's motivation was held to count for nothing. Similarly in *Chandler* v *DPP* (1964),[87] the defendants' conviction for acting 'for a purpose prejudicial to the safety or interests of the State' was upheld by the House of Lords. They had infiltrated a military airfield, and this was regarded as prejudicial to the state's interests. The defendant's argument that their own purpose was to promote the safety and interests of the state (by promoting peace), rather than to prejudice them, was discounted.

What these decisions and others[88] demonstrate is that the courts do not adhere to a single definition of intention. Various observations may be made about this. One common reaction is to treat it as evidence for a 'realist' interpretation of how courts behave: they decide on the desired

---

[84] [1986] AC 122.   [85] See the discussion in Ch 4.9(b) above.
[86] [1960] 2 QB 423; see also *Yip Chiu-cheung* [1994] 2 All ER 924, discussed in Ch 11.5 below.   [87] [1964] AC 763.
[88] See *Hyam* and *Walker and Hayles*, discussed in (iii) next.

result, and then define the law in whatever way happens to achieve it. But the evidence is limited to a small number of appeal court decisions, and may not reflect the everyday operation of the criminal courts. Even if it were true to some degree (and few suggest that the courts have an absolute freedom in these matters), what is it that leads courts to adopt these reasons for reaching these particular results? Judges in the appellate courts are fond of referring to 'ordinary language' as a justification for their decisions, but this claim has not been subjected to rigorous empirical analysis. Critical writers have made much of the tensions revealed by the varied judicial approach. Thus Nicola Lacey scrutinizes the shifting language of the appellate judges and argues that this reflects their attempt to keep the law fairly close to popular conceptions (and thereby to enhance its legitimacy) while trying to ensure that the interests of the powerful are not significantly challenged.[89] Alan Norrie, focussing on the way in which courts sometimes regard the defendant's motive as relevant (*Steane, Gillick*) and sometimes do not (*Smith, Chandler*), concludes that 'the shifting between narrow and broad definitions [of intention] is at the same time a shifting between the poles of individual justice and state policy. Logic remains no more than a potential intermediary in this constant conflict.'[90] The two poles described by Norrie are evident at many stages in the practice and the rhetoric of law. But concepts such as intention are surely central to systems of criminal liability, and the striking features of English law are that there is no statutory definition, and that judges have tended to exploit this by deploying inconsistent definitions of intention rather than keeping the definition constant and developing defences to criminal liability, such as duress (*Steane*), clinical necessity (*Gillick*), and even the apprehension of offenders (*Smith*).

Finally, it may be noted that one effect of the recent murder decisions has been to narrow the concept of intention for that offence, since the leading case previously was *Hyam* v *DPP* (1975),[91] which suggested that a person could be held to intend a result which he had foreseen as probable (or highly probable) to occur. This was much wider than 'virtual certainty' (and probably much further from ordinary language). The argument in its favour would be that, if D realizes that a consequence probably will occur if a particular act is done, and, when the act is done, the consequence does occur, D should be rendered criminally liable for that consequence. There are various difficulties with this. First, it swallows up a large part of the species of fault known as recklessness, which typically involves the realization that a given consequence may ensue. Secondly, it does so in a

---

[89] N. Lacey, 'A Clear Concept of Intention: Elusive or Illusory?' (1993) 56 MLR, 621.
[90] A. Norrie, *Crime, Reason and History* (1993), 57.
[91] [1975] AC 55.

rather vague way, so that the distinction between intention and reckless-ness detracts significantly from the principle of maximum certainty. If the law is to draw the distinction between intention and recklessness, as a major device of classification, it should be clearly done. The *Hyam* test of probability or high probability fails to achieve this. It might be argued that foresight of 'virtual certainty' also leaves room for an element of doubt, as indeed does the draft Code's formulation of 'being aware that it will occur in the ordinary course of events'.[92] However, absolute certainty is rare in human affairs, and there is an unavoidable margin of open texture. Open texture increases judicial power. Thus the Court of Appeal has upheld a judicial direction in terms of 'a very high degree of probability' or a 'very high degree of possibility'.[93] Any leeway left by terms such as 'virtual' in the context of 'virtual certainty' might be exploited so as to pass judgment on D's background and general behaviour rather than to express a prediction of the degree of probability involved.[94]

(iii) *Intention Concluded*: This discussion of intention has given a glimpse of the working of the appellate criminal courts, and of the gap that may appear between judicial practice and a principled approach to the definition of intention. Yet the latter leaves us with a paradox, to which, in a sense, the courts have been trying to respond. The criminal law often uses the distinction between intention and recklessness as a means of grading the seriousness of offences. But since the definition of recklessness includes the requirement that the risk be socially unjustified (see below),[95] whereas the definition of intention includes no reference to social justification, there may be cases of intention that are adjudged less heinous than cases of recklessness. At least, that will be so unless some defences are developed to cover likely cases of intended-but-justified conduct.

(c) Recklessness

Much of the preceding discussion about the proper limits of the concept of intention in the criminal law has inevitably concerned the dividing line between recklessness and intention. The argument was that there are some cases in which D knows the risk of the prohibited consequence to be so very high (i.e. practically certain) that it is more appropriate to classify his mental attitude within the highest category of culpability (intention) rather than in the lesser category of recklessness. We also noted that some would draw the dividing line lower, arguing that if D foresaw the prohibited consequence as a *probable* result, this should be classified as intention,

[92] See above, n. 74.
[93] *Walker and Hayles* (1990) 90 Cr App R 226 (attempted murder).
[94] Norrie, *Crime, Reason and History*, 47–57.
[95] See 5.3(c).

leaving only the lesser degrees of risk within the category of recklessness.[96] We will now move away from these arguments, but they do remind us that debates about the boundaries of intention relate to the grading of culpability and so of offences. The same is true of the boundary between recklessness and negligence: when criminal lawyers refer to offences as requiring *mens rea*, they usually mean that either intention or recklessness will suffice for liability but that negligence will not. Thus, once again, the debate concerns not so much language as the limits of criminal liability.

An abiding difficulty in discussing the legal meaning of recklessness is that the term has been given several different shades of meaning by the courts over the years. In the law of manslaughter, 'reckless' has long been regarded as the most appropriate adjective to express the degree of negligence needed for a conviction:[97] in this sense, it means a high degree of carelessness. In the late 1950s the courts adopted a different meaning of recklessness in the context of *mens rea*, referring to D's actual awareness of the risk of the prohibited consequence occurring:[98] we shall call this 'advertent recklessness'. Controversy was introduced into this area in the early 1980s, when the House of Lords purported to broaden the meaning of recklessness so as to include those who failed to give thought to an obvious risk that the consequence would occur:[99] we shall call this *inadvertent* or *Caldwell* recklessness. A further shade of meaning emerged during the 1980s in the particular context of indecent assault and rape.[100] The law of manslaughter will be left for discussion later:[101] here we will focus on the other meanings of recklessness.

(i) *Advertent Recklessness.* It was in *Cunningham* (1957) that the Court of Criminal Appeal held that, in a statute, the term 'malicious' denotes intention or recklessness, and that recklessness means that 'the accused has foreseen that the particular kind of harm might be done and yet has gone on to take the risk of it'.[102] There are essentially three elements in this definition, and they are the same ones found in the Model Penal Code's definition of recklessness as 'the conscious taking of an unjustified risk'.[103] First, it requires D's actual awareness of the risk; this is why it is referred to as 'advertent recklessness', and it is regarded as the key element in

---

[96] This was one of the views expressed in *Hyam v DPP* [1975] AC 55, by Lord Diplock (not dissenting on this point); see J. Buzzard, 'Intent' [1978] Crim LR 5, with reply by J. C. Smith at [1978] Crim LR 14; cf. also Bentham, *Introduction to the Principles of Morals and Legislation.*

[97] See *Andrews v DPP* [1937] AC 576 and *Adomako* [1994] 2 All ER 79, discussed below in Ch 7.5.

[98] *Cunningham* [1957] 2 QB 396, adopting the definition offered by C. S. Kenny, *Outlines of Criminal Law* (1st edn, 1902; 16th edn 1952).

[99] *Caldwell* [1982] AC 341, and *Lawrence* [1982] AC 510.

[100] *Kimber* [1983] 1 WLR 1118, *Satnam S. and Kewal S.* (1983) 78 Cr App R 149.

[101] Ch 7.5(b).   [102] See above, n. 98.

[103] Model Penal Code, s 2.02(s)(c).

bringing recklessness within the concept of *mens rea*. A person should only be held to have been reckless about a particular result if the court is satisfied that he or she was aware of the risk at the time. The second element is that a person may be held to have been reckless if he or she was aware of any degree of risk: we have seen that when the risk is so high as to be a practical certainty, D may be classed as intending the consequence, but any risk, however slight, may be sufficient for recklessness, so long as D is aware of it and it materializes. The third element is that the risk which D believes to be present must be an unjustified or unreasonable one. This is an objective element: courts have rarely discussed it, but it exerts a significant background influence. A typical example of the objective element is the surgeon who carries out an operation knowing that death will probably result.[104] Thus 'the responsibility line is drawn according to an evaluation of the nature of the activity and the degree of the risk'.[105] This evaluative task has rarely been performed by the courts but, as Alan Norrie rightly points out, this is because prosecutors have often made their own evaluations at an early stage and no prosecution (or at least no prosecution for a serious offence such as manslaughter) has been brought.[106] Evaluations of the reasonableness of risks taken by transport operators may go some way towards explaining the rarity of prosecutions following large-scale transportation disasters. Thus the objective element does exert an effect, but does so in a way that usually prevents the evaluations being spelt out and challenged.

The justifications for the advertent definition of recklessness are grounded in the principle of individual autonomy and the importance of respecting choice, outlined above.[107] The distinction between recklessness and negligence turns on D's awareness or unawareness of the risk. In both cases there is an unreasonable risk taken, but D should only be held to have been reckless if he or she was aware of the risk. A person who is aware of the risk usually chooses to create it, and therefore chooses to place his or her interests above the wellbeing of those who may suffer if the risk materializes. Choosing to create a risk of harmful consequences is generally much worse than creating the same risk without realizing it. Moreover, holding a person reckless despite unawareness of the risk would result in a conviction in a case like *Stephenson* (1979).[108] D, a schizophrenic, made a hollow in a haystack in order to sleep there; he felt cold, and so lit a small fire, causing the whole haystack to go up in flames, and resulting in damage of some £3,500. The defence relied on medical evidence that D may not have had the same ability to foresee the risk as a

---

[104] Criminal Law Revision Committee, 14th Report, *Offences against the Person* (1980), 8.
[105] D. J. Galligan, 'Responsibility for Recklessness' (1978) 31 CLP, 55, at 70.
[106] Norrie, *Crime, Reason and History*, 81.   [107] See above, 5.2(a).
[108] [1979] QB 695.

mentally normal person. The Court of Appeal, quashing D's conviction, held that the definition of recklessness clearly turned on what this defendant actually foresaw, and the medical evidence should have been taken into account on this point. This decision, then, affirms the element of individual fairness in the advertent or subjective definition. As entirely objective test would exclude this.

Does concentration on the element of awareness always produce decisions in accord with fairness? There are at least two types of awkward case for a test of liability which requires the court to be satisfied that the defendant actually saw the risk, however briefly. One is where a person acts impulsively in the heat of the moment. This is often expressed in ordinary speech by saying 'I acted without thinking', or 'I just didn't think'. D denies that he or she was aware of the risk at the time of acting. In *Parker* (1977)[109] D tried unsuccessfully to make a telephone call from a kiosk; in his frustration he slammed down the receiver and broke it. The Court of Appeal upheld his conviction for causing criminal damage recklessly, despite his defence that it did not occur to him that he might damage the telephone. The Court held that he must have known that he was dealing with breakable material, even if that fact was not at the forefront of his mind when he slammed the received down. He had 'closed his mind to the obvious', or suppressed this knowledge at the time of act.[110] It is quite evident that this decision involves some stretching of the awareness element which is thought to be central to advertent recklessness. In effect, it broadens the time frame from the moment of the act itself to an earlier and calmer time, when D would almost certainly have answered the question: 'What might happen if you slammed down a telephone receiver?', by saying: 'It might break.' The reason for thus broadening the time frame is presumably to prevent bad temper resulting in an acquittal, since this would be socially undesirable: people should control their tempers. But it does sully the subjective purity of this definition of recklessness.

The second problem is the 'couldn't care less' attitude: D might not have thought about a particular consequence, because it was irrelevant to his interests. If this version of events is accepted, D must be acquitted on the advertent definition of recklessness. Antony Duff has argued that these cases can and should be included within the meaning of recklessness, by invoking the concept of 'practical indifference'. This is 'a matter, not of feeling as distinct from action, but of the practical attitude which the action

---

[109] [1977] 1 WLR 600.
[110] See the discussion by Geoffrey Lane LJ, in *Stephenson* [1979] QB 69, and M. Wasik and M. P. Thompson, 'Turning a Blind Eye as Constituting Mens Rea' (1981) 32 NILQ, 328, at 339.

itself displays'. Moreover, it may include cases in which D fails to advert to certain aspects of the situation: 'what I notice or attend to reflects what I care about; and my very failure to notice something can display my utter indifference to it'.[111] The argument is that people who are practically indifferent to certain key features of a situation may be just as much to blame as those who do advert to them. This argument is at its strongest in relation to rape, and to those defendants who contend that they never really considered whether the woman was consenting. The law has adopted the 'couldn't care less' test here but not elsewhere. Duff's argument is that requiring practical indifference is just as subjective, and just as respectful of individual autonomy, as requiring awareness of risk. The question is what D's attitude was towards the victim's interests: D's words and acts provide the basis for determining that attitude. However, Duff's view that the test of practical indifference is no more objective than the test of awareness of risk is unconvincing, for, at least in the rape cases that Duff discusses,[112] judgments of practical indifference are apparently made by others on the basis that men *ought* to consider the victim's interests in such cases. Wholly acceptable that approach may be,[113] but it is not a subjective approach because some defendants apparently do not think in those terms. The objective element of 'unreasonableness' would play a far more dominant role in the test of practical indifference than it now plays in advertent recklessness, and it is preferable to recognize this explicitly.[114]

Thus there are at least two types of situation in which the 'awareness' requirement, the centrepiece of advertent recklessness, may fail to yield an acceptable grading of blameworthiness. One is the person who acts impulsively or in a temper, 'without thinking'. The other is the person who fails to think about the consequences out of callous indifference to them. A third possibility would be where D states that he was so preoccupied with other aspects of what he was doing as to give no thought to a particular consequence (although the courts might be reluctant to accept such a defence).[115]

(ii) *Caldwell Recklessness*. It may or may not be true historically that the *Caldwell* test grew out of dissatisfaction with the limitations of the subjective or advertent definition, but it certainly suceeds in encompassing the three situations just discussed (acts during loss of temper, acts due to callous indifference, and acts done while preoccupied). In the House of Lord decision in *Caldwell* (1982),[116] Lord Diplock formulated the

---

[111] R. A. Duff, *Intention, Agency and Criminal Liability* (1990), 162–163.
[112] Ibid., 167–173. [113] See below, Ch 8.5.
[114] See Norrie, *Crime, Reason and History*, 71–7.
[115] See Williams, 'The Unresolved Problem of Recklessness' (1988) 8 *Legal Studies*, 74, at 82.
[116] [1982] AC 341. The case of *Lawrence* (next note) was decided on the same day.

following model direction: a person is guilty of causing damage recklessly if:

(i) he does an act which in fact creates an obvious risk that property would be destroyed or damaged and (ii) when he does the act he either has not given any thought to the possibility of there being any such risk or has recognized that there was some risk involved and has nonetheless gone on to do it.

It will be noticed that this definition includes the advertent element (by referring to the person who recognizes the risk and takes it), but then goes further, extending to all those who fail to give any thought to the possibility of a risk which may de described as obvious. The formulation in the reckless driving case of *Lawrence* goes a little further by requiring proof that the risk was 'obvious and serious', the latter term implying that the ordinary prudent person would not have considered the risk negligible.[117] Returning to the *Caldwell* formulation quote above, it appears that the requirement that the risk be 'obvious' has to be satisfied independently, no matter which of the two conditions in (ii) is relied upon. However, the House of Lords held in *Reid* (1992)[118] that the 'obviousness' requirement applies only when the 'failing to give thought' condition is relied upon. If it is established that the defendant was actually aware of 'some risk of the relevant kind', there is no need for the prosecution to go on and prove that it was 'obvious'. Lord Diplock's speech in *Caldwell* was unclear on the question of to whom the risk must be obvious. At one stage he suggested that it was necessary to show that it would have been obvious to D if D had stopped to think:[119] this version of *Caldwell* might have allowed the acquittal of a person such as *Stephenson*,[120] whose mental disturbance meant that he might not have been able to see a risk which other people would regard as obvious. However, as we shall see presently, subsequent decisions have left this point without authoritative resolution.

What is the justification for this extension of recklessness beyond the advertent definition? Lord Diplock offered three reasons. One was that the dividing line between awareness and unawareness or risk is so narrow and so difficult to prove that juries and magistrates should not be required to labour over it. The factual basis of this must be accepted: it may be virtually impossible to know whether or not a person was fleetingly aware of the consequences of his action. The same is true of intention, mistake,

---

[117] [1982] AC 510 at 527, reiterated in the reckless driving case of *Reid* (1992) 95 Cr App R 391.   [118] (1992) 95 Cr App R 391.
[119] See G. Williams, 'Recklessness Redefined' [1981] CLJ 252; E. Griew, 'Reckless Damage and Reckless Driving: Living with *Caldwell* and *Lawrence*' [1981] Crim LR 743; G. Syrota, 'A Radical Change in the Law of Recklessness?' [1982] Crim LR 97; R. A. Duff, 'Professor Williams and Conditional Subjectivism'.
[120] However, *Caldwell* overruled *Stephenson:* see n. 108 above.

and other questions which turn on the contents of another person's mind at some time past. But it does not follow from this that the distinction must be abandoned; it is right to persist with it if it is regarded as crucial to the grading of culpability—that is the question. Indeed, this distinction is maintained in many areas of the law, including non-fatal offences against the person, as the House of Lords itself has confirmed.[121] Another reason given by Lord Diplock was that, in ordinary speech, the term 'reckless' is wider than awareness of risk, and includes lack of care and lack of thought. That may be true, but it does not solve the question of how wide the law's definition should be. The third reason given by Lord Diplock is the only one worthy of being called a justification: that it may be no less blameworthy for a person to fail to foresee an obvious risk than it is to see the risk and knowingly to take it. In other words, Lord Diplock challenged the common law distinction between recklessness and negligence on the ground that it fails to draw the line in the right place. It will be observed that Lord Diplock did not appear to be altering the balance between individual responsibility and social protection. He did not argue that the definition of recklessness should be widened because a person who fails to give thought to an obvious risk is just as *dangerous* as the person who realized the risk. Rather, he attacked fundamental conceptions of responsibility by arguing that the ideas of *mens rea*, as encompassing intention and subjective recklessness, is unsatisfactory because it omits some equally culpable cases.[122] As we have seen, some of the supporters of advertent recklessness accept that it is under-inclusive, in that they have attempted to stretch it to include actions during fits of temper and actions out of indifference.

One criticism of *Caldwell* recklessness which must be faced at the outset is that it cannot properly be terms *mens rea*, because it is not a state of mind. A person who fails to give thought to a consequence does not have a state of mind in relation to that consequence. But this presupposes that the only proper ground for ascribing blame for serious offences is advertence— in other words, that the minimum requirement for criminal culpability should be that the harmful consequence passed through D's mind. This is exactly what *Caldwell* is attacking, and this substantive challenge cannot be defeated by the procedural or linguistic device of saying that this is not *mens rea*. *Mens rea* is just a Latin term which is used as a shorthand reference to the requirements of intention, recklessness, knowledge, and reckless knowledge which have generally been thought to set the

---

[121] *Savage, Parmenter* [1992] 1 AC 299, below, Ch 8.3.
[122] Lord Goff in *Reid* (1992) 95 Cr App R at 405–6 took the same view, arguing that unawareness of risk stemming from drink, rage, an attitude of indifference or wilful blindness, ought to be regarded as culpable and as reckless.

appropriate conditions for liability for serious offences. That could be changed if it were agreed that the *Caldwell* test is a more accurate representation of social judgments of blame.

A true objection is that, whereas advertent recklessness is under-inclusive, *Caldwell* recklessness is over-inclusive. Lord Diplock's test of what would have been obvious to the reasonable person appears to admit of no exceptions. Thus *Stephenson* (1979)[123] was overruled as a decision on the Criminal Damage Act by *Caldwell*: this suggests that Stephenson would now be convicted despite his inability, stemming from schizophrenia, to foresee a risk which others would have foreseen. If he is not within the defence of insanity, then he must be judged by the standard of mentally normal people. The point emerges even more strongly from *Elliott* v *C* (1983),[124] where a backward girl of 14 who had not slept all night wandered into a shed, poured white spirit on to the floor, and dropped lighted matches on to it. The shed was destroyed; apparently D did not know about the inflammable properties of white spirit. The Divisional Court held that she should none the less be convicted of criminal damage, since she should be judged on the basis of whether the risk would have been obvious to the reasonable adult. The court held that it was bound by precedent, unable to modify the test either for her age or for her mental condition. Shortly after this, in *Stephen Malcolm R* (1984),[125] the Court of Appeal was invited to amend the test to 'an ordinary prudent person of the same age and sex as the defendant', but it felt unable to do so. The judges in these cases appeared uncomfortable with the strictness of the *Caldwell* test, and there are now dicta in *Reid* (1992)[126] which suggest that exceptions can be made. Lord Goff referred to a person 'afflicted with illness or shock',[127] Lord Browne-Wilkinson to 'reasonable misunderstanding, sudden disability or emergency',[128] and Lord Keith to circumstances in which the 'capacity to appreciate risks was adversely affected by some condition not involving fault on his part'.[129] Although their Lordships were careful to confine their remarks to the offence of reckless driving, the *Caldwell* test is closely similar and these dicta raise the hope that exceptions based on diminished capacity may be recognized in future cases.[130]

Another difficulty with *Caldwell* is that the model direction makes no mention of the person who recognizes the risk but believes that it can be

---

[123] See above, n. 108 and accompanying text.   [124] (1983) 77 Cr App R 103.
[125] (1984) 79 Cr App R 334.
[126] (1992) 95 Cr App R 391; see S. *Gardner* (1993) 109 LQR 21.
[127] Ibid., at 409.   [128] Ibid., at 414.   [129] Ibid., at 393.
[130] See S. Field and M. Lynn, 'The Capacity for Recklessness' (1992) 12 Legal Studies, 74; K Oliphant, 'Mind the Gap' (1993) 4 KCLJ, 69; and S. Field and M. Lynn, 'Capacity, Recklessness and the House of Lords' [1993] Crim LR 127.

eliminated. This has led commentators to argue that there is a gap or loophole which may be exploited to gain an acquittal in appropriate cases: if D has recognized the risk, he is not in Lord Diplock's category of failing to give thought to it; and if D believes the risk has been eliminated, he has not gone on to take the risk. The argument was run before the Divisional Court in *Chief Constable of Avon and Somerset* v *Shimmen* (1987),[131] where D, an exponent of a martial art, was showing his friends how close to a shop-window he could kick without damaging it. In fact, he broke the window. The Divisional Court did not gainsay the loophole argument, but they directed that D should be convicted because he had said in evidence that he 'thought [he] had eliminated as much risk as possible'. This means that he did not think he had eliminated *all* risk, which in turn means that he knew there was a slight risk, and that is enough for subjective recklessness (without the need to rely on the *Caldwell* extension).[132] True cases of the *Caldwell* loophole will be rare and, as Lord Goff observed in *Reid*, a defendant would in practice have to 'point to some specific fact as to which he was mistaken and which, if true, would have excluded the possibility of risk'.[133] If the loophole argument is assessed morally, however, can it be maintained that there is less culpability in erroneously believing that one has eliminated all risk than in failing to give thought to the risk at all? The difference is merely that between mistake and accident: in the former case D is under a misapprehension which leads to harm; in the latter case D fails to consider the consequences of actions and causes harm. The former amounts to an omission to discover the true nature of the risk; the latter amounts to an omission to think about the existence of the risk. It is by no means clear that the *Caldwell* test is logically consistent in excluding the former and including the latter.

(iii) *Application of the Two Tests.* The *Caldwell* definition is now of little practical significance. It applies only to the crime of criminal damage (including arson) and to a few other statutory offences.[134] It formerly applied to reckless driving, as the decisions in *Lawrence* and *Reid* demonstrate, but that offence was abolished in 1991 and replaced with dangerous driving. It is no longer applicable to manslaughter.[135] *Caldwell* is now unlikely to be extended to other crimes, and so advertent recklessness remains the dominant test. The approach to recklessness in rape continues to be the 'couldn't care less' test.[136] The respective merits of the different tests are discussed again in 5.3(g).

---

[131] (1987) 84 Cr App R 7.
[132] See D. J. Birch, 'The Foresight Saga: the Biggest Mistake of All?' [1988] Crim LR 4, and *Goodfellow* (1986) 82 Cr App R 23.
[133] (1992) 95 Cr App R at 410.
[134] E.g. *Large* v *Mainprize* [1989] Crim LR 213 (sea fishing regulations).
[135] See *Adomako*[1994] 2 All ER 79, discussed in Ch 7.5 below.
[136] See *Satnam S. and Kewal S.*(1983) 78 Cr App R 149, and below, Ch 8.5(d).

(d) Knowledge and Belief

In general terms, the requirement of knowledge is regarded as having the same intensity as that of intention, except that knowledge relates to circumstances forming part of the definition of the crime, and intention relates to the consequences specified in the definition of the crime. This is probably acceptable as a dividing line, even though the distinction between circumstances and consequences is not without difficulty when applied to the definitions of some offences.[137] Let us consider the basic definition of the offence of criminal damage: a person is guilty if he or she damages property belonging to another with intent to damage property belonging to another (Criminal Damage Act 1971, section 1(1)).[138] One can argue, of course, that the only fault element required here is intention—does D intend to damage property belonging to another? But it is also possible to divide the fault element into two: Does D intend to damage property? Does D know that the property belongs to another? The knowledge relates to a fact or circumstance: although it will usually be relevant to D's reasons for acting, it may be separated analytically from the result which D intends. Such an analysis is essential for those crimes which require no result or conduct, such as possessing a controlled drug, where knowledge becomes the key element in the crime.[139] The matter is absolutely clear in the many offences which include the term 'knowingly' in their definition, such as being knowingly concerned in the importation of prohibited goods into the country.[140] There are also some offences in which the requirement is extended slightly, such as handling stolen goods knowing or believing them to be stolen, where the reference to 'believing' is taken to include people who may not *know* that the goods are stolen but may have no substantial doubt that they are.[141]

It is at this point, however, that a significant difference opens up between intention and knowledge as fault requirements. One can intend a result, whether or not it actually occurs: D can intend to kill by, say, shooting at V; if D's shot missed, then D still intended to kill and may be convicted of attempted murder. If the intention fails to come to fruition, it is none the less an intention. But this does not apply to knowledge. If we return to the basic offence of criminal damage as described above, we can

---

[137] For discussion of the potential problems, see G. Williams, 'The Problem of Reckless Attempts' [1983] Crim LR 365, R. J. Buxton, 'Circumstances, Consequences and Attempted Rape' [1984] Crim LR 25, and R. A. Duff, 'The Circumstances of an Attempt' (1991) 50 Camb LJ, 100. The issue is discussed in Ch 11.3 below.

[138] The offence may also be committed recklessly, but that is not relevant here. See more fully D. W. Elliott, 'Criminal Damage' [1988] Crim LR 403.

[139] See the discussion of possession offences above, Ch 4.3(b).

[140] Customs and Excise Management Act 1979, s 170; see e.g. *Taaffe* [1984] AC 539.

[141] See *Hall* (1985) 81 Cr App R 260, and the discussion below, Ch 9.6.

consider the facts of *Smith (D R)* (1974):[142] D was renting a flat, and during the course of his tenancy he fixed some panelling to the walls to conceal the wires of his stereo equipment. When his tenancy ceased, he took down and destroyed the panelling—which he had put up for his own convenience. He was charged with criminal damage, on the basis that, in law, the panelling became the property of the landlord once it was fixed to the walls. The Court of Appeal quashed his conviction for criminal damage, pointing out that although he did intend to damage property, he believed that the property was his own, and therefore he lacked the fault element for the crime. If D had been asked whether the panelling was his own, he would surely have replied: 'Yes'. Yet it would be inaccurate to say that he *knew* this, since it was not in fact true. It is more accurate to say the he *believed* the panelling to be his own; this belief should not be described as knowledge, because it does not accord with the true position. Therefore, although one can intend something which does not come to fruition, one cannot know something which is not in fact (or in law) true.

It is relatively unusual for the element of 'knowledge of circumstances' to be contested in serious crimes. Neither murder nor manslaughter is committed if D does not know that the object against which he uses force is a human being, but it is rare for a defendant to argue that the target was believed to be a dummy.[143] In some cases of rape the defendant argues that he believed that the victim was consenting, even though it subsequently transpires that she was not. Absence of consent is an element in the definition of rape, and so it must be proved either that D knew that the victim was not consenting or that he was reckless[144] as to the absence of consent. Where D argues that he mistakenly believed her to be consenting, and the jury is left in reasonable doubt about this, he should be acquitted of rape, as the law stands, because the prosecution has failed to prove that he had the requisite knowledge of absence of consent. This is what is sometimes called 'the defence of mistake', but it should be clear that it cannot properly be termed a defence in this context. A defendant who argues that he was mistaken about consent may succeed in creating a reasonable doubt in the minds of the jury, but the defendant does not have to prove anything: the prosecution has to establish knowledge or reckless knowledge as to the absence of consent, as the House of Lords held in the landmark case of *DPP* v *Morgan* (1976).[145] Lawyers tend to refer loosely to 'the defence of mistake', but in most cases this means, strictly speaking, that it will be argued that the prosecution has failed to prove that D had the

[142] [1974] QB 354.
[143] See G. Williams, 'Homicide and the Supernatural' (1949) 65 LQR, 491.
[144] For the relevant meaning of recklessness, see below, Ch 8.5(d).
[145] [1976] AC 182.

required knowledge of the elements in the definition of the crime. It is not a defence in the sense that D must prove anything; and mistaken belief is simply an explanation of why knowledge was lacking.[146]

Although it is rare in offences against the person for the defendant to claim that he did not know he was striking another human being, mistaken beliefs are occasionally raised in these cases in a different way. Offences of assault and wounding are defined not just in terms of the use of force against another, but the *unlawful* use of force. As we saw in Chapter 4.7, force may be lawful if it is used in self-defence or the prevention of crime, for example. The 'logical' argument is that, if D used force in the belief that he was preventing a crime, when in reality this was not so, D would lack the knowledge that the use of force was unlawful and should therefore be acquitted of the offence. An example here is *Williams* (1984):[147] V saw a man, X, snatch a bag from a woman in the street; V ran after X and forcibly detained him; D then came upon the scene and asked V why he was punching X; V said, untruthfully, that he was a police officer; D asked V for his warrant card, and when V failed to produce the card, D struck V. D was charged with assaulting V, and his defence was that he had mistakenly believed that his actions were justifiable in the prevention of crime. It is plain that his actions were not in fact justified, since V was acting lawfully in trying to detain X. In Uniacke's terms D's conduct was agent-perspectivally justified but not objectively justified.[148] The law requires the prosecution to satisfy the court that D was aware of the facts which made his action unlawful, and he was not. He was mistaken. The Court of Appeal held that his conviction should be quashed: 'The mental element necessary to constitute guilt is the intent to apply unlawful force to the victim. We do not believe that the mental element can be substantiated by simply showing an intent to apply force and no more.'

The emphasis thus far in the discussion of knowledge and mistake has been upon the 'inexorable logic', as Lord Hailsham put it,[149] that if an offence requires knowledge of a given circumstance, a person who is mistaken about that circumstance should be acquitted for lack of knowledge. Logic it may be, but that should not be taken to mean that there is no place for objective requirements of reasonableness in this realm of the law. There are two ways of arguing for objective restrictions.[150] First, it can be pointed out that there is a long standing defence of reasonable mistake, which applies to all criminal offences.[151] This defence

[146] A true defence of mistake is discussed in Ch 6.6 below.
[147] (1984) 78 Cr App R 276.
[148] S. Uniacke, *Permissible Killing* (1994), discussed in Ch 4.7 above.
[149] In *DPP* v *Morgan* [1976] AC 182, at 214.
[150] See A. P. Simester, 'Mistakes in Defence' (1992) 12 Oxford JLS, 295, and the fuller discussion in Ch 6.6 below.
[151] *Prince* (1875) LR 2 CCR 154, *Tolson* (1889) 23 QBD 168.

is discussed in Chapter 6.6. Of course a defence of this kind is unlikely to be found satisfactory by full-blooded subjectivists, who applaud the wider ground of exculpation in *Morgan* and *Williams*. They might contend, for example, that the reasonableness requirement has historically been little more than a device to overcome difficulties of proof and to prevent bogus defences from succeeding. The reason for mentioning it here is that to some extent the courts had a choice between two approaches. In *DPP* v *Morgan*[152] the House of Lords could have upheld the doctrine of reasonable mistake: after all, the 'inexorable logic' does not affect the courts' approach to intoxication, as we shall see,[153] and so the House could have declared that mistakes would be treated on a special footing too. Likewise in *Williams*,[154] the Court of Appeal could have re-asserted the doctrine of reasonable mistake, adopting the view of earlier years that the existence or implication of the term 'unlawful' in all offences against the person has no particular effect on the law of mistake.[155] A second argument is that the courts should have been more sensitive to the rights and wrongs of the situations to which the 'inexorable logic' was being applied. Thus one could argue that the very offence with which the leading decision of *DPP* v *Morgan*[156] was concerned—rape—should incorporate a requirement of reasonable grounds for the belief in consent: the two parties are physically so close that there is every opportunity for D to find out whether or not the woman is consenting by asking her,[157] and it is reasonable to require him to do so. Similarly, where a case concerns the use of force by a trained law enforcement officer, is it not right to expect the officer to make reasonable checks on the facts (if time permits, of course) before using considerable force?

The appellate courts have taken considerable strides towards subjectivism in cases such as *Morgan* and *Williams*, and yet the judges do not seem to be thoroughly convinced. In respect of the defences of duress and necessity, the courts have required D's belief that dire threats were being made or that circumstances of necessity had arisen to be based on reasonable grounds if it is to excuse.[158] That divergence of approach to mistakes relating to duress and necessity occurred during the same decade (1980s) as the establishment of the principle that mistakes in relation to

---

[152] [1976] AC 182.
[153] As decided by the House of Lords in *DPP* v *Majewski* [1977] AC 443. On intoxication, see Ch 6.3 below. For a juxtaposition of judicial statements for and against 'logic', see A. Norrie, *Crime, Reason and History* (1993), 10–11.
[154] (1984) 78 Cr App R 276.
[155] A view taken three years earlier by Hodgson J in *Albert* v *Lavin* (1981) 72 Cr App R 178. For fuller discussion of this 'redefinition' argument, see R. Tur, 'Subjectivism and Objectivism: Towards Synthesis' in Shute, Gardner, and Horder (eds), *Action and Value in Criminal Law* (1993).   [156] [1976] AC 182.   [157] See below, Ch 8.5.
[158] See Ch 6.6 on putative defences.

self-defence and prevention of crime must be genuine but need not be reasonable. While it is possible to discern theoretical differences between the two kinds of defence, the difference of legal approaches is more likely to reflect ambivalence about the proper treatment of mistakes. The 'logical' approach was urged on the judges as irresistible when, as the two reasons given in the previous paragraph show, it is not. This may be similar to the ambivalence about the parameters of culpability shown by *Caldwell* and the ensuing debate.[159] Just as one might argue that there are circumstances in which a person who fails to give thought to an obvious risk of harm is sufficiently blameworthy for criminal liability, so one might argue that there are circumstances in which a person who acts on an unreasonable belief about facts or circumstances may also deserve criminal conviction.

(e) Reckless Knowledge

'Reckless knowledge' bears the same relation to knowledge as recklessness to intention. Thus, the general, common law meaning of reckless knowledge is that D believes that there is a risk that the prohibited circumstance exists, and goes on to take that risk. In the rare offences to which *Caldwell* applies, reckless knowledge is extended to cover those who fail to give thought to the existence of the prohibited circumstances, when a reasonable person would have done so. An example might be provided by the facts of *Smith* (D R), discussed above.[160] The Criminal Damage Act 1971 penalizes anyone who damages property either intending to damage property belonging to another or being reckless as to whether property belonging to another is damaged. When the case was decided in 1974, the common law meaning applied and D would have been found reckless if he thought there was a risk that the panelling now belonged to his landlord: he did not. If the case arose now *Caldwell* would apply, and he would be convicted if he failed to give any thought to the possibility that his landlord owned the panelling and if a reasonable person would have seen that risk. In fact, D would not be convicted, since he falls into the *Caldwell* gap:[161] he had thought about the matter and believed that the panelling belonged to him.

The tendency in the modern cases has been to draw no distinction between circumstances and consequences, and therefore to regard reck-lessness as something which applies in the same way to all elements of the offence. Thus in *Kimber* (1983)[162] D was convicted of indecent assault on a woman. The question arose of whether D was reckless as to the fact that she was not consenting, and the Court of Appeal held that 'his attitude to

---

[159] See above, 5.3(c).   [160] See above, n. 142 and accompanying text.
[161] See above, nn. 131–133 and accompanying text.
[162] (1983) 77 Cr App R 225.

her was one of indifference to her feelings and wishes. This state of mind is aptly described in the colloquial expression, "couldn't care less". In law this is recklessness.' The court did not say that it was dealing with reckless knowledge, but clearly this is what the crime of indecent assault requires—that D was reckless as to the woman's non-consent. The use of the phrase 'couldn't care less' is somewhat equivocal as between advertent reckless-ness and *Caldwell*.

One other point on reckless knowledge is the proper approach to what is termed 'wilful blindness'. This occurs where D knows that there is a risk that a prohibited circumstance exists, but refrains from checking it. An example is *Westminster City Council* v *Croyalgrange Ltd* (1986),[163] where D was charged with knowingly permitting the use of premises as a sex establishment without a licence. The House of Lords held that:

it is always open to the tribunal of fact, when knowledge on the part of a defendant is required to be proved, to base a finding of knowledge on evidence that the defendant had deliberately shut his eyes to the obvious or refrained from enquiry because he suspected the truth but did not want to have his suspicion confirmed.[164]

It will be seen that Lord Bridge used the language of inference here, suggesting that a court might infer knowledge from wilful blindness in the same way as he suggested that intention might be inferred from foresight of virtual certainty.[165] The true meaning of the passage is surely that wilful blindness is treated as actual knowledge, which has long been the law.[166] Although, strictly speaking, D does not *know*, since he has refrained from finding out, he may have an overwhelmingly strong belief (he may believe it is virtually certain) that the prohibited circumstance exists. Thus, wilful blindness may be treated not as reckless knowledge, but as a form of actual knowledge.

(f) Negligence

Traditionally, books dealing with English criminal law afford an extremely brief discussion to negligence as a standard of liability. Among the common law crimes, only manslaughter rests on liability for (gross) negligence,[167] and careless driving is perhaps the only common offence based on negligence. Yet there are many offences of negligence among the statutory offences regulating various commercial and other activities, often

---

[163] (1986) 83 Cr App R 155; see also the draft Criminal Code, Law Com No. 177, clause 18(a).
[164] *Westminster City Council* v *Croyalgrange Ltd* (1986) 83 Cr App R 155; see generally Wasik and Thompson, 'Turning a Blind Eye'.
[165] See *Moloney* [1985] AC 905, and above, n. 80.
[166] The classic statement is that of Devlin J, in *Roper* v *Taylor's Garages Ltd* [1951] 2 TLR 284, at 288.   [167] See below, Ch 7.5(c).

taking the form of an indictable offence of doing an act 'with intent' to contravene the regulations, supported by a summary offence of negligence in committing an act in such a way as to 'have reason to believe' that the regulations will be contravened.[168] Moreover, other systems of law tend to have a larger group of offences of negligence, and might look askance at a set of laws which penalizes negligence where death is caused but does not penalize it where serious injury or suffering is caused or risked.

One reason for the opposition of many English text-writers to criminal liability for negligence is that it derogates from the subjective principles stated at the beginning of this chapter.[169] The doctrine of *mens rea*, as expressed in the requirements of intention and recklessness (apart from *Caldwell*),[170] makes liability depend on proof that D chose the harm, in the sense of intending it or at least being aware that it might result. These elements are missing where mere negligence is admitted: there is no need to prove that D adverted to the consequences at all, so long as the court is satisfied that a reasonable person would have done so. To have negligence as a standard of liability would therefore move away from advertence as the foundation of criminal responsibility and, in doing so, might show insufficient respect for the principle of autonomy. Thus it would dilute the element of individual culpability which justifies the public condemnatory element in a criminal conviction, as distinct from a judgment of damages in tort or contract.

The counter-argument to this might be a form of 'capacity theory', the origins of which might be found in the proposition that human actions are sufficiently free, rather than determined, as to make blame and punishment defensible. This proposition underlies most of the criminal law,[171] and it might be argued that a person who negligently causes harm could have done otherwise—he could have taken the care necessary to avoid the harm. So long as the individuals have the capacity to behave otherwise, it is fair to impose liability in those situations where there are sufficient signals to alert the reasonable citizen to the need to take care. Autonomy is a fundamental principle, but this does not mean that advertence should always be required so long as there is fair warning and a fair opportunity to conform with the required standard.

Three features of this counter-argument should be noted. First, its focus on capacity should not be dismissed as 'objective', for that would be an undiscriminating use of the term. As Hart has shown, it is perfectly possible to make exceptions for those who cannot be expected to attain the standard of foresight and control of the reasonable citizen. One only has to

---

[168] Some examples are collected at [1980] Crim LR 1.
[169] See above, Ch 5.2(a).   [170] Discussed above, Ch 5.3(c).
[171] Discussed above, Ch 4.2.

supplement the question, 'Did D fail to attain a reasonable standard of care in the circumstances?', with the further question; 'Could D, given his mental and physical capacities, have taken the necessary precautions?'[172] Negligence liability need be 'objective' only in so far as it holds liable those who fail to take precautions when they could reasonably have been expected to do so. Secondly, negligence liability may also derogate from any principle of contemporaneity, in the sense that the culpable failure to take precautions often pre-dates the causing of the harm: the railwayman failed to check the signals or the track, so that a crash occurred later; D misunderstood the mechanism of the gun, so that when he later pulled the trigger it killed someone. The enquiry into capacity and opportunity necessitated by negligence liability widens the time frame of the criminal law, giving precedence to the doctrine of prior fault over the principle of contemporaneity.[173] Thirdly, the argument is in favour of negligence liability, not strict liability. Existing law imposes obligations on people who engage in various activities: the obligations of those operating systems of public transport; or the obligations of driving a motor vehicle; or the obligations of owning or managing a factory; or the obligations of engaging in a particular trade or business. Strict liability has been criticized in 3(a) above. Negligence liability, on the other hand, is not open to the same objections.

The discussion thus far should have established that people who cause harm negligently may be culpable, in the sense that they fail to take reasonable precautions when they have the capacity to do so. What it does not establish is that negligence is an appropriate standard for criminal liability, for it must be borne in mind that criminal liability is the law's most condemnatory form, and it should be reserved for serious wrongs. How might it be argued that the English doctrinal tradition of drawing the line of criminal liability below intention and recklessness, and above negligence (at least for 'conventional' crimes, such as those in the draft Criminal Code),[174] is ill-founded? One approach would be to establish that some cases of negligence manifest greater culpability than some cases of subjective recklessness. Thus it could be claimed that a person who knowingly takes a slight risk of harm is less culpable than another person who fails to think about or recognize a high risk of the same harm: D, a shotgun champion, fires at a target, knowing that there is a slight risk that the bullet will ricochet and injure a spectator, which it does; E, who rarely handles guns, is invited to participate in a shooting party and fires wildly into bushes, failing to consider the possibility of others being there, and one is injured. Is D manifestly more culpable than E? A different

---

[172] This is the argument of Hart, *Punishment and Responsibility*, Chs 2 and 5.
[173] See above, 5.2(f).
[174] See above, nn. 39 and 40, and accompanying text.

comparison would be between someone who knowingly takes the risk of a small harm occurring and someone who fails to recognize the risk of a serious harm occurring: a criminal law which convicts the former and not the latter could be said to be transfixed by the notion of a 'consistent' general part. Why maintain that negligence is never an appropriate standard of criminal liability, even where the harm is great and the risk obvious?

The argument is therefore moving towards the conclusion that negligence may be an appropriate standard for criminal liability where: (i) the harm is great; (ii) the risk is obvious; and (iii) the defendant has the capacity to take the required precautions. This opens up further debates on various points. The thesis is that negligence may be an appropriate standard where there are well-known risks of serious harm. This argues in favour of negligence as a standard of liability for certain serious offences against the person, including some serious sexual offences,[175] and also for some serious offences against the environment and property. Critics would be able to attack decisions to draw the line at certain levels of seriousness, but these would be essentially practical criticisms which would not undermine the argument in favour of negligence liability. The spread of negligence liability would not have to result in the broadening of the traditional category of *mens rea*, and would not mean that intention, recklessness, and negligence would henceforth be bracketed together. It would be perfectly possible for a Criminal Code to provide separate crimes of negligence, with lower maximum sentences, at appropriate points in the hierarchy of offences. This, in turn, raises the possibility of defendants who foresaw the risk of the harm (and were therefore subjectively reckless) pleading guilty to the lesser offence of negligence, whereas if there were no such offence, they would be duly convicted of the 'intentionally or recklessly' higher offence. But this is a systemic problem in criminal justice, and cannot be a conclusive argument against spreading the net of the criminal law in respect of serious harms. A further issue is whether the offences of negligence should be in the inchoate mode, 'failing to take reasonable precautions', or should be tied to the occurrence of the particular harm. Careless driving is of the former type, manslaughter of the latter, and this point will be pursued further in connection with crimes of endangerment.[176]

Even granting this argument in favour of criminalizing certain instances of negligence, what would be the point of doing so? This takes us back to the aims of the criminal law, discussed earlier.[177] It might be tempting to maintain that the general preventive aim of the criminal law cannot be

---

[175] See the discussion of rape in Ch 8.5.   [176] See Chs 7.6, 7.7, and 8.3(f).
[177] See Ch 1.3.

served by offences of negligence: the notion of deterrence presupposes rational reflection by D at the time of offending, whereas the distinguishing feature of negligence is that D failed to think (when a reasonable person would have done). However, it can be argued that crimes of negligence may exert a general deterrent effect, by alerting people to the need to take care in certain situations. The practical prospects of deterrence here seem no less propitious than in relation to offences requiring intention or recklessness. The principal justification, however, would be that negligent harm-doers deserve criminal conviction because they are sufficiently culpable. This is a question of degree and of judgment, on which views may differ. But it is certainly not resolved by stating that persons found to have acted with the form of *mens rea* known as recklessness are always more culpable than those who act negligently. Once the falsity of this proposition is demonstrated, the argument about the appropriate level of culpability for criminal conviction cannot be concluded simply by drawing a line based on *mens rea* and awareness.

(g) Objective versus Subjective

Much of the discussion of the law in section 3 of this Chapter has concerned the interplay of subjective and objective factors in the definition of the core fault terms. It has been suggested that in crimes where strict liability is imposed on individual defendants, the courts have generally placed insufficient emphasis on respect for individual autonomy and the importance of requiring fault. When dealing with recklessness and mistake, however, the tendency of many text writers and judges has been to accept the advertent or subjective approach, thus excluding from conviction certain people who may be no less culpable than those who are convicted. The decision in *Caldwell* might be seen as a reaction to this narrow subjectivism, but there are various objections to that development in the law. Successful as it might be in convicting unthinking, bad-tempered, and callously indifferent defendants, it does not yet have an established exception for people who lack the capacity to attain its objective standard.[178] Furthermore, *Caldwell* now occupies a somewhat isolated position in English law: what possible reason can there be for having a separate and rather elaborate test of recklessness that is essentially confined to one crime, criminal damage?

The *Caldwell* test is not the only way of supplementing the narrow conception of moral fault embodied in advertent recklessness. An alternative is Duff's test of practical indifference, which relies considerably on objective judgments as evidence of a person's attitude when behaving in a particular way. A further alternative would be to introduce more

[178] See the discussion of *Reid*, above, n. 133 and text.

offences of negligence and, in respect of mistake, more objective limitations on defences to criminal liability. The fact is that in many cases examined in this chapter, focussing solely on advertence fails to capture moral distinctions and to satisfy social expectations. Subjective tests heighten the protection of individual autonomy, but they typically make no concession to the principle of welfare and the concomitant notion of duties to take care and to avoid harming the interests of fellow citizens. However, if we are to move towards greater reliance on objective standards, at least two points must be confronted. First, objective tests must be applied subject to capacity-based exceptions. This preserves the principle of individual autonomy by ensuring that no person is convicted who lacked the capacity to conform his or her behaviour to the standard required. Failure to recognize this in the *Caldwell* decision was a major blemish that drew subsequent discussions away from the moral basis of the test itself. Secondly, any improved moral 'fit' obtained by moving more towards objective standards must be weighed against the greater detraction from the principle of maximum certainty that is likely to result.[179] Objective standards inevitably rely on terms such as reasonable, ordinary, and prudent. They appear much more malleable and unpredictable than subjective tests that ask whether or not a defendant was aware of a given risk, and they explicitly leave room for courts and even prosecutors to make social judgments about the limits of the criminal sanction.

5.4 THE VARIETY OF FAULT TERMS

Although the focus so far has been upon intention, recklessness, and knowledge, an examination of criminal legislation in force—some modern, some from the nineteenth century—reveals a diversity of fault terms. Even if the draft Criminal Code were to be enacted, its provisions would not be restricted to the core fault terms discussed so far. Moreover, the Code would cover only some 200 out of nearly 8,000 criminal offences, so the diversity would inevitably remain for some years. No survey of the different fault terms can be offered here, but some general remarks may be worthwhile.

Nineteenth-century legislation such as the Offences against the Person Act 1861 makes considerable use of the term 'maliciously'.[180] It is now settled that this term should be interpreted to mean intention or advertent recklessness, which simplifies the criminal lawyer's task.[181] Unfortunately, certain other terms have not been interpreted consistently in line with the core terminology. Many statutory offences, both ancient and modern, rely

[179] Norrie, *Crime, Reason and History*, 66.
[180] See the discussion of specific offences in Ch. 8.3.
[181] *Cunningham* [1957] 2 QB 396; *Savage, Parmenter* [1992] AC 699; above, Ch 5.3(c).

on the term 'wilfully': although in *Sheppard* (1981)[182] the House of Lords held that the term meant 'intentionally or recklessly' in the context of the crime of wilful neglect of a child, there are other offences in which 'wilfully' has been held not to require full mens rea.[183] Many offences are defined in terms of 'permitting', a word that has usually been interpreted as requiring full knowledge but has sometimes been held to impose strict liability, even on individuals.[184]

More to the point, however, is the fact that many major criminal offences rely on fault terms that bear little relation to any of those discussed so far. Theft and several other Theft Act offences rely on the term 'dishonestly', which, as we shall see,[185] may include a mixture of elements of subjective awareness and motivation with elements of objective moral judgment. Some fraud offences turn on whether the act or omission was done 'fraudulently'. And a number of public order and racial hatred offences impose liability where a certain consequence is 'likely' to result from D's conduct, without reference to whether D is aware of this likelihood. Thus, for example, a person commits the offence of 'fear or provocation of violence' by threatening, abusive or insulting words or behaviour *either* with intent to cause another person to believe that immediate unlawful violence will be used, *or* 'whereby that person is likely to believe that such violence will be used or it is likely that such violence will be provoked'.[186] Similarly, the offence of publishing or distributing racially inflammatory material is committed if *either* D intends thereby to stir up racial hatred *or* 'having regard to all the circumstances racial hatred is likely to be stirred up thereby'.[187] Offences that rely on the court's assessment of the probable effect of certain conduct may be said to impose a form of strict liability, or at least liability for negligence if it is assumed that the defendant ought to have known what effect was likely. However, suffice it to say that criminal offences in English law vary in their use of fault terms. The arguments for and against the core terms, examined in this Chapter, should provide a framework for considering the justifications for most other fault terms that may be encountered.

5.5 THE REFERENTIAL POINT OF FAULT

To say that a certain crime should require intention, wilfulness, knowledge or recklessness, is not enough. One must enquire: intention (or recklessness) as to what? It might be said loosely that 'the crime of manslaughter

---

[182] [1981] AC 394.
[183] See J. A. Andrews, 'Wilfulness: a Lesson in Ambiguity' (1981) 1 Legal Studies, 303.
[184] Compare, e.g., *James and Son* v *Smee* [1955] 1 QB 78 with *Baugh* v *Crago* [1976] Crim LR 72. [185] In Ch 9.2. [186] Public Order Act 1986, s 4(1); see Ch 8.3.
[187] Public Order Act 1986, s 19(1).

requires proof of intention or recklessness': the reason why this is a loose statement is that the intent or recklessness required is the same as that for assault or some other criminal act, whereas the liability imposed is that for homicide. Close analysis of the elements of the crime will show that the required fault and the result specified in the definition fail to correspond. This is what the principle of correspondence, outlined above, aims to eliminate.[188] Whenever one is discussing intent or recklessness, its referential point should always be established.

(a) Fault, Conduct, and Result

The argument may be carried further by considering the breadth or narrowness of the definitions of offences. A law which included a general offence of intentionally causing physical harm to another would make it far easier to establish the intent than it is in a system with a series of graded offences, such as causing serious injury intentionally, causing injury intentionally, and so forth. Similarly, a law which includes a general offence of intentionally causing damage to property belonging to another makes it far easier to establish the intent than a law with a series of offences differentiated according to the type of property damaged. Do these different legislative techniques have significant implications for the subjective doctrines of fault? Surely they do: one could argue that a single broad offence of 'intentionally causing a physical harm to another' obliterates the distinction between intending a minor assault and intending a major injury, and that a single broad offence of 'intentionally damaging property belonging to another' obliterates the distinction between intending damage to a cheap item and intending damage to an expensive item. The trend towards broader offence definitions, evident in criminal damage[189] but not in offences against the person in England,[190] gives greater weight to the principle of taking the consequences of any wrongdoing (5.2(b) above) than to the principle of correspondence (5.2(a) above). To that extent, it detracts from the elements of choice and control which are fundamental to the subjective approach. But how should this problem be solved?[191] It is hardly practical to allow each person to nominate those factors which he or she regarded as significant in any particular event: who is to say whether fidelity to individual choice and

---

[188] See above, 5.2(b).

[189] *Offences of Damage to Property*, See Law Com No. 29 (1970), and the Criminal Damage Act 1971; also above, n. 138.

[190] See Criminal Law Revision Committee, 14th Report, *Offences against the Person* (1980, Cmnd 7844), discussed below, Ch 8.3(k).

[191] See A. Ashworth, 'The Elasticity of Mens Rea' in C. Tapper (ed), *Crime, Proof and Punishment* (1981), and M. Moore, 'Intention and Mens Rea', in R. Gavison (ed), *Issues in Contemporary Legal Philosophy* (1987).

control requires two or 20 grades of criminal damage, or two or four grades
of offences of violence? At least, the implications for fault principles of
these labelling decisions[192] should be kept firmly in mind.

The argument may be taken still further, for there are cases where, as
everyone agrees, D intended to cause a different result from the one which
actually occurred. How ought the law to deal with such cases? Should it
respect D's choice, and provide for a conviction of attempting to do X
(which was what D intended to do)? Or should it regard the result as the
dominant factor, ignore the difference in D's intention, and convict on the
basis of 'sufficient similarity' between the intention and the result? English
law adopts the latter, more pragmatic approach. The Law Commission, in
introducing a provision into the draft Criminal Code which follows the
traditional approach, confirms the emphasis on results by stating that a
conviction for attempt would be 'inappropriate as not describing the *harm
done* adequately for labelling or sentencing purposes'.[193] The traditional
English approach rests on three doctrines—unforeseen mode, mistaken
object, and transferred fault.

(b) Unforeseen Mode

When D sets out to commit an offence by one method but actually causes
the prohibited consequence in a different way, the offence may be said to
have been committed by an unforeseen mode. Since most crimes
penalizing a result (with fault) do not specify any particular mode of
commission,[194] it is easy to regard the difference of mode as legally
irrelevant. D intended to kill V; he chose to shoot him, but the shot
missed; it hit a nearby heavy object, which fell on V's head and caused his
death. Any moral distinction between the two modes is surely too slender
to justify legal recognition. To charge D with *attempting* to kill V when he
did kill him seems excessively fastidious. Pragmatism is surely the best
approach here, and English law is generally right to ignore the unforeseen
mode.[195]

(c) Mistaken Object

When D sets out to commit an offence in relation to a particular victim but
makes a mistake of identity and directs his conduct at the wrong victim, the
offence may be said to have been committed despite the mistaken object.
The same would apply if D intends to steal one item of property but
mistakenly takes another. So long as the two objects fall within the same

---

[192] See the discussion of the principle of fair labelling in Ch 3.4(s).
[193] Law Com No. 177, ii, para 8.57 (my italics).
[194] The offences of obtaining by deception form an exception: see below, Ch 9.7.
[195] See Ashworth, 'The Elasticity of Mens Rea', 46–7.

legal category, it may be said that any moral distinction between them is too slender to justify legal recognition. In English law, mistake of object within the same offence is ignored. Two questions may be raised, however. First, there is one other area of criminal law where as change in the identity of the victim is regarded as crucial, namely, the law of complicity.[196] One may therefore ask whether there really is inadequate moral significance in the plea: 'I intended to help to kill my enemy, X, and never meant any harm to the poor innocent, Y.' Secondly, much depends on the breadth of definition of the relevant offence: there is surely some moral significance in the plea: 'I thought the picture I damaged was just a cheap copy; I had no idea that a valuable painting would be kept in that place.'[197] English law favours the pragmatic answer of taking the defendant's mistake into account in sentencing, which incidentally is much simpler for prosecutors.

(d) Transferred Fault

When D sets out to commit an offence in relation to a particular person or particular property but his conduct miscarries and the harm falls upon a different person or different property, D's intent may be said to have been transferred and the offence to have been committed against the actual victim or property. When the fault is transferred, any defence which D might have is transferred with it.[198] As with unforeseen mode and mistaken object, the fault may only be transferred within the same offence.[199] Thus, if D throws a brick at some people, intending to hurt them, and the brick misses them and breaks a window, the intent to injure cannot be transferred to the offence of damaging property.[200] In this situation, the possible offences are an attempt to cause injury, and recklessly damaging property. As with the doctrine of mistaken object, the breadth of definition of the offence has some importance here. It is one thing to accept that D, who swung his belt at W and struck V, should be convicted of injuring V;[201] it is quite another thing, in moral terms, to accept that E, who threw a stone at a window, should be convicted of intentionally damaging a valuable painting which, unbeknown to him, was hanging inside. Yet English law would convict E, probably by reference to the broad wording of the Criminal Damage Act 1971 (any 'property belonging to another'), without any need to rely on the doctrine of transferred

---

[196] See Law Com No. 177, ii, para 8.31, and below, Ch 10.5(a).
[197] See Ashworth, 'The Elasticity of Mens Rea', 47.
[198] *Gross* (1913) 23 Cox CC 455 (qualified defence of provocation transferred).
[199] See A. Ashworth, 'Transferred Malice and Punishment for Unforeseen Consequences', in P. Glazebrook (ed), *Reshaping the Criminal Law* (1978).
[200] *Pembliton* (1874) 12 Cox CC 607.
[201] As in the leading case of *Latimer* (1886) 17 QBD 359.

fault.[202] Thus the more broadly offences are defined, the less resort there will be to these three doctrines.

(e) Establishing the Referential Point

A system of criminal law which succeeded in reflecting the varying degrees of importance which people attribute to aspects of their intention (the mode of execution, the identity of the victim, the value of the property) might be a 'law professor's dream', but it is clearly not practical. The law is right to regard some aspects as relevant and others as irrelevant. But that does not establish that the traditional English approach is the most appropriate. The draft Criminal Code provides for the continuance of the pragmatic approach, arguing that this is simpler for prosecutors and that an attempt conviction would ignore the harm actually done.[203] Does its pragmatism stretch too far? Would it not be better to analyse some of these cases in terms of an unfulfilled intention, combined with an accidental (or perhaps reckless) causing of harm? Some would argue that the present law of inchoate offences would not ensure a conviction in all these cases of miscarried intent and miscarried recklessness:[204] according to this view, the three doctrines are not merely effective in returning convictions and symbolically right in their emphasis on results,[205] but also necessary if justice is to be done in all cases. There is, it may be argued, no serious distortion of 'desert' or proportionality involved in the three doctrines, since the doctrines do not misrepresent the class of harm that D set out to commit. Yet there remains the law's ambivalence about the importance of a victim's identity: if this really is significant to offenders and people's judgments of them, should not prosecutors make more use of the law of attempts, where it is clearly applicable?

This chapter has outlined only part of the picture of fault requirements in criminal law, since the negative fault requirements (to be discussed in Chapter 6) have a significant bearing on general conceptions of 'desert', responsibility, and culpability. However, a few points should be made at this stage.

First, it is always necessary to analyse the elements of each offence, so as to be clear exactly what fault requirements apply to which conduct elements. The focus here on a few core fault terms should not obscure the great variety of English criminal offences. Secondly, there is the manifest flexibility of the borderlines between the various gradations of fault: the penumbra of vagueness in the extent to which 'intent' is wider than purpose,

---

[202] See Ashworth, 'Transferred Malice and Punishment', 89–93.

[203] In effect, cl 24 of the draft Criminal Code is a 'deeming' provision: see Law Com No. 177, ii, paras 8.57–8.59.

[204] G. Williams, 'Convictions and Fair Labelling' [1983] CLJ 85.

[205] Cf. the discussion of luck and results in Ch 5.2(b) above.

in the distinction between recklessness and negligence, and even in the notion of strict liability, not only breaches the principle of maximum certainty but also places considerable discretion in the hands of the courts. Thirdly, and most importantly, warnings have been sounded about the variable use of social defence arguments and the principle of welfare. Judges and some text writers have placed too much emphasis on social defence arguments in relation to strict liability, and yet there has been too little emphasis on the principle of welfare in the debate about liability for recklessness or negligence. Moreover, there is a widespread assumption that the same standard of liability should operate throughout the criminal law, that standard being *mens rea* defined in terms of intention, knowledge, and subjective recklessness. Yet if the potential harm is great and the precautions needed to avoid it are well-known or should be known to someone engaged in the particular activity, the argument for departing from the supposed orthodoxy may be a powerful one.

6

Negative Fault Requirements

6.1 GROUNDS OF EXCUSE

Criminal lawyers sometimes speak and write as if criminal guilt consists of the presence of *mens rea*, but observations in previous chapters have already hinted that matters are not so simple. The notions of fault and culpability go beyond *mens rea* and require a discussion of other doctrines which are sometimes referred to as 'excuses' or 'defences'. It is technically incorrect to use the term 'defence' when referring to the 'defence of mistake' or the 'defence of accident', since these (along with intoxication and, to some extent, insanity) are simply 'failure of proof' arguments; 'mistake' or 'accident' is merely a way of explaining why the prosecution has failed to prove knowledge, intention, or recklessness.[1] Beyond these, there is a range of possible excuses which contain elements which do not correspond to the positive requirements of criminal liability (e.g. duress, mistake of law), and they are discussed here with a view to assessing whether they have any general characteristics in common. They are termed 'negative fault requirements' in order to indicate that they are generally matters which the prosecution does not have to disprove unless the defence raises some credible issue on one or more of them. In other words, it is assumed that D has no excuse on any of these grounds unless some evidence of it is adduced in court. It therefore follows that many of these excuses are not inconsistent with *mens rea*: duress and mistake of law, for example, may be perfectly compatible with an intention to commit the prohibited act. However, the first two conditions to be discussed—insanity and intoxication—might well exclude *mens rea* in particular cases, and we shall see that the law has evolved doctrines which prevent or restrict the avoidance of liability by this means. The law takes such a serious view of harm caused by an insane or intoxicated person that not only does it invoke social defence arguments to justify special provisions for these cases, but it also goes some way towards ensuring that these special provisions also apply to other conditions created by insanity or intoxication (e.g. automatism, mistake).

---

[1] See Paul Robinson, 'Criminal Law Defenses: A Systematic Analysis' (1982) 82 Columbia LR, 199, and his *Criminal Law Defences* (1984), for a fivefold classification of defences: (i) failure of proof defences; (ii) offence modifications (e.g. withdrawal in complicity); (iii) justifications; (iv) excuses; and (v) non-exculpatory public-policy defences (e.g. time limitations). This chapter is concerned with (iv) and with some forms of (i).

6.2 MENTAL DISORDER[2]

One of the fundamental presumptions of the criminal law and criminal liability is that the defendant is 'normal', i.e. is able to function within the normal range of mental and physical capabilities. We have seen that many of the principles of individual fairness presuppose an individual who is rational and autonomous: otherwise he does not deserve to be liable to criminal punishment. A person who is mentally disordered may fall below these assumed standards of mental capacity and rationality, and this may make it unfair to hold him responsible for his behaviour. It is for this autonomy-based reason that most systems of criminal law introduce tests of 'insanity' which result in the exemption of some mentally disordered persons from criminal liability. Once again, however, there are conflicts between the principle of individual autonomy and the principle of welfare, since some of those who succeed on a defence of insanity are thought so dangerous that they must be detained. Until 1991 this was the rule: the insanity verdict could only be followed by an order for detention without limit of time. This led to the paradox that a defence to crime resulted in compulsory loss of liberty. The Criminal Procedure (Insanity and Unfitness to Plead) Act 1991 has now given courts a discretion at this stage. The judge may decide that detention in a mental hospital is required—thus preserving the possibility of protective measures—but there are also lesser alternatives.

(a) Unfitness to Stand Trial

Before considering the defence of insanity, some attention should be devoted to the procedural provisions for dealing with persons who are unfit to stand trial through mental disorder or (in some cases) through being deaf mutes. The basis for the law was laid in *Pritchard* (1836)[3], where Alderson B held that the question was whether the defendant 'was of sufficient intellect to comprehend the course of the proceedings in the trial so as to make a proper defence . . .'. Pritchard was deaf and dumb, and not surprisingly the court's statement dwelt on matters of cognition and understanding. The modern version is that the defendant must be capable of giving, receiving, and understanding communications relating to a criminal trial—on matters such as challenging jurors, deciding on a plea, understanding the evidence, instructing counsel, and so forth.[4] However, it has been argued that the law is wrong to confine its criteria of unfitness to these cognitive matters, and that a person may be just as unfit if he suffers from delusions and is unable to act in his own best interests (e.g. by

---

[2] See R. D. Mackay, *Mental Condition Defences in Criminal Law* (1995), Ch 2.
[3] (1836) 7 C&P 303.
[4] *Robertson* [1968] 1 WLR 1767.

pleading guilty when it appears unlikely that he committed the offence).[5] This suggests that the criteria ought to be broadened and reformulated.[6]

The procedure in these cases is as follows. Under the Criminal Procedure (Insanity) Act 1964, when there are doubts about a defendant's fitness to plead, this should be the first issue to be determined, before any evidence about the alleged offence is heard. However, the 1964 Act gave the judge a discretion to postpone the issue of fitness to plead until the end of the prosecution case, and this discretion would tend to be exercised where there was doubt about whether the defendant had committed the offence anyway. The Criminal Procedure (Insanity and Unfitness to Plead) Act 1991 now engrafts a further procedure on to those established by the 1964 Act.[7] It provides that, wherever a court has decided that a defendant is unfit to plead, it must then conduct a 'trial of the facts'. The judge's discretion to postpone the issue of fitness to plead remains, but it seems likely that almost all cases will now adopt the 1991 Act's approach. Evidence of fitness to plead will be examined first. If the defendant is found fit to plead, the case will proceed. If the defendant is found unfit to plead, another jury will be empanelled and there will be a trial to determine whether the defendant 'did the act or made the omission charged against him as the offence'. This formula seems to separate the conduct or *actus reus* from the fault elements of an offence, even though such a distinction is often unsatisfactory.[8] If the court is not satisfied that D did what was alleged, he will be discharged. If the court is satisfied, the judge now has a choice of disposals in all cases other than murder (where indefinite committal to hospital remains mandatory). The 1991 Act gives a choice between: admission to hospital with or without a restriction order; a guardianship order; a supervision and treatment order; or an absolute discharge.

In the 1980s the annual total of findings of unfitness to plead declined markedly, from some 33 per year during 1980–82 to some 13 per year during 1987–89. At the same time, the proportion of defendants found unfit to plead who were remitted to court for trial, on the basis that their condition had improved, increased to around one-half by the end of the decade.[9] It appears that the 1991 Act has not had any discernible effect on

---

[5] D. Grubin, 'What Constitutes Fitness to Plead?' [1993] Crim LR 748.

[6] Compare Grubin, ibid., advocating judicial discretion on this issue, with R. A. Duff, 'Fitness to Plead and Fair Trials' [1994] Crim LR 419 and reply by Grubin [1994] Crim LR 423.

[7] For the origin of the reforms, see *Report of the Committee on Mentally Abnormal Offenders* (chairman: Lord Butler), 1975, Ch 3.

[8] For analysis of this and other provisions of the 1991 Act, see S. White, 'The Criminal Procedure (Insanity and Unfitness to Plead) Act' [1992] Crim LR 4.

[9] R. Mackay, 'The Decline of Disability in Relation to the Trial' [1991] Crim LR 87.

the low numbers of findings of unfitness to plead, although the courts have begun to use their new range of alternative disposals.[10]

(b) The Special Verdict of Insanity

If the defendant is thought fit to stand trial, then the issue of mental disorder may also be raised as a defence; namely, that at the time of the alleged offence D was too disordered to be held liable. Medical evidence will be crucial in determining this,[11] but it is for the law to lay down the appropriate test. Mental disorder is a broad concept under the Mental Health Act 1983,[12] and few would maintain that all those who fall within one of the four classes of disorder under that Act should be exempted from criminal liability. The criminal law has settled on a much narrower conception of 'insanity', proof of which should lead to a verdict of 'not guilty by reason of insanity'. In order to understand how this defence functions, however, it is important to bear in mind that until the Criminal Procedure (Insanity and Unfitness to Plead) Act 1991 came into force, the result of a successful defence of insanity was mandatory and indefinite commitment to mental hospital. While research revealed that about 20 per cent of defendants thus committed were released within nine months,[13] the inevitable consequence of the insanity verdict was enough to lead many defendants to plead guilty and to hope for a more favourable disposal at the sentencing stage.[14] The 1991 Act now gives the court the same discretion after an insanity verdict as it has after a finding of unfitness to plead (hospital order, guardianship, supervision, absolute discharge). This still leaves the possibility that the court will order deprivation of liberty, even though the defendant has 'succeeded' on a 'defence', but it seems likely that in due course the use of the insanity defence will increase.[15]

The possible legal consequences of the insanity verdict show the tension between considerations of individual autonomy and policies of social welfare in this sphere, and the same tension is manifest in the evidential and procedural provisions. Insanity is the only general defence where the burden of proof is placed on the defendant, a paradox when one reflects that the consequence of a successful defence may be a court order

[10] R. Mackay and G. Kearns, 'The Continued Underuse of Unfitness to Plead and the Insanity Defence' [1994] Crim LR 576.

[11] The Criminal Procedure (Insanity and Unfitness to Plead) Act 1991, s 1(2), requires the evidence of two doctors, at least one of them an experienced psychiatrist.

[12] See s 1 of the Act, discussed by A. Ashworth and L. Gostin, 'Mentally Disordered Offenders and the Sentencing Process' [1984] Crim LR 195, at 195–8.

[13] R. D. Mackay, 'Fact and Fiction about the Insanity Defence' [1990] Crim LR 247.

[14] See P. Fennell, 'Diversion of Mentally Disordered Offenders from Custody' [1991] Crim LR 333, at 341–6.

[15] Cf. Mackay and Kearns, 'The Continued Underuse of the Insanity Defence', showing that there was no such increase in the first year after the 1991 Act came into force.

favouring social welfare rather than the defendant's own interests. The prosecution may raise insanity if the defendant pleads diminished responsibility in response to a murder charge,[16] and, according to one view, can do so in all cases where D puts state of mind in issue.[17] The prosecution bears the burden of proving insanity here, which is much more appropriate given the consequences of the verdict of 'not guilty by reason of insanity'.

The requirements of the defence of insanity were laid down by the judges in *M'Naghten's Case* as long ago as 1843:[18]

to establish a defence on the ground of insanity, it must be clearly proved that, at the time of committing the act, the party accused was labouring under such a defect of reason, from disease of the mind, as not to know the nature and quality of the act he was doing; or, if he did know it, that he did not know he was doing what was wrong.

A 'defect of reason' means the deprivation of reasoning power, and does not apply to temporary absent-mindedness or confusion.[19] It is, however, limited to cognitive defects, and therefore excludes from the insanity defence those forms of mental disorder that involve significant emotional or volitional deficiencies. Although in that respect the definition of insanity is very narrow, in other respects it is so wide as to go well beyond even the broad definition of mental disorder in the Mental Health Act 1983. Thus the phrase 'disease of the mind' has been construed so as to encompass any disease which affects the functioning of the mind—whether its cause be organic or functional, and whether its effect be permanent or intermittent—so long as it was operative at the time of the alleged offence.[20] This means, as we saw in Chapter 4.2(c), that any condition which affects the functioning of the mind and which results from an 'internal' rather than an 'external' cause will be deemed to be a 'disease of the mind', and if D relies on it in his defence he will be held to be raising the defence of insanity. This 'internal factor' doctrine has resulted in epilepsy,[21] sleepwalking,[22] and hyperglycaemia[23] being classified as insanity. This shows that the policy of social protection has gained the upper hand, and that the judiciary has been prepared to overlook the gross unfairness of labelling these people as insane in order to ensure that the court has the power to take measures of social defence against them. Even

---

[16] Criminal Procedure (Insanity) Act 1964, s 6.

[17] Per Watkins L. J., in *Dickie* (1984) 79 Cr App R 213, at 219.

[18] (1843) 10 Cl & Fin 200; see generally N. Morris, *Madness and the Criminal Law* (1982), and I. Potas, *Just Deserts for the Mad* (1985).

[19] *Clarke* (1972) 56 Cr App R 225.

[20] Per Lord Diplock, in *Sullivan* [1984] AC 156.   [21] *Sullivan* [1984] AC 156.

[22] *Burgess* [1991] 2 QB 92.   [23] *Hennessy* (1989) 89 Cr App R 10.

then, the policy of protection has not been carried to its logical conclusion, since the law now perpetrates the absurdity of classifying *hyper*glycaemia as insanity (protective measures possible under the 1991 Act) while, because of the external/internal distinction, classifying *hypo*glycaemia as automatism (resulting in an outright acquittal unless prior fault can be shown).[24] More will be said about this below.

Where it is established that there was a defect of reason due to disease of the mind, it is then necessary to show that it had one of two effects. First, the defence is fulfilled if D did not know the nature and quality of the act—in other words, did not realize what he was doing. In most cases this would show the absence of intention, knowledge or recklessness; but since this mental state arises from insanity, considerations of welfare are held to require the special verdict rather than an ordinary acquittal. Secondly, the defence is fulfilled if D did not know that he was doing wrong. In English law 'wrong' has been given the narrow meaning of 'legally wrong'[25] although in practice it seems that some cases veer towards the Australian interpretation of 'failure to appreciate that the conduct was morally wrong' (usually, where D believes that he must, for some distorted reason, do the act).[26]

(c) Reform

Two major issues concerning defences of mental disorder emerge from the above discussion: the question of definition, and the question of protective measures. In the past they have been closely connected, so that the definition has often been expanded to include persons against whom compulsory measures are thought to be necessary. The 1991 Act alters the balance somewhat, since commitment to a mental hospital is now only a possible and not an inevitable consequence of a special verdict of not guilty by reason of insanity. But the label 'insane' remains, and it is manifestly unsuitable for those whose behaviour stemmed from epilepsy, somnambulism, or diabetes. Not only does this confirm that the definition of insanity is too wide in some respects and too narrow in others, but it also suggests that the English rules and procedure are so at odds with 'objective medical expertise' as to infringe Article 5 of the European Convention on Human Rights.[27]

The enormous advance in medical science in the last 150 years makes a

---

[24] See, more fully, Ch 4.2 above.

[25] *Windle* [1952] 2 QB 826, followed by the majority of the Supreme Court of Canada in *Schwartz* (1979) 29 CCC (2d) 1.   [26] *Stapleton v R* (1952) 86 CLR 358.

[27] For full discussion, see P. Sutherland and C. Gearty, 'Insanity and the European Court of Human Rights' [1992] Crim LR 418, and E. Baker, 'Human Rights, M'Naghten and the 1991 Act' [1994] Crim LR 84.

powerful case for re-examining the M'Naghten Rules.[28] They refer only to mental disorders which affect the cognitive faculties, i.e. knowledge of what one is doing, or of its wrongness, whereas some forms of mental disorder impair practical reasoning and the power of control over actions. This is now recognized in the 'diminished responsibility' doctrine in manslaughter,[29] which includes cases of 'irresistible impulse', and it should clearly be recognized as part of a reformed mental disorder defence. The Model Penal Code accomplishes this by referring to mental disorders which result in D lacking 'substantial capacity either to appreciate the wrongfulness of his conduct or to conform his conduct to the requirements of the law'.[30] The Butler Committee proposed to take this into account in a different way—by ensuring that one ground for a mental-disorder verdict is that, at the time of the alleged offence, D was suffering severe mental illness or handicap.[31] In other words, if the mental disorder was severe in degree, there should be no need to establish that it affected D's cognition: so long as the court is satisfied that the conduct was attributable to that disorder, the special verdict should be returned. It therefore includes both cognitive and volitional deficiencies, and places the insanity verdict more squarely on the ground of incapacity. In doing so, however, it takes a somewhat static view of mental disorder, confining it more or less to the major psychoses. It fails to recognize the variety of mental disorders, and the fact that some of them may substantially impair the patient's practical reasoning even though the diagnosis contains some prominent evaluative elements. Psychiatry has been attacked for these inevitably contestable elements of evaluation, but the proper response is to recognize and discuss the evaluations rather than to deny their relevance to criminal liability.[32]

Only to a small extent is this conservative approach to mental disorder mitigated by the second limb of the Butler proposals, also to be found in a revised form in the draft Criminal Code.[33] This provides for evidence of mental disorder to be adduced to show that D lacked the mental element for the crime. The Law Comission, unlike the Butler Committee, limits the type of mental disorder that may be relied upon here to 'severe mental illness' and 'incomplete development of mind'. The Commission cites the danger of allowing too wide a definition, which would sweep in too many defendants.[34] However, the proposed definition does include cases of 'pathological automatism that is liable to recur', and again classifies diabetes and epilepsy within mental disorder for reasons of social

---

[28] C. Wells, 'Whither Insanity?' [1983] Crim LR 787.

[29] Homicide Act 1957, s 2; see below, Ch 7.4(e).

[30] Model Penal Code, s 4.01.   [31] Butler Report, para 18.30.

[32] K. W. M. Fulford, 'Value, Action, Mental Illness, and the Law', in S. Shute, J. Gardner, and J. Horder (eds), *Action and Value in Criminal Law* (1993).

[33] Law Com No. 177, cls 34–40.   [34] Law Com No. 177, para 11.27.

defence.[35] If there is a need for criminal courts to retain compulsory powers in respect of this small group of harm-doers, respect for the principle of fair labelling[36] should surely mean that they be dealt with under a separate provision from those suffering from mental disorder. Diabetes, somnambulism and epilepsy do not normally fall within the definition of mental disorder, and they should not do so for the purposes of the criminal law. Of course this leads to the problem of drawing a definitional line between 'insanity' and 'automatism', and it was the difficulty of doing so that led the Law Commission to bring these cases within the mental disorder defence, believing that this would be less 'offensive' and 'preposterous' than the insanity label.[37] Fair labelling surely demands that a definition be devised.

6.3 INTOXICATION

Research confirms that many of those who commit crimes of violence and burglary (at least) have taken some kind of intoxicant beforehand.[38] Alcohol is probably the most widely used of intoxicants, but narcotic or hallucinogenic drugs are involved in some cases, too, and our discussion will relate to those who have taken alcohol, drugs, or a combination of the two. The usual effects are a loosening of inhibitions and, perhaps, a feeling of well-being and confidence. It is well known that people who have taken intoxicants tend to say or do things which they would not say or do when sober, and, in that sense, intoxicants may be regarded as the cause of such behaviour. But, as we saw in Chapter 5 and in the discussion of the insanity defence, the criminal law's conception of fault has tended to concentrate on cognition rather than on volition. One would therefore expect the law to be more concerned with the question of whether D's intoxicated state negatived *mens rea* than with the question of whether D's power to choose to cause the prohibited harm was substantially reduced, and this is so. However, as with insanity, arguments of social defence have been used to prevent the simple acquittal of those who cause harm and who lack awareness at the time because of intoxication. This, as we shall see, has caused various doctrinal difficulties for English criminal law.

(a) The English Intoxication Rules

From what was said earlier about the doctrine of prior fault,[39] it is not surprising to find that a person who deliberately drinks himself into an

---

[35] Law Com No. 177, ii, para ii, 28.   [36] See above, Ch 3.5(s).

[37] Ibid., para 11.28(c).

[38] See the circumspect findings of R. Walmsley, *Personal Violence*, Home Office Research Study No. 89 (1986), 15–17.   [39] See Ch 5.2(d) above.

intoxicated state in order to carry out a crime will have no defence. As Lord Denning declared in *Attorney-General for Northern Ireland* v *Gallagher* (1963):[40]

If a man, while sane and sober, forms an intention to kill and makes preparation for it . . . and then gets himself drunk so as to give himself Dutch courage to do the killing, and while drunk carries out his intention, he cannot rely on this self-induced drunkenness as a defence to a charge of murder.

Cases such as this are rare and hard to believe: can a person be totally drunk and yet carry out a plan? More frequent are cases in which D has become intoxicated 'voluntarily', i.e. where there is no reason to regard it as 'involuntary',[41] and has then done something which, he argues, he would not have done but for the alcohol or drugs. Here English law has trodden a fine (but not straight) line between the 'inexorable logic'[42] of the doctrine of *mens rea* and restrictive rules based on considerations of welfare. Where the crime charged is an offence of specific intent, intoxication may amount to a defence if it is sufficient to negative intention. This is the rule established by the decision in *DPP* v *Majewski* (1977),[43] which divides crimes into 'offences of specific intent' and 'offences of basic intent', and allows intoxication as a 'defence' to the former but not to the latter. Murder and wounding with intent are crimes of specific intent, and there is no great loss of social defence in allowing intoxication to negative the intent required for those crimes when the amplitude of the basic intent offences of manslaughter and unlawful wounding lies beneath them—ensuring D's conviction and liability to sentence. Various theories have been advanced in an attempt to explain why those offences (together with theft, handling, and all crimes of attempt, for example) are crimes of 'specific intent' whereas others are not, but none is satisfactory.[44] For example, to argue that all these crimes require some form of further intent is unconvincing, since that is not true of murder.[45] Moreover, many crimes contain some elements for which only intent will suffice and others for which recklessness is sufficient.[46] However, this rather ramshackle law has proved workable. The courts have thus restricted the operation of the 'inexorable logic' of *mens rea* to the few offences of specific intent and, since most of them are underpinned by a lesser offence of 'basic intent', no great loss of social defence has occurred.

---

[40] [1963] AC 349, at 382.   [41] See the discussion in 6.3(d) below.
[42] The phrase of Lord Hailsham in *DPP* v *Morgan* [1976] AC 182, at 214, criticized in Ch 5.3(d) above and 6.6 below.   [43] Ibid.
[44] Their inadequacy is demonstrated by G. Williams, *Textbook of Criminal Law* (2nd edn, 1983), 428–30, and A. Ward, 'Making Some Sense of Self-Induced Intoxication' [1986] CLJ 247.   [45] See Ch 7 below.
[46] S. White, 'Offences of Basic and Specific Intent' [1989] Crim LR 271.

The policy expressed in *Majewski* through the idea of 'offences of basic intent' was expressed slightly differently in *Caldwell* (1982)[47] in terms of 'recklessness'. Thus, where recklessness is a sufficient fault element for the crime, evidence of intoxication is irrelevant because anyone who was intoxicated is deemed to have been reckless. This is a simpler rule to apply, although it may not have entirely displaced the *Majewski* test.[48] It is subject to an exception, as we shall see in 6.3(d), in cases where the intoxication can be regarded as to some degree 'involuntary'. Section 6(5) of the Public Order Act 1986, which applies only to that Act, reads as follows:

. . . a person whose awareness is impaired by intoxication shall be taken to be aware of that of which he would be aware if not intoxicated, unless he shows either that his intoxication was not self-induced or that it was caused solely by the taking or administration of a substance in the course of medical treatment.

This provision, though couched in the terminology of awareness instead of advertent recklessness, may be thought to express the law's general approach.

The effect is that voluntary intoxication rarely functions as a ground of exculpation. The courts have also placed weight on considerations of welfare and social defence when determining the impact of intoxication on other 'defences,' such as automatism and mistake. Thus where it is alleged that intoxication induced a state of automatism, the case is treated as one of intoxication (the cause) rather than automatism (the effect).[49] The same approach has been quite vigorously pursued in cases of intoxicated mistake, bringing them under the rules of intoxication (the cause) rather than mistake (the effect). In *O'Grady* (1987),[50] where the defence took the form of a drunken mistaken belief in the need for self-defence, the Court of Appeal held that D could not rely on his mistake if it stemmed from intoxication. This means, in effect, that where the subjective rule for mistake clashes with the objective rule for intoxication, the latter takes priority. The same view was taken in the rape case of *Fotheringham* (1989),[51] where the Court declared roundly that 'in rape self-induced intoxication is no defence, whether the issue be intention, consent, or, as here, mistake as to the identity of the victim'. This is perfectly consistent with the approach sketched earlier. However, it does lead to the extraordinary result in crimes of specific intent that intoxication alone may negative *mens rea* whereas an intoxicated mistake must be discounted. The

---

[47] [1982] AC 341.   [48] See White, 'Offences of Basic and Specific Intent'.
[49] *Lipman* [1970] 1 QB 152; see Ch 4.2 above.
[50] (1987) 85 Cr App R 315, followed by the Court of Appeal in *O'Connor* [1991] Crim LR
135.   [51] (1989) 88 Cr App R 206.

O'Grady approach should be confined to crimes of basic intent or recklessness, although one of the few decisions on such crimes went the other way. This was *Jaggard* v *Dickinson* (1980),[52] where the Divisional Court was so mesmerized by the wording of the Criminal Damage Act 1971 (which does not deal expressly with intoxication) that it paid no heed to the general principles relating to defences of intoxication. At least *O'Grady* recognized the clash of approaches between mistake and intoxication.

(b) The Attack on the English Approach

The approach of the English courts has been attacked on several grounds. The absence of a definition of 'specific intent', which enables lawyers to assign offences to that category or to 'basic intent', is a familiar source of criticism.[53] Nor has the approach of deeming intoxicated persons to be reckless been any better received. Any 'deeming' is plainly a fiction, and the attempts of Lord Elwyn-Jones in *DPP* v *Majewski* to argue that intoxicated persons really are reckless because 'getting drunk is a reckless course of conduct'[54] involve a manifest confusion between a general, non-legal, use of the term 'reckless' and the technical, legal term, which denotes (for almost all offences)[55] that D was aware of the risk of the result which actually occurred. In most cases it is far-fetched to argue that a person who is getting drunk is aware of the type of conduct he or she might later indulge in.

These criticisms of the courts' attempts to stretch the established meaning of 'intent' and of 'recklessness' in order to deal with the problems of intoxication have been joined by other arguments. Some have held that the intoxication rules are inconsistent with the Criminal Justice Act 1967, section 8, which requires courts to take account of all the evidence when deciding whether D intended or foresaw a result:[56] but the effect of *DPP* v *Majewski* is to deny that evidence of intoxication is relevant unless the crime is one of specific intent, and section 8 extends only to legally relevant evidence.[57] Another argument is that the intoxication rules are inconsistent with the principle of contemporaneity, in that they base D's conviction (of an offence of basic intent) on the antecedent fault of voluntarily taking intoxicants:[58] but the principle of contemporaneity itself conflicts with the doctrine of prior fault, as we have noted,[59] and there

---

[52] [1981] QB 527.   [53] See above n. 44.   [54] [1977] AC 443, at p. 475.
[55] See above, Ch 5.3(c), for discussion. Cf. the few offences to which *Caldwell* recklessness applies, above, Ch 5.3(c).
[56] See J. C. Smith, 'Intoxication and the Mental Element in Crime', in P. Wallington and R. Merkin (eds), *Essays in Honour of F. H. Lawson* (1987).
[57] [1977] AC 443, at 475; see C. Wells, 'Swatting the Subjectivist Bug' [1982] Crim LR 209.
[58] Voiced by majority judges in the High Court of Australia, in *O'Connor* (1980) 54 ALJR 349.   [59] See Ch 5.2(d) and (e).

seems no reason why contemporaneity should be an absolute principle. The question is whether it is appropriate to apply the rival doctrine of prior fault to intoxication cases.

Whatever the merit of these criticisms, it is undeniable that the intoxication rules in English law rest on fictions and apparently illogical legal devices. Is it the policy of restricting the defence of intoxication which is wrong, or merely the legal devices used to give effect to the policy?

(c) Intoxication, Culpability, and Social Policy

One may concede that, in fact, a person may be so drunk as not to know what he or she is doing when causing harm to others or damage to property, and yet maintain that there are good reasons for criminal liability. What might these reasons be? At the root of the 'social defence' or 'public protection' arguments is the proposition that one of the main functions of the criminal law is to exert a general deterrent effect so as to protect major social and individual interests, and that any legal system which allows intoxication to negative *mens rea* would present citizens with an easy route to impunity. Indeed, the more intoxicated they became, the less likely they would be to be held criminally liable for any harm caused. As a matter of human experience, it is far from clear that this argument is soundly based. There are several common law jurisdictions which have declined to follow the English approach and which allow intoxication to negative *mens rea*,[60] and yet there do not appear to have been untoward social effects in those countries. Two comments might be made here. First, these jurisdictions can be taken to be reinforcing the important and often neglected point that it is extremely rare for a defendant to be able to raise even a reasonable doubt that he was unaware of what he was doing. All that is required for proof of intent or recklessness is a momentary realization that property is being damaged or that a person is being assaulted, etc. Thus, even if evidence of intoxication were relevant, it would not usually be acute enough to prevent conviction. Secondly, and alternatively, the rarity of acquittals based on intoxication in these jurisdictions may simply be because juries and magistrates are applying a normative test rather than a purely factual test. Thus the confidence of the majority judges in the High Court of Australia that juries and magistrates will not be too readily persuaded to acquit in these cases[61] might derive less from the rarity of acutely intoxicated harmdoers than from a belief that the courts will simply decline to return verdicts of acquittal where D is

---

[60] See *Keogh* [1964] VR 400, and *O'Connor* (1980) 54 AJLR 349, in Australia, and *Kamipeli* [1975] 2 NZ LR 610 in New Zealand, discussed by G. Orchard, 'Surviving without *Majewski*—a view from down under' [1993] Crim LR 26.

[61] *Keogh* [1964] VR 400, and *O'Connor* (1980) ALJR 349.

regarded as unworthy or culpable in some general way. This would suggest that both the English and the Australian approaches are unsatisfactory in their method—the English because it deems intoxicated harmdoers to be 'reckless' when they are not, the Australian because it relies on juries to make covert moral assessments and not simply the factual assessment that the law requires—even if they usually produce socially acceptable outcomes.

There remains the question of individual culpability. What distinguishes evidence of intoxication from many of the other explanations for D's failure to realize what most ordinary people would have foreseen is the element of prior fault. It was D's fault for taking drink or drugs to such an extent as to lose control over his behaviour. Does this mean that, in order to support a finding of culpability, it must be established that D knew of the likely effects of the intoxicants upon behaviour? Probably not, for it would be regarded as perfectly fair to assume that all people realize the possible effects of taking alcohol or drugs (apart from the exceptional situations to be discussed in 6.3(d) below). 'It is common knowledge that those who take alcohol to excess or certain sorts of drugs may become aggressive or do dangerous or unpredictable things.'[62] This is plainly an objective standard, but it is so elementary that it should not be regarded as unfair on anyone to assume such knowledge. Thus there is an element of culpability in intoxication cases which serves to distinguish them not only from insanity cases (which arise without fault) but also from many cases of simple absence of *mens rea*. The point was put more strongly and more directly in early modern times, when temperance was regarded as a virtue and excessive drinking as an 'odious and loathsome sin'.[63]

But in what does the culpability consist? Specifically, is D to blame for becoming intoxicated or for causing the proscribed harm? It is fairly simple to establish culpability for becoming intoxicated if there is no evidence that it was 'involuntary'. It is fairly difficult to establish culpability for causing the proscribed harm if we follow normal principles: we must assume acute intoxication at the time of the act, and if we look back to the period when D was becoming intoxicated, it is unlikely that one could establish actual foresight of the kind of harm eventually caused. Perhaps some people who regularly assault others when drunk might realize that there is a risk of this occurring, but in order to encompass the majority of cases, it would be necessary to rewrite the proposition about 'common knowledge' so as to maintain that people realize that, when intoxicated, they are likely to cause damage or to assault others. The culpability, in other words, is somewhat unspecific—as in many instances where prior fault operates to bar a

[62] *Bailey* [1983] 1 WLR 760, per Griffiths L. J. at 864.
[63] J Horder, 'Pleading Involuntary Lack of Capacity' [1993] Camb LJ, 298, at 308-9.

defence.[64] Sentencing decisions suggest that intoxication might mitigate on the first occasion it is raised, if the offence can be portrayed as 'out of character', but it will not mitigate any subsequent offences committed in an intoxicated state.[65]

(d) Voluntary and Non-Voluntary Intoxication

We have already noted that non-voluntary intoxication may constitute an exception to the general intoxication rules, and we saw that section 6(5) of the Public Order Act 1986 recognizes some such exception. There is, however, no sharp distinction between the voluntary and the non-voluntary: rather, there is a continuum of states in which D has more or less knowledge about the properties of what he is consuming. The English courts, consistently with their generally restrictive approach, have been reluctant to exempt defendants from the intoxication rules. Thus in *Allen* (1988),[66] D's argument was that he had become intoxicated because he had not realised that the wine being given to him had a high alcohol content. The Court of Appeal held that, so long as a person realizes that he is drinking alcohol, any subsequent intoxication is not rendered non-voluntary simply because he may not know the precise strength of the alcohol he is consuming. In some circumstances this might be quite a harsh ruling, but in broad terms it is compatible with judicial statements about the unpredictability of alcohol. A slightly different problem arose in *Hardie* (1985),[67] where D took a quantity of valium tablets 'for his nerves' and later set fire to an apartment. The Court of Appeal quashed his conviction. The main distinguishing factor here was that valium was re-garded as a sedative or soporific drug, and was not thought likely 'to render a person aggressive or incapable of appreciating risks to others'. This suggests that one basis for the distinction between voluntary and non-voluntary intoxication is the division of intoxicants into those that are sedative and others that may have aggressive effects. The Court in *Hardie* added that nonetheless D would be treated as reckless if he had known, contrary to general beliefs, that valium might have disinhibiting rather than sedative effects.[68] It should be noted that section 6(5) of the Public Order Act 1986, set out above, allows D a defence where the intoxication 'was

---

[64] See P. H. Robinson, 'Causing the Conditions of One's Own Defence' (1985) 73 Virginia LR 1, at 50–1, discussed above in Ch 5.2(e).

[65] A typically resolute Court of Appeal decision against allowing intoxication to mitigate is *Bradley* (1980) 2 Cr App R(S) 12.   [66] [1988] Crim LR 698.

[67] (1985) 80 Cr App R 157.

[68] This follows the reasoning in *Bailey* (1983) 77 Cr App R 76 on diabetes and automatism: see above, Ch 4.2.

caused solely by the taking or administration of a substance in the course of medical treatment'. In line with the general approach, this should be confined to cases where D was not warned of the possible effects, or where those effects were not widely known.

The question of non-voluntary intoxication is raised most directly by *Kingston* (1994).[69] The evidence suggested that certain sedative drugs had been introduced into D's coffee, and that he had then carried out indecent sexual acts on a sleeping boy. The Court of Appeal quashed D's conviction, holding that if D had been placed in an altered mental state by the stratagem of another and this led him to form an intent that he would not otherwise have formed, he should have a defence. This approach accepts that D may have had the mental element required for the crime, but looks to the *cause* of that condition: in effect, a doctrine of prior lack-of-fault. The House of Lords restored the conviction. If non-voluntary intoxication negatives *mens rea*, then it may lead to an acquittal of any offence requiring *mens rea*, whether of specific or basic intent. Where non-voluntary intoxication is not so acute as to negative *mens rea*, Lord Mustill held that there is no basis for an acquittal unless the courts created a new defence.[70] This the House was unwilling to do, because their Lordships could see no significant moral difference between this case and *Allen*, and because the opportunity for false defences was considerable. The matter was one for the Law Commission and Parliament.

What, then, is the position? If the intoxicant is in the soporific category, it seems from *Hardie* that D may have a defence if he can show that he lacked the mental element required for the crime. The general rule would prevent evidence of intoxication being adduced to show that he was not reckless but, if the intoxication was non-voluntary, evidence of the intoxication should be admitted. However, where the intoxicant is not so powerful as to remove D's awareness of what he is doing, it seems immaterial whether it is in the soporific or the 'aggressive' category. *Kingston* holds that there is no defence available and D is therefore convicted on the basis of his intention or recklessness. Even if D can establish that the intoxicant was administered without his awareness—the 'laced' or 'spiked' drink[71]—this appears insufficient to alter the analysis, even though one might think that this presents a stronger argument than *Hardie*. The House of Lords in *Kingston* overlooks D's absence of fault in bringing about the condition: it prefers the proposition that, since D was

---

[69] [1994] 3 All ER 353.
[70] His Lordship concluded that the few distant authorities in favour of the defence were unpersuasive, and so the House of Lords (rightly) considered the issue afresh.
[71] For an example, see *Blakely and Sutton* [1991] Crim LR 763.

aware of what he was doing, he should have desisted. This assumes that D had the capacity to desist: paradoxically, that might be harder to establish for 'aggressive' than for soporific drugs.

(e) Finding a Legal Solution

The simplest solution is to regard evidence of intoxication as relevant on issues of *mens rea*, as do the courts in New Zealand and the non-Code states of Australia.[72] There will only rarely be acquittals, and these may be regarded as part of a small price for respecting the principle of individual autonomy—like occasional acquittals of clumsy and thoughtless individuals. In practice the behaviour of most defendants who allege intoxication will show some elements of intention, knowledge, or awareness.[73] The objection to the Antipodean approach is that it seems to yield the antisocial maxim 'more alcohol, less liability', and gives no weight to the elements of choice and risk involved in getting drunk. Usually the choice is to loosen one's self-restraint rather than to commit a crime, let alone a particular kind of crime, but the retention of control over one's behaviour might fairly be regarded as a social duty. This argument is considerably weakened where D is addicted to alcohol or drugs, since the element of choice may have been exhausted long ago.[74]

There is a strong argument for maintaining elements of social defence against intoxicated harmdoers, however. One crucial issue is the relevance of the resulting harm: should the conviction of an intoxicated person reflect the harm done? Does D deserve to be labelled as that kind of harmdoer, or only as a person who became drunk and dangerous? The criminal law manifests considerable ambivalence on this kind of issue. It punishes reckless harms, but not generally recklessness which happens not to result in harm.[75] It punishes driving with excess alcohol, but not simple drunkenness except in the form of a summary 'nuisance' offence of being drunk and disorderly.[76] Since the culpability in most intoxication cases lies in becoming drunk, perhaps in the knowledge that there is a risk of harmful behaviour, it might be logical to criminalize the drunkenness irrespective of whether any harm actually results. But this would be a widely resented law; it would be thought to be unduly restrictive of individual liberty, unduly oppressive in terms of police power, and unnecessary in terms of

---

[72] See n. 60 above.

[73] R. Shiner, 'Intoxication and Responsibility' (1990) 13 Int J Law & Psychiatry, 9, C. N. Mitchell, 'The Intoxicated Offender—Refuting the Legal and Medical Myths' (1988) 11 Int J Law & Psychiatry, 77.

[74] Cf. H. Fingarette, 'Addiction and Criminal Responsibility' (1975) 84 Yale LJ, 413.

[75] See above, Ch 5.2(b), on resulting harm.

[76] Cf. A. Ashworth, 'Intoxication and the General Defences' [1980] Crim LR 556.

the relative infrequency of harm caused by people who are completely intoxicated. The compromise, then, is to impose criminal liability only where harm results.

The Law Commission made a tentative proposal that the law be changed along these lines:[77] courts would have been allowed to take account of evidence of intoxication whenever they had to decide whether or not a fault element was present. This would have been combined with a new offence of causing harm whilst intoxicated, a new 'state of affairs' offence that would clearly have been an exception to general principles of criminal liability.[78] However, in its final report the Law Commission abandoned this approach and decided to recommend the codification of the existing law based on the *Majewski* decision.[79] No reasons of principle were given for this sudden reversal: the argument is that many judges and practitioners regard the present law as workable and fear that the changes might render it less workable. The Law Commission's report also contains some ambitious and complex recommendations on intoxicated mistakes and related matters.

6.4 DURESS AND NECESSITY

This part of the chapter deals with cases in which D's behaviour fulfils the conduct element and the positive fault requirements of an offence, but in which D acted as a result of threats from another person (sometimes called *duress per minas*) or in order to avert dire consequences (called 'necessity' or 'duress of circumstances'). We have already seen, in Chapter 4.9, that some cases of necessity might give rise to a claim that the use of force was justified, but those are likely to be rare cases of a net saving of lives. In dealing here with the general defences of duress and necessity, we will find that the development of the common law has been characterized by the interplay of reasons of excuse and justification, and by conflicts between recognizing the pressure to which D was subject and upholding the rights of victims.

(a) Requirements of the Defences in English Law

The courts have generally held that the requirements of duress by threats and of duress of circumstances (which has largely taken over from

---

[77] Law Commission Consultation Paper No. 127, *Intoxication and Criminal Liability* (1993).
[78] Cf. N. Lacey, C. Wells and D. Meure, *Reconstructing Criminal Law* (1990), 199.
[79] Law Com. No. 229, *Legislating the Criminal Code: Intoxication and Criminal Liability* (1995), on which see E. Paton [1995] Crim LR (May).

necessity) are in parallel.[80] The defences arise, however, in different factual circumstances, and it might be best to illustrate this by contrasting two cases. In *Hudson and Taylor* (1971)[81] two teenagers were prosecution witnesses at a trial for wounding. They testified that they did not know the man charged and could not identify him as the culprit. The man was acquitted but the young women were charged with perjury. They admitted that they gave false evidence, but said that they were under duress, having been threatened with violence by various men, one of whom was in the public gallery at the original trial. The Court of Appeal quashed their convictions because the defence of duress had been wrongly withdrawn from the jury. In *Conway* (1989)[82] two men approached D's car, whereupon D, urged on by his passenger, drove off at great speed and in a reckless manner. D's explanation was that he knew that his passenger had recently been threatened by two men who had fired a shotgun. D feared that these two men intended harm, and his driving was in response to that emergency. The Court of Appeal quashed the conviction for reckless driving because the trial judge had failed to leave the defence of duress of circumstances to the jury. The difference emerging from these two cases, then, is that for the defence of duress itself there should typically be a direct threat aimed at persuading D to commit a particular offence, whereas for duress of circumstances there will typically be a situation of emergency (not involving direct threats) that leads D to do something that would otherwise be an offence.

What, then, are the general requirements of the two defences? They appear to be restricted to cases where the threat or danger is of death or serious injury.[83] Threats to property or to reputation have been held to be insufficient,[84] but there was a dictum in *Steane* (1947)[85] that a threat of false imprisonment would suffice. In a sense it seems strange that the degree of threat or danger should be fixed in this way, since the seriousness of the crimes in respect of which duress is raised may vary considerably. A dire threat should be necessary to excuse a person who caused a grave harm, but it does not follow that some lesser threat should not be sufficient to excuse a lesser offence. However, the courts have continued to insist on this requirement and, additionally, that the threats must be such that 'a sober person of reasonable firmness' would not have resisted them.[86] This

---

[80] See *Willer* (1986) 83 Cr App R 225, *Conway* (1988) 88 Cr App R 159, *Martin* (1989) 88 Cr App R 343, discussed by D. W. Elliott, 'Necessity, Duress and Self-Defence' [1989] Crim LR 611.   [81] [1971] 2 QB 202.   [82] [1989] 3 All ER 1025.

[83] See *DPP for Northern Ireland* v *Lynch* [1975] AC 653.

[84] In, respectively, *DPP* v *Lynch* [1975] AC 653 AT 687, and *Valderrama-Vega* [1985] Crim LR 220.   [85] [1947] KB 997.

[86] *Graham* (1982) 74 Cr App R 235, confirmed by the House of Lords in *Howe* [1987] AC 417.

objective condition has been tested in recent cases in which the defence has sought to introduce evidence to the effect that D was particularly susceptible to threats because of mental instability[87] or undue pliability and vulnerability to pressure.[88] In both these cases the Court of Appeal held that such evidence was rightly excluded and that to admit it would be to undermine the essentially objective test of reasonable firmness. The full test is that of a 'sober person of reasonable firmness sharing the characteristics of the defendant': that allows courts to take account of age, sex, and physical health while excluding factors that have a direct bearing on the ability to resist threats.[89] This raises the question whether a defence based on concessions to human weakness does not operate harshly against relatively timorous people caught up in desperate situations, and whether it should not be possible to modify the standard to deal fairly with defendants incapable of attaining it.[90]

Another objective element is that the defendant is not entitled to be judged on the facts as he believed them to be. Contrary to the general approach to mistaken beliefs,[91] the Court of Appeal in *Graham* (1982)[92] held that the test for duress is whether, as a result of what D *reasonably* believed that the duressor had said or done, he had *good cause* to fear death or serious injury. In some cases the question of mixed threats and mixed motives has arisen: in *Valderrama-Vega* (1985)[93], a case in which D was also under severe financial pressure and subject to blackmail threats, the Court of Appeal held that duress would be available if the jury found that D would not have acted as he did, but for the death threats he had received. The other pressures may have exerted an influence, but so long as the threats were causally significant, this was sufficient.

The threats need not have been addressed to D personally:[94] they may be against D's family, or friends, or perhaps anyone. The threat must be 'present' and not a remote threat of future harm: the significance of *Hudson and Taylor*,[95] the facts of which were outlined above, is that the Court of Appeal held that it is not necessary that the threat would be

[87] *Hegarty* [1994] Crim LR 353.

[88] *Horne* [1994] Crim LR 585; see also *DPP* v *Davis, Pittaway* [1994] Crim LR 600.

[89] Cf. the discussion of provocation in Ch 7.4 below. The distinction was stretched in *Emery* (1993) 14 Cr App R (S) 394, a sentencing appeal in which the Court of Appeal approved of the trial court having heard evidence of the abuse that D had allegedly received in the past from the person who was said to have exerted the duress.

[90] See the discussion of negligence above, Ch 5.3(f). On duress itself, see P. Alldridge, 'Developing the Defence of Duress' [1986] Crim LR 433, and K. J. M. Smith, 'Must Heroes Behave Heroically?' [1989] Crim LR 22.   [91] See Ch 5.3(d) above.

[92] (1982) 74 Cr App R 235.   [93] [1985] Crim LR 220.

[94] *Valderrama-Vega*, ibid., *Gill* (1963) 47 Cr App R 166, and Law Com No. 83, *Defences of General Application* (1977), 2–3.

[95] See above, n. 61, and accompanying text.

carried out immediately, so long as its implementation was imminent. That case also raised the question of whether the defence is barred if D fails to take an opportunity to alert the police. The Court of Appeal thought that a rule of that kind would be too severe a restriction, and held that D loses the defence by failing to:

avail himself of some opportunity which was reasonably open to him to render the threat ineffective . . . having regard to his age and circumstances, and to any risks to him which may be involved in the course of action relied upon.

This test, with its mixture of objective factors and subjective elements, ensured that the two young women in that case did not forfeit the defence by failing to notify the police.[96]

Both duress and necessity are subject to the doctrine of prior fault. In *Sharp* (1987)[97] D joined a gang of robbers, participating in crimes where guns were carried, but when he tried to withdraw he was himself threatened with violence. The Court of Appeal held that the defence of duress is unavailable to anyone who voluntarily joins a gang 'which he knows might bring pressure on him to commit an offence and was an active member when he was put under such pressure'. Although this is phrased subjectively, 'which he knows . . .', the principle here is surely an objective one. In the later case of *Shepherd* (1987)[98] it was added that 'There are certain kinds of criminal enterprises the joining of which, in the absence of any knowledge of propensity to violence on the part of one member, would not lead another to suspect that a decision to think better of the whole affair might lead him into serious trouble.' Phrased again in subjective language, the possibility of running a defence of duress should remain open in such cases.

(b) Theoretical Foundations for the Defences

Why should defences of duress be allowed? One argument is that acts under duress or necessity are justified in the sense that they constitute a lesser evil than the carrying-out of the threat: the credentials of this rather narrow justification were discussed in Chapter 4.9. In general the courts have tended to mix arguments of justification with those of excuse, without noticing the distinction. How strong are the arguments for excusing D rather than justifying the act? It is fairly clear that duress and necessity do not negative intent, knowledge, or recklessness: D will know only too well the nature and consequences of the conduct. It also seems unlikely that they negative the voluntary nature of D's conduct: the elements of unconsciousness and uncontrollability of bodily movements which are

---

[96] Cf. *Gill* (1963) 47 Cr App R 166 and *Cole* [1994] Crim LR 582.
[97] [1987] QB 853.   [98] (1988) 86 Cr App R 47.

regarded as the hallmark of involuntary behaviour[99] are not typically to be found in duress cases. However, conduct in response to duress or necessity may be described as *non*-voluntary, even if not *in*voluntary. There is a much lower degree of choice and free will in these cases than in the normal run of actions. George Fletcher has termed this 'moral or normative involuntariness', arguing that the degree of compulsion in these cases is not significantly less than in cases of physical involuntariness.[100] The phrases used by the Court of Appeal in *Hudson and Taylor*—'effective to neutralize the will of the accused', and 'driven to act by immediate and unavoidable pressure'—show that the courts also have this in mind, although 'neutralising the will' puts it rather too strongly.

If the defence of duress is based on 'pressure' which is 'immediate and unavoidable', why should these factors be regarded as so powerful? Surely people frequently act in a certain way because they feel under intense pressure, but that does not mean that we treat them as not responsible for those actions. Moreover, the criminal law generally presumes free will and disregards the possibility that our acts are determined to any significant degree. Perhaps one element which marks out circumstances of duress and necessity is that they cast D as the innocent—often, chance—victim, and another person or some natural phenomenon as the primary causal force. Emotional, financial, or social pressures may be felt just as intensely by many people at certain times, and the resulting acts might be equally 'determined', but perhaps it is regarded as difficult to treat D as entirely innocent in their production,[101] or at least there may be no other person who can be identified as the cause of the wrongdoing (as in duress). It must be conceded that this distinction is not compelling if one looks only to the degree of pressure felt by D: a confluence of economic and social pressures may occasionally lead a person to believe that there is no choice but to act in a certain way. The courts have always resisted this line of argument,[102] but there is no easy distinction (in terms of pressure experienced) between direct threats, dangerous emergencies, and other forms of moral non-voluntariness.[103] Perhaps the argument is that there is a social duty to resist ordinary financial and emotional pressures, but no absolute duty in cases of threat or emergency. This might fit with the 'person of reasonable firmness' test, on the argument that it is unfair to expect D to resist

[99] See Ch 4.2.

[100] G. P. Fletcher, *Rethinking Criminal Law* (1978), 803, adopted by Dickson J. in the Supreme Court of Canada in *Perka* v *R* (1984) 13 DLR (4th) 1. For discussion, see C. Wells, 'Necessity and the Common Law' (1985) 5 Oxford JLS, 471.

[101] The proposal for a defence based on 'social deprivation' is discussed below, Ch 6.9(b), text at n. 157.

[102] For recent examples, see *DPP* v *Davis*; *DPP* v *Pittaway* [1994] Crim LR 600.

[103] See Norrie, *Crime, Reason and History*, 113–17.

pressure which a reasonably steadfast citizen would not have resisted.[104] But in a sense that begs the question of how much resistance it is fair to expect. It also leaves untouched the problem of defendants who lack the capacity to conform to the law's expectations, and who give way to pressure because of weaknesses in their psychological make-up: a suggestion for dealing with these cases was made earlier.[105]

The Law Commission has recommended a significant shift in the approach to duress defences.[106] Many of the objective restrictions developed by the courts would be dismantled. Although the law would still require a threat of death or serious injury, the basis of the defence would be D's belief that such a threat has been made (no reasonableness requirement), D's belief that the threat would be carried out before he could obtain 'effective official protection' (no requirement to avail himself of a reasonable opportunity), and proof that the threat was one 'which in all the circumstances (including any of his personal characteristics that affect its gravity) he cannot reasonably be expected to resist'. The last requirement focusses on what this defendant could reasonably be expected to do, and suggests that defendants who lack the 'normal' capacity to resist threats could be acquitted. These changes might well lead to the success of many more duress defences, although the counterweight in the Law Commission's scheme is to place the burden of proof on the defendant. Reversal of the onus of proof is wrong in principle,[107] but the challenge thrown down by the Law Commission is to distinguish between objective rules combined with the normal prosecution burden of proof and subjective rules combined with a defence burden of proof. However, this challenge should not distract attention from the proposal to remove from the defence the judgmental elements: it may be right to extend the defence to those incapable of attaining reasonable standards, but is it right to accord it to those who could and should have made the effort?[108]

The Law Commission's approach is only one of the radical possibilities for dealing with cases of duress. The existing law circumscribes the defences rather tightly, and relies on mitigation of sentence to deal with less strong excuses. A radical approach in the opposite direction would be to argue that, since there are so many questions of degree in duress and necessity cases (degree of threat, degree of immediacy, seriousness of crime), they are much more appropriate for the sentencing stage than the

---

[104] See J. Dressler, 'Reflections on Excusing Wrongdoers: Moral Theory, New Excuses and the Model Penal Code' (1988) 19 Rutgers LJ, 671, at 708–15, and below, Ch 6.9(c).

[105] See above, nn. 89–90 and text thereat.

[106] Law Com No. 218, *Legislating the Criminal Code: Offences against the Person and General Principles* (1993).   [107] See Ch 3.5(m) above.

[108] See J. Horder, 'Occupying the moral high ground? The Law Commission on Duress' [1994] Crim LR 343.

liability stage.[109] On that view, the duress defences should be abolished altogether. At present English law takes the view (except in murder cases) that there is a point at which threats or an emergency may place so much pressure on an individual that it is unfair to attribute criminal responsibility at all, although the courts have then circumscribed the defence tightly and many claims of duress sound only at the sentencing stage. Mitigation may be right if 'desert' is the basis for sentence, but supporters of deterrent sentencing have a particular problem. Their general approach is to maintain that the stronger the temptation or pressure to commit a crime, the stronger the law's threat should be in order to counterbalance it.[110] The law and its penalties should be used to strengthen the resolve of those under pressure. Yet Bentham also accepted that criminal liability and punishment are inefficacious where a person is subject to such acute threats (e.g. death, serious injury) that the law's own threat cannot be expected to counterbalance it: in these cases, he said, there should be a complete defence.[111] The difficulty with this analysis is that it suggests heavy deterrent sentences for all cases except the most egregious, where it prescribes no penalty at all—a distinction with momentous effects but no clear reference point. There is surely a sliding scale of intensity of duress and necessity, and 'desert' theory can reflect the gradations by providing a complete defence, or perhaps a qualified defence (e.g. murder to manslaughter), and variable mitigation of sentence.

(c) Duress, Necessity, and the Taking of Life

Although most of the elements of these defences seem to be based on a rationale of excusing a person's understandable submission to the threat, the troubled issue of whether the defences should be available to murder has led the courts to draw on justification-based rationales. The tone was set in the late nineteenth century with *Dudley and Stephens* (1884),[112] where two shipwrecked mariners killed and ate a cabinboy after 17 days adrift at sea. Lord Coleridge C. J. held that no defence of necessity was available in a case of taking another person's life. In the first place, he argued, there is no *necessity* for preserving one's own life, and there are circumstances in which it may be one's duty to sacrifice it. Then, secondly, if there were ever to be a similar case, who would judge which person is to die? (This point might be overcome by drawing lots.) So he concluded that, terrible as the temptation might be in this kind of case, the law should 'keep the judgment straight and the conduct pure'. The sentence of death

---

[109] See below, Ch 6.9(a), and M. Wasik, 'Duress and Criminal Responsibility' [1977] Crim LR 453.
[110] J. Bentham, *Introduction to the Principles of Morals and Legislation*, Ch XIV, para 9.
[111] Ibid., para 11. [112] (1884) 14 QBD 273.

was later commuted to 6 months' imprisonment, thus emphasising the obvious conflict between the desire to reaffirm the objective standard of the sanctity of life, and the widely felt compassion for people placed in an extreme situation.

In *DPP* v *Lynch* (1975)[113] the House of Lords accepted, by a majority of three to two, that duress by threats should be available as a defence to an accomplice to murder, reflecting the law's compassion towards a person placed under such extreme pressure. But then the Privy Council in *Abbott* v *R* (1977)[114] held that duress was unavailable as a defence to the principal in murder, and in *Howe* (1987)[115] the House of Lords had to decide whether to perpetuate this distinction between principals and accomplices. Their Lordships decided not to do so, unanimously favouring a rule which renders duress and necessity unavailable as defences in all prosecutions for murder. The primary reason for their decision was that the law should not recognize that any individual has the liberty to choose that one innocent citizen should die rather than another. All duress cases involve a choice between innocents, D and the intended victim, and the law should not remove its protection from the victim. Thus D is required to make a heroic sacrifice. A secondary argument, similar to that employed a century earlier in *Dudley and Stephens*, was that executive discretion could take care of deserving cases—either by releasing D on parole at an early stage or even by refraining from prosecution.[116]

Both these arguments are open to criticism. The argument based on protection for the innocent victim seems to assume that duress is being advanced as a justification for killing: this enables the judges to assume that, because the killing of an innocent person is unjustified, duress should not be a defence. It was argued earlier that a killing under duress might be justifiable if there were a net saving of lives,[117] but that is not the question here. Where it is a question of liability for taking one innocent life to save another, the issues concern excuse, not justification. It can therefore be put alongside other situations in which a killing may be excused in whole or in part (e.g. mistaken self-defence, intoxication, insanity), without being justified.[118] Utilitarians might argue that a rule denying duress as a defence to murder is preferable because through the years it might achieve a net saving of lives:[119] this not only fails to take the defendant's interests into account, but also assumes that persons under duress will know of the law's approach and will be influenced by it, an assumption which will rarely be fair (except perhaps in some terrorist cases). Not all of those who

---

[113] [1977] AC 653.
[114] [1977] AC 755; cf. I. Dennis, 'Duress, Murder and Criminal Responsibility' (1980) 96 LQR 208.   [115] [1987] AC 417.
[116] Per Lords Griffiths and Mackay, at 446 and 457.   [117] Above, Ch 4.9.
[118] P. Alldridge, 'The Coherence of Defences' [1983] Crim LR 665.
[119] A. Kenny, *Freewill and Responsibility* (1978), 38.

respect the principle of individual autonomy would agree with the Law Commission's recommendation, which is that duress should be available as a defence to murder (with the defence bearing the burden of proof): there are some who argue that a directly intentional killing of another human being can never be excused.[120] The second argument, in favour of convicting the person under duress and then invoking executive clemency to reduce the punishment, also smacks of an unrealistic utilitarian solution. For one thing, there can be no certainty that the Parole Board will view these cases more favourably than others. For another, if we are satisfied that D was placed under extreme pressure, we ought to declare that publicly, either by allowing a defence or, if not, by allowing a qualified defence to murder on an analogy with provocation. The argument in favour of merely a qualified defence should not be understated: as Chapter 7.4(c) will show, it is possible both to recognize the sanctity of life as a fundamental value and to demonstrate compassion.

On the basis of the decision in *Howe* that duress cannot be a defence to murder, the House of Lords in *Gotts* (1982)[121] held that duress cannot be a defence to attempted murder either. Their Lordships found no justification in logic or in morality for drawing a distinction between the two, especially since the mental element in attempted murder (intent to kill) is higher than that for murder itself (intent to kill or do grievous bodily harm). The same 'logical' approach might lead the court to rule that duress can be no defence to causing grievous bodily harm with intent. But what is this 'logic'? The House of Lords seemed greatly impressed by the fact that it might be 'pure chance' that an attempted murderer did not succeed in committing murder. But there are many other parts of the criminal law where, logically or not, matters of luck and chance make considerable impact.[122]

6.5 PROVOCATION[123]

Should the criminal law provide a defence of provocation in certain circumstances? The context of the question differs from mental disorder, intoxication, and duress, since provocation is not generally regarded as a defence to criminal liability.[124] Many legal systems allow it as a qualified defence to murder which reduces the crime to manslaughter or culpable homicide, and provocation will be discussed in this connection in Chapter

---

[120] J. Horder, 'Occupying the moral high ground', at 335 and 339.
[121] [1992] 2 AC 412.   [122] See Ch 3.5(r) and 5.2(b) above.
[123] See generally J. Horder, *Provocation and Responsibility* (1992).
[124] In the Code states of Australia provocation is a defence to assault: see Queensland Criminal Code, s 269.

7.4(b). Here the questions are whether it should ever be a complete defence, or, if not, how if differs from those conditions which are admitted as compete defences. The details of provocation in English law are reserved for Chapter 7: it is enough to state that provocation is generally taken to include both a subjective condition (was D provoked to lose self-control?) and an objective condition (was the provocation enough to cause a reasonable person in D's position to lose self-control?).

(a) Elements of Excuse in Provocation

One way of enquiring whether provocation should be regarded as negativing the fault element is to ask whether it excludes either *mens rea* or voluntariness. It is generally assumed that loss of self-control does not negative intention: indeed, this is part of the logic of provocation as a qualified defence to murder, since no such defence might be required if it simply negatived intention. One might argue, however, that in some cases D would act in such a blind rage, after being provoked, that he would be unaware of what he was doing. Such an extreme condition might be difficult to prove, as distinct from lesser degrees of anger, but that is a quite separate argument for refusing to admit a defence. This is merely a manifestation of the general assumption that people who are not drunk or mentally disordered know what they are doing and cannot be heard to say otherwise.

Might loss of self-control negative voluntariness? Since unconscious behaviour is not an issue here, the question is whether behaviour during loss of self-control is 'uncontrollable' rather than simply 'uncontrolled'. There is ambiguity in the law at this point: the law clearly does not require *total* loss of self-control as a precondition of allowing provocation as a partial defence to murder, but quite what it means by 'loss of self-control', and how great a loss is required, remains uncertain. It is not difficult to conceive of conditions of extreme rage in which a person would find it virtually impossible to control his actions, although, again, it would be difficult to prove this. Provocation may therefore be one of those areas in which the elements of choice and control are significantly reduced: they might be regarded as cases of 'moral non-voluntariness', although whether more or less so than duress cases may be difficult to state.[125] Probably there is enough in the argument that loss of self-control may occasionally negative *mens rea* or voluntariness to suggest that its claim to be treated as a complete defence should be considered seriously.[126] However, as with

---

[125] See 6.4(b) above.

[126] J. Horder, 'Autonomy, Provocation and Duress' [1992] Crim LR 706, 712. Cf. F. McAuley, 'Anticipating the Past: The Defence of Provocation in Irish Law' (1987) 50 MLR, 133, and J. Dressler, 'Provocation: Partial Justification or Partial Excuse?' (1988) 51 MLR, 467, at 472–3.

intoxication, it might be decided on a principle of welfare that citizens have a duty to learn to control their passions and tempers to the extent of not inflicting criminal harms, and thus the law might adopt the view that loss of self-control should never be allowed to negative the fault requirements for an offence. This would be a strong policy, presumably exempting only the mentally disordered, and not those who have abnormal difficulty in controlling themselves. Indeed, in English law the policy seems to be stronger than that in intoxication cases, since intoxication is allowed as a defence to the wider (though illogical) category of 'specific intent' crimes, whereas provocation is currently a defence to murder only. Is there not a case, based on fairness to individual defendants, for arguing that extreme loss of self-control should be capable of acting as a defence to crimes of specific intent, at least? Would not the response to this argument be based on practicalities, such as the dangers of making trials even more complex, rather than principle?

(b) Elements of Justification in Provocation

There are cases in which D pleads provocation on a charge of murdering a bullying father or husband and receives so light a sentence as to suggest that the court regards the killing as not far short of justifiable.[127] Indeed, it has been argued that in some cases where women kill a spouse or partner who has battered them, the elements of self-defence may be made out. This requires some reinterpretation of the existing law, viewing the woman's reaction as an instinctive and reasonable reaction to a situation to which she believes there is no realistic alternative.[128] Even if few cases could be brought convincingly within self-defence, the comparison is sufficiently plausible to serve to raise questions about possible elements of justification in provocation cases. The answer may be sought in various directions. The objective condition in the provocation defence to murder is whether the provocation was enough to cause a reasonable person to lose self-control. The element of reasonableness may be discerned in the paradigm of provocation as a wrongful act towards D, and in the assumption that lawful acts should not be regarded as provocation.[129] Thus Aristotle argued that anger is a socially respectable emotion which may, within limits, be a proper response to certain behaviour by others.[130] It is

[127] M. Wasik, 'Cumulative Provocation and Domestic Killing' [1982] Crim LR 29, and J. Horder, 'Sex, Violence and Sentencing in Domestic Provocation Cases' [1989] Crim LR 546.
[128] A. McColgan, 'In Defence of Battered Women who Kill' (1993) 13 Oxford JLS, 508, also discussed in Ch 4.7(f) and Ch 7.4(b).
[129] See A. Ashworth, 'Self-Induced Provocation and the Homicide Act' [1973] Crim LR 483.
[130] Aristotle, *Nicomachean Ethics*, Bk V 8; cf. the discussions by Ashworth, 'The Doctrine of Justification', and Dressler, 'Provocation'.

therefore necessary to consider both D's feelings and the moral basis: the principle is that culpability is reduced where D acts in anger towards the victim, and has good reason for being angry in virtue of some apparent wrong or impropriety suffered at the victim's hands.[131] A further way of answering the question would be to argue that a provoked offence is caused by the provoker rather than by D, which suggests that D's responsibility for the outcome is less than it would otherwise be.[132]

None of these arguments is sufficient to establish that provocation should be a complete justification. It is one thing to state that the victim 'asked for it' by what he or she did; it is quite another thing to suppose that the victim asked to die. It may have been morally appropriate for D to feel outraged and angry, but it is morally inappropriate for D to have killed V.[133] The element of wrongdoing by the victim (or another)[134] might therefore be combined with the excusatory element of loss of self-control to provide grounds for a (partial) defence. The point now is not merely that D lost control at the time of the offence, but that D was understandably and with some justification *provoked* to lose self-control at the time of the offence. Is there an analogy here with duress and necessity as defences? It is certainly true that duress, though predominantly an excuse, contains elements of justification. A person under duress is presented with an urgent situation, not of his or her own making, and then acts in an understandable response to these extreme pressures. The analogies between provocation and duress cases are: (i) that the situations are not of D's own making; and (ii) that the acts are not regarded as freely willed. The differences are: (i) that there is no element of necessity in D's reactions to provocation: it is not a matter of acting prospectively to avert a threat, but rather retaliating in a retrospective fashion, which is surely more culpable;[135] therefore (ii) that the severe restrictions on choice of action found in duress cases are not present in provocation. D will not suffer serious physical harm if he fails to respond to the provocation. The argument is that, while it is unfair to expect citizens to withstand threats sufficient to affect even a person of reasonable firmness, it is not unfair to expect citizens to control their behaviour when provoked. We might recognize that such control is abnormally difficult in certain extreme situations by allowing a circumscribed defence of provocation to reduce the

---

[131] This adapts the 'principle of resentment' proposed by A. von Hirsch and N. Jareborg, 'Provocation and Culpability', in F. Schoemann (ed), *Responsibility, Character and the Emotions* (1988); the adaptation is the insertion, following Aristotle, of the word 'apparent'.

[132] Dressler, 'Provocation', 477–80.

[133] von Hirsch and Jareborg, 'Provocation and Culpability'.

[134] See R. S. O'Regan, 'Indirect Provocation and Misdirected Retaliation' [1968] Crim LR 319.   [135] Horder, 'Autonomy, Provocation and Duress', 709.

grade of offences (murder to manslaughter; but why not also 'causing serious injury with intent' to 'causing serious injury recklessly'?[136]), but still maintain the general social proposition that citizens who are not mentally disordered can be expected to control their tempers. On this reasoning the emotional difficulties which people encounter in provocative circumstances are not so strong as to suggest that fairness demands no criminal liability at all.

(c) Extreme Mental or Emotional Disturbance

In its Model Penal Code the American Law Institute includes a partial defence of 'extreme mental or emotional disturbance . . . for which there is reasonable explanation or excuse'.[137] The defence is confined to murder, like provocation and diminished responsibility in English law, and seeks to cover broadly the same conditions (together with duress) in a single doctrine. It dispenses with any technical definition of what might amount to adequate provocation by simply requiring 'reasonable explanation', a formulation which retains some normative element. Like provocation, it directs attention to earlier or pre-existing circumstances by way of exculpation rather than adhering strictly to the principle of contemporaneity. It covers cases of cumulative provocation,[138] since there is no specification of the origins of the disturbance: so long as the court finds a reasonable explanation or excuse, that is sufficient. It channels the mentally abnormal and the mentally normal into a single doctrine, by focussing on the element of disturbance, and, in so doing, it obscures the element of partial justification which at present separates provocation cases. Two points may be made in the present context. First, is it preferable to forgo the labelling distinctions which would be achieved by separate qualified defences to murder of provocation, diminished responsibility, and duress in favour of a test which might prove simpler for trial courts to deal with? Secondly, if there is a case for such a broadly drawn partial defence based on emotional or mental disturbance, is it right that it should only be available in murder cases, and not available to reduce the grade of other offences in the same way as the 'specific intent' rule in intoxication?

---

[136] One direct counter-argument is that a provoked wounding might be intentional rather than reckless, and so conviction for the recklessness offence would be mislabelling. The proper label should perhaps be 'wounding in the second degree'.

[137] Section 210.3.1(b); see Robinson, *Criminal Law Defenses*, and Dressler, 'Reflections on Excusing Wrongdoers', 704–5.

[138] This refers to provocation behaviour which occurs over a period of time: see Wasik, 'Cumulative Provocation'.

6.6 REASONABLE MISTAKE AND PUTATIVE DEFENCES

For the first three-quarters of the twentieth century, the approach of the common law to mistake was that if the defendant wished to rely on this defence it must be shown that he had reasonable grounds for his mistaken belief. The leading case was *Tolson* (1889),[139] where the Court for Crown Cases Reserved held that a mistake of fact on reasonable grounds would be a defence to any criminal charge. Despite being cited as the leading case, the ambit and status of *Tolson* was never clear, since Stephen J devoted much of his judgment to the proposition that if the mental element of the crime is proved to have been absent, the crime so defined is not committed.[140] Certainly it is authority for the proposition that reasonable mistake is a defence to crimes of strict liability.[141] It is also authority on the crime of bigamy, and was expressly preserved by the House of Lords in *Morgan* when it introduced (or, in the light of Stephen J's judgment, reintroduced) the proposition that if the mental element is missing in respect of one of the conduct elements specified in the definition of the crime, then as a matter of inexorable logic D should be acquitted even if the mistake was wholly unreasonable.

The 'inexorable logic' argument was criticized in the previous chapter:[142] this part of the criminal law should be founded on considerations of moral fault rather than dictated by 'logic', as our discussions of intoxication and duress have already shown. When the House of Lords in *Morgan* opted for the 'inexorable logic' approach, treating the claim of mistake as a mere denial of the required mental element, it expressly left undisturbed both the *Tolson* principle and the requirement that mistakes relating to a defence should be reasonable. This requirement developed more through assumption and repetition than by dint of principled argument. Its chief application had been in cases of self-defence, where courts had tended to require that any mistake about the circumstances should be based on reasonable grounds.[143] But this reasonable mistake doctrine, left intact in *Morgan* itself, was swept away by decisions of the Court of Appeal and

---

[139] (1889) 23 QBD 168.

[140] Compare E. Griew, 'States of Mind, Presumptions and Inferences', in P. F. Smith (ed), *Criminal Law: Essays in Honour of J. C. Smith* (1987), with A. P. Simester, 'Mistakes in Defence' (1992) 12 2Oxford JLS 295, and R. H. S. Tur, 'Subjectivism and Objectivism: Towards Synthesis', in S. Shute, J. Gardner and J. Horder (eds), *Action and Value in Criminal Law* (1993).

[141] Confirmed by the House of Lords in *Sweet* v *Parsley* [1970] AC 132.

[142] See the discussion in Ch 5.3 above.

[143] The leading cases were probably *Rose* (1884) 15 Cox CC 540 and *Chisam* (1963) 47 Cr App R 130. The only careful analysis was that of Hodgson J in the Divisional Court in *Albert* v *Lavin* (1981) 72 Cr App R 178.

Privy Council in the 1980s.[144] A putative defence, i.e. a mistaken belief in circumstances which (if true) would form the basis of a defence, will succeed wherever D raises a reasonable doubt that he actually held the mistaken belief, no matter how outlandish that belief may have been. The courts in *Williams* and *Beckford*[145] presented this as an application of the 'inexorable logic' approach in *Morgan* (overlooking the fact that *Morgan* left this aspect of the law unchanged), reasoning as follows: (i) unlawfulness is an element in all crimes of violence; (ii) intent, knowledge, or recklessness must be proved as to that element; and therefore (iii) a person who mistakenly believes in the existence of circumstances which would make the conduct lawful should not be criminally liable. The crucial step is the first: how do we know that unlawfulness is a definitional element in all crimes?[146] Not all crimes are defined explicitly in this way. So it is, rather, a doctrinal question. Andrew Simester has argued that unlawfulness cannot be an ingredient of the *actus reus*, since only when there is *actus reus* with *mens rea* can we conclude that conduct was unlawful.[147] Might this not be a question of terminology? Some would argue, as we saw in Chapter 4.7, that there is no *actus reus* where the conduct is justified. If 'absence of justification' is substituted for 'unlawfulness' in the above reasoning, does not the difficulty claimed by Simester disappear? A stronger argument is that, irrespective of the definitional boundaries of the *actus reus*, there is a need to confront the moral issue whether there should not be some duty to reflect before using force against another. Using force is *prima facie* wrongful and should put a citizen on notice to examine—if, of course, time and circumstances permit—the grounds for doing so. This distinguishes cases of putative defence from other cases of mistake in which D does not think what he is doing is wrongful or dangerous.[148] Rather than relying on the logic of steps (i), (ii) and (iii), the law should adopt this more context-sensitive approach.

Although English judges may seem to be firmly in the embrace of the 'inexorable logic' approach to mistake,[149] there have been some deviations which perhaps suggest recognition of the complexity of the issues. In *Graham* (1982)[150] Lord Lane C. J. held that, if D is mistaken about the existence or nature of a threat, the mistake must be a reasonable one if the defence of duress is to be available; and in *Conway* (1989)[151] the Court

---

[144] *Kimber* (1983) 77 Cr App R 225, followed by *Gladstone Williams* (1984) 78 Cr App R 276 and by *Beckford* [1988] 1 AC 130.

[145] Last note.

[146] Cf. the discussion by S. Yeo, *Compulsion in the Criminal Law* (1991), 198–208.

[147] Simester, 'Mistakes in Defence'.   [148] Simester, ibid., 307.

[149] This seems, strangely, to have been true of mistake in provocation for some time: *Letenock* (1917) 12 Cr App R 221; see also *Wardrope* [1960] Crim LR 770.

[150] (1982) 74 Cr App R 235.   [151] [1988] 3 All ER 1025.

of Appeal held that 'a defence of duress of circumstances is available only if from an objective standpoint the defendant can be said to be acting in order to avoid a threat of death or serious injury'. The reasoning in these two cases appears to be that, since defences of duress and necessity are available only where a person of *reasonable* steadfastness would have yielded to the threat, it follows that mistakes must be based on *reasonable* grounds if they are to excuse.

Is this a sound course of reasoning? Surely the 'person of reasonable firmness' standard is, like the limitation of 'reasonable force' in self-defence cases,[152] a form of words designed to ensure some proportionality between threat and response. It sets the legal standard for the magnitude or quantum of threat or response. The issue of mistaken belief concerns perception, and we have seen that the English courts' general approach to questions of perception embodies the belief principle[153]—a subjective enquiry, not an objective standard. However, once the confusion between issues of proportionality and perception has been dispelled, we should return to the question of whether the belief principle should be regarded as the absolute doctrinal solution to these cases. It focusses on D's attitude of mind at the time, but includes no reference to the circumstances of the act, to D's responsibilities, or to social expectations of conduct in that situation. As argued above, the law on mistake should be more context-sensitive. Thus in rape cases those considerations militate in favour of a requirement of reasonable grounds for any mistake;[154] and a similar argument might be developed in relation to the responsibilities of a police officer with firearms training, as in *Beckford* v *R* (1987).[155] Of course, any such infusion of objective principles must recognize the exigencies of the moment, and must not expect more of D than society ought to expect in that particular situation. That is a necessary safeguard of individual autonomy. The general point, however, is that there may be good reasons for society to require a certain standard of conduct if the conditions were not such as to preclude it, particularly where the potential harm involved is serious. These arguments may be no less strong in cases of rape, indecent assault, and some cases of self-defence (where the courts have pursued a subjective approach) than they are in many cases of putative defences of duress and necessity (where a reasonableness requirement has been imposed).[156]

---

[152] See above, Ch 4.7(e).   [153] See Ch 5(2)(a) above.

[154] See Ch 5.3(d) above and Ch 8.5(c) below.

[155] [1988] AC 130; cf. J. Horder, 'Cognition, Emotion and Criminal Culpability' (1990) 106 LQR, 469. The High Court of Australia has required 'reasonable grounds' in all cases of mistaken self-defence: *Zecevic* v *R* (1987) 61 AJLR 375.

[156] As discussed in 6.4(c) above, the Law Commission has recommended a subjective test of mistake for duress.

6.7 IGNORANCE OR MISTAKE OF LAW

(a) The English Rules

English criminal law appears to pursue a relatively strict policy against those who act in ignorance of the true legal position, but the maxim *ignorantia juris neminem excusat* (ignorance of the law excuses no one) is too strong as a description. Ignorance or mistake as to civil law, rather than criminal law, is capable of forming the basis of a defence; indeed, the crimes of theft and criminal damage explicitly provide for defences where D believes that he has a legal right to take or to damage property.[157] But it would be unsafe to state the rule by reference to a distinction between matters of civil law and criminal law, because offences are often defined in such a way as to blur the two. Whether goods are classified as 'stolen' for the purposes of the offence of handling stolen property seems to be a question of criminal law, so if D knows all the facts but misunderstands their legal effect this is irrelevant. Whether an auditor is disqualified from acting for a certain company seems to be a question of civil law, so where D was unaware of the relevant law, his conviction for acting as an auditor knowing that he was disqualified was quashed.[158] One difference between these two offences is that the latter contains the word 'knowingly', whereas the crime of handling includes the words 'knowing or believing'; it is certainly true that a number of English decisions have allowed mistake or ignorance of the law to negative 'knowingly',[159] but this cannot explain all the decisions.[160] English law does recognize that the obligations are not all on one side. The state has duties to declare and to publicize laws and regulations, and these appear as exceptions to the general rule. Thus non-publication of a Statutory Instrument will usually afford a defence to any crime under that Instrument to a person unaware of its existence,[161] and failure to publish a government Order in respect of a particular person will also afford a defence to that person if he or she is unaware of the Order.[162]

(b) Individual Fairness and Public Policy

It could be argued that individual fairness demands the recognition of ignorance or mistake of law as an excuse: a person who acts in the belief that conduct is non-criminal, or without knowing that it is criminal, should not be convicted of an offence. In order to support such a fairness

---

[157] Theft Act 1968, s 2(1)(a); Criminal Damage Act 1971, 2.5(2)(a).
[158] *Secretary of State for Trade and Industry* v *Hart* [1982] 1 WLR 481.
[159] Williams, *Textbook of Criminal Law*, Ch 20.
[160] E.g. *Grant* v *Borg* [1982] 1 WLR 638, *Jones, The Times*, 19 Aug. 1994.
[161] Statutory Instruments Act 1946, s 3(2).
[162] *Lim Chin Aik* v *R* [1963] AC 160.

principle, one might wish to argue that ignorance or mistake as to the law should be recognized as an excuse in the same way (though for different reasons) as duress. It may not negative the fault requirements of a particular offence, but respect for individual autonomy supports the excuse in its own right: a person who chooses to engage in conduct without knowing that it is criminal makes a choice which is so ill-informed as to lack a proper basis. The counter-arguments are based on conceptions of social welfare. One is the utilitarian argument that it is desirable to encourage knowledge of the law rather than ignorance, and any rule which allowed ignorance as a defence would therefore tend to undermine law enforcement.[163] This does not establish that ignorance of the law is wrong, merely that it is socially harmful. Another is the argument that, if we judge defendants on their particular *view* of the law rather than on the law as it is, we are contradicting the essential objectivity of the legal system.[164] This is, to say the least, an exaggeration: so long as the court stated what the law is, the law's objectivity would remain unimpaired. It would also seem to suggest that for a court to allow any excuse amounts to a denial of the offence. This not only confuses the element of excuse with the element of wrongdoing,[165] but also overlooks the value of a publicized trial, where reasonable mistake of law is allowed, as a means of public education.

What is needed here, if the policy is to be supported, is an argument that it is wrong to be ignorant or mistaken about the law. This can be found in the conception of duties of citizenship. Thus, to argue that a person might be convicted despite ignorance of the law is not to attack the principles of choice and individual autonomy which were identified earlier as fundamental to the principles of fairness;[166] it is to forsake the atomistic view of individuals in favour of a recognition of persons as social beings, with both rights and responsibilities within the society in which they live.[167] It has already been argued that in many situations it is fair to expect citizens to take care to enquire into the surrounding circumstances before they act, and the case for requiring some mistakes to be reasonable has been put.[168] A similar line of argument might support a duty on each citizen to take reasonable steps to become acquainted with the criminal law. There are few problems in making the duty known, since 'ignorance of the law is no excuse' is a widely-known principle even now.[169] The duty

---

[163] O. W. Holmes, *The Common Law* (1881), 48.
[164] J. Hall, *General Principles of Criminal Law* (2nd ed., 1960).
[165] G. P. Fletcher, *Rethinking Criminal Law* (1978), 734, and above, Ch 4.1.
[166] See above, Ch 5.2(a).
[167] J. Raz, *The Morality of Freedom* (1987), 206–7, and above, Ch 2.2 and 2.3.
[168] In Ch 5.3(d) and in 6.6 of this Chapter.
[169] Cf. D. Husak, 'Ignorance of Law and Duties of Citizenship' (1994) 14 Legal Studies, 105, 110: 'the problem arises from the fact that few persons are likely to be aware of the existence of the alleged duty to know the law'.

should not be an absolute one, however. First, there is often uncertainty in the ambit of the law. Sometimes the legislature acknowledges the difficulty of stating the law by allowing D's own standards as a benchmark of lawfulness, as in the crime of blackmail.[170] Sometimes it resorts to a broad standard such as 'reasonable' or 'dishonest', leaving it to the courts to concretize after each event, which goes against the principle of maximum certainty.[171] This is not to suggest that every case in which the courts change the law should inevitably give the defendant a defence of ignorance of the law; but it does at least recall some of the issues of principle and policy which had to be resolved in the case of *Shaw* v *DPP* (1962).[172] A second reason for not making the policy absolute is the possibility that the state has not fulfilled its duties in respect of making a new offence known and knowable. The state clearly has this duty when it seeks to impose criminal liability for an omission,[173] and the duty applies generally to the publication of laws. This, indeed, is an aspect of the principle of legality, as embodied in the principle of fair warning.[174]

One way of maintaining the general duty to know the law, while allowing exceptions based on respect for individual autonomy, would be to provide that a mistake of law might excuse if it is reasonable. This, in combination with the argument in 6.6 above, would have the advantage of narrowing down the present gulf, wide and difficult to defend, between the effects of ignorance of law (no general defence) and ignorance of fact (frequently negativing liability).[175] Ignorance of the law would clearly be reasonable if fair warning of a prohibition had not been given: this would accommodate the second point above. Mistake or ignorance of law might also be reasonable if D had no cause to suspect that certain conduct was criminal, or if D had been misinformed or wrongly advised about the law (see (c) below), or perhaps in other circumstances.[176] Ignorance and mistake would be unlikely to be held reasonable if D was engaging in a business or an activity (such as driving a car) that is known to have changing rules; but the merit of a reasonableness requirement is that it would not absolutely rule the defence out. A defendant would be able to argue that there were special circumstances warranting exculpation. To rebut the claim that such an excuse might be raised so often as to impede the administration of the

---

[170] Theft Act 1968, s 21(1), discussed below, Ch 9.4.
[171] See above, Ch 3.4(h).
[172] [1962] AC 220, discussed above, in Ch 3.4(g).
[173] See the American case of *Lambert* v *California* (1957) 355 US 225, and above, Ch 4.4(c).   [174] Above, Ch 3.4(i).
[175] Cf. D. Husak and A. von Hirsch, 'Culpability and Mistake of Law', in Shute, Gardner, and Horder, *Action and Value*.
[176] See Husak and von Hirsch, ibid., proposing that the only way of avoiding unfairness is to allow courts to assess the moral legitimacy of D's beliefs.

criminal law, one has only to refer to the lengthy experience of Scandinavian countries in allowing defences of this kind.[177]

The provision in the draft Criminal Code is that 'ignorance or mistake as to a matter of law does not affect liability to conviction for an offence except (a) where so provided, or (b) where it negatives the fault element of the offence'.[178] This is traditional, inflexible, and unsatisfactory: it relegates most of these matters to mitigation of sentence. Moreover, exception (b) hardly corresponds with any general moral distinction. The legislature has not pursued a consistent policy in deciding whether or not 'knowingly' should form part of the definitions of offences, and it certainly cannot be assumed that Parliament had considered whether particular offences justify an exception in favour of ignorance or mistakes of criminal law (including unreasonable ones). In recent years courts have veered between allowing ignorance of law to negative 'knowingly' and declaring that this approach would be 'wholly unacceptable'.[179] There is a need to adopt a clear, autonomy-based principle and then to interpret statutory offences in the light of it. The same approach should be adopted where the offence includes a phrase such as 'without lawful excuse' or 'without reasonable excuse'.[180]

(c) The Reliance Cases

Another benefit of moving away from the relatively strict English policy against defences based on mistake or ignorance of criminal law towards a 'reasonable grounds' defence is that the 'reliance' cases could also be accommodated. In *Cooper* v *Simmons* (1862)[181] an apprentice absented himself from his apprenticeship after the death of his master, having sought the advice of an attorney and having been counselled that he was no longer bound. The court nevertheless convicted him of unlawfully absenting himself from his apprenticeship, and Pollock C. B. stated that 'it would be dangerous if we were to substitute the opinion of the person charged . . . for the law itself'. In *Arrowsmith* (1974)[182] D had, on occasions, distributed leaflets urging British soldiers not to serve in Northern Ireland. In the past, the Director of Public Prosecutions had declined to prosecute her under

---

[177] J. Andanaes, '*Error Juris* In Scandinavian Law', in G. Mueller (ed), *Essays in Criminal Science* (1961); cf. generally P. Brett, 'Mistake of Law as a Criminal Defence' (1966) 5 Melb U LR, 179.   [178] Law Com No. 177, cl 21.

[179] Cf. *Secretary of State for Trade and Industry* v *Hart* [1982] 1 WLR 481, with *Grant* v *Bord* [1982] 1 WLR 638, two decisions of the House of Lords in the same year; see generally A. T. H. Smith, 'Error and Mistake of Law in Anglo-American Criminal Law' (1984) 14 Anglo-American LR, 3.

[180] See R. Card, 'Authority and Excuse as Defences to Crime' [1969] Crim LR 359 and 415.

[181] (1862) 7 H&N 707, discussed by Brett, 'Mistake of Law as a Criminal Defence'.

[182] (1974) 60 Cr App R 211.

the Incitement to Disaffection Act 1934, but now she was charged with an offence under that Act. One line of defence was that she reasonably believed, as a result of a letter from the Director, that her conduct did not contravene the Act. The Court of Appeal upheld her conviction, stating that 'a mistake as to the law would not avail the appellant except perhaps in mitigation of sentence'. Both these cases would surely be better analysed in terms of reasonable reliance. If it is established that D relied on advice from officials with regard to the lawfulness of the proposed conduct, that ought to be sufficient to support reasonable grounds for the mistake of law. Arguably, this ought also to extend to reliance on a lawyer's advice, although the Model Penal Code stops short of this.[183] Confusion may arise about the entitlement of a particular agency or official to advise a member of public about the law, as one English case vividly demonstrates,[184] but since reasonable mistake of law would be an excuse, the key question is whether D reasonably assumed that the person giving the advice was duly authorized. In the element of reliance, these cases can call upon a kind of estoppel reasoning—the state and the courts should not convict a person whom they or their officers have advised otherwise.[185] Also, D's effort to ascertain the legal position is surely a strong indication against conviction. The Control of Pollution Act 1974, section 3(4), specifically creates a defence to the crime of unlicensed waste-disposal where D 'took care to inform himself from persons who were in a position to provide information'. This ought to foreshadow wider recognition of these grounds for a defence. Indeed, one reason why the defence is so rarely raised in English courts is the prevalence of crimes of strict liability in some fields: such offences leave no more room for a mistake of law defence than for one based on mistake of fact.[186]

6.8 ENTRAPMENT

There are cases in which the police arrange either for one of their own officers or for some other person to approach D and tempt him to commit an offence. If D commits the offence, should there be a defence of entrapment? Many jurisdictions admit such a defence, within limits, but English law has already rejected it. What are the main arguments?[187]

No such defence would be available if it were a private individual who,

---

[183] Model Penal Code, s 2.04(3).

[184] *Cambridgeshire and Isle of Ely CC v Rust* [1972] 1 QB 426.

[185] Ashworth, 'Excusable Mistake of Law' [1974] Crim LR 652.

[186] Another reason may be that defendants who are mistaken about the law may not be prosecuted: see below, 6.9(a).

[187] The classic article is by J D Heydon, 'The Problems of Entrapment' [1973] Camb LJ 268.

on his or her own initiative, incited D to commit the offence: the fact that one person incites another does not relieve the other of criminal liability, since the law regards each of them as autonomous individuals who are able to choose what to do. Yet one might wish to argue that, if the person incited was an ordinary citizen, and not someone predisposed to committing such offences, that person's offence might fairly be said to have been caused by the temptations proffered by the *agent provocateur*. This would seem to shift the enquiry back towards the character and previous record of the person incited—and, perhaps, into dangerous ground, in the sense that persons with previous convictions would be unable to take advantage of any defence of entrapment. To this problem we will return.

Is it the involvement of the state, through its law-enforcement officers or their agents, which alters the complexion of the event? Can it be said that this State involvement affects D's culpability, when incitement by a private individual would not? In one sense there is no difference at all. However, it might be argued that the State should not stultify itself by creating the very offences which it then goes on to punish. If it is granted that D would not have committed this offence on this occasion had it not been for the entrapping conduct of the State's agents, the element of entrapment may be said to create a potential contradiction in criminal justice which can only be prevented by excluding D from criminal liability. A counter-argument to this is that techniques amounting to entrapment are sometimes necessary if the police are to make significant progress towards detecting certain forms of crime, particularly so-called 'victimless' crimes such as drug offences. Of course the police should be controlled in these activities, but that is a separate matter from the question of D's liability to conviction. This counter-argument suggests that there may be sufficient social justification for entrapment, but under what conditions?

An outline of the changing attitude of the English courts may help to answer this question. Although in *Sang* (1980)[188] the House of Lords declared that there is no defence of entrapment, the enactment and judicial interpretation of section 78 of the Police and Criminal Evidence Act 1984 have led to the exclusion of some entrapment evidence on the ground that its admission would have an adverse effect on the fairness of the proceedings. In *Smurthwaite and Gill* (1994)[189] the Court of Appeal set out guidelines on factors relevant to the exclusion of entrapment evidence, including:

1. whether the offence was already afoot;
2. whether D would have committed the offence but for the *agent provocateur*'s conduct; and
3. whether D already had a propensity to commit such offences.

[188] [1980] AC 402.   [189] (1994) 98 Cr App R 437.

In *Smurthwaite and Gill* undercover police officers had posed as 'hit-men' and were hired to kill the defendants' spouses; it was held that they had not over-stepped the line by encouraging the commission of the offence. In any event, one might wish to argue that encouragement to hire a killer, or even someone to inflict serious injury, is something that citizens ought to resist.[190] In other cases, the Court of Appeal has drawn a distinction between passive entrapment, where the defendants apply themselves to a 'trick' set up by the police, and active entrapment.[191]

It must be said, however, that the English courts have been rather less assertive in this field than those in some other jurisdictions. The Supreme Court of Canada has stated that 'there are inherent limits on the power of the state to manipulate people and events for the purpose of attaining the specific objective of obtaining convictions,' and has chosen to grant a stay of the prosecution in such cases.[192] The Supreme Court of the United States still upholds an entrapment defence, but the exclusion of those who have a disposition (previous similar conviction) affords little protection to some defendants and considerable licence to the police.[193] Out of fairness, the law should ensure that individuals who have been induced to commit crime by law enforcement officers or their agents are not liable to conviction. Whether the law achieves this by providing a defence, or by exclusion of evidence, or by stay of the prosecution for abuse of process, is perhaps a secondary matter. If there were to be a defence, it would have to be defined in legislation and the result might be a tightly circumscribed defence in the English tradition, leaving other cases to be reflected by mitigation of sentence. The other routes, *via* exclusion of evidence or stay of the prosecution, would probably leave considerable discretion to the courts. Guidelines such as those in *Smurthwaite and Gill* would then be needed to ensure consistent protection of defendants' rights. Before new guidelines were drawn up, a proper survey of the conflicting interests and considerations would be necessary.[194]

6.9 FAULT AND THE EXCUSES

This chapter and Chapter 5 have discussed the fault requirements for criminal liability; both the positive ones which the prosecution must

[190] G. Robertson, 'Entrapment Evidence: Manna from Heaven or Fruit of the Poisoned Tree?' [1994] Crim LR 805.

[191] Compare *Christou and Wright* (1992) 95 Cr App R 264 with the less convincing judgment in *Williams* (1994) 98 Cr App R 209; see S. Sharpe, 'Covert Police Operations and the Discretionary Exclusion of Evidence' [1994] Crim LR 793.

[192] *Mack v R* (1988) 44 CCC (3d) 513; cf. also *Amato v R* (1982) 69 CCC (2d) 31. For discussion, see A. Choo, *Abuse of Process and Judicial Stays of Criminal Proceedings* (1993), Ch 6. [193] *Jacobson v US* (1992) 112 S Ct 1535.

[194] Cf. the rather unsatisfactory treatment by the Law Commission in 1977: Law Com No. 83, *Defences of General Application*, Ch 5.

establish in order to fulfil the definition of the offence, and the negative ones which may be raised by evidence and which the prosecution then (with the exception of insanity) bears the burden of disproving. The discussion of the conduct element in criminal liability in Chapter 4 dealt with some matters of defence (justifications for the use of force) and also with involuntary conduct, which may be said to function as an excuse. The reason for placing involuntariness (automatism) in Chapter 4 was that it has generally been thought to strike at one of the fundamental requirements of criminal liability—proof of a voluntary act by the defendant. From the functional point of view, however, it tends to operate as an excuse, and the accompanying doctrine bears many of the elements (e.g. prior fault, concern for social defence) seen in the discussion of insanity in 6.2 above. Strong arguments can be made for moving both automatism and the justifications out of Chapter 4 into Chapter 6,[195] but the more important point is to recognize the necessary fluidity of classifications, apparent particularly in 6.6 above on mistake and putative defences.

Matters raised in defence in criminal trials may be provisionally divided into denials, justifications and excuses. Denials consist of evidence suggesting that one of the fault elements required for the offence is not present: when reference is made to the 'defence of accident', this is essentially a denial of intent or recklessness. We noted in 6.6 the controversy about whether the 'defence of mistake' should be regarded as a mere denial or developed as an excuse. This may appear to be a strange proposition—either it is a denial or it is not—but some of the excuses, such as insanity and intoxication, already have their basis in the denial of fault and have then been elaborated and restricted. Others, such as duress and mistake of law, plainly do not correspond to any of the positive fault requirements. There is, for example, no express requirement that a person should have acted 'unconstrained by threats' as a condition of criminal liability; the issue only arises when there is evidence of threats which affected D. However, the fact that the 'negative fault requirements' do not all correspond to, or amount to a negation of, the positive fault requirements should not lead us to regard these excuses as a separate group from cases where there is a denial of a positive fault requirement. It is important to keep in view the conflicts between the principle of individual autonomy and the principle of welfare that pervade all questions of defence, whether denial, excuse, or justification.

This concluding section will raise some general issues about fault and the

---

[195] P. Robinson, 'Should the Criminal Law abandon the Actus Reus–Mens Rea Distinction?', in S. Shute, J. Gardner, and J. Horder (eds), *Action and Value in Criminal Law* (1993).

excuses. First, we shall examine the implications of the threshold question: should a suggested excuse be recognized as a defence or merely as a mitigating factor in sentencing? Then we consider the roots of fault and the excuses in conceptions of individual responsibility, from which we go on to examine the arguments in favour of elements of social responsibility and policies of social defence. Whether it is possible to travel beyond a demonstration of the conflicting policies and principles and to achieve a unifying theory is then the question which remains.

(a) The Recognition of the Excuses

In moral and social terms there is probably a scale of excuse, running from the most acute form of (physical) involuntariness at one extreme to mere matters of difficulty and extra pressure at the other extreme. Most of the forms of excuse considered above can be manifested to a different degree (strong or weak circumstances of duress, mild or acute mental disorder), and it might even be possible to rank the excuses themselves in some order of intensity. During the course of the chapter it has often be remarked that the courts strive to keep the ambit of a particular defence as narrow as possible, so as to capture only the full or extreme cases of excuse. This approach leaves other cases, which have elements of excuse, to be dealt with in some other way. In some spheres of criminal law it is not simply a question of whether there is a defence or not. Provocation and diminished responsibility[196] are available as qualified defences to murder, reducing the crime to manslaughter, and there is no procedural reason why they and other qualified defences should not be granted a wider application—wherever there is a graduation of offences, the qualified defence might serve to reduce the higher to the lower.[197] There are obvious counter-arguments, grounded in the increased complexity and length of trials of cases where the unique stigma of 'murder' is not present,[198] but these concede rather than weaken the moral/social arguments for allowing the reduced culpability in, say, provocation cases to be signified by a reduction in the offence of conviction. This may be regarded as an example of fair labelling:[199] just as there is a 'scale of excuse, running downwards from excusing conditions. through partial excuses to mitigating excuses',[200] so the law should reflect these gradations through complete defences, partial defences, and then mitigation of sentence.

In some spheres, English courts have faltered and have refused to

---

[196] See below, Ch 7.4(b) and (e), and above, Ch 6.5.

[197] This was proposed by the Criminal Law Revision Committee in its 1976 Working Paper, 'Offences against the Person'.

[198] Cf. M. Wasik, 'Partial Excuses in the Criminal Law' (1982) 45 MLR, 515, with S. Morse, 'Diminished Capacity', in Shute, Gardner, and Horder (eds) *Action and Value in Criminal Law*.   [199] See above, Ch 3.4(l).   [200] Wasik, 'Partial Excuses', 524.

recognize a defence at all, leaving all degrees of exculpation to be reflected at the sentencing stage. This has been the predominant approach to entrapment,[201] and for many years it was the courts' approach to excuses based on necessity.[202] Indeed, the House of Lords recently went further and invoked executive discretion as a desirable way of mitigating the effective punishment of those who kill under duress.[203] In principle this is an unsatisfactory position. It would be possible to deal with all excuses, and, indeed, with all fault requirements, in this way: as we saw in Chapter 5.2(a), one could create a strict liability system in which proof of conduct and causation was sufficient for conviction, and fault would then be considered as a pointer to the most appropriate means of state intervention to ensure any repetition. The objection to this is that a criminal conviction is rightly regarded as condemnatory: it is unfair to apply this label when the absence of fault is so high on the 'scale of excuse' that there should be no formal blame. Supporters of strict liability, such as Baroness Wootton, would reply that on their system a conviction would not carry such a stigma, since it would not imply culpability.[204] Such an approach would sacrifice the underlying deterrent and censuring elements of the criminal law, as well as reducing the protection of individual autonomy by reducing the individual citizen's ability to plan and to predict the law's interventions.

Even if defences to criminal liability are recognized for 'strong' excuses, it will remain necessary to deal appropriately with 'weak' or imperfect cases of excuse. Mitigation of sentence must be the principal tool here. Unless the penalty is mandatory (as, in English law, for murder), courts will be able to reflect the strength of the excuse in the sentence they pass. However, there are two difficulties in treating this as an ideal way of reflecting the defendant's desert. First, there is the question of establishing the factual basis for mitigation. Sometimes this will have emerged during a trial, if a trial has taken place,[205] but more often it will be necessary to lay a foundation after conviction and before sentence. Procedures to ensure proper fact-finding are still developing, and there has been no clear recognition of the importance of ensuring that defendants have the same evidential safeguards as they would have had in a criminal trial.[206] Secondly, there is no clear recognition that mitigation of sentence is a right. It is often presented as discretionary, suggesting that courts may withhold a reduction in sentence if they wish to do so.[207] This is unsatisfactory, and the problems then shade into the general lack of

---

[201] See above, Ch 6.8.   [202] See above, Ch 6.4(c).
[203] *Howe* [1987] AC 417; see above, Ch 6.4(a).
[204] The views of Baroness Wootton are discussed above, Ch 5.3(a).
[205] See Ch 1.4 above on the prevalence of guilty pleas.
[206] See A. Ashworth, *Sentencing and Criminal Justice* (2nd edn, 1995), Ch 11.1.
[207] Ibid., Ch 5.7.

structure in English sentencing. There is little firm guidance on matters of mitigation, which leaves individual judges and magistrates' courts with considerable leeway. It is right that imperfect excuses should sound in mitigation, but English law provides no clear structure for them to do so.

Lastly, some excuses might be reflected in the exercise of prosecutorial discretion. The range here is enormous. Prosecutors are expected to take account of the likely line of defence in a particular case, and they might therefore bring no prosecution if convinced that a certain defence is probable to succeed. Where they are not so convinced, they might still decide that a prosecution would not be 'in the public interest'. The *Code for Crown Prosecutors* mentions cases where 'the offence was committed as a result of a genuine mistake or misunderstanding', and cases where 'the defendant is elderly or is, or was at the time of the offence, suffering from significant mental or physical ill health'.[208] Both of these factors are to be weighed against the seriousness of the offence. In practice, non-prosecution and discontinuance of prosecution take place in many cases involving mentally disordered persons, who may then be admitted to hospital or a treatment programme informally.[209]

(b) Individual Responsibility

It was shown in Chapter 5.2(a) that the roots of the conception of individual responsibility which underlie the principle of *mens rea* lie in respect for the autonomy of the individual: criminal liability should be imposed only where D chose the conduct and had the capacity and a fair opportunity to choose otherwise. As developed by Joshua Dressler, the principle is that there is only sufficient freedom of choice for criminal liability if D had 'the substantial capacity and a fair opportunity to (1) understand the pertinent facts relating to his conduct, (2) appreciate that his conduct violates society's morals/norms, and (3) conform his conduct to the law'.[210] What are the measures of fairness of an opportunity? The test which seems to emerge in English law, particularly from the excuses of duress and necessity, is whether a person of reasonable firmness might have been expected to withstand the pressures placed on D. Now in one sense this might be thought to be indulgent to D—there is no requirement that he should have felt totally deprived of his freedom of action, merely that a reasonably steadfast citizen would have found the pressure

---

[208] Crown Prosecution Service, *Code for Crown Prosecutors* (1994), discussed in Ch 1.4 above.

[209] D. Carson, 'Prosecuting People with Mental Handicap' [1989] Crim LR 87.

[210] J. Dressler, 'Reflections on Excusing Wrongdoers: Moral Theory, New Excuses and the Model Penal Code' (1988) 19 Rutgers LJ, 671 at 675, developing H. L. A. Hart, *Punishment and Responsibility* (1968), 181.

intolerable.[211] The answer to this is that in the demands it imposes on individuals the criminal law should prefer minimalism rather than perfectionism.[212] It should not expect more than it is reasonable to expect in a given situation. In another sense, however, the standard of reasonable firmness may be thought insufficiently indulgent to D: it precludes actual enquiry into the pressures experienced by this defendant. Even if D felt totally overwhelmed by the pressures, the law would not allow a defence of duress unless a reasonably steadfast person would also have been seriously affected. By this means, the idea of individual responsibility (how impaired was the choice and freedom of this person?) is compromised—perhaps for fear of false defences if the law were totally subjective, perhaps for fear of a significant loss in the deterrent effect of the law, or perhaps for other social reasons. One way of preventing harsh convictions of weak or vulnerable defendants would be to allow an exception to the standard for those lacking the capacity to conform, as proposed in Chapter 5.3(d) and (g).

We have also noted that the notions of free will and choice do not retain their full vigour within the excuses. Granting a complete defence in extreme cases of duress and necessity is clear recognition that D's behaviour was determined to a considerable degree by the circumstances. Behaviour in these cases is not *physically in*voluntary, as in cases of automatism,[213] but it can certainly be described as *non*-voluntary or morally involuntary. The same might sometimes be said of acts done during a provoked loss of self-control.[214] Most of these cases arise suddenly and place D under pressure of an emergency. Why is the law—probably following everyday assumptions on this point—so much more willing to accept diminished capacity when there is an 'explosive event' than where there has been a longer-term 'corrosion of the will' by fear or other pressures?[215] As Keith Smith and William Wilson comment, we need 'a better justification than that the doctrine . . . reflects a slice of incoherent moral etiquette, rather than a rational and consistent principle'.[216] The difficulty of determining the degree of pressure on others, and the possibility of false defences, are two poor justifications. Apart from the fact that they should apply to all fault requirements if to any, the proposition is unduly pessimistic and philosophically doubtful.[217]

---

[211] See the decisions in *Graham* (1982) 74 Cr App R235, and *Conway* [1988] 3 All ER 1025, and the theoretical discussion by A. Brudner, 'A Theory of Necessity' (1987) 7 Oxford JLS, 338.

[212] E. Colvin, 'Exculpatory Defences in Criminal Law' (1990) 10 Oxford JLS, 381, 395.

[213] See above, Ch 4.3.   [214] See above, Ch 6.5(a).

[215] See the argument of K. J. M. Smith and W. Wilson, 'Impaired Voluntariness and Criminal Responsibility' (1993) 13 Oxford JLS, 69, at 79–80.   [216] Ibid., 81.

[217] See the arguments against dualism in R. Shiner, 'Intoxication and Responsibility' and in R. A. Duff, *Intention, Agency, and Criminal Liability* (1990), Ch 6.

A more coherent justification might be found by focussing on the causal significance of other people's acts, in cases of duress and provocation at least. It is possible to point to someone else who was originally or ultimately to blame, and this is easy to understand.

If we could establish that there are other types of case in which the capacity of defendants to conform with the law was no less diminished than in many cases of duress and provocation, why should the law decline to accept them as excuses? Consider the proposal for a defence of 'social deprivation', based on the assertion that many offenders fail to acquire the capacity to resist offending because society fails to provide the conditions, facilities, and resources for their proper moral and social development. In arguing this case in the United States, Judge Bazelon referred to such individuals as 'the ignorant, the ill-educated and the unemployed and often unemployable', adding, in connection with their offending: 'I cannot believe that this is coincidental.'[218] The argument is that some of these people are trapped in a criminal lifestyle, with scarcely more capacity for free choice than the person under duress. They have not had a fair opportunity to conform their behaviour to the law. Critics suggest that this confuses explanation with excuse: research may demonstrate a causal link between social deprivation and offending behaviour, but this does not deny a fair opportunity to behave otherwise.[219] Not all persons from these backgrounds commit serious offences, and many other citizens from different circumstances suffer from personal problems and pressures which make it difficult for them to do the right thing at the right time. Yet this does not rule out the possibility that the pressures on some defendants are so great as to diminish capacity significantly. It seems to be because the effect of social deprivation is less urgent and more diffuse (insufficiently 'explosive') that it is widely assumed that this matter is better taken into account in mitigation of sentence.[220]

Together with lack of 'fair opportunity', the other criterion of excuse was lack of 'capacity' or 'substantial capacity'. One example of this is that children under the age of criminal responsibility (10, in Britain) are incapable of committing offences—not because they are incapable of doing acts intentionally or recklessly, but rather because they are assumed not to have developed the ability to evaluate their behaviour morally.[221] Until

[218] D. Bazelon, 'The Morality of the Criminal Law' (1976) 49 S Cal LR, 385.

[219] M. Moore, 'Causation and the Excuses' (1985) 73 Cal LR, 1091; S. Kadish, *Blame and Punishment* (1987), 102–6; Dressler, 'Reflections on Excusing Wrongdoers'.

[220] See M. Tonry, 'Racial Disproportion in US Prisons' (1994) 34 Brit J Criminol, 97, 112; S. J. Morse, 'Culpability and Control' (1994) 142 U Pa LR, 1587, 1652–4.

[221] See Horder, 'Pleading Involuntary Lack of Capacity', 300–2. There may also be other reasons, such as the wish to shield them from the criminal process until they are older: see next note.

recently this was extended by the presumption of *doli incapax* in respect of children aged 10 to 13 (inclusive), but the requirement that the prosecution show that such a child knew that the act was seriously wrong has now been abrogated.[222] Another example of the capacity rationale is provided by the defence of insanity. We saw in 6.2 above, that in English law the insanity defence is tied firmly to cognitive criteria, whereas other jurisdictions have extended it to volitional deficiencies. Another approach is to regard the matter rather as a question of status: mentally disordered persons lack the capacity for rational thought and direction of behaviour which normal citizens generally have, and they should therefore not be subjected to criminal liability and punishment.[223] But the tendency in English law has been to try to link the insanity defence with the positive fault requirements, such as *mens rea*, and this poses the questuion of where other personal conditions might form the basis of a defence. For example, should pre-menstrual syndrome should be accepted as a defence? It has been contended that hormonal imbalance can so unhinge a woman for a few days every month as significantly to impair her capacity to conform her conduct to the law. If the medical credentials of this condition and its effects are established, then there would seem to be good reason for recognizing an excuse in those cases where its effects reach an appropriate level of incapacitation.[224]

One way of dealing with several of these possible excuses would be to introduce either a complete defence or a partial defence based on 'diminished capacity'.[225] This would keep faith with Hart's doctrine of fair opportunity, and would either exculpate or reduce the grade of liability for defendants who to a significant extent felt coerced, compelled, or 'pressured' to do what they did. Although it is easy to think of possible practical problems in introducing such a defence,[226] its theoretical justification should also be considered with care. It might be preferable to articulate as many discrete defences as possible before turning to a broad, catch-all defence of this kind. While there is no need for citizens to have fair warning of its existence,[227] it is important to ensure that the courts exercise their power fairly and consistently between similarly or equivalently situated defendants.

---

[222] *C v DPP* [1995]

[223] See M. Moore, *Law and Psychiatry* (1985); R. A. Duff, *Trials and Punishments* (1986).

[224] Taylor and Dalton, 'Pre-Menstrual Syndrome: A New Criminal Defense?' (1983) 19 Cal WLR, 269; *Sandie Smith* [1982] Crim LR 531; and Dressler, 'Reflections on Excusing Wrongdoers', 707.

[225] S. J. Morse, 'Diminished Capacity', in S. Shute, J. Gardner, and J. Horder (eds), *Action and Value in Criminal Law*.   [226] Ibid., 268–73.

[227] See Ch 3.4(i) above.

(c) Social Responsibilities and Social Defence

This chapter can have left little doubt about the influence of considerations of welfare and social defence on the shaping of the law relating to excuses. Fear that individuals will raise, and succeed with, false defences is never far from the minds of judges and legislators, and goes some way towards explaining the presence of restricting conditions in duress and necessity (the 'person of reasonable firmness'), in intoxication (the restriction to crimes of 'specific intent'), and in ignorance or mistake of law (the virtual denial of such a defence). However, it was suggested above that this fear is an unsatisfactory reason for objective requirements.[228] There are stronger social arguments for restrictions. One is the importance of taking compulsory measures against persons shown to be capable of causing harm in their condition. This is a major plank of the 'special defence' in insanity cases, where absence of capacity leads to a special verdict which, in turn, may give rise to compulsory measures of social protection.[229] Yet we saw in 6.2 that the terms of the defence are not designed to demonstrate that D is a dangerous person, likely to cause further serious harm if given a simple acquittal. Moreover, the fragility of predictions of dangerousness is well known,[230] and the present English system depends on the ability of judges to select cases in which hospitalization or treatment in the community is necessary.

Prediction of future dangerousness may also play some part in the prevailing English approach to intoxication as a defence, but probably the chief reason for restricting the defence is the belief that people who do harm while intoxicated are blameworthy. This is a strong application of the doctrine of prior fault. Australian and other jurisdictions reject both the dangerousness and the prior fault reasoning in intoxication cases, maintaining an approach based purely on *mens rea* at the time of the act. No loss of social defence appears to have resulted, but it was argued in 6.3(d) above that abolition of the artificial and restrictive English rules ought to be accomplished, as the Law Commission at one time proposed, by the creation of a new offence of causing harm while intoxicated. Reasoning of this kind has been generalized by Eric Colvin, who argues that those who raise defences based on mental impairment 'are proper subjects for coercive measures' even though their 'mental condition makes them unsuited to handling within the standard structure of criminal liability'.[231]

One argument often mobilized against the infiltration of objective requirements into excusing defences is 'logic'. We have noted this in

---

[228] See n. 176 above. [229] See above, Ch 6.2.
[230] For a summary, see Ashworth, *Sentencing and Criminal Justice*, Ch 6.8.
[231] Colvin, 'Exculpatory Defences', 392.

relation to intoxication (6.3(b) above) and particularly mistake of fact (6.6). Consistency of approach to excusing conditions would certainly seem to be an element in fairness, but it does not follow that the excuses should be consistently and utterly subjective in their requirements. The subjective principles have their foundation in the principle of individual autonomy, and its emphasis on choice, control, and fair warning. But we have seen that modern liberal philosophy has begun to emphasize that individuals should be viewed as members of society with mutual obligations rather than as abstracted and isolated individuals. The subjective principles and the contemporaneity principle,[232] ingrained as they are in much academic writing in the common law world, in some judicial pronouncements and in many Law Commission proposals, seem premised on an atomistic view of individual behaviour.[233] An alternative approach would spell out certain duties of citizenship which should form part of membership of a legal community and which might have some bearing on issues of criminal responsibility. One such duty might be to avoid uncontrolled behaviour that might lead to harm to others. This might apply specifically to cases of intoxication, based on the general social proposition that persons who take large amounts of alcohol or certain drugs constitute a greater risk of causing harm. A similar argument might be used to justify the refusal to admit provocation as a general defence—if we are satisfied that no exceptions should be admitted to the principle that citizens should control their tempers. However, it was argued above that certain provocation cases contain strongly exculpating elements, which at the very least make a convincing case for provocation as a qualified defence.[234]

This line of reasoning may also be applied, in a critical fashion, to mistake cases. Citizens may surely be expected to make reasonable efforts to acquaint themselves with the contours of the criminal law, but this does not support the refusal of the English courts and legislature to recognize a general excuse based on ignorance or mistake of law. On the contrary, the citizen's duty is fulfilled by reasonable enquiries, and this would support a defence of reasonable ignorance or mistake of law (including reasonable reliance on official advice).[235] Strangely, the English courts have erred in the opposite direction in cases of mistake of fact, seduced by the allure of what Lord Hailsham described as 'inexorable logic'. The courts have failed to show proper sensitivity to the rights of others in particular situations which ought to alert the citizen. Thus, rather than regarding the defendant in a rape case as abstracted from the situation of close proximity to the

---

[232] See above, Ch 5.2(a) and (d).

[233] M. Kelman, 'Interpretive Construction in the Substantive Criminal Law' (1981) 33 Stanford LR, 591.   [234] See above, Ch 6.5(b).

[235] See above, Ch 6.7(b) and (c).

victim and subject only to the momentary and 'inexorable' logic of the question: 'did he at that time realise that there was a risk that she was not consenting?', the law might fairly ask whether he took care to ensure that his sexual partner was willing.[236] Similarly, rather than regarding a police officer as abstracted from his or her training and knowledge of alternative means of resolving a situation and subject only to the momentary and 'inexorable' logic of the question: 'did he at that time believe that his life was in danger from V?', the law might perhaps ask whether he took care to ensure that V was armed, before injuring V or taking V's life.[237]

The drift of this argument is towards the idea of duties of citizenship which relate in part to control of one's own passions or 'vices'[238] and in part to one's respect for the rights of others in situations which obviously concern those rights (e.g. sexual intercourse, the use of deadly force). The doctrine of prior fault should prevail over the principle of contemporaneity, as the various duties tug the enquiry away from the momentary conduct towards a broader consideration of the situation and its antecedents. Those wedded to traditional theory will doubtless regard this as the spread of negligence liability, and so it is. In this sense, it is compatible with much of what was said by Lord Diplock in *Caldwell*,[239] in that failure to give thought to those matters which the reasonable citizen might regard as obvious may be just as culpable as momentary advertence to such matters. But the idea of duties of citizenship does not require full adherence to the *Caldwell* doctrine. Two modifications are particularly important. First, the general notion that citizens with ordinary powers of perception and self-control should exercise those powers must be subject to an exception in favour of persons incapable of attaining that general standard. The greater flexibility shown by the House of Lords in *Reid* was welcomed on this point.[240] Secondly, a full-blown notion of individual responsibility in a social context should lay greater emphasis on the avoidance of greater harms. The paradox of *Caldwell* is that it applies chiefly to criminal damage, an offence which is, in most instances,[241] well down the scale of seriousness. A socially sensitive doctrine would impose greater duties of care on citizens in situations where harm is widely known to be possible (e.g. use of firearms, fire-raising, irregular driving), where great harm is a possibility (e.g. the operation of transport systems, sports stadiums), and particularly where the means of avoiding harm are

---

[236] C. Wells, 'Swatting the Subjectivist Bug' [1982] Crim LR 209 and below, Ch 8.5(c).
[237] Horder, 'Cognition, Emotion and Criminal Culpability'.
[238] Fletcher, *Rethinking Criminal Law*, 514.
[239] [1982] AC 341, discussed above, Ch 5.3(c).
[240] *Reid* (1992) 95 Cr App R 391, discussed in Ch 5.3(c) above.
[241] Cf. criminal damage by fire (arson), which is often serious.

relatively simple (as in sexual intercourse, enquiring about the other's willingness). It will be evident that these arguments do not promise a simplified system of fault and excuses, but Chapters 5 and 6 should have demonstrated that the present system is far from simple. Conflicts between 'pure' individual responsibility and questions of social responsibility are endemic in this sphere. The torch of orthodox subjectivism, carried by Glanville Williams, by Smith and Hogan, and then by the Law Commission, should be doused. The conflicts of autonomy and welfare must be recognized, examined, and constantly reappraised.

In order to avoid the arguments for social responsibility being seen as placing too great an onus on individuals, it is important not to neglect the duties of the state in these matters. The obligation to publicize new criminal laws is obviously one such duty, particularly strong in respect of duties to act. The obligation not to entrap citizens into committing offences might be another.[242] And then there is the more general issue of the state's responsibility for social conditions which foster crime. This is not an outrageous notion: the preamble to the European Convention on Compensation for Victims of Crimes of Violence refers to the idea that the state's duty to provide compensation arises from its failure to prevent crimes,[243] and this suggests at least an obligation to take reasonably determined measures to reduce crime. One such measure is to relieve those criminogenic social conditions of poverty, bad housing, unemployment, lack of social facilities, and so forth which have an established link with law-breaking.[244] Even if we are not prepared to go so far as to accept social deprivation as an excuse for crime,[245] it may be regarded as significantly reducing an offender's 'desert', and also as an example of state neglect of a duty towards its citizens.[246]

(d) Fault, Excuse, and 'Desert'

Modern writings on the criminal law have made substantial advances in uncovering and criticizing the reasons for admitting, rejecting, and shaping the various fault requirements in criminal liability. Some defences are essentially denials (usually of intention, recklessness, or knowledge), others are of a 'confession-and-avoidance' type in that they concede the

---

[242] See above, Ch 6.8.

[243] Council of Europe, *European Convention on Compensation for the Victims of Crimes of Violence* (1984).

[244] Cf. S. Box, *Recession, Crime and Unemployment* (1987), 30–1, with J. Q. Wilson and R. Herrnstein, *Crime and Human Nature* (1983), esp. Pt VI. See also S. Field, *Trends in Crime and their Interpretation*, Home Office Research Study, No. 119 (1990).

[245] See above, n. 218 and accompanying text.

[246] See Lacey, *State Punishment*, Ch 3 and 140–1, and A. Ashworth, 'Justifying the Grounds of Mitigation' (1994) 13 *Criminal Justice Ethics* 5.

existence of the required positive fault elements and point to other reasons for exculpation. These other reasons are, in most instances, varieties of justification and/or excuse. Awareness of the conceptual difference between justification and excuse improves the clarity of analysis and might avert confusions in the courts.[247] However, sharp distinctions between justificatory and excusatory defences are sometimes unproductive,[248] and the idea that the communicative and labelling functions of the criminal law would be better served by special verdicts ('not guilty on grounds of justification'; 'not guilty because excused')[249] seems to overlook the extent to which many defences contain elements of both. Equally, it is probably true that defendants would prefer to be acquitted on grounds of justification (recognising that the conduct was acceptable in the circumstances) rather than on grounds of excuse (conduct unacceptable, but D insufficiently culpable). There is a strong moral argument that the 'serial view' of defences—whereby courts should always consider denials before justifications, and justifications before excuses—should be preferred, but the extent to which it is forensically workable is another issue.[250]

The search for a unifying theory of excuses has been less productive. Proposed theories of excuse seem to offer conclusory descriptions rather than criteria which may be used to admit or reject possible excuses. Hart's doctrine of fair opportunity has been particularly influential, and yet it leads us into uncharted waters. His argument that a person should only be held criminally liable if he or she had the capacity and a fair opportunity to act in conformity with the law[251] has been widely accepted. It captures the essence of individual autonomy in the importance of having fair warning and being able to plan and predict. However, it leaves much work to be done on appropriate criteria of the 'fairness' of opportunities. For example, in disputed areas such as ignorance and mistake of law, the cutting edge of this theory is rather blunt.[252] Some have assumed that Hart's approach followed the subjective principles entirely, yet he was prepared to accept the punishment of negligent harm-doers.[253] Moreover, as argued throughout this chapter, respect for the principle of autonomy does not require purely subjective criteria. In some instances where the

---

[247] See the discussion of *Howe* above, Ch 6.4(d).

[248] See Fletcher, *Rethinking Criminal Law* Ch 10, K. Greenawalt, 'The Perplexing Borders of Justification and Excuse' (1984) 84 Columbia LR, 1897; J. Dressler, 'Justifications and Excuses; A Brief Review of the Concept and the Literature' (1987) 33 Wayne LR, 1155; G. Williams, 'The Theory of Excuses' [1982] Crim LR 732; Alldridge, 'The Coherence of Defences'.

[249] See the discussion by Colvin, 'Exculpatory Defences', 385–6.

[250] D. Husak, 'The Serial View of Criminal Law Defences' (1992) 3 Crim LF, 369.

[251] H. L. A. Hart, *Punishment and Responsibility* (1968), Chs 2 and 7.

[252] Cf. Dressler, 'Reflections on Excusing Wrongdoers', 703–15.

[253] See Ch 5.3(e) above.

onset of a certain mental condition was caused by D's prior fault, it is not a negation of autonomy to suggest that D should not be exculpated. The idea of duties of citizenship, aired in the previous section, can and should be developed to broaden out the concept of desert. Although some of the objective requirements mentioned in this chapter are based on principles of welfare, it should not be thought that all of them are derogations from a properly social theory of individual autonomy.[254]

Desert theory—maintaining that individuals should be liable to punishment only when they deserve it, and to the extent that they deserve it[255]—takes one of two forms in most modern writings. One is the character theory, which argues that D's 'desert' is 'gauged by his character' and therefore that 'a judgment about character is essential to the just distribution of punishment'.[256] Behaviour should be excused when it does not reflect D's true character, but D should be held responsible whenever the behaviour can be regarded as genuinely expressive of his dispositions.[257] The Court of Appeal came close to espousing this theory in *Kingston* (1993),[258] when it held that D should not be held liable for acts done while involuntarily (but not totally) intoxicated. Full espousal of the theory would have excused D if he had no general disposition to paedophilia but would have convicted him if paedophilia was part of his general character. There are several difficulties with this approach, one of which is the breadth of the conception of character it employs (although that, in turn, raises the question of one's responsibility for one's character), and another is its lack of sharpness in distinguishing between acceptable and unacceptable excuses.[259] Fletcher's attempt to limit the theory to the particular act charged, by reference to the principle of legality and the value of privacy, is unconvincing.[260] It also brings the theory close to the second manifestation of 'desert' theory, which focusses more explicitly on the act or omission charged, and argues that liability is undeserved where D's practical reasoning capacities were impaired.[261] Again, it is unclear whether this provides a sufficient criterion for dealing with controversial areas such as mistake of law and provocation. Moreover, there is a difficulty with such a momentary conception of 'desert', which appears inconsistent with the morally powerful doctrine of prior fault. It is

---

[254] See Ch 4.1 above for discussion.   [255] See Ch 1.5 above.

[256] Fletcher, *Rethinking Criminal Law*, 800.

[257] Cf. M. Bayles, 'Character, Purpose and Criminal Responsibility' (1982) 1 Law and Philosophy 5, and Lacey, *State Punishment*, 65–78, with R. A. Duff, 'Choice and Character' (1993) Law and Philosophy.

[258] See G. R. Sullivan, 'Involuntary Intoxication and Beyond' [1994] Crim LR 272. For the House of Lords decision, see n. 69 above and text thereat.

[259] Dressler, 'Reflections on Excusing Wrongdoers', 692–701.

[260] See Fletcher, *Rethinking Criminal Law*, 800, criticized by Brudner, 'A Theory of Necessity', 344–7.   [261] Moore, 'Causation and the Excuses'.

one thing to join with Nozick in asserting that 'desert' does not have to go 'all the way down',[262] so that it is unnecessary to investigate whether every element of the situation can be said to be deserved; it is quite another to abstract D's 'desert' from the situation which confronted him at that time, which may have been 'determined causally and (therefore) not according to desert'.[263] Arguments about desert have a powerful intuitive appeal and yet, because of these difficulties, are thought open to the charge of incoherence.[264] It is certainly necessary to explore relevant moral principles and intuitions and not to accept the traditional categories of defence as conclusive. To reject desert, however, would be to reject the foundations for many of the safeguards and protections for individuals that are constructed out of respect for autonomy, and that is not the road we should go down.

[262] R. Nozick, *Anarchy, State and Utopia* (1974), 225, quoted by Weinreb, 'Desert, Punishment and Criminal Responsibility' (1986) 49 Law and Contemporary Problems (No. 3), 47.
[263] Weinreb, 'Desert, Punishment and Criminal Responsibility', 75.
[264] E.g. Norrie, *Crime, Reason and History*.

7

Homicide

This chapter deals with the approach of the criminal law to behaviour which causes death or risks causing death. Murder, manslaughter, and several other offences are discussed, and one recurrent issue here is fair labelling: does English law respond proportionately to the different degrees of culpability manifested in cases where death is caused?

7.1 DEATH AND FINALITY

For practical purposes, the culpable causing of another person's death may fairly be regarded as the most serious offence in the criminal calendar. There is an argument that treason is a more serious offence, since it strikes at the very foundations of the state and its social organizations, but in any event treason is rarely prosecuted. The harm caused by homicide is absolutely irremediable, whereas the harm caused by many other crimes is remediable to a degree. Even in crimes of violence which leave some permanent physical disfigurement or psychological effects, the victim retains his or her life and, therefore, the possibility of further pleasures and achievements, whereas death is final. This finality makes it proper to regard death as the most serious harm that may be inflicted on another, and to regard a person who chooses to inflict that harm without justification or excuse as the most culpable of offenders.

Although many deaths arise from natural causes, and many others from illnesses and diseases, each year sees a large number of deaths caused by 'accidents', and also a number caused by acts or omissions which amount to some form of homicide in English law. In 1987, for example, the statistics showed that there were some 20,000 accidental deaths, of which some 7,000 occurred in the home, 6,000 at work, and 5,000 on the roads.[1] By comparison, the number of deaths recorded as criminal homicide varied within a range of 500 to 600 per year during the 1980s. This includes all the murders and manslaughters, and a typical year would be 1990: 182 cases ended in a murder verdict, 81 manslaughter by diminished responsibility, and 162 other manslaughters.[2] This figure is relatively small when compared with many American cities, but that is no cause for satisfaction.

---

[1] *Social Trends 1987* (HMSO, 1988).
[2] *Criminal Statistics England and Wales 1992*, Table 4.2.

There are still awkward questions to be confronted. For example, are we satisfied that the 600 deaths recorded as homicide are in fact more culpable than all, or even most, of the deaths recorded in other categories? In other words, does English criminal law pick out the most heinous forms of killing as murders and manslaughters, or are the boundaries frozen by tradition? For example, during the years 1982–84 the average annual number of cases of causing death by reckless driving was 227, whereas during 1990–92 it was 371—a significant increase at a time when the 'homicide rate' (so called) remained fairly stable. Another question is whether the criminal law ought not to be wider in its application to activities which carry some risk of causing death than in other spheres. Thus, even if it would be excessive to sweep large numbers of the deaths now recorded as 'accidents' into the law of homicide, there may be sufficient justification for creating or enforcing offences designed to ensure safe conditions of work, safe goods, safe buildings, and so on. It was argued in Chapter 2 that the criminal law ought to spread its net wider where the potential harm is greater. It will be seen that English law does this up to a point, and in the process seems to accept social defence arguments as reasons for departing from several of the principles set out in Chapter 3.

7.2 REQUIREMENTS OF CRIMINAL HOMICIDE

English law distinguishes between the offences of murder and manslaughter, as we shall see, but the two crimes do have certain common elements. It must be proved that the defendant's act or omission caused the death of the victim within a year and a day.[3] (The requirements on causation in the criminal law were discussed in Chapter 4.6.) The 'year and a day' rule is a legacy of times when medical science was so rudimentary that, if there was a substantial lapse of time between injury and death, it was unsafe to pronounce on whether the defendant's conduct or some other event caused the death. Nowadays the problem is quite the reverse: medical science is able not only to help determine whether D's conduct caused the death, but also to prolong life for years by the use of life-support machines.[4] The Law Commission has reviewed the operation of the rule, which no longer exists in many other common law jurisdictions, and has recommended its abolition.[5] If this recommendation is followed by legislation, prosecutors will be able to bring a murder charge if a victim

---

[3] Rule affirmed in *Dyson* [1908] 2 KB 454, and in *R* v *West London Coroner, exp, Luca* [1988] Crim LR 541; see D. E. C. Yale, 'A Year and a Day in Homicide' [1989] Camb LJ, 202.
[4] See Ian Kennedy, *Treat Me Right* (1989), Ch 18, *Airedale NHS Trust* v *Bland* [1993] 1 All ER 831.
[5] Law Commission No. 230 *Legislating the Criminal Code: The Year and a Day Rule in Homicide* (1995), on which see [1995] Crim LR 353.

dies months or even years after D had already been convicted of a non-fatal offence. The Criminal Law Revision Committee supported the existing rule on the ground that a defendant should not be left in peril of a homicide conviction indefinitely.[6] Abolition of the rule would mean reliance on prosecutorial discretion to prevent unfair convictions years after the event, and so the Law Commission recommends a requirement for the consent of the Attorney-General's consent in certain cases. In one case an inquest returned a verdict of unlawful killing in respect of a man who died from septicaemia and pneumonia some eight years after being stabbed with scissors. His assailant had originally been convicted of causing grievous bodily harm with intent and served a sentence of six years' imprisonment.[7] Should a homicide prosecution be brought on these facts?

7.3 DEFINING MURDER: THE INCLUSIONARY QUESTION

(a) The Procedural Context

If causing death is to be regarded as the most serious harm that can be inflicted, it would seem to follow that the most blameworthy form of homicide should result in the highest sentences imposed by the courts. Indeed, many systems of criminal law impose a mandatory sentence for murder (or whatever the highest form of homicide is called in that system). In some jurisdictions this is a mandatory sentence of death. In others, such as those in the United Kingdom, it is the mandatory sentence of life imprisonment. Why should this penalty be mandatory, and not at the discretion of the court as in other offences? One argument in favour of the mandatory life sentence is that it amounts to a symbolic indication of the unique heinousness of murder. It places the offender under the state's control, as it were, for the remainder of his or her life. This is often linked with a supposed denunciatory effect—the idea that the mandatory life sentence denounces murder as emphatically as possible—and with a supposed general deterrent effect, in declaring that there is no mitigation of sentence available for this crime. It might also be argued that the mandatory life sentence makes a substantial contribution to public safety.

None of these arguments is notably strong, let alone conclusive. The mandatory penalty does indeed serve to mark out murder from other

---

[6] Criminal Law Revision Committee, Fourteenth Report, *Offences against the Person* (1980, Cmnd 7844), paras 39–40.

[7] As reported in *The Rochdale Observer*, 6 August 1994.

crimes, but whether the definition of murder is sufficiently refined to capture the worst killings, and only the worst killings, remains to be discussed below. Whether the life sentence is regarded as a sufficient denunciation in society depends on the public's perception of what life imprisonment means: if it is widely believed that it results in an average of nine or 10 years' imprisonment, the effect will be somewhat blunted, even if the belief is untrue. The same applies to the general deterrent argument: its effectiveness depends on whether the penalty for murder affects the calculations of potential killers at all, and, if it does, whether the prospect of life imprisonment affects them more than the alternative of a long, fixed-term sentence. As for public protection, this depends on executive decisions with regard to release; it raises the question whether it is necessary for public protection to keep 'lifers' in for so long.[8]

This brings the discussion to a crucial point: what does the mandatory sentence of life imprisonment mean in practice, and what would be the alternative? What it means is that the time of release from prison is determined by the Home Secretary, on the advice of the Parole Board and the Lord Chief Justice, rather than by the judge at the trial. In procedural terms, therefore, the life sentence involves a transfer of function: normally it is the judge who determines the sentence (or at least its upper limit, since earlier release on parole may be possible), whereas a life sentence entrusts that function to the Home Secretary and his advisers, having first ascertained the opinions of the Lord Chief Justice and the trial judge. The Home Office is not bound by those opinions, and appears to depart from them frequently.[9] While the mechanism for determining the length of time actually served by an offender sentenced to a *discretionary* life sentence (i.e. for an offence other than murder) has now been altered following a ruling of the European Court of Human Rights, release from a *mandatory* life sentence for murder remains in the hands of the Home Secretary.[10]

The result of this is that decisions to release murderers—some after only a few years, others after extremely long periods or not at all—are taken by members of the executive, in private, without representations on behalf of the prisoner, without the need to give reasons, without the possibility of appeal, and sometimes on blatantly political grounds.[11] Surely decisions of this nature should be taken by the courts, or at least subject to an

---

[8] On this, see the cautious words of S. Brody and R. Tarling, *Taking Offenders out of Circulation*, Home Office Research Study No. 64 (1980), 33.

[9] HL Select Committee on Murder etc., paras 154–6.

[10] For discussion, see Lord Windlesham, 'Life Sentences: law, practice and release decisions, 1989–93' [1993] Crim LR 644, discussing the decision in *Thynne, Wilson and Gunnell* v *UK* (1991) 13 EHRR 666, and the Criminal Justice Act 1991, s 34.

[11] See the speech of Rt Hon Michael Howard as Home Secretary in July 1993, reported in [1994] Crim LR 81.

appealable 'tariff' period set by the judge, in the same way as for discretionary life sentences. The answer sometimes given is that murderers should be treated differently because they are particularly dangerous: anyone who chooses to kill once can choose to kill again. But this argument will seem less persuasive when we have discussed cases of manslaughter by reason of diminished responsibility: where a murder is reduced to manslaughter, the judge has a wide sentencing discretion and may, according to the facts of the case, select a determinate prison sentence, a hospital order, or life imprisonment. Those who kill and are convicted of manslaughter by reason of diminished responsibility are no less dangerous than those convicted of murder, and yet the judge has sentencing discretion in one case and not in the other. Considerations of this kind led the House of Lords Committee on Murder and Life Imprisonment to recommend the abolition of the mandatory sentence for murder.[12] A committee chaired by the former Lord Chief Justice, Lord Lane, reached the same conclusion in 1993, with blunt criticism of successive Home Secretaries for ignoring the European Convention on Human Rights and 'turning a blind eye to the merits of any change until it can no longer be avoided or postponed'.[13] Both committees favoured judicial sentencing discretion to mark the relative heinousness of the murder, subject to review on appeal. In cases where life imprisonment was thought to be the appropriate sentence, the trial judge would still specify—in open court—the number of years to be spent in prison, taking the gravity of the offence into account, and release would be determined by a judicial tribunal. Such a reform would bring improvements in natural justice without loss of public protection, but the government has refused to contemplate any relaxation of the Home Secretary's control over these decisions.

(b) Degrees of Homicide

English criminal law has two degrees of homicide: murder and manslaughter. Many American jurisdictions have three degrees of murder—first-degree murder, requiring premeditation, and second- and third-degree murder, covering lesser shades of culpability.[14] In England there has been a proposal that we should do away with all these distinctions, leaving a single offence of criminal homicide.[15] That proposal,

---

[12] HL Select Committee on Murder etc., paras 101–22, adopting the reasoning of D. A. Thomas, 'Form and Function in Criminal Law', in P. R. Glazebrook (ed), *Reshaping the Criminal Law* (1978); cf. also M. D. Farrier, 'The Distinction between Murder and Manslaughter in its Procedural Context' (1976) 39 MLR, 414.

[13] *Committee on the Penalty for Homicide* (Prison Reform Trust, 1993).

[14] See further P. Low, J. Jeffreys, and R. Bonnie, *Criminal Law, Cases and Materials* (2nd edn, 1986), Ch 6.

[15] Per Lord Kilbrandon, in *Hyam* v *DPP* [1975] AC 55, at 98.

if implemented, would shift almost all the decision-making in homicide cases from the trial to the sentencing stage: the only issue of any consequence in most cases would be the sentence to be imposed, and all the distinctions now drawn at the stage of criminal liability would be reflected in the sentence alone. The jury would have no role in most homicide cases, since a plea of guilty would be the norm. Contrast this with the position in jurisdictions where there are three or more degrees of homicide: pleas of guilty to first- and second-degree murders would be less frequent, since there would be the possibility of argument in court (if no bargain was struck beforehand between prosecution and defence), and the defence might succeed in persuading the jury to reduce the degree of the killing. Moreover, the borderlines between the various degrees would raise questions of law, which would provide many opportunities for legal argument and for appeals. The result would be that killings were classified and labelled in a more refined way, but at the cost of lengthy trials and mounting legal aid bills. That cost is not difficult to justify where capital punishment is the penalty for first-degree murder. Is it any easier to justify when conviction for murder (as distinct from manslaughter) results in a mandatory sentence of life imprisonment which leaves release in the hands of a politician, the Home Secretary? Or it is a question of weighing the principle of fair labelling (see Chapter 3.5(s)) against the cost and time arguments mobilized by the policy of efficient administration (see Chapter 3.5(t))?

The structure of the English law of homicide is rather strange. Although there are two offences, murder and manslaughter, the latter includes two distinct varieties: 'voluntary' manslaughter (killings which would be murder but for the existence of defined extenuating circumstances); and 'involuntary' manslaughter (killings for which there is no need to prove any awareness of the risk of death being caused, but for which there is thought to be sufficient fault to justify criminal liability). The arguments therefore tend to focus on three borderline questions: What is the minimum fault required for conviction of murder? In what circumstances should murder be reduced to manslaughter? And what is the minimum fault required for a conviction of manslaughter?

(c) Requirements for Murder

In English criminal law there are now two alternative fault requirements for murder: an intent to kill, or an intent to cause grievous bodily harm. What do these requirements mean? Do they extend the definition of murder too far, or are they too narrow?

Intent to kill may be regarded as the most obvious and indisputable form of fault element for murder, but to some extent that depends on the meaning of 'intent'. This has been the subject of a number of House of

Lords decisions,[16] and yet the definition is still not clear and settled. Probably the most accurate statement would be that a person *intends* to kill if it is his or her purpose to kill by the act or omission charged, or if he or she foresees that death is practically certain to follow from that act or omission. In this way, both purpose and foresight of practical certainty are regarded as part of the definition of intent, although there are other statements suggesting that foresight of practical or 'virtual' certainty is merely evidence from which intent may be inferred.[17] How would this test be applied? The 'golden rule' is that intention should be left without description or definition in most cases, and the full definition should be reserved for cases where D claims that his purpose was something other than to cause injury. A fairly typical set of facts is provided by *Nedrick* (1986),[18] where D had a grudge against a woman and had threatened to 'burn her out'. One night he went to her house, poured paraffin through the letter-box and on to the front door, and set it alight. One of the woman's children died in the ensuing fire. When asked why he did it, D replied: 'Just to wake her up and frighten her.' A defence of this kind, a claim that the purpose was only to frighten and not to cause harm, requires the full definition to be put to the jury. The question is: granted that D's purpose was to frighten, did he nonetheless realize that it was practically certain that his act would cause death or grievous bodily harm to someone? The jury should answer this, as in all criminal cases, by drawing inferences from the evidence in the case and from the surrounding circumstances.[19]

What about the alternative element in the definition, an intent to cause grievous bodily harm? This has considerable practical importance, since this is all that the prosecution has to prove in order to obtain a verdict of guilty of murder. It must be shown that the defendant intended (which, again, includes both purpose and awareness of practical certainty) to cause really serious injury to someone. The House of Lords confirmed this rule in *Cunningham* (1981):[20] D struck his victim on the head a number of times with a chair, causing injuries from which the victim died a week later. D maintained throughout that he had not intended to kill, but there was evidence from which the jury could infer—and did infer—that he intended to cause grievous bodily harm. The House of Lords upheld D's conviction for murder: an intent to cause really serious injury is sufficient for murder, without any proof that the defendant intended, or even contemplated, the possibility that death would result.

---

[16] Apart from *Hyam* (ibid.), now overruled, there is *Moloney* [1985] AC 905, and *Hancock and Shankland* [1986] AC 455, both discussed in Ch 5.3(b) above.

[17] Such statements are to be found in *Moloney* and *Hancock and Shankland* (last note) and *Nedrick* (next note).   [18] [1986] 3 All ER *1*.

[19] See the discussion of inferences by R. Shiner, 'Intoxication and Responsibility' (1990) 13 Int J of Law & Psychiatry, 9.   [20] [1982] AC 566.

Does the 'grievous bodily harm' rule extend the definition of murder too far? If the point of distinguishing murder from manslaughter is to mark out the most heinous group of killings for the extra stigma of a murder conviction, it can be argued that the 'grievous bodily harm' rule draws the line too low. The rule departs from the principle of correspondence (see Chapter 5.2(a)), namely that the fault element in a crime should relate to the consequences prohibited by that crime. By allowing an intent to cause grievous bodily harm to suffice for a murder conviction, the law is turning its most serious offence into a constructive crime. Is there any justification for 'constructing' a murder conviction out of this lesser intent? There are some arguments in favour, death is final, and there is no significant moral difference between someone who chooses to cause really serious injury and someone who sets out to kill. No one can predict whether a serious injury will result in death—that may depend on the victim's physique, on the speed of an ambulance, on the distance from the hospital, and on a range of other medical and individual matters. If one person chooses to cause serious injury to another, he or she has already crossed one of the ultimate moral thresholds and has shown a sufficiently wanton disregard for life as to warrant the label 'murder' if death results. The counter-arguments, which would uphold the principle of correspondence, are that breach of that principle is unnecessary when the amplitude of the crime of manslaughter lies beneath murder, and also that the definition of grievous bodily harm includes a number of injuries which are most unlikely to put the victim's life at risk. In the leading case of *Cunningham*, Lord Edmund-Davies (dissenting) gave the example of breaking someone's arm: that is a really serious injury, but one which is unlikely to endanger the victim's life.[21] So in practice the 'grievous bodily harm' rule goes further than the arguments of its protagonists would support.

Nonetheless, it must be recognized that many other legal systems also have a definition of murder that goes beyond an intent to kill. What other approaches might be taken? The fault element for many serious offences is intent or recklessness: why should this not suffice for murder? The question is whether all killings in which the defendant is aware of the risk of death are sufficiently serious to warrant the term 'murder'. One answer sometimes given is that they are not, because a driver who overtakes on a bend, knowingly taking the risk that there is a car travelling in the opposite direction, should not be labelled a murderer if a collision and death happen to ensue.[22] This example assumes that a sympathy for motorists will overwhelm any tendency to logical analysis. One might ask whether

---

[21] [1982] AC 582; see also *Donnelly* [1989] Crim LR 739.
[22] One of the examples given by Lord Goff, 'The Mental Element in the Crime of Murder' (1988) 104 LQR, 30, at 48.

motorists are ever justified in knowingly taking risks with other people's lives. Yet if the example is modified a little, so that the overtaking is on a country road at night and the risk is known to be slight, it becomes questionable whether the causing of death in these circumstances should be labelled in the same way as intentional killings. This is not to suggest that motorists should be treated differently. The point is rather that, even though knowingly taking risks with other people's lives is usually unjustifiable, taking a slight risk is less serious than intentionally causing death. In discussing the boundaries of murder, we are concerned with classification, not exculpation.

To classify all reckless killings as murder might be too broad, but the point remains that some reckless killings may be thought no less heinous than intentional killings. Can a satisfactory line be drawn here? One approach would be to draw the line by reference to the degree of probability. Murder is committed in those situations where D caused death by an act or omission which he knew had death as the probable or highly probable result. A version of this test of foresight of high probability is used in several other European countries;[23] it was introduced into English law by the decision in *Hyam* v *DPP* (1975),[24] but abandoned in *Moloney* (1985)[25] on grounds of uncertainty.

A second approach is to frame the law in such a way as to make it clear that the court should make a moral judgment on the gravity of the defendant's conduct. The Model Penal Code, section 210.2, includes within murder those reckless killings which manifest 'extreme indifference to the value of human life'. Scots law treats as murder killings with 'wicked recklessness', a phrase which directs courts to evaluate the circumstances of the killing.[26] Both the Model Penal Code test and the Scots test may be reduced to circularity, however, for when one asks how extreme or how wicked the recklessness should be, the only possible answer is: 'wicked or extreme enough to justify the stigma of a murder conviction'. Admittedly, the Model Penal Code does contain a list of circumstances which may amount to extreme indifference, which assists the courts and increases the predictability of verdicts in a way that Scots law does not, but the essence of both approaches is that there is no precise way of describing those non-intentional killings which are as heinous as intentional killings. Their protagonists argue that the law of murder is so important socially that derogation from the principle of maximum certainty should be allowed in favour of more accurate labelling by the courts. Opponents argue that the principle of maximum certainty is needed here specifically to reduce

---

[23] See the formulations listed by HL Select Committee on Murder etc., App 5.
[24] [1975] AC 55.   [25] [1985] AC 905.
[26] For discussion, see G. H. Gordon, *Criminal Law of Scotland* (2nd edn, 1978), 736–41.

the risk of verdicts based on discriminatory or irrelevant factors, such as distaste for the defendant's background, allegiance, or other activities, not least because the mandatory life sentence is at issue.[27]

A third, more precise formulation derives from the recommendations of the Criminal Law Revision Committee in 1980, namely, that a killing should be classified as murder in those situations where there is an intention to cause serious injury coupled with awareness of the risk of death.[28] Neither an intention to cause serious injury nor recklessness as to death should be sufficient on its own, but together they restrict one another, producing a test which both satisfies the criterion of certainty and marks out some heinous but non-intended killings.

A fourth approach, adopted by English law until 1957 and still in force in many American jurisdictions, is some form of felony-murder rule: anyone who kills during the course of a felony (or, more restrictively, a serious crime of violence) or while resisting arrest should be convicted of murder.[29] Thus stated, there is no reference to the defendant's intention or awareness of the risks: the fact that D has chosen to commit rape, robbery, or another serious offence, and has caused death thereby, is held to constitute sufficient moral grounds for placing the killing in the highest category. Plainly, this is a form of constructive criminal liability: the murder conviction is constructed out of the ingredients of a lesser offence. Presumably the justification is that D has already crossed a high moral/social threshold in choosing to commit such a serious offence, and should therefore be held liable for whatever consequences ensue, however unforeseeable they may be. The objections would be reduced if awareness of the risk of death was also required: in other words, if the test were the commission of a serious offence of violence plus recklessness as to death. The effect of that test would be to pick out those reckless killings which occurred when D had already manifested substantial moral and legal culpability, and to classify them as murder.

Four alternative approaches have been described, and many others could be listed. The point is that the traditional concepts of intention and recklessness do not, of themselves, appear to be sufficiently well focussed to mark out those killings which are the most heinous. The law must resort

---

[27] This is particularly relevant to killings resulting from the activities of terrorist, or allegedly terrorist, groups. HL Select Committee on Murder etc., para 76, concluded that 'It is neither satisfactory nor desirable to distort [general principles] in order to deal with the reckless terrorist and other "wickedly" reckless killers, who will, in any event, be liable to imprisonment for life [i.e. for manslaughter].'

[28] 14th Report (1980), para 31, adopted in the draft Criminal Code cl 54(1), and supported by HL Select Committee on Murder etc., para 71.

[29] For discussion of American formulations, see G. P. Fletcher, *Rethinking Criminal Law* (1978), Ch 4.4., and P. Robinson, *Fundamentals of Criminal Law*, Ch 5, 2.19.

to some kind of moral and social evaluation of conduct if it is to identify and separate out the gravest killings. Many people might think that a person who causes death while using an unlawfully held firearm or explosive ought to be convicted or murder because there is, generally speaking, no excuse for using such dangerous equipment. Some of the people thus covered would be armed robbers, others would be terrorists. The armed robber might say that he had no intention of using the firearm, that he carried it with him simply to frighten the victim, and that it went off accidentally:[30] if the jury believes that, should he be convicted of murder? The terrorist might say that he gave sufficient warning of the bomb for the area to be cleared, and that it was unforeseeable that a deaf person should remain on the premises and be killed in the explosion, which was intended only to cause damage. If the jury believes that, should he be convicted of murder?[31] It is possible that juries would prefer to convict of murder in such cases so as to register their abhorrence of the defendant's activities in general. If so, this would suggest a social preference for regarding killings of these kinds as among the worst, because of the circumstances in which they occur (which may include considerations of distaste and prejudice), rather than because of the defendant's awareness of the possible consequences. However, both the Royal Commission on Capital Punishment, which reviewed the matter thoroughly in the early 1950s, and later law reform committees have accorded preference to the 'general principle' that 'persons ought not to be punished for consequences of their acts which they did not intend or foresee'.[32] A conviction for manslaughter would be sufficient to mark the gravity of those cases in which D was not aware of the risk of death, and the court would have ample discretion in sentencing to reflect the blameworthiness of D's conduct. Thus matters which were excluded at the liability stage would filter back into court at the sentencing stage, and it would be important to ensure that there were proper safeguards for fact-finding and guidelines for sentencing in these cases.

To summarize: the existing English law classifies as murder those killings where there was an intent to kill or an intent to cause grievous bodily harm. The reason for distinguishing between murder and manslaughter must be to identify and to label the most heinous killings as murder. It has been questioned whether English law succeeds in this: should the law depart from the principle of correspondence and admit an intent to do grievous bodily harm? Should the law go beyond intention as

[30] In *Donnelly* [1989] Crim LR 739, the defence was that D used the gun to strike V on the head, and never intended to fire the gun, but it went off accidentally.
[31] See the discussion by Lord Goff, 'The Mental Element in Murder', and Glanville Williams, 'The *Mens Rea* for Murder: Leave it Alone' (1989) 105 LQR, 387.
[32] Report of the Royal Commission on Capital Punishment (1953, Cmd 8932), para 76.

purpose, and include cases of foresight of virtual certainty? Is English law right in excluding all situational and motivational factors from the murder/manslaughter borderline? There can be no *absolutely right* place in which to draw the line, but the severe consequences of being convicted of murder (especially so long as the mandatory life sentence remains) make a powerful case for scrupulous adherence to the principles of correspondence, maximum certainty, and fair labelling.

7.4 DEFINING MURDER: THE EXCLUSIONARY QUESTION

Even in a legal system which has the narrowest of definitions of murder—say, premeditated intention to kill—there would still be an argument that some cases which fulfil that criterion should have their label reduced from murder to manslaughter because of extenuating circumstances. Just as the discussion of the *inclusionary* aspect of the definition of murder travelled beyond the concepts of intent and recklessness, so the discussion of the *exclusionary* aspect (i.e. which killings fulfilling the definition should be classified as manslaughter rather that murder?) must consider the circumstances in which the killing took place and other matters bearing on the culpability of the killer.

(a) The Mandatory Penalty

It is sometimes argued that the main reason for allowing such matters as provocation to reduce murder to manslaughter is to avoid the mandatory penalty for murder. Thus, if the mandatory penalty were abolished, it would be sufficient to take account of provocation when sentencing for murder.[33] This argument neglects the symbolic function of the labels applied by the law and by courts to criminal conduct. Surely it is possible that a jury might decline to convict of murder a person who intentionally killed under gross provocation, even though they knew that the judge could give a lenient sentence, because they wished to signify the reduction in the defendant's culpability by using the less stigmatic label of manslaughter. Since there are two offences—and particularly in jurisdictions where the are three or more grades of homicide—surely it is right and proper to use the lesser offence to mark significant differences in culpability. This may be seen as an application of the principle of fair labelling. When a jury takes the decision between the two grades of homicide, this may also assist the judge in sentencing, and help the public to understand the sentence imposed.[34] However, this reasoning is not

---

[33] See the proposals discussed by C. Wells, 'The Death Penalty for Provocation?' [1978] Crim LR 662.

[34] This was the view taken by HL Select Committee on Murder etc., paras 80–3, agreeing with the CLRC, 14th Report (1980), para 76.

accepted in English law for non-homicide offences, and provocation is not generally allowed to reduce a more serious offence to a less serious offence—probably for reasons associated with the policy of efficient administration (see Chapter 3.5(t)), which the significance of death is thought to outweigh in homicide cases.

(b) Manslaughter upon Provocation

Provoked killings are generally thought to be less heinous than unprovoked killings, and provocation has long been accepted as a ground for reducing to manslaughter a killing which would otherwise fulfil the definition of murder.[35] From time to time there are cases where the provocation is so gross and so strong that a court imposes a very short prison sentence or even a suspended sentence for the manslaughter—typically, cases where a wife, son, or daughter kills a persistently bullying husband or father—and such cases raise the more general question of whether provocation should ever be a complete defence to homicide or to other crimes. That question was discussed in Chapter 6.5. The issues here are whether provocation should remain a qualified defence to murder, and, if so, how far it should extend.

In English law the doctrine of provocation has two main elements, which emerge from the Homicide Act 1957, section 3:

Where on a charge of murder there is evidence on which the jury can find that the person charged was provoked (whether by things done or by things said or by both together) to lose his self-control, the question whether the provocation was enough to make a reasonable man do as he did shall be left to be determined by the jury; and in determining that question the jury shall take into account everything both done and said according to the effect which, in their opinion, it would have on a reasonable man.

This is not intended to be a complete statement of the law on provocation, but it settles the form of the two main requirements. First, there must be evidence that D was provoked to lose self-control and kill. Secondly, the jury must decide whether the provocation was enough to make a reasonable man do as D did. D is not required to prove any of this: in a murder trial, if there is sufficient evidence that D was provoked to lose self-control, the judge is bound to leave provocation to the jury, even if D has not raised this defence,[36] and the burden of disproving it beyond reasonable doubt lies upon the prosecution.

(i) *The Subjective Requirement.* The first requirement of the qualified defence of provocation is predominantly subjective—evidence that D was

---

[35] See generally J. Horder, *Provocation and Responsibility* (1992).
[36] See *Cambridge* (1994) 99 Cr App R 142, following a line of decisions since *Hopper* [1915] 2 KB 431.

provoked to lose self-control and kill. This requirement contributes to the excusing element in the provocation doctrine, the idea being that a person who has lost self-control is less responsible for subsequent conduct. Without this element, there would be no way of excluding planned revenge killings, and the argument is that they should be excluded from the defence because a person who coolly plans a response to an affront or a wrong ought to ensure that the response conforms with the law. The genuinely provoked killer, on the other hand, is in such a disturbed state of mind that such calculation does not occur.

How disturbed does that state of mind have to be? The concept of loss of self-control has received little close attention from lawyers.[37] Such phrases as 'loss of temper' or 'heat of passion' are treated as useful synonyms, for which angry or apparently uncontrolled reactions may be treated as evidence. For centuries courts have distinguished between revenge killings and others where D was not 'the master of his own understanding' and where there had not been 'time for the blood to cool and for reason to resume its seat'.[38] In *Duffy* (1949),[39] Devlin J. appeared to draw the same contrast but phrased the law's requirement as 'a sudden and temporary loss of self-control'. The word 'sudden', which does not appear in the Homicide Act 1957, section 3, narrows the effect of the doctrine considerably. It suggests that the retaliation must occur fairly quickly after the provocation has been received, rather than asking whether D was still in a disturbed state at the time of the killing. Clearly the length of time that elapses is of evidential importance. Thus in *Ibrams* (1982)[40] there had been considerable ill-treatment and violence by the deceased towards D and his girlfriend, and this led them eventually to plan and carry out a night-time raid on the deceased's flat, during which they attacked and killed him. The Court of Appeal confirmed that the defence of provocation was unavailable: even if D had lost his self-control at the time, it was hardly a sudden and temporary response to an act of the deceased, who was asleep when D struck him. Differing slightly from *Ibrams* are the many cases where 'cumulative provocation' has been directed towards D over a period of time, and then some minor act sparks off the loss of self-control and killing.[41] In cases of this kind the last act of the provoker, even though minor in itself, may be placed in the context of the previous provocation,

---

[37] Compare P. Brett, 'The Physiology of Provocation' [1970] Crim LR 634, with Ashworth, 'The Doctrine of Provocation' [1976] CLJ 303–6.

[38] *Hayward* (1833) 6 C&P 157, per Tindal CJ For detailed discussion of the historical development, see Horder, *Provocation and Responsibility*, Chs 4 and 5.

[39] [1949] 1 All ER 932.   [40] (1982) 74 Cr App R 154.

[41] See M. Wasik, 'Cumulative Provocation and Domestic Killing' [1982] Crim LR 29, and J. Horder, 'Sex, Violence and Sentencing in Domestic Provocation Cases' [1989] Crim LR 546.

and may itself be treated as sufficient to show that the loss of self-control was 'sudden and temporary'. However, in *Thornton* (1992),[42] the Court of Appeal applied the 'sudden and temporary' test strictly so as to withhold the defence of provocation from a woman who had suffered years of physical abuse and had just been threatened again, on the ground that she had first gone to the kitchen and sharpened the carving knife. The killing was therefore not 'sudden', even though it is doubtful whether (in the words of Tindal CJ in *Hayward*) 'reason had resumed its seat'. The greater indulgence shown to some defendants re-emerged in *Pearson* (1992),[43] where the Court of Appeal allowed the qualified defence of provocation in a case where D took a sledgehammer, asked his brother to switch the light on, and then bludgeoned their sleeping father to death. The trial judge's direction to the jury to take account of the father's violent bullying over the preceding years was not questioned. A final example of this judicial ambivalence is *Ahluwalia* (1992),[44] where Lord Taylor CJ held that the subjective requirement 'would not as a matter of law be negatived simply because of the delayed reaction'. In each case it would be a matter of evidence.

The development of the law relating to the subjective requirement is most unsatisfactory. First, the idea that loss of self-control must be 'sudden' arrived in *Duffy* without support from the precedents, and perhaps without realizing that it is not the only alternative to allowing all revenge killings. Secondly, some judges plainly do not accept the suddenness test, as *Pearson* and many sentencing cases demonstrate. Thirdly, the suddenness test is objectionable in principle because it favours those with quick tempers over others with a slow-burning temperament (but no less intensity of emotion), it favours the strong who can retaliate immediately over the weak who dare not, and it often favours men over women. It is one thing to exclude cases like *Ibrams* from the defence—the gap of some five days between provocation and killing savours of considered revenge; it is another thing to exclude defendants with slow-burning temperaments, who do not react straight away to an insult or wrong, but go away and then react after minutes or even hours of festering anger. Why should a court be prevented from hearing and acting on evidence that, despite the lapse of a few hours, a defendant's temperament was such that it is fair to say that he or she was provoked to lose self-control, and that it was not calculated revenge?

The Homicide Act requires that D was *provoked* to lose self-control: this is wide enough to include things said or done by persons other than the

---

[42] [1992] 1 All ER 306.   [43] [1992] Crim LR 193.
[44] [1992] 4 All ER 889, on which see D. Nicholson and R. Sanghvi, 'Battered Women and Provocation: the Implications of *Ahluwalia*' [1993] Crim LR 728.

deceased,[45] and acts done against persons other than D (e.g. where D is provoked to kill someone who has just committed a sexual offence upon D's son, daughter, wife, etc.). But the word 'provoked' does seem to require a human act rather than a natural event which leads D to lose self-control. Thus, in *Doughty* (1986),[46] the crying of a 17-day-old child was held to be sufficient to fall within the requirement (even though such an infant is not aware of the significance of what he or she is doing), whereas someone who loses self-control after a storm or explosion has destroyed his property would be outside the requirement. These restrictions show that the subjective element is merely preparing the ground for the objective element; it is not part of a broader defence of emotional pressure of the kind discussed in Chapter 6.5(c).

(ii) *The Objective Condition.* Once the court is satisfied that there is evidence that D was provoked to lose self-control, it must go on to consider the second requirement: was the provocation enough to make a reasonable man do as D did? This is English law's rather clumsy attempt to reflect the element of partial justification in the doctrine of provocation. The clumsiness is evident in the standard of 'the reasonable man', an anthropomorphic (and male) standard which might be taken to suggest a paragon of virtue if it were not for the context of partially exculpating a killing by such a person. The underlying point is that it is not every act of provocation which should be allowed as the basis of this qualified defence, but only those serious enough to unbalance the behaviour of a person with reasonable self-control. As we saw in Chapter 6.5, the elements of partial excuse and partial justification should both be required.

In earlier times the judge would rule on the sufficiency of the provocation, and the result of this was rather narrow and legalistic categories of sufficiency (e.g. violence or finding a spouse in adultery was enough, but words or a confession of adultery were not). The Homicide Act 1957 deprived judges of their power to give authoritative rulings on the sufficiency of provocation, and the question must now be left to the jury in the terms of section 3 (set out above), even where the judge is strongly of the opinion that there is no basis for the defence.[47] There appears to be no time limit on the matters to be considered, so that not only the final act but a whole course of conduct may be taken into account.[48] This should ensure that those cases of cumulative provocation that satisfy the subjective requirement (see above) are seen and judged in their proper context.

---

[45] *Davies* [1975] QB 691.

[46] (1986) 83 Cr App R 319, on which see J. Horder, 'The Problem of Provocative Children' [1987] Crim LR 654.

[47] E.g., *Doughty*, ibid., and *Cambridge* (1994) 99 Cr App R 142.

[48] *Burke* [1987] Crim LR 336, *Pearson* [1992] Crim LR 193, *Ahluwalia* [1992] 4 All ER 889.

How has the 'reasonable man' test been interpreted by the courts? In *Bedder* v *DPP* (1954),[49] D, who was sexually impotent, was taunted about his impotence and kicked in the groin by a prostitute with whom he had been attempting to have sexual intercourse, whereupon he lost self-control and killed her. The House of Lords held that the jury should consider the effect of these acts on a reasonable man, without regard to the sexual impotence. The court seemed to be afraid that if it allowed the jury to take account of one characteristic, such as sexual impotence, then it would be illogical to direct them not to take account of another characteristic, such as irascibility or bad temper. It is no less illogical, however, to ask a jury to consider the effect of taunts of impotence on a reasonable person who is *not* impotent, and the *Bedder* approach was overruled by the House of Lords in *DPP* v *Camplin* (1978).[50] A court should now consider the effect of the provocation on 'a person having the power of self-control to be expected of an ordinary person of the sex and age of the accused, but in other respects sharing such of the accused's characteristics as they think would affect the gravity of the provocation to him'.

This test demonstrates that the illogicality alleged in *Bedder* does not exist: some characteristics of each individual defendant must be considered by the jury in assessing the gravity of the provocation, but the level of self-control must be kept fairly constant. In fact the standard of self-control was probably lowered in *Camplin* itself, since D was only 15 years old and the House of Lords held that the standard of a reasonable boy of 15 was appropriate. More significant is *Newell* (1980),[51] where the Court of Appeal developed the *Camplin* test in two ways. First, it held that only permanent characteristics such as race, ethnic origin, disability and, probably, religion may be taken into account, whereas transient conditions such as intoxication and exhaustion may not. Secondly, it held that for a characteristic to be relevant the provocation must have been aimed at it. These requirements were adopted from New Zealand, whose Court of Appeal has now abandoned the second one.[52] The English Court of Appeal has, however, further tightened the *Newell* criteria in *Morhall* (1993).[53]

In this case D, a glue-sniffing addict, was taunted about his glue-sniffing by the victim, whom D subsequently stabbed. The Court of Appeal held that the test is not simply that of a person with the self-control of a reasonable man. The word 'reasonable' has another function, which is to prevent defendants from relying on self-induced addictions or (it seems)

[49] [1954] 2 All ER 201.   [50] [1978] AC 705.
[51] (1980) 71 Cr App R 331, on which see A. T. H. Smith (1980) 43 MLR, 441.
[52] *McCarthy* [1992] 2 NZ LR 550, reinterpreting *McGregor* [1962] NZ LR 1069.
[53] (1994) 98 Cr App R 108, on which see J. C. Smith [1993] Crim LR 958.

other discreditable characteristics. This is a corruption of the function of the objective requirement, which is to keep constant the standard of self-control while allowing juries to assess the intensity of the effect of the provocation on an ordinary person with these characteristics. It must be recalled that provocation is not a complete defence. The underlying idea is that citizens are expected to keep control over their behaviour, but that in circumstances where even a person with normal self-control might be provoked, the offence may be reduced from murder to manslaughter.

This is not to deny that there ought to be some normative element in the reasonableness standard. It was the rule at common law that lawful acts could not amount to provocation, and this is surely right. On this view, a jury might justifiably decline to extend the qualified defence to a person who was provoked to kill a police officer by an arrest that was perfectly lawful. However, it seems that a judge cannot withdraw the issue from the jury in these circumstances or direct them not to take account of lawful acts or of self-induced provocation: the jury must decide.[54] Jeremy Horder puts the case of a racist who believes that 'it is the gravest of insults for a coloured person to speak to a white man unless spoken to first', and asks whether the test of a reasonable person with those racist views would not be 'an outrageous compromise of society's commitment to racial tolerance'.[55] The dilemma is how to strive to reflect proper social values without having unduly high expectations of ordinary people who develop characteristics that are thought to be discreditable (e.g. glue-sniffing, previous convictions).

What personal characteristics ought not, then, to be taken into account? Bad temper should be left out of account for that is plainly inconsistent with the standard of reasonable self-control. Mental imbalance should also be excluded, since that may also be inconsistent with reasonable self-control, and the defence of diminished responsibility is more appropriate.[56] It is probably right to leave intoxication outside the test: if the provocation was not enough to lead an ordinary sober person to do as D did, then the cause of the loss of self-control is assumed to be the intoxication rather than the provocation.[57] A difficult but crucial issue is whether the 'reasonable man' test should take account of whether a female defendant was suffering from battered woman syndrome. In *Ahluwalia* no evidence that D suffered from the syndrome had been adduced, but Lord

---

[54] *Johnson* (1989) 89 Cr App R 148.

[55] Horder, *Provocation and Responsibility*, 144.

[56] For discussion of the possibility that provocation and diminished responsibility couldapply to the same case, see below, 7.4(e).

[57] For discussion of the 'causal' approach to provocation, see Horder, *Provocation and Responsibility*, 113–27.

Taylor CJ commented that, if it had been, 'different considerations may have applied'.[58] In so far as this suggests that BWS should be worked into the reasonableness test, it creates two problems. One is that the provocation is unlikely to have been directed at this condition: this means either that this 'directed at' requirement is dispensable, as proposed above, or that the courts are handing down inconsistent decisions. The second problem is that a test of 'the reasonable woman suffering from battered woman syndrome' will, at the very least, need to be put to a jury only after it has heard expert evidence on the typical causes and effects of this condition.

There remain doubts about the appropriateness of the qualified defence of provocation for battered women. In *Ahluwalia* itself the case was treated as one of diminished responsibility at the re-trial, perhaps reflecting an understandable belief that BWS is more a form of mental abnormality. However, this approach has been criticized. Donald Nicholson and Rohit Sanghvi are among those who have argued that the haste to stereotype women and to medicalize their condition must be resisted. Instead, we should recognize that the existing law of provocation is biassed towards men, being founded on the idea of a swift violent response to a supposed insult. There is no recognition of the long periods of violence and abuse suffered by many of the women who become defendants, no recognition of their relative powerlessness compared with the man, and no recognition of the countervailing impulses often felt by women to keep a family together. They are sceptical of a test for provocation based on 'the reasonable woman suffering from BWS', and propose the test of 'a reasonable person in the shoes of the defendant, having suffered the same level of violence and abuse'.[59] Others have gone further and have proposed that some battered women should be able to rely on self-defence to secure a complete acquittal. Thus Aileen McColgan argues that there may be cases in which a battered woman should not call evidence of battered woman syndrome but should rather construct a case out of her fear of imminent serious injury, the fact that she was in her home and therefore should not be expected to retreat, and the right of pre-emptive strike.[60] To succeed on self-defence would require the courts to re-think their concept of 'imminent harm' and to adapt the notion of 'reasonableness of response' to accord with the circumstances of a history of abuse within the home.[61] The Supreme Court of Canada has shown a

[58] [1992] 4 All ER at 898.
[59] Nicholson and Sanghvi, 'Battered Women and Provocation', 738. See also, e.g. Horder, *Provocation and Responsibility*, 186–94, and sources cited there.
[60] A. McGolgan, 'In Defence of Battered Women who Kill' (1993) 13 Oxford JLS, 508; see also C. Wells, 'Battered Woman Syndrome and Defences to Homicide: where now?' (1994) 14 Legal Studies, 266.   [61] See Ch 4.7 above.

willingness to move in this direction,[62] and for some defendants this would be a fair outcome.

(iii) *A Further Requirement?* At common law the famous case of *Mancini* v *DPP* (1942)[63] held that the retaliation must bear a reasonable relationship to the provocation. The idea was that only an extremely grave provocation ought to mitigate a killing with a deadly weapon, whereas a lesser provocation might be allowed to mitigate other killings. This rule seemed to be modelled on the proportionality requirement in self-defence, and was criticized as quite unsuitable for cases of provocation, where loss of self-control intervenes between the provocation and the retaliation. Is it not both illogical and unreasonable to require a person who has lost self-control to ensure, none the less, that his response is not disproportionate? This counter-argument has been given some recognition by the courts, in that the 'reasonable relationship rule' is no longer a rule of law.[64] But traces of it remain: the Homicide Act 1957, section 3, contains the words 'do as he did', and the model direction in *Camplin* requires the judge to ask the jury not merely whether the reasonable man would be provoked to lose self-control, but also 'whether he would react to the provocation as the accused did'.[65] The precise meaning of this formulation is unclear: does it mean 'lose self-control and kill', or 'lose self-control and kill in the way D did'? The second alternative ought to be ruled out on the ground that acts done after loss of self-control should not be measured. However, in *Clarke* (1991)[66] D had strangled the victim and had then electrocuted her: the defence argued that death was probably caused by the strangulation and that therefore the jury should have been instructed to ignore the electrocution, which was probably performed on a corpse. The Court of Appeal was unmoved by this argument, observing that 'there are no limiting words to the phrase "do as he did", such as "in causing the death of the accused".' This is an indiscriminate approach, which fails to draw a proper distinction between the provoked act which causes death and D's subsequent behaviour.

(iv) *Provocation and Murder.* The two key questions here are: first, whether provocation ought to reduce murder to manslaughter; and, secondly, how wide the qualified defence should be. The answer to the first question is closely related to issues of stigma and labelling. It was argued above that it is unacceptable to claim that the mandatory penalty for murder supplies the *raison d'être* for the qualified defence of provocation:

---

[62] *Lavallee* v *R* [1990] 1 SCR 852, on which see the essay by C. Boyle in R. Hinch (ed), *Readings in Critical Criminology* (1994), 383.   [63] [1942] AC 1.

[64] *Brown* [1972] QB 229.   [65] *Camplin* [1978] AC 705, 718.

[66] [1991] Crim LR 383; see J. C. Smith, ibid., 384, and Horder, *Provocation and Responsibility*, 147–50.

the label 'murder' should be reserved for the most heinous of killings, and most people would accept that provoked killings are not in this group.[67]

The second question, the proper ambit of the provocation defence, is more troublesome. It would be possible to absorb provocation into a wider notion of 'extreme emotional disturbance', as the American Model Penal Code does, so that the key to mitigation would be the extent of the defendant's psychological disturbance at the time of the killing rather than the reasons for it.[68] In effect, this would be to merge provocation into a widened doctrine of diminished responsibility. One advantage would be that 'extreme emotional disturbance' would eliminate the tendency of the existing law of provocation to favour male rather than female defendants and would 'medicalize' women no more than men. One disadvantage would be that this would submerge the element of partial justification that has been so central to the provocation defence. If the explanation for the violent outburst lies in something which understandably led a person to be so angry as to lose self-control, then this supplies an added reason for mitigating the offence, and ought to be recognized in the label applied.[69] Indeed, one might argue that adoption of the qualified defence of 'extreme emotional disturbance' would transfer many issues from the liability stage (since contested cases might be rare, as they are when diminished responsibility is pleaded)[70] to the sentencing stage. Courts would still have to ascertain the basis for the qualified defence, in order to determine whether a medical disposal, a custodial sentence, or some other order ought to follow. This would place considerable weight on fact-finding processes prior to sentencing.[71] In addition, attention ought to be paid to the wide divergence between sentences for manslaughter on provocation, which are generally no longer than eight years and usually around four to seven years, and sentences for other offences—such as armed robberies of post offices and betting shops—which result in sentences in the same range even where serious injury is not caused. Is life being valued too cheaply, and provocation being accorded too great a mitigating effect?[72]

(c) Duress as a Qualified Defence

In 1987 the House of Lords in *Howe*[73] held that duress should not be available as a defence to murder. Their Lordships devoted little of their speeches to the possibility of allowing duress to function as a qualified defence to murder, reducing the crime to manslaughter and leaving the

---

[67] Cf. M. Goode, 'The Abolition of Provocation', in S. Yeo (ed), *Partial Excuses to Murder* (1991).   [68] *Model Penal Code*, s 210.3.1(b); see above, Ch 6.5(c).
[69] See the discussion in Ch 6.5 above.   [70] See below, 7.4(e).
[71] See the discussion in Ch 6.9 above.
[72] For discussion, see A. Ashworth, *Sentencing and Criminal Justice* (2nd ed, 1995, Ch 4.4(d).   [73] [1987] AC 417, above, p. 199.

judge to pass an appropriate sentence. This would preserve the principle that a person who is threatened must be prepared to undergo heroic self-sacrifice rather than take the life of a third party, just as the provocation doctrine preserves the principle that citizens ought always to retain self-control. However, the House of Lords preferred to see a conviction for murder in these cases, with the use of executive discretion to secure an early release from the mandatory sentence of life imprisonment for offenders who killed when under duress, and thus appear to have reduced culpability.[74] This is surely an unsatisfactory way of dealing with these cases, where the degree of emotional disturbance is likely to be no less than that involved in most provocation cases. The normative requirements of the defence of duress (discussed in detail in Chapter 6.4) ensure that it is restricted to dire and realistic threats which a citizen of reasonable firmness could not be expected to resist. The degree of emotional pressure on the defendant can almost be taken for granted in these cases. 'If murder is to be reserved for those homicides which are most deserving of stigma, this does not seem to be one of them.'[75] If duress is not to be allowed as a complete defence to murder, the reduction in culpability should surely be reflected by reducing the conviction to manslaughter.

(d) Killings by the Use of Excessive Force on a Justified Occasion

Just as it seems strange and unnecessary that the law should have to choose between duress as a complete defence to murder, and duress as no defence at all, so it seems strange and unnecessary that a killing which narrowly fails to come within the requirement of self-defence or other justifiable force should then be classified as murder.[76]

The Australian case of McKay (1957)[77] involved a chicken farmer who, when he found an intruder stealing chickens, shot at him five times, killing him. The farmer's defence was that he intended only to wound the thief, and thought he was entitled to do so. In another Australian case, Howe (1958),[78] D was attacked by a man, in an isolated place, whom he believed was trying to force him to commit sodomy. D took a gun and, fearing that this stronger man would renew his attack, shot and killed him. In both cases it was held that the alternative of a manslaughter verdict ought to be left to the jury where the occasion justified action in self-defence, or to prevent a crime, or to apprehend an offender, but where the defendant acted beyond the necessity of the occasion. Three reasons may be advanced

---

[74] See particularly the speeches of Lord Hailsham and Lord Griffiths.

[75] HL Select Committee on Murder etc., para 88; the remark referred to cases of excessive defence, but its force is surely general.

[76] For discussion, see the essays in Part III of Yeo, *Partial Excuses to Murder*.

[77] [1957] VR 560.   [78] (1958) 100 CLR 448.

for labelling these cases as manslaughter rather than murder: first, there is the presence of an element of legal justification; second, the defendant's purpose was a lawful one; and third, an element of emotional disturbance or instinctive reaction may go some way towards explaining the over-reaction.

The Australian initiative was rejected both by the Privy Council and the English courts,[79] largely on the grounds that the common law precedents were not compelling, that the full defence of self-defence should be applied indulgently in favour of those who use such force as they instinctively think necessary, and that the doctrine of provocation might be used to accommodate other cases. The Criminal Law Revision Committee disagreed, recommending that a verdict of manslaughter should be possible where the use of some force was justified by the occasion and where D honestly believed that the force he used was reasonable in the circumstances.[80] History then took a strange twist, for in *Zecevic v DPP* (1987)[81] the Australian High Court denounced the doctrine of excessive force as too complicated for juries and removed it from Australian law.

The question came before the House of Lords in *Clegg* (1995)[82], where a soldier in Northern Ireland had been convicted of murder as a result of shooting at a car which drove through a checkpoint. The House upheld the conviction and stated that the introduction of a doctrine of excessive defence to reduce murder to manslaughter was a matter for the legislature, not for the courts. The House seemed sympathetic towards the argument that those who kill by using *excessive* force on an occasion which justified the use of *some* force should be recognised as less culpable than the ordinary run of murderers. There was some suggestion that the question is linked with that of the mandatory sentence for murder, but that overlooks the principle of fair labelling (see Chapter 3.5(s)). It is assumed here that juries and others do attach considerable importance to the label when it is a question of homicide, and therefore that the excessive use of force in self-defence is a matter which is properly reflected by a separate qualified defence, rather than being left to sentencing (which means executive discretion, if the mandatory penalty for murder remains) or forced artificially into the doctrine of provocation (when there may be no real evidence of loss of self-control). The problem encountered in Australia, of the doctrine being too complicated for juries, was the result of a six-stage

[79] See *Palmer R* [1971] AC 814, and *McInnnes* (1971) 55 Cr App R 551.
[80] 14th Report (1980) para 288.   [81] (1987) 61 ALJR 375
[82] [1995] 2 WLR 80; see also Ch 3.4(g) above.

direction which the courts developed; surely the essence of the doctrine can be conveyed more simply than that, and its thrust retained.[83]

(e) Manslaughter by Reason of Diminished Responsibility[84]

Of the qualified defences to murder in English law, diminished responsibility is the most frequently used. Roughly speaking, there are each year around 80 convictions for manslaughter on grounds of diminished responsibility compared with some 200 murder convictions. The precise number of provocation cases is not known, since the verdict is simply manslaughter. Diminished responsibility was only introduced into English law in 1957, in response to long-standing dissatisfaction with the insanity defence. Insanity was, and still is, a complete defence to crime, as we saw in Chapter 6.2, but its confines are narrow, and on a murder charge a verdict of not guilty by reason of insanity still results in indefinite committal to mental hospital.[85] Diminished responsibility has a wider ambit, but its effect is merely to reduce murder to manslaughter, giving the judge discretion on sentencing which may result in a prison sentence.

The wording with which the Homicide Act 1957 introduced diminished responsibility is rather unsatisfactory, but judges, counsel, doctors, and juries have approached it with a compassionate pragmatism rather than with the rarefied verbal analysis too frequently encountered in English criminal law. Section 2(1) of the 1957 Act reads:

Where a person kills or is party to the killing of another, he shall not be convicted of murder if he was suffering from such abnormality of mind (whether arising from a condition of arrested or retarded development of mind or any inherent causes or induced by disease or injury) as substantially impaired his mental responsibility in doing or being a party to the killing.

The mainstay of section 2 is a wide concept of 'abnormality of mind', interpreted in the leading case of *Byrne* (1960)[86] as 'wide enough to cover the mind's activities in all its aspects', including 'the ability to exercise will-power and to control physical acts' in accordance with rational judgment. This makes it clear that the test is not purely cognitive, as it is

---

[83] Cf. cl 59 of the draft Criminal Code with the complexity of the Australian position revealed in *Zecevic* (ibid.) and discussed by D. J. Lanham, 'Death of a Qualified Defence?' (1988) 104 LQR, 239.

[84] For detailed discussion, see R. D. Mackay, *Mental Condition Defences in Criminal Law* (1995), Ch 4.

[85] This was left unaltered by the Criminal Procedure (Insanity and Unfitness to Plead) Act 1991; cf. Ch 6.2 above.　　　　　　　　　　　　　　　　　　　　　[86] [1960] 2 QB 396.

for M'Naghten insanity, and that it extends to so-called irresistible impulse.

The words in brackets in section 2(1) specify three ways in which the abnormality of mind may be found to arise if it is to fall within diminished responsibility. 'Arrested or retarded development of mind' includes the categories of mental impairment and severe mental impairment. 'Any inherent causes' seems wide enough to cover virtually all cases in which the mental disorder does not have a clear external cause. Mental abnormality 'induced by disease or injury' refers to organic mental disorders, including disease of the brain. These distinctions emerge from the Court of Appeal's judgment in *Sanderson* (1994),[87] a case in which there was a conflict of psychiatric evidence. Both psychiatrists concluded that D suffered from paranoid psychosis. The prosecution psychiatrist stated that the abnormality of mind arose from taking cocaine. The defence psychiatrist stated that it arose from a childhood characterized by violent abuse and drug-taking since he was 11, an 'inherent cause' perhaps exacerbated by later drug abuse. Reducing D's conviction from murder to manslaughter, the Court held that a jury should only be directed on the part of section 2(1) that is relevant in the case—i.e. no reference to 'arrested or retarded development' was necessary here—and it went on to suggest that the phrase 'any inherent cause' would cover functional mental disorders, while 'induced by disease or injury' applies to organic disorders.

Two further requirements must be satisfied before a case is brought within section 2(1), and the burden of proof lies on D as it does for insanity. First, D must show that the abnormality of mind 'substantially impaired' his mental responsibility. This is plainly a question of degree for the jury in those cases which are contested. In practice, some 80 per cent of diminished responsibility defences are accepted by the prosecution, and only in around 13 per cent of cases does the prosecution contest the defence evidence and thus require the jury to apply section 2.[88] Finally, it has often been observed that the wording of section 2(1) is clumsy when it refers to 'impairing mental responsibility'. It should refer to the substantial impairment of D's capacity, which then results in reduced culpability that is reflected in a reduction of liability from murder to manslaughter.[89]

One class of case where diminished responsibility is quite frequently contested is where alcohol or drugs are involved. Where the evidence is that D is suffering from alcoholism, the Court of Appeal has held that this can be recognized as an abnormality of mind arising from disease or injury

---

[87] (1994) 98 Cr App R 325.
[88] See the study by Suzanne Dell, *Murder into Manslaughter* (1984), 25–7.
[89] Griew, 'The Future of Diminished Responsibility' [1988] Crim LR 75.

(to the brain). However, in *Tandy* (1988)[90] the Court of Appeal added that, for a defence of diminished responsibility to succeed on this ground, D must also establish that the first drink on the day of the killing was involuntary. This is an extremely demanding test, manifesting deep judicial suspicion of any defence based on alcohol or drugs, and it is hardly appropriate when the question is one of reducing murder to manslaughter rather than a complete acquittal. Where the medical evidence is that D was suffering from an abnormality of mind and had taken drink or drugs on the day in question, the judicial approach has been different but equally restrictive. In *Gittens* (1984)[91] the Court of Appeal held that a jury should be directed to disregard the effects of the alcohol or drugs and to decide whether the combined effect of any abnormalities of mind falling within section 2(1) was substantially to impair D's responsibility. This hypothetical test is difficult to satisfy and probably difficult to apply. It was repeated in *Egan* (1992),[92] although in that case the abnormality of mind was mental impairment or subnormality which, as an 'arrested or retarded state of mind', was a permanent condition not related to D's powers of control. Since section 2(1) does not require proof that the abnormality of mind resulted in the killing, but merely that D was suffering from it at the time of the killing, *Egan* may be wrongly decided.[93]

In some cases defendants run the two qualified defences of provocation and diminished responsibility in tandem. These will be cases where there is evidence of abnormality of mind falling within section 2(1), combined with some evidence that D was provoked to lose self-control and kill.[94] In theory the two qualified defences seem incompatible. Provocation depends on whether a reasonable man would have provoked to do as he did, and we have seen that the concept of the reasonable man has been interpreted restrictively so as to exclude defendants with abnormal temperaments.[95] Despite this theoretical incompatibility, courts do allow defences advanced on this joint basis, although the widely publicized case of *Thornton* (1992)[96] shows the possible pitfalls of this.[97]

What is the practical effect of a successful section 2 defence? In the three years from 1990–92 there were some 184 such cases, of which just over half were dealt with by a hospital order under the Mental Health Act 1983 (with

---

[90] (1988) 87 Cr App R 45; see also *Inseal* [1992] Crim LR 35.
[91] (1984) 79 Cr App R 272, on which see J. C. Smith [1984] Crim LR 553.
[92] [1992] 4 All ER 470.
[93] G. R. Sullivan, 'Intoxicants and Diminished Responsibility' [1994] Crim LR 156.
[94] R. D. Mackay, 'Pleading Provocation and Diminished Responsibility Together' [1988] Crim LR 411.   [95] See 7.4(b) above.   [96] (1993) 96 Cr App R 112.
[97] Cf. *Ahluwalia* (1993) 96 Cr App R 133, discussed above, 6.4(b), where the defences at the original trial were lack of intent and provocation, but one reason for allowing her appeal was fresh evidence of diminished responsibility.

or without restrictions). 12 per cent received life imprisonment, 16 per cent were given determinate prison sentences of 4–10 years, 8 per cent were given prison sentences below four years, and 12 per cent were given probation orders (with or without a condition of psychiatric treatment). These figures show the diversity of the cases dealt with under section 2, and they also represent a significant shift from policy in the 1960s, when around 70 per cent of diminished responsibility offenders were given hospital orders. The decline in hospital orders and the rise of prison sentences are traceable formally to the practice of modern psychiatrists of recommending fewer hospital orders, and in reality to the more restrictive policy on admission to special hospitals being pursued by the Department of Health, and also to the higher proportion of defendants who are declared to have 'recovered' by the time of the trial. No hospital order will be made where the defendant is said to have recovered, and the courts often feel it necessary to impose a prison sentence in such cases. Delays before trial can therefore affect the result, for a defendant who is committed to hospital and recovers there would usually be released back into the community fairly swiftly.

Should the qualified defence of diminished responsibility be retained? In answering this question, one has to contend with two muddles in English law: a general muddle about mental disorder and criminal responsibility, and a specific muddle about murder and manslaughter. The general muddle was discussed in Chapter 6.2(c): in principle, a person whose conduct was caused by mental disorder should not be liable to criminal conviction at all, but in practice the narrow and antiquated defence of insanity is rarely invoked in England (a handful of cases each year), and the courts normally proceed to conviction and then select a medical disposal where appropriate. The muddle could, and should, be cleared by introducing a broader mental disorder defence, along the lines recommended by the Butler Committee in 1975.[98] If such a defence were available in murder cases—and the consequences of a successful plea would be to give the court a limited discretion as to the order to be made— the case for a separate doctrine of diminished responsibility would be weak. However, some of the cases now brought within section 2 result in prison sentences, and the courts might be reluctant to accept a verdict that made any punitive disposal impossible.

The second muddle concerns murder and manslaughter specifically, namely that since there is no workable defence of insanity, it is often assumed that the existence of the mandatory penalty for murder is the essential reason for the section 2 defence. The Butler Committee argued

[98] For discussion, see S. Dell, 'Wanted: An Insanity Defence that Can Be used' [1983] Crim LR 341, and E. Griew, 'The Future of Diminished Responsibility' [1988] Crim LR 75.

that relatively minor mental disorders may be regarded as falling within section 2 simply because this outcome is thought to be preferable to mandatory life imprisonment. 'The medical profession is humane', commented the Butler Committee, 'and the evidence is often stretched.'[99] That may be so, but it may be suggested that as much depends on the surrounding legal rules as on the mandatory penalty. If there is no workable defence of insanity, it is surely wrong to convict a grossly disordered killer of murder when the less stigmatic offence of manslaughter is at hand. And if the law of homicide makes no special provision for mercy killings (see Chapter 7.4(h)) or for killings during extreme emotional disturbance, despite a widely held view that such cases ought to be treated as less culpable than 'ordinary' murders, this supplies a strong argument for retaining diminished responsibility as a qualified defence. The problems of definition inherent in the existing section 2 would be swept away with a broad reference to 'such mental abnormality as is a substantial enough reason to reduce his offence to manslaughter'.[100]

(f) Infanticide

This is a separate offence from manslaughter, but it is relevant here because of its close links with diminished responsibility. By the Infanticide Act 1922 Parliament created this new offence to mitigate the application of the law of murder to mothers who killed their new-born babies while suffering from the effects of childbirth. Doubts arose over the length of time which might elapse before the child ceased to be regarded as 'newly born', and the Infanticide Act 1938 extended the definition to the killing of a child within 12 months of its birth by a mother whose mind is disturbed either by reason of her not having fully recovered from the effect of giving birth to the child, or by reason of the effect of lactation consequent upon the birth of the child. Infanticide is a defence to murder, but it is more usual to charge infanticide in the first place. The maximum penalty remains life imprisonment, although almost all the cases each year (10–20) are dealt with non-custodially, usually by a probation order.[101] This leniency appears to be uncontroversial, even though children under 12 months old are the age-group most vulnerable to criminal homicide, with a rate of victimization four times that of the general population.[102]

We have seen that infanticide depends on a finding of 'mental disturbance'—not clinical mental disorder—resulting either from the effect of giving birth or from the effect of lactation. Three interconnected

---

[99] Report of the Committee on Mentally Abnormal Offenders (1975, Cmnd 6244), para 19.4. [100] Law Com No. 177, draft Criminal Code, cl 56(1).
[101] See the decisions in *Sainsbury* and *Lewis* [1990] Crim LR 348.
[102] D. Maier-Katkin and R. Ogle, 'A Rationale for Infanticide Laws' [1993] Crim LR 903.

criticisms of the law may be considered here. First, the medical basis of the Infanticide Act 1938 is now discredited: the reference to the effect of lactation is without foundation, and it is acknowledged that the social pressures consequent upon the arrival of a new child (such as financial demands, unsuitable housing, effects on family relationships) may be just as likely to lead to the mental disturbance manifest in these cases as any condition linked specifically with the event of giving birth. That is not to deny that some of the women do suffer from psychiatric disorders connected with the after-effects of giving birth.[103] However, in their evidence to the Criminal Law Revision Committee, the Royal College of Psychiatrists pressed for legal recognition of the wider social and situational factors which cause stress and mental disturbance in many cases. The Committee was equivocal on this, but recommended a formulation which would be broad enough to encompass these wider factors—'the balance of the women's mind was disturbed by reason of the effect of giving birth or circumstances consequent upon that birth'.[104]

A second criticism is that the law is gender-specific, singling out women for more lenient treatment. Some people take exception to this on the ground that it may imply that women generally have weaker characters and are less responsible for their behaviour. There is evidence that some women who have given birth do suffer from forms of mental disorder unique to this (female) condition.[105] Moreover it seems likely, from the statistical evidence, that women are treated more leniently than men if they kill their children; and so the question arises whether the critics are proposing that women be sentenced more harshly.[106] A third and related criticism is that the definition of infanticide is limited to the killing of the child most recently born, which means that when a mother in a disturbed state kills both her last-born child and another slightly older child, the one killing is infanticide and the other may be murder, whereas D's culpability is surely the same in both cases. If the essence of infanticide lies in the effects of the stresses consequent upon recent childbirth, then it is this, and not the age of the victim, which should be the basis of the law. Similarly, fathers of children may kill while overwhelmed by the stress consequent upon the arrival of a new child, and it is questionable whether they should be left outside the law of infanticide.[107]

---

[103] See the analysis by Maier-Katkin and Ogle, 'Rationale for Infanticide Laws', 905–9.

[104] 14th report (1980), paras 100–14, incorporated in the draft Criminal Code, Law Com No. 177, cl 64.

[105] Cf. Maier-Katkin and Ogle, 'Rationale for Infanticide', with K. O'Donovan, 'The Medicalisation of Infanticide' [1984] Crim LR 259.

[106] A. Wilczynski and A. Morris, 'Parents who Kill their Children' [1993] Crim LR 31.

[107] The case of *Doughty* (see above, n. 46 and accompanying text) might be an example here.

Would it not be preferable to absorb infanticide into the doctrine of diminished responsibility and allow the prosecution to charge manslaughter in such cases? This would have the advantage of removing both the restriction as to the victim, and the limitation to women, but the Criminal Law Revision Committee thought that this would lead to an effective narrowing of the scope of infanticide. There might be cases of killings by mothers burdened by 'social and emotional pressures' which would not be brought within the definition of mental disorder which would be the basis of a reformed defence of diminished responsibility.[108] There remains a difference between clinical mental disorder and the mere mental disturbance required for infanticide.[109] Of course, doctors might be prepared to stretch those definitions in order to bring such cases within diminished responsibility, but that is an unsatisfactory basis on which to reform the law, and it provides the defendant with no legal protection against a murder verdict. The Committee's solution was to persist with a separate offence of infanticide. If the defence of diminished responsibility were to be broadened, or even a qualified defence of extreme emotional disturbance adopted, this would overcome the definitional problems and any discrimination between sexes in the written law, but it would transfer considerable power to the jury and to the judge in sentencing, without any guarantees that the existing policy of leniency towards mothers who kill young children would be maintained. Is this too high a price for flexibility?

(g) Killing in Pursuance of a Suicide Pact

Section 4 of the Homicide Act 1957 provides that a person who kills another in pursuance of a suicide pact is guilty of manslaughter not murder. A suicide pact exists where two or more people, each having a settled intention of dying, reach an agreement which has as its object the death of both or all. This may be regarded as the highest expression of individual autonomy, by means of a mutual exercise of the individuals' rights of self-determination. Cases are infrequent, tending to occur in circumstances which evoke compassion rather than condemnation. The Criminal Law Revision Committee recommended that killings in pursuance of a suicide pact should be a separate offence, on the ground that the stigma and maximum penalty for manslaughter are inappropriate in these cases.[110]

Suicide and attempted suicide ceased to be a crime when the Suicide Act 1961 became law, in recognition of the right to self-determination, but there remains an offence of aiding, abetting, counselling, or procuring the

[108] CLRC 14th Report (1980), para 102.
[109] See the cases discussed by R. D. Mackay, 'The Consequences of Killing very young Children' [1993] Crim LR 21.   [110] CLRC 14th Report (1980), para 132.

suicide of another which carries a maximum penalty of 14 years' imprisonment. Many of the cases involve compassionate assistance, of the kind which may be necessary and justifiable if the right to self-determination is to have any meaning for those who are weak or bedridden (e.g. responding to a request to bring pills), but not all are like this. In *McShane* (1977)[111] a woman was convicted of an attempt to counsel her mother's suicide by encouraging her repeatedly to take an overdose, and it was shown that the mother's death would greatly alleviate the defendant's financial problems. It is for cases of this kind, where the evidence shows that there was active persuasion rather than compassionate assistance to someone already determined to commit suicide, that a substantial maximum penalty is thought necessary. For this offence and for the proposed suicide-pact offence, the Criminal Law Revision Committee (CLRC) recommended a maximum of seven years' imprisonment.[112] This grading of the offences may be seen as a compromise between the elements of compassion connected with the right to self-determination, and the need to protect the vulnerable from persuasion on such a crucial matter as the ending of life, an argument also derived from the right to self-determination.

(h) Mercy Killing

This concept has no special significance in English criminal law. Where there is a clear case of mercy killing by a doctor, he or she is likely to avoid prosecution or to benefit from Devlin J's concession to good motive in the *Adams* case.[113] The usual response to a 'genuine' case involving a non-professional defendant is that 'legal and medical consciences are stretched to bring about a verdict of manslaughter by diminished responsibility'.[114] The Criminal Law Revision Committee regarded this bending of the law as unsatisfactory, and tentatively proposed a new offence of mercy killing where a person, out of compassion, unlawfully kills another who is, or is believed by him to be, permanently helpless or in great pain. The proposal attracted strong opposition, some arguing that it might withdraw legal protection from the weak and vulnerable, others arguing that the fundamental ethical problems could not be satisfactorily resolved by legal definition. The difficulty with the counter-arguments is that the practice of 'stretching' diminished responsibility gives a *de facto* defence to mercy killers already. Thus, in Dell's sample of diminished responsibility cases there were some 10 cases with a mercy-killing element. Most of them involved 'killings committed impulsively with whatever

---

[111] (1977) 66 Cr App R 97.   [112] 14th report (1980), paras 136–7.
[113] See Ch 4.5(a) above, at n. 113.
[114] CLRC 14th Report, para 115; cf. *Cocker* [1989] Crim LR 740.

means were at hand', usually by 'men in their 60s or 70s [who] had reached breaking point under the continuing strain of looking after wives with severe mental or physical illness'.[115] In some of these cases the defendant appeared mentally normal when examined by the doctor, but the doctor was none the less willing to infer from the circumstances that there had been abnormality of mind at the time of the killing, and to write a report which brought this within section 2. Practitioners seem to accept that worthy cases of mercy killing invariably have this outcome, but this informal approach provides the defendant with no legal basis for a defence—he or she is truly at the mercy of the psychiatrists, the prosecutor, and the judge.

The House of Lords Select Committee on Medical Ethics examined the issues and decided against recommending a defence of mercy killing, largely on the ground that existing provisions are sufficiently flexible to allow appropriate outcomes to be achieved.[116] Is this 'blind eye' approach defensible? The chief difference in protection of the vulnerable between the present system and the CLRC's proposed offence is that the latter had a maximum penalty of two years' imprisonment, whereas life imprisonment is available where a defence of diminished responsibility succeeds; and the fundamental ethical problems are now swept under the carpet by a combination of a stretched diagnosis of 'abnormality of mind' and the ample judicial sentencing discretion, whereas the CLRC's proposal attempted to make the issues justiciable. If, however, the CLRC's proposal were altered so as to make mercy killing into a new qualified defence to murder, with the normal maximum sentence of life imprisonment, the central plank of the opposition to an explicit recognition of this mitigation in English law would disappear.[117]

Beneath these arguments about legal form lie the wider issues of self-determination. English law might be said to recognize a right to self-determination, inasmuch as suicide is no longer a crime, but that right does not yield a clear answer to the present difficulty. The right to self-determination might realistically be extended to cover those who desire their own death but lack the resources or the strength to accomplish it: this is a strong argument for a mercy-killing defence or offence. Yet, recognition of that extension might at the same time open up the possibility

[115] Dell, *Murder into Manslaughter*, 35–6. Figures produced by the Home Office for the HL Select Committee (next note) show that between 1982 and 1991 there were 22 homicide cases involving 'mercy killing', and a murder verdict was returned in only one.

[116] House of Lords Select Committee on Medical Ethics, Report (Session 1993–94), vol I, paras 259–260; cf. I. J. Keown, 'The Law and Practice of Euthanasia in the Netherlands' (1992) 108 LQR, 51.

[117] Such a proposal was put to the HL Select Committee on murder by the Law Commission, but the Committee made no recommendation on the subject: See HL Select Committee on Murder, etc., paras 94–100.

that vulnerable people who do not desire death, despite their suffering, might be killed by others for reasons of their own: this would subvert the right to self-determination, and is an argument against a mercy-killing defence or offence. Doctors who carry out mercy killings may be protected from liability, but such trust is not shown towards relatives and friends who assist suffering people in this way: they must run the gauntlet of a legal process which accords no formal recognition to the circumstances under which they killed.

(i) Conclusion: The Murder–Manslaughter Boundary

The basic legal distinction between murder and manslaughter lies in the mental element, but English law has now developed qualified defences to murder which mark out cases where, despite the presence of the mental element for murder, culpability is thought to be sufficiently reduced to warrant a reduction in the class of offence. Our discussion has taken a broad view of qualified defences, commenting also on some qualified defences which might be recognized but which do not feature in contemporary English law. Various reasons have been advanced for recognizing qualified defences to murder. Some regard the mandatory penalty for murder as the chief, even the sole, reason for these doctrines. It has been suggested here that the mandatory penalty is relevant but not critical. The key issues are, on the one hand, the proper legal classification of an offence which contains some exculpatory features, and, on the other, the distribution of decision-making power between the judge, the jury, and the executive. The label 'murder', and the stigma thought to accompany it, should be reserved for the most heinous group of killings; there is a well-recognized offence of manslaughter beneath murder, and this should be used for offences where the culpability is significantly lower. The mandatory penalty of life imprisonment for murder makes issues of relative culpability non-justiciable at present, since the length of imprisonment is 'determined or partly determined behind the scenes by someone who has not heard any representations by or on behalf of the prisoner on grounds which the prisoner does not know'.[118] If, on the other hand, Lord Kilbrandon's suggestion of a single offence of unlawful homicide were adopted, the crucial questions of culpability would be decided solely at the sentencing stage by the judge. The jury would have no role in this; the judge would derive no assistance from their verdict.

   What, then, should be the proper division of functions between judge and jury in homicide cases? The arguments in favour of some seven qualified defences have been considered above. Since it is possible that

---

[118] The words of Lord Lane C. J., giving evidence to the HL Select Committee on Murder etc., para 151.

more than one defence might be raised in each case, sometimes in combination with a defence of lack of intent, a system of criminal law which offers seven qualified defences to murder risks undue complication and confusion in contested cases. The merit of separate qualified defences is that they focus the evidence and the legal argument, giving the jury (in contested cases) an opportunity to assess the defence, and giving the judge fairly precise guidance on the basis for sentencing. This might be thought to ensure that each defendant is dealt with more fairly, while the risk of confusing the jury in a contested case might tend to erode that protection. One approach would be to consider amalgamating some of the defences. This is not to condone 'stretching' defences, using diminished responsibility to cover mercy killing, for example, or provocation to cover excessive defence, but rather to examine whether the defences have common rationales which can be drawn together. Three of the qualified defences discussed above have an element of justification—provocation, excessive defence, and some cases of duress. Most of the qualified defences have an element of excuse—provocation, diminished responsibility, most duress cases, infanticide, mercy killing, and suicide pacts.

One possibility would be to evolve a qualified defence of killing under extreme emotional disturbance, following the lead of the Model Penal Code. This might encompass all those qualified defences with an element of excuse in them. A provoked loss of self-control could fall within this new doctrine—as, indeed, could losses of self-control stemming from non-human sources such as a natural disaster or financial ruin. Diminished responsibility could also be accommodated, although a general defence of mental disorder remains a better way of labelling and dealing with cases of clinical mental disorder. Cases now treated as infanticide often involve extreme emotional disturbance, as do mercy killings, suicide pacts, and cases of duress. One advantage of this amalgamation might be that there would be less potential for the jury to become confused, and yet the jury would still be empowered to reduce murder to manslaughter in appropriate cases. One disadvantage of the change might be that the more precise moral distinctions currently incorporated within the law would become submerged within the sentencing discretion, where the signposts are less clear and the arguments less structured. This might be the case with provocation, for example: there may be objections to some of the distinctions now drawn by the law of provocation, but a broader defence of extreme emotional disturbance might provide for reduction of the offence in cases of loss of self-control when caring for a baby or when arrested by a police officer known to be acting lawfully, and some might feel that there are strong arguments against this.[119] However, such disadvantages could

[119] See Ashworth, 'The Doctrine of Provocation'.

be minimized by elaborating the definitions of extreme emotional disturbance so as to clarify its extent and its limitations, and by evolving sentencing guidelines which set out the major determinants of culpability. This would show respect for the principle of maximum certainty (see Chapter 3.4(i)) in this important area of the law. Yet there would undoubtedly remain a considerable amount of discretion, both for judges and juries applying the law, if the words 'sufficient to reduce the offence from murder to manslaughter' were retained, and at the sentencing stage, in response to the particular combination of factors in each case. Such a reformulated qualified defence would not encompass cases of excessive self-defence, since they may involve a genuine and unhurried misjudgment of the amount of force permissible, and so they would have to be the subject of a separate qualified defence. Fair labelling and proper scrutiny of the issues (at least in contested cases) suggest that the several separate qualified defences should be retained: are the practical arguments against this compelling?

7.5 'INVOLUNTARY MANSLAUGHTER'

The category of killings which has come to be known as involuntary manslaughter has nothing to do with involuntariness, properly so called. These are not cases where the accused has caused death while in an involuntary state.[120] These are cases where death has been caused with insufficient fault to justify labelling it as murder, but with sufficient fault for a manslaughter verdict. The word 'involuntary' is therefore used merely to distinguish these killings from ones which have the necessary intent for murder but which are reduced to manslaughter by one of the doctrines just considered, such as provocation or diminished responsibility. The legal debate in involuntary manslaughter is over the lower threshold of homicide liability—where to draw the line between manslaughter and cases of death caused by misfortune which are not serious enough to deserve a manslaughter conviction.

In practice the category of involuntary manslaughter contains a large variety of killings. As we will see, a killing in which D merely pushed a person during an argument in the street and the person fell backwards, cracking his head on the kerb and dying from a brain haemorrhage, might fall within involuntary manslaughter. The sentence for such an offence would be low, whereas a killing in which D knew there was a risk of death, but was held not to have intended death or grievous bodily harm, would also fall within involuntary manslaughter and might justify a high sentence. The offence, as now defined in English law, covers a wide spectrum of culpability which stretches up to the boundary with murder.

[120] Discussed in the context of automatism in Ch 4.2 above.

Beneath the law of involuntary manslaughter lie some deep issues of general principle. For example, the offence includes a species of constructive liability, which was criticized in Chapters 3.5(r) and 5.2(b). In none of these cases was death or grievous bodily harm intended. Can constructive liability be justified by reference to the magnitude of the harm resulting, i.e. death? Or would it be fairer to convict the harm-doer of a lesser offence, thus ignoring the chance result? Another problem is the more general one of liability for negligence: as we saw in Chapter 5.3(f), this is regarded as insufficient for liability for most serious offences, and yet it may be sufficient for manslaughter. Is it right that liability for the second most heinous crime in English law, which carries a maximum penalty of life imprisonment, should be satisfied by this relatively low grade of fault? These questions will be discussed in more detail once the elements of the offence have been outlined.

(a) Manslaughter by Unlawful and Dangerous Act

This species of involuntary manslaughter is based upon constructive liability. In broad terms, the law constructs liability out of the lesser crime which D was committing, and which happened to cause death. In fact, the courts have progressively narrowed this species of manslaughter over the last century or so:[121] there was a time when the mere commission of a tort or civil wrong sufficed as the 'unlawful act', and when there was no additional requirement of 'dangerousness' to be satisfied. What the prosecution must now prove is that D was committing a crime (not being a crime of negligence or a crime of omission), that in committing this crime he caused V's death, and that what he did when committing this crime was objectively dangerous. Let us examine each of these requirements in turn.

First, D must have been committing a crime. In many cases the crime which constitutes the 'unlawful act' will be a battery or an assault occasioning actual bodily harm, arising from a push, a punch, or a kick. The prosecution must establish that all the elements of the crime relied upon as the unlawful act were present, and this includes the mental elements of intent or recklessness in assault or battery. This point had been overlooked by the trial judge in *Lamb* (1967),[122] in assuming that an assault had taken place when two young men were joking with a revolver, without noting that fear was neither caused nor intended to be caused.[123] The point appears to have been overlooked by all the courts, including the House of Lords, in *Newbury and Jones* (1977):[124] two boys caused the death of a railman by pushing a paving stone off a railway bridge on to a train below,

---

[121] R. J. Buxton, 'By Any Unlawful Act' (1966) 82 LQR, 174.
[122] [1967] 2 QB 981.   [123] For the law on assault, see Ch 8.3(e) below.
[124] [1977] AC 500.

but none of the judges identified the precise crime which constituted the 'unlawful act'. No doubt the boys' act was a crime, and so this case does not call into question the proposition that all the elements of the crime relied upon must be established. To this extent there may be said to be a mental element required for this variety of manslaughter, but it is a manifestly low mental element compared with the death which results. Indeed, if the unlawful act is arson (criminal damage by fire), the fault element will be intention or *Caldwell* recklessness, and the latter does not require any subjective awareness on the defendant's part.[125]

The 'unlawful act' requirement also means that D must not have any defence to the crime relied upon. Intoxication would supply a defence to a crime of specific intent in this context,[126] but in most cases the prosecution will rely on a crime of basic intent or recklessness and therefore intoxication would be no defence.[127] In a case where the prosecution relies on assault or battery as the 'unlawful act' and D claims that it was a justifiable use of force, the court must be satisfied beyond reasonable doubt that the force was not justified if it is to proceed to a manslaughter conviction.[128]

There appear to be two types of crime which will not suffice as the unlawful act—crimes of negligence and crimes of omission. The reasons for excluding crimes of negligence were stated in *Andrews* v *DPP* (1937),[129] where a driver had killed a pedestrian while overtaking another car. There was little dispute that D had committed the offence of dangerous driving, but did that automatically make him guilty of manslaughter when death resulted? The House of Lords held that it did not: since the essence of dangerous driving was negligence, a driver should only be convicted of manslaughter if his driving was so bad as to amount to the gross negligence required under the second head of involuntary manslaughter (see below). Whether or not the decision was motivated by tenderness towards motorists is hard to tell, but there is certainly some logic in keeping offences of negligence out of the 'unlawful act' doctrine when a separate head of manslaughter by gross negligence exists. The logic of the second exception is less evident, and cases of omission have not always been treated differently. In *Senior* (1899)[130] a man who belonged to a religious sect called the Peculiar People refused to call a doctor to his child, who subsequently died; he was held guilty of manslaughter on the ground that he had committed an unlawful act (wilful neglect of the child) which caused death. However, this very reasoning was abjured in *Lowe* (1973),[131]

---

[125] *Goodfellow* (1986) 83 Cr App R 23.
[126] *O'Driscoll* (1977) 65 Cr App R 50.
[127] *Lipman* [1970] 1 QB 152, and generally Ch 6.3 above.
[128] *Scarlett* [1993] 4 All ER 629.   [129] [1937] AC 576.
[130] [1899] 1 QB 283.   [131] [1973] QB 702.

where D failed to ensure that medical help was summoned to his child, and it died. The Court of Appeal held that a manslaughter verdict would not necessarily follow from a conviction for wilful neglect:

if I strike a child in a manner likely to cause harm it is right that if the child dies I may be charged with manslaughter. If, however, I omit to do something with the result that it suffers injury to health which results in death, we think that a charge of manslaughter should not be an inevitable consequence, even if the omission is deliberate.

This passage suggests that the law should, and does, draw a distinction between the blameworthiness of acts and omissions, even where the omission is deliberate. Yet the connection between withholding medical aid and subsequent death is surely closer than that between striking a child once and subsequent death. The father's duty in *Senior* and in *Lowe* is manifest and incontrovertible. If the 'unlawful act' doctrine is thought sound, these cases should fall squarely within it. If the doctrine is thought unsound, it should be abolished. This distinction between acts and omissions is morally untenable.

Once it has been established that D was committing a criminal offence, the second step is to establish that this caused the death. In most cases of battery or actual bodily harm the causal connection will be plain, but cases involving drugs have presented difficulties. In *Cato* (1976)[132] the Court of Appeal was prepared to hold that the offence of possessing controlled drugs was sufficient, together with the act of injecting another with these drugs, even though it is difficult to see how mere possession (which is the offence) can cause death. In *Dalby* (1982)[133] the unlawful act was the supplying of controlled drugs to V, who then took them. The Court of Appeal quashed the manslaughter conviction, holding that the supply was insufficient as an unlawful act because it was not 'directed at' V. This attempt to narrow the ambit of 'unlawful act' manslaughter seems no longer to represent the law. It was distinguished in *Mitchell* (1983),[134] and the Court of Appeal in *Goodfellow* (1986)[135] interpreted the 'directed at' requirement as meaning only that 'there must be no fresh intervening cause between the act and the death'. As such, it adds nothing to ordinary causal principles. The question remains whether the extravagant decision in *Cato* remains good law: the judgment reads more as a response to 'drug culture' than as a balanced application of general principles.

The third requirement is that the defendant's conduct in committing the crime must have been objectively dangerous. This was seen as a slight restriction of the doctrine when it was imposed in *Church* (1966)[136], where

---

[132] [1976] 1 WLR 110.   [133] [1982] 1 WLR 425.   [134] [1983] QB 741.
[135] (1986) 83 Cr App R 23.   [136] [1966] 1 QB 59.

the court held that 'the unlawful act must be such as all sober and reasonable people would inevitably recognize must subject the other person to, at least, the risk of some harm resulting therefrom, albeit not serious harm'. The House of Lords has declined to restrict this test by requiring that D recognized the risk.[137] The test remains largely objective but not entirely so. The dangers inherent in the situation should be judged on the basis of a reasonable person in that position, endowed with D's knowledge of the surrounding circumstances. Thus an ordinary person who burgled the house of an elderly resident would realise the possible dangers as soon as the age and frailty of the householder became apparent,[138] whereas the ordinary person would not know (if D did not know) that a petrol station attendant had a weak heart.[139] However, the reasonable person does not make unreasonable mistakes, and so the mistake of D, who carelessly loaded a gun with a live cartridge thinking that it was blank, was not taken into account.[140] One element of the *Church* test—'some harm . . . albeit not serious harm'—has been construed restrictively. In *Dawson* (1985) D, wearing a mask and carrying a pickaxe handle, approached a petrol-station attendant and demanded money; D fled when the attendant pressed the alarm bell, but the attendant then suffered a heart attack and died.[141] The Court of Appeal held that the unlawful act would only be regarded as 'dangerous' if it was likely to cause physical harm, not if mere emotional shock (unaccompanied by physical harm) was foreseeable. The manslaughter conviction was quashed, partly because the trial judge had given the impression that conduct likely to produce emotional disturbance would be sufficient.

(b) Manslaughter by Gross Negligence

This second variety of 'involuntary' manslaughter has suffered no fewer changes of direction than the first. Gross negligence became well established as a head of manslaughter in the nineteenth century, and then all but disappeared from the law in the 1980s. Thus in *Finney* (1874)[142], where an attendant at a mental hospital caused the death of a patient by releasing a flow of boiling water into a bath, the test was whether he had been grossly negligent. In *Bateman* (1925),[143] where a doctor had attended the confinement of a woman who died while giving birth, the Court of Criminal Appeal held that there must be negligence over and above that which is sufficient to establish civil liability, and which shows 'such

---

[137] *DPP* v *Newbury and Jones* [1977] AC 500.
[138] *Watson* [1989] 1 WLR 684.   [139] *Dawson* (1985) 81 Cr App R 150.
[140] *Ball* [1989] Crim LR 730.
[141] (1985) 81 Cr App R 150; cf. the strange interpretation of this decision in *Ball* [1989] Crim LR 730 and in *Watson* [1989] 1 WLR 684.
[142] (1874) 12 Cox CC 625.   [143] (1925) 94 LJKB 791.

disregard for the life and safety of others' as to deserve punishment. This test was approved by the House of Lords in *Andrews* v *DPP* (1937).[144] In *Lamb* (1967)[145] two young men were joking with a gun; D pointed it at V and pulled the trigger, believing that it would not fire because neither bullet was opposite the barrel. The gun was a revolver, however, and it did fire, killing V. The Court of Appeal held that D might properly be convicted if his belief that there was no danger of the gun firing was formed in a criminally negligent way.

The beginnings of a change of direction appeared in *Stone and Dobinson* (1977),[146] where two people were convicted of manslaughter for allowing a sick relative, whom they had permitted to live in their house, to die without medical attention. The Court of Appeal's grounds for finding a duty of care in this case are scrutinized elsewhere.[147] The fault element required was expressed as recklessness, and defined thus: 'a reckless disregard of danger to the health and welfare of the infirm person. Mere inadvertence is not enough. The defendant must be proved to have been indifferent to an obvious risk of injury to health, or actually to have foreseen the risk but to have determined nevertheless to run it.' This passage contrasted 'mere inadvertence' with 'indifference to an obvious risk', perhaps fore-shadowing the change that was about to take place. In the 1980s it was the concept of recklessness, in the *Caldwell* sense,[148] that came to dominate this variety of manslaughter. Both the House of Lords in *Seymour*[149] and the Privy Council in *Kong Cheuk Kwan*[150] propounded this as the proper test, and it was widely assumed that manslaughter by gross negligence had been absorbed into and replaced by reckless manslaughter.

The House of Lords in *Adomako* (1995)[151] has now re-established manslaughter by gross negligence, and has jettisoned manslaughter by *Caldwell* recklessness. At one time it was thought that the category of 'motor manslaughter' might remain separate and subject to *Caldwell* recklessness, but Lord Mackay in *Adomako* made it clear that the House of Lords was overruling its previous decision in *Seymour*. There is now a single test for manslaughter by gross negligence, requiring the prosecution to prove: (i) that D was in breach of a duty of care towards the victim; (ii) that the breach of duty caused the victim's death; and (iii) that the breach of duty amounted to gross negligence. The first step is to find that a duty existed. Certain duty situations are well established, such as parent–child and doctor–patient. Others have been recognized in previous decisions: there are the omissions cases where D has undertaken to care for V by

---

[144] [1937] AC 576.   [145] [1967] 2 QB 981.   [146] [1977] QB 354.
[147] A. Ashworth, 'The Scope of Criminal Liability for Omissions' (1989) 105 LQR 440–5.
[148] Discussed in Ch 5.3(c) above.   [149] [1983] 1 AC 624.
[150] (1985) 82 Cr App R 18.   [151] [1995] 1 AC 171.

agreement[152] or by assumption of responsibility,[153] where D has a contractual duty to ensure safety,[154] and where D was initially responsible for creating a hazardous situation.[155] The categories of duty-situations are not closed, however. In *R v West London Coroner, ex p Gray* (1988)[156] the Divisional Court recognized that police officers have a duty of care towards persons they arrest, particularly persons who are intoxicated. In *Prentice* (1994)[157] the Court of Appeal recognized the duty of an electrician to leave the house safe for the householder who employed him. No doubt the proprietors of an activity centre would be found to have a duty towards children, and probably adults, for whom they organize activities.[158] It seems likely that the courts would also recognize more general duties of care, such as the duty of a driver towards other road users and the duty of anyone in possession of a firearm that is or may be loaded.[159]

Once it is established that there was a duty, that it was breached, and that this caused the death, there is the question of the terms in which the test of gross negligence is to be put to the jury. Lord Mackay LC in *Adomako* held that gross negligence depends:

on the seriousness of the breach of duty committed by the defendant in all the circumstances in which he was placed when it occurred and whether, having regard to the risk of death involved, the conduct of the defendant was so bad in all the circumstances as to amount in the jury's judgment to a criminal act or omission.[160]

Lord Mackay did not rule out the use of the word 'reckless' to explain the degree of negligence required, despite the fact that the recent history of that word in legal discourse should counsel caution. Lord Taylor CJ in the Court of Appeal had earlier stated that there were other types of case that might justify a finding of gross negligence, notably cases where there was actual awareness of a risk combined with indifference to it or a grossly negligent attempt to avoid it.[161] It does not seem difficult to encompass these other cases within the *Adomako* test, but one question that is raised is the nature of the risk. In *Prentice* Lord Taylor CJ referred to a 'risk of injury to health', which sets the threshold rather low for such a serious offence as manslaughter, whereas in *Adomako* Lord Mackay referred to 'the risk of death'. If such a risk was reasonably foreseeable, then the jury

---

[152] *Instan* [1893] 1 QB 450.
[153] *Stone and Dobinson* [1977] QB 354; cf. *Smith* [1979] Crim LR 251, where D had undertaken the care of his wife but she had expressed the wish to be left alone.
[154] *Pittwood* (1902) 19 TLR 37, the operator of a railway level crossing.
[155] *Miller* [1983] 2 AC 161.   [156] [1988] QB 467.
[157] [1994] QB 302; this was the case that became *Adomako* in the House of Lords, the other three defendants having their convictions quashed by the Court of Appeal.
[158] See the conviction reported in *The Times*, 9 December 1994.
[159] *Jones* (1874) 12 Cox C.C 628, *Lamb* [1967] 2 QB 981, *Gray v Barr* [1971] 2 All ER 949.
[160] [1995] 1 AC at 187.   [161] *Prentice* [1994] QB 302, at 323.

must decide whether D's conduct fell so far below the expected standard as to justify conviction for manslaughter. It has often been observed that this test, formulated in *Bateman*,[162] is circular: if the jury asks how negligent D must have been if they are to convict of manslaughter, the answer is 'so negligent as to deserve conviction for manslaughter'. In paragraph (d) we will discuss whether the standard can be made more certain. In the meantime, the decision in *Adomako* can be welcomed for returning the law of manslaughter to its pre-*Seymour* state, even though there are several dicta that may need further interpretation.

(c) Corporate Manslaughter

The general question of the criminal liability of corporations was discussed in Chapter 4.5. One particular problem in recent years has been whether a company can be convicted of manslaughter. It is not a crime for which only a prison sentence is possible (like murder), nor is it an offence peculiarly applicable to natural persons (like bigamy). Therefore, as Bingham LJ put it, there is 'no reason in principle why such a charge should not be established'.[163] No appellate court has gone further than this, but in the prosecution of P&O Ferries following the Zeebrugge ferry disaster, Turner J heard extensive argument on the point and ruled that the indictment for manslaughter could stand.[164] The Law Commission has proposed that the law of manslaughter should apply to companies no less than to individuals, the test of gross negligence being whether 'the corporation's conduct fell seriously and significantly below what could reasonably have been demanded of it in dealing with that risk'.[165]

(d) The Contours of Involuntary Manslaughter

The English law of manslaughter exhibits a tension between the significance of the harm caused and various principles of fairness such as the principles of correspondence and fair labelling. It is the resulting harm (death) which still dominates, as is evident from the fact that many forms of conduct fall within the law of manslaughter if death happens to result, whereas if death does not occur there can be no conviction of a serious offence (manslaughter by unlawful act) and in some cases no conviction of any offence (manslaughter by gross negligence). Much is made of the unique significance of human life and the need to mark out,

---

[162] (1925) 94 LJKB 791; see n. 143 above and text.
[163] *R v HM Coroner for East Kent, ex p Spooner* (1989) 88 Cr App R 10, 16.
[164] *P&O European Ferries (Dover) Ltd* (1991) 93 Cr App R 72. The prosecution failed for other reasons: see C. Wells, *Corporations and Criminal Responsibility* (1993), 68–72. An activity company, OLL Ltd, was convicted of manslaughter in 1994: *The Times*, 9 December.
[165] Law Commission Consultation Paper No. 135, *Involuntary Manslaughter* (1994), Part IV.

and to prevent, conduct which causes its loss. But does this really justify the present law of involuntary manslaughter?

It is important not to neglect the fact that some offences of manslaughter lie well above the lower boundaries of liability and fall little short of murder. There is no doubting the substantial culpability of the person who embarks on a course of conduct knowing that there is a risk of death or serious injury to another (e.g. the man who administered carbon tetrachloride to the woman in *Pike*,[166] knowing the danger of physical harm to her). The offence of murder is restricted to intent, and it would seem natural that recklessness as to the same consequences should amount to the lesser offence of manslaughter. The offence of murder breaches the principle of correspondence by requiring an intent to cause death or grievous bodily harm, and an offence of reckless manslaughter would do so too. Both the Criminal Law Revision Committee and the Law Commission, despite their criticisms of other aspects of the English law of manslaughter, argued that there is a need for a homicide offence beneath murder to encompass those who cause death when reckless as to death or serious injury.[167]

But what about the lower threshold of manslaughter, where its minimum requirements form the boundary with accidental (non-criminal) homicide? Surely, to apply the label 'manslaughter' to the conduct of a person who envisaged no more than a battery, e.g. by a single punch, is both disproportionate and unfair. It is only luck that makes the difference between the summary offence of common assault (maximum, six months' imprisonment) and the grave offence of manslaughter (maximum, life imprisonment). The manslaughter label grossly exaggerates the amount of culpability, producing an extreme form of constructive liability.[168] Statistically speaking, the risk of death from a single punch is far too remote to enter into reasonable contemplation. The present law attributes too much weight to chance: 'the offender's fault falls too far short of the unlucky result. So serious an offence as manslaughter should not be a lottery.'[169] Moreover, the existing law has become technical and uncertain, and gives rise to anomalies (e.g. a burglar who happens to cause death may fall within unlawful act manslaughter, whereas a driver who causes death through committing motoring offences may be excluded).[170] If D's conduct was not serious enough to constitute reckless manslaughter (as described in

---

[166] [1961] Crim LR 547.

[167] CLRC 14th Report (1980), paras 123–4; Law Commission Consultation Paper No. 135, paras 5.16–5.21. 'Reckless' in these formulations means advertent recklessness, not *Caldwell*.

[168] See Ch 3.5(r).   [169] CLRC 14th Report, para 120.

[170] Law Commission, ibid., paras 5.1–5.7; see A. McColgan, 'The Law Commission Consultation Document on Involuntary Manslaughter—Heralding Corporate Liability?' [1994] Crim LR 547. See also *Creighton* (1993) 105 DLR 4th 632 at 665.

the previous paragraph), and does not amount to manslaughter by gross negligence, the proper course is simply to convict D of whatever other offence he has committed and to pass sentence for that.

This assumes that manslaughter should remain capable of commission by gross negligence. Since negligence is not usually a sufficient fault element for serious offences, can this be justified? The Law Commission has argued that a justification can be found. In the first place there is the special value attached to human life and hence to the causing of death. Then there is the argument that cases of gross negligence are unlike 'unlawful act' cases in that the death is hardly an accident: it usually stems from a distinct breach of duty. The Commission accepts that an offence that steps beyond intention and advertent recklessness ought to be narrowly confined and, recognising the special significance of death, proposes that any new offence should be limited to cases where there is a risk of death (or, perhaps, of serious injury). The two-part test proposed is:

1. The accused ought reasonably to have been aware of a significant risk that his conduct could result in death or serious injury.
2. His conduct fell seriously and significantly below what could reasonably have been demanded of him in preventing that risk from occurring or in preventing the risk, once in being, from resulting in the prohibited harm.[171]

The first requirement recognizes that this is an objective test. The second requirement specifies the nature of the objective judgment. It encompasses both cases where D has created the risk (e.g. the electrician, the motorist, or transport operator) and cases where D has a duty to respond to a risk created by others (e.g. the doctor, the lifeguard). The Law Commission emphasized that the appropriate standard has two aspects. Since it refers to what could reasonably be expected *of D*, the standard will differ according to whether D is an ordinary citizen or a trained professional. It appears to leave no possibility of lowering the standard for persons suffering from some incapacity, such as learner drivers, youngsters with air rifles, etc.[172] In referring to what could be *reasonably expected*, the test encourages the court to look, not at common practice in the profession or industry, but rather at what those practices ought to be. 'The jury must retain the right to say that, where a significant risk of death or serious injury exists, the industry's practice is just not good enough.'[173] In general the Law Commission's proposed test achieves greater certainty than the direction

---

[171] Law Commission Consultation Paper No. 135, para 5.57.
[172] See the discussion of negligence in Ch 5.3(d) above.
[173] Ibid., para 5.61. Cf. the comments in para 5.62 on the possible effect of this test on the prosecution of P&O Ferries following the Zeebrugge disaster.

on gross negligence approved by the House of Lords in *Adomako*,[174] but it is fair to say that the possibility of courts judging the adequacy of safety precautions taken by companies and individuals introduces a margin of uncertainty. In formulating a test that is to apply in so many different types of situation, it seems inevitable that a degree of judgment is left to the court.

This discussion of the lower boundary of manslaughter should not neglect the possibility of prosecutions for other offences. There are various endangerment offences in English law, and there is a cluster of offences of causing death with a motor vehicle, which are now considered.

7.6 ENDANGERMENT ON THE ROADS

English law contains a number of offences which penalize the driving of a motor vehicle on a road in circumstances or in a manner which may cause harm. Five of the most serious offences of this kind may be considered here in brief terms:

1. dangerous driving, contrary to section 2 of the Road Traffic Act 1988;
2. causing death by dangerous driving, contrary to section 1 of the 1988 Act;
3. careless driving, contrary to section 3 of the 1988 Act;
4. driving with excess alcohol, contrary to section 5 of the 1988 Act; and
5. causing death by careless driving when under the influence of drink or drugs, contrary to section 3A of the 1988 Act.

Most of these provisions were substituted into the 1988 Act by the Road Traffic Act 1991, which broadly implemented the reforms recommended in the North Report.[175]

The offence of dangerous driving replaces the former offence of reckless driving and, unlike that offence, is defined in the legislation. This is a considerable step towards greater certainty in the criminal law. In outline, section 2A(1) provides that a person drives dangerously if: '(a) the way he drives falls far below what would be expected of a competent and careful driver; and (b) it would be obvious to a competent and careful driver that driving in that way would be dangerous'. Section 2A(2) adds that a person also drives dangerously if it would be obvious to a competent and careful driver that driving the vehicle in its current state would be dangerous—for example, driving an obviously defective vehicle or driving with an unsteady load.[176] Section 2A(3) defines 'dangerous' in terms of danger either of injury

---

[174] [1994] 2 All ER 79, above n. 151.

[175] Report of the Road Traffic Law Review (1988), discussed by J. R. Spencer, 'Road Traffic Law: a Review of the North Report' [1988] Crim LR 707.

[176] Cf. *Crossman* (1986) 82 Cr App R 333.

to any person or serious damage to property, and provides that any special knowledge possessed by the driver should be taken into account. The new offence of dangerous driving therefore establishes a firm objective standard, the 'competent and careful driver,' and requires conduct on the road that falls 'far below what would be expected'. The standard may therefore be higher than that of negligence in the law of tort, and is approaching the standard of gross negligence used in manslaughter. There is no concession for lack of capacity on the part of the driver: in this sense, anyone who drives on a public road does so at his or her peril.

The offence of causing death by dangerous driving replaces the former offence of causing death by reckless driving, previously linked with manslaughter.[177] The definition of dangerous driving in section 2A of the 1988 Act applies. The extra element is that D's dangerous driving must cause death, although that merely means that it must be a significant or perhaps substantial cause, and not the sole cause.[178] While the maximum penalty for dangerous driving stands at two years, the maximum for this offence was increased from five to ten years by the Criminal Justice Act 1993.

Careless driving lies further down the scale of seriousness from dangerous driving. With a fine as its maximum sentence, this offence is defined as driving 'without due care and attention, or without reasonable consideration for other persons using the road'. Once again the offence establishes a wholly objective standard, with no concession to those who are merely learning to drive.[179] The standard is that of the reasonable and prudent driver: this appears to be the same as the test of the 'competent and careful driver' adopted for dangerous driving in section 2A of the Road Traffic Act 1988, and so the difference between the two offences lies in the degree to which a particular driver fell below the required standard. Turning now to the drink-driving offences, section 5 of the 1988 Act creates the crime of driving while having an excessive proportion of alcohol in the breath, blood, or urine. The maximum punishment is six months' imprisonment. Both careless driving and driving with excess alcohol are relatively long-established crimes, but elements from them have now been drawn together to form the new offence of causing death by careless driving when under the influence of drink or drugs or having consumed excess alcohol. This offence now carries a maximum sentence of 10 years' imprisonment[180]—not high for a homicide offence, but spectacularly higher than the maxima for the two constituent offences put together. What is the reasoning behind this strange structure of offences, with its enormous premium for offences that happen to result in death?

[177] *Seymour* [1983] 2 AC 493.
[178] See above, Ch 4.6, and also *Hennigan* [1971] 3 All ER 133.
[179] *Preston JJ, ex p Lyons* [1982] Crim LR 451.
[180] Raised by s 67 of the Criminal Justice Act 1993.

The first offence of causing death by dangerous driving was introduced in 1956, largely because juries were unwilling to convict culpable motorists of such a serious-sounding offence as manslaughter. Ever since its introduction there have been those who have pointed to its 'illogicality'.[181] The difference in practice between an offence of dangerous driving (maximum penalty of 2 years) and one of causing death by dangerous driving (maximum penalty of 10 years) may simply be one of chance. Bad driving may or may not lead to an accident, depending on the chance conjunction of other factors and other people's behaviour. And an accident may lead to death (in which case the more serious offence is committed) or merely to serious injuries or to minor damage. The response to this 'illogicality'—which is, of course, the very problem with the law of involuntary manslaughter too—has varied in recent English proposals. Both the James Committee in 1976[182] and the Criminal Law Revision Committee in 1980[183] recommended the abolition of the offence of causing death by dangerous driving, thereby accepting the 'illogicality' argument. This accords with the CLRC's proposal that 'unlawful act' manslaughter should be abolished.[184] However, the North Report on road traffic law reversed this trend. The report accepted the principle that, in general, persons should be judged according to the intrinsic quality of their driving rather than its consequences, but argued that the law should depart from this in cases where death is caused and the driver's culpability is already high.[185] Public opinion was adjudged to support this, and undoubtedly there is a conflict between reflecting the degree of culpability and signalling recognition of the occurrence of the supreme harm (death). There is a well-known risk in motoring that certain kinds of driving may cause accidents, and that accidents may cause death. The rules of the road are designed not only to produce the orderly and unhampered movement of traffic, but also to protect property, safety, and lives. One who deviates so manifestly from these rules as to drive dangerously ought to realize— because the driving test requires a driver to realize—that there is a considerable risk of an accident. If an accident happens as a result of driving which falls well below the proper standard, then that may well be a case of culpable negligence even if the driver had never thought of the risk in that particular case, because the driver is presumed to know the Highway Code.

The North Report pursued these arguments further when it

---

[181] Sir Brian McKenna, 'Causing Death by Reckless or Dangerous Driving: a Suggestion' [1970] Crim LR 67.
[182] Report of the Interdepartmental Committee on the Distribution of Criminal Business between the Crown Court and the Magistrates' Courts (1975, Cmnd 6323), App K.
[183] 14th Report (1980), paras 140–8.   [184] Ibid., paras 116–23.
[185] Road Traffic Law Review (1988), Ch 6.

recommended the creation of an offence of causing death by careless driving while intoxicated. Here the divergence between the terrible consequences and D's fault seems particularly wide. Careless driving itself is such a non-serious offence that it cannot result in a prison sentence of any length. Driving with excess alcohol or while unfit through drink or drugs carries a maximum prison sentence of six months. Yet when death results, even though the intrinsic fault in D's driving is no higher, the maximum penalty is raised to 10 years. If 'public opinion' is to be the justification for this wide divergence, then it is surely appropriate to question the power of public opinion here. This is pure constructive crime: the legislature has created a serious offence, with a high maximum penalty, out of two offences that are rather low on the scale. One possible answer to this is that the two constituent offences, particularly drunk driving, ought to carry higher maxima themselves. But this would still leave a considerable gap, for which the chance occurrence of death is the only possible reason. In the law of torts this is a good reason for awarding a particular level of damages, but it does not increase the fault of D's driving, and that is what should be crucial in criminal law. This is not simply an academic point of view. It was the view of the Criminal Law Revision Committee, whose chairman (Lawton LJ) and many of whose members would have been affronted to be described as academic.

Yet the CLRC was perhaps somewhat equivocal. Firm as the Committee was in its view that the 'accident of death' should not change the label of a bad driver's offence from dangerous driving to causing death by dangerous driving, it seemed to expect that the sentence would, to some degree, reflect the result that had occurred. Current sentencing guidelines for the offence of causing death by dangerous driving recognize that the degree of fault in an offender's driving is a key issue, but also expect the judge to reflect both the fact of death and the number of deaths that happen to ensue.[186] The Court of Appeal has recognized that it is 'rather illogical . . . that a given piece of driving which causes three deaths should be punished more heavily than the identical piece of driving causing one death, or indeed causing no death at all'. The answer was said to be that 'people do regard killing three as more criminal than killing one. That is a fact of life which this court recognizes'.[187] This approach has now been applied to the new offence of causing death by careless driving while intoxicated: 'although it may be fortuitous, the fact that more than one death was caused is an aggravating feature'.[188] The Court of Appeal was

---

[186] *Boswell* (1984) 79 Cr App R 277, revised in *Attorney-General's References Nos. 14 and 24 of 1993* [1994] Crim LR 305.

[187] *Pettipher* (1989) 11 Cr App R (S) 321, per Schiemann J at 323.

[188] *Attorney-General's References Nos. 14 and 24 of 1993* [1994] Crim LR 305. Cf. the approach to careless driving itself in *Krawec* (1984) 6 Cr App R (S) 367.

responding to the lead given by Parliament, not merely in creating the new offence but also in doubling the maximum penalty to 10 years in 1993. The same approach appears likely to be adopted when sentencing for an offence of aggravated vehicle-taking which results in death, although the maximum penalty for that offence remains five years' imprisonment.[189]

There are powerful arguments against the legislature's approach both in terms of labelling offenders and in terms of sentencing them. Far too much emphasis is now placed on the occurrence of death despite the fact that these are not cases in which death is intended or knowingly risked. These are cases of negligence, to a greater (dangerous) or lesser (careless) degree. The great significance attributed to the accident of death is more appropriate to a compensation scheme than to a system of criminal law. Yet if the criminal law were to focus entirely on the intrinsic fault in a defendant's driving, it would probably come down much harder on many people who by good fortune did not cause any or much harm even though their driving fell appallingly below the required standard. Those who think it wrong that the courts should respond so readily to the 'accident of death' would equally have to harden themselves to reject the pleas of drivers who say 'at least I did no harm'. If the courts were to focus on the intrinsic fault in a defendant's driving, sentencing would become more difficult in itself and more controversial in the view of the mass media.

It will therefore be seen that many of the issues involved here are similar to those raised by the law of involuntary manslaughter, save for the fact that driving offences constitute deviations from a code of conduct on which all persons are tested before they are granted driving licences. This factor serves to distinguish driving cases from those of deaths resulting from a single punch, and also to bolster the argument that the penalties for the former should be higher than for the latter.

7.7 ENDANGERMENT IN OTHER SITUATIONS

Our discussion so far has stressed the relationship between endangerment on the roads and the detailed rules of the road, including the driving test. Some preventive rules, together with endangerment offences, can be seen in a variety of other situations, but nowhere is there such a detailed and fairly widely known set of standards as that applicable to drivers on the roads. For example, there are regulations about the storage of explosives, and the dangers of handling explosives are well known. The main thrust of the Explosives Act 1883, however, is contained in the offences of causing an explosion likely to endanger life (section 2), and the possession of explosives with intent to endanger life (section 3). The latter offence is an

---

[189] Aggravated Vehicle-Taking Act 1992, and *Ore and Tandy* [1994] Crim LR 304.

inchoate offence of a familiar kind:[190] possession with intent, in circumstances where an innocent reason for possessing explosives is fairly hard to
come by (unless the defendant is engaged in quarrying or another business
in which explosives are used). The justification for the possession offence is
preventive, and there is little difficulty in holding that a person caught in
possession of explosives with intent to endanger life has sufficiently crossed
the threshold of criminality to justify punishment. True, there may yet be
the possibility of repentance as the time for using the explosives draws
near, but the very step of taking explosives into one's possession with this
intent is culpable. As for the endangerment offence itself, two features in
section 2 of the 1883 Act stand out. One is that no actual endangerment is
required: the explosion need only have been inherently likely to endanger
life, and the offence is committed whether or not anyone's life was put in
danger. In its style of labelling, therefore, this differs from the present
driving law, with its separate offences of dangerous driving and causing
death by dangerous driving: the equivalent would be a single offence of
driving in a manner likely to endanger life. The second feature of the
offence of causing an explosion likely to endanger life is that there appears
to be no distinct fault requirement. So long as the prosecution proves that
D caused the explosion, and that the explosion was likely to endanger life,
that would suffice for conviction. Presumably the reason for this is that one
can hardly cause an explosion without realizing that one is about to do so,
and that explosions usually create danger and must be known to do
so, unless they are carefully controlled in an area away from members of
the public. However, these arguments are not particularly strong: if the
inference of fault is so great, why not comply with principle and include a
requirement of proof of fault, at least at the level of advertent
recklessness?

Further offences of endangerment may be found in the Firearms Act
1968. Section 16 contains an offence of possessing a firearm with intent to
endanger life, which corresponds to the offence under section 3 of the
Explosives Act. Again, the circumstances of the possession are likely to
raise an inference of intent, unless the possession was clearly connected
with some authorized shooting activity. There are then three possession
offences of a slightly different type. Section 18 penalizes the possession of a
firearm with intent to commit a crime or to resist arrest: this is a more
specific variation of section 16, catering for the defence that the firearm
was being carried for use in a robbery but with no intention that it would
actually be used to endanger anyone, only to frighten—that would be a
section 18 offence. Section 19 penalizes possession of a loaded firearm in a
public place, presumably in circumstances where the section 16 offence

[190] See below, Ch 11.1 and 11.9.

cannot be proved, but on the argument that the mere possession is sufficiently dangerous because accidents can happen with loaded guns, and the consequences might be life-endangering. Section 20 penalizes possession of a firearm when trespassing: again, there might be a defence to a section 16 charge if D was merely intending to shoot animals or fowl, but the gun could be turned on a human being and therefore represents a source of danger. What these firearms offences appear to amount to is a criminalization of the carrying of firearms in all but the most innocent of contexts. If the firearm is discharged and property is damaged, then an offence of criminal damage may be committed. If it is discharged and a person is injured or killed, the appropriate offence against the person can be charged. What the Firearms Act provides is a series of inchoate or preventive offences which criminalize conduct even before it has reached the stage of an attempt to commit some substantive offence. The offences do not require any endangerment at all: that is taken to be inherent in the carrying of firearms, since their potential effects are grave and the risk of accidents as well as deliberate use is well known.

Offences relating to the operation of aircraft, ships, and railways have not been prominent in the practice of English criminal law. But the law does contain such offences, and it is more a matter of prosecutors making little use of them. It is true that over the years a few railmen have been convicted of manslaughter for wrongful acts and omissions leading to fatal train crashes,[191] but there is not the natural resort to the criminal law which is now a feature of road traffic cases. In a sense, greater values are at stake in the operation of aircraft, ships, and railways, because many lives are involved, more than would normally be risked by the bad driving of a motor vehicle (although there is an important exception here in the operation of buses and coaches, which are more akin to planes, boats and trains). The extra responsibilities of mass transportation were recognized legislatively soon after the Zeebrugge ferry disaster in 1987, and ss 30 and 31 of the Merchant Shipping Act 1988 contain offences penalising the operation of an unsafe ship (maximum penalty, two years imprisonment and unlimited fine). These provisions also recognize another significant difference between the individual driving a car or a lorry and all these other forms of transport: the chain of responsibility. Both ss 30 and 31 of the 1988 Act attempt to reach charterers and managers of ships as well as owners. More generally, a company's management policies might be just as much to blame for a particular 'accident' as the actions of the driver, pilot, or captain, and the state of the law on corporate manslaughter was discussed in 7.4(c).

---

[191] E.g. *Morgan* (1990) 12 Cr App R (S) 504 (driver caused train crash at Purley killing five people and injuring 87).

It is not just the operation of systems of transport which is a source of endangerment: the actions of individuals may be designed to take advantage of the possibility of causing several deaths at once. The longest determinate prison sentence ever upheld by English courts was the sentence of 45 years' imprisonment in the case of *Hindawi* (1988),[192] a man who took his pregnant girlfriend to an airport with a bag in which he had concealed a bomb timed to destroy the aircraft and its 350 passengers in mid-flight. The offence charged was 'an attempt to place on an aircraft a device likely to destroy or damage the aircraft, contrary to the Aviation Security Act 1982'—an inchoate offence, and one worded without any express reference to the endangerment of lives. The sentence, however, was intended to reflect the attempt to kill so many people.

Injuries and deaths at work are a significant and reducible source of danger to the citizen, and the Health and Safety at Work Act 1974 provides the framework for the regulation of safety in workplaces with an offence of failing to ensure that, 'so far as is reasonably practicable', employees are not exposed to risks to their health or safety.[193] In support of that general duty is a mass of regulations relating to particular industries. For example, in the construction industry the leading statutes are the 1974 Act and the Factories Act 1961, but under those statutes are such provisions as the Construction (General Provisions) Regulations 1961, the Construction (Lifting Operations) Regulations 1961, the Construction (Health and Welfare) Regulations 1966, the Control of Substances Hazardous to Health Regulations 1988, the Construction (Head Protection) Regulations 1989, the Noise at Work Regulations 1989, the Dangerous Substances (Notification and Marking of Sites) Regulations 1990, and various European directives.[194] Technical as they are, these detailed regulations may be said to give fair warning to those engaged in the construction industry.

Other fragmentary legislation is to be found in recent years, e.g. the Safety of Sports Grounds Act 1975. However, in addition to all these specific offences of endangerment, English law does contain one fairly wide-ranging offence, and that is the aggravated offence of criminal damage. Under section 1(2) of the Criminal Damage Act 1971 it is an offence—punishable with life imprisonment—to damage property 'intending by the destruction or damage to endanger the life of another or being reckless whether the life of another would be thereby endangered'. Criminal damage itself is an offence carrying up to 10 years' imprisonment,

---

[192] (1988) 10 Cr App R(S) 104.
[193] See *Austin Rover Group Ltd* v *HM Inspector of Factories* [1990] AC 619.
[194] D. Levine, 'Health and Safety at Work: the Statutory Framework in Construction Matters' (1992) 8 Construction LJ, 10.

but this is a more serious offence—more of an offence against the person. One might well ask how important the element of criminal damage is to the rationale of the aggravated offence. One answer could be that, where the damage is caused by fire, the consequent danger to life may be similar to that created by an explosion, and the inferences may be the same: who could cause such a fire in such a place without appreciating the danger to others?

The major question raised by section 1(2) of the Criminal Damage Act is why English law does not have a general offence of endangerment. Why should the fact that D was engaged on causing damage to property at the time (even damage to D's own property) make his conduct into an offence punishable with life imprisonment when, if D were engaged in some other activity, it would not be punishable as such and would only amount to manslaughter if a death happened to result? Section 211.2 of the Model Penal Code has been enacted into the laws of many American states, providing a general endangerment offence. The offence is committed where a person recklessly engages in conduct which places another person in danger of death or serious bodily injury.[195] It does not require any result, although it does require actual danger. Its great merit is that it is not confined to particular activities, and therefore has an across-the-board application to different sources of endangerment—in effect, a preventive or inchoate version of subjectively reckless manslaughter. On the other hand, such a general offence does not fulfil the educative or 'fair warning' function of singling out situations which carry a particular risk of danger. For that reason, it would be wise to retain a special offence for road-traffic cases, and there may be merit in retaining offences with particular labels in other spheres. The chief difference between the English approach and that of the Model Penal Code is that English law has (and, under the Law Commission's proposals, will continue to have) a test of gross negligence when the result of death occurs, but no generalized preventive or inchoate offences, whereas the Model Penal Code sets a higher standard for liability (advertent recklessness) but extends it to cases where there is actual danger, even if it does not materialize.

---

[195] See below, Ch 8.3(j) and K. J. M. Smith, 'Liability for Endangerment: English *Ad Hoc* Pragmatism and American Innovation' [1983] Crim LR 127.

8

Non-Fatal Violations of the Person

8.1 VARIETIES OF PHYSICAL VIOLATION

In this chapter we shall be discussing two main forms of physical violation: the use of physical force, and sexual assaults. There may be considerable variations of degree: physical force can be anything from a mere push to a brutal beating which leaves the victim close to death, and a sexual assault may be anything from a brief touching to a gross form of sexual violation. One problem which the criminal law has to confront, therefore, when dealing with physical violation, is how to grade the seriousness of the conduct. The variations are so wide that it would contravene both the principle of fair labelling (see Chapter 3.5(s)) and the principle of maximum certainty (see Chapter 3.4(i)) if there were just a single offence of non-fatal harm and a single offence of sexual assault: this would often leave little to be decided at the trial and would transfer the effective decision to the sentencing stage. Given that it would be unsatisfactory to have a single offence, the question is how best to divide up the forms and degrees of physical violation and of sexual assault.

We shall look first at physical violation. Although many cases of sexual assault also involve significant physical violation, this is not always so, and the essence of many sexual assaults lies in their destruction of the freedom of choice in the most intimate area of personality, and in psychological damage. By considering physical violations first, this will enable us to identify more accurately the distinctive element in sexual assaults. The general term 'sexual assault' is used here to include non-consensual sexual offences: there are various forms of sexual activity which are criminal even if they are indulged in consensually by adults of sound mind, and there was a brief discussion of these in Chapter 2.6.

8.2 REPORTED PHYSICAL VIOLATIONS

Crimes of violence constitute a mere 5 per cent of all crimes reported to, and recorded by, the police. Although crimes of violence continue to increase, the British Crime Survey shows that the increase of 24 per cent between 1981 and 1991 is around half the increase for crimes in general (49 per cent).[1] Increases have tended to be lowest in the most serious forms of

[1] P. Mayhew, N. Aye Meung, and C. Mirrlees-Black, *The 1992 British Crime Survey* (1993), 99 and Table A2.4.

violent offences, and highest in the less serious offences of violence and in robbery.[2] Three-quarters of these offences of violence each year are 'cleared up'. Of the incidents uncovered in the 1992 British Crime Survey, some 20 per cent were 'domestic' assaults, involving partners, ex-partners or other household members. Nearly half of the female victims were victims in their home. This trend may in fact be more marked, since it is acknowledged that victims have been reluctant to report, and police to record, offences of violence committed in the home. Studies are beginning to uncover the true extent of so-called 'domestic' violence,[3] and many police forces have now adopted more consistent policies of recording such incidents and dealing with them as true offences of violence.[4] Some 19 per cent of violent incidents took place in the street, and a further 16 per cent in pubs and clubs, the vast majority of both involving young men.[5] It seems that the use of a weapon is important in determining the legal classification of offences (not surprisingly, since offences involving weapons may tend to have more serious consequences): some three-quarters of the serious woundings involved a weapon, whereas the proportion was only one-fifth for the less serious offences.[6]

Two particular points may be made about offences of physical violation. First, there is evidence of a strong correlation between drinking and violence: the 1992 British Crime Survey found that the victim said the offender was drunk in 4 out of 10 cases overall. It may be added, of course, that most of those who drink alcohol do not commit offences of violence thereafter.[7] But the first point remains, and means that the special rules relating to fault and intoxication, discussed in Chapter 6.3, may come into play. A second general point is that many offences of violence have consequences for the victim which extend well beyond any injury caused. There are psychological effects of fear and depression, which may significantly impair the victim's enjoyment of life long after the physical wounds have healed. Such effects are well documented in the case of female victims of 'domestic' violence,[8] but many victims of violence suffer lasting social and psychological effects stemming from the offence and from other circumstances (e.g. intimidation, long periods off work) that may follow it.[9]

[2] R. Walmsley, *Personal Violence*, Home Office Research Study No. 89 (1986), 3.
[3] E.g. S. S. M. Edwards, *Policing Domestic Violence* (1989).
[4] L. J. F. Smith, *Domestic Violence*, Home Office Research Study No. 107 (1989), Ch 7, and the Government Reply to the Third Report from the Home Affairs Committee, *Domestic Violence* (1993).   [5] Mayhew *et al.*, 'The 1992 British Crime Survey', xi–xii.
[6] Walmsley, *Personal Violence*, 8.
[7] Walmsley, *Personal Violence*, 16; cf. the perceptive study by Mary Tuck, *Drinking and Disorder: A Study of Non-Metropolitan Violence*, Home Office Research Study No. 108 (1989).   [8] Smith, *Domestic Violence*, 18–20.
[9] J. Shapland, J. Willmore, and P. Duff, *Victims in the Criminal Justice System* (1985), Ch 6, esp. at 99.

The values which underlie the offences of physical violation are not far to seek. They are the values of physical autonomy and freedom from molestation. The value of privacy is central here: the body is part of one's private identity, and, apart from any physical hurt inflicted by violence, a violent assault constitutes a challenge to one's personal identity, peace, and well-being. Yet there is another aspect of individual autonomy which comes into play: the liberty to decide for oneself the level of pain to which one subjects one's body (e.g. in sport, or for pure recreation). This raises the question of the extent to which individuals may lawfully consent to the infliction of harm or injury on their bodies, which is for discussion later.

8.3 OFFENCES OF NON-FATAL PHYSICAL VIOLATION

We have seen something of the various situations in which non-fatal physical harm might occur. How does the law classify its offences? How should it respond to these various invasions of physical integrity, a quality which is highly valued by most citizens? One approach would be to create separate offences to cover many of the situations in which violence occurs, and to single out those situations in which there is some element of aggravation, such as attacks on law-enforcement officers. This was the nineteenth-century English approach, and many such offences still survive in the Offences against the Person Act 1861 (relating, for example, to injuries caused by gunpowder, throwing corrosive fluid, failing to provide food for apprentices, setting spring guns). A second approach would be to attempt to rank the offences by reference to the degree of harm caused and the degree of fault in the person causing it. The 1861 Act also contains some offences of this kind, but, as we shall see below, its ranking is impaired by obscure terms, uncertainties in the fault requirements, and some overlapping. Thorough reform of the law is long overdue, and will be discussed in 8.3(l) below. Perhaps the most important development in practice is the drawing up, by the police and the Crown Prosecution Service, of 'Charging Standards' for the various offences against the person.[10] The expressed aim is to improve fairness to defendants, through greater uniformity of approach to charging, and to make the criminal justice system more efficient by ensuring that the appropriate charges are laid at the outset. The standards will be referred to as each offence is discussed; it is too soon to say what effect the new standards will have.

(a) Attempted Murder

If we were to construct a 'ladder' of non-fatal offences, starting with the most serious and moving down to the least serious, the offence of

[10] Crown Prosecution Service, *Charging Standards for Criminal Offences* (1994), outlined at [1994] Crim LR 777.

attempted murder should be placed at the top. There is an immediate paradox here: attempted murder may not involve the infliction of any harm at all, since a person who shoots at another and misses may still be held guilty of attempted murder. What distinguishes this offence is proof of an intent to kill, not the occurrence of any particular harm. The fault element for attempted murder is therefore high—higher than for murder, under English law, since murder may be committed by someone who merely intended to cause really serious injury and not death.[11] An intention to kill must be proved in order to convict someone of attempted murder.[12] Beyond that, all that is necessary is proof that D did something which was 'more than merely preparatory' towards the murder.[13] Although a conviction is perfectly possible where no harm results—and such a case might still be regarded as a most serious non-fatal offence, since D tried to cause death, and the subjective principles[14] confirm the high guilt—there are also cases where D's attempt to kill results in serious injury to the victim. In such cases a prosecution might be brought for attempted murder—and will succeed if the intention to kill can be proved. However, the court might not be satisfied of that 'beyond reasonable doubt', and might find that D only intended to cause grievous bodily harm. In that event, the conviction will be for the offence of causing grievous bodily harm, but both offences carry the same maximum punishment—life imprisonment.

(b) Wounding or Grievous Bodily Harm (GBH) with Intent

Section 18 of the Offences against the Person Act 1861 creates a serious offence which may be committed in a number of different ways. There are two alternative forms of conduct, and either of two forms of intent will suffice. The conduct may be either causing a wound or causing grievous bodily harm. A wound has been defined as an injury which breaks both the outer and inner skin. A bruise or a burst blood vessel in an eye would not amount to a wound,[15] but it is clear that this requirement of the offence may be fulfilled by a rather minor cut. Grievous bodily harm is much more serious, although it has never been defined with any precision and the authoritative description is 'really serious harm'.[16] The Court of Appeal has recently quashed a conviction for causing grievous bodily harm with intent by making persistent indecent telephone calls, causing psychiatric injury.[17] The Court did not decide the question whether this type of injury

---

[11] See the discussion above, Ch 7.3(c), where this is viewed as one argument against the 'gbh' rule for murder.
[12] Recently confirmed in *Fallon* [1994] Crim LR 519.
[13] This is the conduct requirement of all attempted crimes: see below, Ch 11.3(b).
[14] See above, Ch 5.2(a).   [15] *C v Eisenhower* [1984] QB 331.
[16] *DPP v Smith* [1961] AC 290.   [17] *Gelder, The Times*, 16 Dec. 1994.

could amount to grievous bodily harm, but it is arguable that the causing of severe psychiatric symptoms ought to suffice.[18] The Charging Standards state that 'when psychiatric injury is alleged, appropriate expert evidence is essential'. More broadly, the Charging Standards refer to injuries resulting in permanent disability or loss of sensory function, non-minor permanent visible disfigurement, broken or displaced limbs or bones, injuries which cause substantial loss of blood, and injuries resulting in lengthy treatment or incapacity.

Turning to the fault requirements, the one most commonly relied on in prosecutions is 'with intent to cause grievous bodily harm'. The meaning of 'intention' here is the same as outlined earlier.[19] It was observed above that most serious woundings involve the use of a weapon,[20] and that may make it easier to establish intention. Where the prosecution fails to establish intention, the offence will be reduced to the lower category, to be considered in 8.3(c), so long as recklessness is proved. But there is an alternative fault element: 'with intent to prevent the lawful apprehension or detainer of any person'. While the policy of this requirement—classifying attacks on persons engaged in law enforcement as especially serious—is perfectly understandable, one result of the wording of section 18 of the 1861 Act is that D can be convicted of this offence (with a maximum penalty of life imprisonment) if he intends to resist arrest and is merely reckless as to causing harm to the police officer.[21] There is no requirement that consequences so serious as grievous bodily harm should have been foreseen or foreseeable in this type of case,[22] and so this seems to be a stark example of constructive criminal liability.[23]

(c) Recklessly Inflicting a Wound or Grievous Bodily Harm

Section 20 of the Offences Against the Person Act 1861 creates the offence of unlawfully and maliciously wounding or inflicting grievous bodily harm. The conduct element in this offence is similar to that for the more serious offence under section 18, and the meanings of 'wound' and 'grievous bodily harm' are no different. Considerable attention has been focussed on the distinction between *causing* grievous bodily harm (section 18) and *inflicting* grievous bodily harm (section 20). Critics have long argued that it is illogical for the more serious offence to have the wider causal basis, but John Gardner has argued that it is perfectly rational to allow a wide causal basis (cause) when the fault element is narrow (intent) while restricting the

---

[18] Extending the decision in *Chan-Fook*, below, n. 38.
[19] See above, Ch 5.3(b).   [20] See above, n. 2 and accompanying text.
[21] *Morrison* (1989) 89 Cr App R 17; cf. *Fallon* [1994] Crim LR 519.
[22] The decision in *Morrison* did not clarify this; cf. *Mowatt*, below, n. 32 and accompanying text.   [23] On which, see Ch 5.2(b) above.

causal basis (inflict) when the fault element is much wider (recklessness).[24]
The exact meaning of the more restrictive word 'inflict' in section 20 is
controversial. For many years it was believed to require proof of a
sufficiently direct action by D to constitute an assault. This was held in the
leading case of *Clarence* (1888),[25] where D had communicated venereal
disease to his wife during intercourse that was held to be consensual.[26] As
she consented, there was no assault, and so there could be no 'inflicting'
within section 20. A number of other decisions overlooked this requirement: convictions were returned in *Martin* (1881)[27] for harm caused by
placing a bar across the exit to a theatre and shouting 'Fire!', and in
Cartledge v *Allen* (1973)[28] for a hand injured when a man threatened by D
ran off and smashed into a glass door, although in neither case was there a
clear assault. However, the House of Lords in *Wilson* (1984)[29] decided that
there can be an 'infliction' of grievous bodily harm without proof of an
assault. The decision is unsatisfactory in its reasoning,[30] but it may be
explained as an attempt by the judiciary to improve the workability of an
ageing legal structure.

The main difference between ss 18 and 20 lies in the fault element, and it
is a considerable difference. Section 18 requires intention. Section 20
requires recklessness, in the advertent sense of the conscious taking of an
unjustified risk.[31] The fault element in section 20 was further broadened by
the decision in *Mowatt* (1968):[32] there is no need to prove recklessness as to
wounding or grievous bodily harm, so long as the court is satisfied that D
was reckless as to some physical harm to some person, albeit of a minor
character. Not only has this unduly broad fault element been approved by
the House of Lords,[33] but any attempt to narrow it down by requiring that
D foresaw that the conduct *would* cause some minor physical harm now
seems precluded by the courts' insistence of foresight that it *might* do so.[34]
The *Mowatt* extension is another example of constructive liability, and it is
particularly inappropriate here, in so far as the law is aiming to produce a

---

[24] J. Gardner, 'Rationality and the Rule of Law in Offences against the Person' [1994]
Camb LJ 502.   [25] (1888) 22 QBD 23.
[26] For discussion of liability for transmitting diseases, see S. Bronitt, 'Spreading Disease
and the Criminal Law' [1994] Crim LR 21.   [27] (1881) 8 QBD 54.
[28] [1973] Crim LR 530.
[29] *Wilson; Jenkins* [1984] AC 242, followed by the House of Lords in *Savage, Parmenter*
[1992] 1 AC 699, and again in *Mandair* (1994) 99 Cr App R 250.
[30] The decision has important procedural as well as substantive implications: see J. C.
Smith [1983] Crim LR 37–9; Glanville Williams, 'Alternative Elements and Included
Offences' [1984] CLJ, 290.   [31] See above, Ch 5.3(c).
[32] [1968] 1 QB 421.   [33] *Savage, Parmenter* [1992] AC 699.
[34] *Mowatt* [1968] 1 QB 421, confirmed in *Rushworth* (1992) 95 Cr App R 252. This accords
with the normal definition of advertent recklessness: see Ch 5.3(c). Diplock LJ's judgment in
Mowatt also includes the phrase, 'should have foreseen', which wrongly suggests an objective
criterion. The Court of Appeal has pointed this out, but judges occasionally fall into the error.

'ladder' of offences graded in terms of relative seriousness. However, even without the *Mowatt* extension, one might ask whether the distinction between intention (section 18) and recklessness (section 20) is so wide in crimes of violence, which are often impulsive reactions to events, as to warrant the difference in maximum penalties between life imprisonment and five years' imprisonment.

(d) Aggravated Assaults

Common assault is the lowest rung of the 'ladder' of non-fatal offences, with a maximum penalty of six months' imprisonment, and it is discussed in more detail below.[35] But certain aggravated assaults are singled out by the law for higher maximum penalties, and three of them may be mentioned here. One is assault with intent to rob, which, like robbery, carries a maximum of life imprisonment;[36] it is, in effect, an offence of attempted robbery. Another aggravated offence is assault with intent to resist arrest or to prevent a lawful arrest, contrary to section 38 of the 1861 Act and carrying a maximum penalty of two years' imprisonment. The third, which is usually regarded as representing the rung of the 'ladder' below recklessly inflicting a wound or grievous bodily harm (contrary to section 20) but above common assault, is assault occasioning actual bodily harm (contrary to section 47).

The conduct element of 'actual bodily harm' has been given the wide definition of 'any hurt or injury calculated to interfere with the health or comfort of the victim' so long as it is not merely 'transient or trifling'.[37] However, in *Chan-Fook* (1994)[38] the Court of Appeal held that in most cases the words 'actual bodily harm' should be left undefined. Where there is no bodily contact it may be necessary to elaborate somewhat, but it should be made clear that any psychological effect on the victim must amount to psychiatric injury before it can fall within section 47. Merely causing a hysterical or nervous condition is no longer sufficient.[39] This is an unfortunate restriction, even if it is arguably inherent in the word 'bodily', since research shows that immediate fright and lasting fear are produced by many attacks,[40] and it is important that this be given some recognition. The Charging Standards state that section 47 should be charged where there is loss or breaking of a tooth, temporary loss of sensory function, extensive or multiple bruising, broken nose, minor fractures, minor cuts requiring

---

[35] In 8.3(e).
[36] Theft Act 1968, s 8(2); note that robbery itself (discussed in the context of property offences in Ch 9.3 below) may also be classified as an offence of violence.
[37] *Donovan* [1934] 2 KB 498.   [38] [1994] Crim LR 432.
[39] Disapproving dicta in *Miller* [1954] 2 QB 282.
[40] Shapland, Willmore, and Duff, *Victims of the Criminal Justice System*, Ch 6; M. Maguire and C. Corbett, *The Effects of Crime and the Work of Victim Support Schemes*(1987), Ch 7.

stitches, and, reflecting *Chan-Fook*, psychiatric injury which is more than fear, distress, or panic.

The fault requirement for the offence of assault occasioning actual bodily harm reveals that it is an offence of constructive liability. All that needs to be established is the fault required for common assault, i.e. intent or recklessness as to the application of some unlawful touching or use of force. This clearly breaches the principle of correspondence (above, Chapter 3.5(q)). The Court of Appeal tried to remedy this deficiency, but the House of Lords overruled them.[41] Constructive liability therefore remains: a person who risked a minor assault may be held guilty of a more serious offence if 'actual bodily harm' happened to result. Moreover, the maximum penalty for the section 47 offence is five years' imprisonment, with no apparent justification for the strange approach of making the *penalty* equivalent to the higher offence on the 'ladder' (the section 20 offence), and the *fault requirement* equivalent to the lower offence on the 'ladder' (common assault, with a maximum of six months' imprisonment).[42]

Section 51 of the Police Act 1964 contains the offence of assaulting a police officer in the execution of his or her duty. Procedurally speaking, this is not an aggravated assault, since it carries the same maximum penalty as common assault (six months' imprisonment) and is also triable summarily only. However, in practice the courts tend to impose higher sentences for assaults on the police, and it is therefore worth noting that this offence is committed even though D was unaware that he was striking a police officer. A decision by a single trial judge in 1865[43] is still regarded as authority for this proposition, but there is surely little justification for this today. The draft Criminal Code is right to require actual or reckless knowledge that the person being assaulted is a constable,[44] leaving the possibility of conviction for common assault in other cases.

(e) Common Assault

The lowest offence on the 'ladder' is what is known as common assault. Strictly speaking, the term 'assault' is used here in its generic sense, as including two separate types of offence, assault and battery. In simple terms, battery is the touching or application of unlawful force to another person, whereas assault consists of causing another person to apprehend or expect a touching or application of unlawful force. Most batteries involve an assault, and in both popular and legal language the term 'assault' is

---

[41] *Savage, Parmenter* [1992] 1 AC 699.

[42] Gardner, 'Rationality and the Rule of Law', argues that this is not irrational: someone who has chosen to assault or risk assaulting another has crossed a moral threshold and is rightly held liable if more serious consequences result.

[43] *Forbes and Webb* (1865) 10 Cox 362, *Blackburn v Bowering* [1994] 3 All E.R. 380.

[44] Law Com No. 177, cl 76; awareness that the constable is or may be acting in the execution of duty is not required.

often used generically to include batteries. However, the Divisional Court in *DPP* v *Little* (1992)[45] held not only that the two offences are separate in law but also that they are statutory offences and not, as had often been assumed, still offences at common law. Each offence is now properly charged under section 39 of the Criminal Justice Act 1988, which provides that they are triable summarily only with a maximum penalty of six months' imprisonment.

The essence of a battery is any touching or application of unlawful force to another. Examples might include a push, a kiss, touching another's hair, touching another's clothing,[46] or throwing a projectile or water which lands on another person's body. Is it right that the criminal law should extend to mere touchings, however trivial? The traditional justification is that there is no other sensible dividing line, and that this, at least, declares the law's regard for the physical integrity of citizens. As Blackstone put it: 'the law cannot draw the line between different degrees of violence, and therefore totally prohibits the first and lowest stage of it; every man's person being sacred, and no other having a right to meddle with it, in any the slightest manner'.[47] It is strange that the draft Criminal Code defines assault in terms of applying force to, or causing an impact on the body of, another.[48] Would that include or exclude stroking another's hair or clothing? Individuals have a right not to be touched if they do not wish to be touched, since the body is private. Someone who knowingly touches another without his consent violates this personal right as surely as if he had taken his property. This is most evident in cases of indecent assault, which may be committed by the least unwanted touching or stroking of one person's body by another. These are culpable acts, often regarded as being more serious than thefts of property. Should it be made clear that the offence really concerns the invasion of another's right not to be touched or violated in any way—an aspect of the right to privacy—and is not necessarily an offence of 'violence'?[49] One consequence of defining the offence so widely would be reliance on prosecutorial discretion to keep minor incidents out of court. The Charging Standards now attempt to structure that discretion, but focus more on the dividing line between section 39 and section 47. They state that 'although any injury can be classified as actual bodily harm, the appropriate charge will be contrary to section 39 where injuries amount to no more than the following—grazes,

[45] (1992) 95 Cr App R 28.
[46] *Thomas* (1985) 81 Cr App R 331 (touching the hem of a skirt and rubbing it).
[47] Blackstone, *Commentaries*, iii. 120.
[48] Law Com No. 177, cl 75; assault and battery are combined in a single offence under the code.
[49] See also Gardner, 'Rationality and the Rule of Law', and the discussion of indecent assaults, below, 8.6(c).

scratches, abrasions, minor bruising, swellings, reddening of the skin, superficial cuts, a "black eye" '.

One disputed point about the ambit of the offence of battery is whether it can be committed by the indirect application of force, such as by digging a hole into which people subsequently fall. There are longstanding judicial dicta in favour of liability in these circumstances,[50] and the decision in *DPP* v *K* (1990)[51] now supports them. In this case a schoolboy, frightened that he might be found in possession of acid that he had taken out of a laboratory, concealed it in a hot air drier. Before he could remove it, another boy used the drier and suffered burns on his face. Parker LJ held that K had 'just as truly assault[ed] the next user of the machine as if he had himself switched the machine on'.[52]

Another problem is that, if the offence is defined so as to include all touchings to which the victim does not consent, it seems difficult to exclude everyday physical contact with others. This could be resolved by assuming that all citizens impliedly consent to those touchings which are incidental to ordinary everyday life and travel; but the judicial preference seems to be to create an exception for 'all physical contact which is generally acceptable in the ordinary conduct of daily life'.[53] The cases decide that this exception extends to touching a person in order to attract attention, although there can be no exception when the person touched has made it clear that he or she does not wish to be touched again. The problem arose in *Collins* v *Wilcock* (1984),[54] where a police officer, not empowered to arrest D, touched D in order to attract her attention and then subsequently took hold of D's arm. D proceeded to scratch the police officer's arm, having previously made it clear—in colourful language—that she did not wish to talk to the police officer. The Divisional Court quashed D's conviction for assaulting a police officer in the execution of her duty, on the ground that the officer herself had assaulted D by taking hold of D's arm. The key issue here was D's obvious refusal of consent to any touching; in other cases there might be a question of whether the touching goes 'beyond generally acceptable standards of conduct'.[55] A number of decisions have suggested what appears to be an alternative approach: to ask whether D's touching was 'hostile'. This seems to be an inferior method of identifying the question of the boundaries of permissible conduct. There has been

---

[50] See *Clarence* (1888) 22 QBD 23, per Stephen and Wills JJ.

[51] (1990) 91 Cr App R 23 (reversed on other grounds by the House of Lords in *Savage, Parmenter* [1992] 1 AC 699).

[52] Ibid., at 27; although it was not mentioned, the analysis might have been linked to the principle in *Miller* [1983] 2 AC 161, above, Ch 4.4.

[53] Per Goff LJ, in *Collins* v *Willcock* (1984) 79 Cr App R 229, at 234.

[54] Ibid.   [55] Ibid., 234; cf. *Donnelly* v *Jackman* (1969) 54 Cr App R 229.

disagreement whether this requirement forms part of the criminal law,[56] but the House of Lords applied it in *Brown*[57] while emptying it of much significance.

The essence of the crime of assault, as distinct from battery, is that it involves an apprehension of an immediate touching or application of unlawful force. It is therefore possible to have a battery without an assault (e.g. where D touches V from behind), as well as an assault without a battery (e.g. where D threatens to strike V but is prevented from doing so), but most cases involve both. One disputed question is whether words alone can constitute an assault. It has long been accepted that words may negative what might otherwise be an assault, as when in the course of a quarrel D placed his hand on his sword (a potential assault) and said 'if it were not assize time, I would not take such language from you' (denying any intention to use the sword).[58] The preponderance of authority is probably that mere words, unaccompanied by any threatening conduct, cannot amount to an assault,[59] but if the point of the offence is to penalize the creation of fear of imminent attack, it is difficult to see why utterances such as 'Get out the knives' or 'Let's hit them' should be regarded more indulgently than a raised hand. Another disputed issue concerns the ambit of immediacy. In one case the Divisional Court held that assault was committed where a women was frightened by the sight of a man looking in through the window of her house,[60] although there seems to have been little suggestion that the man was threatening to apply force either immediately or at all. The decision might be explained as a pragmatic attempt to remedy the absence of an offence which penalizes such *voyeurs*. Similarly in *Logdon v DPP* (1976)[61] D showed the victim a pistol in his desk drawer and said that it was loaded, and the Divisional Court held that this was an assault even though D had not handled the gun or pointed it. Presumably the threat was thought sufficiently immediate. Also in this case, D knew that the gun was a replica and was unloaded, but his actions and words caused the victim to believe otherwise. The fact that no harm was likely is immaterial, since the essence of the offence is the causing of apprehension in the victim.[62]

---

[56] A requirement of hostility was reasserted in the civil case of *Wilson v Pringle* [1986] 2 All ER 440, although the criminal cases of *Collins v Wilcock* (1984) 79 Cr App R 229, and *Faulkner v Talbot* (1981) 74 Cr App R 1, are against it.

[57] [1993] 2 WLR 556, discussed in (f) below.

[58] *Tuberville v Savage* (1669) 1 Mod Rep 3.

[59] Cf. *Meade and Belt* (1823) 1 Lew CC 184 with *Wilson* [1955] 1 WLR 493, and the discussion by Glanville Williams, 'Assaults and Words' [1957] Crim LR 216.

[60] *Smith v Chief Superintendent of Woking Police Station* (1983) 76 Cr App R 234.

[61] [1976] Crim LR 121.

[62] Thus if the victim also believes that the gun is a toy or is unloaded, there can be no assault: see *Lamb* [1967] 2 QB 981, above, Ch 7.5(a).

What fault element is required for assault and battery? The law is now
settled that either intention or recklessness as to the respective conduct
elements is sufficient.[63] The term 'reckless' is used here in its advertent
sense, and the *Caldwell* test has no place in this part of the law.[64]

(f) Questions of Consent

In order to explain why offences of violence are regarded so seriously,
reference has been made to the values of privacy and physical integrity.
However, if individual autonomy is to be regarded as one of the
fundamental values, the question arises of whether individuals might
consent to the infliction of physical harm on themselves. The owner of
property can consent to someone destroying or damaging that property.[65]
We shall see below that consent may constitute the difference between the
sexual expression of shared love between two people and the serious
offence of rape.[66] If a person wishes to give up her or his physical integrity
in certain circumstances, or to risk it for the sake of sport or excitement,
should the criminal law allow the consent to negative what would otherwise
be a crime?

A preliminary point in answering this question, material to all crimes
where consent is relevant, is whether the absence of consent is an element
in the offence or the presence of consent is a defence. It seems more
sensible to adopt the former alternative in relation to sexual offences—it
would seem odd to suggest that every act of heterosexual intercourse
constitutes the whole conduct element of rape, to which the consent of the
'victim' then provides a defence.[67] The same ought surely to be true of
touchings between lovers, whether or not they might be labelled
'indecent'. Thus battery might be defined as any (unlawful) touching or
application of force without the consent of the person touched. The
defence would normally raise the issue of consent, where relevant, but it
should be for the prosecution to disprove it beyond reasonable doubt. The
same burden of proof is borne where the defence argue that the force was
lawful, e.g. in self-defence, but there is a significant difference between the
two doctrines. Self-defence is one of the justifications, which imply that the
conduct was right or acceptable in the circumstances.[68] Consent does not

---

[63] *Venna* [1976] QB 421.

[64] *Spratt* (1990) 91 Cr App R 362, overruling *DPP* v *K* (1990) 91 Cr App R 23. *Spratt* seems
to have been confirmed by the House of Lords in *Savage, Parmenter* [1992] 1 AC 699.

[65] Criminal Damage Act 1971, except in circumstances where life is endangered: see
above, Ch 7.7.   [66] See above, 8.5(c).

[67] Likewise, it would seem strange to say that every appropriation of another's property
amounts to theft unless there is the defence that the owner consents—although, as we shall
see in Ch 9.2(a) below, the courts appear to have gone even further than that.

[68] See Ch 4.7 above.

have the same philosophical underpinning: it embodies a recognition that the autonomy of the other person ('victim') is involved, and that if that person agrees to the conduct there should be no offence. One might relate this to the idea of justification by arguing that the state regards it as right and acceptable that the criminal law should not extend to (most kinds of) conduct to which individuals freely consent; but, even if one is persuaded by that link, all it claims is that respect for individual autonomy is right, not that the conduct which then takes place is right. Some judges have fallen into the error of believing that recognition of consent implies approval of the conduct involved.[69]

The ambit of effective consent in non-fatal offences remains a matter of common law, and it has been determined by the answer of the judges to two questions. First, in what offences is the absence of consent an element? Secondly, even when it is not an element in an offence, can consent be relevant in limited circumstances? The answer to the first question has been considered in a number of cases, of which three merit attention here. In *Attorney-General's Reference (No. 1 of 1980)*,[70] the reference concerned a fight in the street between two youths to settle an argument. The essence of the Court of Appeal's answer was that 'it is not in the public interest that people should try to cause or should cause each other actual bodily harm for no good reason'. In other words, the Court held that, if the fight merely involves assault or battery, consent can be effective as a defence. But if the results constitute actual bodily harm—which, as we saw in (d) above, extends to 'any hurt or injury calculated to interfere with the health or comfort of the victim'[71]—consent cannot be a defence. The Court developed this in a rather strange way in *Boyea* (1992),[72] holding on the one hand that it was sufficient if the act was likely to do bodily harm even if D did not advert to this consequence, and on the other hand that the requirement that 'actual bodily harm' should be more than 'transient or trifling' must be interpreted in the light of the higher 'level of vigour in sexual congress which is generally acceptable' in the modern day. Both those decisions placed the dividing line between assault and battery (absence of consent an element) and actual bodily harm (presence of consent generally irrelevant). This dividing line was attacked by counsel for the appellants in *Brown* (1993),[73] but by a majority of three to two the House of Lords confirmed it. While Lords Mustill and Slynn (dissenting) took the view that the absence of consent should be an element in any offence not

---

[69] Compare the remark of Lord Lowry in *Brown* [1993] 2 WLR 556, at 588, to the effect that allowing consent would give a 'judicial imprimatur' to what the defendants had done, with the more thoughtful approach of Lord Mustill.   [70] [1981] QB 715.
[71] *Donovan* [1934] 2 KB 498.   [72] (1992) 156 JP 505.
[73] [1993] 2 WLR 556.

involving grievous bodily harm, the majority rejected this change as unwise and unworkable.[74]

In what circumstances can consent be relevant, exceptionally, in relation to harms that might otherwise amount to assault occasioning actual bodily harm or even a more serious offence? The best known modern statement of the position is that of Lord Lane CJ in *Attorney-General's Reference (No. 6 of 1980)*:

Nothing which we have said is intended to cast doubt on the accepted legality of properly conducted games and sports, lawful chastisement or correction, reasonable surgical interference, dangerous exhibitions, etc. These apparent exceptions can be justified as involving the exercise of a legal right, in the case of chastisement or correction, or as needed in the public interest, in the other cases.[75]

The closing words of this passage demonstrate the unsatisfactory basis of the prevailing judicial approach. How can it be said that dangerous exhibitions such as circus acts or trying to vault over 12 buses on a motorcycle are 'needed in the public interest'? The Supreme Court of Canada has attempted to answer this question by suggesting that stuntmen who agree to perform dare-devil activities are engaged 'in the creation of a socially valuable cultural product', with benefits 'for the good of the people involved, and often for a wider group of people as well'.[76] This is far less convincing than an approach that begins with the high value placed on individual autonomy and liberty, and then examines reasons why particular consensual activities should be criminalized by way of exception to the general principle. This would require judges to look for distinct reasons for criminalizing consensual conduct rather than taking refuge in overblown claims about what is 'needed' in the public interest.

If we examine the exceptional categories in turn, cases of the lawful chastisement of children are better treated separately.[77] Cases of reasonable surgical interference encompass all the usual medical operations, but questions may be raised about non-essential interference such as plastic surgery. Presumably such cases must be justified as expressions of the general principle of individual choice and autonomy. The exceptional category of sport has attracted many prosecutions in recent years arising from rugby and association football.[78] It is accepted that not every 'foul' committed in breach of the rules amounts to a crime, and it seems to be assumed that players do, and may lawfully, consent to physical force over and above the minimum permitted by the rules. But this does not exclude

[74] For discussion, see D. Kell, 'Social Disutility and the Law of Consent' (1994) 14 Oxford JLS 121; M. J. Allen, 'Consent and Assault' (1994) J Crim Law, 183.
[75] [1981] QB 715, at 719.
[76] *Jobidon* [1991] 2 SCR 714, cited in the discussion by Kell, 'Social Disutility and the Law of Consent'.   [77] See Ch 4.8 above.
[78] See the cases cited by S. Gardiner, 'The Law and the Sports Field' [1994] Crim LR 513.

the possibility of convictions for the use of physical force well beyond that which may reasonably be expected in a game: the borderline is vague, but presumably the courts decide particular cases by reference to the degree of violence used, its relation to the play in the game, any evidence of intent, and so on. It is sometimes thought that an intent to cause injury carries a case across the threshold into criminality, but there are examples (such as some short-pitched bowling in cricket) where this might lead to unexpected liability. Moreover, in boxing this is surely what each boxer is trying to do. However, it would be wrong to take the legality of boxing as a benchmark: as more is known about the incidence of brain damage among boxers, and as more deaths result from boxing, the question of why boxing is still lawful needs to be approached with circumspection and without preconceptions.

We now turn to two categories that were not mentioned in the passage from Lord Lane's judgment, 'horseplay' and sado-masochism. In *Jones* (1986)[79] the Court of Appeal held that schoolchildren could validly consent to 'rough and undisciplined play' so long as there was no intention to cause injury thereby. In that case boys were tossed in the air by others, and injuries were sustained when the others failed to catch them as they fell. This 'horseplay' exception was taken much further in *Aitken* (1992),[80] where officers in the RAF had been drinking and then began various mess games and pranks. At one stage they poured white spirit on the flying suits of some officers who were asleep and set fire to them, dousing the flames with no ill effects. They then seized V, who resisted only weakly, and poured white spirit on his flying suit. When they lit it, he was engulfed in flames and suffered 35 per cent burns. The Courts-Martial Appeal Court quashed their convictions for inflicting grievous bodily harm, contrary to section 20 of the 1861 Act. The reason for the decision was chiefly the judge advocate's failure to direct the jury clearly that a mistaken belief in consent would provide a defence. This implies that actual consent would have provided a defence to conduct that would otherwise amount to inflicting grievous bodily harm.

Before commenting on the 'horseplay' exception recognized in *Jones* and *Aitken*, it is appropriate to move on to the leading case on sado-masochism, *Brown* (1993).[81] Here five men were convicted of assault occasioning actual bodily harm, and three of them also of unlawful wounding. They were found to have indulged in various homosexual sado-masochistic practices in private, involving the infliction of injuries on one another but not requiring medical treatment. Having failed to persuade a majority of the House of Lords to accept that the absence of consent should be an element in actual bodily harm or unlawful wounding,[82] the appellants' second argument was that consensual sado-masochism should

---

[79] (1986) 83 Cr App R 375.　　　　　　　[80] (1992) 95 Cr App R 304.
[81] [1993] 2 WLR 556.　　[82] Discussed above, n. 72 and accompanying text.

be recognized as an exceptional category. This received a tart response from the Court of Appeal—'the satisfying of sado-masochistic libido does not come within the category of good reason'[83]—and fared no better with a majority of the House of Lords. Lord Templeman condemned the 'violence' and 'cruelty' of what the defendants had done;[84] Lord Lowry referred to their desire to 'satisfy a perverted and depraved sexual desire;'[85] Lord Jauncey was particularly exercised by the possibility that others might follow the defendants' example if their convictions were not upheld. What emerges from these three speeches is an overwhelming distaste for the defendants' activities, and a determination to describe it in language designed to produce the conclusion that it should be criminalized. However, a court that looked for good reason for regarding the conduct as lawful might well find the task more difficult than one which looked for good reason to criminalize conduct that was private, consensual, and imposed no burden on the health service. This point emerges with clarity from the dissenting speech of Lord Mustill, who argued that the case was really about the criminalization of 'private sexual relations', and that the proper question was whether the public interest required this. He, like his fellow dissentient Lord Slynn, found no compelling reasons for criminal liability.

Beneath all these particular situations there are conflicting values which claim the law's attention. Respect for the principle of individual autonomy suggests that the liberty to submit to (the risk of) injury, however serious, ought also to be respected. It is an aspect of self-determination: the point is conceded in the fact that suicide is no longer an offence, and it should therefore follow that consent to injury should negative any offence. That argument is not watertight, however, because existing law does not allow euthanasia. What distinguishes suicide from euthanasia is that the former is the individual's own act, whereas the latter involves the direct act of another. Why should this make so great a difference? It seems that problems of proof loom large here: there is a fear that the unscrupulous would manipulate any law permitting 'mercy killings', and the argument is presumably that there would be greater overall benefits to autonomy from criminalizing euthanasia (thereby protecting unwilling parties) than from legalizing it (thereby allowing willing parties to do as they wish). Some empirical support would be needed for this proposition, but it also presents a problem of conflicting rights. There are those, however, who find it objectionable that one person should ever be permitted intentionally to take the life of another.[86]

---

[83] (1992) 94 Cr App R 302, at 309.   [84] [1993] 2 WLR at 564.
[85] Ibid., at 583.
[86] A. Kenny, *Freewill and Responsibility* (1978); J. Finnis, 'Intention and Side-Effects', in R. G. Frey and C. W. Morris (eds), *Liability and Responsibility* (1991); and above, Ch 7.4(h).

If we bring the argument back to consent to non-fatal physical harm, we may recall that the predominant judicial approach has been to maintain a low threshold for consensual harm (only common assault), and to promote two criteria ('good reason', 'needed in the public interest') for recognizing exceptions that allow consensual harms. Even if the low threshold is accepted, the approach to exceptions is manifestly unsatisfactory, for at least three reasons. First, the two criteria adopted by the judges fail to explain, let alone to justify, the categories of conduct included and excluded. There has been no attempt to explain why 'horseplay' should be recognized as an exception when sado-masochism is not. Possible explanations suggest themselves—the disgust of the judges for sado-masochism, the notion that the armed forces contain 'decent people' who sometimes act in 'high spirits'—but there has been no judicial attempt to explain the different treatment. Plainly it is not a matter of the degree of injury caused: in both the 'horseplay' cases there were serious injuries requiring hospital treatment, and of course in boxing this results quite frequently, whereas in *Brown* no medical treatment was required. Even if we move away from those controversial areas, the attempt to justify daredevil stunts as 'needed in the public interest' is hardly persuasive. The justifications advanced by the judges are both incoherent in theory and incapable of embracing the categories of the common law.

The second reason why the judicial approach is unsatisfactory is its failure to recognize the values at stake. In *Brown* the House of Lords was forced to make some reference to values because the appellants based their argument partly on the right of privacy in Article 8 of the European Convention on Human Rights. While the majority's handling of this argument does not inspire confidence, the important point is that it focusses attention on recognition of the values involved. If there is any merit in the judicial formula 'for no good reason', it must be to raise the question of what ought to qualify as a 'good reason'. The answer should be that individual rights such as privacy and autonomy ought to be recognized. This is not an inevitable starting point: one could begin instead with the proposition that it is the courts' duty to maintain the moral fabric of society and to protect the 'common morality', following the approach of Lord Devlin.[87] But the argument in Chapter 2.2 was that the principle of individual autonomy ought generally to be given preference, unless there are strong arguments from welfare. On this approach, respect for individual autonomy should mean that the law does not restrict consensual harms unless distinct and well-founded reasons can be found for doing so. In relation to *Brown* this rejects the approach of the majority in favour of that of the minority: the burden of finding strong arguments should lie on

---

[87] Discussed in Ch 2.6 above, and adopted in *Brown* by Lord Templeman at [1993].

those who wish to criminalize consensual conduct, not on those who wish it to be lawful. This would mean that it is no longer necessary for judges to affirm that dare-devil stunts are 'needed in the public interest' or that 'manly sports' help to keep people fit to fight for their country if necessary.[88] Instead, the question should be whether consensual boxing and 'horseplay', in so far as they are both expressions of individual autonomy, do not go too far if there is a high risk of serious injury resulting. This leads on to the third criticism of the law, which is that there are no clear boundaries to the exceptions. The exceptional categories plainly apply to offences more serious than common assault, but no court has ever decided how far they go. If boxing is to remain lawful, then it seems that the exceptions apply even to the causing of grievous bodily harm with intent. There is scope for considerable argument about the role of paternalism and the justification for criminalizing conduct in order to protect citizens from allowing themselves to be injured seriously. The sanctity of life is also a weighty value, and preservation from serious injury may not be far behind as a principle of welfare. Justifications of this kind are already accepted in the minor offences of failing to wear a safety helmet when riding a motor cycle or failing to wear a seatbelt when travelling in a car; in relation to horseplay and some sports it may be as much a question of protecting individuals from peer pressure to join in dangerous activities—if 'protection' it be.

The Law Commission has tentatively proposed that the threshold for criminalizing consensual harm should be raised from actual bodily harm to 'injury', and that it should be irrelevant whether the harm is caused in private or in public.[89] The Commission proposes that the 'horseplay' exception should be abolished, and suggests that any intentional or reckless infliction of injury during the course of sport should be an offence, although boxing is left out of the discussion.

(g) Offences under the Public Order Act 1986

Despite its title, the Public Order Act creates three serious offences which apply whether the conduct takes place in a public or a private place.[90] Of particular relevance here are those offences which involve violence or the threat of violence. The Act provides a 'ladder' of offences, of which the most serious is riot (section 1). The essence of riot is the use of unlawful violence by one or more persons in a group of at least 12 persons who are

---

[88] Sir Michael Foster, *Crown Law* (1762), 260.

[89] Law Commission Consultation Paper No. 134, *Consent and Offences against the Person* (1994), discussed by R. Leng, [1994] Crim LR 480.

[90] For general analysis, see A. T. H. Smith, *Offences against Order* (1987), and R. Card, *Public Order: the New Law* (1986).

using or threatening violence. The maximum penalty is 10 years' imprisonment, compared with a maximum of five years for the lesser offence of violent disorder. The essence of violent disorder (section 2) is the use or threat of unlawful violence in a group of at least three persons who are using or threatening violence. Beneath violent disorder comes the crime of affray (section 3), now defined in terms of threatening or using unlawful violence towards another, and carrying a maximum of three years' imprisonment. Affray may be committed by one individual acting alone, and, like the other offences, it may be committed in a private place. The term 'violence' includes conduct intended to cause physical harm and conduct which might cause harm (such as throwing a missile towards someone); and, for the two most serious offences of riot and violent disorder, 'violence' bears an extended meaning which includes violent conduct towards property.[91]

The breadth of these offences should be noted. The extended definitions of 'violence' are one example of this, and it is apparent that only one person need use this 'violence' while the remainder (11 others for riot, two others for violent disorder) must be involved in threatening it. There is no barrier to convicting only one person of riot or violent disorder, so long as there is evidence that others were also present and threatening 'violence'.[92] Moreover, the three serious offences are under-pinned by three summary offences: causing fear or provocation of violence (section 4) and causing harassment, alarm, or distress (section 5). These summary offences do not involve violence, and the offence under section 4 is inchoate in nature.[93] A new section 4A penalises those who do cause harassment, alarm or distress and who intend to do so, with a maximum sentence of six months' imprisonment.[94]

Is it necessary to have an extra ladder of offences so closely linked with the general ladder of offences against the person? One reason might be the unsatisfactory state of the law under the Offences against the Person Act 1861; that Act fails to provide either a clear and defensible gradation of offences or any general offences of threatening violence against another.[95] A more frequent argument is that the provisions of the Public Order Act are needed to cope with 'group offending', which causes fear in ordinary citizens, and causes extra difficulties for the police and for prosecutors (in obtaining persuasive evidence). Offences committed by groups may well occasion greater fear than offences committed by individuals, and it may

---

[91] Public Order Act 1986, s 8.
[92] Cf. *Mahroof* [1989] Crim LR 72 and comment by J. C. Smith.
[93] Cf. Ch 2.1 above for discussion of the use to which s 5 has been put.
[94] Inserted by s. 154 Criminal Justice and Public Order Act 1994.
[95] It does contain the offence of threatening to kill (s 16), and common assault may be committed by threatening unlawful force, but there are no general offences: see P. Alldridge, 'Threats Offences—a Case for Reform' [1994] Crim LR 176.

also be true that groups have a tendency to do things which individuals might not do: there may be a group bravado, fuelled by peer pressure, which may lead to excesses.[96] On the other hand, the criminal law already makes some provision for such cases. The law of conspiracy is aimed at group offending, but that branch of the law is itself open to criticism.[97] The law of complicity enables the conviction of people who aid and abet others to commit offences, and spreads a fairly wide net in doing so.[98] However, the law of complicity is technical, and the 1986 Public Order Act may be seen as a response to the call for a simplified and more 'practical' scheme of offences for dealing with group disorder. Thus the Act goes a long way in smoothing the path of the prosecutor. It is indeed an element of all three offences that the conduct must be such as would cause a person of reasonable firmness, present at the scene, to fear for this personal safety; and yet it is provided, for each offence, that 'no person of reasonable firmness need actually be, or be likely to be, present at the scene'. This not only removes the need for the prosecutor to prove this element, but also removes part of the rationale for the offences. It may be 'practical' in the sense that the prosecution need not rely on members of the public to come forward and give evidence, which there is often a reluctance to do. But it is manifestly impractical from D's point of view, since it limits the opportunities for the defence to contest the issue.

The most prominent justification for having separate 'public order' offences is that group activities of this kind may, over and above the features discussed above, constitute a special threat to law enforcement and the political system. Control and stability are challenged. This argument comes close to a constitutional paradox—that people who are protesting against the fairness of the political system may find themselves convicted of serious offences if they adopt a vigorous mode of protest which may be the best one available to them because of their relative powerlessness.[99] Article 11 of the European Convention on Human Rights declares a right of peaceful assembly, and where the bona fide exercise of this right happens to lead to some form of disorder it is wrong to visit the perpetrators with severe sanctions. The counter-argument is that peaceful protest is one thing but violent protest crosses the boundaries of acceptability; the value of physical integrity is such that violence and threats of violence ought not to be downgraded simply because their origins lie in some political protest. However, it should be recalled that the two most serious offences include violence against property, so that conviction may result from mere threats against a person's property, and that various provisions in the 1986 Act dispense the prosecutor from

[96] Cf. E. Trivizas, 'Sentencing the "Football Hooligan" ' (1981) 21 BJ Criminology, 342.
[97] See below, Ch 11.5.   [98] See below, Ch 10.3.
[99] See N. Lacey, C. Wells, and D. Meure, *Reconstructing Criminal Law* (1990), 50.

proving key elements. Moreover, an argument based on control and stability fails to account for the selective concept of 'public order' that is used in these contexts,[100] evidenced again by the use of the term in the title of the Criminal Justice and Public Order Act 1994 to cover some cases of trespass on private property. An incident may be labelled as public disorder on account of the social position of those taking part rather than the intrinsic seriousness of the violence used: the 'high spirits' of the well-connected might not result in prosecution when a fight between consenting parties involving no greater harm might well.[101]

One beneficial aspect of the breadth of the new provisions is that, since they apply to conduct on private property, they might assist in reducing the different perception of abuse and violence in the family compared with street violence. However, there may be better ways of achieving that goal. The question whether the broad pro-prosecution offences in the Public Order Act can be justified or, alternatively, whether they could be justified if the general non-fatal offences were well drafted, remains pressing.

(h) Causing Illness

The Offences against the Person Act 1861 contains a number of crimes concerned with the administration of noxious or toxic substances. Section 22 penalizes the use of any overpowering drug or substance 'with intent to enable the commission of an arrestable offence' (maximum sentence of life imprisonment). Section 23 penalizes the intentional or reckless administration of any poison or noxious thing which results in danger to the victim's life or grievous bodily harm (maximum sentence of 10 years' imprisonment). Section 24 penalizes the administration of any poison or noxious thing, 'with intent to injure, aggrieve or annoy the victim' (maximum sentence of five years). This section has been applied so as to cover the administration of a drug which causes harm to the victim's metabolism by over-stimulation, if D's motive for this is malevolent rather than benevolent.[102] It has also been held that a substance may be noxious when administered in a large quantity even if it would be harmless in a smaller dose.[103]

The three offences seem to provide a 'ladder' but, once again, the distinctions between them vary considerably, with section 23 being more concerned about the result than about D's fault. Indeed, this section was applied in *Cato* (1976)[104] to the injection of heroin into a consenting adult

---

[100] Ibid., 47, 72.

[101] The occurrences in *Aitken* (above, 8.3(f)) were not characterized as a public order problem, despite the fact that the 1986 Act extends to private premises.

[102] *Hill* (1986) 83 Cr App R 386.   [103] *Marcus* (1981) 73 Cr App R 49.

[104] (1976) 62 Cr App R 41.

who was well accustomed to taking it: it was no defence, the Court of Appeal held, that the heroin might not be noxious to a particular person. It seems likely that a redefinition of the principal crimes of physical violation would cover most of these cases anyway, and the Criminal Law Revision Committee saw the need to supplement those general offences with only one special offence—administering to another, without his consent, any substance which D knows to be capable of interfering substantially with the other's bodily functions.[105]

(i) Torture

In order to comply with its international obligations, the government introduced an offence of torture in 1988. Its essence is the intentional infliction of severe pain or suffering by an official or by someone else with the consent or acquiescence of an official, and the maximum penalty is life imprisonment.[106] The offence is committed whether the pain or suffering is physical or mental, and whether it was caused by an act or an omission. In almost all cases this would amount to the general offence of wounding or causing grievous bodily harm, but the reason for the separate offence is to mark the distinctive character of official violence, and also to give the offence a wider extra-territorial effect.

(j) Neglect of Duty

Several of the offences discussed above may be committed by omission. One can cause grievous bodily harm by omission, and a person who does so intentionally in a case where a duty of care exists may be convicted under section 18 of the 1861 Act. An example would be starving a child for whom one has parental responsibility, with the result that the child suffers serious harm.[107] It is unclear whether battery can be committed by omission,[108] but it is certainly possible to convict of battery someone who accidentally causes the unlawful application of force to another and then intentionally desists from stopping that application of force. The example is the famous case in which a man unintentionally drove his car on to a police officer's foot and then declined to remove it, for a minute or two, when asked.[109]

There are also cases in which the criminal law creates special offences attached to certain duties of care, of which the parent's duty towards a child is one example. Section 1 of the Children and Young Persons Act 1933 contains an elaborately worded offence which may be termed 'child

---

[105] CLRC, 14th Report, *Offences against the Person* (1980, Cmnd 7844), 84–7, and the draft Criminal Code, Law Com No. 177, cl 73.
[106] Criminal Justice Act 1988, s 134.
[107] *Gibbins and Proctor* (1918) 13 Cr App R 134; see above, Ch 4.4.
[108] *Fagan* v *Metropolitan Police Commissioner* [1969] 1 QB 439.
[109] Ibid.

neglect'. It consists, essentially, of wilfully assaulting, ill-treating, neglecting, abandoning, or exposing a child in a manner likely to cause unnecessary suffering or injury to health. The maximum penalty for child neglect is now 10 years' imprisonment, which should be sufficient to deal with cases involving considerable fault and actually or potentially serious consequences. The Mental Health Act 1983 contains a somewhat similar offence of ill-treating or wilfully neglecting a patient in a mental hospital, which has a maximum penalty of two years' imprisonment.[110]

(k) Weapons, Motor Vehicles, and Endangerment

Most of the offences considered above involve the occurrence of physical harm plus intention or recklessness. It may also be justifiable, however, for the criminal law to penalize conduct which may lead to the causing of physical harm, particularly in situations where the conduct has little social utility or where the risk is well known. In fact, English criminal law has a wide range of such offences, of which those involving firearms, offensive weapons, motor vehicles, and other endangerment will be outlined here.

The Firearms Act 1968 sets out to control the possession of firearms and ammunition, and contains several offences. The basic offence in section 1 is that of possessing a firearm without a certificate, an offence which (despite elements of strict liability[111]) carries a maximum of three years' imprisonment. The Act also contains a number of aggravated offences of possessing a firearm with various intents, and these were set out in Chapter 7.7.[112] Lower down the scale comes the offence of possessing an offensive weapon without lawful authority or reasonable excuse, contrary to the Prevention of Crime Act 1953. This offence, with its maximum penalty of two years' imprisonment, encompasses two classes of weapon; first, an article made or adapted for use as a weapon; and secondly, any article intended for such use. Much attention has been focussed on the concept of 'reasonable excuse', where the courts have attempted to impose a fairly stringent test on persons whose reason for carrying a weapon is said to be fear of attack.[113]

Where motor vehicles are concerned, the problems are different. Although they are no less lethal than firearms in their potential to cause

---

[110] Section 127, and the decision in *Newington* [1990] Crim LR 593; cf. Offences against the Person Act 1861, s 27, an obsolete offence of neglect in providing for apprentices.

[111] See *Howells* [1977] QB 614, discussed above Ch 5.3(a).

[112] For further discussion, see P. J. Clarke and J. W. Ellis, *The Law relating to Firearms* (1981). Substantial sentences of imprisonment for offences of possessing an unlicensed shotgun with a sawn-off barrel are frequent: see e.g. *Parkinson* (1990) 12 Cr App R (S) 159, *Yates* (1994) 15 Cr App R (S) 400.

[113] See above, Ch 4.7 and, more generally, A. Ashworth, 'Liability for Carrying Offensive Weapons' [1976] Crim LR 725.

injury or even death, their considerable social utility (indeed, the dependence on much social interaction on them) indicates the need for a different approach. That approach consists of a code of good practice (The Highway Code), a requirement that drivers pass a qualifying test, and a network of offences to penalize those who deviate from proper standards. The more serious offences, from causing death by dangerous driving down to careless driving, were discussed in Chapter 7.6, and will not be taken further here. Instead, two general points will be made. The first is that the offences already discussed are underpinned by a multitude of less serious offences directed at road safety. One of these is exceeding the speed limit, an offence designed to prevent dangers of physical harm from occurring and, in that sense, somewhat analogous to possession of an offensive weapon.[114] Other examples would be disobeying a traffic signal and crossing double white lines. The second point is that the relationship between the conventional non-fatal offences and road traffic offences needs further examination. The tendency is often to regard the former as 'real crime' and the latter as mere regulations whose breach should carry little stigma. However, both types of offences may result in fairly serious physical harm, and so the main ground of distinction must be that many of the conventional offences are committed intentionally or recklessly, whereas the motoring offences tend to be committed negligently. Even if this is true—and it seems possible that some serious motoring offences may involve a form of recklessness—it brings the argument back to the justifications for punishing negligent harmdoing.[115]

The question of endangerment has already been raised in a general fashion in Chapter 7.7. English criminal law contains a number of discrete offences of endangerment, created in particular circumstances to deal with particular problems. For example, in addition to the road-traffic offences, there are offences under ss 32 and 33 of the Offences Against the Person Act 1861 of endangering railway passengers; there are the offences under section 1(2) of the Criminal Damages Act 1971 of endangering the lives of others by causing damage to property (usually by fire); the Health and Safety at Work Act 1974 penalizes employers for failure to ensure that employees are not exposed to risks to their health and safety; there are offences, such as that under section 12 of the Consumer Protection Act 1987, of selling goods in contravention of safety regulations. These are all offences of endangerment, in the sense that no harm need have resulted from the dangerous behaviour. Their importance lies in the value of the interest in freedom from physical violation. However, perhaps even more than motoring offences, they are out of accord with traditional conceptions

---

[114] See J. R. Spencer, 'Motor Vehicles as Weapons of Offence' [1985] Crim LR 29.
[115] See above, Ch 5.3(f).

of crime—many of them being committed in 'normal' situations. This may tend to obscure their direct relation to the issue of physical safety. Social attitudes may be more influential than legal form, but changing the law may have an effect. The apparent transformation of social attitudes towards drinking and driving in the last 10 years, assisted by publicity campaigns, shows the possibility of changing attitudes. So far as the law is concerned, chapter 7.7 commended the approach of the American Model Penal Code in creating a general offence of endangerment.[116] An alternative would be to extend criminal liability for negligence in dangerous situations.[117] Such reforms would only be effective if they were accompanied by changes in policing practice and prosecution policy.[118] The point of principle they raise is whether the degree of harm and the amount of culpability involved are sufficient to justify the creation of offences of this kind.

(l) The Structure of the Non-Fatal Offences

In this part of the chapter we have seen that, generally speaking, the existing range of offences seems to emphasize the result, the degree of foresight, and the status of the victim as the critical issues in grading crimes of physical violation. The crimes in the 1861 Act form a somewhat shakily constructed ladder, with rather more overlapping of offences than is necessary and more elements of constructive liability than are justifiable.[119] Factors which undoubtedly influence judgments of seriousness, such as the existence of provocation, or the difference between premeditated and impulsive violence, are accorded no legal significance and are left to the sentencing stage.[120] The main exception to this concerns the status of the victim, with separate offences for assaults on police officers and wilful neglect of children, for example.

There is an overwhelming case for reform of the 1861 Act. It is unprincipled, it is expressed in unhelpful language, and it leads judges to perpetrate manifest distortions in order to secure convictions in cases where there is 'obvious' guilt but where the Act falls down.[121] How might the non-fatal offences be reformed? It is important to start by affirming the

---

[116] Model Penal Code, s 211.2; see, generally, K. J. M. Smith, 'Liability for Endangerment: English *Ad Hoc* Pragmatism and American Innovation' [1983] Crim LR 127.

[117] For discussion, see Ch 5.3(f) and (g).   [118] See above, Ch 2.10.

[119] For some doubts on the latter point, see J. Gardner, 'Rationality and the Rule of Law'.

[120] See T. Hadden, 'Offences of Violence: The Law and the Facts' [1968] Crim LR 521.

[121] For example, to compound the distortions already manifest in *Wilson, Jenkins* [1984] AC 242, the House of Lords in *Mandair* (1994) 99 Cr App R 250 managed to uphold a verdict of '*causing* grievous bodily harm contrary to section 20', only Lord Mustill dissenting and insisting that this is not an offence known to the law.

principle of maximum certainty, the principle of correspondence, and the principle of fair labelling, and in particular to ensure that the new scheme of offences is not so dominated by concerns about efficient administration (usually, prosecutorial convenience) as to produce wide, catch-all offences.[122] The approach of the Law Commission, broadly adopting the proposals of the Criminal Law Revision Committee, illustrates the difficulties.[123] The Law Commission's draft Bill includes three major offences in the field between attempted murder and common assault: causing serious injury with intent to cause serious injury; causing serious injury recklessly; and causing injury either with intent or recklessly. Beneath these three offences would be assault. Two forms of aggravated assault would be retained: assault on a police officer, and assault with intent to resist arrest.[124] The scheme depends chiefly on the seriousness of the harm caused and the degree of foresight, though in a much more structured fashion than the 1861 Act. There are three obvious problems. First, what is the meaning of 'injury'? Clause 18 of the Law Commission's draft Bill defines it as '(a) physical injury, including pain, unconsciousness, or any other impairment of a person's physical condition; (b) impairment of a person's mental health'. This seems to leave a wide and relatively indeterminate dividing line between causing injury and the lesser offence of assault. Minor cuts and bruises would be included, although the test of impairment of mental health is intended to exclude such conditions as alarm, distress, or anxiety and to be limited to clinical disorders.[125] The Law Commission's general approach is that the law must be broadly stated and that prosecutors can be relied upon to select appropriate charges. Such an approach ensures that defendants have little room for arguing that they have been wrongly charged, since the law is so open-textured. It is possible, however, that the 'Charging Standards' recently established may lead to greater consistency in police and prosecutorial practice.[126] Secondly, what is the distinction between injury and serious injury? Once again, no attempt is made to achieve certainty of any kind, let alone maximum certainty, and a great deal is left to prosecutorial and judicial discretion. Those who maintain that this scheme would 'cause little problem of interpretation' are surely giving way to unwarranted optimism and prosecution-mindedness.[127] Thirdly, why are these two separate

---

[122] See Ch 3.4 and 3.5 above for discussion of the principles mentioned here.

[123] *Legislating the Criminal Code: Offences against the Person and General Principles*, Law Com No. 218 (1993), adopting CLRC, 14th Report (1980), Part IV.

[124] For discussion of the report, see C. M. V. Clarkson, 'Violence and the Law Commission' [1994] Crim LR 324.

[125] Cf. the existing test in *Chan-Fook*, n. 38 above and accompanying text.

[126] See n. 10 above and accompanying text.

[127] CLRC, 14th Report (1980), para 154; cf. p. 71, n. 1.

offences of causing serious injury—with intent, or recklessly—when the two mental states are combined in a single offence for mere injury? The Committee's view was that there is 'a definite moral and psychological difference' between causing serious injury with intent and causing serious injury recklessly, and that this difference should be reflected in separate offences. However, since it is 'not an easy distinction for the police, magistrates and juries to have to make', no attempt should be made to draw such a legal distinction at the lower level of 'injury' offences.[128] In order to support this position, one has to accept (i) that the intention-recklessness distinction is the most significant dividing line for serious injuries, more relevant than such factors as premeditation, provocation, or the use of a weapon; (ii) that this is a workable distinction for the courts, especially in impulsive crimes, where the definition of intention may be fulfilled by a momentary realization of what is happening; (iii) that it is so significant that a difference in maximum penalties between life imprisonment and five years' imprisonment is appropriate; and (iv) that there is not a strong case for phrasing the offences in terms of endangerment rather than of causing physical harm.

The Law Commission's draft Bill is a distinct improvement on the anomalies of the 1861 Act, and if it could be enacted immediately it should be. However, it should not be treated as the most appropriate basis for the law of the next 20 years, for the reasons given above. Jeremy Horder has gone further and has argued that proper respect for the principle of fair labelling militates against having a small number of 'morally sterilized' offences, as proposed by the Law Commission.[129] He suggests that the law should seek to capture ordinary moral distinctions by adopting more descriptive definitions. The law should avoid the two extremes of undue particularism and moral vacuity, and the new Bill should create separate offences for such conduct as causing mental cruelty (as it already does for torture, assaults on the police, administering substances, etc.). He also proposes that the main offences should spell out separate modes of commission (e.g. 'castrates, disables, disfigures, or dismembers'). There are obvious objections based on the possibility of technical unmerited acquittals and on inefficiency (i.e. losses on time-saving and prosecutorial convenience, compared with the Law Commission's scheme), but these counter-proposals do raise the question whether too much weight has not been given to prosecutorial convenience and too little to principle. If the new Charging Standards are successful, could they not be made the basis of a re-shaped law?

[128] Ibid., para 152.
[129] J. Horder, 'Rethinking Non-Fatal Offences against the Person' (1994) 14 Oxford JLS, 335.

Even more important than the shape of the law is the shape of its enforcement. By bringing certain 'public order' offences into the discussion, it has been argued that the concept of violence is being expanded (to include not simply threatening behaviour but also damage to property) and that considerable discretion is being bestowed on the police in respect of certain groups of (relatively powerless) people.[130] In addition, there is the longstanding difference of approach to violence on the streets and violence in the home: improvements have been made in the treatment of child abuse and 'domestic' violence, but there remains some distance to go. In some cases, as the Bristol research showed,[131] it is the victims who decline to co-operate by not reporting the offence or not 'making a complaint'. Once evidence has been gathered, the Charging Standards may structure the discretion of the police and prosecutors. What the law should aim to do is to reflect the relative seriousness of the offence, in terms of harm, culpability, and any other significant features. What it cannot do, however, is to alter patterns of reporting and the perspectives of enforcement officers. This must be tackled by other means.

8.4 REPORTED SEXUAL ASSAULTS

The kinds of sexual assault reported to the police cover an enormous range of conduct. Among the most serious are rapes of women, and about one-sixth of these cases involve not merely non-consensual sex but also further sexual indignities perpetrated upon the victim. Reported rapes of women have increased considerably in recent years,[132] but it is difficult to tell to what extent this represents a real increase in the number of rapes or an increase in the reporting of them. The approach of the police to the investigation of rape cases has been subject to much criticism—and then to considerable improvement[133]—and it seems quite possible that this improvement, together with the advent of rape crisis centres and victim support facilities, have led more women to report rapes than did so formerly. Reporting a rape may still be a strenuous and harrowing experience, however, and it is likely to continue as an under-reported offence. Many of the other forms of sexual assault on females do not take the form of sexual intercourse as defined in the offences of rape, and English law classifies these as indecent assaults. This offence, with a

---

[130] Cf. D. Brown and T. Ellis, *Policing Low-Level Disorder* (1994).

[131] Clarkson *et al.*, 'Assaults: Seriousness and Criminalisation'.

[132] There were 1,300 rapes reported in 1980, 2,900 rapes reported in 1988, and 4,600 rapes reported in 1993: *Criminal Statistics: England and Wales 1993*, Table 2.9. This amounts to an annual average increase of 13 per cent, compared with 5.5 per cent for all crimes.

[133] L. J. F. Smith, *Concerns about Rape*, Home Office Research Study No. 106 (1989), Chs 2 and 4.

maximum penalty of 10 years' imprisonment, covers a wide range of conduct, from a stolen kiss to forced fellatio (oral sex). Offences against men include male rape and gross indecency. Then there is a group of offences which prohibit sexual activities with young people, whether they appear to consent or not: while there is little dispute about the need for some such offences, there is room for disagreement on the proper boundaries of the criminal law and on the role of prosecutorial discretion. The offence of incest prohibits certain sexual relations within the family, thus providing a distinct label for some forms of child sexual abuse by parents and grandparents, although it also covers brother–sister relationships.

Before we consider each of these offences in outline, let us examine the practical and theoretical foundations for them. The practical effects of sexual assault can be considerable. There are well-documented consequences of rape for many female victims: some authors write of a 'rape trauma syndrome', signifying deep disruption of the victim's life-pattern and thought-processes not just in terms of the physical effects of rape (physical pain, inability to sleep, prolonged distress), but also in terms of the effects on well-being (new-found fears, mistrust of surroundings and other people, embarrassment, and so on).[134] Young's New Zealand report concludes that 'rape is an experience which shakes the foundations of the lives of the victims. For many its effect is a long-term one, impairing their capacity for personal relationships, altering their behaviour and values and generating fear.'[135] The effects of sexual abuse of young children may be similar and long-lasting.[136] Indeed, there is no reason to suppose that such effects are confined to the victims of rape as traditionally defined: although sexual assaults vary in their degree, there may be many other forms of sexual assault which are serious enough to create such profound physical and psychological after-effects. Those effects may also tend to spread to the family and close friends of the victim, and then to reflect back on to the victim.[137]

What, then, are the interests typically threatened or destroyed by sexual assaults? They may be described generally in terms of sexual autonomy and sexual choice. The argument must begin from the proposition that our body is our own: it is our private zone, and respect for privacy and personal autonomy both support this. Since these values are high among those which the criminal law ought to respect, no further demonstration of this

---

[134] See the discussion by J. Temkin, *Rape and the Legal Process* (1987), 1–6.
[135] W. Young, *Rape Study: A Discussion of Law and Practice* (1983), 34.
[136] J. Morgan and L. Zedner, *Child Victims* (1992), Ch 3.
[137] J. Shapland, J. Willmore, and P. Duff, *Victims in the Criminal Justice System* (1985), 107–8.

starting-point is necessary. Each citizen may be said to have the right not to have others' sexual choices imposed on him or her;[138] whether the law should go further, and hold that each citizen has the right to pursue his or her sexual choices consensually with another (subject to public decency laws and to the protection of the young), is a question to be considered separately. Is respect for sexual choice any more important than respect for another's property rights? The answer to this requires us to assess the relative centrality of sexual choice to life choices and living standards. It may be argued that sexuality has a certain uniqueness which is absent from much property: sexuality is an intrinsic part of one's personality, it is one mode of expressing that personality in relation to others, and it is therefore fundamental that one should be able to choose whether to express oneself in this way—and, if so, towards and with whom. The essence of such self-expression is that it should be voluntary. Thus, even where a sexual assault involves no significant physical force, it constitutes harm in the sense that it invades a deeply personal zone, gaining non-consensually that which should only be shared consensually. In case this formulation of 'taking without permission' sounds too close to an analogy with theft, it must be emphasized that the crucial element in sexual assault resides in the close interrelationship between the body and the personality. This close relationship, some would say identity, emphasizes that central values such as autonomy and privacy are bound up in all sexual cases. It is the threat to these values which brings the real, deep, and sometimes long-lasting effects of sexual assaults. There can therefore be little doubt that, in general, sexual assaults constitute a substantially more serious form of harm than mere property offences—which is not to deny that some forms of theft or destruction of property can be more serious than some minor sexual assaults.

There is much to suggest that the attitudes of society towards sexual offences, particularly the attitudes of many men (who hold most of the leading posts in the making of policy and law), have tended to undervalue the seriousness of sexual assaults. Among the manifestations of these attitudes are the statements of some defendants in rape trials, which may show an indifference towards the wishes of women, or a belief that the wearing of attractive clothes or an invitation to coffee is a sure sign of willingness to engage in sex; and the attitudes of some police officers in the early 1980s, influenced by any one of a number of assumptions about the prevalence of false complaints of rape, about the 'typical' rape as an attack by a stranger, about the presence of injuries or bruises in 'genuine' rapes,

---

[138] See S. J. Schulhofer, 'Taking Sexual Autonomy Seriously: Rape Law and Beyond' (1992) 11 Law and Philosophy, 35, for a discussion in the context of US rape laws, which generally require force as an element of the offence.

and so forth.[139] Recent years have seen a growing awareness that most of these assumptions about rape are myths. The police have improved both their procedures and their training, but it is not known whether social attitudes in general have changed greatly. Studies of rape in England and Wales suggest that two-thirds of rapes take place in the home of the victim or the offender, and that only one-third involve strangers; that two-fifths of victims suffer physical violence as well as rape, and one-sixth suffer additional sexual indignities;[140] that recent years have seen an increase in the reporting of rapes between acquaintances; and that rapes are increasing a little in their intrinsic seriousness (i.e. in terms of the violence used, other sexual acts, etc.), but that the most significant rise has been in the average length of sentences imposed on rapists by the courts.[141] Longer sentences may be applauded by some,[142] but it is doubtful whether they will make any significant contribution to the protection of women. A Home Office survey concludes that there is no simple solution to the prevention of rape, other than 'the willingness both to question and to change the pattern of social life'.[143] The argument is that serious sexual assaults, and the attitude of many men towards them, derive from a male-dominated approach to sexuality in which aggressive sexual behaviour by males is praised or condoned while women are associated with passivity. To alter this cluster of attitudes to one in which sexuality is seen as an expression of an equal, sharing relationship will require a widespread change in social attitudes through education and other media.

8.5 NON-CONSENSUAL SEXUAL INTERCOURSE

The structure of sexual offences in English criminal law places rape at the top of the 'ladder', carrying a maximum of life imprisonment, with the offences of attempted rape (maximum penalty of life imprisonment) and indecent assault (maximum penalty of 10 years) beneath them. The definition of rape was changed fundamentally by the Criminal Justice and Public Order Act 1994, s 142 of which substituted s 1 of the Sexual Offences Act 1956 as follows:

[139] See the Scottish research by G. Chambers and A. Millar, *Investigating Sexual Assault* (1983). [140] Smith, *Concerns about Rape*, Ch 3.

[141] C. Lloyd and R. Walmsley, *Changes in Rape Offences and Sentencing*, Home Office Research Study No. 105 (1989), 40.

[142] One purpose of the guideline judgment in *Billam* (1986) 82 Cr App R 347, was to increase the length of sentences for rape, in the belief that the crime was being undervalued in proportion to other offences; but the relativities are still unsatisfactory; see Ashworth, *Sentencing and Criminal Justice* (2nd edn, 1995), Ch 4.

[143] Smith, *Concerns about Rape*, 36. For further argument, see F. Olsen, 'Statutory rape: A Feminist Critique of Rights Analysis' (1984) 63 Texas LR, 387, and S. Estrich, 'Rape' (1986) 94 Yale LJ, 1087.

(1) It is an offence for a man to rape a woman or another man.
(2) A man commits rape if—
    (a)   he has sexual intercourse with a person (whether vaginal or anal) who at the time of the intercourse does not consent to it; and
    (b)   at the time he knows that the person does not consent to the intercourse or is reckless as to whether that person consents to it.

There are three notable changes in this definition. First, it removes the word 'unlawful' from the previous definition, thereby confirming that rape can be committed by a man who is married to the woman victim (see paragraph (b) below). Secondly, the new definition includes not only vaginal intercourse, as before, but also anal intercourse. The latter, previously classified as buggery,[144] may involve no less pain and humiliation than vaginal rape. Thirdly, the new definition is gender-neutral, in that the offence is classified as rape whether the victim is a woman or a man. This is perhaps a reflection of the currency of the term 'male rape', even though male rape can only involve anal intercourse whereas rape of a woman may involve vaginal and/or anal intercourse. Before 1994 the maximum sentence for buggery of a woman without consent was life imprisonment, compared with the maximum of 10 years for buggery of a man without consent, and one effect of the 1994 amendment is to provide a single maximum of life imprisonment.

(a) The Concept of 'Sexual Intercourse'

Rape is only committed where the man has sexual intercourse with the victim without her or his consent. Until 1993 there was a conclusive presumption that a male under 14 could not commit an offence of which sexual intercourse was an element, but that presumption has been abolished.[145] We have seen that, under the 1994 amendment, either vaginal or anal intercourse may constitute the conduct element required for rape. Intercourse is defined as the penetration of the penis into the vagina or anus: ejaculation is not required, and the offence is committed as soon as penetration takes place, with the required fault element. It has also been held that the offence continues throughout the penetration, so that if the victim revokes consent during intercourse, and the man fails to withdraw, he commits rape.[146] This has been criticized on the two grounds: if the initial act of penetration is done with consent and without fault, mere continuation by D does not amount to the act of penetration; and if the withdrawal of consent by V turns consensual conduct into criminal conduct, how quickly must the man withdraw in order to avoid committing

---

[144] That offence still exists: see paragraph 6(a) below.
[145] Sexual Offences Act 1993, s 1.
[146] *Kaitamaki v R* [1985] AC 147, *Cooper and Schaub* [1994] Crim LR 531.

the offence?[147] The first argument seems no stronger than the same point in relation to assault and battery: if the application of force to the constable's foot in *Fagan* v *Metropolitan Police Commissioner* was a continuing act, is there any reason to classify penetration in rape differently?[148] The second argument points to a problem of degree, but there will certainly be clear cases of continued penetration. A deeper question is whether continued penetration in these circumstances ought to be classified as rape: if there was initial consent, should D's conduct be condemned as the highest form of sexual assault?

This leads to more general questions about English law's definition of rape. Is it right to exclude from this offence such conduct as forced oral sex (fellatio), and cunnilingus? It can be argued that these offences may be no less traumatic for the victim than 'conventional' rape,[149] and therefore that any attempt to classify sexual offences by reference to their seriousness should place these forms of sexual assault in the highest category. Some years ago the Criminal Law Revision Committee argued in favour of preserving the definition of rape based on the popular meaning of vaginal penetration, adding that the distinguishing feature was the risk of pregnancy. However, this failed to take account of the fact that rape is committed even if there is no ejaculation, and even if the woman is infertile. English law has now broken away from that limited definition by extending the definition to anal intercourse, moving closer to Jennifer Temkin's argument that any 'penetration involving the penis, vagina or anus is perceived differently and regarded more seriously than other forms of penetration'.[150]

(b) Marital Rape

For many years the common law held that a husband could not be convicted of the rape of his wife. The origins of this marital rape exemption seemed to lie in the notion that the wife was the husband's property, or at least in Hale's view that a wife gave irrevocable consent to sexual intercourse with her husband,[151] but it has been defended in modern times on the basis that such cases raise essentially family matters, better suited to examination in a non-criminal court, and that in any case proof would be difficult.[152] However, the common law rule was gradually eroded by the courts in case there had been a separation order, a decree nisi for

---

[147] Sir John Smith [1984] Crim LR 565, [1994] Crim LR 532.
[148] See 5.2(c) and 8.3(j).
[149] See the evidence of victims collected by the Law Reform Commission of Ireland, *Rape*, Law Reform Commission No. 24 (1988).
[150] Temkin, *Rape and the Legal Process*, 33.   [151] See Hale, 1 PC. 629.
[152] CLRC, 15th Report, *Sexual Offences* (1984, Cmnd 9213), paras 2.64–2.70 (the view of a narrow majority of the Committee).

divorce, a non-molestation order, or a separation agreement between the parties.[153] Eventually the rule itself was challenged in the House of Lords and, as we have seen in Chapter 3, the House abolished it in *R* (1992).[154] The main reason for the decision was that social conditions and expectations had changed, and that 'in modern times any reasonable person must regard [Hale's view, above] as quite unacceptable'. The main legal difficulty to be overcome was that the word 'unlawful', which before 1994 was part of the statutory definition, had long been taken to refer to sexual intercourse outside marriage. Parliament was assumed to have confirmed this meaning when it repeated the phrase in the Sexual Offences (Amendment) Act 1976. The rather cavalier and unconvincing manner in which the House of Lords disposed of this objection, and held that the word 'unlawful' was mere surplusage in the statutory definition, exhibits at once two unsatisfactory features of judicial decision-making—the ability to choose between two interpretations of different strengths on largely extra-legal grounds, and the absence of any settled understanding of the proper relationship between the legislature and the judiciary.

The decision in *R* now represents the law and there have been several convictions of husbands, suggesting that the counter-argument based on difficulty of proof was overdone.[155] The Law Commission has recommended that the abolition of the marital rape exemption be placed on a statutory footing,[156] and the 1994 Act does this to some extent by omitting the word 'unlawful'. It is preferable to have such a declaration of married women's autonomy and freedom of choice in sexual matters enshrined in legislation rather than in a judicial decision which, however laudable in its aims, is unacceptable in its methods.

(c) Mistaken Belief in Consent

The fault element in rape is that the man knows that the woman is not consenting or is reckless as to whether or not she or he is not consenting. It would seem to follow from this that a man who *believes* that the victim is consenting, even though he is wrong, ought to be acquitted. Lord Hailsham, in the leading decision of *DPP* v *Morgan* (1976)[157] held that this follows as a matter of 'inexorable logic'. It is not, then, a question of deciding on the elements of a 'defence' of mistake, because, where the man is mistaken, this means that he quite simply lacks the fault element

---

[153] See the decisions in *Clarke* [1949] 2 All ER 448; *Miller* [1954] 2 QB 282; *O'Brien* [1974] 3 All ER 663; *Steele* (1977) 65 Cr App R 22; *Roberts* [1986] Crim LR 188; and *Sharples* [1990] Crim LR 198; and discussion by R. Brooks, 'Marital Consent in Rape' [1989] Crim LR 877.
[154] [1992] 1 AC 599.
[155] See, e.g. *W* [1992] Crim LR 905, *T* (1994) 15 Cr App R (S) 318.
[156] 'Rape within Marriage', Law Com No. 205, 1992.
[157] [1976] AC 182, discussed above Ch 5.3(d).

required for the offence. It is not a 'defence' so much as the negation of the elements of the crime. So where, as in *Morgan*, defendants claim that they believed the woman was consenting, because her husband (who was present) had told them that she enjoyed a struggle, their case is simply that they lacked the fault element required for the crime.

The decision in *Morgan* has already been criticized on two occasions above.[158] It is possible to accept the general principle that defendants should be judged on the facts as they believe them to be, and yet to argue in favour of an exception in rape cases. This would be a bold argument, since its thrust would be that, even if *Morgan* is correct as a case on general principles, it is wrong as a rape decision. How might the argument run? One could argue that there are certain situations in which the risk of serious harm is so obvious that it would be right for the law to impose a duty to take care to ascertain the facts before proceeding. In other words, mistakes must be based on reasonable grounds where the offences are serious—which would cover not only rape but also cases involving a risk of death or serious injury, such as the use of force in self-defence. One drawback of this style of argument is that not only is the harm serious for the victim, but conviction of such an offence is serious for the defendant: a single class of offenders (rapists, serious wounders) would contain not only those with subjective fault but also those who merely failed to take proper care, all of whom would be convicted of a grave offence carrying a maximum of life imprisonment. Perhaps a more fruitful line of argument is to emphasize that not only is rape a serious matter for the victim, but the ascertainment of one vital fact—consent—is a relatively easy matter for the man. There is a clear contrast here between cases of the use of serious force in self-defence, where there may be a need to act instantaneously on a hastily formed view of the situation, and sexual intercourse with another, where consent or non-consent is the essence of the crime and can be ascertained by asking a plain question of the victim. Thus the argument is that the victim's right to autonomy and freedom of sexual choice does not need to yield to the principle that a defendant should be judged on the facts as he believes them to be; it would be so simple (because of the inevitable physical proximity of the two parties) for the man to ascertain the facts here. Of course, this involves a departure from the general subjective principle of criminal liability, since it involves imposing a duty on the defendant to ask about the victim's consent before continuing with his conduct. But compared with the potential sacrifice of victims' rights, this duty is so undemanding that the arguments in its favour are powerful.[159]

---

[158] Ch 5.3(d) and Ch 6.6.
[159] For elaboration, see E. M. Curley, 'Excusing Rape' (1976) 5 *Philosophy and Public Affairs*, 325.

Critics will say that it converts rape into an offence of negligence, in one respect at least. The answer is that it does, and that the justifications for doing so have been set out above—not so much because rape is a serious offence, but rather because ascertainment of the facts is so easy that there should be little substantive unfairness to defendants.[160]

If the criminal law is to impose further duties on citizens, it is important to take account of the legality principles, particularly the principles of maximum certainty and fair warning (see Chapter 3.4(i) and (g)). There is no shortage of examples of defendants in rape cases who assumed that a woman who said no really meant yes, or who inferred from other supposed clues (make-up, clothing, accepting a drink) that the victim had consented, despite her apparent protests. Changing the law on mistake in rape could help to change these social attitudes, but it would do so by convicting some men of rape largely on account of an unreflective assumption of ingrained attitudes towards women.[161] This would mean some sacrifice of the principle of fair warning, a sacrifice that some writers would doubtless think justified as a necessary element in challenging the way in which men have used their power in society.[162] However, changing the criminal law may not be the most effective, or even an effective, way of bringing about changes in social attitudes. Reform of the law of mistake as to consent in rape would be symbolically significant, but it must be preceded and accompanied by a vigorous programme of social education.

(d) Reckless Rapes

We have seen that, according to the statutory definition, a man commits rape if, at the time he has sexual intercourse with a non-consenting victim, 'he is reckless as to whether that person consents to it'. The meaning given by the judges to the term 'reckless' in this context differs from both advertent and inadvertent (*Caldwell*) recklessness. The prevailing view in the Court of Appeal is that a man commits rape recklessly if he 'could not care less' whether or not V consents.[163] An alternative formulation is that D 'carried on regardless' of whether V was consenting.[164] This definition of recklessness has an unusual feature, in that it refers more to D's attitude than to his knowledge or awareness. Courts have occasionally used the term 'indifferent' in this context: subjectivists have criticized the use of this term on the ground that it is unclear whether a person who is 'indifferent'

---

[160] See T. Pickard, 'Culpable Mistakes' (1980) 30 U Toronto LR, 75 and C. Wells, 'Swatting the Subjectivist Bug' [1982] Crim LR 209.
[161] D. Husak and G. Thomas, 'Date Rape, Social Convention, and Reasonable Mistakes' (1992) 11 Law and Philosophy, 95.
[162] C. MacKinnon, *Towards a Feminist Theory of the State* (1989), 174–6.
[163] *Breckenridge* (1984) 79 Cr App R 244, *Taylor* (1985) 80 Cr App R 327.
[164] *Gardiner* [1994] Crim LR 455.

needs to be aware of the risk that the woman is not consenting, but there is considerable support for the 'couldn't care less' formula among those who are not thoroughgoing subjectivists.[165] However, there is a rival formulation in *Satnam and Kewal S.* (1984),[166] a decision that supported the 'couldn't care less' test and also held a man is guilty if he had no genuine belief that the woman was consenting. This formulation appears in the draft Criminal Code, which holds that a man is reckless if he 'does not believe that she is consenting'.[167]

(e) Fraud, Deception, and Consent

How should the law deal with cases where the victim's consent to sexual intercourse stemmed from a mistake on her or his part? English law has tended to confine narrowly the situations in which a mistake is held to negative the consent apparently given by V: only where V was made to believe that the man was her husband,[168] or where V thought that the act consented to was not sexual intercourse, is the mistake sufficiently fundamental to convert the apparently consensual sex into rape. The latter question has arisen where young girls have been invited to submit to acts in order to train their voice or to improve their breathing[169]—unbeknown to them, the act which they were permitting was sexual intercourse. Other types of fraud and mistake are held to be insufficient for the offence of rape, and bring the case within the lesser offence of procuring a woman by false pretences or false representations to have sexual intercourse (Sexual Offences Act 1956, section 3, carrying a maximum penalty of two years' imprisonment).[170]

The identity of one's sexual partner may be assumed to be of fundamental significance, and it is surely unjustified to give effect to this only where the mistake concerns whether the man is the woman's husband. The Court of Appeal has now extended the defence to cover mistake as to a partner.[171] But there are wider issues here, too, implicit in the promiscuous use of the words 'mistake', 'false representations', 'fraud', and so on. Analogies with the effect of mistake in the law on contract may appear obvious, but it is questionable whether they are appropriate. The issues are: when the defendant should be convicted of a crime; how the

---

[165] E.g. R. A. Duff, *Intention, Agency and Criminal Liability* (1990), 167–73; S. Gardner, 'Reckless and Inconsiderate Rape' [1991] Crim LR 172.

[166] (1984) 78 Cr App R 141.   [167] Law Com No. 177, cl 89(1)(b).

[168] 'A man also commits rape if he induces a married woman to have sexual intercourse with him by impersonating her husband': s 1(3) Sexual Offences Act 1956 as amended.

[169] *Flattery* (1877) 2 QBD 410; *Williams* [1923] 1 KB 340.

[170] The offences in ss 2, 3, and 4 of the Sexual Offences Act 1956 still only apply to vaginal intercourse with a woman.

[171] *Elbekkay* [1995] Crim LR 163; cf. CLRC, 15th Report (1984) para 2.25, recommending abolition of the limitation now contained in the Sexual Offences Act 1956, s 1(2).

crime should be labelled; and how seriously it should be viewed. It could be argued, therefore, that the focus should not be the victim's mental state but the defendant's intentions. If D set out to trick V into having sex, realizing that she probably would not consent otherwise, are not his intention and his method sufficient to condemn him for rape, as they would be for obtaining property by deception? Similarly if D, in order to have sex with V, knowingly takes advantage of the fact that V is labouring under a mistaken belief, when (as he realizes) V probably would not consent otherwise, should this not be sufficient? The answer to those questions may be said to depend on whether it is generally as serious to obtain sex by deception as it is by other means (threats, force, fear). In England the Criminal Law Revision Committee took the view that it is not,[172] and therefore supported the division between fundamental deceptions (as to identity or the nature of the act) and lesser deceptions, placing the latter within the less serious category of procuring sex by deception. According to this view, the woman who agrees to have sex with D only when he promises to marry her (never intending to keep this promise)—and because he has promised to marry her—is a victim not of rape but of the lesser offence of procuring sexual intercourse by false representations. The Committee proposed to raise the maximum penalty for this offence to five years, but limited its recommendation to cases where D actively deceives V. No provision was proposed for cases where D takes advantage of a known mistake.

(f) Threats, Fear, and Consent

More frequent in practice, and more problematic, are the cases involving threats and fear. At one time it was the law that rape is committed only where the woman submits through force, fear, or fraud. This is no longer a requirement, because decisions in the nineteenth century made it clear that rape can be committed whenever the victim does not consent—is asleep, for example, or too drunk to consent.[173] However, there are both practical and legal problems in cases where V says that she consented through fear only: she did not resist, because she thought that it would be hopeless in the circumstances, she was terrified, or she feared serious violence. The practical problem is that there may be no evidence of violence on V's body, which usually means that the case will be a question of the victim's word against the defendant's. This may lead the police to be sceptical of the complaint, or may incline the prosecutor to accept a plea of guilty to the lesser charge of indecent assault. The contrast between fear and threats is parallel to that between mistake and deception. Thus the key question is:

---

[172] Ibid.; cf. Temkin, *Rape and the Legal Process*, 63–7 and 69–71.
[173] *Camplin* (1845) 1 Car & Kir 746; *Mayers* (1872) 12 Cox CC 311.

are all threats serious enough to justify regarding the crime as a rape, or should some threats be accommodated within a lesser offence? English law has the lesser crime of procuring sexual intercourse by threats or intimidation, and appears to limit rape to those cases where there is a threat of violence.[174] However, there is a wider dimension to the question, which encompasses fear as well as threats, and this hinges on the distinction between submission and consent.

In the case of *Olugboja* (1982)[175] two girls were picked up by two men and taken to a remote house. The victim was already distressed after being raped by the other man when D announced his intention to have sex with her. She asked him why he could not leave her alone, in view of what the other man had already done to her, but he turned off the light and told her to undress. She did not resist. The Court of Appeal rejected the defence argument that there must be actual violence or threats of violence for the offence to be classified as rape. It also rejected the Crown's argument that the issue of consent should be left to the jury—in the same way as the question of dishonesty is left to them in theft cases—but its actual decision comes fairly close to this position. Thus, the jury should be instructed that the term 'consent' covers a whole range of situations from actual desire to reluctant acquiescence, and that the dividing line between real consent and mere submission must be drawn by the jury, applying its knowledge of human nature to the facts of the case. An example of the difficult decisions sometimes required is provided by *McFall* (1994),[176] where D had kidnapped V with a gun and yet claimed that some signs of enthusiasm during later sexual intercourse led him to believe that it was consensual. It is possible for a woman captured at gunpoint to consent to sex later, but rarely will either the consent or mistaken belief in consent be plausible on such facts.

The law of rape may therefore extend to threats other than threats of violence, but its boundaries are most uncertain. Resort to such concepts as 'common sense' and 'knowledge of human nature' is little more than a veiled admission that no satisfactory criteria have been found. The narrowest approach is to say that rape is committed only where D threatens violence or knows that V is in fear of violence, and that any other threat must fall within the lesser offence of procuring sex by threats.[177] A broader approach would be to hold that any threat may negative consent, and this might include a threat to send a compromising photograph to someone, a threat to report a driver for exceeding the speed

---

[174] Sexual Offences Act 1956, s 2. [175] [1982] QB 320.
[176] [1994] Crim LR 226.
[177] The CLRC would restrict the offence of rape to threats of 'immediate' violence: 15th Report (1984), para 2.29.

limit, and so on. Among intermediate approaches, one possibility is to draw an analogy with the offence of blackmail, holding that any unwarranted demand for sex with menaces should amount to rape, the menaces being either sufficient to influence an ordinary person or sufficient to influence the mind of this victim.[178] A promise that D will procure some advantage for V should not generally be sufficient to negative consent, but there will be situations in which the difference between a threat and a promise may be hard to draw. Thus, if a male tutor makes it known to female pupils that sexual intercourse with him is the gateway to high grades, would it not be too refined to suggest that it is a threat if he says that it is the only way to higher grades, and a promise if he says it is one way to higher grades?[179]

A fundamental problem with this discussion is that it lacks a firm point of reference because it cannot be taken for granted that there should be two levels of offence, rape and procuring sex by threats. If there is to be a single offence of serious sexual assault, there are arguments for including all cases of obtaining sex by fear or threats within that. If the present division is regarded as desirable, the next step is to ensure that the maximum penalty for the lesser offence is sufficient to deal with cases of serious threats which are not enough to negative consent in rape. Then one can address the question of whether rape should be confined to cases where submission arises from a threat or fear of violence, or whether it should be phrased more widely. At that stage, questions about the appropriateness of labels, sentencing powers, and the principle of legality (in terms of certainty requirements) come to the fore. These questions will be considered on a broader canvas in 8.7.

8.6 OTHER NON-CONSENSUAL SEXUAL OFFENCES

So far the discussion has focussed on the offence of rape in English law, which now extends to vaginal or anal intercourse. Other kinds of sexual assault are classified in English law as buggery, attempted buggery or rape, or indecent assault, and there are also offences against young people and the mentally disordered. These will be considered briefly before the general subject of sexual offences is re-examined.

(a) Male Rape and Buggery

Section 12 of the Sexual Offences Act 1956 states that it is an offence 'for a person to commit buggery with another person or with an animal'. The

---

[178] See Temkin, *Rape and the Legal Process*, 67–9.
[179] Cf. the analogous discussion of the concept of threat in blackmail in Ch 9.5 below.

meaning of buggery is anal intercourse, and we have seen that offences of anal intercourse without consent now amount to rape, on the revised 1994 definition of that offence. Thus the maximum penalty for rape of a man or woman is life imprisonment, as is the maximum for buggery of an animal. However, the effect of section 12 is that it remains an offence to commit buggery with the victim's consent, save in exempted cases. Section 143 of the Criminal Justice and Public Order Act 1994 inserts a new section 12(1A) into the 1956 Act, creating two main exceptions. The first exception is where the act takes place in private and both parties are aged 18: this, in effect, decriminalizes consensual anal intercourse, which until 1994 was an offence even if the parties were married. The second exception applies directly to consensual buggery between males, and provides that the offence is not to be treated as taking place in private if more than one person is present or if it takes place in a public lavatory. It seems likely that in future section 12 will be used only in consensual cases either in public or involving one or more under-age participants (see paragraph (e) below), and for cases involving animals.

(b) Attempted Rape or Attempted Buggery

If a defendant fulfils the other requirements for the offence of rape or buggery but failed to achieve penetration, liability for attempted rape or attempted buggery may be possible. A survey in the 1970s showed that almost one-third of rape charges resulted in conviction of attempted rape.[180] Accordingly to the law of attempts, the least that a defendant must be proved to have done is something 'more than merely preparatory' to sexual intercourse, with intent to have unlawful sexual intercourse without the victim's consent.[181] Whether the prosecution can prove attempted rape rather than the lesser offence of indecent assault will often depend on proof of the defendant's intention to go beyond the indecent acts already committed. A man who 'could not care less' whether the victim was not consenting can be convicted of rape in cases where penetration is achieved; but if he failed to achieve penetration and clearly intended to do so, there is the problem that conviction for an attempted crime requires an *intent* to commit the full offence. The Court of Appeal managed to uphold a conviction for attempted rape based on recklessness as to V's consent in *Khan* (1990),[182] and the Law Commission has recognized the arguments in favour of this approach in its draft Criminal Code.[183]

---

[180] R. Wright, 'A Note on the Attrition of Rape Cases' (1984) 24 BJ Criminology, 399.
[181] Criminal Attempts Act 1981, 1.1(1); see below Ch 11.2.
[182] (1990) 91 Cr App R 29, discussed below, Ch 11.3(a).
[183] Law Com No. 177, ii, 244.

(c) Indecent Assault

In English law the offence of indecent assault is widely used as a residual offence, beneath rape and attempted rape. Until 1985 the maximum penalty for indecent assault on a female was two years' imprisonment, compared with 10 years for indecent assault on a male—a legacy of the horror with which homosexuality was viewed, and of the undervaluing of female sexual and physical autonomy—but the maximum penalty for both forms of indecent assault is now 10 years.[184] This is a far more realistic maximum for cases involving forced oral sex and other indignities, but the real question is whether such serious forms of sexual assault should be classified differently. At present they 'share' the offence of indecent assault with many minor forms of misconduct, such as giving an unwanted kiss or fondling clothes being worn by someone else, for which the penalty is likely to be a long way down the scale. This suggests that there is a strong argument for having two grades of indecent assault in English law, or for moving some of the more serious forms of the crime (such as forced fellatio or cunnilingus) into a broadened crime of rape or 'serious sexual assault'.

Most of the technical legal controversy has concerned not the more serious varieties of indecent assault but the more ambiguous forms, where the element of indecency is used to separate the sexual offence from the non-sexual. In *Court* (1988)[185] the House of Lords upheld the conviction of a man who had spanked a young girl several times on the seat of her shorts. The House distinguished, in effect, three types of case. First, where the conduct would not be thought indecent by any right-minded observer, there can be no conviction of indecent assault, whatever D's motivation. This confirms the ruling in *George* (1956),[186] to the effect that a man who derived sexual pleasure from removing women's shoes could not be convicted of indecent assault since his acts were not objectively indecent. Secondly, where right-minded observers would agree that the conduct was indecent, that would be an indecent assault whatever D's actual motivation. In a third class of cases, where the right-minded observer would be unsure, the court would look at the defendant's motive: only if that was indecent would the offence be made out. One result of this is that much will turn on the court's initial characterization of the incident, using the 'right-minded person' test. The test is vague, and in *Court* Lord Ackner's application of it to the case of *Pratt* (1984)[187] made matters less rather than more clear. In that case D came upon two boys fishing at night, threatened them with a gun, told them to undress and ordered them to shine a torch at each other while naked. His defence to indecent assault was that he was

---

[184] Sexual Offences Act 1985, s 3.   [185] (1988) 87.
[186] [1956] Crim LR 52, Streatfeild J.   [187] [1984] Crim LR 51.

merely searching for cannabis that he thought the boys had stolen. The Recorder directed that the prosecution needed to prove an indecent intention, and Lord Ackner signified his approval of this. Yet many 'right-minded' people would regard D's conduct as indecent in itself, and would therefore place this case in the second category in *Court* rather than the third.

Could a more precise and acceptable test be found? Is it possible to list the types of conduct regarded as indecent? Should the defendant's motive be so crucial in cases where the act is not obviously indecent, in the sense that 'right-minded persons' would not unhesitatingly classify it as such? (One might argue against the concept of 'right-minded persons', which moves away from a statistical concept such as 'most people' or 'the ordinary citizen' and seems to seek a moral plane which is 'right-minded', a question-begging approach in this context). If a person derives some kind of sexual satisfaction from an act which most people or 'right-minded persons' would not regard as clearly indecent, should this be sufficient? There is no parallel here with punishment for attempts and other inchoate offences, because there is no proof that the defendant was aiming to do something harmful: the harmfulness of the action is supposedly constituted by the indecent motive, not by anything actually done, or about to be done, to the victim.

The two main issues in the crime of indecent assault are therefore (i) whether the crime ought to be divided into two grades so that the more serious forms of sexual assault can be labelled separately; and (ii) how to draw the line between indecent and non-indecent contact with another. There is no indecent assault where the other party consents to the conduct, as we saw above.[188] The fault element for the crime includes knowledge or recklessness as to whether the other party is consenting. Here, as with rape, it seems sufficient to show that D 'could not care less' whether the other party was not consenting.[189] However, a person under the age of 16 cannot give valid consent. Thus, if a woman were to have sexual intercourse with a boy under 16, this would be the offence of indecent assault by the woman even if the boy consented to, or instigated, the act.[190] This restriction on consent is designed for the protection of the young, to which we will now turn.

(d) Sexual Intercourse with Girls under 16

A male commits an offence if he has sexual intercourse with a girl under 16. The extended definition of sexual intercourse in rape does not apply

---

[188] See 8.3(f), and *Boyea* [1992] Crim LR 574.
[189] *Kimber* (1983) 77 Cr App R 225.
[190] Sexual Offences Act 1956, ss 14 and 15; *Faulkner v Talbot* (1982) 74 C App R 1.

here, so this offence is confined to vaginal intercourse. Even if the girl consents in fact, this has no effect in law and the offence is still committed. If she is under 13, the maximum penalty is life imprisonment, since a girl of 12 or under cannot have sufficient knowledge of the consequences of sex, or sufficient maturity of judgment to take decisions on those consequences. Where the girl is aged 13 to 15 the maximum penalty is two years: this creates an anomaly, since the maximum for indecent assault on a girl under 16 is 10 years, thus treating it as more serious than intercourse itself. In practice, the vast majority of reported offences of unlawful sexual intercourse with a girl of 16 involve young men of a similar age or a few years older, and the general trend is to administer a formal caution to such persons rather than to prosecute them. Prosecution is thus reserved for the cases in which some unfair advantage has been taken of the girl, particularly where the man is considerably older than the girl or where there is some element of deception involved. The law does not specify any of these elements: everything is left to prosecutorial discretion. The Criminal Law Revision Committee took the view that, if the law did try to restrict the offence in this way, it would inevitably legalize some cases which should remain contrary to the law.[191] Thus the law continues to sacrifice the principle of maximum certainty (see Chapter 3.4(i)) to the supposed dictates of practicality. The law is framed widely, in the expectation that it will be enforced selectively. In one particular sphere, however, other legal systems seem to disagree with the practicality argument: namely, cases of sexual intercourse with a girl under 16 committed by a person in a position of trust towards her. Many countries have an offence of 'abuse of authority' to differentiate these crimes, in accord with the principle of fair labelling (Chapter 3.5(s)), but anxieties about the problem of listing the types of authority (should it include persons undertaking voluntary responsibility, such as choirmasters and youth-club leaders?) have led to the continuation of the pragmatic all-encompassing provisions in England and Wales. However, the higher maximum penalty in cases where the girl is under 13 (when lack of proper understanding is assumed) does mark out these cases for aggravation of sentence.

There are sharp divisions about the fault element for the offence of unlawful sexual intercourse with a girl under 16. There is a defence for a young man under 24 who has not previously been charged with a similar offence and who believes that the girl is 16 years old.[192] Apart from this limited 'defence', it appears that the crime does not require any fault element as regards the girl's age. For many years the decision in *Prince*

---

[191] CLRC, 15th Report (1984), paras 5.19–5.21.
[192] Sexual Offences Act 1956, s 6(3).

(1875), in effect that the man is strictly liable when the girl is under 16, has been paraded by academic lawyers as the acme of injustice.[193] The decision may certainly be said to be out of line with the recent trend, that a defendant should be judged on the facts as he believes them to be; and this led the Criminal Law Revision Committee to recommend that the rules should be harmonized and that the prosecution should prove that the man realized that the girl was under 16.[194] Once again, one must question whether consistency is the highest value here. Critics argue that the whole point of this offence is to provide protection for young girls, and that this will be undermined if it is open to men to seek an acquittal on the ground that the girl looked 16. Without directly embracing the 'protection' element in this argument, it can be suggested that there should be a duty on the man to ask the girl about her age before entering into sexual relations, even though the answers may be untruthful in some cases.

(e) Other Rules against Exploitation of the Vulnerable

The criminal law contains several special rules relating to the involvement of vulnerable persons in sexual activity. The *Prince* rule of strict liability as to age, which applies equally to indecent assault, has already been noticed. Another judge-made rule is that in *Tyrrell* (1894), which provides that a person cannot be convicted as a party to an offence if the offence was created for the protection of such persons.[195] Thus, in cases where a young girl or young boy of 15 leads an adult into sexual activity, the youth cannot be convicted as an accomplice to either unlawful sexual intercourse with a girl under 16 or indecent assault (as the case may be). The adult commits the offence; the law imposes on him or her the duty to resist whatever temptation is offered, and leaves the young person to be the subject of civil proceedings under the Children Act 1989 where appropriate.

Among the offences designed to protect the vulnerable, four may be singled out here. First, there is the offence under section 7 of the Sexual Offences Act 1956 of sexual intercourse with a woman who is a 'defective', i.e. suffering from mental handicap.[196] Section 7(2) provides that no offence is committed if D did not know and had 'no reason to suspect' that the woman was a defective, and it has been held that a court should take account of D's own mental limitations in deciding whether he had 'reason to suspect'.[197] Secondly, section 23 of the 1956 Act makes it an offence to

---

[193] (1875) LR 2 CCR 154, on which see R. Cross, 'Centenary Reflections on Prince's Case' (1975) 91 LQR 540.   [194] CLRC, 15th Report (1984), paras 5.5–5.15.
[195] [1894] 1 QB 710.
[196] See also Sexual Offences Act 1956, s 9 (procuring a woman who is a defective to have sexual intercourse); Mental Health Act 1959, s 128 (offence for employee of mental hospital or guardian to have sexual intercourse with mentally disordered patient).
[197] *Hudson* [1966] 1 QB 448.

procure a girl under 21 to have sexual intercourse with a third party in any part of the world. This little-used section ensures that English law complies with international conventions against what was known as the 'white slave trade', i.e. tempting young women to work abroad when the result is a form of forced sexual labour.[198] Thirdly, there is a crime of gross indecency with or towards a child under 14, which may be committed even though there is no indecent assault on the child by the adult—by inviting the child to touch the genitalia of the adult, for example.[199] However, there seems little reason for limiting the offence to cases involving children under 14 when the general age of consent to sexual activity stands at 16. And fourthly, it is an offence for a man to commit gross indecency with another man: this offence usually concerns mutual masturbation or oral sex between two males (there is no equivalent offence between females). Under the Sexual Offences Act 1967 the offence was not committed where the act was done in private, between consenting males, both aged 21 or over. Section 145 of the Criminal Justice and Public Order Act 1994 reduces the age to 18, and we have already noted (in 8.6(a)) that this is also now the minimum lawful age for consensual buggery. The age of 18 may be said to recognize that the person has the right to vote and therefore ought to be able to express his sexual preferences in private, but it leaves the anomaly that the age of consent for other sexual conduct is 16. The CLRC took the view that young men of 16 and 17 need protection from this kind of behaviour, whereas they do not from other kinds of sexual contact.[200] The evidence for this is not strong, and the argument begs the question why young women of 16 and 17 do not 'need protection' from the attentions of older men. The anomaly is increased by the fact that, under the present law, two young men under 18 who consensually commit 'gross indecency' are both liable to conviction for the offence; the rule in *Tyrrell* is inapplicable here, although the maximum penalty is two years' imprisonment where the offender is under 18, compared with five where he is over 18.[201]

8.7 INCEST

A parent or grandparent who has sexual contact with a child or grandchild may well be guilty of one of the offences already considered—rape, if there is sexual intercourse without consent; unlawful sexual intercourse or

---

[198] See CLRC, 15th Report.
[199] Indecency with Children Act 1960, s 1; see the discussion of *Speck* (1977) 65 Cr App R 161 above, Ch 4.4.   [200] CLRC, 15th Report (1984), para 6.18.
[201] Ibid., paras 6.13–6.15; see J. C. Hindley, 'The Age of Consent for Male Homosexuals' [1986] Crim LR 595.

indecent assault, if there is sexual contact with a child under 16; and even gross indecency with or towards a child, if the child is under 14. These offences do not cover all eventualities, and, moreover, it may be argued with some force that child sexual abuse at home ought to be labelled separately. It is not merely a sexual offence, but one of the deepest breaches of trust which can take place in a family-based society. The home ought to be a safe haven, the place where people go to get away from fear and violence, and it is this fundamental feeling of safety which can be destroyed by child sexual abuse. Incest was introduced into English law as a distinct offence by the Punishment of Incest Act 1908.[202] Although the eugenic risk (that the child of an incestuous relationship between father–daughter or brother–sister will have congenital defects) was known at the time and was probably a factor, most of the arguments of the reformers were based on the protection of children from sexual exploitation. Those arguments have great force today, as increasing evidence of child abuse within the family comes to light. Fathers may use their considerable power within the home to lead a daughter into sexual activity from a relatively early age. All kinds of pressure may be exerted on the child to keep quiet about the behaviour, with sometimes disastrous effects on his or her emotional development. Indeed, the primacy of this anti-exploitation rationale over eugenic reasons makes it desirable to extend the offence to cover adopted children as well as blood-relationships.[203]

The offence of incest is committed by a man who has sexual intercourse with a person whom he known to be his granddaughter, daughter, sister, or mother, and by a woman aged 16 or over who 'permits' her grandfather, father, brother, or son to have sexual intercourse with her.[204] The first thing to notice about this definition is that, unlike the offence of rape, it remains restricted to vaginal sexual intercourse. Within the logic of incest this seems indefensible—first, because eugenic reasons no longer provide the main grounds for criminalization; and second because the primary rationale of punishing the sexual exploitation of children within the family applies no less to other serious sexual behaviour, such as oral and anal sex or homosexual activity.

Another feature of the offence is that it applies irrespective of the ages of the parties (save that a woman cannot commit the offence quaintly termed 'permitting' intercourse unless she is aged 16 or over). Thus the crime of incest covers sexual relations between mature adults, in situations where

---

[202] See V. Bailey and S. Blackburn, 'The Punishment of Incest Act 1908: A Case Study in Law Creation' [1979] Crim LR 708, and S. Wolfram, 'Eugenics and the Punishment of Incest Act 1908' [1983] Crim LR 308.   [203] CLRC, 15th Report (1984), para 8.28.
[204] Sexual Offences Act 1956, ss 10 and 11; sentencing guidelines for the offences were laid down in *Attorney-General's Reference No. 1 of 1989* (1989) 11 Cr App R(S) 409.

the rationale of punishing exploitation of the young should no longer apply. One question, therefore, is whether the age should be reduced to 16, which is the general age of consent for heterosexual activity. There might appear to be an argument in favour of consistency here, but it is surely eclipsed by the need to recognize that many children remain dependent on their parents until they are at least 18. The CLRC recommended that the age should be no lower than 21, but that raises questions about the conflict between sexual self-expression and protection from exploitation.[205] Another issue is whether brother–sister incest should remain criminal. It is quite wrong that it should be criminalized where both parties are adults, as the CLRC accepted. However, adulthood begins at 18, whereas the CLRC proposed decriminalization where both parties were aged 21.[206] It is arguable that, by and large, brother–sister incest is less exploitative than incest involving a parent, step-parent, or grandparent. Brother–sister cases might be dealt with adequately under the general law of sexual offences, whereas there are powerful arguments for retaining the special crime of incest for the other relationships.[207]

8.8 PARAMETERS OF THE LAW ON SEXUAL ASSAULT

It is evident from this survey of English law on sexual assault that the parameters are open to considerable argument. In these concluding paragraphs, four central issues will be raised for discussion—the inter-relationship of the criminal law, the law of evidence, procedure, and sentencing; the structure of the law of sexual assault; the role of arguments based on consistency; and the criminalization of consensual sexual conduct.

There can be little doubt that the administration of criminal justice has paid insufficient attention to problems of sexual abuse over the years, and recent improvements in police procedures and in services for victims are to be welcomed. For too long, insufficient attention has been paid to the considerable psychological effects of sexual victimization. However, changes designed to signal a new awareness of these matters must be approached with circumspection, because in practice there are close links between the law, evidence, procedure, and sentencing. Thus changes which make it easier to convict men of sexually assaulting women, or parents of the sexual abuse of children, cannot be welcomed unless one has a clear conception of the rights of defendants as well as the rights of victims. It is one thing to maintain that victims of sexual assault have in the past suffered oppressive questioning by the police and oppressive cross-examination in

---

[205] CLRC, 15th Report (1984), paras 8.15–8.17.   [206] Ibid., para 8.22.
[207] J. Temkin, 'Do we need the Crime of Incest?' (1991) 44 CLP, 185.

court. It is quite another thing to suggest that it is therefore proper to place higher burdens of proof on defendants, and to restrict the presentation of the defence.[208] Even the introduction of video links and screens into courts may raise questions of fairness.[209] A possible example of the interrelationships between sentencing changes and bringing cases to court is provided by the argument that children might refrain from reporting or at least giving evidence if they know that a substantial prison sentence for a member of their family is the probable outcome. Another effect is that defendants might defend cases more vigorously, causing greater trauma to child witnesses, if substantial imprisonment is probable. It can therefore be argued that, serious as the offence usually is, a policy of non-custodial treatment might be preferable in view of the effects on child victims.[210]

Notwithstanding that argument, the structure of the law on sexual assaults ought surely to reflect their relative seriousness. The starting-point must be the empirical evidence of the effects of sexual assaults. These are variable, of course, but in many cases there are severe psychological after-effects—trauma, fear, and mistrust—which deeply affect the victim's ability to lead a normal life for some time to come. It is not suggested that each offence should be ranked according to the seriousness of its after-effects on the particular victim—although there is an argument for assuming that young victims will be particularly damaged by unwanted sexual experiences, and therefore, for regarding such offences as more serious—but some general propositions ought to be reflected. For example, why should English law exclude from its offence of rape such conduct as forced oral intercourse and penetration of the vagina by other objects? The recent extension of rape to cover non-consensual anal intercourse upon a man or woman is welcome, but there is a strong argument for extending the offence of rape to cover other sexual indignities, or for restructuring the law so that there are degrees of sexual assault. The sentencing decision in *Billam* (1986)[211] marks out some of the more serious varieties of sexual assault, and this could be used as a basis for introducing a new scheme of three or four graded offences.

Jennifer Temkin, adapting the Canadian approach, suggests that first-degree sexual assault should be defined so as to include penetration involving the penis, vagina, or anus, together with the threat or infliction of serious injury; then a second-degree offence of the same nature involving a threat or infliction of injury; then a third-degree offence covering all other sexual assaults involving penetration, and a fourth offence to cover

---

[208] Temkin, *Rape and the Legal Process*, 119–49.
[209] *Cooper and Schaub* [1994] Crim LR 531.
[210] See D. Glaser and J. R. Spencer, 'Sentencing, Children's Evidence and Children's Trauma' [1990] Crim LR 371.   [211] (1986) 82 Cr App R 347.

indecent assaults not involving penetration.[212] This might better reflect the principle of fair labelling than the existing legal structure.[213] In recent years English law has shied away from the grading of offences on 'practical grounds', for example the argument that it would lead to plea-bargaining, and thus to offenders escaping with lesser convictions and lesser sentences. The fact is that this is a prominent feature of the existing law, in which there are three major offences (rape, attempted rape, and indecent assault) and the vast majority of those charged with rape have a plea of guilty to one of the lesser offences accepted by the court.[214] A more refined gradation of offences could hardly be worse in this respect, and might improve the structure of sentencing for sexual offences. Another welcome consequence of a fresh gradation of sexual offences might be that they would cease to be gender-specific: there are some strange inconsistencies in the law at present, and the 1994 Act has shown that it is not at all difficult to draft gender-neutral offences.

A third point, already raised on various occasions above, is to challenge the use of the concepts of consistency and 'inexorable logic' as unanswerable standards of appraisal of the law. This is not to suggest that consistency is an unworthy value: the argument is rather that there is a need to decide upon the categories to which the argument of consistency is being applied, and above all to recognize that simple resort to the allegation of inconsistency might serve to conceal the conflict between a number of social interests or principles. One example is the doctrine of mistake in rape: it might appear to be 'inexorable logic' that if the offence of rape is only committed where D knew that V was not consenting or was reckless as to her non-consent, a mistaken belief that she was consenting should lead to an acquittal. The inexorable logic does not, however, establish that the result is morally or socially desirable. There is a powerful argument that as far as sexual behaviour is concerned, an area in which consent makes the difference between gross violation and shared pleasure, and in which physical proximity makes it relatively easy to ask about consent, the law should in effect impose a duty to enquire. This would be done by limiting exculpatory mistakes to those based on reasonable grounds. It would partly alter the definition of rape or serious sexual assault; it would introduce an element of negligence liability; and it would also make D liable for an omission. But all those changes could be justified out of respect for the principle of freedom of choice in sexual matters, particularly where the enquiry is so straightforward. A similar argument

---

[212] Temkin, *Rape and the Legal Process*, 95–109; see now J. V. Roberts and R. Mohr (eds), *Confronting Sexual Assault: a Decade of Legal and Social Change* (Toronto, 1994).

[213] For an analogous argument in another field, see Horder, 'Rethinking Non-Fatal Offences', discussed in 3(1) above.

[214] Wright, 'A Note on the Attrition of Rape Cases', 400.

could be mounted in relation to mistakes about age in the offences against girls and boys under 16: the basic principle of fairness to defendants underpins the subjective requirement of fault, but there is also the social policy against exploitation of the young and vulnerable. This social policy might support a duty to enquire about age wherever there might be room for doubt, and the ease of compliance (because of the inevitable physical proximity of the parties) again favours the requirement. In practice, there might be situations of doubt; a man might claim that there was nothing to alert him to the girl's age (e.g. a 15-year-old girl, who looks much older, soliciting in a street with other prostitutes). Moreover, if the criminal law is to impose duties of these kinds, it should publicize them widely, so as to ensure compliance with the principle of legality. The point of this argument is not to maintain that there would be no practical problems, but to demonstrate that there are weighty issues of principle on both sides. Appeal to 'inexorable logic' or consistency cannot conclude the argument: it over-simplifies the issues.

Finally, there is the role of consent in sexual relations. It has already been observed that the presence or absence of consent to sexual intercourse makes the difference between shared pleasure and rape. Respect for sexual autonomy and self-determination supports this. But there remain some spheres in which the law criminalizes consensual sexual relations between people of full age and sound mind. One example is the offence of doing homosexual acts in private with a young man aged under 18: as we have seen, the law still 'protects' young men of 16 and 17 by criminalizing them and those engaged in homosexual acts with them. Another example is sado-masochism which, following the decision of the majority of the House of Lords in *Brown* (1994),[215] is criminal wherever it involves the causing of actual bodily harm to any of the participants. The reasoning in this decision flows from the assumption that the conduct of the parties should be regarded as physical violence. There is a paradox here, since some women have been pressing the law and its institutions to recognize that many sexual offences are forms of violence and to treat them accordingly.[216] However, the conduct in *Brown* was wholly consensual and was intended for the purpose of sexual gratification. It can therefore be argued that it should be treated as consensual sexual activity and, out of respect for sexual autonomy and privacy, should not be brought within the criminal law.[217] A similar approach should be considered in

---

[215] [1994] 1 AC 212, above 8.3(f).

[216] See, e.g., the readings collected in N. Lacey, C. Wells, and D. Meure, *Reconstructing Criminal Law* (1990), 314–30, and L. Zednes, 'Sexual Offences' in I. Loveland (ed), *Frontiers of Criminality* (1995).

[217] N. Bamforth, 'Sado-Masochism and Consent' (1994) Crim LR 661, drawing on the classic article by L. H. Leigh, 'Sado-Masochism, Consent and Reform of the Criminal Law' (1976) 39 MLR, 130.

relation to brother–sister incest and indeed other forms of incest where both parties are of full age and sound mind: at present, prison sentences may still be imposed where the 'victim' is an adult.[218] Before there is any proposal to put before Parliament that part of the draft Criminal Code relating to sexual offences,[219] there is a need for some fundamental rethinking about the rationale, structure, and content of this field of law.

[218] E.g. *Murphy* (1981) 3 Cr App R (S) 285, three months for repeated incest with daughter aged 30; cf. *P* (1993) 15 Cr App R (S) 116, incest with sister aged 28, suspended sentence reduced to conditional discharge.

[219] Law Com No. 177, draft Bill, Part II, Ch II.

9

Offences of Dishonesty

9.1 INTRODUCTION

The principal statute in this part of the criminal law is the Theft Act 1968, and the principal offence is referred to as theft or stealing. These terms seem to convey the idea of permanently taking another's property, but in fact the definitions in the Theft Act extend the notion of stealing to a wide variety of dishonest violations of another's property rights. The Theft Act shifted the emphasis of the offence from protecting possession to protecting ownership, and also encompassed a much wider range of property rights than the old law of larceny.[1] Now it is more a question of infringing another's property rights than of taking their property. There is no requirement that D should have permanently deprived V of the property, although it must be proved that D *intended* to do so. D's conduct does not have to amount to a potential destruction of V's ability to use the property or act as owner: on the contrary, the courts have held that the merest interference with any right of an owner may suffice, so long as it is accompanied by dishonesty and an intention permanently to deprive. One might therefore say that these are crimes of dishonesty rather than property crimes as such. But this is not a true characterization of the whole field, since dishonesty is often not criminalized when it merely involves temporary deprivation,[2] and the criminal law is somewhat less extensive where the dishonesty does not relate to some corporeal thing but only to, for example, the fruits of one's labour (e.g. not paying for a taxi fare, or for the work of a house painter).[3]

Indeed, it is the great variety of offences of dishonesty, and the breadth of their definitions, which raises problems of proportionality and the proper limits of the criminal sanction. The proportionality issues revolve partly round the problem of deciding what concept of property rights should be employed (discussed in the next paragraph) and partly round the prevalence of 'white-collar crime'. For many years there has been criminological interest in the notion of 'white-collar crime,'[4] particularly

---

[1] For discussion, see A. T. H. Smith, *Property Offences* (1994), 1–17.
[2] Cf. the discussion in 9.3 below.
[3] Cf. the offence of obtaining services by deception, discussed in 9.8(e) below.
[4] See e.g. E. H. Sunderland, *White Collar Crime* (1949); M. Levi, *Regulating Fraud: White Collar Crime and the Criminal Process* (1987); H. Croall, *White Collar Crime* (1992); D. Nelken, 'White-Collar Crime', in M. Maguire, R. Morgan, and R. Reiner (eds), *Oxford Handbook of Criminology* (1994).

deprivations of property perpetrated in commercial settings, but this has not really been reflected by changes in the law or in enforcement practice. The police have traditionally concerned themselves more with stealing from shops and burglary than with embezzlement and the various forms of frauds upon and by companies. And, although the modernization of property offences achieved by the Theft Act 1968 did have the effect of freeing the law from such constricting notions as thieves having to 'take and carry away' property in order to be convicted, the Act provides little indication of a determination to treat white-collar offences as equivalent to other forms of theft: only ss 17 and 19, on false accounting and on false statements by company directors, point in this direction. It is true that the 1980s saw the creation of several new offences in the spheres of white-collar crime and 'city fraud', but these offences remain outside the Theft Acts and the proposed Criminal Code,[5] making it difficult to claim that they have been integrated into a new scheme of property offences which achieves a realistic proportionality among the degrees of offending. There remains more than a suggestion that the Theft Acts are 'real crime', whereas the Companies Acts, Financial Services Acts, and other legislation are 'regulatory' in nature, despite the indictable offences they contain, and despite some maximum penalties (e.g. seven years for misleading statements or practices contrary to section 47 of the Financial Services Act 1986, and for fraudulent inducement to make a deposit contrary to section 35 of the Banking Act 1987) which are the same as for theft[6] and only slightly less than the maximum for obtaining property by deception (10 years' imprisonment). This chapter's discussion of the 'traditional' property offences will attempt to keep the 'new' offences of dishonesty well in sight.

The idea of dishonesty, explored in the context of the crime of theft (see Chapter 9.2(e)), seems to be the notion which binds these offences together. But they are also often grouped together as 'property offences', since they involve some violation of the property rights of another. Personal property is one of the basic organizing features of many modern societies, and it may be defended as an institution on grounds of individual autonomy and rights.[7] Individuals should generally be free to decide how to spend their money; if they choose to purchase property with it, this should be respected in the same way as their own physical integrity. This liberal political philosophy does not exclude the compulsory payment of taxes, and the approach should therefore find room for the notion of

---

[5] See Law Com No. 177, cls 139–77, which cover only the offences under the Theft Act and forgery.
[6] S.26(1) of the Criminal Justice Act 1991 reduced the maximum for theft from 10 to 7 years.   [7] See e.g. J. Waldron, *The Right to Private Property* (1988).

state property—property in public ownership, which no individual citizen is free to take for his or her exclusive use. So, the foundation of these property or dishonesty offences is that it is wrong for any person to take more than his or her rightful share—'rightful' being interpreted in the light of legally ordained methods of property distribution (including, at present, such things as earned income, inherited wealth, public funds derived from taxation, state benefits paid to certain citizens, etc.)

Agreement with the proposition that the law should uphold and respect property rights leaves the question of proportionality: what priority should it give to them? There has long been an allegation that English criminal law is too concerned with property offences—at the expense of offences against the person and against the environment. Whether, or to what extent, this allegation is factually accurate cannot be tested fully here, but two points should be made. First, the allegation may concern enforcement as much as the written laws. The police investigate and prosecute relatively fewer crimes within business and commercial circles. This may, in turn, be because offences are dealt with informally in other ways, by dismissing an employee who has been caught committing an offence, for example.[8] Recent years have seen the creation of the Serious Fraud Office as part of a stated determination to pursue commercial frauds more vigorously.[9] The SFO will only accept a case for investigation if it involves £5 million or more: of the 79 cases on which it worked during 1993, 25 were frauds on the creditors of companies, 20 were frauds on banks or other institutions, 11 were frauds on investors and nine were frauds involving the manipulation of financial markets.[10] The Department of Trade and Industry also investigates and prosecutes some offences relating to the financial markets, including the crime of 'insider dealing' in shares. Significant as these developments may be, they are on such a comparatively small scale that they do little to redress the imbalance in law enforcement between 'crime in the streets' and 'crime in the suites'. Second, there is the question of whether the threshold of the criminal law is lower in property offences than elsewhere. Civil law has a far greater involvement in offences of dishonesty than in violent or sexual offences; the very questions of property ownership and property rights are the subject of a complicated mass of rules relating to contracts, trusts, intellectual property, restitution, and so forth. Many property losses could be tackled through the civil courts, by suing under one of these heads of civil law. It may be true that the amounts concerned are often too small to justify the time and expense of civil proceedings, but

---

[8] See Levi, *Regulating Fraud*, and id., 'Suite Justice: Sentencing for Fraud' [1989] Crim LR 420; see also L. H. Leigh, *The Control of Commercial Fraud* (1982).

[9] J. Wood, 'The Serious Fraud Office' [1989] Crim LR 175; G. Staple, 'Serious and Complex Fraud: a New Perspective' (1993) 56 MLR, 127.

[10] *Serious Fraud Office: Annual Report* 1993–1994, 9.

should that not make us pause to consider whether the criminal sanction is being properly deployed here, and whether adequate weight is being given to the policy of minimum criminalization discussed in Chapter 2.4(b)? If the criminal law is to be reserved for significant challenges to the legal order, should there not be vigilance about the extension of the criminal sanction into spheres in which civil remedies exist, or where some non-criminal procedures might be more proportionate? Is it not true that many dishonest dealings which amount to criminal offences are in practice the subject of nothing more than regulatory action or civil penalties, from commercial frauds to income tax frauds? How, then, can one justify prosecuting ordinary people for the relatively petty thefts that are the everyday business of the criminal courts? These are questions to which we will return at the end of this chapter.

Attention should also be drawn at this introductory stage to the respective roles of the legislature and the courts in property crimes. Parliament has, through the Theft Acts of 1968 and 1978, provided some fairly broad offences. The appellate courts have, in dealing with appeals, developed the law in ways which often extend the ambit of already wide offences in order to criminalize persons whose conduct seems wrongful. Although the decisions have not been all one way, there is much evidence here of the relative impotence of the principle of maximum certainty in relation to legislators and the principle of strict construction in relation to judges.[11] The Law Commission has now embarked on a full review of dishonesty offences, which is likely to cover many of the issues raised in this chapter.

9.2 THE OFFENCE OF THEFT[12]

Theft is not the most serious of the English offences against property, but it must be discussed first, because it is an ingredient of some more serious offences, notably robbery and burglary. The offence of theft, contrary to section 1 of the Theft Act 1968, may be divided into five elements. The three conduct elements are that there must be: (i) an appropriation; of (ii) property; which (iii) belongs to another. The fault elements are that this must be done: (iv) with an intention of permanent deprivation; and (v) dishonestly. Discussion of each of these five elements in turn will demonstrate just how extensive the English law of theft is in some directions, and how restrictive in other directions.

---

[11] See the examples given above, Ch 3.4(i) and (k).

[12] In addition to the work by A. T. H. Smith on *Property Offences* (see n. 1 above), there are two shorter monographs: J. C. Smith, *The Law of Theft* (7th edn, 1993), and Edward Griew, *The Theft Acts* (6th edn, 1990).

(a) Appropriation

Before the Theft Act 1968, English law used to require proof that D had taken and carried away the property, a requirement far too stringent for some types of property (e.g. bank balances), and yet a requirement which at least ensured that certain overt physical acts had to be established before conviction. The Theft Act broadens the law's basis by requiring merely an appropriation. In most cases this will involve taking possession of someone else's property without consent. Section 3(1) of the Act begins by defining an appropriation as 'any assumption by a person of the rights of an owner', and then extends the concept to cover a case where D has come by the property without stealing it and where D subsequently assumes 'a right to it by keeping or dealing with it as owner'. This includes cases where D finds property which he does not initially intend to keep (perhaps intending to report the finding), but later decides to do so. The wording of section 3(1) seems to allow a simple change of mind, unaccompanied by any overt act, to constitute appropriation. Put another way, the mere omission to return the goods or to report the finding constitutes (together with the change of mind) the keeping which amounts to an appropriation. This is a dramatic demonstration of how far the law has retreated from the requirement of 'taking and carrying away' which characterized the previous law, and of how little is required in order to constitute the conduct element of theft. It also raises questions about the justification for this omissions liability, and whether citizens have fair warning of it.

Let us explore the ambit of appropriation by returning to the main defining words, 'any assumption of the rights of an owner'. Does this mean that one can appropriate property even if one obtains it with the consent of the owner? On the face of it, this might seem absurd: surely one cannot be said to steal property if the owner consents to part with it. But the House of Lords has pointed out that the definition of theft does not include the phrase 'without the consent of the owner', as did the previous offence; and in *Lawrence* (1972)[13] it held that a taking can amount to theft, even though the owner consents. The facts in that case were that V, an Italian who spoke little English, arrived in England and wished to hire a taxi to take him to an address in London. He offered D, the taxi-driver, enough money to cover the lawful fare, but D asked for more and, as V held his wallet open, D took more notes from it. The defence argued strenuously that this could not be theft because V consented to D taking the extra money, but the House of Lords held this irrelevant. The definition of theft does not expressly *require* the taking to be without the owner's consent, and the House of Lords held that the term 'appropriates' does not imply an

---

[13] [1972] AC 626.

absence of consent. Thus D had appropriated V's property dishonestly and with the intention of depriving V permanently of it. This decision has given rise to much controversy and to diverse interpretations.[14] One technical question is whether the money still belonged to V when D took it from V's wallet: if it was V's intention that ownership should pass to D, maybe the second element in theft was missing. But perhaps the most regrettable fact is that D was prosecuted for theft at all, since the case seems to be an obvious example of obtaining by deception. An English appeal court cannot alter the charge or order a retrial on the different charge, and so the choice lay between quashing the conviction of a manifestly dishonest person and reaching a decision which might well destabilize the law of theft. The courts preferred the latter course to the former.

Apparently inconsistent with *Lawrence* was the later decision in *Morris* (1984).[15] The essence of the two cases consolidated in the appeal was that D took goods from a supermarket shelf, replaced their existing price-labels with labels showing lower prices, and then took them to the checkout, intending to buy them at the lower price. As in *Lawrence*, the cases proceeded on theft charges rather than on obtaining or attempting to obtain by deception. The House of Lords upheld the convictions, but propounded a more restrictive idea of appropriation. Lord Roskill stated that the concept of appropriation involves 'an act by way of adverse interference with or usurpation of' the owner's rights, and that this will generally require D to have committed some unauthorized act. This was clearly fulfilled in *Morris*, since the attaching of price-labels by customers is unauthorized. However, if the case had proceeded on the *Lawrence* basis that consent is irrelevant, the customers would have been held to have appropriated the goods as soon as they took hold of them, and before tampering with the price labels.

The conflict between these two decisions was resolved by the House of Lords in *Gomez* (1993).[16] D, an employee at an electrical store, persuaded his manager to sell goods to a friend in exchange for cheques which he knew to be worthless. As in the two previous cases (and several others over the years), facts which obviously supported a charge of obtaining property by deception resulted in a prosecution for theft. The House of Lords, by a majority, preferred *Lawrence* to *Morris* on the ground that the remarks on appropriation in the latter were *obiter dicta* whereas in the former they were part of the *ratio decidendi*. Not only did the House of Lords therefore hold that whether the act was done with the owner's consent or authority is immaterial, but they also stated this as a general proposition on 'appropriation', not confined to cases in which there is an element of deception.

[14] See especially G. Williams, 'Theft, Consent and Illegality' [1977] Crim LR 127.
[15] [1984] AC 320.   [16] [1993] AC 442.

The result of *Gomez* is that the offence of theft is now astoundingly wide. Any act in relation to property belonging to another constitutes an appropriation of that property, and liability for theft then turns on the presence of dishonesty and of an intention permanently to deprive the owner. The breadth of this test is emphasized by one dictum from *Morris* that was incorporated into the *Gomez* formulation: that 'the assumption of *any* of the rights of an owner in property amounts to an appropriation of the property'.[17] Thus all that D needs to do is to assume any one right of an owner, and the conduct element in theft is complete. A customer who touches a tin of beans in a supermarket has appropriated them, even though the owners of the supermarket are quite content for customers to take goods from the shelves and even to replace them later, provided that when they reach the checkout they pay for the goods that are to be taken away.

The Court of Appeal found it difficult to come to terms with the breadth of the new test when deciding *Gallasso* (1994).[18] D was a nurse, whose responsibilities included the receipt of cheques on behalf of mentally handicapped patients and payment into accounts in their names. On one occasion, although there were already two accounts in the name of a particular patient, D opened a new account in that patient's name and paid cheques into it. The prosecution's case was that these acts constituted an appropriation and that, since in their view D intended to deprive the patient of the money by transferring it out of the new account, theft had already been committed. The Court of Appeal, quashing the conviction, held that *Gomez* dispenses only with any consent requirement, and not with the requirement of a taking. Some might applaud this decision for narrowing *Gomez*, but it does so in an unsatisfactory and confusing way. The Theft Act 1968 was intended to remove the requirement of 'taking' and all the restrictions to which it had led, and no post-1968 decision had sought to revive it. No doubt the Court in *Gallasso* was uneasy about holding that a person who does an authorized act (opening a trust account for a patient and paying a cheque into it) has thereby 'appropriated' it for the purposes of the offence of theft, but that is what *Gomez* decided.

A number of other questions arise about the ambit of appropriation, some affected by *Gomez*, others not. First, is appropriation an instantaneous or a continuing act? There is no definite answer, but if the question itself is analysed a plausible answer might be found. The question is not whether the appropriation continues throughout the time when the thief is in possession of the property, and whenever he uses it. That is implausible. The question ought to be whether appropriation is complete as soon as D does an act in relation to the property and, if so, whether it can also be said

[17] [1984] AC 320, per Lord Roskill at 332.   [18] (1994) 98 Cr App R 84.

that the appropriation continues throughout the period when D is engaged on that act. It follows from *Gomez* that D could be convicted of theft on the basis of his first act (e.g. seizing a victim's jewellery, getting into a car hired to him). Is it then inconsistent to hold that the appropriation continues while D is engaged on that particular piece of conduct (e.g. while D is in the victim's house after seizing the jewellery, while D is driving the car hired to him)? There is authority to support the view that appropriation does continue throughout the act or 'transaction',[19] not being exhausted by the first act in relation to the property, and this corresponds with the courts' approach to the conduct element in rape.[20]

Connected with this is a second point about the time factor in appropriation. The result of *Gomez* is that a person appropriates property even if the owner's consent is given. Thus where D goes to a restaurant, orders food and eats it, D has appropriated the food. Likewise, where D goes to a petrol station and fills up with petrol, D has appropriated the petrol. In both cases the owner intends ownership of the food or petrol to pass to D. However, ownership has passed by the time D finishes eating or filling the tank with petrol, and so has the relevant act of appropriation. If, therefore, D then decides to leave without paying for the food or petrol, there can be no conviction of theft because the appropriation has ceased before the dishonest intention was conceived.[21] A court might adopt the reasoning in the previous paragraph and hold that the act or 'transaction' should be construed so as to include paying for the property, so that the dishonest intent would be contemporaneous with the appropriation, but since D did not pay either the restaurant or the petrol station this argument would be based on hypothetical, rather than real, facts.

A third, related point is that the act which constitutes the appropriation does not need to be the act which is intended to deprive the owner permanently. The act of appropriation need only be an act done in relation to the property: so long as it was done with the dishonest intent required, theft has been committed at that point. It does not matter that D's act of swapping the price labels on two items was part of a plan to offer the higher-priced goods to the cashier with the lower price label on them, and that that plan had not been executed. *Morris*[22] holds that D does not have to intend permanent deprivation by the act of appropriation; he may intend to deprive by some act in the future. This confirms that the offence of theft in English law criminalizes people at a much earlier point than they

---

[19] *Hale* (1978) 68 Cr App R 415 (below, 9.3); *Atakpu and Abrahams* (1994) 98 Cr App R 254; J. C. Smith, *Law of Theft*, 26–7.

[20] *Kaitamaki* [1985] AC 147 and *Cooper and Schaub* [1994] Crim LR 531, discussed in Ch 8.5(a) above.

[21] *Edwards* v *Ddin* (1976) 63 Cr App R 218, *Corcoran* v *Whent* [1977] Crim LR 52.

[22] [1984] AC 320.

would generally suppose. A stark example is provided by *Chan Man-sin* v
A.G. for Hong Kong (1988),[23] where D wrote unauthorized cheques on his
employers' accounts. It was argued that this was not an appropriation
since, when the bank discovered that the cheques were forged, it would
have to make good the companies' accounts. The Privy Council upheld the
theft conviction, stating that D had assumed a right of the owner and that it
is not necessary to show that the appropriation would be 'legally
efficacious'. The decision penalizes dishonesty, but reduces appropriation
to a will o' the wisp.[24]

In exploring the concept of appropriation, the phrase 'act in relation to
the property' has been used above. We have already noted that an
omission (or, at least, a private decision) can suffice, as in the case of a
person who finds property and subsequently decides to keep it: section
3(1). What is the minimum conduct that might suffice? In *Pitham and Hehl*
(1976)[25] it was held that a person who went to the house of a man who was
in prison and offered to sell that man's furniture to the two defendants had
thereby appropriated the furniture: he 'showed them the property and
invited them to buy what they wanted'. The Court of Appeal held that it
was clear that this amounted to 'assuming the rights of the owner,'
untroubled by the fact that no hands may have been laid on the furniture.
Should it be necessary to show a touching? Surely the facts of *Pitham* are
strong enough without that. No more convincing is the criticism that the
person who offered to sell the furniture did not purport to be the owner,
and the offerees knew that the offeror had no title to pass on:[26] surely the
offeror was in control of the furniture, in the sense that he had brought
the others to the house, and he certainly assumed a right of the owner in
what he did.

Before re-assessing the concept of appropriation, mention should be
made of the exception in section 3(2) of the Theft Act. If a person acquires
property for value in good faith, no later assumption of the rights D
believed he had acquired can amount to an appropriation, even if D then
knows that he has not acquired good title. This applies when D keeps the
goods or gives them away, but if D sells them and represents expressly or
impliedly that he has the title to do so, he will commit the offence of
obtaining the purchase price from the purchaser by deception.[27]

Leaving aside this exception, what is the ambit of appropriation? As a
result of *Gomez*,[28] any act in relation to property that can be said to
assume a right of the owner of the property constitutes appropriation, and

---

[23] (1988) 86 Cr App R 303.
[24] See the criticism by A. T. H. Smith, *Property Offences*, 162.
[25] (1976) 65 Cr App R 45.
[26] G. Williams, *Textbook of Criminal Law* (2nd edn, 1983), 764.
[27] Smith, *Law of Theft*, 24.   [28] [1993] AC 442.

the consent of the owner is irrelevant. Sir John Smith lampoons the state of the law with this summary of its effect:

anyone doing anything whatever to property belonging to another, with or without the authority or consent of the owner, appropriates it; and, if he does so dishonestly and with intent, by that act or any subsequent act, permanently to deprive, he commits theft.[29]

What are the objections to such a definition? Four lines of criticism may be mentioned. First, the definition is not faithful to the intentions of the Criminal Law Revision Committee or of Parliament. That the CLRC intended the concept of appropriation to cover only unauthorized acts is set out plainly in the dissenting speech of Lord Lowry in *Gomez*. A person can now be guilty of theft even though the transaction was effective in passing ownership to D.[30] As a matter of statutory interpretation the decision of the majority of the House of Lords in *Gomez* is untenable; but it is the law. A second and related criticism is that the new definition violates the principle of fair labelling by lumping together thieves and swindlers. One effect of *Gomez* is that all cases of obtaining property by deception are also cases of theft, except those relating to land. Once again this contradicts the intentions of the CLRC and Parliament: 'obtaining by false pretences is ordinarily thought of as different from theft . . . To create a new offence of theft to include conduct which ordinary people would find difficult to regard as theft would be a mistake.'[31] The distinction between the two kinds of conduct is morally relevant: there are situations in which one would think differently of a thief and a swindler,[32] and the law ought to attach different labels to people who violate property rights in such different ways. This is particularly so in view of the difference in maximum penalties between obtaining property by deception (10 years) and theft (now seven years).

Thirdly, the new definition is so broad that it exhibits no respect for the principle of maximum certainty, makes conduct criminal when it would not even amount to a civil wrong, and thus fails to give fair warning to citizens about the boundaries of the law of theft. For example, there is no civil wrong involved in eating a restaurant meal or filling a car's tank with petrol before paying, but both acts amount to appropriation and, if accompanied by a dishonest intent at the time, may result in a conviction for theft. The point about fair warning might be thought to be overdone: after all, a

---

[29] *Law of Theft*, 11.
[30] Cf. *Kaur* v *Chief Constable of Hampshire* [1981] 1 WLR 578.
[31] CLRC, *Theft (General)* (1965), para 38.
[32] S. Shute and J. Horder, 'Thieving and Deceiving: What is the Difference?' (1993) 56 MLR, 548; C. M. V. Clarkson, 'Theft and Fair Labelling' (1993) 56 MLR, 554.

person who acts dishonestly takes the risk that the conduct will be held to be criminal. But that is an unsatisfactory basis for the criminal law. In everyday life, in business and in financial dealings, there is often a fine line between unlawful dishonesty and merely exploiting gaps in the law—in taxation matters, this is expressed as the distinction between evasion and avoidance. While it is often impossible to frame a criminal provision precisely, without excluding a number of cases that ought to be included and without rendering the law unintelligible, the result of *Gomez* is that the law of theft incorporates no attempt at precision at all. Every objective benchmark is rejected: the appropriation need not be a civil wrong, or involve an unauthorized act, or be an overt act, etc. This fails not only to give any guidance to citizens and their legal advisers but also to lay down any clear guidance for the courts. It is, as it were, a prosecutor's dream.

A fourth and related criticism is that the judicial approach severely reduces the amount of manifest criminality in the offence of theft.[33] In other words, liability is imposed for conduct that is not manifestly theftuous: section 3 of the Theft Act 1968 contains elements of this, in its reference to a later assumption of rights by a finder of property, but the three House of Lords decisions (*Lawrence, Morris, Gomez*) take it much further by labelling as a thief any person who assumes a right of the owner in respect of another's property, with or without that other's consent, provided that the two fault elements (dishonesty, intention to deprive permanently) can be proved. Some would say that this proviso is sufficient to rebut the criticism, since the dishonest intent should be the key factor. But this raises questions about the ambit of the criminal law: quite apart from the fact that it often exceeds the ambit of the civil law here, the offence of theft now has the breadth and the characteristics of an inchoate offence, and yet it is extended further by the crime of attempted theft. The result is an extremely wide conduct element, not distinguished from ordinary honest transactions save by the intent, and rendered especially threatening to citizens, and powerful for prosecutors, by the need for defendants to explain their conduct to the police on peril of adverse inferences being drawn.[34]

This fourth criticism is an argument against the judicial expansion of the conduct element in theft, rather than against the assimilation of deception to theft achieved in *Gomez* itself. The two points are treated differently by Peter Glazebrook, who applauds *Gomez* on the grounds that:

---

[33] M. Giles and S. Uglow, 'Appropriation and Manifest Criminality in Theft' (1992) 56 J Crim Law, 179, adapting G. Fletcher, *Rethinking Criminal Law* (1978).

[34] Criminal Justice and Public Order Act 1994, ss 34–7, on which see I. Dennis, 'The Evidence Provisions' [1995] Crim LR 4.

Holding swindlers to be thieves does no injustice, will save much inconvenience in cases where it transpires only late in the day that a crook has resorted to deception, and avoids the extreme absurdity of denying the name of thief to those who misappropriate property received as a result of a mistake that they have induced while according it to those who had done nothing to bring about the mistaken transfer: Theft Act 1968, section 5(4).[35]

The point about section 5(4), which is discussed in (c) below, is that no absolutely satisfactory line can be drawn between theft and deception in all instances. But that does not establish the folly of making the effort to draw that distinction in many other clear cases. Holding swindlers to be thieves obscures a clear category difference in many cases. What has exercised the judges, particularly in appellate courts, has been the prospect of quashing a theft conviction simply because the police and the Crown Prosecution Service have alleged the wrong offence. This is largely a procedural error: it ought to be remediable by procedural means either at the trial or on appeal, rather than being allowed to distort the development of the law.

While procedural change is needed to avoid the acquittal of swindlers simply because they have been wrongly charged as thieves, the substantive definition of theft ought to be reconsidered too. Glazebrook, following Glanville Williams, argues that since theft is an offence of dishonesty 'legal logic requires that the conduct constituting its external elements be unlawful—either tortious, or a breach of trust, or, if the property belongs to a company, a fraud on its creditors or shareholders'.[36] One desirable effect of this definition would be to state clearly that there can be no theft if the owner consented to D dealing with the property as D has done.[37] Although there are those who maintain that the criminal law should avoid civil law distinctions at all costs, since juries and magistrates' courts would have to grapple with recondite points of civil law, the answer is surely that the criminal law must be tied to the civil law of property (to do otherwise makes no social sense), that this is inevitable, and that awkward cases would be rare.[38]

(b) Property

In order to be stolen, the object concerned must be 'property' within the meaning of the Theft Act 1968. Section 4(1) appears to be couched in very broad terms—'property includes money and all other property, real or personal, including things in action and other intangible property'—and it

---

[35] P. R. Glazebrook, 'Revising the Theft Acts' [1993] Camb LJ, 191.
[36] Ibid., 192.
[37] For Glazebrook, however, it would be subject to the rider 'unless that consent is obtained by duress or by deceit, that is, tortiously'. This would perpetuate the overlap between theft and deception, argued against in the text.
[38] A. T. H. Smith, *Property Offences*, 6–8 and 146.

is certainly apt to include some forms of property with which the previous law could not cope. For example, one can steal from another person's bank account by transferring money out of it. The property which one appropriates here is not the account-holder's *money*, strictly speaking, but the account-holder's *right to be paid that amount by the bank or, ultimately, the right to sue the bank* for whatever money stands to credit in the account.[39] The same analysis is possible where the account-holder has an overdraft arrangement with the bank, and someone else dishonestly draws money out.[40]

But there are limits. There is no property capable of being stolen in a dead body or its parts.[41] Nor does electricity fall within the definition of 'property', although section 13 of the Theft Act 1968 provides an offence of dishonestly abstracting electricity. More importantly, there is no property in confidential information, such as business secrets and examination papers. Thus, if D purloins a confidential document of this kind, photocopies it and replaces it, he cannot be charged with theft: not only is it difficult to argue that D has an intention to deprive the owner permanently of the information, but what has been taken does not constitute property.[42] Injunctions may be obtained in the civil courts to prevent interference with, or the abuse of, such secrets, but the criminal offence of theft does not extend so far. The problem has become more pertinent with the increasing use of computers as means of storing information: if D 'hacks into' V's computer system, retrieving from it some confidential information which is then noted down, it appears that no 'property' has been stolen. The House of Lords was invited to extend the law of forgery to cover cases of 'hacking' in *Gold and Schifreen* (1988),[43] and its refusal to extend the law in this direction helped to precipitate specific legislation on the subject. The Computer Misuse Act 1990 created three offences of unlawfully entering another's computer system, with dishonest intent.[44] It is right that this form of property violation should be the subject of special provisions: and artificial extension of the present structure of the law of theft to cover such cases, which lie far from the ordinary stealing of tangible property, would probably be less successful and might have unexpected side-effects. It is also right that the law should criminalize this kind of property violation, which might be much more serious financially than many of the takings which fulfil the basic definition of theft. This is one instance in which there was judicial self-restraint and

---

[39] See the discussion by E. Griew, 'Stealing and Obtaining Bank Credits' [1986] Crim LR, 356.   [40] See J. C. Smith, *The Law of Theft*, 55.

[41] See the discussion by A. T. H. Smith, *Property Offences*, 46–9.

[42] *Oxford v Moss* (1978) 68 Cr App R 183, and generally R. G. Hammond, 'Theft of Information' (1984) 100 LQR, 252.   [43] [1988] AC 1063.

[44] M. Wasik, *Crime and the Computer* (1991); A. T. H. Smith, *Property Offences*, Ch 11.

strict construction, in *Gold and Schifreen*, and it was followed by remedial legislative action.[45]

There are further limitations in section 4. In the first place, the general proposition is that land cannot be stolen. There are some exceptions to this, and of course it is quite possible to convict someone of theft of title-deeds or of obtaining them by deception, but the land itself, being of a certain permanence, remains. Section 4(3) effectively excludes from the law of theft the picking of mushrooms or of flowers, fruit, or foliage from plants growing wild, unless the picking is 'for reward or for sale or other commercial purpose'. It should be noted that this exception is confined to wild mushrooms, flowers, etc., and that the term 'picking' would seem to exclude a person who digs up a wild plant or cuts down a tree. Section 4(4) provides that a wild creature cannot be stolen, unless it is ordinarily kept in captivity (e.g. at a zoo) or has already been reduced into possession (e.g. game birds already shot and retrieved by a landowner). Much of the conduct thus excluded from the law of theft falls within longstanding offences of poaching.

(c) 'Belonging to Another'

The old law of larceny was concerned mainly to penalize those who took possession of property from those in possession, whereas there are many other ways of depriving a legal owner of property. How far should the law go in criminalizing appropriations of property from persons other than the legal owner? Section 5 of the Theft Act 1968 succeeds in spreading the net wide: property is regarded as belonging 'to any person having possession or control of it, or having in it any proprietary right or interest (not being an equitable interest arising only from an agreement to transfer or grant an interest)'. The first phrase, 'possession or control', may be wide enough to enable D to be convicted of theft of, say, suits from a dry-cleaning shop even though the suits had only been placed there temporarily by their owners. There is no need to establish the precise legal relationship between the possessor and the supposed owner of the goods; for Theft Act purposes, the goods are treated as belonging to the temporary possessor, too.

The second phrase of the definition encompasses various situations in which D might regard himself as owner or part owner of the property. Only three years after the enactment of the Theft Act, section 5(1) led the Court of Appeal in *Turner (No. 2)* (1971)[46] to affirm the conviction of a man who had seized his own car back from a garage that had just repaired it. D certainly intended to avoid paying for the repairs, but the question was whether he had appropriated 'property belonging to another'. The Court

---

[45] See Ch 3.4(k) above.   [46] (1971) 55 Cr App R 336.

held that the garage was clearly in 'possession or control' of the car. It was parked outside the garage, and they had a set of keys for it. However, D would only have appropriated property belonging to another if the garage had a lien over the car, and the Court of Appeal held, unsatisfactorily, that the issue of a lien should be disregarded. Section 5(1) certainly provides that one part-owner of property can be convicted of theft from the other part-owner. For example, a partner who appropriates property in order to deprive the other partner of partnership property may be liable to theft so long as the other elements (notably dishonesty: there must be no claim of right) are present.[47] A controversial question is whether company controllers may be convicted of stealing the property of the company—meaning by 'company controllers' one or more persons who, between them, own the entire shareholding in a company. If D and E (being the sole shareholders) transfer money from the company's account to their personal accounts, it might seem strained to say that the company's property 'belongs to another' when the sole shareholders are the very persons who are doing the appropriating. However, it has been held[48] that such cases may in principle amount to theft because the company is a separate legal entity from its controllers, and this view has been reinforced by the decision in *Gomez* (1993)[49] to the effect that the owner's consent does not prevent an appropriation in law. Thus in this sphere, too, theft liability turns largely on proof of dishonesty. Whether the same applies to transfers of company property by the controllers in order to put it out of the reach of creditors, in circumstances of actual or pending insolvency, remains doubtful.[50]

In view of the gain and of the dishonesty, company cases are surely as proper a concern of the criminal law as shoplifting. Whether they should be classified as theft, or dealt with under the Companies Act offence of fraudulent trading,[51] bears on such matters as the stigma of conviction (theft may be more stigmatic than a 'breach' of the Companies Act) and the mode of enforcement. Thus there are arguments in favour of criminalization—and against the marginalization of such offences—by placing them within the Theft Act. Whether the troubled concept of appropriation and the existing definitions within section 5 are adequate to the purpose is doubtful, and legislative amendment seems desirable.

Section 5 of the Theft Act also elucidates, and perhaps extends, the definition of 'belonging to another' in two distinct ways. Section 5(3)

---

[47] *Bonner* (1970) 54 Cr App R 257.

[48] *Attorney-General's Reference (No. 2 of 1982)* [1984] QB 624, and *Philippou* (1989) 89 Cr App R 290.

[49] [1993] AC 442, particularly the speech of Lord Browne-Wilkinson.

[50] Cf. G. R. Sullivan [1991] Crim LR 929, replying to D. W. Elliott, 'Directors' Thefts and Dishonesty' [1991] Crim LR 732.   [51] Companies Act 1989, s 41.

expressly includes property received 'from or on account of another' where the person receiving it is under an obligation to the other to retain and deal with that property or its proceeds in a particular way'. This applies to the treasurer of a sports club or a holiday fund who misappropriates some of the funds; it does not extend, in the ordinary way, to the travel agent or other trader who receives a deposit for a purchase and then fails to fulfil the contract.[52] Section 5(3) provides only for those cases where D is responsible for a particular sum of money or its proceeds on another's behalf:[53] the former case involves an obligation to deal with the money received in a particular way, as part of a distinct fund, whereas payments to a business are usually payments into the general funds of that business. It has also been held that the manager of a public house who made secret profits by selling beers not brewed by his employers fell outside section 5(3), since he was merely accountable for the profits of the public house and was under no obligation to 'retain and deal with' them.[54] Some might argue that this is an arbitrary way to draw the line between criminal liability and mere civil liability, but it tends to be justified on the basis that a remedy for breach of contract is usually sufficient for the latter type of case. However, the civil law has now been altered by the Privy Council:[55] a secret profit is now deemed to be held on constructive trust for the principal, and so it seems that the manager of the public house would be convicted of theft since section 5(3) would apply.

Section 5(4) extends the definition of 'belonging to another' to cases where D 'gets property by another's mistake and is under an obligation to make restoration (in whole or in part).' The obvious example of this is the mistaken overpayment: if money is credited to D's bank account in error, and D resolves to keep it, this amounts to theft of the overpaid sum.[56] If the overpayment is by a bookmaker, there is no legal obligation involved and so section 5(4) cannot be invoked to support a theft conviction.[57]

(d) 'The Intention Permanently to Deprive'

It must be proved that D intended that the person from whom he appropriated the property should be deprived of it permanently. We have already seen that permanent deprivation itself is not necessary for theft: a temporary appropriation will suffice. But the ambit of the offence is

---

[52] *Hall* [1973] QB 126; *aliter* if the contract provides that the money must be held specifically for this purpose.

[53] In most such cases a trust would be created, and s 5(1) itself could be applied.

[54] *Attorney General's Reference (No. 1 of 1985)* (1986) 83 Cr App R 70.

[55] *Attorney-General for Hong Kong* v *Reid* [1994] 1 AC 324, noted by Sir John Smith at (1994) 110 LQR 180.

[56] *Attorney-General's Reference (No. 1 of 1983)* [1985] QB 182; it is arguable whether s 5(4) is needed to achieve this result after the civil case of *Chase Manhattan Bank NA* v *Israel-British Bank* [1981] Ch 105.   [57] *Gilks* (1972) 56 Cr App R 734.

restricted by the need for an *intention* permanently to deprive. Thus, the essential minimum of the offence becomes temporary appropriation with the intention of permanent deprivation.

The Theft Act does not define 'intention permanently to deprive'. Intention presumably bears the same meaning as elsewhere in the criminal law,[58] and therefore covers cases where D knows that a virtually certain result of the appropriation will be that the other is deprived of the property permanently. Most cases will fall into place fairly easily, but the requirement of intention 'means that it is still not theft to take a thing realising that the owner may not, or probably will not, get it back'.[59] Thus there will be no theft where D takes property and then abandons it where it might be found, and the description 'stolen car' is inaccurate if it refers to a car taken from its owner and abandoned some distance away, since it is well known that cars are normally returned to their owners by the police. Section 12 of the Theft Act 1968 provides a special offence of taking a car without the owner's consent, which does not require proof of an intention permanently to deprive (discussed in 9.3). A car *would* be stolen, however, if it were taken with a view to changing its identity marks and then reselling it.

Is there an 'intention permanently to deprive' if D takes someone else's money, intending to repay it before the owner notices its absence? At first sight it would appear not: an intention to repay surely negatives an intention to deprive permanently. Yet if the property taken is money, it is highly unlikely that D intends to replace exactly the same notes (or coins) that were taken. It would therefore be correct to hold that D did intend to deprive the owner permanently of the notes and coins that were taken, and the Court of Appeal confirmed that this is the law in *Velumyl* (1989).[60] A manager had taken money from his company's safe, intending to repay it the following day when a debt was repaid to him. The Court held that an intention to return objects of equal value is relevant on the issue of dishonesty, but does not negative the intention to deprive the owner permanently of the original notes and coins. The Court added that taking someone else's property in these circumstances amounts to forcing on the owner a substitution to which he or she does not consent.[61] Some would argue that this is both pedantic and unrealistic, since money is fungible and one £10 note is for all purposes the same as another. On the other hand, there may be situations in which the owner wants particular coins (£1 coins for a slot machine, whereas D takes ten and leaves a £10 note) or needs to use the money earlier than expected. One merit of the strict rule here is

---

[58] See above, Ch 5.3(b). [59] A. T. H. Smith, *Property Offences*, 187.
[60] [1989] Crim LR 299.
[61] Adopting the words of Winn LJ in *Cockburn* (1968) 52 Cr App R 134.

that, by foreclosing what might otherwise be a defence of lack of intent to deprive permanently, it ensures that the wider rights and wrongs are assessed in the context of the dishonesty requirement.

Does it matter if the intention is conditional? One answer to this is that most intentions in theft are conditional in some respect, and so it should not matter greatly. Particular difficulty has been caused in cases of attempted theft, where D has not yet appropriated any property but is searching a container (a pocket, handbag, suitcase, car boot) in order to find something worth stealing. In these circumstances it would be unsatisfactory to convict D of attempting to steal a purse, for example, if D had already examined the purse and decided not to take it. This may explain the rather sweeping statement of the Court of Appeal in *Easom* (1971)[62] that 'a conditional appropriation will not do'. Subsequently the Court of Appeal held that the correct form of indictment in these 'container' cases would be to charge D with attempting to steal 'all or any of the contents' of the bag, vehicle, or other container.[63] However, it has been pointed out that this is hardly more satisfactory in a case like *Easom*, where D had examined all the contents of the handbag and had found nothing worth taking. It is an offence to attempt something that turns out to be impossible,[64] and so the better wording is to charge D with simply attempting to steal from the container.[65]

Neither of the two problems just discussed is mentioned in the Theft Act itself. The Act does not define 'an intention permanently to deprive', but it does provide, in section 6, an extension of the concept. It states, in a poorly drafted compromise provision,[66] that persons are to be treated as having an intention permanently to deprive in certain circumstances. The general principle is that where D's intention is 'to treat the thing as his own to dispose of regardless of the other's rights', this is equivalent to an intention permanently to deprive. Sir John Smith quotes the *Shorter Oxford Dictionary*'s definition of 'dispose of' as 'to deal with definitely; to get rid of; to get done with, finish; to make over by way of sale or bargain; sell'.[67] One example of this is the ransom principle, where D takes V's property, telling V that he will return it only if V pays the asking price. D is clearly treating the property as 'his own to dispose of regardless of the other's rights', in that he is bargaining with the owner (in effect) to sell them

---

[62] [1971] 2 QB 315; for analysis, see K. Campbell, 'Conditional Intention' (1982) 2 Legal Studies, 77.

[63] *Attorney-General's References (Nos 1 and 2 of 1979)* [1980] QB 180, *Smith and Smith* [1986] Crim LR 166.   [64] See Ch 11.3(c).

[65] J. C. Smith, *Law of Theft*, 69.

[66] See J. R. Spencer, 'The Metamorphosis of Section 6 of the Theft Act' [1977] Crim LR 653.

[67] J. C. Smith, *Law of Theft*, 70, quoted with approval in *Cahill* [1993] Crim LR 141.

back.[68] It is right to bring such cases within theft, inasmuch as they are takings where, as section 6 puts it, D does not mean 'the other permanently to lose the thing itself', and yet where the substance of D's intended taking and V's intended loss is little different from permanent deprivation. However, the Divisional Court has effectively broadened section 6(1) in *DPP* v *Lavender* (1994),[69] where D had taken two doors from a council house undergoing repair and had fitted them to another council house to replace damaged doors. The Court did not refer to the dictionary definition of 'dispose of', but appeared to hold that 'dealing with' the doors could amount to 'disposing of' them. The Court therefore held that D should be convicted of stealing the doors, even though they had simply been transferred from one council property to another. This is unsatisfactory.

Section 6 goes on to deal with two specific types of case. One, set out in section 6(2), is where D parts with V's property under a condition as to its return which D may be unable to fulfil; the obvious example of this is pawning another's property, hoping to be able to redeem it at some time in the future. The other example, in section 6(1), is where D borrows or lends V's property: this may amount to D treating it as his own to dispose of 'if, but only if, the borrowing or lending is for a period and in circumstances equivalent to an outright taking or disposal'. Although this is an extension of the idea of intending permanent deprivation, the final few words may prove fairly restrictive. Their scope was considered by the Court of Appeal in *Lloyd* (1985),[70] where a cinema employee removed films from the cinema for a few hours, thereby enabling others to copy the films with a view to selling 'pirate' copies. The employee always intended to return the films, and always did. Clearly, his conduct in allowing others to make copies did significantly reduce the value of the films, but it is not possible to say, as section 6(1) requires, that his borrowing constituted an outright taking. He did not render the films valueless, even though he did reduce their commercial value by enabling the production of copies. Fewer people might pay to watch the films at the cinema. Lord Lane CJ stated the effect of section 6(1) in these terms: 'A mere borrowing is never enough to constitute the necessary guilty mind unless the intention is to return the 'thing' in such a changed state that it can truly be said that all its goodness or virtue has gone.'[71]

The application of this test may be illustrated by D, who takes V's railway season ticket, which expires on 31 January, and maintains that it

---

[68] *Coffey* [1987] Crim LR 498; cf. *Chan Man-Sin* v *R* [1988] 1 All ER 1.
[69] [1994] Crim LR 297. [70] [1985] QB 928.
[71] Ibid., 836; in *Bagshaw* [1988] Crim LR 321, the Court of Appeal commented that this restrictive reading of s 6(1) was obiter.

was always his intention to return it on 1 February. His intention clearly is to return the ticket, which may be physically unchanged, but, since it will no longer be valid, it is fair to describe it as being in a 'changed state'. 'All its goodness' will have gone by 1 February and so D is liable to conviction. But if D maintains that it was always his intention to return the ticket on 30 January, it will still be valid for one more day and, on the *Lloyd* test, D would have to be acquitted (if the court believed the story). Thus, by using the word 'all', Lord Lane made it clear that few borrowings will amount to theft. Some might argue that the wording of section 6 is slightly more flexible—'in circumstances making it *equivalent* to an outright taking'—but the only way of introducing greater flexibility would be to hold that an intention substantially to reduce the value of the property would suffice, and such a broad reading would go against the principle of maximum certainty (see Chapter 3.4(i)). The real problem here is that, without a general offence of temporary deprivation, judicial attempts to stretch an offence based on an intention permanently to deprive are likely to produce difficulties.

Any review of the law of theft ought to consider whether there is not a strong case for dispensing with the requirement of an intention permanently to deprive. At present there are only two such offences in the Theft Act—Section 12, penalizing the taking of cars, bicycles, etc. without the owner's consent; and section 11, penalizing the removal of an article on display in places open to the public, such as museums and galleries. Among the arguments for penalizing temporary deprivation generally,[72] probably the strongest are that the chief value of many items lies in their use and that many modern objects are intended for fashion or for a relatively short active life. If someone obtains an item for a period and deprives the other of its use for the same period, there may be far more gain and loss involved than in many cases of theft in which there is an intention permanently to deprive. In many similar cases where deception is used, there will be an offence of obtaining services by deception;[73] but if the advantage is gained boldly, without deception, the criminal law is rarely broken. The usual counter-argument is that the criminal law would be extended to many trivial 'borrowings' without consent, and that the police and courts would be flooded by such cases. However, this does not appear to have occurred in those European and Commonwealth jurisdictions which have extended their law of theft in this way. The real question is whether a sufficiently strong case for extending the ambit of the criminal law has been made: police and prosecutorial discretion might

---

[72] See G. Williams, 'Temporary Appropriation Should Be Theft' [1981] Crim. LR 129; A. T. H. Smith, *Property Offences*, 191; *Conspiracy to Defraud*, Law Com No. 228 (1994), 32–4.   [73] See below, Ch 9.7(a).

serve to eliminate minor cases, but does the existence of major cases justify criminalization? Could these major cases, such as unauthorized copying of materials and other commercial malpractices, be covered adequately by specific offences? Would this approach not have the further advantage of removing the need for the over-complicated provisions in section 6? These issues will doubtless be canvassed in the Law Commission's review of dishonesty offences.

(e) The Element of Dishonesty

Perhaps the core concept in the Theft Acts of 1968 and 1978 is dishonesty. The breadth of the definition of appropriation means that the finding of dishonesty may often make the difference between conviction and acquittal. In most cases, the presence or absence of dishonesty turns not so much on D's view of the situation but on the characterization of D's conduct by the jury or magistrates—and that characterization may be grounded in social attitudes and moral judgments which proceed from a particular social perspective. Let us consider the details.

The 1968 Act does not provide a definition of dishonesty, but it does stipulate in section 2 that, in each of three instances, an appropriation may *not* be considered dishonest for the purposes of the crime of theft.[74] The first instance, in section 2(1)(a), is where D believes that he has the legal right to deprive V of it. An example of this is where D seizes money from V, believing that V owes him the money.[75] In many cases under this provision there will be a mistake of law (usually, of civil law), and the main question will be whether the court is satisfied that D actually had the mistaken belief claimed—or, to reflect the burden of proof, whether the prosecution has established beyond reasonable doubt that this was not D's actual belief. The second instance, in section 2(1)(b), is where D believes that V would have consented if V had known of the circumstances. The third, in section 2(1)(c), is where D believes that the owner of the property cannot be discovered by taking reasonable steps. This applies chiefly to people who find property and conclude that it would be too difficult to trace the owner.

The main feature of section 2, then, is that it removes three types of case from the possible ambit of 'dishonesty', making it clear that it is the personal beliefs of defendants which are crucial here. The only other legislative clue to the meaning of 'dishonesty' is the declaration in section 2(2) that an appropriation may be dishonest even though D is willing to pay for the property. Apart from that, the definition of dishonesty is at large,

---

[74] Section 2 does not apply to the term 'dishonesty' as used in other offences under the Theft Act such as the deception offences and handling, nor to conspiracy to defraud.

[75] *Robinson* [1977] Crim LR 173.

and the courts have been left to develop an approach. They have insisted that the meaning of dishonesty is a matter for the jury or magistrates and not a matter of law, but the judges have gone on to lay down a proper approach to the question. It seems that there are three stages. First, the court must ascertain D's beliefs in relation to the appropriation—the reasons, motivations, explanations. Secondly, the jury or magistrates must decide whether a person acting with those beliefs would be regarded as dishonest according to the current standards of ordinary decent people. Thirdly, if there is evidence that D thought that the conduct was not dishonest according to those general standards, D should be acquitted if the court is left in reasonable doubt on the matter.

The first and second stages in the test were laid down in *Feely* (1973),[76] where D had 'borrowed' money from his employer's safe despite a warning that employees must not do so. D's explanation was that he intended to repay the sum out of money which his employer owed him (which amply covered the deficiency). The Court of Appeal held that the key question for the court should have been whether a person who takes money in those circumstances and with that intention is dishonest according to the current standards of ordinary decent people. The third stage was added by *Ghosh* (1982),[77] where the Court of Appeal tried to reconcile two lines of earlier cases. The example given by the court was of a foreigner failing to pay when travelling on English public transport in the belief that it is free. However, as has been pointed out,[78] this is a poor example, which would render the third stage superfluous. D's own beliefs are already considered at the first stage, so that, in the example given, the court would then consider at the second stage whether a foreigner with that belief would be dishonest according to the current standards of ordinary decent people. The answer would surely be no. Moreover, even though the third stage does not provide a defence where D acts on strong moral or social beliefs which he knows are not shared by 'ordinary decent people', it may provide a defence for the person who thinks that 'ordinary decent people' would not regard his conduct as dishonest. Whether people who are so out of tune with current standards should be acquitted is a difficult issue. But the overall complexity makes it hardly surprising that the Court of Appeal has declared that the third stage should not be mentioned to a jury unless the facts specifically raise it.[79]

The three-stage test of dishonesty evolved by the courts is complex and controversial. Moreover, its sphere of operation is enormous: around one-half of all indictable charges tried by the courts include a requirement

---

[76] [1973] QB 530.   [77] [1982] QB 1053.
[78] See K. Campbell, 'The Test of Dishonesty in *R v Ghosh*' [1984] Camb LJ 349.
[79] *Roberts* (1985) 84 Cr App R 177, *Price* [1990] Crim LR 200.

of dishonesty. The few specific instances covered by section 2 are relevant only to a few theft charges. Where the charge is deception or any other offence covered by the Theft Act, it is the three-stage judicial test which governs completely. Yet that test is open to serious objections.[80] The root of the problem has been the assumption, first stated by the Criminal Law Revision Committee[81] and then espoused by the courts in the 1970s,[82] that dishonesty is easily recognized and that the concept should therefore be treated as an ordinary word. Neither part of this assumption is well founded. Dishonesty may be easily recognized in some situations, but it is far more difficult in situations with which a jury or magistrates are unfamiliar—such as alleged business fraud or financial misdealing. Moreover, much depends on who is responsible for characterizing conduct as dishonest. In a multicultural society with widely differing degrees of wealth, it may often happen that someone who is poor or is a member of a minority community may have his or her conduct characterized as honest or dishonest by people who are relatively wealthy and are members of the majority community. There may also be an element of hypocrisy in this, since it is well known that practices which are strictly dishonest abound in the business or private lives of people at all levels.[83] Many, or most, forms of employment have their 'perks' according to which some practices of employees taking or using company property have become so traditional as to be thought of almost as an entitlement, and employers are content to 'turn a blind eye' to this. This all tends to suggest that there are situations in which dishonesty cannot be regarded as an ordinary word with a clear, shared meaning. On the other hand, it might be thought better that such an issue is resolved by a jury or lay magistrates than on a judge's direction.[84]

There are further objections to using the 'current standards of ordinary decent people' as a test for establishing dishonesty. It embodies a derogation from the principle of maximum certainty in the criminal law.[85] It also increases the risk of different courts reaching different verdicts on essentially similar sets of facts, and leaves room for the infiltration of irrelevant factors. The *Feely* problem of borrowing money without permission is not unusual, but differently constituted juries might take a different view of its dishonesty. The inherent uncertainty of the test might

[80] E. Griew, 'Dishonesty: The Objections to *Feely* and *Ghosh*' [1985] Crim LR 341; N. Lacey, C. Wells, and D. Meure, *Reconstructing Criminal Law* (1990) 469–71.

[81] Criminal Law Revision Committee, 8th Report, *Theft and Related Offences* (1966, Cmnd 2977), para 39.

[82] But strongly criticized in Australia: see e.g. *Salvo* [1980] VR 401.

[83] For details from the most specific to the most general, see e.g. S. Henry, *The Hidden Economy* (1978); G. Mars, *Cheats at Work* (1982); and M. Levi, *Regulating Fraud: White-Collar Crime and the Criminal Process* (1987).

[84] R. Tur, 'Dishonesty and Jury Questions', in A. Phillips Griffiths (ed), *Philosophy and Practice* (1985).   [85] See above, Ch 3.4(i) and (j).

also work against the efficiency of the system, by encouraging defendants to contest charges in the hope of finding a tribunal which is either sympathetic in its view of current standards or confused by the complexity of the three-stage test.

It is far easier to criticize the test, however, than to propose a replacement which overcomes all the objections. Some years ago D. W. Elliott proposed that the requirement of dishonesty should be jettisoned; that the three types of case now covered by section 2(1) should be declared not to be theft; and that the statutory definition of appropriation should exclude all appropriations 'not detrimental to the interests of the owner in a significant practical way'.[86] This would have the advantages of greater simplicity than *Ghosh* and of confining the decisions of juries and magistrates to whether the taking was too trivial to justify conviction, but it would fall well below the principle of maximum certainty until the courts had developed some specific criteria. Somewhat similar are the proposals of Peter Glazebrook, which stem from the proposition that no conduct that is not legally wrongful should be sufficient for theft.[87] From this starting-point, Glazebrook assumes the presence of dishonesty unless the case can be brought within one of a number of listed exceptions. The first three exceptions correspond to those in the existing section 2(1), and two others correspond to section 3(2) (purchasers in good faith) and section 4(3) (pickers of wild produce not for a commercial purpose). While Glazebrook does not list a *de minimis* exception of the kind proposed by Elliott, he deals explicitly with one group of cases that Elliott assumed would be excluded by his *de minimis* exception. Thus one of Glazebrook's exceptions is that a person who appropriates property is not to be regarded as dishonest if:

the property is money, some other fungible, a thing in action or intangible property, and is appropriated with the intention of replacing it, and in the belief that it will be possible for him to do so without loss to the person to whom it belongs.

What convinces both Elliott and Glazebrook that these 'borrowing' cases should not be theft? They are cases of wrongdoing, in terms of civil law, but Elliott would exclude them because and in so far as they are not serious enough to justify criminalization. Presumably D's belief in the ability to make repayment is one central factor in this judgment, along with surrounding circumstances about the significance of the event for the owner which may suggest that it is sufficient to treat it as a civil matter.

---

[86] D. W. Elliott, 'Dishonesty in Theft: A Dispensable Concept' [1982] Crim LR 395, adapting the words of McGarvie J., in the Australian case of *Bonollo* [1981] VR 633, at 656.
[87] Glazebrook, 'Revising the Theft Acts' [1993] Camb LJ 191.

This may, however, mean that the differential treatment of employee 'pilfering' and ordinary small-value shoplifting is perpetuated, though this time under the guise of judgments about relative significance. In theory Elliott's test could become the gateway to the decriminalization of much shoplifting, on the basis that a small-value taking is hardly likely to be detrimental in a significant practical way to the interests of Tesco, Sainsbury, or other major retailers, but courts are unlikely to adopt this reading. Glazebrook's formula is concerned more directly with the 'borrower' of money, and would lead to an acquittal in cases such as *Feely*.[88] Presumably the argument here is similar to Elliott's—that these cases are not serious enough to justify criminalization. The provision is narrower in scope, but would be easier to administer since it requires no normative judgment from the court.

9.3 TAKING A CONVEYANCE WITHOUT CONSENT

Although an appropriation of another's property without an intention to deprive the other of it permanently does not normally amount to an offence under English law, there are a few exceptions. The best known and most frequently invoked is the offence of taking a conveyance without the owner's consent, contrary to section 12 of the Theft Act 1968. In the early 1990s there was growing public concern over 'joy-riding' by young drivers who took cars in order to race them and to give 'displays', and this concern was heightened when some of the offences ended in the deaths of pedestrians or other road users. In 1992 Parliament passed the Aggravated Vehicle-Taking Act, empowering courts to impose harsher sentences in many such cases. The Act was mentioned in Chapter 7.6 during the discussion of serious motoring offences, but its structure will be examined here since it is an aggravated form of the basic offence under section 12 of the Theft Act.

The offence created by section 12(1) applies to the taking of any 'conveyance', which includes any contraption for carrying one or more persons by land, water, or air. There is a distinct offence in section 12(5) relating to pedal cycles. The offence may be committed in three separate ways: taking a conveyance, driving a conveyance that has been taken, and allowing oneself to be carried in a conveyance that has been taken. The conduct of a passenger in a 'stolen' car will often amount to aiding and abetting the driver (see Chapter 10), but section 12 dispenses with the need to prove any encouragement by the passenger and penalizes anyone who 'allows himself to be carried in or on' the conveyance. This is an example of treating offences committed by two or more people as more serious than

---

[88] Above, n. 76 and accompanying text.

offences committed by one person acting alone: as in conspiracy,[89] the assumption is that mutual reinforcement and group dynamics will often result in the causing of greater harm.

The offence requires a taking, which is constituted by moving the vehicle but not by merely getting into it.[90] A vehicle can be 'taken' by a person authorized to drive it—for example, an employed van-driver or lorry-driver—if that person deviates significantly (in time or place) from the permitted use.[91] The taking must be 'for his own or another's use': this will easily be fulfilled in most cases, but it has been held that pushing a car round a corner as a prank, to induce the owner to believe that it has been stolen, falls outside section 12.[92] The taking must be 'without having the consent of the owner or other lawful authority,' and the controversial issue concerns the obtaining of permission by deception. The wording of section 12 makes no reference to cases of deception, and the courts have vacillated on the issue. Two decisions suggest a rather unconvincing distinction between the person who drives the car on a permitted journey and then subsequently takes the car on an unauthorized jaunt—guilty, according to *Phipps and McGill* (1970)[93]—and the person who obtains permission for one journey but instead goes on a completely different journey—not guilty, according to *Peart* (1970).[94] The Court of Appeal's ability to find a fresh 'taking' in the first case and not the second seems an insubstantial difference, although it must be said that the statutory provision itself is unhelpful. In *Whittaker and Whittaker* v *Campbell* (1983)[95] the Divisional Court applied the general principles of contract law and took the firm line that section 12 does not extend and was not intended to extend to cases in which consent was obtained, but was obtained by some deception. Thus D, who obtained the hire of a van by pretending to be another person (whose driving licence he had found), was held not to have taken the van without the owner's consent, since this would not be grounds for holding a contract void in English law. This is a rare instance of the courts recognizing that the law of theft presupposes the general civil law relating to property. That, however, raises the question of whether it is property law, or the criminal law's general approach to consent (e.g. in sexual offences and non-fatal offences against the person),[96] that should supply the guiding principles.

The fault elements required for this offence are few. Taking another person's vehicle can hardly be done by accident, but section 12(6) provides that there is no offence where D believes 'that he has lawful authority to do it or that he would have the owner's consent if the owner knew of his doing

[89] See Ch 11.4 below.
[91] *McKnight* v *Davies* [1974] RTR 4.
[93] [1970] RTR 209.
[95] (1983) 77 Cr App R 267.

[90] *Bogacki* [1973] QB 832.
[92] *Stokes* [1982] Crim LR 695.
[94] [1970] 2 QB 672.
[96] See above, Ch 8.3(f) and 8.5(e).

it and of the circumstances of it'. This test, similar to section 2(1) of the Act on dishonesty in theft, is entirely subjective. Where the charge is that D drove a vehicle or allowed himself to be carried in it, the prosecution must prove that D knew that the conveyance had been taken without authority.

The offence under section 12 is triable summarily only and has a maximum penalty of six months' imprisonment. All the elements of the basic offence must be proved if D is to be convicted and sentenced under the provisions of the Aggravated Vehicle-Taking Act 1992, technically a separate offence in view of its higher maximum penalties.[97] The 1992 Act inserts a new section 12A into the Theft Act 1968, which has the effect of imposing strict liability on a person who commits the basic section 12 offence and where 'at any time after the vehicle was unlawfully taken (whether by him or another) and before it was recovered, the vehicle was driven, or injury or damage was caused, in one of more of [four] circumstances'. It will be noted that no causal connection is required between D's involvement and the causing of injury or damage, a form of criminalization that goes even beyond the ordinary bounds of strict liability. The four circumstances are:

(a) that the vehicle was driven dangerously on a road or other public place;
(b) that, owing to the driving of the vehicle, an accident occurred by which injury was caused to any person;
(c) that, owing to the driving of the vehicle, an accident occurred by which damage was caused to any property, other than the vehicle; and
(d) that damage was caused to the vehicle.

The maximum penalty is two years' imprisonment or, where death results under (b) above, five years' imprisonment. This makes clear the impact of the strict liability—an enormous increase in the maximum penalty without proof of any fault other than that required for the basic offence. As a matter of sentencing, a court would be expected to take account of D's culpability, but it is plain from the different maxima that the mere fact of death resulting is an aggravating feature.[98] Where D is convicted on the basis of being carried in the vehicle, a substantial custodial sentence has been approved on the basis that 'the presence of a passenger in a stolen vehicle of this sort, while it is driven in this manner [at high speed and dangerously], amounts, in our judgment, to encouragement'.[99] Much of the conduct at which the new provision is aimed is seriously irresponsible

[97] This procedural point emerges from *Courtie* [1984] AC 463. On the 1992 Act generally, see J. N. Spencer, 'The Aggravated Vehicle-Taking Act 1992' [1992] Crim LR 699.
[98] See the guideline judgment in *Bird* (1992) 14 Cr App R (S) 343, and the decision in *Ore and Tandy* [1994] Crim LR 304, with commentary by D. A. Thomas.
[99] *Sealey* (1993) 15 Cr App R (S) 189, nine months' imprisonment upheld.

and ought clearly to be criminalized. There is already a wide array of road traffic offences, but prosecutors were encountering difficulties in proving the elements of serious offences against defendants in this type of case—particularly where the car was driven dangerously and then abandoned in circumstances in which it was impossible to prove which one of two or more occupants was driving. Such problems of proof are not unique to this type of case,[100] and it is questionable whether they justify such egregious strict liability as is imposed by the 1992 Act.

9.4 ROBBERY

Robbery can be one of the most serious offences in the criminal calendar, and average sentences are higher than for any other crime apart from rape and murder. The definition of the offence is within the Theft Act 1968, but it is largely an offence of violence and is triable only in the Crown Court. Some 4,500 persons are convicted of robbery each year, and many of these offences are planned attacks on persons in charge of money or other valuables at banks, building societies, or in security companies. However, as we shall see in the paragraphs that follow, many fairly minor forms of bag-snatching can be charged as robbery. This creates a problem of fair labelling: a major armed robbery falls into the same legal category as a sudden, impulsive bag-snatching. The offence is extremely wide, and its drafting owes more to efficiency of administration than to fairness of labelling. Thus the starting-point when sentencing someone convicted of robbery of a bank or security vehicle in which firearms were carried and no serious injury done has been held to be 15 years' imprisonment,[101] with smaller scale robberies of building society branches often sentenced in the range from four to seven years, and bag-snatching at a much lower level.[102] However, the detection rate for robbery is rather low, with fewer than 25 per cent 'cleared up' in recent years.

The legal elements of robbery contrary to section 8 of the Theft Act 1968 are theft accompanied by the use of force. It follows from this that if D has a defence to theft, there can be no conviction for robbery. Thus where D brandished a knife at V in order to get V to hand over money which D believed he was owed, it was held that this could be neither theft nor robbery if the jury found that D did believe that he had a legal right to the money (and so was not dishonest: section 2(1)(a)).[103] Conviction for another offence, such as possessing an offensive weapon or blackmail,

---

[100] See Ch 10.2. [101] *Turner* (1975) 61 Cr App R 67, at 89–92.

[102] For discussion, see Ashworth, *Sentencing and Criminal Justice* (2nd edn, 1995), Ch 4.4(b).

[103] *Robinson* [1977] Crim LR 173; cf. *Forrester* [1992] Crim LR 793.

might be possible on these facts. But if there is no theft, there can be no robbery.

The legal definition of robbery has given rise to little case law. The only noteworthy development has been the courts' interpretation of the minimum amount of force needed to convert a theft into a robbery. Section 8 of the Act requires it to be proved that, immediately before or at the time of stealing, and in order to steal, D 'used force on a person or put or sought to put any person in fear of being then and there subjected to force'. Several points of interpretation arise here. The force or threat of force must take place immediately before or at the time of the theft: this seems to exclude the use of force immediately after the offence, but the Court of Appeal has circumvented this limitation by holding that the appropriation element in theft continues while the thieves are tying up their victims so as to make good their escape.[104] The force must be used in order to steal, not merely on the same occasion as the stealing. Where there is a threat of force, the threat must be to subject a person (not necessarily the victim of the theft) to immediate violence—a threat to injure at some time in the future would be insufficient for robbery.

One question which has engaged the attention of the courts is, at first sight, a perfectly simple one: what does the phrase 'uses force on a person' mean? *Dawson and James* (1976)[105] seems to hold that bumping into someone so as to knock him off balance may be sufficient force. The result of *Clouden* (1987)[106] seems to be that pulling V's handbag in a way which causes her hand to be pulled downwards amounts to using force on a person. None of the defendants in these cases could claim any social or moral merit in their activities, but should they be classified as robbers rather than mere thieves? Of course it is difficult to draw the line between sufficient and insufficient force, but if robbery is to continue to be regarded as a serious offence, triable only on indictment and punishable with life imprisonment, surely something more than a bump, a push, or a pull should be required. There is a case for requiring at least the threat or the actual causing of injury, together with theft, as constituents of robbery. This would leave lesser cases to be dealt with by means of the laws on theft and assault, reserving the label 'robbery' for non-minor cases, and thereby promoting the principle of fair labelling (Chapter 3.5(s)).

---

[104] *Hale* (1978) 68 Cr App R 415, above p. 366.
[105] (1976) 64 Cr App R 150.
[106] [1987] Crim LR 56; the decision also goes directly against the Criminal Law Revision Committee's view (8th Report (1966), para 65), that 'we should not regard mere snatching of property, such as a handbag, from an unresisting owner as using force for the purpose of the definition, though it might be so if the owner resisted'.

9.5 BLACKMAIL[107]

It was noted earlier that the criminal law does not penalize all threats of violence,[108] although it does criminalize threats made in order to obtain sexual intercourse.[109] We have just seen that robbery is committed if a person uses a threat of immediate violence in order to steal property. The essence of blackmail contrary to section 21 of the Theft Act 1968 is the making of a demand, reinforced by menaces, with a view to making a gain or inflicting a loss. Blackmail is therefore wider than the other offences committed by threats, since it is not confined to threats of violence. The word 'menaces' has been held to extend to threats of 'any action detrimental to or unpleasant to the person addressed',[110] and may involve a threat to disclose some compromising information. On the other hand, blackmail is narrower than some other 'threat' offences, in that the offence is only committed where D makes the demand 'with a view to gain for himself or another or with intent to cause loss to another'. The definitions of 'gain' and 'loss'[111] are supposed to establish blackmail as a property offence, although the notion of 'gain' has been applied to the obtaining of a pain-killing injection from a doctor.[112]

What, then, are the elements of blackmail as a property offence? First, there must be a demand: this is a question of substance not form, and, in an appropriate context, the politest words can amount to a demand.[113] Secondly, the exact nature of the demand does not matter, but there must be the elements of gain or loss, discussed above. Thirdly, the demand must be accompanied by menaces. The broad definition of 'menaces' already quoted suggests that this is an objective question, but what approach should be taken to the person who knowingly exploits another's timidity? This point was raised in *Garwood* (1987),[114] and Lord Lane CJ held that there are two situations in which a court may need to go beyond the test of whether the menaces would affect a person of normal stability. One is where the menaces would affect a person of normal stability but did not influence the particular victim: that is sufficient. The other is where the menaces would not affect a person of normal stability but did influence

---

[107] See the symposium of articles on blackmail in (1993) 141 U Pa LR.
[108] See above, Ch 8.3(e).   [109] See above, 8.5(f).
[110] *Thorne* v *Motor Trade Association* [1937] AC797.
[111] In s 34(2)(a) of the Theft Act 1968.
[112] *Bevans* (1988) 87 Cr App R 64.
[113] *Treacy* v *DPP* [1971] AC 537. For philosophical discussion of the difference between a demand and a promise, see Lamond, 'Coercion, Threats, and the Puzzle of Blackmail', in Simester and Smith (eds), *Harm and Culpability* (forthcoming 1995).
[114] (1987) 85 Cr App R 85.

the actual victim: that is sufficient if it is established that D was aware of the likely effect of his conduct on this victim.[115]

Fourthly, it must be established that the demand was 'unwarranted', within the special definition in section 21: 'a demand with menaces is unwarranted unless the person making it does so in the belief—(a) that he has reasonable grounds for making the demand; and (b) that the use of menaces is a proper means of reinforcing the demand'. It will be noticed that this definition incorporates a fault element which focusses on the presence of two beliefs in D's mind. The first element classifies a demand as unwarranted unless D thinks there are reasonable grounds for making the demand. This will usually mean that D believes that he has a right to whatever he is demanding—a provision roughly parallel to section $2(1)(a)$ of the Theft Act 1988, which holds that there is no dishonesty in theft if D believes that he has a legal right to the property taken. The second element classifies a demand as unwarranted unless D believes that the menaces are a 'proper' means of reinforcing the demand. This element plugs a gap which we noticed in the definition of robbery: someone who threatens another in order to obtain what be believes to be his rightful property is not guilty of robbery—he is not being dishonest—but he may be guilty of blackmail if the second element is fulfilled.

The wording of this second element might seem to be 'doubly subjective' again—in that D's own moral standards seem to set the standard of liability. If D was brought up to think that it was proper to threaten those who do not pay their debts, he would be immune from conviction for blackmail. But it is not certain that this is the correct meaning of this element. The Committee which proposed the test intended the word 'proper' to refer to what was thought to be morally and socially acceptable.[116] This would move away from D's own standards towards a test similar to Ghosh (on dishonesty): did D believe that people in general would regard the use of menaces as proper? It seems that both elements should be left to the jury, but that does not settle the issue of whether it is D's own standards or general social standards which are the focus of the second element. One decision went so far as to lay down that if D knows that a threatened act is unlawful, it cannot be maintained that it was believed 'proper'.[117] That favours the view that it is general social standards which apply here, but one might then go on to ask how one discovers what they are. As with the Ghosh test of dishonesty, there is much ambiguity and potential for inconsistent verdicts. It would be clearer and simpler to place the matter entirely on D's own belief as to what was

[115] Ibid., at 88, applying Lawrence and Pomroy (1971) 57 Cr App R 64 and Clear [1968] 1 QB 670.   [116] CLRC, 8th Report (1966), para 123.
[117] Harvey, Vylett and Plummer (1981) 72 Cr App R 139.

'proper': the issue will rarely arise, and where the courts have doubts about D's understanding of what was proper, there is a case for avoiding criminal liability. Of course, this amounts to a deviation from the policy of presumed knowledge of the law[118]—by allowing one individual's standard to set the bounds of the criminal sanction—but it does so at a point where clear objective standards peter out. Any objective standard would inevitably be uncertain, thus derogating from the 'rule of law' principles of maximum certainty and fair warning.

9.6 BURGLARY

One of the aims of the Theft Act 1968 was to reduce the earlier mass of prolix offences to a reasonable minimum. The law thus abandoned a definition which distinguished between burglaries of dwellings and other premises, although sentencers continue to reflect the widely felt difference in seriousness by imposing more severe sentences on those who break into dwellings. The psychological effects of residential burglary are well documented: Maguire and Bennett found that about a quarter of victims 'are, temporarily at least, badly shaken by the experience', and that a small minority of victims suffer longer-lasting effects.[119] By virtue of a change in sentencing law, there are now separate offences of burglary in a dwelling and other burglaries again. The Criminal Justice Act 1991 reduced the maximum penalty for non-residential burglary to 10 years, retaining the 14-year maximum for burglary in a dwelling. This separation of maximum penalties has the procedural effect of creating separate offences,[120] and the prosecution must specify which form of burglary is being charged. However, the legal definition continues unchanged, with no reference to the psychological harm which constitutes the gravamen of burglary in a dwelling.

The offence of burglary contrary to section 9 of the Theft Act 1968 has a wide ambit, but its essence may be summarized thus: it may be committed either by entering a building as a trespasser with intent to steal, or by stealing after entering a building as a trespasser. 'Entry', does not require entry of the whole body: it is sufficient if, say, an arm is put through a broken window to take goods from within.[121] What must be entered is a building or part of a building: this is drafted so as to cover the person who enters the building itself lawfully, but then trespasses by going into a forbidden part of the building. The forbidden part does not have to be a separate room: it has been held that a customer in a shop who goes into

---

[118] See above, Ch 6.7(a).
[119] M. Maguire and T. Bennett, *Burglary in a Dwelling* (1982), 164.
[120] *Courtie* [1984] AC 463.   [121] *Brown* [1985] Crim LR 611.

the area behind a service counter enters part of a building as a trespasser.[122] The requirement of trespass places a civil law concept at the centre of the offence. There is no general offence of trespass in English law—it is regarded as merely a civil matter between the parties—but a stealing or intent to steal converts trespass into the serious offence of burglary. In broad terms, someone who trespasses in another person's building is one who enters it without permission. Usually the permission will take the form of a direct invitation, but there may be cases of implied permission which raise difficulties of interpretation.

Two Court of Appeal decisions have been responsible for developing the requirement of entry as a trespasser in different, and possibly inconsistent, ways. In *Collins* (1973)[123] it was held that it is not enough that D would be classified as a trespasser in civil law: the criminal offence of burglary requires that D knew that, or was reckless as to whether, he was a trespasser. This protects from conviction the person who enters at the invitation of the householder's daughter, without realizing that she is unauthorized to give such permission. This decision kept the offence fairly narrow, by insisting on a fault element on this point, but the decision in *Smith and Jones* (1976)[124] broadened it by suggesting that the fault element is sufficient in itself. The defendants here had entered the house of Smith's father and stolen two television sets. The father maintained that his son would never be a trespasser in his house, but this did not prevent the Court of Appeal from upholding the convictions. The Court reasoned that Smith had entered 'in excess of the permission' given by his father, since the father's general permission surely did not extend to occasions when his son intended to commit a crime on the premises. The result of this decision seems to be that anyone who enters another person's building with intent to steal is a trespasser by virtue of that intention. This approach has what some would see as the great merit of removing questions of civil law from the centre of the offence and replacing them with a straightforward test more appropriate to criminal trials: did D enter the building with the intention of stealing? More turns on D's intent than on the technicalities of trespass.

Simplicity is a virtue in the criminal law, and yet *Smith and Jones* introduces difficulties. In the first place, it seems inconsistent with *Collins*, where D had a (conditional) intent to rape the woman who invited him in, but this was not held to invalidate her permission. More importantly, the boundaries of burglary are being pushed wider than is necessary or appropriate. Surely the proper label for what was done in *Smith and Jones* is theft, and the availability of the charges of theft and attempted theft

---

[122] *Walkington* (1979) 68 Cr App R 427.
[123] [1973] QB 100.
[124] (1976) 63 Cr App R 47.

makes it unnecessary to strain the boundaries of trespass by inserting unstated reservations into general permissions given by householders. There is no element of suspicion, fear, or threat when the person who enters is someone who is generally permitted to do so. Of course, part of the problem here is that the present definition of burglary includes no reference to the factors which make it such a serious crime in some cases. Convictions for the offence might be rare if the prosecution had to prove that D intended to cause, or was reckless as to causing, fear, alarm, or distress—a burglar might try to avoid such effects by entering a house when the occupier is out and taking property without damaging or ransacking the premises—but even then the crime can cause considerable distress and fear (feelings that one's property has been sullied by another, for example, or that one's home is no longer a safe place).[125] The difficulty is that the real gravamen of many burglaries lies in an unintended, unforeseen, or even unwanted effect upon the victim. It is fair to fix the general level of sentences by reference to that element,[126] since the psychological effects ought to be widely recognized, but it is more problematic to make it a requirement in the definition of the offence.

Section 9 creates two forms of burglary. The first, contrary to section 9(1)(a), is a truly inchoate offence: entering a building as a trespasser with intent to steal, etc. The offence is complete as soon as D has entered with the requisite intent. What ordinary people might regard as an 'attempted burglary', since D has not yet stolen anything, is in fact the full offence. The section refers to entry with intent to steal 'anything therein', and in most cases it will not matter that D's intent was a conditional one, to steal only if something worth stealing were found.[127] The second form is, having entered as a trespasser, stealing or attempting to steal etc. (section 9(1)(b)). Either form of the offence becomes the more serious crime of aggravated burglary (section 10, punishable with life imprisonment) if D is carrying any firearm or imitation firearm, any weapon of offence or any explosive. In most of these instances there could, in any event, be a conviction for an additional offence in respect of the weapon. Section 10 incorporates the aggravating element into the label, but in one recent decision the Court of Appeal took this too far when extending the offence to D who, having used a screwdriver to effect entry, then prodded the householder in the stomach with it.[128]

Burglary also has another unexpected element. Not only does it have the inchoate form of entering a building with intent, but it also covers four

---

[125] See Maguire and Bennett, *Burglary in a Dwelling*, Ch 5.
[126] Cf. *Mussell* (1990) 12 Cr App R (S) 607 with *Bennett* (1994) 15 Cr App R (S) 213.
[127] See Smith, *Law of Theft*, 181, arguing that D might fall outside the section if his intention was only to steal a specific item if, on examination, it had certain characteristics.
[128] *Kelly* (1994) unreported.

different intents. The discussion thus far has concentrated on the intent to steal, since that is what one would expect. But, in fact, burglary is also committed by entering a building as a trespasser with intent to rape, to inflict grievous bodily harm or to commit criminal damage. This means that section 9(1)(a) burglary functions as an inchoate sexual offence and an inchoate violent offence: the intending rapist who enters, say, a nurses' home has not yet committed attempted rape, but he may well have committed burglary or (if armed) aggravated burglary. This illustrates the considerable reach of section 9(1)(a) burglary, going beyond that of an attempt to commit the substantive crime (e.g. rape). If it can be justified, it is on the ground that entering a building as a trespasser is a non-innocent act which should be sufficient (when combined with evidence of a proscribed intent, often inferred from surrounding circumstances or from the absence of any other plausible explanation) to warrant criminal liability. D has crossed the threshold between conceiving an intent and taking steps to translate the intent into action. It should also be noted that, where the charge is burglary contrary to section 9(1)(b), only two types of further offence convert the crime into burglary: D must have entered as a trespasser and then have either stolen or inflicted grievous bodily harm, or attempted either offence. Criminal damage and rape are not relevant to this form of burglary.

We have seen that what makes most residential burglaries more serious than most thefts is the element of invasion of privacy, with all the possible psychological effects which make it a more personal offence. It should therefore be mentioned that there are other offences which 'protect' the home: the Protection from Eviction Act 1977 (as amended) criminalizes the unlawful eviction or harassment of a residential occupier, and there are various offences in Part II of the Criminal Law Act 1977, which penalize the adverse occupation of residential premises. These offences are re-stated in the draft Criminal Code.[129]

9.7 HANDLING STOLEN GOODS

If has often been said that if there were fewer receivers of stolen goods, there would be fewer thieves.[130] This may well be true—there are professional 'fences' who act as outlets for stolen goods, and goods are sometimes stolen 'to order'[131]—although it is doubtful whether this is a sufficient justification for keeping the maximum penalty for handling stolen goods at 14 years, double the maximum for theft. Section 22 of the

---

[129] Law Com No. 177, cls 187–96.
[130] E.g. *Battams* (1979) 1 Cr App R(S) 15.
[131] See C. B. Klockars, *The Professional Fence* (1975), and Maguire and Bennett, *Burglary in a Dwelling*, 70–5.

Theft Act 1968 considerably extended the liability of persons concerned in dealing with stolen goods, creating a broad offence which covers many minor acts of assistance which might more naturally fall within inchoate offences or complicity. The aim was 'to combat theft by making it more difficult and less profitable to dispose of stolen property'.[132]

The essence of the offence of 'handling' is dealing with stolen goods. The concept of stolen goods includes goods obtained by means of theft (including robbery and burglary), deception, or blackmail, and it often covers the proceeds of such goods. Goods may, however, lose their classification as stolen if returned to their owner or to police custody, even temporarily.[133] The fault elements required for handling are dishonesty, and that D must 'know or believe' that the property is stolen, terms which include 'wilful blindness'[134] but not suspicion, even strong suspicion. The prohibited conduct may take one of four forms, but merely touching stolen property does not amount to the offence. 'Handling' is simply the compendious name for the four types of conduct. Type (i) is 'receiving' stolen property, which means taking control or possession of it. This is the most usual form of the offence, and applies to the 'fence' who takes the property from the thief for resale, and to the person who knowingly buys stolen goods from another. Type (ii) is 'arranging to receive' stolen goods, and here we meet the broadening of the offence. If D agrees to buy stolen goods from the thief, who is to deliver them later, D has 'arranged to receive' even before the thief has taken any action to bring the goods to him. Type (iii) is 'undertaking or assisting in their retention, removal, disposal or realization by or for the benefit of another person'. This is an extremely wide provision designed to criminalize those who help a thief or a receiver. It is rendered even wider by type (iv), which penalizes arrangements to do an act or omission within (iii). Thus, a person who does, assists in, or arranges to do or assist in any of the acts or omissions within type (iii) is criminally liable—on one condition. The condition is that it must be 'by or for the benefit of another person'. In the leading case of *Bloxham* (1983)[135] D bought a car, subsequently realizing that it was stolen. He then sold the car to someone else and was charged with type (iii) handling. The House of Lords quashed his conviction, on the ground that he sold the car for his own benefit, not for the benefit of another. He did not sell the car for the benefit of the original thief or handler, of whom he knew nothing; and it would be ridiculous to suggest that he sold it for the buyer's benefit. Moreover, D was originally a purchaser in good faith, and

---

[132] CLRC, 8th Report (1966), para 127.

[133] For an example, see *Attorney-General's Reference (No. 1 of 1974)* [1974] QB 744.

[134] Discussed above, Ch 5.3(d).

[135] [1983] 1 AC 109, responding to the promptings of J. R. Spencer, 'The Mishandling of Handling' [1981] Crim LR 682.

the policy of the Theft Act is not to criminalize such purchasers, even if they later discover the unwelcome truth about their purchases.[136]

The offence of handling is therefore drafted widely so as to cast a net around the main Theft Act offences. 'Since thieves may be helped not only by buying the property but also in other ways such as facilitating its disposal, it seems right that the offence should extend to these kinds of assistance.'[137] But in doing so the offence assumes the role normally played by the doctrine of complicity and the inchoate offences—while those doctrines then apply so as to widen the scope of criminal liability still further. The definition of handling eschews maximum certainty in favour of flexibility for prosecutors. And any impact of the policy of minimum criminalization is obviously muted where there are offences so wide as to cover attempting to arrange the removal of stolen goods, or counselling the retention of such property.

9.7 DECEPTION OFFENCES

(a) The Range of Deception Offences

Stealing and swindling seem to be nothing more than two means of obtaining the same thing. And, as we saw earlier, English law has developed in such a way that the same event can fulfil the definitions both of theft and of obtaining property by deception.[138] However, it was argued in 9.1(a) that the criminal law should continue to draw a distinction between the two types of offence, although it should be procedurally easier to substitute one charge for the other. Theft is typically a non-consensual taking of property. Deception, on the other hand, is a means of securing another's consent to the taking of property: deceptions may be practised for a whole range of purposes (e.g. obtaining consent to sexual familiarities, or obtaining consent to a surgical operation). There seems to be no general assumption that, in relation to property, deception is more heinous that a simple taking; it is just a different method. The maximum penalty for obtaining property by deception remained at 10 years when that for theft was reduced to seven years, but it would be unwise to draw inferences from this.

The criminal law provides a broad range of deception offences related to property, only a few of which are in the Theft Acts 1968 and 1978. The basic offence is obtaining property by deception (section 15 of the 1968

---

[136] Sections 3(1) and (2) of the Theft Act; and see the exchange on 'Handling, Theft and the Purchaser who Takes a Chance' between J. R. Spencer [1985] Crim LR 92, Glanville Williams [1985] Crim LR 432, and J. R. Spencer [1985] Crim LR 440.

[137] CLRC, 8th Report (1966), para 127.

[138] *Gomez* [1993] AC 442, discussed in 2(a) above.

Act), and it is supplemented by the offences of obtaining services by deception (section 1 of the 1978 Act), evasion of liability by deception (section 2 of the 1978 Act), and obtaining a pecuniary advantage by deception (section 16 of the 1968 Act). Beyond these offences lie several fraud offences, some of them in the Theft Act 1968 (section 17, false accounting; section 10, false statements by company directors; section 20(2), procuring the execution of a valuable security by deception); others in the Forgery and Counterfeiting Act 1981; fraudulent trading in the Companies Act 1985; these and several others surrounded by the ample girth of common law conspiracy to defraud.[139] More will be said about the control of fraud below, but first we will explore the essence of these deceptions.

(b) The Meaning of 'Deception'

The classic definition here is that 'to deceive is . . . to induce a man to believe that a thing is true which is false'.[140] That involves proof of causation, which is discussed further below. For the moment, we must consider what representations may amount to a deception (or attempted deception, in cases where causation is not established). Section 15(4) of the Theft Act 1968 casts the net wide: deception 'means any deception (whether deliberate or reckless) by words or conduct as to fact or as to law, including a deception as to the present intentions of the person using the deception or any other persons'. The breadth of this definition makes plain the legislature's purpose of avoiding doubt about whether misstatements of the law or deceptions as to intention should fall within the reach of the criminal law. Deceptions may, of course, be express or implied, and this is where the notion of deception as to conduct becomes important. Many everyday transactions are conducted on certain assumptions which it would be tedious to spell out or to check on every occasion. We assume that the woman wearing a police uniform is a policewoman, or that the woman wearing a nurse's uniform is a nurse. We also assume that when a person pays by cheque there will be the funds to meet the cheque. The representations implied by giving a cheque in payment have now been formalized in a number of decisions: it is implied (i) that the drawer has an account at the bank; and (ii) that the cheque will be met on presentment, which may mean that in practice that there are sufficient funds in the account, or that sufficient funds will be paid in before the cheque is presented, or that there is an arrangement with the bank for a sufficient overdraft facility.[141]

---

[139] Discussed at pp. 401–3 below.
[140] Per Buckley J., in *Re London and Globe Finance Corporation Ltd* [1903] 1 Ch 728, at 732.   [141] Discussed at pp. 398–9 below.

The courts have adopted a particularly zealous approach to cases involving a cheque card or credit card. In *Metropolitan Police Commissioner* v *Charles*[142] it was held that the use of a cheque card with a cheque implies not only that the bank will meet the cheques (provided they fall within the relevant conditions), but also that D has the authority to use the cheque card in this way or to this extent. Similarly, in *Lambie* (1982)[143] it was held that the use of a credit card implies not only that the credit card company will ensure that the money is paid, but also that D has the authority to use the credit card in this way or to this extent. Thus, in both these decisions a person was convicted because he or she had knowingly exceeded the borrowing limit imposed by the bank or credit card company. The key question here should be whether it is generally implied in such transactions that D has the authority (from the bank or credit card company) to use the card for this transaction: in practice, it seems doubtful whether that implication is conveyed to most traders, since the whole point of the card is to ensure that, if the proper formalities are observed, the trader will be paid.

Can silence on a particular point amount to a deception? According to the House of Lords in *DPP* v *Ray* (1974),[144] a person who enters a restaurant and orders a meal is impliedly representing that payment will be made. If the person then has a change of mind and decides not to pay, the very act of remaining there (eating the meal, drinking coffee, etc.) amounts to an implied misrepresentation and therefore a deception. A person who obtains property under such circumstances will be obtaining property by deception. (Where the change of mind occurs after the meal has been consumed, no further property is obtained by the deception: but there is a special offence under section 3 of the Theft Act 1978 of making off without payment.[145]) A further example would be where D, a builder, had done work for V and her family over the years and, on request, gave her a quotation for building work which was excessively high. In *Silverman* (1988)[146] the Court of Appeal held that this might amount to a deception by silence: V had grown to trust D by virtue of their previous dealings, and so when D quoted a price for the work to be done, D assumed (and D knew that she would assume) that it was a fair price. These do not seem to be objectionable extensions of the notion of deception: indeed, in view of the commercial significance of assumptions, it would be artificial to exclude deception by silence. Where D is under a duty to supply information to V as the basis for charging D money, and D refrains from supplying the information so that no charges are made, the omission can properly be held to amount to deception.[147]

---

[142] [1977] AC 177.   [143] [1982] AC 449.   [144] [1974] AC 370.
[145] Discussed in paragraph (e) below.
[146] (1988) 86 Cr App R 213.   [147] *Firth* [1990] Crim LR 326.

(c) Causation and Deception

It is axiomatic in deception offences that the deception must cause the obtaining. In practical terms, this means that the deception must precede the obtaining, and that it must be an operative cause of V's allowing D to obtain the property, services, or whatever. In most cases these propositions cause no difficulty: D says he is an investment agent when he is not, and V hands over a sum of money; D tricks V into believing that she is a student and therefore entitled to a student discount on a purchase or on entry to a concert. Let us take *Metropolitan Police Commissioner* v *Charles*, for instance:[148] in evidence the casino manager said that, when he saw that D had a cheque card, he had no hesitation in cashing the cheques because he knew that his employers would be assured of payment by the bank. So, even if (as the House of Lords held) there was an implied representation by D that he was authorized to use the cheque card to this extent, no such representation made an impact on V's decision to cash the cheques. Yet, later in his evidence, V stated that he would not have cashed the cheques if he had known that D was acting beyond the bank's authority. Does this mean that, in *Metropolitan Police Commissioner* v *Charles*, the deception caused the obtaining? The answer is: only if causation is established by holding that V would not have acted as he did, if he had known the facts of the situation. This may seem to be a difficult proposition to accept, since V clearly knew all the facts relevant to his decision to accept the cheques—he said so, regarding only the validity of the cheque card as relevant. So the causation test which the courts appear to be using here is not one of actual causation, asking the factual question of whether any mistaken belief implanted or encouraged by D operated on V's mind at the crucial time, but a test of hypothetical causation, asking whether V would have acted in the same way if he or she had known the true position.

Some have condemned this hypothetical test of causation as wrong and inappropriate.[149] However, it was argued in Chapter 4.6(c) that omissions cases cause no insuperable problems of causation, once a duty has been established. For example, where D fails to reveal a key fact relevant to a claim under an insurance contract, few would dispute the appropriateness of holding that D deceived V. There is a clear duty on the claimant to disclose all material facts in such a situation,[150] and it is therefore possible

---

[148] [1977] AC 177, above, p. 397.

[149] J. C. Smith, commentary [1977] Crim LR 617; A. T. H. Smith, 'The Idea of Criminal Deception' [1982] Crim LR 721.

[150] See the discussion by the Law Commission in *Insurance Law: Non-Disclosure and Breach of Warranty*, Law Com No. 104 (1988).

to say that, but for D's failure to fulfil his duty, the obtaining would not have taken place. The question then is whether this analysis of deception by omission can fairly be extended to many of the 'assumption' cases, where V acts on the basis of the usual assumptions and D hopes that V will do so. One might argue that, if it can be assumed that the shopkeeper or cashier would not wish to facilitate a breach of contract,[151] and if D is at least reckless as to whether this is so, there might be a deception by omission. However, opponents of the courts' broad approach in *Metropolitan Police Commissioner* v *Charles* and *Lambie* say that this is inconsistent with the legislature's use of the concept of deception, as distinct from 'fraud' or 'false pretences': the Criminal Law Revision Committee proposed the term 'deception' because it has 'the advantage of directing attention to the effect that the offender deliberately produced on the mind of the person deceived',[152] whereas the two House of Lords decisions effectively negate this requirement. Thus, although good arguments for finding operative deceptions in these cases were suggested above, it does seem that proper reference to legislative purpose would have led to the opposite conclusion.

It is the jury who must be satisfied that 'the deception was a material cause of the victim's parting with his property', and to this question it is 'irrelevant that other factors were operating on his mind at the same time'.[153] In *King and Stockwell* (1987)[154] the defendants told an old lady that they worked for a reputable firm of tree surgeons, that tree surgery was needed in order to avoid damage to the foundations of her house, and that it would cost some £500. The tree surgery was not necessary, and they knew it. In the Court of Appeal it was argued that the men had been wrongly convicted of attempting to obtain the money by deception because the money would have been paid for work done, but the Court held that the jury had rightly considered whether the defendants' false statement that the work was necessary would have been an operative cause of the obtaining of the money.

(d) The Fault Element in Deception Offences

Broadly speaking there are three fault elements in the deception offences. The first is dishonesty. The important point to note here is that section 2 of the Theft Act 1968 applies only to theft (and to offences of which theft is an element). It does not apply to deception offences, which are therefore governed solely by the *Ghosh* test, considered in 9.1(e) above. The second

---

[151] See *Doukas* [1978] I WLR 372, *Cooke* [1986] AC 909.

[152] CLRC, 8th Report (1966), para 87, although the 1968 penalizes reckless as well as deliberate deception; see also ibid., pp. 50–1 on the question of deception by omission.

[153] A. T. H. Smith, *Property Offences*, 523.   [154] [1987] QB 547.

fault element is to be found in section 15(4) of the Act, which brings within the offence 'any deception (whether deliberate or reckless) by words or conduct as to fact or as to law'. Thus a deception offence can be committed by someone who knows that there is a risk that a certain representation may be untrue, as well as by a person who deliberately lies. The third element is an intention to deprive the owner permanently of the property.

(e) Forms of Obtaining[155]

For the offence of obtaining *property* by deception, contrary to section 15 of the 1968 Act, it must be proved that D obtained, either for himself or for another, some property belonging to another. Section 16(1) of the 1968 Act creates an offence of obtaining *a pecuniary advantage* by deception. A pecuniary advantage is obtained where D is allowed to borrow by way of overdraft, or to take out an insurance contract (or obtain improved terms), or to earn remuneration or greater remuneration in an office or employment, or to win money by betting. Section 1 of the Theft Act 1978 creates the offences of obtaining *services* by deception. The definition of services is somewhat abstract—'where the other is induced to confer a benefit by doing some act, or causing or permitting some act to be done, on the understanding that the benefit has been or will be paid for'—but rather surprisingly the Court of Appeal held in *Halai* (1983)[156] that a mortgage advance is not a service. The making of a mortgage advance would seem to amount to an act done on the understanding that it would be paid for, and the Court's view that a lending of money is not appropriately termed a 'service' seems to fly in the face of the statutory definition. The Law Commission has recommended that the decision in *Halai* be legislatively overruled.[157]

· Section 2 of the Theft Act 1978 creates three offences of evading liability by deception. The essence of the first one, under section 2(1)(a), is that D dishonestly by deception *secures the remission* of a debt or liability, in whole or in part, as by persuading V to transfer to a credit card company the liability to pay for goods or services.[158] Section 2(1)(b) creates an offence of *inducing a creditor to wait for or forgo payment*, but this offence is only committed where there is an 'intent to make permanent default in whole or in part' on the debt: merely using a deception in order to postpone payment is insufficient. The third offence, contrary to section 2(1)(c), consists of *obtaining exemption from or abatement of liability*: this

---

[155] For the details of the offences summarized briefly below, references should be made to the relevant sections of the monographs by J. C. Smith, *Law of Theft*, Griew, *The Theft Acts*, and A. T. H. Smith, *Property Offences*.   [156] [1983] Crim LR 624.
[157] *Conspiracy to Defraud*, Law Com No. 228, 37–40.
[158] *Jackson* [1983] Crim LR 817.

offence extends to a liability not yet incurred, and would be committed by the person who pretends to be under 18 or over 65 in order to obtain a reduction in the admission price to some event.

Passing mention may be made here of the offence created by section 3 of the Theft Act 1978, *making off without payment*. This is closely connected with the offences just discussed, but it is not a deception offence. It is aimed at people who simply leave without paying. The prohibited conduct is 'making off without having paid as required or expected'. The fault elements are dishonesty, knowledge that payment 'on the spot' is required or expected, and an intention to avoid payment permanently.[159]

9.9 FRAUD OFFENCES

In addition to the deception offence in the Theft Acts, there are a considerable number of offences of fraud scattered through the statute-book and at common law. Among the statutory offences are several under the Forgery and Counterfeiting Act 1981, the offence of fraudulent trading (Companies Act 1985, section 458), and various offences of false and misleading statements under the Financial Services Act 1986 and the Banking Act 1987. Among the common law offences are cheating the public revenue (which is based on fraud, and does not require deception[160]) and conspiracy to defraud, to which we shall now turn.

The elements of the common law crime of conspiracy to defraud were restated in *Scott* v *Metropolitan Police Commissioner* (1975).[161] The offence may take one of two forms. If it is directed at a private person, what is proscribed is an agreement between two or more persons 'by dishonesty to deprive' that person of something to which he or she is or may be entitled, or to injure some proprietary right of that person, with intent to cause economic loss. It seems that an intention to do acts which will defraud is sufficient, and a 'good motive' cannot negative that.[162] If the offence is directed at a public official, what is proscribed is an agreement between two or more persons 'by dishonesty' to cause the official to act contrary to his or her public duty. There seem to be few prosecutions for conspiracy to defraud directed at public officials.[163] The controversies mainly concern the first form of the offence.

It is, in the first place, a crime of conspiracy. Conspiracy is one of the three inchoate offences in English criminal law, to be discussed in Chapter 11, but conspiracy may also be charged when the acts agreed upon have

---

[159] *Allen* [1985] AC 1029.
[160] *Mavji* (1987) 84 Cr App R 34; *Redford* (1989) 89 Cr App R 1.
[161] [1975] AC 819.　　　　　[162] *Wai Yu-tsang* [1992] 1 AC 269.
[163] Cf. *Moses* [1991] Crim LR 617.

actually been committed. The definition of conspiracy to defraud is so wide that it criminalizes agreements to do things which, if done by an individual, would not amount to an offence. The Law Commission accepts that in principle this is objectionable, but in its recent report it advances the view that there are 'compelling' practical reasons for retaining the offence, at least until its general review of dishonesty offences is completed.[164] Among the practical reasons on which the Law Commission relies are the utility of the charge in portraying the 'overall criminality' more effectively than several individual charges, the simplification of trials, and the probable saving of public money. However, to set against this there is the wide and uncertain scope of the offence, leaving considerable prosecutorial discretion which might be structured by published guidelines for prosecutors but no longer is.[165] Thus the offence contravenes the 'rule of law' principles of maximum certainty and fair warning, and may well breach Article 7 of the European Convention on Human Rights.[166] The Law Commission recognizes that in its present form conspiracy to defraud goes beyond the standard offences of theft, deception, etc. in several respects. An agreement temporarily to obtain someone's property may amount to a conspiracy to defraud, even though there is no general offence of temporary deprivation. There is no offence of deceiving a machine, but there may be a conspiracy to defraud a machine's owner. Conspiracy charges may also be brought for some gambling swindles, for 'long firm' frauds, and, in the area of commercial counterfeiting, for making and selling goods which are copies of famous branded goods.

The Law Commission has decided to wait until the completion of its review of dishonesty offences before reconsidering the position of conspiracy to defraud. Clearly it will wish to consider the case for and against creating specific offences to cover the types of conduct mentioned at the end of the previous paragraph. In previous recommendations for reform of conspiracy law,[167] which Parliament followed in enacting the Criminal Law Act 1976, it adopted the approach that if new forms of conduct were to arise that required criminalization, it should be left to Parliament to move swiftly. This was not a sufficient reason, the Commission believed, for retaining broad residual conspiracy offences. However, it is often assumed that it is bound to be 'necessary' to retain a

---

[164] *Conspiracy to Defraud*, Law Com No. 228, summarized at [1995] Crim LR 97 and discussed by Sir John Smith at [1995] Crim LR 209.

[165] The relevant guideline, originally recommended by the Criminal Law Revision Committee, 18th Report, *Conspiracy to Defraud* (1986), has been excluded from the 1994 edition of the Code for Crown Prosecutors: see [1994] Crim LR 901.

[166] See Ch 3.2 and Ch 3.4(i) above.

[167] *Conspiracy and Criminal Law Reform*, Law Com No. 76 (1976), discussed below, Ch 11.5.

general and residual offence of fraud, since it will be acutely difficult to cover the ground with specific offences.[168] The Law Commission's tentative proposal in 1988 was as follows: 'Any person who dishonestly causes another person to suffer [financial] prejudice, or a risk of prejudice, or who dishonestly makes a gain for himself or another, commits an offence.'[169] This would be an offence of staggering breadth, applicable to conduct by an individual as well as to agreements by two or more people. Is there really sufficient justification for furnishing prosecutors with such a blunderbuss? Is there any reason why fraud cases cause special difficulties that warrant derogation from the principles of maximum certainty and fair warning? Perhaps the strongest argument is that the invocation of those principles would shelter people who are often in powerful commercial positions or are otherwise able to call upon substantial financial resources. The law generally favours such people by imposing civil and adminstrative penalties rather than criminal prosecution. In respect of criminal law it has been argued that, the more specific and certain the law is, the easier it is for those with resources to manipulate, to slip between its provisions, and to draw fine distinctions.[170] Is this a satisfactory reason for contravening the principles and Article 7? Surely not: the problem of inequity, formidable as it is, must be tackled by other means.

9.10 DISHONESTY, DISCRETION, AND 'DESERT'

There is no shortage of issues of principle raised by the approach of the legislature and the courts to offences of dishonesty. The most obvious of these is the virtual abandonment of the principle of maximum certainty in relation to the offences of conspiracy to defraud, and, more generally, in the reliance on 'dishonesty' as the key element in most offences. Apart from the three exceptions in section 2 of the 1968 Act, which apply only to offences of theft, the meaning of 'dishonesty' is left at large, with only the 'current standards of ordinary decent people' to steer the jury or magistrates towards a conclusion. This ample discretion—which is what it amounts to, since there is no touchstone of social honesty—opens the way to inconsistent decisions (which detract from the rule of law) and discriminatory decisions (which detract from equality before the law). No doubt, prosecutors and some judges regard flexibility as a great virtue in the law, but it runs counter to any principles which regard the principle of

---

[168] *Conspiracy and Criminal Law Reform*, Law Com No. 76 (1976), discussed below, Ch 11.5.

[169] Law Commission Working Paper 104, *Conspiracy to Defraud* (1988).

[170] See D. McBarnet and C. Whelan, 'The Elusive Spirit of the Law: Formalism and the Struggle for Legal Control' (1991) 54 MLR, 848, describing mechanisms of 'creative compliance'.

legality and respect for individual autonomy as a central value.[171] Efforts must be made to redefine at least some of the property offences in a way which cuts down or structures this wide discretion. It is a great irony that the Criminal Law Revision Committee, in the report that preceded and proposed the Theft Act, accorded recognition to 'the principle of English law to give reasonable guidance as to what kinds of conduct are criminal'.[172]

The definitions of some of the offences under the Theft Act are notable for their breadth. Theft and robbery cover wide areas of major and minor wrongdoing, without differentiation in the label. Some offences spill over into areas normally occupied by inchoate offences or by law of complicity. The inchoate mode of definition is used with regard to burglary contrary to section 9(1)(a), 'entering as a trespasser with intent to steal', and—more significantly—it is adopted for the crime of theft itself: the main conduct element is an 'appropriation', which may be fulfilled by any assumption of the right of an owner, even if it is with the owner's consent.[173] One consequence is to push back the crime of attempted theft even further, so that in *Morris*[174] theft was constituted by swapping labels on goods in the supermarket, and attempted theft would presumably be committed by such acts as trying to peel off the labels prior to swapping them. This presses criminal liability too far. Another example is provided by the offence of handling, for which the legislature has cast the net so wide (assisting in, or arranging to assist in, the retention, removal, disposal, or realization of stolen goods) as to cover conduct which would normally be charged as aiding and abetting, etc.[175] Again, one consequence of this is that the law of complicity applies so as to extend the boundaries of the wide offence of handling still further. Just as attempted theft might be termed a doubly inchoate offence, so aiding and abetting an offence of handling stolen goods might be called a doubly secondary offence.

The historical explanation for the broad drafting of offences in the Theft Act is that the earlier law of larceny consisted of many technically worded offences covering fairly similar forms of conduct, an approach which had attracted technical interpretations and which resulted in a complex law often quite removed from its original purposes. The drive to eschew technicality was laudable. Some would prefer it to have been taken further—by amalgamating theft and deception into a single offence for example—but in the conclusions to section 9.1 above, it was argued that this has more disadvantages than advantages. However, among the results

[171] See the fairness principles discussed above, Ch 3.4.
[172] CLRC, 8th Report (1966), para 99(i).
[173] See 9.1(a) above, discussing *Gomez*.   [174] [1984] AC 320.
[175] See above, Ch 9.9.

of the new 'broad band' offence-structure have been (i) some difficulty in predicting the precise boundaries of the criminal law, which gives more power to prosecutors; (ii) greater discretion in the administration of the law by juries and magistrates; and (iii) wider discretion in sentencing, an intended result of the pattern of fewer offences with relatively high maximum penalties.[176] Yet the picture is blurred by the fact that the Theft Act 1978 reverts to a more particularistic style of drafting.

The property offences both within and outside the Theft Acts do not form a readily comprehensible scheme, based on relative seriousness and proportionality. It was noticed earlier that the fairly serious offence of burglary is defined without any reference to the element of psychological harm to the victim, which is such a key factor in determining its relative seriousness. The piecemeal nature of the law's development is betrayed by several anomalies: it is an offence to obtain services by deception, but not to help oneself to them brazenly; temporary deprivations are criminal in some circumstances and not in others, irrespective of the loss inflicted on the victim; various commercial swindles are offences if done by two or more people (conspiracy to defraud), but not if done by an individual; and so forth.

The flexibility of the 'broad band' approach to definitions in the Theft Act 1968, together with the anomalous contours of criminalization, has meant that the outer boundaries of the law (and particularly the lower boundaries) are uncertain and shifting. This problem is compounded by the variable approaches to statute interpretation taken by the appellate courts. The concept of 'appropriation' is central to the offence of theft, yet the definition in section 3 of the Act was interpreted in quite extraordinary fashion by the House of Lords in *Gomez*,[177] with the minority judge (Lord Lowry) pointing out quite clearly what the legislative intention was, and the majority of their Lordships simply refusing to recognize it. Moreover, the consequence of this decision in particular, and of several other 'stretching' decisions too, is that the focus of the law of theft has been moved from the misappropriation of others' property towards the punishment of dishonesty even where there has been no significant infringement, or at least no non-consensual infringement, of another's property.

A particularly objectionable feature of the many cases of stretching dishonesty offences is that they have stretched the law downwards, so that relatively minor acts render persons liable to conviction for offences with fairly serious labels. It is important to note here that English law has no provision equivalent to the *de minimis* section of the Model Penal Code, allowing a defence where the conduct was not serious enough to warrant

---

[176] See above, Ch 3.4(l) and (m).   [177] [1993] 1 All E.R.1.

conviction.[178] There is a provision in the Code for Crown Prosecutors in England which states that it is not in the public interest to bring a prosecution where only a nominal penalty would be likely;[179] but that consigns the matter to discretion once more, leaving the boundaries of the criminal law in a distinctly uncertain state. The point is strengthened by the presence of civil remedies for many acts of dishonesty concerning property. In the two House of Lords decisions, *Metropolitan Police Commissioner* v *Charles* and *Lambie*[180], the court strove to bring the defendants' behaviour within the criminal law rather than leaving the banks to pursue civil remedies against customers with whom they had regular and considered contractual arrangements. In *Clarke*[181] the Court of Appeal made strong criticisms of the banks for their poor precautions against the fraudulent use of credit cards. Unusually, in *Navvabi*[182] the Court of Appeal stopped short of convicting of theft a person who opened bank accounts in false names, and then passed cheques in excess of the balance in the accounts. There are some cases where the courts have taken a strong stance against the importation of civil law concepts into the criminal law,[183] and others where they have either embraced or distorted civil law reasoning in order to reach a desired conclusion.[184] Behind these inconsistencies of approach lies the fundamental question of principle—for the legislature rather than for the courts—about the proper division between criminal prosecution and civil suits.

The legislative and judicial development of dishonesty offences charted in this chapter shows little attachment to a policy of minimum criminalization, and ready resort to the criminal sanction as 'social defence' against relatively minor forms of dishonesty.[185] Otherwise, efforts would have been made to remove many of the lesser appropriations and handlings from the criminal law. The problem appears to be that it is hard to find a workable distinction between these minor forms of dishonesty and dishonest appropriations of property which are quite serious. One approach is to regard the value of the appropriated goods or services as the crucial element, and to place all cases below a certain sum into a separate category—cancellation of the offence if the taker repays what was taken within seven days, for example, like the French bad-cheque law;[186] or a fixed

---

[178] *Model Penal Code*, s 212.
[179] Code for Crown Prosecutors (3rd edn, 1994), para 6.5(a).
[180] *Metropolitan Police Commissioner* v *Charles* [1977] AC 177, and *Lambie* [1982] AC 449, discussed above, pp. 397–9.   [181] (1982) 75 Cr App R 119.
[182] (1986) 83 Cr App R 371.
[183] E.g. *Morris* [1984] AC 320, and *Attorney-General's Reference (No. 1 of 1985)* [1986] QB 491.   [184] E.g. *Metropolitan Police Commissioner* v *Charles* [1977] AC 177.
[185] Cf. Ch 3.2(b) with Ch 3.2(a).
[186] For an outline, see C. Anyangwe, 'Dealing with the Problem of Bad Cheques in France' [1978] Crim LR 31.

penalty offence;[187] or a new category of civil infractions.[188] Of course, there are possible objections against each of these alternatives, not least the claim that offences of dishonesty have a significance in one's judgment of people which transcends the sum involved. But this is where we meet serious problems of proportionality and of social hypocrisy. Many forms of conduct amounting to dishonesty offences are routinely dealt with in some non-criminal manner—large companies required to repay money on government contracts, for example, executives dismissed from employment, tax fraudsters required to pay double the underpaid tax rather than being prosecuted, and so forth. A Law Commission Working Paper argued that there is no need to criminalize those who deliberately use another person's profit earning property in order to make secret profits, since it is generally adequate to leave the owner to sue the malefactor; yet restaurant bilkers who make off without paying a few pounds are routinely subjected to the criminal sanction.[189] Moreover, as argued above, there are few social standards of dishonesty which do not vary according to the background and circumstances of the group of citizens who are making the judgment. The argument is clearly one of social fairness: the present legal definitions and enforcement practices are failing to ensure equality before the law, by subjecting many minor offenders to conviction while adopting a different approach to some major offenders.

There are, then, at least four conflicting principles in dishonesty offences. The principle of proportionality militates in favour of a more clearly structured restatement of these offences so as to integrate crimes from the Companies Acts and elsewhere into the general framework and emphasize their seriousness. The principle of maximum certainty urges that such a restatement should be less reliant on such discretionary terms as 'dishonesty'. The principle of minimum criminalization argues in favour of a reconstruction of these offences so as to exclude some minor forms of dishonesty and to include some major ones. On the other hand, the same principle would support the exploration of non-criminal means of dealing with some forms of dishonesty: this has been the pattern for many years, but it has generally meant that companies and well-connected persons have succeeded in avoiding the criminal sanction, when others of lowlier status have been convicted. This goes against the principle of equality before the law, since it discriminates on grounds of wealth and

---

[187] For a radical proposal, see A. Ashworth, 'Prosecution, Police and the Public: A Guide to Good Gatekeeping' (1984) 23 Howard JCJ, 621.

[188] See the discussion by B. Huber, 'The Dilemma of Decriminalization: Dealing with Shoplifting in West Germany' [1980] Crim LR 621.

[189] Pointed out by A. T. H. Smith, 'Conspiracy to Defraud' [1988] Crim LR 508, at 513, commenting on the Law Com WP 104.

social position. Some propose to resolve this conflict by maintaining non-criminal means of dealing with commercial fraud, since these can be more effective,[190] but redoubling efforts to narrow down the ambit of the criminal sanction for minor forms of dishonesty. Unfortunately, the present tendency is towards the former but not the latter.[191]

[190] Cf. J. Braithwaite and B. Fisse, 'The Allocation of Responsibility for Corporate Crime' (1988) 11 Sydney LR, 468, with Levi, *Regulating Fraud*.

[191] Royal Commission on Criminal Justice, *Report* (1993, Cm 2263), para 7.63; Serious Fraud Office, *Annual Report 1993–94*.

Complicity

10.1 INTRODUCTION

The question of complicity arises when two or more people play some part in the commission of an offence. It has already been noted, in discussing the various public order offences,[1] and will be emphasized later, when discussing conspiracy,[2] that the criminal law regards offences involving more than one person as particularly serious—sometimes because they suggest planning and determination to offend and make it difficult for an individual to withdraw, and sometimes because group offences against an individual tend to be more frightening. There are, of course, different degrees of involvement in a criminal enterprise, and one of the main issues in the law of complicity is the proper scope of criminal liability: how much involvement should be necessary, as a minimum?

Let us take a hypothetical example of a burglary, in which A and B plan to raid a country house: they approach C, who has worked at the house, for information which will help them to gain entry; they arrange for D to drive them to the house in a large van and to transport the stolen goods after the burglary; and they agree with E that he should come and position himself near the main gates of the house in order to warn them if anyone approaches. If A, B, C, D, and E all do as planned, what approach should the law take to their criminal liability?

It is apparent that A and B are the only ones to have fulfilled the definition of the crime of burglary, by entering the house as trespassers and stealing property from it.[3] They are guilty as co-principals. It should then be asked whether there is sufficient justification for bringing C, D, and E within the ambit of the criminal law at all. Would the law not be more effective if it concentrated on the major offenders? The main difficulty in answering this question is that, in some crimes, the conduct of the accomplices, urging and threatening, is no less serious than that of the principals. As a general reason for bringing accomplices within the ambit of criminal liability, one might say that culpably assisting one or more persons in a criminal enterprise deserves the criminal sanction; the culpability implies a decision to support the commission of the principal's crime, and the assistance is a practical manifestation of that support. A

---

[1] See above, Ch 8.3(g). [2] See below, Ch 11.4.
[3] Theft Act 1968, s 9; see above, Ch 9.5.

consequentialist reason for convicting those who help and support a criminal enterprise can also be found: penalizing helpers and other participants should act as a deterrent, thereby making offences less likely to occur.

What contribution to a crime must be made before the law regards a person as an accomplice? The neutral word 'assistant' was used in the previous paragraph, but must it be proved that the conduct of persons such as C, D, and E actually *caused* A and B's offence, in the sense that it would not have happened as it did but for their help? One practical answer to this question is that A and B might well have found others willing to help. The theoretical answer would begin by pointing out that A and B are responsible, autonomous individuals—one cannot, in general, trace causal responsibility through the voluntary act of another person[4]—so it will not usually be possible to hold that the accomplices *caused* the principals to act, save in a rather diluted form of 'causing'.[5] The law of complicity does not require causation, then, but it does require certain conduct by the accomplice, perhaps more as evidence of the accomplice's commitment to furthering the criminal enterprise, in a similar way to the conduct requirement in attempts and other inchoate offences,[6] than as evidence that the crime would not have happened but for the accomplice's assistance. Broadly speaking, the rather loose conduct requirements for complicity are in practice narrowed down by the fault requirements: a small act of assistance may suffice, but only if it is done with intent to assist or encourage the commission of the principal's crime. The English rules on complicity have been shaped almost entirely at common law, since the only statutory provision is vague and limited in scope, and the courts have developed the law—often stretching it, occasionally restricting it—in their endeavour to ensure that it applies to new forms of behaviour thought sufficiently reprehensible.[7]

10.2 DISTINGUISHING PRINCIPALS FROM ACCESSORIES

The simplest way of drawing this distinction is to say that a principal is a person whose acts fall within the legal definition of the crime, whereas an accomplice (sometimes called an 'accessory' or 'secondary party') is anyone who aids, abets, counsels, or procures a principal. It does not follow from this that where two or more persons are involved in an offence,

---

[4] See above, Ch 4.6(a) and (b).
[5] Cf. H. L. A. Hart and T. Honoré, *Causation in the Law* (2nd edn, 1985), 388.
[6] See below, Ch 11.3(b) and 11.6.
[7] For a full study, see K. J. M. Smith, *A Modern Treatise on the Law of Criminal Complicity* (1991).

one must be the principal and the others accomplices. Two or more persons can be co-principals, so long as each of them satisfies the definition of the substantive offence, for example, by each inflicting wounds upon the victim with the required fault. Indeed, English law goes further, holding that two or more persons can be co-principals if each of them satisfies some part of the conduct element of the offence, if all their acts together fulfil all the conduct elements, and if each of them has the required mental element.[8] This is an unusual example of the attribution of one person's acts to another, and is probably connected with the idea of a 'joint enterprise' or 'common purpose' which binds together the several acts of persons who are acting in pursuance of an agreement (discussed in 10.5).

Some criminal offences are so defined that they can only be committed by two or more co-principals. The public order offences of riot and violent disorder are clear examples of this.[9] There can also be accomplices to such offences, but one result of the broad definitions of the offences is that such cases rarely arise. A related rule, which operates only in the United States, is that all members of a conspiracy are deemed to be co-principals in the offence if it is committed. The rule eliminates from such cases the distinction between principals and accessories, and has led to the conviction, as principal in an offence, of someone who was in prison at the time for another crime. The result is that the conviction misrepresents the nature of the person's participation in the crime: a conspirator is labelled as a perpetrator, which is hardly fair or necessary.[10]

English law maintains the distinction between principals and accessories, but the practical implications of holding a person to be an accomplice rather than a principal are not greatly significant. The leading statute is the Accessories and Abettors Act 1861, which provides that anyone who 'shall aid, abet, counsel or procure the commission of any indictable offence . . . shall be liable to be tried, indicted and punished as a principal offender'. This means that, in practice, the prosecution can succeed against a defendant without specifying in advance whether the allegation is that D is a principal or an accomplice, or what form the alleged complicity took. This is undoubtedly a great convenience for the prosecution, particularly in cases where they can prove that each of the two defendants was at least an accomplice but cannot prove which one was the principal. Thus, in a case of a child's death caused by drugs, if it can be shown that one or other parent administered methadone to their young child, and that both were

---

[8] K. J. M. Smith, *Modern Treatise on Complicity*, 27–30.

[9] See above, Ch 8.3(g).

[10] It conflicts with the principle of fair labelling (discussed in Ch 3.5(s)) and the principles of 'desert' (Ch. 5.2(b)). The leading American decision is *Pinkerton* v *United States* (1946) 328 US 640.

present throughout, it matters not that the prosecution cannot establish which parent administered it because the other parent must at least be an accomplice, having failed to intervene to save the child.[11] On the other hand, if in such a situation it cannot be established that both parents were present throughout, it cannot be proved that both of them were at least accomplices, and the prosecution must fail.[12] The Royal Commission on Criminal Justice registered public concern about such cases and pointed out that the abolition of the 'right to silence' would not necessarily assist if both parents decided to remain silent.[13] It is surely right that some means be found of minimizing the extent to which defendants can escape criminal liability by blaming one another, if they were clearly involved in some way. On the other hand, in cases where it cannot be proved that both defendants were involved in some way, the presumption of innocence ought to be accorded respect, and the law currently ensures this.

What the 1861 Act does not ensure, however, is that individual defendants receive fair warning of the case against them, although the House of Lords has encouraged prosecutors to frame indictments in as much detail as possible.[14] One must ask whether the present system is not more concerned with minimizing the opportunities for avoiding criminal liability by resort to procedural rules which conceal the normal elements of criminal guilt.

The 1861 English statute is sometimes compared unfavourably with such systems as the German, which restricts the maximum penalty for an accomplice to three-quarters that of the principal.[15] The comparison is not a straightforward one, however. It is true that accomplices are normally less blameworthy than principals and therefore deserve less severe sentences. It is also true that a law which produces a conviction of murder and a sentence of life imprisonment for giving relatively minor assistance to a murderer is unjust (though the injustice stems as much from the mandatory penalty for murder as from the law of complicity). But systems like the German seem not to provide for those, admittedly rare, cases in which the accomplice is no less culpable, even more culpable, than the principal—as where a powerful figure orders a weak-willed person to commit a certain crime. One way of providing for all degrees of complicity would be to retain the legal power to impose any relevant sentence on the principal; to respect the accomplice's right not to be punished more

---

[11] *Russell and Russell* (1987) 85 Cr App R 388; *Emery* (1993) 14 Cr App R (S) 394.

[12] *Lane and Lane* (1986) 82 Cr App R 5.

[13] Royal Commission on Criminal Justice, *Report* (1993), Ch 4, para 25. For further discussion, see E. Griew, 'It Must Have Been One of Them' [1989] Crim LR 129, and G. Williams, 'Which of You Did It?' (1989) 52 MLR, 179.

[14] *Maxwell v DPP for Northern Ireland* [1979] 1 WLR 1350.

[15] See Fletcher, *Rethinking Criminal Law* (1978) 634 ff.

severely than is proportionate to the gravity of his contribution by declaring a general guideline that accomplices should receive no more than half the sentence of the principal; and to permit courts to exceed this normal level in cases where the accomplice's role was unusually influential, and to sentence below it if the accomplice's contribution was minor. Some such approach would sacrifice the notion that the legal labels ought to reflect the different degrees of involvement in favour of a more flexible, yet regulated, response through sentencing.

10.3 THE CONDUCT ELEMENT IN COMPLICITY

We have seen that the 1861 Act refers to those who 'aid, abet, counsel or procure' a crime. As a matter of history, it seems that this Act was intended only to declare the procedure whereby accomplices could be convicted and sentenced as principals, and not to provide a definition of complicity. Earlier statutes had used a wide range of terms—contriving, helping, maintaining, directing—and it seems likely that the wording of the 1861 Act was intended merely as a general reference to the existing common law on accomplices. However, the words have taken on an authority of their own. There have been many decisions on the meaning of each term, and in 1976 the Court of Appeal declared that each of the four verbs should be given its ordinary meaning.[16] In general this 'ordinary language' approach to the interpretation of statutes now seems to be receding,[17] and since the 1976 decision paid no heed to the historical development of the law, its authority is open to doubt.

One factor which used to have considerable importance was presence during the commission of the crime. So long as the other conditions for liability were fulfilled, presence turned the accomplice into an aider or abettor, absence into a counsellor or procurer.[18] However, it appears that the distinction no longer has any practical consequences in English law.[19] Whether an accomplice is described as an aider, abettor, counsellor, or procurer seems to depend partly on ordinary language, and partly on specific judicial decisions.

(a) Aiding and Abetting

It has been traditional to consider the modes of complicity in terms of the two time-honoured pairings: 'aid or abet', and 'counsel or procure'. In

---

[16] *Attorney-General's Reference (No. 1 of 1975)* [1975] QB 773.

[17] *Maginnis* [1987] AC 303, discussed by D. W. Elliott, 'Brutus v Cozens: Decline and Fall' [1989] Crim LR 323.

[18] See e.g. Lord Goddard CJ in *Ferguson* v *Weaving* [1951] 1 KB 814, and generally J. C. Smith, 'Aid, Abet, Counsel or Procure', in P. R. Glazebrook (ed), *Reshaping the Criminal Law* (1978). [19] *Howe* [1987] AC 417, overruling *Richards* [1974] QB 776.

fact, the concept of abetment seems to play no independent role now. Abetting involves some encouragement of the principal to commit the offence' and this usually accompanies, or is implicit in, an act of aiding. Aid may be given by supplying an instrument to the principal, keeping a lookout, doing preparatory acts, and many other forms of assistance given before or at the time of the offence. The disappearance of the old requirement of presence may be illustrated by two cases. In *Bainbridge* (1959)[20] a man who provided equipment for use in a burglary was treated as a counsellor and procurer, because the burglary was to take place some days hence, whereas it would now be more natural to refer to him as an aider since he gave assistance by supplying the equipment. In *Attorney-General* v *Able* (1984)[21] the discussion of D's criminal liability for supplying a booklet explaining various ways of committing suicide was conducted on the basis that this would be aiding and abetting, whereas in former times this would have been regarded as counselling, since the author of the book was not present at the suicides.

Once it has been shown that the accomplice's conduct helped or might have helped the principal in some way, it does not have to be established that the accomplice caused the principal's offence. But that leaves us with the problem of deciding on the lower boundaries of 'aiding and abetting'. Causation requirements often function so as to fix the threshold of legal liability. Since causation is not a requirement here, how can the boundaries be drawn? It has been argued that there is still a form of causation requirement here: the courts must be satisfied that the accomplice's help *might* have made a difference to whether the principal's offence was actually committed, in the sense that one could not be sure that it would have been committed but for the accomplice's assistance.[22] Even according to this view, which is not supported by the explicit reasoning of the courts, the causal connection is rather tenuous and might fall within the *de minimis* range normally excluded from legal causation (see Chapter 4.6(a)). Surely the search for a causal connection should be abandoned. There would then be two options. One would be for the law to formulate an objective test, such as 'did the act or omission make some actual or potential contribution to the principal's offence?'. This would leave the law well short of the principle of maximum certainty, and would not exclude the criminalization of minimal acts of assistance. The other option would be to focus on the accomplice's conduct as an outward manifestation of his or her willingness to be associated with the crime and to support its perpetrator. According to this view, the fault element in complicity is the main justification for

---

[20] [1960] 1 QB 129.   [21] [1984] 1 QB 795.

[22] S. Kadish, *Blame and Punishment* (1987), 162.

imposing liability on accomplices, and it would also define the outer boundary of accessorial liability. This second option would tend to assimilate accomplice liability within the criteria for attempts liability, discussed in Chapter 11.3(b).

This raises the question of intended contributions by would-be accomplices. If we return to the hypothetical example given earlier, let us suppose that D had agreed with A and B that he would bring the van to a certain place, would carry them to the house, and would then bring them back with the proceeds of their crime. So, D drives the van to the meeting-place, ready to play his part, but A and B, having decided that they do not wish to rely on D, have obtained a van for themselves and have carried out the burglary without D's assistance. D's culpability remains the same as if A and B had relied upon his help. Yet there is no shadow of a causal link between D's assistance and A and B's offence. One suggestion is that D should be liable to conviction for attempting to aid and abet the burglary by A and B, but English law draws the line here: there is no offence of attempted complicity, on the ground that this lies too remote from the occurrence of the harm.[23] It would be possible to penalize D if English law included a general offence of assisting or encouraging a crime. However, it does not: it places limits on accomplice liability, largely through its basic doctrine that the liability of the accomplice derives from the liability of the principal, of which more will be said as the chapter proceeds.

Two further situations illustrate these difficulties over the link between an accomplice's aiding and the principal's offence. In *Wilcox* v *Jeffery* (1951) a jazz enthusiast attended a concert, applauding the decision of an American jazz musician to give an illegal performance. No point was taken in court about whether the musician was actually encouraged by the defendant's acts.[24] Indeed, in cases where several people applaud or encourage some kind of unlawful spectacle, it would be difficult to maintain that the performer(s) drew actual encouragement from the acts of any one of the spectators. One might say that a form of causal connection is assumed, but once again this is patently weak. Another type of situation occurs where the principal is unaware of the help given by the secondary party. In the famous American case of *State* v *Tally* (1894),[25] Judge Tally, knowing that his brothers-in-law had set out to kill the deceased, and knowing that someone else had sent a telegram to warn the victim, sent a telegram to the telegraph operator telling him not to deliver the warning

---

[23] Criminal Attempts Act 1981, s 1(4), and J. C. Smith, 'Secondary Participation and Inchoate Offences', in C. Tapper (ed), *Crime, Proof and Punishment* (1981).
[24] [1951] 1 All ER 464.   [25] *State* v *Tally* (1894) 15 So 722.

telegram. The telegraph operator complied, and the brothers-in-law committed the offence. The judge was convicted of aiding and abetting murder, even though the brothers-in-law were unaware of the judge's assistance when they killed the victim. It could be said that there was a causal connection in this case, but surely it should have been enough that the judge's act was more than minimal and he intended to aid.

(b) Accomplice Liability and Social Duties

We saw in Chapter 4.4 how accomplice liability has been used in English law to establish criminal liability for certain omissions, and the relevant authorities must now be considered in their adopted legal habitat. The cases raise issues of constitutional and social importance, but the key question in accessorial liability is simple to state: can a person be convicted as an accomplice merely for standing by and doing nothing while an offence is being committed?

If mere presence at the scene during the principal's offence were sufficient for accomplice liability, this would amount to recognizing a citizen's duty to take reasonable steps to prevent or frustrate any offence which is witnessed. The citizen's choice would lie between taking some preventive action or being deemed to be an accomplice. The courts have responded by drawing some fine lines. Non-accidental presence, such as attending a fight or an unlawful theatrical performance, is not conclusive evidence of aiding and abetting.[26] It seems that the prosecution must establish both that D intended to encourage and that this encouragement had some effect on the principal.[27] The factual questions are for the jury or magistrates. The inference of an intention to encourage might readily be drawn if D has gone to the place where the performance is taking place, especially if payment were made;[28] also if D remained in a vehicle that was being used to obstruct the police, in circumstances showing that he supported the actions of the driver.[29] The position of spectators who happen upon an illegal fight or event and stay to watch it is different: simply sitting or standing nearby is unlikely to be sufficient for liability, but any cheering or applause would probably tip the balance in favour of conviction. The problems are particularly acute in cases of public disorder. To impose duties on bystanders, even the duty to move away, might be regarded as an incursion on a citizen's right to freedom of movement. On the other hand, to remain at the scene might strengthen the resolve of the aggressors, increase the fear of victims, and make it difficult for the police to separate the involved from the uninvolved, but it is questionable

---

[26] *Coney* (1882) 8 QBD 534.   [27] *Clarkson* [1971] 1 WLR 1402.
[28] *Wilcox* v *Jeffery* [1951] 1 All ER 464.
[29] *Smith* v *Reynolds et al.* [1986] Crim LR 559.

whether these considerations are sufficient to justify the imposition of criminal liability.

Are there arguments in favour of the law going further and imposing a duty to take steps to prevent crime? The public disorder example may be complicated by the impotence of individuals to do anything to stop the disturbance, and, indeed, the imprudence of their trying to do so. But is it not arguable that there should be at least a duty to alert the police? If so, should failure to do so constitute a distinct offence (as in French law[30]) or complicity in the public disorder? Another example, which does not involve public disorder, occurs where a woman is living with a man who, she discovers, is dealing in drugs. If the police raid the dwelling and find drugs on the premises, should the law treat her as an accomplice even if there is no evidence of active assistance or encouragement of the drug-dealing? In the case of *Bland* (1988)[31] the Court of Appeal quashed the woman's conviction as an accomplice. Cases such as this demonstrate a vivid conflict between individuals' rights of privacy in their personal relationships and the social interest in suppressing serious crime. Would it be right for the law to co-opt husbands against wives, parents against children, house-sharing friends against friends in order to increase public protection?[32]

Probably the only way to answer this question is to balance the relative centrality of the right against the seriousness of the offence involved—not a simple exercise, but an inevitable one if the true nature of the problem is to be confronted. The same applies to the situation in *Clarkson* (1971):[33] two soldiers happened to enter a room where other soldiers were raping a woman. It was not found that they did anything other than watch, but they certainly did nothing to discourage continuance of the offence. The Court of Appeal quashed their conviction for aiding and abetting, because the judge had not made it clear that there should be proof of both an intent to encourage and actual encouragement. Nothing was said about a duty to alert the authorities immediately in the hope of preventing the crime's continuance. What if three persons came upon one man raping a woman? If it was within their power to put a stop to the offence and to apprehend the offender, should they have a duty to do so—or at least a duty to inform the police? The particular situation will vary from case to case, but the real issue is whether there is to be a principle that citizens ought to take reasonable steps to inform the police when they witness an offence. The

[30] Article 63(1) of the French Penal Code, discussed by A. Ashworth and E. Steiner, 'Criminal Omissions and Public Duties: the French Experience' (1990) 10 Legal Studies, 153.
[31] [1988] Crim LR 41.
[32] Cf. Police and Criminal Evidence Act 1984, s 80, which makes a husband or wife compellable as a witness on a charge of a sexual or violent offence towards a child under 16 in the household.   [33] [1971] 1 WLR 1402.

decision in *Allan* (1965)[34] is against this, emphasising the requirement of encouragement and adding that, even if D would have joined in if necessary, it would be unacceptable 'to convict a man on his thoughts, unaccompanied by any physical act other than the facts of mere presence'. However, variations in the facts of cases could be accommodated by requiring only 'reasonable steps',[35] and no court should require a person to place his or her own safety in jeopardy. Even if this were accepted, there would remain the question of whether it is fairer to convict the defaulting citizen of a new offence of failing to inform the police rather than making the citizen into an accomplice to the principal crime. The former is surely more appropriate in terms of fair labelling.

Can a person be said to aid an offence by an omission?[36] There would surely be no awkwardness in describing the cleaner of a bank who, in pursuance of an agreed plan, purposely omits to lock the doors when leaving as 'aiding' a burglary of the bank. In such a case, there is a clear duty and a failure to perform it, and the causation question is answered (in so far as it is relevant to aiding) in the same way as for omissions generally.[37] Another example would be the driving instructor who is supervising a learner-driver and who realizes that the learner is about to undertake a manoeuvre which is dangerous to other road-users: if, as in *Rubie* v *Faulkner* (1940),[38] the instructor fails to intervene, either by telling the learner not to do it or by physically acting to prevent it, then this failure in the duty of supervision is rightly held to be sufficient to support liability for aiding and abetting the learner-driver's offence.

From these cases of duty we turn to cases of legal power, and the so-called 'control principle'. The owner of a car who is a passenger when the car is being driven by another has the legal power to direct this other person not to drive in certain ways;[39] the licensee of a public house has the legal power to require customers to leave at closing-time;[40] the owners of a house have the legal power to direct the behaviour of their children and of visitors to their premises. In the first two cases the courts have held the car owner and the licensee liable as accomplices to the crime of the offender who drives carelessly or remains drinking after hours. What is unusual about these cases is that they rest on a legal power of control and not, like *Rubie* v *Faulkner*, on the existence of a legal duty to ensure compliance with the law. The cases seem to transgress the principle that there should

---

[34] [1965] 1 QB 130.   [35] See n. 30 above.
[36] K. J. M. Smith, *Modern Treatise on Complicity*, 39–47.
[37] See above, Ch 4.6(c).
[38] [1940] 1 KB 571, discussed by M. Wasik, 'A Learner's Careless Driving' [1982] Crim LR 411, and D. J. Lanham, 'Drivers, Control and Accomplices' [1982] Crim LR 419.
[39] *Du Cros* v *Lambourne* [1907] 1 KB 40.
[40] *Tuck* v *Robson* [1970] 1 WLR 741.

be no liability for an omission unless a clear duty exists.[41] What the courts have done, in effect, is to assimilate these cases of 'power of control' to cases of duty, thereby creating a new class of public duty.[42] Even though English law does not impose liability for failing to take reasonable steps to prevent an offence which occurs in the street, these cases hold that a property owner will be liable for failing to take reasonable steps to prevent an offence which occurs on or with that property and in the owner's presence. The law has, in effect, co-opted property owners as law enforcement agents in respect of their own property.

Does it amount to aiding if a shopkeeper sells an item to P knowing that P intends to use it in a crime, or if a borrower returns an article to its owner knowing that the owner intends to use it in crime? These could be said to be acts of assistance, in the sense that the physical conduct of selling or returning goods helps an offender: should they, if accompanied by the required mental element, amount to aiding the principal? The problem is that both acts are 'normal': the shopkeeper is simply selling goods in the normal course of business, and the borrower is merely fulfilling a duty to restore the goods to their owner. If the law were to regard either of these acts as 'aiding', it would be requiring the defendants to do something abnormal in the circumstances, and—in effect—punishing them for the omission to do the abnormal thing.

Three approaches to this problem may be considered. The first was described by Devlin J in *National Coal Board* v *Gamble* (1959): 'If one man deliberately sells to another a gun to be used for murdering a third, he may be indifferent whether the third man lives or dies and interested only in the cash profit to be made out of the sale, but he can still be an aider or abettor.'[43] This view criminalizes the shopkeeper as an accomplice in every case where the customer's intention to commit that kind of offence is known. It might be justified by arguing that a small sacrifice may be required of shopkeepers in order to benefit the potential victims of crime. Surely, where an offence against the person is a possibility, it is right to place the potential victim's right not to be subjected to assault or injury above the shopkeeper's liberty to sell to allcomers. After all, the shopkeeper is not being required to intervene or even to notify the police of the customer's intentions. The requirement is not to sell goods when the customer is known to be bent on crime.

---

[41] The Law Commission's view is that the breach of duty must also have actually amounted to assistance or encouragement (Law Commission Consultation Paper No. 131, *Assisting and Encouraging Crime* (1993), para 2.29), but the decisions seem to regard this requirement as easily fulfilled.

[42] Cf. the debate between G. Williams, 'Which of you did it?' (1989) 52 MLR, 179, and D. J. Lanham, 'Three Cases of Accessorial Absurdity' (1990) 53 MLR, 75.

[43] *NCB* v *Gamble* [1959] 1 QB 11.

Despite the decision in *Gillick* v *West Norfolk and Wisbech Health Authority* (1986),[44] the statement in *NCB* v *Gamble* that selling goods in the ordinary course of business can satisfy the conduct element of 'aiding' remains good law. But English law as a whole now seems to be moving towards a second approach, long upheld in many American jurisdictions, namely, that a shopkeeper should only be liable as an accomplice where it was his or her purpose to further the customer's offence.[45] This stresses the notions of free trade and individual autonomy, treating the shopkeeper as a mere trader rather than as a fellow citizen's keeper. A third approach would not involve the law of complicity, but would treat the shopkeeper's liability as a matter of general criminal law—either by creating a special offence of selling goods which are likely to be used in the commission of crime (of which there are some examples now, such as the sale of flick-knives), or through a general offence of facilitating crime.

The situation of someone who has borrowed goods and who is asked by the owner to return them so that they may be used for a crime is slightly different. In *NCB* v *Gamble* it was held by Devlin J that returning goods in these circumstances is a 'negative act' rather than a 'positive act': 'A man who hands over to another his own property on demand, although he may physically be performing a positive act, in law is only refraining from detinue'.[46] Thus the return of the goods is not an act of aiding, because, according to this sophistry, it is not a positive act. In one sense the case is weaker than that of the shopkeeper, since the borrower has a duty to return goods to their owner, whereas a shopkeeper has no duty to sell; but in another sense it is just as strong, since a court would be reluctant to find liability in tort for failing to return goods in such circumstances, and would be more likely to recognize a defence if it was known that a crime was contemplated. Devlin J's analysis, despite the fragility of the positive–negative distinction, may appear to offer a pragmatic solution, but it is inadequate when it comes to dealing with a case where the borrower is returning a gun which is then to be used for killing someone. The potential victim's rights must count for more than the borrower's duty to return goods to their owner. Rather than concealing these conflicts behind Devlin J's unconvincing analysis, a preferable course would be either to allow a defence of 'balance of evils' to any apparently criminal complicity,[47] or to state that D should not be liable for returning property to its owner unless

---

[44] *Gillick* v *West Norfolk and Wisbech Area Health Authority* [1986] AC 112, criticized in Ch 4.9(b) and Ch 5.2(b) above.
[45] Model Penal Code, s 2.06(3).
[46] [1959] 1 QB 11, at 20, discussing *Lomas* (1913) 9 Cr App R 220.
[47] See above, Ch 4.9.

D shares the owner's criminal purpose or unless a crime of violence is known to be in contemplation.[48]

(c) Counselling and Procuring

The characteristic contribution of the counsellor or procurer is to incite, instigate, or advise on the commission of the substantive offence by the principal. One way of expressing this is to describe the role as 'encouraging' the perpetrator. Some European legal systems provide a higher maximum penalty for an accomplice who incites or instigates than for a mere helper, and a general justification for this can readily be found. No offence might have taken place at all but for the instigation, and this is surely more reprehensible than assisting someone who has already decided to commit a crime. In practice, however, there are many shades of culpability between helpers and instigators, a point which strikes the English lawyer more forcefully, because of the uncertain limits of the terms 'counselling' and 'procuring'. The ordinary meaning of 'counselling' may fall well short of inciting or instigating an offence, and covers such conduct as advising on an offence and giving information required for an offence. The ordinary meaning of 'procuring' is said to be 'to produce by endeavour',[49] which goes beyond mere instigation.

The forms of counselling and procuring recognized by English law probably stretch from the giving of advice or information, through encouraging or trying to persuade another person to commit the crime, to such conduct as threatening or commanding that the offence by committed. Generally speaking, the accomplice's culpability increases as one proceeds towards the extreme of a command backed by threats. In that extreme situation the principal may have the defence of duress,[50] and may be regarded as an innocent agent of the threatener, who then becomes the principal.[51] There are also cases in which the principal does not realize that someone is trying to bring about an offence: for example, if D surreptitiously laces P's non-alcoholic drink with some form of alcohol and P subsequently drives a car, unaware of the consumption of alcohol, P would be liable to conviction for drunken driving and D could be convicted of procuring the offence, so long as it was shown that D knew P was intending to drive. Such conduct fulfils the ordinary definition of procuring: 'you procure a thing by setting out to see that it happens and

---

[48] G. Williams, 'Obedience to Law as a Crime' (1990) 53 MLR, 445; an alternative advanced by G. R. Sullivan, 'The Law Commission Consultation Paper on Complicity: Fault Elements and Joint Enterprise' [1994] Crim LR 252, is to exempt crimes triable only on indictment.

[49] *Attorney-General's reference (No. 1 of 1975)* [1975] QB 773.

[50] See above, Ch 6.4.

[51] See *Bourne* (1952) 36 Cr App R 125, discussed below, Ch 10.6.

taking appropriate steps to produce that happening'.[52] P's case may also
look like one of innocent agency, but that doctrine could not be invoked
unless it could be shown that it was D's purpose to bring about the
offence.[53]

The ordinary meaning of procuring, 'to produce by endeavour', is not
restricted to cases where the principal is unaware of the accomplice's
design. One can take the appropriate steps to bring about a crime by
persuading another to do the required acts—for example, by shaming
someone into committing an offence by taunts of cowardice—but conduct
such as hiring 'hit men' to carry out an offence is probably better described
as counselling.[54] It can be said that in cases of procuring there is a causal
relationship between the accomplice's procuring and the principal's act,
and it is proper to say that the principal acts *in consequence of* the
accomplice's conduct.[55] These cases, then, represent the high-water mark
of causal connection among the various types of accessorial conduct,
headed by the case of procuring an unwitting principal (where D laces P's
drink), in which there is no meeting of minds between principal and
accomplice. Such a strong causal connection is not found in counselling,
which may merely involve the supply of information, advice, or encouragement. This has led Professor Sir John Smith to conclude that: 'Procuring
requires causation but not consensus; encouraging requires consensus but
not causation; assisting requires actual help but neither consensus nor
causation.'[56] If cases of hiring hit-men are classified as counselling or
encouraging, then all that is required is that accomplice and principal
reached some kind of agreement on what was to be done, with the
accomplice encouraging the principal (usually by offering money) to carry
out the crime.[57]

(d) Reform

The uncertain and, indeed, vanishing quality of causation in the law of
complicity is not the only difficulty with the conduct element required.
There is undue complexity involved in retaining the four separate terms,
'aid, abet, counsel or procure,' and the law has been developed by the
courts largely as a series of pragmatic responses to particular sets of facts.
Without anticipating the discussion in the final part of this chapter, it is
appropriate to mention here that the Law Commission now appears to

---

[52] See *Attorney-General's Reference (No. 1 of 1975)* [1975] QB 773.
[53] Cf. P. Alldridge, 'The Doctrine of Innocent Agency' (1990) 2 Criminal Law Forum 45.
[54] As on the facts of *Richards* [1974] QB 776, and of *Calhaem* [1985] QB 808.
[55] H. L. A. Hart and T Honoré, *Causation in the Law* (2nd edn 1985), 51–9, and Ch 4.6(d)
above.
[56] Smith, 'Aid, Abet, Counsel or Procure', 134; perhaps the words 'actual or potential
help' might be preferable.   [57] *Calhaem* [1985] QB 808.

accept that the forms of complicity ought to be reduced to two: assisting, and encouraging.[58] Both forms of conduct are defined broadly: assisting would include any act that D knows or believes assists or will assist the principal, and encouraging would apply to anyone who 'solicits, commands or encourages' another to do acts that amount to a crime. As in the existing law of complicity, however, the breadth of these terms is somewhat restricted when combined with the fault requirements.

10.4 THE MENTAL ELEMENT IN COMPLICITY

The fault required before a person can be convicted as an accomplice differs from that required for all other forms of criminal liability. This is because it concerns not merely the defendant's awareness of the nature and effect of his own acts, but also his awareness of the intentions of the principal. It is a form of two-dimensional fault, which brings with it various complexities: the would-be accomplice's knowledge of the principal's intentions may be more or less detailed, and in any event the principal might not do exactly as planned.

Two basic fault requirements may be outlined. First, the accomplice must intend to do whatever acts of assistance or encouragement are done, and must be aware of their ability to assist or encourage the principal.[59] Secondly, the accomplice must know the 'essential matters which constitute the offence', i.e. all the relevant circumstances.[60] These requirements apply whether the principal's crime is one of recklessness, negligence, or strict liability. Why is the higher degree of fault required for the accomplice than for the principal? The answer, as for inchoate offences (see 11.3(a)), is that as the form of criminal liability moves further away from the actual infliction of harm, so the grounds of liability should become narrower. Otherwise, the law would spread its net wide indeed, and all kinds of people who did acts which, unbeknown to them, helped others to commit crimes of strict liability or negligence, might find themselves liable to conviction. In fact, the two basic fault requirements are put under strain largely in cases of assisting crime in which D is not present at the commission of the offence, and in cases of encouraging (counselling, procuring) when there is a change of plan. Both these situations reinforce the feature of complicity that differentiates it from other forms of liability: it is not merely that the accomplice must have some awareness of what the principal is doing, but in cases where the accomplice acts before the principal starts to commit the crime there is also the problem of awareness

---

[58] LCCP, *Assisting and Encouraging Crime*, Part IV.
[59] K. J. M. Smith, *Modern Teatise on Complicity*, 141.
[60] *Johnson v Youden* [1950] 1 KB 544.

of what will happen in the future. In effect, this is a question of prediction rather than knowledge—or to put it another way, a question of reckless knowledge, being aware that there is a risk of one or more offences occurring.

In its recent discussion of complicity, the Law Commission states the negative proposition that 'there is no case which rejects the awareness of a mere possibility of the commission of the principal offence as a ground of accessory liability, and at least some authority that seems to support that analysis.'[61] One recent authority is *Blakely and Sutton* v *Chief Constable of West Mercia* (1991):[62] the defendants had laced P's soft drinks with vodka, intending to inform him of this and thus lead him to stay the night with the first defendant rather than driving home. P left before they could inform him, and was convicted of driving with excess alcohol. The two defendants were charged with procuring P's offence and, although their convictions were quashed, it emerges from McCullough J's judgment in the Divisional Court that it is sufficient for other forms of complicity, if not for procuring, that D contemplated that his act 'would or might' bring about or assist the commission of the principal offence.[63] There is no evidence that prosecutors have exploited this great and new-found width in the law of complicity, but it could lead to the conviction of most people who host parties at which alcohol is consumed and after which guests drive their cars, unless the host keeps a careful check on the drinks consumed by potential drivers.[64]

The interaction of the conduct element and the fault element in complicity has not always operated so as to broaden liability. Cases in which recklessness is relied upon have been rare, and greater attention has been given to the conflict of authority between two leading cases on intention and knowledge. The first is *National Coal Board* v *Gamble* (1959),[65] where a weighbridge operator issued a ticket to a lorry driver certifying the lorry's weight and thus allowing him to take his lorry out of the colliery and on to a public road. The Divisional Court held that the weighbridge operator was liable for aiding and abetting the driver's offence so long as he knew that the lorry was overweight and that it was about to be driven on a public road,[66] with Devlin J explaining that 'mens rea is a matter of intent only and does not depend on desire or motive'. Thus, it was irrelevant that the weighbridge operator was 'only doing his job' and had no personal interest in what the lorry driver might do thereafter. His

---

[61] LCCP, *Assisting and Encouraging Crime*, para 2.58.   [62] [1991] RTR 405.

[63] This case was unusual in that the prosecution only alleged 'procuring'. Cf. the aiding and abetting case of *Carter* v *Richardson* [1974] RTR 314.

[64] The attempt of Lord Widgery CJ in *Attorney-General's Reference (No. 1 of 1975)* [1975] QB 773 to argue that the 'generous host' would not be liable was unconvincing then, and is more unconvincing since the *Blakely* case.   [65] [1959] 1 QB 11.

knowledge of what the lorry driver *was about to do* was sufficient. This approach would also lead to the conviction of a shopkeeper who knows that his customer plans to use a certain item for a crime and who nevertheless sells the item, and it is dissatisfaction with this outcome which led the framers of the American Model Penal Code to impose the more stringent requirement that the accomplice should have acted with the purpose of promoting or facilitating the offence.[67] The effect of that narrower doctrine is to ensure that citizens are not treated as their fellow citizens' keepers, a sturdy individualist approach. The wider doctrine of *NCB* v *Gamble*, which imposes accomplice liability wherever a person knows that the recipient intends to commit a certain crime with the property delivered, has the effect of placing a seller, a weighbridge operator, etc. under a duty not to make the sale or issue the ticket in these circumstances. Not only is this consistent with the general assimilation of foresight of practical certainty within intention,[68] but it also supports a more social and less individualistic notion of responsibility.

English courts have not always felt comfortable with the propositions that knowledge of the principal's intention (without purpose) should suffice for accomplice liability—indeed, Slade J dissented on the point in *NCB* v *Gamble*—and in the unusual circumstances of *Gillick* v *West Norfolk and Wisbech Health Authority* (1986)[69] the House of Lords held that a doctor who supplies contraceptives to a girl under 16, knowing that this will assist her boyfriend to commit the offence of unlawful sexual intercourse with a girl under 16, is not an accomplice to the boyfriend's offence. The reason for this decision seems to be that the doctor's purpose would not be to assist the boy but to protect the girl. This runs directly counter to *NCB* v *Gamble*, where it was held that mere knowledge of assistance is enough and that purpose is not required. *Gillick* should probably not be treated as conclusive on the issue of accomplice liability, since their Lordships did not trouble to examine the existing authorities in their speeches. The doctor's motive evidently overshadowed the case,[70] and a preferable way of dealing with that emerges from *Clarke* (1985).[71] Here the Court of Appeal held that a person who knowingly assists others in a burglary, with the intent of ensuring that the police capture both burglars and the stolen property, does satisfy the mental element of complicity (in that he knows that the principals will commit the offence) but may have a defence based on his purpose of assisting law enforcement. That decision

---

[66] See also *Attorney-General* v *Able* [1984] 1 QB 795.

[67] Model Penal Code, s 2.06(3).

[68] As in *Moloney* [1985] AC 905, *Hancock and Shankland* [1986] AC 455, and the draft Criminal Code, cl 18(b), discussed above, Ch 5.3(b). [69] [1986] AC 112.

[70] For discussion of a possible defence of medical necessity, based on *Gillick*, see above, Ch 4.9(b). [71] (1985) 80 Cr App R 344.

keeps the question of the accomplice's knowledge separate from the question of whether there is any defence.

Much more could be written about the conflict between the cases of *Gamble* and *Gillick*. There are legal precedents in favour of each view,[72] and a further possibility is that the broader *Gamble* requirement of knowledge should be applied in cases of aiding and abetting, whereas the narrower *Gillick* concept of purpose is more appropriate in cases of counselling and procuring.[73] What is regrettable is that the issue of principle has been obscured by confusions of terminology (e.g. different meanings of intention) and by a failure to discuss the matter as one of principle. The real issue concerns the proper scope of the criminal law in this sphere: one might argue that the difficulty in finding a reasonably certain definition of the conduct element in complicity renders it desirable to maintain a narrow fault requirement, and yet the decision in *Blakely and Sutton* v *Chief Constable of West Mercia*[74] has the opposite effect by recognizing advertent recklessness as sufficient.

Further problems on fault arise from the fact that at least two people are involved, the accomplice and the principal, and so it is often a question of one person's knowledge of another person's intentions. Some issues can be resolved by basic propositions. If the aider knows the nature of the offence which the principal intends to commit but does not know when it is to occur, that should be immaterial: time is rarely specified as an element in the definition of an offence. The same applies to the location of the offence: so long as the aider knows that the principal plans to burgle a bank, ignorance as to the particular bank is immaterial to accomplice liability.[75] The real difficulties begin when the aider or counsellor does not know precisely what offence the principal intends to commit, and has only a general idea. Should this be sufficient?

Let us suppose that D lends P some mechanical cutting equipment, knowing full well that P intends to use it in connection with a forthcoming crime but having no precise idea of the crime intended: D does not ask, and P does not tell. In fact, D uses the equipment in a burglary. On facts similar to these, the decision in *Bainbridge* (1960)[76] held that neither mere suspicion nor broad knowledge of some criminal intention is sufficient: the minimum condition for accomplice liability is knowledge that the principal intends to commit a crime of the *type* actually committed. This decision clearly goes against, or beyond, the basic requirement that the accomplice

---

[72] See I. H. Dennis, 'The Mental Element for Accessories', in P. F. Smith (ed), *Criminal Law: Essays in Honour of J. C. Smith* (1987); G. R. Sullivan, 'Intent, Purpose and Complicity' [1988] Crim LR 641, with reply by Dennis, *ibid*, 649.

[73] G. Williams, 'Complicity, Purpose and the Draft Code, I' [1990] Crim LR 4.

[74] Above, n. 62 and accompanying text.

[75] *Bainbridge* [1960] 1 QB 219.   [76] Ibid.

should know the essential matters that constitute the principal's crime.[77] Should this extension of liability be opposed—knowledge of the particular crime committed ought to be required, because the theory is that the accomplice's liability derives from the principal's offence—or should it be accepted as a pragmatic solution which avoids the acquittals of those who assist willingly without knowing the precise form of offence envisaged? This might depend on the breadth of the term 'type', and some light is thrown on this by the decision of the House of Lords in *Maxwell* v *DPP for Northern Ireland* (1978).[78] Maxwell was persuaded to drive a car for a group of terrorists, knowing broadly what offences they *might* commit, but not knowing which one or ones they *would* commit. It was held that he was liable as an accomplice to the offence of planting explosives, so long as he contemplated that offence as one of the possible offences and intentionally lent his assistance. As Lord Scarman put it: 'An accessory who leaves it to his principal to choose is liable, provided always the choice is made from the range of offences from which the accessory contemplates the choice will be made'.

It is not difficult to see why the courts reached the decisions in *Bainbridge* and in *Maxwell*. They probably believed that a narrow view of the mental element in complicity might open the door to acquittal for some persons believed to be sufficiently culpable, and in *Maxwell* there was the additional factor of the defendant's knowing involvement in terrorism which may have led the court to avoid a narrow view. Both courts appear to have decided to propound a test which stops short of proclaiming that a general criminal intent is sufficient (i.e. knowledge that the principal was going to commit some crime), and yet which goes wider than a requirement of full knowledge. The effect of the *Maxwell* test is to introduce reckless knowledge as sufficient: the accomplice knows that one or more of a group of offences is virtually certain to be committed, which means that in relation to the one(s) actually committed, there was knowledge only of a *risk* that it would be committed—and that amounts to recklessness. Since our discussion began with the principle that accomplice liability should be restricted to cases of full knowledge, and since the effect of *Gillick* may be to restrict it further to cases of purpose, the ruling in *Maxwell* does appear to be a significant departure. Yet there is surely no merit in acquitting a person who willingly gives assistance, knowing that one of a group of crimes will be committed but now knowing exactly which one. Such a person has surely crossed the threshold of blameworthiness, both in conduct and in the accompanying fault. The difficulty arises not so much

---

[77] See *Johnson* v *Youden*, above, n. 60; the Law Commission is prepared to describe the *Bainbridge* judgment as an 'evasion' of this basic requirement: LCCP, *Assisting and Encouraging Crime*, para 3.22.   [78] [1978] 3 All ER 1140.

from the *Maxwell* ruling itself as from English law's insistence that the liability of the accomplice should be derived from, and tied to, the precise offence committed by the principal. In situations like *Maxwell*, the main justification for convicting the defendant is the willing assistance to persons known to be involved in serious crime.

A preferable way of dealing with this, as will be argued in 10.8 below, would be to create a separate crime of facilitation, to be committed by anyone who assists a person known to be involved in a crime, with a maximum sentence tied to the level of seriousness of the crime contemplated by the facilitator.[79] In the absence of such an offence, the courts have created another *ad hoc* adaptation of the prevailing complicity doctrine, by extending the referential field of the accomplice's 'knowledge' to deal with the problems raised by *Bainbridge* and *Maxwell*. The Law Commission proposes a test based on *Maxwell*, founded on D's knowledge or belief 'that the principal intends to commit one of a number of offences,' but not including the elastic concept of the same 'type' of offence.[80]

10.5 COMMON PURPOSE AND LIABILITY FOR THE UNEXPECTED

Most complicity cases involve some kind of agreement between principal and accomplice. This is not necessarily the case where the accomplice's contribution is a form of 'aiding': as we saw earlier, 'aiding' can be effected without any consensus between the two parties—and, indeed, without the principal knowing about the accomplice's contribution.[81] However, many of the cases can be interpreted as involving some kind of common purpose, sometimes termed 'joint enterprise' or 'common design'. The courts have tended only to discuss cases in these terms where there has been some unexpected turn of events which calls into question the liability of a secondary party for what the principal has done. Historically it is unclear whether the doctrine of common purpose or joint enterprise amounts to an additional form of complicity liability (beyond aiding, abetting, counselling, or procuring), or is merely grafted on to each of them.[82] Without attempting to explore that issue here, we focus on some specific questions: what view does the law take if the plan goes wrong and unexpected consequences ensue? What is the accomplice's liability if the principal deliberately deviates from the plan? What principles should govern these questions?

---

[79] A precedent for this would be s 4 of the Criminal Law Act 1967; see further R. J. Buxton, 'Complicity in the Criminal Code' (1969) 85 LQR, 252.
[80] LCCP, *Assisting and Encouraging Crime*, para 4.99.
[81] See above, Ch 10.3(a), and the case of *State* v *Tally* (1894) 14 So 722.
[82] See K. J. M. Smith, *Modern Treatise on Complicity*, Chs 7 and 8.

(a) Same Offence: Different Result

In one group of cases the law takes the same approach for joint enterprises as it does for offences by individuals. Thus, where the intended result occurs by an unexpected mode (e.g. death caused by drowning rather than by beating), this does not affect the accomplice's liability;[83] where the principal makes a mistake of identity and commits the offence against the wrong victim, this is also irrelevant;[84] and where the intended offence falls upon the wrong victim because the principal's attempt to harm one person succeeds only in harming another, this too is irrelevant.[85] In so far as the policies of transferred liability and the other rules are sound for individuals, they should apply to principals and accomplices. The same should presumably be said of constructive liability: thus, if D helps P in an assault on V, as a result of which V unexpectedly dies, a law which renders P liable for manslaughter should also apply so as to render D an accomplice to manslaughter.[86] These propositions all apply the logic of English law's 'derivative' theory of complicity, whereby the accomplice's liability derives from that of the principal. Most of the questions could be approached in other ways—for example, making the accomplice's liability turn on what he or she intended the principal to do, rather than attaching liability to what actually happened.[87]

The common factor in the above group of cases is that the result was unexpected by both principal and accomplice. The problem of the accomplice's liability is different in cases where the principal deviates intentionally from the agreed course of conduct. Causal principles would suggest that this change of mind constitutes a voluntary intervening act which should sever all connection between the accomplice's contribution and the principal's actual offence. This was the approach taken in the old case of *Saunders and Archer* (1573), where D had advised P to kill his wife by means of a poisoned apple; P placed the apple before his wife, but the wife passed the apple to their child, who ate it and died.[88] D was held not to have been an accomplice in the child's murder, on the basis that the events amounted to a deliberate change of plan by P. Although P did not actually give the apple to the child, he sat by and allowed the child to eat the apple when it was his parental duty to intervene, and this failure to prevent the miscarriage of the plan was enough to negative D's complicity in the actual result.

[83] For the unforeseen mode, see Ch 5.4(b) above.
[84] For mistaken victim, see Ch 5.4(c) above.
[85] For transferred fault, see Ch 5.4(d) above.
[86] *Baldessare* (1930) 22 Cr App R 70; cf. *Mahmood* [1994] Crim LR 368.
[87] Discussed further in 10.8 below.   [88] (1573) 2 Plowd 473.

Behind this decision lies a conflict of principle. It seems to establish that an accomplice is relieved of liability if the principal deliberately deviates from the 'common design' by selecting a different victim, and causal reasoning may support that. But this seems inconsistent with English law's general disregard of the identity of the victim and of the method used to effect result-oriented crimes. Would the *Saunders and Archer* approach be used in cases of deliberate change of mode? If D had counselled P to kill his wife with a poisoned apple, and P had decided to use a knife or a gun instead, should D equally be acquitted of complicity in the killing? One might argue that accessorial liability should be determined on the basis that it is for the parties to stipulate which features of their common design are critical, rather than for the law to declare that neither the identity of the victim nor the method employed is legally relevant. For example, in the South African case of *S* v *Robinson* (1968)[89] X and two others agreed with V that V should be killed by X so that V could escape prosecution for fraud and the others could obtain insurance monies. V withdrew his consent to the arrangement, not surprisingly, but X killed him nevertheless. The offence was as planned, the victim was as planned, but the element of consent was crucial to the common purpose, and that was absent: should the two others be convicted as accomplices to X's offence? The South African court held them liable as accomplices to attempted murder only, because their complicity in murder was dependent on the consent. A counter-argument is that this is too precious an approach, in that they had made their intended contributions to a planned murder. Yet English courts, too, might well take the view that because the principal has taken an unexpected decision, and because the common law maintains that the liability of the accomplice derives from that of the principal, there is a logical difficulty. English law has struggled to resolve the problem by holding that a deliberate change of victim releases the accomplice from liability; it has also used the test of whether the principal's conduct was 'beyond the scope of this authority';[90] but it has not directly confronted the question of whether these *ad hoc* adaptations of the derivative approach to liability are satisfactory both in theory and in practice. A preferable approach, again, might be to abandon the derivative theory and to base liability more squarely on what the accomplice set out to do.

(b) Different, More Serious Offence

The cases discussed so far have chiefly concerned deviations by the principals which have none the less resulted in the commission of an

---

[89] 1968 (1) SA 666.
[90] *Calhaem* [1985] 1 QB 808. The draft Criminal Code leaves the issue for judicial solution: Law Com 177, cl 27(1) and para 9.31.

offence in the same legal category as that contemplated by the parties. What if the principal deliberately deviates so as to commit a more serious offence? English law on this point has developed in a curious way. A hundred years ago Sir James Stephen stated the test as whether the crime committed by the principal could be regarded as a 'probable consequence' of the common design—an objective test of foreseeability, to be applied to the point at which the assistance was given or the agreement reached.[91] To allow the accomplice's liability to turn on an objective test of foreseeability was open to criticism on the familiar unfairness grounds,[92] and the modern decisions move away from it. One leading case is *Anderson and Morris* (1966),[93] where Lord Parker CJ held that 'if one of the adventurers goes beyond what has been tacitly agreed as part of the common enterprise, his co-adventurer is not liable for the consequences of that unauthorized act'. The other leading case is probably the decision of the Privy Council in *Chan Wing-Siu* (1985),[94] where the defendants had gone to commit a robbery armed with knives and one of their number used a knife to kill one of the robbery victims. The defendants argued that the agreement was to commit robbery, using the knives to frighten and not to cause death or injury. However, the Privy Council held that there is a doctrine of common purpose that 'turns on contemplation . . . or authorization, which may be expressed but is more usually implied. It meets the case of a crime foreseen as a possible incident of the common unlawful enterprise. The criminal culpability lies in participating in the venture with that foresight.' The element of prior agreement or 'authorization' seems to be rather weak here: in reality, the basis of liability has shifted to (subjective) foresight of a significant possibility, as the Privy Council confirmed when suggesting that a remote possibility would be insufficient but that foresight of a 'real risk' would be enough.[95] In practice this test may be wider than the old objective one: indeed, it bases the accomplice's liability on a restricted form of recklessness, and is therefore similar in spirit to the *Maxwell* decision.[96] At one stage there was a rival line of decisions favouring the narrower view that the accomplice is only liable if he or she had the same degree of *mens rea* as is required for the principal.[97] The reasons for this approach are not difficult to find. If D and E go out to burgle a house, and D hands E a knife on the understanding that it will only be used to frighten

[91] J. F. Stephen, *A Digest of the Criminal Law*, art 20.
[92] See above, Ch 5.2(a) and 5.3(a).
[93] [1966] 2 QB 110, the Court of Criminal Appeal sitting with five judges.
[94] [1985] AC 168.
[95] To similar effect, see *Hyde, Sussex and Collins* [1991] 1 QB 134, *Roberts* (1993) 96 Cr App R 291.   [96] See above, n. 78 and accompanying text.
[97] *Barr et al.* (1989) 88 Cr App R 362; *Wakeley et al.* [1990] Crim LR 119; see M. Giles, 'Complicity: The Problems of Joint Enterprise' [1990] Crim LR 383.

the victim, the broader test (above) would turn D into an accomplice to murder, liable to the mandatory penalty of life imprisonment, if E uses the knife and kills someone. E would be liable for murder only if he had the required intention, but D is liable to conviction of the same offence, with the same mandatory penalty, on the basis of recklessness alone. The narrower test avoids this result by requiring some tacit agreement between the parties about the conduct which took place. This would be very much an *ad hoc* solution, driven by the inflexibility of the English law of murder rather than by policies relevant to complicity. That it does not represent the law was confirmed by the Privy Council in *Hui Chi-Ming* v *R* (1992),[98] which follows *Anderson and Morris* and *Chan Wing-Siu*. All that is required by the doctrine of common purpose is that the jury is satisfied that each defendant contemplated that there was a real possibility that one member of the joint enterprise might go beyond their agreement and do what he did.

(c) Different, Less Serious Offence

The English courts have recently stretched the law of complicity in the opposite direction: the House of Lords decision in *Howe* (1987)[99] holds that where D aids or counsels the principal to commit a certain offence, and the principal deviates by committing a less serious offence, D may be convicted as an accomplice to the intended (more serious) offence. The previous decision in *Richards*[100] laid down a different rule. In that case a woman paid two men to beat up her husband so as to put him in hospital for a few days. Her hope was that this experience would lead her husband to turn to her for comfort, thus repairing their relationship. The hired men inflicted less serious injuries than she had asked them to, and it was held that she could not be convicted as an accomplice to the higher offence unless she was present at the scene (an ancient rule). The effect of *Howe* is to sweep away such restrictions. Yet this new rule involves a patent departure from the derivative theory of accomplice liability: the (intended) higher offence was never committed, and so the accomplice's liability cannot derive from any such offence. The theory underlying the *Howe* ruling is that the culpability of the accomplice should be viewed as a separate issue from that of the principal, and based upon what the accomplice intended to happen or believed would happen. This result could have been achieved in *Richards* by charging the wife with the inchoate offence of incitement (see Chapter 11.6). Where the prosecution uses the law of complicity, the decision in *Howe* suggests that courts sometimes determine liability according to which of two principles—the derivative and the subjective—has the further reach in a given case.

[98] [1992] 1 AC 34.   [99] [1987] AC 417.
[100] [1974] QB 776, discussed by Kadish, *Blame and Punishment*, 184–6.

10.6 DERIVATIVE LIABILITY AND THE MISSING LINK

We now come to another set of cases in which the English courts have departed from, or at least modified, the derivative theory of accessorial liability. If the would-be principal is not guilty of the substantive offence, because of the absence of a mental element or the presence of a defence, does this mean that the accomplice must also be acquitted? A straightforward application of the derivative theory would lead to non-liability; one cannot be said to have aided and abetted an offence if the offence did not take place, for there is nothing from which the accomplice's liability can derive. Yet the would-be accomplice has done all that he or she intended to do in order to further the principal's crime, and, considered in isolation, the accomplice is surely no less culpable than if the principal had been found guilty. It is therefore not surprising that English courts have responded by stretching the doctrine of complicity. In *Bourne* (1952)[101] D threatened and forced his wife to commit bestiality with a dog, and his conviction for aiding and abetting bestiality was upheld despite the fact that his wife would have had a defence of duress if charged as the principal. In *Cogan and Leak* (1976)[102] Cogan had intercourse with Leak's wife, believing, on the basis of what Leak had told him, that Mrs Leak was consenting. Leak knew that his wife was not consenting. Cogan's conviction for rape was quashed because his defence of mistaken belief in the woman's consent had not been put the jury, but Leak's conviction for aiding and abetting rape was upheld. The judgments in these cases contain little elaboration of the theoretical basis for conviction, but they could be defended as a mere extension of the derivative theory. The extension would be that a person may be convicted as an accomplice to the commission of an *actus reus* or 'wrongful act', where the reason for acquitting the would-be principal is the absence of a mental element or the presence of a defence. This approach does have theoretical and practical limitations, however. One requirement of accomplice liability is that the accomplice must know the essential elements of the offence (including the principal's mental element); but in these cases the accomplice usually knows that the would-be principal lacks an element necessary for conviction. Bourne knew that his wife was acting because of his threats; Leak knew that Cogan was acting because of his lies. The same difficulty arises in respect of *Millward* (1994),[103] where D was convicted of procuring the offence of causing death by reckless driving by sending an employee out in a tractor with a defective trailer which led to the death of another motorist. The employee was acquitted of the principal offence, but the

---

[101] (1952) 36 Cr App R 125.　　　　　[102] [1976] 1 QB 217.
[103] [1994] Crim LR 527.

Court of Appeal upheld the employer's conviction for, essentially, procuring the *actus reus*.

This extension of the derivative theory does not, however, give the courts grounds for overturning the decision in *Thornton v Mitchell* (1940).[104] A bus-conductor was directing the driver in reversing a bus when an accident was caused. The driver was acquitted of careless driving, because he was relying on the conductor's guidance, and it was held that the conductor must therefore be acquitted of aiding and abetting. Since the *actus reus* of careless driving was not committed, the suggested extension of the derivative theory would yield the same result.[105] Only a suitably worded offence of facilitation would produce a conviction.

Convictions seem justified for Bourne and Leak, because they both chose to bring about a result which the law prohibits: their behaviour and culpability are as high on the scale of seriousness as many principals. The inchoate offence of incitement might appear to offer a solution, but it may not succeed where the inciter knows that the incitee lacks an element of the full offence.[106] One solution would be to change the law and to deem such persons principals, which the draft English Code proposes;[107] or the law could render the person liable as a principal for causing the prohibited conduct or result—for example, by imposing liability for causing an innocent or non-responsible person to engage in prohibited conduct where the person who causes this has the mental element required for the offence.[108]

Another possible approach is through the doctrine of innocent agency. A clear example would be where an adult urges or orders a child under the age of criminal responsibility to commit crimes, such as stealing from a shop. The young child is deemed 'innocent' in law, and so it is said that the adult commits the crime through the innocent agency of the child. No such notion is possible where two adults are involved, since it is presumed that adults are autonomous beings acting voluntarily, save in exceptional circumstances. One exceptional circumstance would be where the adult is mentally disordered; another would be where the adult is acting under duress. Thus if, as in *Bourne*,[109] a man threatens and forces his wife to commit bestiality with a dog, her defence of duress may be said to establish that her conduct was insufficiently voluntary to be regarded as the cause of the event. In causal terms she 'drops out of the picture' as a mere innocent

---

[104] [1940] 1 All ER 339; cf. R. D. Taylor, 'Complicity and the Excuses' [1983] Crim LR 656.
[105] If D in *Millward* had been prosecuted under the new offence of causing death by dangerous driving, no conviction would have been possible for this same reason: see Sir John Smith [1994] Crim LR 530.   [106] See below, Ch 11.6.
[107] Law Com No. 117, clause 26(1).   [108] Model Penal Code, s 2.06(2)(a).
[109] (1952) 36 Cr App R 125.

agent, leaving the person who uttered the threats as the principal responsible for the offence.[110] How much further can the doctrine of innocent agency be taken? If D gives a bottle to the nurse attending V, telling her that it contains a prescribed medicine when in fact it contains poison, D should surely be liable as the principal when the nurse administers the contents of the bottle to V, who dies. The nurse would be regarded as an innocent agent because, although she did not lack criminal capacity in the sense of being mentally disordered or overborne by threats, she was acting under a mistake which would relieve her of criminal liability for her acts.[111] If this is accepted, it would seem to follow that where (as in *Cogan and Leak*) D persuades P to have sexual intercourse with D's wife by inducing P to believe that she consents to this, P's mistake would mean that he drops out of the picture as an innocent agent and that D should be liable as a principal for rape.[112]

Various objections might be raised against this conclusion. The major counter-argument is that the doctrine of innocent agency should not be used where it is linguistically inappropriate. It is appropriate to describe D as killing (or, at least, causing the death of) V in the case involving the nurse, but it is manifestly inappropriate to describe a person as driving with excess alcohol in his blood, if what he has done is to lace the drink of someone who is about to drive a car,[113] or to describe D as having raped a woman if D tricked another man into having sexual intercourse with that woman,[114] or to describe D as having committed bigamy if she induced someone else to believe (erroneously) that the other person's marriage had been legally terminated and to remarry on the strength of this belief.[115] The conflict here is plain. The law has to be expressed in words, and some verbal formulas are hedged about with linguistic conventions which do not correspond to moral or social distinctions in responsibility. It seems right that D who gives poison to the nurse to administer unwittingly should be convicted as the principal in murder, because D was the cause of the death. That element of causation remains prominent in the other examples of the 'lacer' of drinks, the encourager of non-consensual intercourse, and the orchestrators of bigamy, and the moral/social argument for criminal liability seems no less strong; but the conventions of language erect a barrier. Some offences are phrased in terms which imply personal agency (rape is said to be one) or which apply only to the holder of certain office or

---

[110] See above, Ch 4.6(b), and Alldridge, 'The Doctrine of Innocent Agency'.
[111] *Michael* (1840) 9 C&P 356, and above, Ch 4.6.
[112] See generally the discussion by Kadish, *Blame and Punishment*, Essay 8.
[113] *Attorney-General's Reference (No. 1 of 1975)* [1975] QB 773.
[114] *Cogan and Leak* [1976] 1 QB 217; at this time a husband could not be convicted of the rape of his wife, but that rule has now been abrogated: see above, Ch 8.
[115] *Kemp and Else* [1964] 2 QB 341.

licence. There is no reason why the law should be constrained by this
linguistic barrier. The courts could simply ignore it and stretch the
language.[116] Or Parliament could introduce a special provision which
would make it possible to convict as a principal the person who uttered the
threats, implanted the mistaken belief, or poured the alcohol clandestinely,
on the basis that that person *caused* the wrongful act.[117] Or it could
introduce a special provision which would render D liable as an
accomplice, even though no person could be convicted as a principal.[118]
The difference between the last two alternatives would seem to turn on the
appropriateness of labelling D as a principal or an accomplice: since D
really is the motivator and the cause of the event, it would not seem wrong
to assign the label of principal. This could lead to a woman who tricked a
man into having sexual intercourse with another woman being convicted as
a principal in rape. This is said to be absurd but, as argued above, any
absurdity is linguistic rather than moral or social, and is in any event
dependent on the definition of rape or sexual assault.

10.7 SPECIAL DEFENCES TO COMPLICITY

(a) Withdrawal

Complicity often involves the accomplice in words or deeds prior to the
principal's crime. If the accomplice has a change of heart before the
principal commits the offence, can the accomplice's liability be removed?
If an individual decides to commit an offence on his own, then obviously
that individual can change his mind at will. However once some steps have
been taken towards the commission of the offence, the possibility of
preventing liability by abandoning one's intentions depends in English law
on how far one has gone towards the substantive offence. If the acts done
so far amount to a criminal attempt, then the law states that there can be
no legally effective abandonment—it becomes merely a matter in
mitigation of sentence. Only if the acts done fall short of an attempt can the
person abandon the criminal plan with impunity. This is an over-strict
doctrine which neither reflects culpability nor serves the goal of crime
prevention.[119] If we now turn to complicity cases, where there is a principal
and an accomplice, abandonment or withdrawal by the accomplice raises
slightly different issues. Since the contribution of the accomplice may have
had some influence over the principal either by way of encouragement or

---

[116] See A. Ashworth, 'Interpreting Criminal Legislation: A Crisis of Legality?' (1991) 107
LQR, 419.   [117] See Model Penal Code, s 2.06(2)(a).
[118] Confirming *Cogan and Leak* [1976] 1 QB 21 (above, n. 114), and following the German
law described by Fletcher, *Rethinking Criminal Law*, 664–7.
[119] See further Ch 11.3(a) below.

assistance, one might expect the law to require not merely a change of mind communicated to the principal, but some endeavour to 'undo' the effect of what has been done. The older decisions tend to speak in terms of the principal acting with the authority of the accomplice, and withdrawal as a countermanding of that authority.[120] Modern decisions have emphasized the significance of the stage which the principal's actions have reached. Thus, where D's contribution consists of giving information to the principal about property to be burgled, and then, a week or so before the planned burglary, D tells the principal that he does not wish to take part and does not want the burglary to take place, this may be an effective withdrawal.[121]

In *Becerra and Cooper* (1975),[122] however, the situation was rather different. B had given C a knife to use if anyone disturbed them during the burglary they were carrying out. When B heard someone coming, he told C of this, said 'Come on, let's go', jumped out of a window, and ran off. C did not follow: he stabbed the inquisitive neighbour fatally with the knife. B was convicted as an accomplice to murder, and this was upheld in the Court of Appeal; when events have proceeded so far, an effective withdrawal was held to require far more than a few words such as 'let's go'. The Court did not decide exactly what was required, but it seems clear that if C had already been using or preparing to use the knife against the inquisitive neighbour, B might have had to go so far as to try to restrain C physically. The trial judge framed the general proposition that the withdrawing accomplice must 'take all reasonable steps to prevent the commission of the crime which he had agreed the others should commit,' and the Court of Appeal did not dissent from this. Thus the essence of withdrawal in complicity is that the accomplice must not only make a clear statement of withdrawal and communicate this to the principal, but must also (if the crime is imminent) take some steps to prevent its commission. The closer the principal's offence is to commission, the more active the intervention required of the accomplice for effective withdrawal. In a sense, the argument seems to parallel the *Miller* principle—that one has a duty to prevent harm resulting from a train of events which one has started[123]—but the parallel is imperfect, since on the one hand complicity involves the actions of two autonomous individuals, and the accomplice is not causally 'responsible' for the principal's conduct, and on the other hand the accomplice is knowingly involved in initiating the train of events, whereas Miller did so unknowingly. One cannot go further, and suggest that English law is supporting a limited duty to prevent crime here,[124] since

---

[120] E.g. *Saunders and Archer* (1573) 2 Plowd, 473, at 476.
[121] *Whitefield* (1984) 79 Cr App R 36.
[122] (1975) 62 Cr App R 212; see also *Baker* [1994] Crim LR 444.
[123] [1983] 2 AC 161.   [124] See above, Ch 4.4(c) and Ch 10.3(b).

the accomplice who gives information to the principal and then communicates a withdrawal in good time is not, it seems, required to counteract the effect of that information by informing the police of the planned crime.[125] This seems difficult to justify, given the influence which the accomplice's help or advice may have had on the principal, and it would surely be right ·to require more as a condition of legally effective withdrawal.

(b) The Tyrell Principle

In *Tyrell* (1894)[126] it was held that a girl under 16 could not be convicted as a secondary party to an offence of unlawful sexual intercourse committed with her. Lord Coleridge CJ stated that Parliament could not have intended 'that the girls for whose protection [the Act] was passed should be punishable under it for the offences committed upon themselves.' Although the court's reasoning was based on statutory interpretation, the decision has subsequently been interpreted as authority for a general principle that victims, particularly victims of sexual offences, cannot be convicted of complicity if the offence was created for their protection.[127] Glanville Williams has shown that the principle is uncertain and difficult to state satisfactorily,[128] and the Law Commission has proposed a re-drafting of the defence: the principle of protecting victims from conviction for assisting should be retained, it suggests, but there is room for doubt whether a 'victim' who encourages the commission of the offence should be exempt.

(c) Crime Prevention

There is authority that a form of 'choice of evils' defence may be available to someone who would otherwise be an accomplice.[129] In *Clarke* (1984)[130] D's defence was that he joined other burglars once the offence had been planned, and did so in order to assist the police. The Court of Appeal held that this could form the basis for a defence, if the jury were satisfied that D's conduct was 'overall calculated and intended not to further but to frustrate the ultimate result of the crime'. The draft Criminal Code provides for a defence where D acts 'with the purpose of preventing the commission of the offence' or 'with the purpose of avoiding or limiting any harmful consequences of the offence and without the purpose of furthering its commission'.[131] This is apt to cover the circumstances alleged in *Clarke*,

---

[125] See the draft Criminal Code, Law Com No. 177, cl 27(8); cf. *Hudson and Taylor* [1971] 2 QB 202, and Ch 6.4(c).   [126] [1894] 1 QB 710.

[127] E.g. *Whitehouse* [1977] QB 868.

[128] 'Victims and other Exempt Parties in Crime' (1990) 10 Legal Studies, 245.

[129] For discussion of such defences, see above, Ch 4.9.

[130] (1984) 80 Cr App R 344.   [131] Law Com No. 177, cl 27(6).

and might well serve to exempt police officers and others who act as *agent provocateurs*. However, the Privy Council in *Yip Chiu-Cheung* v *R*. (1994)[132] failed to take this approach in a conspiracy case and treated the whole issue as one of intention.

10.8 CONCLUSIONS

It is apparent that the English law of complicity is replete with uncertainties and conflicts. It betrays the worst features of the common law: what some would regard as flexibility appears here as a succession of opportunistic decisions by the courts, usually extending the law, and resulting in a body of jurisprudence that has little coherence. It has usually been assumed that there are two fundamental principles underlying the English doctrine—that the liability of the accomplice derives from that of the principal, and that the accomplice is required to have intention or knowledge of the principal's offence. Neither proposition can now be advanced without qualifications. The derivative theory has given way in several situations to liability based on causal or subjective principles, and the fault requirements have in some spheres been relaxed so as to include recklessness and in other spheres narrowed to 'purpose' alone. Moreover, the conduct requirements for aiding and abetting remain wide and uncertain. The courts have often extended the law to deal with cases where the principal's conduct differs from the accomplice's expectations, resort- ing frequently but inconsistently to the doctrine of joint enterprise. Indeed, the divergences in recent case law on joint enterprise show that the courts feel conflicting pressures in developing the law, and this has also been evident in their continued espousal of the theory that the accomplice's liability derives from that of the principal—despite the various exceptions that they themselves have created.

The early part of this chapter was concerned with the ambit of complicity liability: what forms of conduct should suffice? The variations in the level of accomplices' contributions is great. Someone who procures another to commit an offence by threats or by implanting a false belief may have substantial causal influence. This suggests, by the way, that a rule restricting the penalty for the accomplice to half or three-quarters of the maximum for the principal would be too crude. In contrast, acts of aiding may be minor and hardly significant. It would be impractical to attempt a legislative listing of all the types of conduct which might amount to complicity. And to require that the accomplice contributed significantly or substantially to the principal's offence would introduce a further avenue

---

[132] [1994] 2 All ER 924, below, p. 461; cf. also the entrapment case of *Smurthwaite and Gill* (1994) 98 Cr App R 437, and the discussion in Ch 6.8 above.

for legal argument, without honouring the principle of maximum certainty. Yet the obvious expedient of leaving prosecutorial discretion to determine (in practice) the lower threshold of criminal complicity not only leaves scope for prosecutors to exert pressure on fringe participants in offences to choose between facing prosecution and testifying in offences against the others, but also accords little weight to the principle of minimum criminalization (see Chapter 3.3(a)).

It is rather strange how the law of complicity has become the focal point for a number of arguments about the duties of citizens. The generally restrictive approach of English law towards liability for omissions has already been discussed,[133] but complicity is one sphere in which the courts have abandoned their general reluctance. In a sense, this may be compatible with the idea that the accomplice may be held in some way responsible for the conduct of the principal, a notion implicit in the terminology of 'authority' which is sometimes used, and also in the requirements for withdrawal from complicity. But the idea of legal responsibility as an accomplice for the acts of those whose conduct one has the power to control—rendering the publican, the car owner, and the house owner liable for the conduct of their guests—is a bold step towards omissions liability under the camouflage of the law of complicity.[134] The debate about the liability of the gun-seller as an accomplice to murder turns on somewhat similar considerations of a citizen's duties towards law enforcement, but it has become wrapped up in an analysis of the distinction between intention and purpose. As suggested in Chapter 4.4, a more open and more principled solution would be to create some discrete offences to cover those situations in which it is felt that citizens ought to take positive action.

Another respect in which English law on complicity is confused is the relationship between the accomplice's conduct and that of the principal. On the one hand the law gives itself extraordinary width by its procedural rule which draws no distinction between principal and accomplice in point of charge, conviction, and maximum sentence. Yet on the other hand it has still not relinquished the idea that the accomplice's liability derives from that of the principal, despite the inadequacies of that theory in dealing with cases where there is a missing link,[135] or where the principal deviates from the agreed or understood course of action.[136] In these two types of case the courts have stretched or abandoned the derivative theory—but why? The reason for wishing to secure convictions here is surely that the accomplice

[133] See above, Ch 4.4(b) and (c).
[134] See A. Ashworth, 'The Scope of Criminal Liability for Omissions' (1989) 105 LQR, 445–7; Law Com No. 177, clause 24(3).   [135] See above, Ch 10.6.
[136] See above, Ch 10.5.

is no less culpable than would have been the case if the principal had done as intended. In terms of culpability and danger the accomplice stands on the same level: should we not regard the accomplice's liability as established independently, rather than making it depend on the liability of the principal?

This is the approach now preferred by the Law Commission.[137] The basis of its proposals is that English law should abandon the derivative theory, which in any event exerts only an intermittent effect on the law, and should establish an inchoate basis for liability. The focus should be on D's conduct and what was expected to result from it, and the non-occurrence of the expected principal offence would not alter the accomplice's liability. The greater fairness of this approach has been emphasized on many occasions,[138] but it represents a significant shift in the law. At a time when considerable emphasis is being placed on the harm resulting from conduct as the basis of liability, the proposal here is to decouple the accomplice's liability from the harm that may or may not result (i.e. the expected principal crime), and to align accomplice liability with the inchoate offences of attempt, conspiracy, and incitement, to be considered in detail in Chapter 11. Thus, for example, cases of hiring 'hit-men' to kill or injure another would lead to prosecutions for incitement, bypassing all the causal complexities raised by the doctrine of complicity, especially where the plan miscarries in some way.[139] This whole approach provides a more satisfactory basis for liability, but it is a bold step for the Law Commission to propose. The Commission also favours a simplification of the law, and the need for this is apparent from the discussion in this chapter. It proposes that the forms of complicity should be reduced to two, assisting and encouraging, again following a body of academic opinion.[140] While this leaves a large number of particular issues to be resolved, it is surely the most promising foundation for a new law.

[137] LCCP No. 131, *Assisting and Encouraging Crime* (1993), reviewed by K. J. M. Smith, 'A Blueprint for Rationalism' [1994] Crim LR 239, and by G. R. Sullivan, 'Fault Elements and Joint Enterprise' [1994] Crim LR 252; cf. J. C. Smith [1994] *New LJ* 679.

[138] E.g. R. J. Buxton, 'Complicity in the Criminal Code' (1969) 85 LQR, 252; J. R. Spencer, 'Helping Others to Commit Crimes', in P. Smith (ed), *Criminal Law: Essays in Honour of J. C. Smith* (1987); in the first edition of this work; and cf. K. J. M. Smith, *Modern Treatise on Complicity*, Ch 4.

[139] Cf. *Calhaem* [1985] 1 QB 808, where a prosecution based on complicity drew forth the contorted judgment discussed in 10.5(a) above. It is, of course, possible to prosecute for incitement on such facts now: *Smurthwaite and Gill* (1994) 98 Cr App R 437.

[140] E.g. S. Kadish, *Blame and Punishment*, Ch 6; G. Williams, 'Complicity, Purpose and the Draft Code' [1990] Crim LR 4, 98; cf. K. J. M. Smith, *Modern Treatise on Complicity*, Ch 2.

II

Inchoate Offences

II.I THE CONCEPT OF AN INCHOATE OFFENCE

The word 'inchoate', not much used in ordinary discourse, means 'just begun', 'undeveloped'. The common law has given birth to three general offences which are usually termed 'inchoate' or 'preliminary' crimes—attempt, conspiracy, and incitement. A principal feature of these crimes is that they are committed even though the substantive offence (i.e. the offence it was intended to bring about) is not completed and no harm results. An attempt fails, a conspiracy comes to nothing, words of incitement are ignored—in all these instances, there may be liability for the inchoate crime. Moreover, as we shall see later in the chapter, there are many substantive offences which are defined in such a way as not to require the actual causing of harm: offences which penalize a person who does a certain act 'with intent to do X' are in reality defined in an inchoate mode, having many of the characteristics of inchoate offences. Crimes of possession are also essentially inchoate:[1] it is not the mere possession, so much as what the possessor might do with the article or substance, which is the reason for criminalization. However, the chapter begins with a discussion of the three traditional inchoate offences of attempt, conspiracy, and incitement, which will show that their ambit and their significance are rather wider than the term 'inchoate' suggests.

II.2 THE JUSTIFICATIONS FOR PENALIZING ATTEMPTS AT CRIMES

(a) Introduction

Let us begin with three examples: (i) X goes to the house of his rival, V, with a can of petrol, some paper, and a box of matches; he soaks the paper in petrol and pushes it through the letter-box, but he is arrested before he can do anything more; (ii) Y drives a car straight at V, but V jumps out of the way at the last moment and is uninjured; (iii) Z is offered money to carry a package of cannabis into Britain; she accepts, brings the package in, but on her arrest it is found that the package contains dried lettuce leaves. These are all cases in which there might be a conviction for attempt.[2] The first feature to be noticed is that no harm actually occurred

---

[1] See Ch 4.3(b) above.
[2] This depends on the accused's intention and beliefs at the time: see 11.3(a) below.

in any of them—no damage was done, no injury caused, no drugs smuggled. Normally, criminal liability requires both culpability and harm: X, Y, and Z might appear culpable, but they have caused no harm. Why, then, should the criminal law become involved? The answer is that harm does indeed have a central place in criminal liability, but that the concern is not merely with the occurrence of harm but also with its prevention. According to this view, the first decision for legislators is exactly which harms should properly be objects of the criminal law (see Chapter 2). Once this has been decided, and taking the aims of the criminal law into account,[3] the law should not only provide for the punishment of those who have culpably caused such harms but also penalize those who are trying to cause the harms. The consequentialist justification for a law of attempts is therefore that it allows law-enforcement officers and the courts to step in *before* any harm has been done, so long as the danger of the harm being caused is clear. There is also a separate justification, stemming from the 'desert' theory of criminal liability, namely that a person who tries to cause a prohibited harm and fails is, in terms of moral culpability, not materially different from the person who tries and succeeds: the difference in outcome is determined by chance rather than by choice, and the criminal law should not subordinate itself to the vagaries of fortune by focussing on results rather than on culpability.

(b) Two Kinds of Attempt

The rationale for criminalizing attempts can best be appreciated by drawing a theoretical distinction (which the law itself does not draw) between two kinds of attempt. First, there are incomplete attempts, which are cases in which the defendant has set out to commit an offence but has not yet done all the acts necessary to bring it about. Our first example, of X putting petrol-soaked paper through the door of V's house, is such a case: he has still to strike a match and light the paper. Contrast this with the second kind of attempt, which will be called a complete attempt. Here the defendant has done all that he intended, but the desired result has not followed—Y has driven the car at V, intending to injure V, but he failed; and Z has smuggled the package into the country, believing it to be cannabis when in fact it is a harmless and worthless substance.

It is easier to justify the criminalization of complete attempts than incomplete attempts, and the two sets of justifications have somewhat different emphases. The justification for punishing complete attempts is that the defendant has done all the acts intended, with the beliefs required for the offence, and is therefore no less blameworthy than a person who is successful in committing the substantive offence. The complete 'attempter'

---

[3] As discussed in Ch 1.3 above.

is thwarted by some unexpected turn of events which, to him, is a matter of pure chance—the intended victim jumped out of the way, or the substance was not what it appeared to be. These arc applications of what were called the 'subjective' principles earlier, the essence of which is that people's criminal liability should be assessed on what they were trying to do, intended to do, and believed they were doing rather than on the actual consequences of their conduct. Rejection of this approach would lead to criminal liability always being judged according to the actual outcome, which would allow luck to play too great a part in the criminal law. Of course luck and chance play a considerable role in human affairs, and we have already seen how important the chance result of death is in the law of involuntary manslaughter.[4] However, there is no reason why a human system for judging and formally censuring the behaviour of others should be a slave to the vagaries of chance. The 'subjective principle' would also be accepted by the consequentialist as a justification for criminalizing complete attempts: the defendant was trying to break the law, and therefore constitutes a source of social danger no less (or little less) than that presented by 'successful' harm-doers.

What about incomplete attempts? The subjective principle does have some application here, inasmuch as the defendant has given some evidence of a determination to commit the substantive offence—though the evidence is likely to be less conclusive than in cases of complete attempts. There is one distinct factor present in incomplete attempts, which is the social importance of authorizing official intervention before harm is done. Since the prevention of harm has a central place in the justifications for criminal law, there is a strong case for stopping attempts before they result in the causing of harm. Detailed arguments about the point at which the law should intervene are discussed in section 11.3(b). Once this point has been reached, then the agents of law enforcement may intervene to stop attempts before they go further. The culpability of the incomplete attempter may be less than that of the complete attempter because there remains the possibility that there would have been voluntary repentance at some late stage: after all, it may take greater nerve to do the final act which triggers the actual harm than to do the preliminary acts. But so long as it is accepted that the incomplete attempter has evinced a settled intention to continue, and to commit the substantive offence by doing some further acts, there is sufficient ground for criminalization.

Although there are sufficient grounds for criminalizing both complete and incomplete attempts, it may be right to reflect some differences between them at the sentencing stage. It may be argued that incomplete attempts should be punished less severely than the full offence—because of

---

[4] Above, Ch 7.5(a).

the possibility of voluntary abandonment of the attempt, because it takes greater nerve to consummate an offence, and because it may be prudent to leave some incentive (i.e. reduced punishment) to the incomplete attempter to give up rather than to carry out the full offence. For complete attempts the case for reduced punishment is less strong, although there may be an argument for some reduction of punishment in order to give the complete attempter an incentive not to try again—otherwise D might reason that there is nothing to lose by this. It will be noticed that these arguments for reduced punishments are utilitarian in nature. Following the principle of 'desert', there is little reason for reducing the punishment of the complete attempter, although there is some reason for recognizing the possibility that the incomplete attempter might yet desist.

11.3 THE ELEMENTS OF CRIMINAL ATTEMPT

The relevant English law is now to be found in the Criminal Attempts Act 1981, which followed a Law Commission report on the subject.[5] It will be discussed by considering three separate aspects of the offence in turn—the fault element, the conduct element, and the problem of impossbility.

(a) The Fault Element

It has been said that, where a person is charged with an attempt, 'the intent becomes the principal ingredient of the crime'.[6] The law on this point rarely causes much difficulty: it must be shown that the defendant intended to cause the proscribed harm, and had the necessary knowledge of facts and circumstances. There have been appeals in cases where D has been charged with attempting to cause grievous bodily harm by driving a car at another person, and the defence has been that D did not intend to injure the other. These appeals have led the courts to establish that purpose is not required for the crime of attempt: what is needed, according to James LJ in *Mohan* (1976),[7] is proof of 'a decision to bring about . . . [the offence], no matter whether the accused desired that consequence of his act or not'. This is supposed to align the meaning of intent here with its meaning in the general law, although there is one decision on attempted murder that appears to accept a wider meaning.[8]

---

[5] *Attempt, and Impossibility in Relation to Attempt, Conspiracy and Incitement*, Law Com No. 102 (1980). For an analysis of the provisions of the 1981 Act, see I Dennis, 'The Criminal Attempts Act 1981' [1982] Crim LR 5. A more general discussion of the English law of attempts may be found in A. Ashworth, 'Criminal Attempts and the Role of Resulting Harm under the Code, and in the Common Law' (1988) 19 Rutgers LJ, 725.

[6] Per Lord Goddard CJ, in *Whybrow* (1951) 35 Cr App R 141, at 147.

[7] [1976] 1 QB 1, applied to the 1981 Act in *Pearman* (1985) 80 Cr App R 259.

[8] *Walker and Hayles* (1990) 90 Cr App R 226, upholding a direction in terms of 'foresight of high probability' That part of the decision must surely be regarded as aberrant: see now *Fallon* [1994] Crim LR 519.

A wider question of principle is whether attempts liability should be taken further. Those wedded to a linguistic approach insist that the word 'attempt' connotes trying, trying connotes purposeful behaviour, and therefore there can be no such thing as a reckless or negligent attempt. The opposite view focusses on the element of luck in whether behaviour results in the commission of a substantive offence or not. How might these views be applied to cases where D intends to do the prohibited act but is only reckless as to the circumstances? This problem might arise on a charge of attempting to obtain property by deception, where D tries to induce V to part with property on the strength of a representation which D thinks may be false (but does not know to be false).[9] The problem is usually debated in the context of attempted rape, where D tries to have sexual intercourse with the victim, not knowing and not caring whether there is consent. The Criminal Attempts Act does not give an unambiguous answer: it uses the phrase 'with intent to commit' the substantive offence, which is silent on the question of whether intent combined with reckless knowledge will suffice. One interpretation, based on the Law Commission report,[10] is that the phrase 'with intent to commit' implies that D knows or believes that the victim is not consenting. Reckless knowledge is not enough, and so there could be no conviction of attempted rape on the above facts. The counter-argument is that the Act makes no reference to the degree of knowledge needed for conviction: it refers only to the requirement on intent as to conduct or consequence, and that is present in the example given. Moreover, the offence of rape itself is satisfied by recklessness as to the victim's consent. If two men set out to have sexual intercourse with two women, not caring whether they consent or not, it would be absurd if the one who achieved penetration was convicted of rape, while the other, who failed to achieve penetration despite trying, was not even liable for attempted rape. It may be true that the latter commits indecent assault, for which the maximum is 10 years' imprisonment, but attempted rape would be a more appropriate label for something so close to the full offence. These strong arguments led the Law Commission to change its mind,[11] and the Court of Appeal in *Khan et al.* (1990)[12] has also accepted that a person can be convicted of attempted rape when only reckless as to

---

[9] This offence was discussed in Ch 9.8 above.

[10] Law Com No. 102 (1980), para 2.15. For subsequent debate, see Glanville Williams, 'The Problem of Reckless Attempts' [1983] Crim LR 365; R. J. Buxton, 'Circumstances, Consequences and Attempted Rape' [1984] Crim LR 25; R. A. Duff, 'The Circumstances of an Attempt' (1991) 50 Camb LJ, 100; G. Williams, 'Intents in the Alternative' (1991) 50 Camb LJ, 120; and J. Horder, 'Varieties of Intention, Criminal Attempts and Endangerment' (1994) 14 Legal Studies, 335.   [11] Law Com No. 177, 244.

[12] (1990) 91 Cr App R 29, referring to the articles in n. 10 above; see also S. White, 'Three Points on *Pigg*' [1989] Crim LR 539.

whether the victim is consenting. The proper approach, therefore, is that the fault element in an attempt may be satisfied by intention as to the consequences combined with recklessness as to the circumstances.[13]

Unfortunately, this distinction was ignored recently by the Court of Appeal:[14] in holding that a person can be convicted of attempted aggravated arson if he intends to commit damage while reckless as to whether the life of another would thereby be endangered, the Court extended the notion of an attempt to cover recklessness as to consequences, and did so in respect of one of the few offences satisfied by *Caldwell* (inadvertent) recklessness.[15] The ease with which this pro-prosecution decision was reached suggests that the courts might not stop short of creating a general law of reckless attempts.[16] No doubt this would be the simplest approach, but it might extend the reach of the criminal law considerably. It ought only to be contemplated after the kind of thorough inquiry that even the best-advised court cannot conduct.[17] Until now, English law has resolved the question pragmatically, by creating a few specific offences of endangerment to deal with reckless behaviour on the roads and in other situations where there is a risk but no actual occurrence, of serious consequences (see Chapter 7.6 and 7.7). Since we are concerned here with preliminary offences which go beyond the definitions of substantive crimes, is it not more judicious to proceed in this piecemeal way, thereby ensuring that the outer boundaries of the criminal are carefully regulated?

(b) The Conduct Element

Since the effect of the law of attempts is to extend the criminal sanction further back than the definition of substantive offences, the question of the minimum conduct necessary to constitute an attempt has great importance. The issue concerns incomplete attempts: when has a person gone far enough to justify criminal liability? Two schools of thought may be outlined here. First, there is the fault-centred approach, arguing that the essence of an attempt is trying to commit a crime, and that all the law should require is proof of the intention plus any act designed to implement that intention. The reasoning is that any person who has gone so far as to translate a criminal intention into action has crossed the threshold of criminal liability, and deserves punishment (though, for the reasons given above—the possibility of abandonment, for example—the punishment

---

[13] See particularly Duff, 'The Circumstances of an Attempt'.

[14] *Attorney-General's Reference (No. 3 of 1992)* (1994) 98 Cr App R 383.

[15] On which see Ch 5.3(c) above.

[16] Note Schiemann J's rather airy reference (ibid., at 392) to 'various articles in legal journals and books'.

[17] See also Ashworth, 'Criminal Attempts and the Role of Resulting Harm', 755–7, and Horder, 'Varieties of Intention'.

would be less than for a complete attempt). On the other hand there are two types of act-centred approach. One type bases itself on the argument that one cannot be sure that the deterrent effect of the criminal law has failed until D has done all the acts necessary, since one could regard the law as successful if D did stop before the last act out of fear of detection and punishment. The other type of act-centred approach is adopted by those who see great dangers of oppressive official action—to the detriment of individual liberties—if the ambit of the law of attempts is not restricted tightly. If *any* overt act were to suffice as the conduct element in attempts, wrongful arrests might be more numerous; convictions would turn largely on evidence of D's intention, so the police might be tempted to exert pressure in order to obtain a confession; and miscarriages of justice might increase, especially when inferences from silence are permissible (see (c) below). To safeguard the liberty of citizens and to assure people that justice is being fairly administered, the law should require proof of an unambiguous act close to the commission of the crime before conviction of an attempt. Otherwise, we would be risking a world of thought crimes and thought police.

The choices for the conduct element in attempts might therefore be ranged along a continuum. The least requirement would be 'any overt act', but that would be objectionable as risking oppressive police practices and as leaving little opportunity for an attempter to withdraw voluntarily. The most demanding requirement would be the 'last act' or 'final stage', but that goes too far in the other direction, leaving little time for the police to intervene to prevent the occurrence of harm and allowing the defence to gain an acquittal by raising a doubt as to whether D had actually done the very last act. In the United States the Model Penal Code requires D to have taken a 'substantial step' towards the commission of the full offence.[18] This might appear to breach the principle of maximum certainty,[19] but the Model Penal Code seeks to avoid this by listing a number of authoritative examples of a 'substantial step'. Thus, the approach recognizes the inevitable flexibility in questions of degree such as this but seeks to give some firm guidance. The Criminal Attempts Act 1981 requires D to have done 'an act which is more than merely preparatory to the commission of the offence'. Opinions differ on whether this is closer to the fault-centred approach than the 'substantial step' test, but it is certainly more vague (since there are no authoritative examples), and the Act leaves the application of the test entirely to the jury, once the judge has found that there is sufficient evidence of an attempt.[20] English judges have used various tests to explain the Act's requirements to juries. Some

[18] Model Penal Code, 2.5.01, discussed by Ashworth, 'Criminal Attempts and the Role of Resulting Harm', 751–3.   [19] Discussed above, Ch 3.4(i).
[20] Criminal Attempts Act 1981, ss 1(1) and 4(3).

courts adopted the so-called Rubicon test, which holds that a person is not guilty of an attempt until he has 'crossed the Rubicon and burnt his boats'.[21] This may be no less demanding than the 'last act' test, since it requires D to have reached a stage from which there is no turning back. It has now, rightly, been rejected as an explanation of the current law.

The proper test is whether D was *still* engaged in merely preparatory acts, in which case he is not guilty of attempt, or whether his conduct was *more* than merely preparatory. This is inevitably a question of degree, but the Court of Appeal has given some indication of how to classify different cases. Thus, in *Gullefer* (1987)[22] a man who placed a bet on a race jumped on to the greyhound track in an endeavour to have the race declared void so that he could recover his stake-money. He was held not have gone past the stage of mere preparation for the crime of theft, and so he had not committed an attempted theft. If his plan was to succeed, it remained for the race stewards to declare the race void and for him to demand his money back. Jumping on to the track was 'mere preparation'. In *Jones* (1990)[23] D bought a gun, shortened its barrel, put on disguise, and then jumped into the back seat of his rival's car. D pointed the loaded gun at his rival and said 'You are not going to like this', but his rival then grabbed the gun. The defence argument was that this could not amount to attempted murder: what D had done was not more than merely preparatory, because he still had to release the safety catch, put his finger on the trigger and pull it. The Court of Appeal dismissed this argument, which was more appropriate to the 'last act' or 'Rubicon' test, and held that once D had climbed into the car and pointed the gun there was ample evidence for a jury to hold that attempted murder had been committed. A more difficult case is *Campbell* (1991)[24] where the police had received information about a planned post office robbery. They watched D in the street outside the post office. They arrested him, and found him to be carrying sunglasses, an imitation firearm, and a threatening note. The Court of Appeal quashed D's conviction for attempted robbery, holding that it is extremely unlikely that a person could be convicted of attempt when he 'has not even gained the place where he could be in a position to carry out the offence'.[25] He had not entered the post office, and was no longer wearing the sunglasses.[26]

[21] *DPP* v *Stonehouse* [1978] AC 55.
[22] [1987] Crim LR 195, affirmed in *Jones* (1990) 91 Cr App R 351.
[23] (1990) 91 Cr App R 351.
[24] (1991) 93 Cr App R 350 cf. *Griffin* [1993] *Crim LR* 515.
[25] D's conduct went beyond 'reconnoitring the place intended for the commission of the offence', which is sufficient for an attempt under the Model Penal Code but was intended to lie outside the English test: Law Com No. 102, para 2.33.
[26] These decisions were considered in *Attorney-General's Reference (No. 1 of 1992)* (1993) 96 Cr App R 298, where the Court of Appeal held that a conviction for attempted rape could be proper even if the man had not yet attempted penetration.

It is difficult to say whether the 'more than merely preparatory' test gives sufficient protection to individual liberties while advancing the social interest in preventing harm. If there is a theme running through the appellate decisions, this is the steering of a 'mid-way course' between the 'last act' test and the penalization of merely preparatory acts.[27] However, the time has now come for a renewed effort to formulate some consolidated guidelines for trial judges on the application of the test, so that English law can follow the example of the Model Penal Code in moving closer to the principle of maximum certainty. So long as it is made clear that the guidelines are non-exhaustive, they ought to provide more help than hindrance.

(c) The Problem of Impossibility

Just as the conduct element in attempts relates chiefly to incomplete attempts, so the problem of impossibility usually arises in connection with complete attempts. Once again, there are fault-centred and act-centred perspectives to be considered, according to whether one takes the view that D's beliefs or the reality of D's conduct should be the primary determinant of liability. The fault-centred approach to impossible attempts is a straightforward application of the subjective principle (see Chapter 5.2(a)): a person should be judged on the facts or circumstances as he or she believed them to be at the time. We have seen how the belief principle operates as a ground of exculpation where D is labouring under a mistake of fact (see Chapter 5.3(c)). Here it operates as a ground of inculpation. In other words, where D *believes* that he is committing an offence, it is justifiable to convict of an attempt to commit that offence. D's state of mind is just as blameworthy as it would be if the facts *were* as they are believed to be. Thus, we are justified in convicting the person who smuggles dried lettuce leaves in the belief that they are cannabis, and the person who puts sugar in someone's drink in the belief that it is cyanide, and the person who handles goods in the belief that they are stolen. In all these cases there is no relevant moral difference between their culpability and the culpability of others where the substances *really* are cannabis, cyanide, and stolen goods.

The act-centred approach points to the absence of actual danger in these cases, and argues that there is a risk of oppression if the law criminalizes people in objectively innocent situations.[28] Part of the concern here is that convictions might be based on confessions which are the result of fear,

---

[27] The words of Lord Lane in *Gullefer*, considered by K. J. M. Smith, 'Proximity in Attempt: Lord Lane's Midway Course' [1991] Crim LR 576.

[28] Three expressions of the act-centred view are J. F. Stephen, *History of the Criminal Law* (1883), ii 225; J. Temkin, 'Impossible Attempts: Another View' (1976) 39 MLR, 55; and Lords Bridge and Roskill in *Anderton* v *Ryan* [1985] AC 560.

confusion, or even police fabrication.[29] Without the need to establish any objectively incriminating facts, the police might construct a case simply on the basis of remarks attributed to the accused person. Anyone carrying a bag might be liable to be arrested and to have attributed to him or her the remark: 'I thought it contained drugs'. These arguments, based on the threat to individual rights, are too important to be dismissed peremptorily, particularly now that the Criminal Justice and Public Order Act 1994 has enacted that adverse inferences may be drawn from a suspect's silence in the face of key questions, without also providing that statements attributed by the police to the suspects, which are unrecorded and which the suspects denies, should be inadmissible in evidence.[30] There has been no shortage of research findings to the effect that new controls on the police tend to be manipulated in practice so that the intended goals may not be achieved.[31] It may therefore be unsafe to expect the laws of criminal procedure to prevent any dangers to individual rights. This leaves untouched the fault-centred argument that there really is no difference in terms of moral culpability or dangerousness between persons who actually do make an impossible attempt and many ordinary attempters. The act-centred approach focusses on the absence of danger in the actual situation, while the fault-centred approach emphasizes the 'desert' or potential dangerousness of the person involved. But if a fault-centred law leads to police malpractice which cannot otherwise be prevented, it ought to be narrowed.

There would be little difference between the two approaches over the case of D, who fired a shot at V and missed because his aim was not good enough. That is a classic criminal attempt. But what is the difference between that and a case in which E puts sugar in X's drink in the belief that it is cyanide? On the act-centred approach there is no social danger in the latter case, because sugar is innocuous; yet it is equally true that there is no danger in the first case, because shooting and missing is innocuous. Some might say that D might try again and the shot might not miss; yet it is equally impossible that E might try again and might choose an ingredient which actually is poisonous. It seems, then, that the act-centred approach incorporates one limb of the subjective principle—that people should be judged on the consequences they intend to happen—but not the other (belief) limb—that people should be judged on the facts as they believe

[29] This is one of the concerns expressed in the lengthy discussion of attempts by G. Fletcher, *Rethinking Criminal Law* (1978), 137 ff.

[30] For discussion of the significance of the new law, see I Dennis, 'The Criminal Justice and Public Order Act 1994: the Evidence Provisions' [1995] Crim LR 4.

[31] See e.g. I. McKenzie, R. Morgan, and R. Reiner, 'Helping the Police with their Inquiries' [1990] Crim LR 22; D. Brown, T. Ellis and K. Larcombe, *Changing the Code: police detention under the revised PACE codes of practice* (Home Office, 1993).

them to be. There is no principled explanation for accepting one and not the other, apart from the argument about police powers and individual liberty, which ought (if possible) to be tackled directly, and not through a distortion of the law of attempts.

The recent history of English law contains evidence of both approaches. The House of Lords in *Haughton* v *Smith*[32] adopted an act-centred stance, but the Law Commission accepted the arguments above and recommended a fault-centred approach, in which impossibility would be no defence to liability. Debate continued during the passage of the new law, and one result of further changes of mind by the government was two strangely worded provisions in section 1(2) and (3) of the Criminal Attempts Act 1981. The Act purported to follow the Law Commission and to criminalize impossible attempts, but the House of Lords interpreted the provisions so as not to achieve this result, and it was only in *Shivpuri* (1986)[33] that it was settled that, in the English law of attempts, D is judged on the facts as he or she believed them to be. Thus, if a person buys a video recorder believing that it is stolen when it is not, that constitutes an attempt to handle stolen goods.

The fault-centred approach here has been limited to beliefs about facts. If D is mistaken about the law, believing that certain conduct is an offence when it is not, there is no liability for an attempt. Thus, where D believed that he was smuggling currency into the country but there is no offence of importing currency, there could be no conviction.[34] This is easily explained: there is no crime to be attempted, only an imaginary crime. But it can also be seen as a corollary of the maxim that ignorance of the law is no excuse:[35] a mistake about the criminal law neither exculpates nor inculpates. By contrast, a mistake as to the facts may exculpate (subject to other policies relevant to mistakes)[36] or inculpate (as an impossible attempt), since the general principle is that D is judged on the facts as he or she believed them to be.[37]

11.4 THE JUSTIFICATIONS FOR AN OFFENCE OF CONSPIRACY

The essence of conspiracy is an agreement between two or more persons to commit a criminal offence. Thus defined, conspiracy takes its place as one of the three inchoate offences at common law, penalizing the conspirators before any substantive offence has been committed. The justification for

---

[32] [1975] AC 476.

[33] [1987] AC 1, overruling the House's own decision of the previous year in *Anderton* v *Ryan* [1985] AC 560. A considerable influence in bringing about this judicial volte-face was the article by Glanville Williams, 'The Lords and Impossible Attempts' [1986] Camb LJ 33.

[34] *Taaffe* [1984] AC 539.   [35] Discussed above, Ch 6.7.

[36] See above, Ch 5.3(d).   [37] See above, Ch 5.2(a).

this is largely preventive, as in the law of attempts, since it enables the police and the courts to intervene before any harm has actually been inflicted. Whereas in attempts the doing of a 'more than merely preparatory' act is required as evidence of the firmness of the intent, in conspiracy it is the fact of agreement with others which is regarded as sufficiently firm evidence that the parties are committed to carrying out the crime. Another part of the justification for an offence of conspiracy is that persons who go so far as to reach an agreement to commit a crime, and are caught before the agreement is carried out, may not be significantly less blameworthy or less dangerous than persons who conspire and succeed in bringing about the substantive offence.

However, this fairly traditional analysis of conspiracy as an inchoate offence neglects the other social functions which conspiracy law has been called upon to perform. In the nineteenth century it was accepted that a conviction for criminal conspiracy could be based on an agreement to do any unlawful act, even though that act was not criminal but only a civil wrong, such as a tort or breach of contract. This gave the criminal law a long reach, particularly with regard to the activities of the early trade unions, and the courts upheld conspiracy convictions for what were, in effect, agreements to strike until the law was changed by the Conspiracy and Protection of Property Act 1875 and the Trade Disputes Act 1906.[38] In social terms, the criminal law lent its authority to those who wished to suppress organized industrial action. In legal terms, the reasoning seemed to be that acts which were insufficiently antisocial to justify criminal liability when done by one person could become sufficiently antisocial to justify criminal liability when done by two or more people acting in agreement. Such a combination of malefactors might increase the probability of harm resulting, might in some cases increase public alarm, and might in other cases facilitate the perpetration and concealment of the wrong.[39] These prosecutions were often brought in cases where the agreement had been carried out and the unlawful acts done, since there was no substantive criminal offence to be prosecuted (in that the conspiracy was to do an unlawful but non-criminal act). Thus the legal definition turned on an 'agreement', but the social reality centred upon the actual commission of the tort or breach of contract, from which a prior agreement was inferred. In these contexts, conspiracy functioned more as an additional substantive offence than as an inchoate crime.

The 1875 and 1906 Acts curtailed, but did not remove, this use of the

---

[38] For a general account of the social history of conspiracy, see R. Spicer, *Conspiracy Law, Class and Society* (1981); see also G. Robertson, *Whose Conspiracy?* (1974).

[39] For further discussion, see R. Johnson, 'The Unnecessary Crime of Conspiracy' (1973) 61 Cal LR, 1137, and I. Dennis, 'The Rationale of Criminal Conspiracy' (1977) 93 LQR, 39.

offence of conspiracy against conduct thought to be antisocial, and the idea of conspiracy as an extra substantive offence experienced a revival in the 1960s and early 1970s. The signal for this was probably the House of Lords decision in *Shaw* v *DPP*,[40] the case which created the offence of conspiracy to corrupt public morals. The high-water mark was the decision in *Kamara* v *DPP*,[41] where students who occupied the High Commission of Sierra Leone in London were convicted of conspiracy to trespass, even though trespass is itself a tort and not a crime. However, a judicial retrenchment was evident in *DPP* v *Withers*,[42] where the House of Lords quashed convictions of conspiracy to effect a public mischief and declared that no such general offence was known to the law. The gist of the decision was that criminal conspiracy should be extended no further than had already been established.

The decision in *Withers* may be seen as a belated gesture towards the principles of non-retroactivity and maximum certainty, after a whole host of earlier decisions had ignored the principles in favour of a broad policy of social defence.[43] In a way, it presaged the Law Commission's report on conspiracy in 1976, which recommended that the offence of conspiracy should be coextensive with the substantive law.[44] Conspiracies should only be criminal if the conduct agreed upon constitutes a crime when done by one person. The principles of non-retroactivity and maximum certainty were accepted, even to the point of asserting that if some new form of wickedness were to arise which did not fall within existing offences, the proper approach would be to await a response from the legislature rather than for the judges to exploit the elasticity of the law of conspiracy.[45] Parliament adopted the substance of the Law Commission's report, and enacted the Criminal Law Act 1977. Part I of the Act creates the new offence of statutory conspiracy, limited to agreements to commit one or more criminal offences; Part II provides a handful of new offences of trespass on residential premises.[46] An agreement to commit one of these distinct trespass offences would be a statutory conspiracy, and the common law offence of conspiracy to trespass, upheld in *Kamara*,[47] was abolished.

The 1977 Act did not, however, accomplish a clean sweep of common law conspiracy. The Law Commission had been unable to complete its examination of conspiracy to defraud and any new offences which might be

---

[40] [1962] AC 220, see Ch 3.4(g).   [41] [1973] 2 All ER 1242.
[42] [1975] AC 842.
[43] Cf. *DPP* v *Bhagwan* [1972] AC 60, where the House of Lords held that there is no general crime of conspiracy to defeat the purpose of an Act of Parliament.
[44] *Conspiracy and Criminal Law Reform*, Law Com No. 76 (1976).
[45] Ibid., paras. 1.8–1.9.
[46] The Criminal Justice and Public Order Act 1994 has now added the offences of aggravated trespass (s 68), trespassory assembly (s 70) and unauthorized camping (s 77).
[47] [1973] 2 All ER 1242.

needed to replace it (see Chapter 9.8); and another committee was engaged in a review of the laws on obscenity, which led the government to exclude from the 1977 Act conspiracies to corrupt public morals and to outrage public decency.[48] Thus the controversial decision in *Shaw*[49] remains authoritative on conspiracy to corrupt public morals, as does the decision in *Knuller*[50] on conspiracy to outrage public decency, and also *Scott v Metropolitan Police Commissioner*[51] on conspiracy to defraud, whose precepts owe more to the 'thin ice' principle (Chapter 3.4(h)) and the policy of social defence (Chapter 3.4(j)) than to any notion of maximum certainty in criminal law (Chapter 3.4(i)).

Leaving aside the common law conspiracies to defraud, to corrupt public morals, and to outrage public decency, is it true to say that statutory conspiracy functions primarily as an inchoate offence? Few conspiracies can be prosecuted at the stage of agreement, because meetings of conspirators usually take place in private and it is rare for sufficient evidence to become available until some acts in furtherance of the agreement have been done and observed. So the rationale of early prevention, even before an attempt has been committed, is often far from the social facts. However, another function of inchoate offences is to criminalize those who try and fail, as well as those who are caught before they have the chance to succeed or fail. Conspiracy does fulfil this function, being used against those who join together to commit a crime in circumstances where it is impossible to do so.[52] Yet there remains a way in which even statutory conspiracy also functions as an extra criminal offence. The rules of evidence in conspiracy cases are somewhat wider than in other trials: for example, the statements of one co-conspirator are admissible in evidence against another if they relate to an act done in furtherance of the conspiracy, by way of exception to the general rule that the admissions of one co-defendant cannot be adduced in evidence against the other.[53] Moreover, all that has to be proved for conspiracy is the agreement, and that may be inferred from behaviour. Prosecutors who wish to take advantage of these rules may prefer to charge conspiracy instead of the substantive crime even in a case where the substantive offence has been committed: it is bad practice for them to charge both conspiracy and the substantive crime,[54] but it is no answer to a conspiracy charge alone that

---

[48] The Williams Committee, which subsequently reported on *Obscenity and Film Censorship* (1979, Cmnd 7772), but whose recommendations were not adopted in legislation.
[49] [1962] AC 220.   [50] [1973] AC 435.   [51] [1975] AC 819.
[52] The 1977 Act contained no provision on impossibility, but s 5 of the Criminal Attempts Act 1981 makes it clear that impossibility is no more a defence to conspiracy than it is to attempt.
[53] For a recent discussion, see *Liggins et al.* [1995] Crim LR 45 and commentary.
[54] See the case of the Shrewsbury pickets, *Jones et al.* (1974) 59 Cr App R 120, and the Practice Direction [1977] 2 All ER 540.

the substantive offence was in fact committed. In the terminology of English criminal procedure, a conspiracy does not 'merge' with the substantive offence. Thus the prosecution may bring a conspiracy charge in order to give a more rounded impression of the nature of the criminal enterprise, in terms of planning and the different roles of the various participants.[55]

Despite this use of the crime of conspiracy as an extra substantive offence, its primary justifications remain those of an inchoate offence. An individual who declares an intent to steal certain property has committed no offence; two or more individuals who agree to do the same thing may be convicted of conspiracy to steal. How strong are the justifications?[56] Many of them stem from the fact that more than one person is involved. Thus one argument is that it may be more difficult to reverse a conspiracy than for an individual to change his or her mind: conspiracies are therefore more likely to result in harm-doing. Against this one could put the comparison of one resolute individual compared with two weak and dithering conspirators. Another argument is that the involvement of several people in an offence creates greater fear in victims and greater public alarm. Against this one could put the comparison of one terrifying individual compared with two incompetent and hesitant bunglers. However, these succeed only in showing that it is problematic to use a numerical division (between one and two persons) to distinguish between serious and less serious criminal activities. They cast little doubt on the qualitative difference between most criminal gangs and the activities of most lone offenders. In many cases group crimes are more terrifying, and sentencers may well be justified in treating this as an aggravating factor.[57] In many cases group behaviour may acquire a momentum of its own, with individuals being afraid to withdraw and participants spurring each other on.[58] Whether considerations such as these justify the creation of special public order offences aimed at group behaviour, with separate rules of proof favouring prosecutors, was questioned earlier.[59]

Even if it is conceded that group offences are often qualitatively more serious than offences by individuals, does it follow that the law needs the offence of conspiracy? What if the doctrine of merger was extended, so that conspiracy ceased to be chargeable if the substantive offence had been committed? No special characteristic of group criminality would be lost,

---

[55] This 'rounded impression' argument is emphasized by the Law Commission in Consultation Paper 135, *Conspiracy to Defraud* (1994), discussed in Ch 9.9 above.

[56] See Johnson, 'The Unnecessary Crime of Conspiracy', and Dennis, 'The Rationale of Criminal Conspiracy'.

[57] See Ashworth, *Sentencing and Criminal Justice* (2nd edn, 1995), Ch 5.3(a).

[58] See the discussion of duress and fault in Ch 6.4(c) above.

[59] See above, Ch 8.3(g).

because there remains the doctrine of complicity. The law of principals and accomplices may lack the evidentiary advantages to the prosecution which conspiracy has, but it does favour the prosecution procedurally by not requiring it to charge defendants separately as accomplices or principals.[60] And there is the same discretion at the sentencing stage to reflect the element of aggravation in planned group offending. A similar question about the dispensability of the offence of conspiracy may be asked in relation to its inchoate function. Many conspiracies will already have been carried far enough to fulfil the test for criminal attempt, at least under the broad 'more than merely preparatory' test of English law. Much of the ground might therefore be covered by the law of attempts and by prosecutions for complicity in attempts. This leaves only the few cases where clear evidence is obtained of an agreement to commit a crime, without any action having yet been taken to implement the agreement. This brings the discussion back to the original, narrow, justification for the crime of conspiracy—does an agreement, without more, go far enough to warrant criminalization?

This question raises issues of principle and policy. On the one hand, there is the principle of maximum certainty: the requirement of an agreement is considerably more certain than the requirement of a 'more than merely preparatory act' for attempts. But agreements usually involve words, and issues of privacy, freedom of speech, and freedom of association may arise here,[61] in the sense that the existence of this offence might encourage the police to use intrusive tactics (such as bugging premises). To advocate freedom to commit crimes would be unsupportable, but one must avoid the risk of inhibiting the development of controversial ideas. Furthermore, there is the danger of conviction based on inference and mere association, which leave opportunities for prosecutions to be brought without much hard evidence. The offence of conspiracy may be defended as a vital tool against organized crime, but the difficulty is that it may bear oppressively on some of the individuals who are caught within its ample net.

11.5 THE ELEMENTS OF CRIMINAL CONSPIRACY

(a) An Agreement between Two or More Persons

Agreement is the basic element in conspiracy. The idea of an agreement seems to involve a meeting of minds, and there is no need for a physical meeting of the persons involved so long as they reach a mutual

---

[60] See further, Ch 10.2 above, and *DPP for Northern Ireland* v *Maxwell* [1978] 3 All ER 1140.
[61] Articles 8, 9, and 10 of the European Convention on Human Rights.

understanding of what is to be done.[62] Whether the understanding amounts to an agreement may be a matter of degree: if the parties are still at the stage of negotiation, without having decided what to do, no criminal conspiracy has yet come into being. But what if the parties have reached agreement in principle, leaving matters of details to be resolved afterwards? What if arrangements have been made, but may be unscrambled later? The judicial tendency is to regard these as conspiratorial agreements, and this is consistent with the rule that there is no defence of withdrawal for a person who has become a party to a conspiracy.[63] Moreover, since all human arrangements are vulnerable to changes in circumstances, the possibility that a planned robbery might be cancelled if there are police in the vicinity at the time does not negate the existence of a conspiracy. Further problems over 'conditional' agreements are discussed in 11.5(b).

Certain agreements are excluded from the law of conspiracy. First, by section 2(2)(a) of the Criminal Law Act 1977, agreements between husband and wife only (without a third person) cannot amount to criminal conspiracies. This rule places the value of marital confidence above the public interest in having conspirators brought to justice, a priority which has been partly abandoned in other areas of the law (e.g. by compelling one spouse to give evidence against the other in certain proceedings).[64] If a husband and wife go so far as to commit an attempt or a substantive offence, they can be convicted jointly of that. Secondly, by section 2(2)(b), agreements in which the only other person is under the age of criminal responsibility cannot result in D's conviction for conspiracy—an application of the rule of criminal capacity. Thirdly, by section 2(2)(c) of the Act, agreements in which the only other person is an intended victim cannot result in D's conviction for conspiracy. This parallels the rule that a person who falls within the class protected by the offence (e.g. persons under a given age) cannot be convicted as a party to that crime.[65] Fourthly, section 4(1) provides that a prosecution for conspiracy to commit one or more summary offences requires the consent of the Director of Public Prosecutions. Although this appears to restrict the practical use of conspiracy charges, it should be noted that the crime of attempt does not apply to summary offences at all. Once again, the 'double life' of conspiracy as an inchoate and a quasi-substantive offence is evident. One argument is that the deliberate planning of numerous offences, even if summary only, may justify prosecution as a conspiracy. Presumably, also, the number of persons involved in an agreement to commit summary

---

[62] G Orchard, ' "Agreement" in Criminal Conspiracy' [1974] Crim LR 297.
[63] E.g. *Mulcahy* (1868) LR 3 HL 306; *Thomson* (1965) 50 Cr App R 1.
[64] Police and Criminal Evidence Act 1984, s 80.
[65] *Tyrell* [1894] 1 QB 710, discussed in Ch 10.7(b) above.

offences might persuade the Crown Prosecution Service that it is in the public interest to prosecute for a single conspiracy rather than bringing various separate small charges.

Agreement is the basic element in criminal conspiracy, but the evidence offered to a court may often be inferences from behaviour rather than direct testimony or recording of a meeting of conspirators. Thus the typical process is to infer a prior agreement from behaviour which appears to be concerted.

(b) The Criminal Conduct Agreed Upon

We move now to the subject-matter of the agreement. The Criminal Law Act 1977, section 1(1), provides, that a conspiracy is criminal if it is agreed that 'a course of conduct will be pursued which, if the agreement is carried out in accordance with their intentions . . . will necessarily amount to or involve the commission of any offence or offences by one or more parties to the agreement'. The essence, therefore, is that two or more persons should agree on the commission of a crime. It is well established that they need not know that the agreed course of conduct does amount to a crime— ignorance of the criminal law does not excuse here.[66] The 'course of conduct' includes not only the acts agreed upon but also the intended consequences: conspiracy to murder requires not only an agreement to shoot at a person but also the intention that the shots should cause death.[67]

In interpreting the section, one's eyes are drawn to the word 'necessarily': can it ever be said that, if an agreement is carried out in accordance with the parties' intentions, it will *necessarily* involve the commission of an offence? This unduly concrete term seems to run counter to the proposition that all agreements are conditional in some way or another, and thus to ignore the possibility of an unexpected failure (the bomb which fails to detonate, the shot which misses, etc.). Does it therefore leave all fallible agreements outside the law of conspiracy? Is it enough for the defence to raise a reasonable doubt that the plan might have miscarried for some reason? Such an argument would put the principles of statutory interpretation to a stern test: should the court apply the plain meaning of 'necessarily' on the principle of strict construction—and acquit—or should it apply the purposive approach and the policy of social defence—and convict? One challenge to the wording was heard in *Jackson* (1985).[68] Four men arranged for one of their number to be shot in the leg; the aim was to provide mitigation in the event of his being convicted at his trial for burglary. He was shot in the leg before the end of the trial. On a charge of

[66] *Churchill* v *Walton* [1967] 2 AC 224.
[67] As for attempted murder, an intention to cause grievous bodily harm is not sufficient: see O'Connor LJ in *Siracusa* (1990) 90 Cr App R 340, at 350.
[68] [1985] Crim LR 442.

conspiracy to pervert the course of justice, it was argued that there was no certainty that he would be convicted and therefore the agreement would not necessarily lead to a perversion of the course of justice. The Court of Appeal rejected the argument, drawing a distinction between the inevitability of the substantive offence being committed (which section 1(1) does not require) and the inevitability that it would be committed if the agreement was carried out in accordance with their intentions. The Court approved the example of two people agreeing to drive from London to Edinburgh within a time that could only be achieved without breaking the speed laws if traffic conditions were particularly favourable:[69] this would not be a conspiracy to exceed the speed limit because it would be possible to do everything agreed upon without breaking the law, whereas that would not have been possible in *Jackson*. The decision must be seen as an affirmation of social defence, since the court did not trouble to consult the Law Commission report as a step towards the purposive approach. It is noticeable that the draft Criminal Code abandons the word 'necessarily', leaving the question to the general rules about conditional intention.[70]

Section 1(1) of the 1977 Act was amended by section 5 of the Criminal Attempts Act 1981 to make it clear that impossibility is no more a defence to conspiracy than to a charge of attempt. It is sufficient to establish that the agreement *would* have involved the commission of an offence but for the existence of facts which rendered it impossible. The justifications for this follow those outlined in 11.3(c).

(c) The Fault Requirements

The basic fault requirements for conspiracy would appear to be twofold: first, that each defendant should have knowledge of any facts or circumstances specified in the substantive offence; and, secondly, that each defendant should intend the conspiracy to be carried out and the substantive offence to be committed, although we will see below that this requirement is in doubt.

Section 1(2) makes it clear that these requirements of full intention and knowledge apply no matter what offence is agreed upon. Thus full knowledge and intent are required, even for conspiracies to commit offences of strict liability, negligence, or recklessness. Why is the fault element for conspiracy kept so narrow? If the substantive offence is satisfied, say, by recklessness as to some elements, why should the crime of conspiracy not likewise be satisfied? The answer seems to be the general principle encountered elsewhere: that inchoate crimes are an extension of the criminal sanction, and the more remote an offence becomes from the actual infliction of harm, the higher the degree of fault necessary to justify

---

[69] *Reed* [1982] Crim LR 819.   [70] Law Com No. 177, cl 48.

criminalization. While an individual may be convicted of selling unsound meat despite ignorance that it is unsound and despite the taking of normal precautions, it is thought wrong to convict suppliers and wholesalers of conspiracy to sell unsound meat if they are unaware of its unsoundness. In fact, the general principle cannot be applied completely to conspiracy, because of its 'double life' as an inchoate and a quasi-substantive offence. Thus, once again the doctrinal position is confused, although on this occasion the confusion works in favour of defendants rather than against them, by requiring full knowledge and intention even where conspiracy is used as a quasi-substantive offence.

Should this principled restriction of the fault requirement in conspiracy apply to offences of intention which may include an element of recklessness? If X and Y agree to go to a woman's room and to have intercourse with her, thinking that she may well consent but not caring whether she will nor not, are they guilty of conspiracy to rape? The wording of section 1(2) of the 1977 Act suggests not. Yet it was argued earlier[71] that there should be a conviction for attempted rape where there is recklessness as to consent, and that argument might apply no less strongly to conspiracy. One might say, pragmatically, that there is no need to extend conspiracy in this way because one can wait until an attempt has been committed and then prosecute for that. But the argument in favour of thus extending conspiracy is surely powerful.

In applying the 1977 Act, the concern of the courts has not been with these arguments but with other questions about the meaning of section 1(1). In *Anderson* (1986),[72] the House of Lords chose to reinterpret the words of the section in order to uphold a conviction. They held, first, that a person may be convicted of conspiracy even without intending the agreement to be carried out; and, secondly, that a person is guilty of conspiracy if, and only if, it is established that he or she intended to play some part in the agreed course of conduct. Both these propositions are open to doubt. It seems extraordinary that a person can be held liable for conspiring to commit an offence when he does not intend it to be committed, particularly since that would mean that none of the conspirators needs to intend the substantive offence to be committed. The Privy Council has now held, in *Yip Chiu-cheung* (1994),[73] that the prosecution must establish that each alleged conspirator intended the agreement to be carried out. This is the better view, although *Anderson* remains a House of Lords decision. The second proposition appears to run

---

[71] See 11.3(a), discussing *Khan* (1990) 91 Cr App R 29 and *Attorney-General's Reference (No. 1 of 1992)* (1994) 98 Cr App R 383.   [72] [1986] AC 27.

[73] [1994] 2 All ER 924. This was not a statutory conspiracy contrary to the 1977 Act, but the common law is surely no different on this point.

counter to one of the rationales of conspiracy, which is to bring those who
plan offences but do not take part in them (the 'godfathers') within the
ambit of the criminal sanction. This was later reinterpreted by the Court of
Appeal in *Siracusa* (1989)[74] so as to mean the opposite of what the House
of Lords said: a passive conspirator, who concurs in the activities of the
person(s) carrying out the crime without becoming involved himself, is
guilty of criminal conspiracy. The precedents are therefore in a mess. In
the longer term, a better approach would be reconsider the distinctions
between conspiracy and complicity, and perhaps to enact a general offence
of facilitating crime,[75] which might be a more appropriate label for minor
participants in conspiracies.

11.6 INCITEMENT

The third of the trio of inchoate offences in English criminal law is
incitement. Its essence is that someone who instigates or encourages
another person to commit an offence should be liable to conviction for
those acts of incitement, both because he is culpable for trying to cause a
crime and because such liability is a step towards crime prevention. The
offence of incitement is committed irrespective of whether the person(s)
incited respond by committing the offence concerned. Indeed, when they
do go on to commit the offence, the inciter becomes an accomplice to that
crime, and is liable to conviction for counselling the offence.[76]
The conduct required for incitement is some form of encouragement or
persuasion to commit an offence, although there is authority which would
regard threats or other forms of pressure as incitement.[77] The terms of the
incitement must be communicated to the person incited or to someone who
may fairly be considered as the object of the incitement: if there is no such
communication, then the offence may be an attempt to incite.[78] Where D
incites P to commit an offence that turns out to be impossible on the facts,
perhaps because of a mistake of fact or circumstances, it appears that the
offence of incitement may not be committed. In making this ruling in
Fitzmaurice (1983),[79] the Court of Appeal took the view that it was keeping
the common law offence of incitement in line with the common law rules
for attempt and conspiracy. However, as we have seen, the offences of
attempt and conspiracy have now been put into statutory form, and
impossibility is no defence to either of them. The result is that incitement is
out of line with the other inchoate offences, so far as impossibility
is concerned. The arguments of principle and policy seem no different for
incitement, and it is therefore desirable that incitement should be put into

[74] (1989) 90 Cr App R 340.
[75] See the discussion above, Ch 10.8.
[76] See above, Ch 10.3(c).
[77] *Race Relations Board* v *Applin* [1973] QB 815.
[78] See Ch 11.8 below.
[79] [1983] QB 1083.

a statutory form compatible with attempt and conspiracy as soon as possible.[80]

The fault element in incitement is that D should intend the substantive offence to be committed, i.e. both the conduct and the fault elements of that offence. This is unlikely to cause a problem in most cases, since someone who either encourages or exerts pressure on another person to commit an offence will usually, by definition, intend that offence to be committed. The courts, however, have made some strange rulings. In *Curr* (1968)[81] D organized a moneylending scheme which involved sending his assistants to collect family allowances owed to other women. The Court of Appeal quashed his conviction because it had not been proved that his assistants knew that they were not entitled so to collect the money. However, all that the offence of incitement should require is that D believed that his assistants knew, not that they actually knew. Again, in *Shaw* (1994)[82] D persuaded a colleague to accept certain bogus invoices and to issue cheques in the normal way. D knew that his colleague would be acting dishonestly in doing this, but the Court of Appeal quashed D's conviction of incitement to obtain money by deception on the ground that D's intention was to demonstrate to the company the laxity of their accounting systems. However, this intention would only be relevant if it had also to be established that D was dishonest, but this is not required for incitement. The offence was surely committed when D incited his colleague to act dishonestly, and D's motive would amount to nothing more than mitigation.[83]

The offence of incitement is not widely used by prosecutors in England. It could serve to close some of the gaps left by the law of complicity and conspiracy, but what is really needed here is a new form of inchoate offence. The problem is that if D helps E to commit a crime by lending equipment or providing information, D is liable as an accomplice if E goes ahead and commits the crime, but he is not straightforwardly liable for any offence if E has a change of mind. As in the cases of impossible attempts, discussed in 11.3(c), D is just as culpable in both situations, and it is a matter of chance whether E commits the principal offence or not. Courts have striven to fill this gap by bending the law of incitement, and by invoking offences of possession, but the preferable approach is to recognize the deficiency in the law and to fill it with an offence of facilitating a crime.[84]

---

[80] In their 1980 report the Law Commission took the view that it was not necessary to state in legislation that impossibility is no defence to incitement (Law Com No. 102, para 4.4), but the decision in *Fitzmaurice* showed otherwise, and the draft Criminal Code includes a general provision on impossibility in attempt, conspiracy, and incitement: Law Com No. 177, cl 50.

[81] [1968] 2 QB 944.   [82] [1994] Crim LR 365.

[83] Cf. the defence to complicity discussed above in Ch 10.7(c).

[84] The proposal was discussed extensively in Ch 10.8 above.

11.7 VOLUNTARY RENUNCIATION OF CRIMINAL PURPOSE

In view of the inchoate nature of attempt, incitement, and many conspiracies, the question arises of the legal effect of a change of mind before the substantive offence is committed. What if D abandons the attempt, or withdraws from the conspiracy, or countermands the incitement? English law has generally taken the view that this cannot alter the legal significance of what has already occurred: there is no defence of voluntary renunciation of criminal purpose, and it is a matter for mitigation of sentence only.[85] On the other hand, many other European systems allow such a defence,[86] and the American Model Penal Code also makes provision for it.[87] What are the main arguments on either side?

The main argument against allowing such a defence is that it contradicts the temporal logic of the law. The definition of attempt, conspiracy, or incitement is fulfilled once D, with the appropriate culpability, does the 'more than merely preparatory' act, or reaches the agreement, or utters the words of incitement. Anything that happens subsequently cannot undo the offence: it has already been committed. The situation is no different from that of the thief who decides to return the stolen property: theft has been committed and the offence cannot be undone, even though voluntary repentance may well justify substantial mitigation of sentence. A subsidiary argument is that it would in any event be difficult for a court to satisfy itself of the voluntariness of the renunciation of criminal purpose, and that such occasions might well involve a mixture of motives of D's part. This makes the matter much more suitable for the sentencing stage than the trial itself.

Against this, and in favour of a defence of voluntary renunciation, may be ranged various moral and prudential arguments. The principal argument is that it is the intent or criminal purpose which is the essence of inchoate offences; that the criminal liability is premised on the firmness and continuance of that purpose until the commission of the substantive crime; and that voluntary renunciation shows that the original criminal purpose was not sufficiently firm. This coincides with the view that it often takes more 'nerve' to go through with a crime than merely to plan or encourage it. Thus, where D voluntarily abandons an attempt, withdraws from a conspiracy, or countermands an incitement, this should be sufficient to negative criminal liability. According to this view, D can be said to 'undo' the offence by a change of mind, because the criminal purpose is a continuing one—not a once-and-for-all mental state—and its effect can be neutralized by subsequent decision or action on D's part. The situation is

---

[85] *Lankford* [1959] Crim LR 209, and Law Com No. 102 (1980), para 2.133; cf. M. Wasik, 'Abandoning Criminal Intent' [1980] Crim LR 785.

[86] Fletcher, *Rethinking Criminal Law*, 184–97.   [87] Model Penal Code, s 5.01(4).

different from that of the thief who voluntarily decided to return the property to its owner, for theft is a substantive offence and is not criminalized simply because it is one stage on the way to another crime. A further argument is that if D renounces before the harm is caused, this may show that the threat of the criminal sanction has had a deterrent effect. To punish D none the less would be needless, and the case should be regarded as a success for the law rather than a failure. Both these arguments depart from the principle of contemporaneity (see Chapter 5.2(d)) in favour of a broader timeframe for criminal liability.[88] We have already observed the abandonment of contemporaneity in cases of prior fault (see Chapter 5.2(e)): this deviation would be on the ground of subsequent non-fault.

The argument for allowing a defence of voluntary renunciation becomes stronger as the conduct element in the inchoate offences is taken further back from the occurrence of the harm. In attempts, for example, the fact that there may be ample time for a change of mind between the commission of a 'more than merely preparatory' act and the completion of the substantive offence surely strengthens the case for a defence. There are prudential arguments as well—first, that a defence may act as an incentive to inchoate offenders to give up before they cause harm; secondly, that the renunciation shows that there was no real social danger from this person— but they are not particularly convincing. Whether inchoate offenders ever do contemplate the legal effect of renunciation, and whether they would be influenced by a complete defence rather than by a substantial sentencing discount, is difficult to say.

Those systems which have a defence of voluntary renunciation do not appear to find it problematic.[89] It is rarely raised, and the issue usually turns on the voluntariness of the change of mind, which may then be explored in a trial setting rather than at the sentencing stage. At a theoretical level, there is a strong argument for reduced culpability, but this does not conclude the case for a complete defence. The allocation of excuses as between the liability and the sentencing stages turns on questions of degree (see Chapter 6.9), and one might well take the view that voluntary renunciation is not sufficiently fundamental to warrant a complete defence to criminal liability.

11.8 THE RELATIONSHIP BETWEEN SUBSTANTIVE AND INCHOATE CRIMES

We have seen that the general function of inchoate crimes is to penalize preparation, planning, or encouragement towards the commission of a

[88] See M. Kelman, 'Interpretive Construction in the Substantive Criminal Law' (1981) 33 Stanford LR, 591, at 611–14 and 628–30.
[89] See the discussion by Fletcher, *Rethinking Criminal Law*, 184–97.

substantive offence. It has also been noted that the crime of conspiracy is sometimes invoked where the substantive offence has occurred, and that 'complete' attempts are cases in which D has done everything intended for the commission of a crime: in both those instances, the inchoate offences come very close to substantive crimes. The same phenomenon also appears the other way round: modern legal systems often define what are essentially inchoate offences in the terms of substantive crimes.

A clear example of this is the offence of doing an act with intent to impede the apprehension of an offender.[90] This is not worded as a crime of attempt, but in essence it is a crime of attempt since it requires the doing of an act with the required intent—no result need be proved, no result need have happened. The standard analysis of a substantive crime is 'harm plus culpability', whereas the standard analysis of an attempt is 'culpability without actual harm'. Clearly, the offence of doing an act with intent to impede the apprehension of an offender resembles the latter rather than the former. We can therefore say that the offence is defined in the inchoate mode. There are many other examples of this type of offence—notably burglary,[91] perjury,[92] and perpetrating a bomb hoax.[93] The prosecution's task is made easier in these offences; they do not have to establish that D caused a certain result if they can persuade the court that he did an act with intent to produce that result. Moreover, since these are substantive offences, inchoate liability can be incurred as well, through the three inchoate offences. Thus there can be an attempted burglary or an attempted bomb hoax, which criminalizes D's conduct at an even earlier point than the doing of an act with intent to cause harm. There is little evidence that these extensions of the criminal law are carefully monitored, or that the implications of applying the inchoate offences to crimes defined in the inchoate mode have ever been systematically considered. It is, for example, possible to convict a person of attempting to incite an offence. The reach of criminal liability is pushed further and further, without a specific justification or an overall scheme.

There is an argument for a fourth strand of inchoate liability, to put alongside attempt, incitement, and conspiracy. English law already contains a miscellany of threats offences,[94] but there has never been a general strategy on threats. Thus, for example, it has long been an offence to threaten to kill,[95] and common assault is committed by causing another to

---

[90] Criminal Law Act 1967, s 4.
[91] Theft Act 1968, s 9(1)(a); see above, Ch 9.5.   [92] Perjury Act 1991, s 1.
[93] Criminal Law Act 1977, s 51.
[94] P. Alldridge, 'Threats Offences—a case for Reform' [1994] Crim LR 176.
[95] Put into statutory form in s 16 Offences against the Person Act 1861.

apprehend the use of force,[96] but there is no structure of offences of threatening to wound, or to cause grievous bodily harm, etc. Sections 4 and 5 of the Public Order Act 1986 now criminalize some threats of harm in some circumstances, but the general issue remains. Peter Alldridge points out that the values of consistency and clarity in the law do not favour the creation of a general inchoate offences of threatening to commit a crime, in place of the present array of *ad hoc* accretions, since one might achieve consistency and clarity by abolishing most threats offences and retaining only a few well-known ones.[97] He identifies two key elements in the making of threats. First, uttering a threat is evidence that D has thought about committing the threatened crime and may be willing to do it. It may therefore appear similar in quality to an attempt and an incitement. However, threats are often conditional, whereas a criminal attempt has gone beyond mere preparation, and incitement is a once-for-all act which leaves no further decision for D to make. In some threats cases it may be plausible for D to argue that he never intended to carry out the threat. This takes us to the second element in threats, the creation of fear. This should be the main target of threats offences. It therefore becomes inappropriate simply to regard threats as a fourth form of inchoate liability: what is necessary is to consider the kinds of fear and of circumstances for which criminalization is necessary. There is already the offence of blackmail, which penalizes the making of unwarranted demands with menaces,[98] and this should be the starting point.

Returning to the existing law, another prominent example of offences defined in the inchoate mode is possession—possessing offensive weapons, possessing drugs, possessing instruments for use in forgery, and possessing articles for burglary or deception. A major difference here is that most of these articles are non-innocent, in the sense that their possession calls for an explanation at least. That certainly cannot be said of offences defined so as to penalize 'any act done with intent', although it can perhaps be said of an offence of burglary, which penalizes the entering of a building as a trespasser with intent to steal. Much depends on the way in which a legal system uses and defines its offences of possession, but there is at least one major objection to them, namely, that they presume a criminal intent from the very fact of possession. We have seen that the concept of possession itself is artificially wide;[99] some possession offences leave no opportunity for D to argue that the possession was for a non-criminal reason;[100] others,

---

[96] See above, Ch 8.3(e). [97] Ibid., 180. [98] Above, Ch 9.5.
[99] Above, Ch 4.3(b).
[100] Cf. s 5(4)(b) of the Misuse of Drugs Act 1971, providing a defence for those who take possession of drugs for the purpose of handing them to the police or other authorities.

like the offensive weapons law, impose on the defendant the burden of proving 'lawful excuse' or 'reasonable excuse' for the possession.[101] Now it is true, and worth bringing into the calculation, that possession offences often have the merit of certainty; there is nothing vague about the warning they spell out to citizens.[102] Yet it must be questioned whether this is enough to outweigh the remoteness from harm and the absence of a need for the prosecution to prove criminal intent which characterize most crimes of possession. One might have thought that, as with the fault element for attempt and conspiracy, the more remote offences should be confined to cases of proven intention that the substantive crime be committed. Many offences of possession have no such requirement at all.

11.9 THE PLACE OF INCHOATE LIABILITY

There appear to be sound reasons for including inchoate offences within the criminal law, both on the consequentialist ground of the prevention of harm and on the 'desert' ground that the defendant has not merely formed a culpable and harm-directed mental attitude but has also manifested it. Indeed, our argument has gone further in suggesting that some inchoate offences are no different, in terms of culpability, from substantive offences. This is true of so-called complete attempts, where D has done everything intended but some unexpected—or at least, undesired—circumstance has prevented the occurrence of the harm, and the same may apply to some impossible conspiracies. The subjective principles (see Chapter 5.2(a)) are fulfilled no less in these cases than in substantive crimes. Various challenges to this approach have been noted, and there are prominent desert theorists who oppose it. Thus Nils Jareborg is sceptical of the prominence given to culpability in this approach, arguing that the criminal law is primarily designed for preventing certain types of harm, that a focus on mental states is inappropriate for the large anonymous communities of modern states, and that the proper role of culpability should therefore be to exculpate and not to inculpate.[103] However, shifting the focus to the occurrence or non-occurrence of harm attributes too much significance to matters of chance. This may be appropriate in a system of compensation, but not in a system of public censure such as the criminal law. There is a respectable conception of fairness, connected to principles of individual autonomy, that favours penalizing people who tried and failed—even if, because of some fact unknown to them, their attempt was

---

[101] Prevention of Crime Act 1953, s 1; see above, Ch 8.3(j).
[102] On the principle of maximum certainty, see above, Ch 3.4(i).
[103] N. Jareborg, 'Criminal Attempts and Moral Luck' (1993) 27 Israel LR, 213.

bound to fail. The moral difference between those who fail and those who succeed in causing the harm is too slender to justify exempting the former from criminal liability. It was recognized in 11.3(c) above that conditions in a particular jurisdiction may be such that a properly-developed law of inchoate offences places too much power in the hands of the police and puts innocent citizens at risk, but the law should only be modified if procedural and other means of rectifying this problem seem unpromising.

This does not mean that harm is an unimportant component of criminal liability. On the contrary, decisions on which harms should attract criminal liability remain a major step in determining the ambit of the law (see Chapter 2). What it does mean is that criminal liability need not be dependent on the occurrence of the harm if it can be related to its intended occurrence. As we have seen in this chapter, this relationship is a difficult one at times. The conduct element in attempts has been drawn so vaguely in English law that it sacrifices values of legality (see Chapter 11.3(a) and Chapter 3.4(i)), and there are also uncertainties over the conduct element in conspiracy (11.5(b)) and in incitement (11.6) which ought to be eliminated.

In principle the reach of the inchoate offences should increase with the seriousness of the harm—meaning, for example, that the law should stretch further against crimes of violence than against mere property offences. Surveys of English law suggest that there is no such scheme,[104] and that inchoate offences (and, more particularly, substantive offences in the inchoate mode) have simply proliferated on an *ad hoc* basis. There is, however, some evidence of a general proposition that the inchoate offences should be subjected to more restrictive principles than other crimes: thus intention and knowledge alone are generally required for the inchoate offences, and recklessness is insufficient,[105] and the crime of attempt does not apply to summary offences (nor does conspiracy, unless the Crown Prosecution Service decides otherwise). The need for an overall consideration of this sphere of criminal liability applies equally to the law of complicity, which overlaps at some points with the inchoate offences. As argued in Chapter 10, there is a case for removing the derivative theory from the English law of complicity and replacing it with liability based on the culpability of the individual concerned. This might be achieved through general offences of facilitating crime and of instigating crime, offences which (if suitably drafted) could encompass much of the behaviour now falling within the inchoate offences and other substantive offences defined

---

[104] See Ashworth, 'Criminal Attempts and the Role of Resulting Harm', 764–6.
[105] Cf. the treatment of recklessness as to circumstances, in 11.3(a) (attempt) and 11.5(c) (conspiracy).

in the inchoate mode. In considering such changes, due account should be taken of such doctrines as the policy of minimum criminalization (see Chapter 3.2(a)), the principle of maximum certainty (see Chapter 3.4(i)), and the various policy arguments drawn together under the banner of social defence (see Chapter 3.2(b) and 3.4(j)).

Bibliography

Alldridge, P., 'The Coherence of Defences' [1983] Crim LR 665.
—— 'Developing the Defence of Duress' [1986] Crim LR 433.
—— 'The Doctrine of Innocent Agency' (1990) 2 *Criminal Law Forum* 45.
—— 'Rules for Courts and Rules for Citizens' (1990) 10 OJLS 487.
—— 'What's wrong with the traditional Criminal Law course?' (1990) 10 Legal Studies 38.
—— 'Threats Offences—a Case for Reform' [1994] Crim LR 176.
Allen, M. J., 'Consent and Assault' (1994) J Crim Law 183.
American Law Institute, *Model Penal Code*, Revised Edn. (with commentaries), Philadelphia American Law Institute, 1980.
Andanaes, J., '*Error Juris* in Scandinavian Law', in G. Mueller (ed), *Essays in Criminal Science* (1961), London: Sweet & Maxwell.
Andrews, J. A., 'Wilfulness: a Lesson in Ambiguity' (1981) 1 Legal Studies 303.
Anyangwe, C., 'Dealing with the Problem of Bad Cheques in France' [1978] Crim LR 31.
Aristotle, *Nicomachean Ethics* Bk V (tr. D. Ross, 1925), London: Oxford University Press.
Ashworth, A., *The Criminal Process: an Evaluative Study* (1994), Oxford: Oxford University Press.
—— *Sentencing and Criminal Justice* (2nd edn, 1995), London: Butterworths.
—— 'Criminal Attempts and the Role of Resulting Harm under the Code, and in the Common Law' (1988) 19 Rutgers LJ 725.
—— 'Criminal Justice and Deserved Sentences' [1989] Crim LR 340.
—— 'Criminal Liability in a Medical Context: the Treatment of Good Intentions' in A. Simester and A. T. H. Smith (eds), *Harm and Culpability* (forthcoming, 1995), Oxford: Oxford University Press.
—— 'Defining Criminal Offences without Harm', in P. F. Smith (ed), *Criminal Law: Essays in Honour of J. C. Smith* (1987), London: Butterworths.
—— 'The Doctrine of Provocation' [1976] CLJ 292.
—— 'The Elasticity of Mens Rea', in C. Tapper (ed), *Crime, Proof and Punishment* (1981), London: Butterworths.
—— 'Excusable Mistake of Law' [1974] Crim LR 652.
—— 'Interpreting Criminal Statutes: a Crisis of Legality?' (1991) 107 LQR 419.
—— 'Intoxication and the General Defences' [1980] Crim LR 556.
—— 'Justifying the Grounds of Mitigation' (1994) *Criminal Justice Ethics* 3.
—— 'Liability for Carrying Offensive Weapons' [1976] Crim LR 725.
—— 'Prosecution, Police and the Public: A Guide to Good Gate Keeping (1984) 23 Howard JCJ 621.
—— 'Reason, Logic and Criminal Liability' (1975) 91 LQR 102.
—— 'The Scope of Criminal Liability for Omissions' (1989) 105 LQR 424.
—— 'Self-Defence and the Right to Life' [1975] CLJ 272.
—— 'Self-Induced Provocation and the Homicide Act' (1973) Crim LR 483.

—— 'Taking the Consequences', in S. Shute, J. Gardner and J. Horder, *Action and Value in Criminal Law* (1993), Oxford: Oxford University Press.

—— 'Towards a Theory of Criminal Legislation' (1989) 1 Criminal Law Forum 41.

—— 'Transferred Malice and Punishment for Unforeseen Consequences', in P. Glazebrook (ed), *Reshaping the Criminal Law* (1978), London: Sweet & Maxwell.

——, and Fionda, J., 'The New Code for Crown Prosecutors: (1) Prosecution, Accountability and the Public Interest' [1994], Crim LR 894.

Ashworth, A., and Gostin, L., 'Mentally Disordered Offenders and the Sentencing Process' [1984] Crim LR 195.

Ashworth, A. and Steiner, E., 'Criminal Omissions and Public Duties: the French Experience' (1990) 10 Legal Studies 153.

Atiyah, P. S., *Vicarious Liability in the Law of Torts* (1967), London: Butterworths.

Austin, J., *Lectures on Jurisprudence* (5th edn, 1885).

Bailey, V., and Blackburn, S., 'The Punishment of Incest Act 1908: A Case Study in Law Creation' [1979] Crim LR 708.

Baker, E., 'Human Rights, M'Naghten and the 1991 Act' [1994] Crim LR 84.

Baldwin, J., *The Role of Legal Representatives at Police Stations*, RCCJ Research Study No. 3 (1992), London: HMSO.

Baldwin, R. 'Why Rules Don't Work' (1990) 53 MLR 321.

Bamforth, N., 'Sado-Masochism and Consent' [1994] Crim LR 661.

Bankowski, Z., and MacCormick, D. N., 'Statutory Interpretation in the United Kingdom', in D. N. MacCormick and R. S. Summers (eds), *Interpreting Statutes: a Comparative Study* (1991), London: Dartmouth.

Bayles, M., 'Character, Purpose and Criminal Responsibility' (1982) 1 *Law and Philosophy* 5.

Bazelon, D., 'The Morality of the Criminal Law' (1976) 49 S Cal LR 385.

Bell, J., *Policy Arguments in Judicial Decisions* (1983), Oxford: Oxford University Press.

Bentham, J., *Introduction to the Principles of Morals and Legislation* (1789).

Beynon, H., 'Causation, Omissions and Complicity' [1987] Crim LR 539.

Birch, D. J., 'The Foresight Saga: the Biggest Mistake of All' [1988] Crim LR 4.

Bittner, E., 'The Police on Skid Row: a Study in Peacekeeping' (1967) 32 Amer Soc Rev 699.

Box, S., *Recession, Crime and Unemployment* (1987), London: Sage.

Braithwaite, J., 'Challenging Just Deserts: Punishing White Collar Criminals' (1982) 73 J Crim Law & Criminology.

—— *Corporate Crime in the Pharmaceutical Industry* (1984), London: Routledge & Kegan Paul.

Braithwaite, J., and Fisse, B., 'The Allocation of Responsibility for Corporate Crime' (1988) 11 Sydney LR 468.

Brett, P., 'Mistake of Law as a Criminal Defence' (1966) 5 Melb U LR 179.

—— 'The Physiology of Provocation' [1970] Crim LR 634.

Brody, S., and Tarling, R., *Taking Offenders out of Circulation*, Home Office Research Study No. 64. (1980), 33.

Bronitt, S., 'Spreading Disease and the Criminal Law' [1994] Crim LR 21.

Brooks, R., 'Marital Consent in Rape' [1989] Crim LR 877.

Brown, D. and Ellis, T., *Policing low-level disorder: Police use of Section 5 of the Public Order Act 1986*, Home Office Research Study No. 135 (1994), London: HMSO.

Brown, D., Ellis, T., and Larcombe, K., *Changing the Code: police detection under the revised PACE codes of practice*, Home Office Research Study No. 129 (1993), London: HMSO.

Brudner, A., 'Agency and Welfare in the Penal Law', in S. Shute, J. Gardner and J. Horder (eds) *Action and Value in Criminal Law* (1993), Oxford: Oxford University Press.

—— 'A Theory of Necessity' (1987) 7 Oxford JLS 338.

Buxton, R. J., 'By Any Unlawful Act' (1966) 82 LQR 174.

—— 'Circumstances, Consequences and Attempted Rape' [1984] Crim LR 25.

—— 'Complicity in the Criminal Code' (1969) 85 LQR 252.

Buzzard, J., 'Intent' [1978] Crim LR 5.

Campbell, K., 'Conditional Intention' (1982) 2 Legal Studies 77.

—— 'Offence and Defence', in I. Dennis (ed), *Criminal Law and Criminal Justice* (1987), London: Sweet & Maxwell.

—— 'The Test of Dishonesty in *R v Ghosh*' [1984] CLJ 349.

Campbell, S., 'Gypsies: Criminalising a Way of Life?' [1995] Crim LR 28.

Card, R., *Public Order: the New Law* (1986), London: Butterworths.

—— 'Authority and Excuse as Defences to Crime' [1969] Crim LR 359.

Carson, D., 'Prosecuting People with Mental Handicaps' [1989] Crim LR 87.

Chambers, G., and Miller, A., *Investigating Sexual Assault* (1983), Edinburgh: HMSO.

Choo, A., *Abuse of Process and Judicial Stays of Criminal Proceedings* (1993), Oxford: Oxford University Press.

Clarke, P. J. and Ellis, J. W., *The Law Relating to Firearms* (1981), London: Butterworths.

Clarke, R. V., 'Situational Crime Prevention: Its Theoretical Basis and Practical Scope' (1983) 4 *Crime and Justice: An Annual Review*, 22.

Clarkson, C., 'Theft and Fair Labelling' (1993) 56 MLR 554.

—— 'Violence and the Law Commission' [1994] Crim LR 324.

Clarkson, C., Cretney, A., Davis, G., and Shepherd, J., 'Assaults: the Relationship between Seriousness, Criminalisation and Punishment' [1994] Crime LR 4.

Coffield, F., and Gofton, L., *Drugs and Young People* (Institute for Public Policy Research, 1994).

Collins, H., *Marxism and Law* (1982), Oxford: Oxford University Press.

Colvin, E., *Principles of Criminal Law* (1986), Toronto: Carswell.

—— 'Exculpatory Defences in Criminal Law' (1990) 10 Oxford JLS 381.

Blackstone, W., *Commentaries on the Laws of England* (1768) iii, 3–4.

Committee on the Penalty for Homicide, Prison Reform Trust (1993).

Council of Europe, *European Convention on Compensation for the Victims of Crimes of Violence* (1984).

Criminal Law Revision Committee.

—— 8th Report, *Theft and Related Offences* (1966, Cmnd 2977).

—— 14th Report, *Offences against the Person* (1980, Cmnd 7844).

—— 15th Report, *Sexual Offences* (1985, Cmnd 9213).
—— 18th Report, *Conspiracy to Defraud* (1986, Cmnd 9873).
Criminal Statistics England and Wales 1992, London: HMSO.
Criminal Statistics England and Wales 1993, London: HMSO.
Croall, H., *White Collar Crime* (1992), Milton Keynes: Open University Press.
Cross, R., 'Centenary Reflections on Prince's Case' (1975) 91 LQR 540.
—— 'The Mental Element in Crime' (1967) 83 LQR 215.
Crown Prosecution Service, *Charging Standards for Criminal Offences* (1994).
—— *Code for Crown Prosecutors* (1994).
Crump D. J., and Crump R. J., 'In Defence of the Felony Murder Doctrine' (1985) Harv JLPP 359.
Cullen, F. T., 'Consensus in Crime Seriousness: Empirical Reality or Methodological Artefact' (1985) 23 *Criminology* 99.
Curley, E. M., 'Excusing Rape' (1976) 5 *Philosophy and Public Affairs*, 325.
Daw, R. K., '(2) A Response' [1994] Crim LR 904.
de Burca, G., and Gardner, S., 'The Codification of the Criminal Law' (1990) 10 Oxford JLS 559
Dell, S., *Murder into Manslaughter* (1984), London: Institute of Psychiatry.
—— 'Wanted: An Insanity Defence that can be used' [1983] Crim LR 341.
Dennis, I., 'The Criminal Attempts Act 1981' [1982] Crim LR 5.
—— 'The Criminal Justice and Public Order Act 1994: the Evidence Provisions' [1995] Crim LR 4.
—— 'The Mental Element for Accessories', in P. F. Smith (ed,) *Criminal Law: Essays in Honour of J. C. Smith* (1987), London: Butterworths.
—— 'Duress, Murder and Criminal Responsibility' (1980) 96 LQR 208.
—— 'The Rationale of Criminal Conspiracy' (1977) 93 LQR 39.
Devlin, P., *The Enforcement of Morals* (1965), Oxford: Oxford University Press.
Dicey, A. V., *Law of the Constitution* (8th edn, 1915).
Dressler, J., 'Justifications and Excuses; A Brief Review of the Concept and the Literature' (1987) 33 Wayne LR 1155.
—— 'Provocation: Partial Justification or Partial Excuse?' (1988) 51 MLR 467.
—— 'Reflections on Excusing Wrongdoers: Moral Theory, New Excuses and the Model Penal Code' (1988) 19 Rutgers LJ 671.
Duff, R. A., *Intention, Agency and Criminal Liability* (1990), Oxford: Blackwell.
—— *Trials and Punishments* (1986) Cambridge: Cambridge University Press.
—— 'Choice and Character' (1993), *Law and Philosophy* 345.
—— 'The Circumstances of an Attempt' (1991) 50 Camb LJ 100.
——'Fitness to Plead and Fair Trials' [1994] Crim LR 419.
Dworkin, R., *A Matter of Principle* (1985), London: Duckworth.
—— *Taking Rights Seriously* (1977), London: Duckworth.
Eaton, M., *Justice for Women?* (1987), Milton Keynes: Open University Press.
Edwards, S. S. M., *Policing Domestic Violence* (1989), London: Sage.
Elliott, D. W., '*Brutus* v *Cozens*: Decline and Fall' [1989] Crim LR 323.
—— 'Criminal Damage' [1988] Crim LR 403.
—— 'Directors' Thefts and Dishonesty' [1991] Crim LR 732.
—— 'Dishonesty in Theft: A Dispensable Concept' [1982] Crim LR 395.
—— 'Necessity, Duress and Self-Defence' [1989] Crim LR 611.

Estrich, S., 'Rape' (1986) 94 Yale LJ 1087.

Evans, R., 'Cautioning: Counting the Cost of Retrenchment' [1994] Crim LR 566.

Farmer, L., ' "The Genius of our Law": Criminal Law and the Scottish Legal Tradition' (1992) 55 MLR 25.

Farrier, M. D., 'The Distinction between Murder and Manslaughter in its Procedural Context' (1976) 39 MLR 414.

Feinberg, J., *Harm to Self* (1986), New York: Oxford University Press.

—— *Harm to Others* (1984), New York: Oxford University Press.

—— *Harmless Wrongdoing* (1988), New York: Oxford University Press.

—— *Offense to Others* (1986), New York: Oxford University Press.

Fennell, P., 'Diversion of Mentally Disordered Offenders from Custody' [1991] Crim LR 333.

Field, S., *Trends in Crime and their Interpretation*, Home Office Research Study, No 119 (1990).

Field, S., and Lynn, M., 'The Capacity for Recklessness' (1992) 12 Legal Studies 74.

——, —— 'Capacity, Recklessness and the House of Lords' [1993] Crim LR 127.

Fingarette, H., 'Addiction and Criminal Responsibility' (1975) 84 Yale LJ 413.

Finnis, J., 'Intention and Side-Effects', in R. G. Frey and C. W. Morris, *Liability and Responsibility* (1991).

Fischer, J., 'Responsibility and Control' (1982) 79 Journal of Philosophy 24.

Fisse, B., and Braithwaite, J., 'The Allocation of Responsibility for Corporate Crime: Individualism, Collectivism and Accountability' (1988) 11 Sydney LR 468.

Fletcher, G., *Rethinking Criminal Law* (1978), Boston: Little Brown.

Foster, Sir M., *Crown Law* (1762).

Fulford, K. W. M., 'Value, Action, Mental Illness, and the Law', in S. Shute, J. Gardner, and J. Horder (eds), *Action and Value in Criminal Law* (1993), Oxford: Oxford University Press.

Galligan, D. J., 'Responsibility for Recklessness' (1978) 31 CLP 55.

Gardiner, S., 'The Law and the Sports Field' [1994] Crim LR 513.

Gardner, J., 'Rationality and the Rule of Law in Offences against the Person' [1994] Camb LJ 502.

—— 'Criminal Law and the Uses of Theory: a Reply to Laing' (1994) 14 Oxford JLS 217.

——, and Jung, H., 'Making Sense of Mens Rea: Antony Duff's Account' (1991) 11 Oxford JLS 559.

Gardner, S., 'Reckless and Inconsiderate Rape' [1991] Crim LR 172.

—— 'Reiterating the Criminal Code' (1992) 55 MLR 839.

Giles, M., 'Judicial Lawmaking in the Criminal Courts; the case of Marital Rape' [1992] Crim LR 407.

—— 'Complicity: The Problems of Joint Enterprise' [1990) Crim LR 383.

Giles, M., and Uglow, S., 'Appropriation and Manifest Criminality in Theft' (1992) 56 J Crim Law 179.

Glaser, D., and Spencer, J. R., 'Sentencing, Children's Evidence and Children's Trauma' [1990] Crim LR 371.

Glazebrook, P. R., *Reshaping the Criminal Law* (1978).

—— 'Criminal Omissions: the Duty Requirement in Offences against the Person' (1960) 56 LQR 386.

—— 'Revising the Theft Acts' [1993] Camb LJ 191.

—— 'Situational Liability', in Glazebrook (ed), *Reshaping the Criminal Law*, 108.

Gobert, J., 'Corporate Criminality: New Crimes for the Times' [1994] Crim LR 722.

Goff, Lord 'The Mental Element in the Crime of Murder' (1988) 104 LQR, 30.

Goode, M., 'The Abolition of Provocation', in S. Yeo (ed), *Partial Excuses to Murder* (1991), Sydney: Federation Press.

Gordon, G. H., *The Criminal Law of Scotland* (2nd edn. 1978), Edinburgh: Green.

Gottfredson, M., *Fear of Crime*, Home Office Research Study No. 84 (1985), London: HMSO.

Home Office Circular 18/94, *The Cautioning of Offenders*.

Home Office, *Digest 2: Information on the Criminal Justice System in England and Wales* (1993), London: Home Office.

Horder, J., *Provocation and Responsibility* (1992), Oxford: Oxford University Press.

—— 'Autonomy, Provocation and Duress' [1992] Crim LR 706.

—— 'Cognition, Emotion and Criminal Culpability' (1990) 106 LQR 469.

—— 'Occupying the moral high ground? The Law Commission on Duress' [1994] Crim LR 343.

—— 'Pleading Involuntary Lack of Capacity' [1993] Camb LJ 298.

—— 'The Problem of Provocative Children' [1987] Crim LR 654.

—— 'Rethinking Non-Fatal Offences against the Person' (1994) 14 Oxford JLS 335.

—— 'Sex, Violence and Sentencing in Domestic Provocation Cases' [1989] Crim LR 546.

—— 'Varieties of Intention, Criminal Attempts and Endangerment' (1994) 14 Legal Studies 335.

House of Lords Select Committee on Medical Ethics, Report (Session 1993–94), vol I, London: HMSO.

Huber, B., 'The Dilemma of Decriminalization: Dealing with Shoplifting in West Germany' [1980] Crim LR 621.

Husak, D., *Drugs and Rights* (1992), Cambridge: Cambridge University Press.

—— Philosophy of Criminal Law (1987), New Jersey: Rowman and Littlefield.

—— 'Ignorance of Law and Duties of Citizenship' (1994) 14 Legal Studies 105.

—— 'The Serial View of Criminal Law Defences' (1992) 3 Crim LF 369.

Husak, D., and Thomas, G., 'Date Rape, Social Convention, and Reasonable Mistakes' (1992) 11 *Law and Philosophy* 95.

Husak, D., and von Hirsch, A., 'Culpability and Mistake of Law', in S. Shute, J. Gardner and J. Horder, *Action and Value in Criminal Law* (1993), Oxford: Oxford University Press.

Hutter, B., *The Reasonable Arm of the Law* (1988), Oxford: Oxford University Press.

Greenawalt, K., 'The Perplexing Borders of Justification and Excuse' (1984) 84 Columbia LR 1897.

Griew, E., *The Theft Acts* (6th edn, 1990), London: Sweet & Maxwell.

—— 'Dishonesty: The Objections to *Feely and Ghosh*' [1985] Crim LR 341.

—— 'The Future of Diminished Responsibility' [1988] Crim LER 75.

—— 'It Must Have Been One of Them' [1989] Crim LR 129.

—— 'Reckless Damage and Reckless Driving: Living with *Caldwell and Lawrence*' [1981] Crim LR 743.

—— 'States of Mind, Presumptions and Inferences', in P. Smith (ed), *Criminal Law: Essays in Honour of J. C. Smith* (1987), London: Butterworth.

—— 'Stealing and Obtaining Bank Credits' [1986] Crim LR 356.

Grubin, D., 'What Constitutes Fitness to Plead?' [1993] Crim LR 748.

Hadden, T., 'Offences of Violence: The Law and the Facts' [1968] Crim LR 521.

Hall, J., *General Principles of Criminal Law* (2nd edn, 1960), Indianapolis: Bobbs-Merrill.

Hall, L., 'Strict or Liberal Construction of Penal Statutes' (1935) 48 Harv LR 748.

Hammond, R. G., 'Theft of Information' (1984) 100 LQR 252.

Hart, H. L. A., *Law, Liberty, and Morality* (1963), Oxford: Oxford University Press.

—— Punishment and Responsibility (1968), Oxford: Oxford University Press.

Hart, H. L. A., and Honoré, T., *Causation in the Law* (2nd edn, 1985), Oxford: Oxford University Press.

Hawkins, K., and Thomas, J., (eds) *Enforcing Regulation* (1984), Oxford: Oxford University Press.

Hedderman, C., and Moxon, D., *Magistrates' Court or Crown Court? Mode of Trial Decisions and Sentencing*, HORS 125 (1992), London: HMSO.

Henry, S., *The Hidden Economy* (1978), Oxford: Martin Robertson.

Heydon, J. D., 'The Problems of Entrapment' [1973] Camb LJ 268.

Holmes, O. W., *The Common Law* (1881).

Hindley, J. C., 'The Age of Consent for Male Homosexuals' [1986] Crim LR 595.

HMSO, *Social Trends* 1987 (1988).

Jackson, J. 'The Evidence Recommendations' [1993] Crim LR 817.

—— 'The Right of Silence; Judicial Responses to Parliamentary Encroachment', (1994) 57 MLR 270.

Jackson, S., *Storkwain*: a Case Study in Strict Liability and Self-Regulation' [1991] Crim LR 892.

Jareborg, N., 'The Coherence of the Penal System' in N. Jareborg, *Criminal Law in Action* (1988), Uppsala: Iustus Vorlag.

——' Criminal Attempts and Moral Luck' (1993) 27 Israel LR 213.

——'What Kind of Criminal Law do we want?', in *Scandinavian Studies in Criminology* (forthcoming, 1995).

Jeffries, J. C. 'Legality, Vagueness and the Construction of Penal Statutes' (1985) 71 Virginia L.R. 189.

Johnson, R., 'The Unnecessary Crime of Conspiracy' (1973) 61 Cal LR 1137.

Jones, T. H., 'Common Law and Criminal Law; the Scottish Experience' [1990] Crim LR 292.

Jones, T., Maclean, D., and Young, J., *The Islington Crime Survey* (1987), London: Gower.

JUSTICE, *Breaking the Rules* (1980).

Kadish, S., *Blame and Punishment* (1987), New York: Macmillan.

Keith Committee on the Enforcement of Revenue Legislation (1983, Cmnd 8822), London: HMSO.

Kell, D., 'Social Disutility and the Law of Consent' (1994) 14 Oxford JLS 121.

Kelman, M., 'Interpretive Construction in the Substantive Criminal Law' (1981) 33 Stanford LR 591.

Keown, I. J., 'The Law and Practice of Euthanasia in the Netherlands, (1992) 108 LQR 51.

Kennedy, I. M., *Treat me Right* (1988), Oxford: Oxford University Press.

Kennedy, I. M., and Grubb, A., *Medical Law: Text and Materials* (2nd edn, 1994), London: Butterworths.

Kenny, A., *Freewill and Responsibility* (1978), Oxford: Oxford University Press.

Klockars, C. B., *The Professional Fence* (1975).

Lacey, N., *State Punishment* (1988), London: Routledge.

—— 'A Clear Concept of Intention: Elusive or Illusory?' (1993) 56 MLR 621.

—— 'Contingency and Criminalisation' in I. Loveland (ed), *The Frontiers of Criminalisation* (1995).

Lacey, N., Wells, C., and Meure, D., *Reconstructing Criminal Law* (1990), London: Weidenfeld & Nicolson.

Laing, J. A., 'The Prospects of a Theory of Criminal Culpability: Mens Rea and Methodological Doubt' (1994) 14 Oxford JLS 57.

Lamond, G., 'Coercion, Threats, and the Puzzle of Blackmail', in A. P. Simester and A. T. H. Smith (eds), *Harm and Culpability* (forthcoming 1995), Oxford: Oxford University Press.

Lanham, D. J., 'Death of a Qualified Defence' (1988) 104 LQR 239.

—— 'Defence of Property in the Criminal Law' [1966] Crim LR 368.

—— 'Drivers, Control and Accomplices' [1982] Crim LR 419.

—— 'Larsonneur Revisited' [1976] Crim LR 276.

—— 'Three Cases of Accessorial Absurdity' (1990) 53 MLR 75.

Law Commission, *Parliamentary Procedures and the Law Commission* (1994).

Law Commission, No. 76, *Conspiracy and Criminal Law Reform* (1976), London: HMSO.

Law Commission, No. 83, *Defences of General Application* (1977),London: HMSO.

Law Commission, No. 102, *Attempt, and Impossibility in Relation to Attempt, Conspiracy and Incitement* (1980), London: HMSO.

Law Commission Consultation Paper 127, *Intoxication and Criminal Liability* (1993), London: HMSO.

Law Commission, No. 104, *Insurance Law: Non-Disclosure and Breach of Warranty* (1988), London: HMSO.

Law Commission Consultation Paper 131, *Assisting and Encouraging Crime* (1993), London: HMSO.

Law Commission Consultation Paper 134, *Consent and Offences against the Person* (1994), London: HMSO.

Law Commission Consultation Paper 135, *Involuntary Manslaughter* (1994), London: HMSO.

Law Commission, No. 143, *Codification of the Criminal Law: A Report to the Law Commission* (1985), London: HMSO.

Law Commission, No. 177, *A Criminal Code for England and Wales* (two vols, 1989), London: HMSO.

Law Commission, No. 205, *Rape within Marriage* (1992), London: HMSO.

Law Commission, No. 218, *Legislating the Criminal Code: Offences against the Person and General Principles* (1993), London: HMSO.

Law Commission, No. 222, *Binding Over* (1994), London: HMSO.

Law Commission, No. 223, *Twenty-Eighth Annual Report* (1993), London: HMSO.

Law Commission, No. 228, *Conspiracy to Defraud* (1994), London: HMSO.

Law Commission, No. 230, *The Year and a Day Rule in Homicide* (1995), London: HMSO.

Law Reform Commission of Ireland, No. 23, *Rape* (1988).

Leavens, A., 'A Causation Approach to Omissions' (1988) 76 Cal LR 547.

Leigh, L. H., *The Control of Commercial Fraud* (1982), London: Heinemann.

—— *The Criminal Liability of Corporations in English Law* (1969), London: London School of Economics.

—— *Strict and Vicarious Liability* (1982), London: Sweet & Maxwell.

—— 'Manslaughter and the Limits of Self-Defence' (1971) 34 MLR 685.

——'The Criminal Liability of Corporations and other groups' (1977) 9 Ottawa LR 237.

—— 'Sado-Masochism, Consent and Reform of the Criminal Law' (1976) 39 MLR 130.

Levi, M., *Regulating Fraud: White Collar Crime and the Criminal Process* (1987), London: Tavistock.

—— 'Suite Justice: Sentencing for Fraud' [1989] Crim LR 420.

Levine, D., 'Health and Safety at Work: the Statutory Framework in Construction Matters' (1992) 8 Construction LJ 10.

Lloyd C., and Walmsley R., *Changes in Rape Offences and Sentencing*, Home Office Research Study No. 105 (1985), London: HMSO.

Low, P., Jeffreys, J., and Bonnie, R., *Criminal Law, Cases and Materials* (2nd edn, 1986), New York: Foundation Press.

Lukes, S., *Individualism* (1973).

MacCormick, D. N., *Legal Right and Social Democracy* (1982), Oxford: Oxford University Press.

Mackay, R. D., *Mental Condition Defences in Criminal Law* (1995), Oxford: Oxford University Press.

—— 'The Consequences of Killing very young Children' [1993] Crim LR 21.

—— 'The Decline of Disability in Relation to the Trial' [1991] Crim LR 87.

—— 'Fact and Fiction about the Insanity Defence' [1991] Crim LR 247.

—— 'Non-Organic Automatism—Some Recent Developments' [1980] Crim L 350.

—— 'Pleading Provocation and Diminished Responsibility Together' [1988] Crim LR 411.

Mackay, R. D., and Kearns, G., 'The Continued Underuse of Unfitness to Plead and the Insanity Defence' [1994] Crim LR 576.

MacKinnon, C., *Towards a Feminist Theory of the State* (1989), Boston: Harvard University Press.

Maguire, M. and Bennett, T., *Burglary in a Dwelling* (1982), London: Heinemann.

Maguire, M. and Corbett, C., *The Effects of Crime and the Work of Victim Support Schemes* (1987), Aldershot: Gower.

Maier-Katkin, D., and Ogle, R., 'A Rationale for Infanticide Laws' [1993] Crim LR 903.

Mars, G., *Cheats at Work* (1982), London: Unwin.

Mayhew, P., Aye Meung, N., and Mirrlees-Black, C., *The 1992 British Crime Survey* (1993), London: HMSO.

McAuley, J., 'Anticipating the Past: The Defence of Provocation in Irish Law' (1987) 50 MLR 133.

McBarnet, D., and Whelan, C., 'The Elusive Spirit of the Law; Formalism and the Struggle for Legal Control' (1991) 54 MLR 848.

—— 'The Law Commission Consultation Document on Involuntary Manslaughter —Heralding Corporate Liability?' [1994] Crim LR 547.

McColgan, A., 'In Defence of Battered Women who Kill' (1993) 13 Oxford JLS 508.

—— 'The Law Commission Consultation Document on Involuntary Manslaughter —Heralding Corporate Liability?' [1994] Crim LR 547.

McConville, M., Bridges, L., Hodgson, J., and Pavlovic, A., (eds) *Standing Accused* (1994), Oxford: Oxford University Press.

McConville, M. and Hodgson, J., *Custodial Legal Advice and the Right to Silence*, RCCJ Research Study No. 16 (1993), London: HMSO.

McKenna, B., 'Causing Death by Reckless or Dangerous Driving: a Suggestion' [1970] Crim LR 67.

McKenzie, I., Morgan, R., and Reiner, R., 'Helping the Police with their Inquiries' [1990] Crim LR 22.

Meldon, A. I., 'Willing', in A. R. White (ed). *The Philosophy of Action* (1968), Oxford: Oxford University Press.

Mill, J. S., *On Liberty* (1859).

Mitchell, C. N., 'The Intoxicated Offender—Refuting the Legal and Medical Myths' (1988) 11 Int J Law & Psychiatry 77.

Moore, M., *Act and Crime: the Philosophy of Action and its Implications for Criminal Law* (1993), Oxford: Oxford University Press.

—— *Law and Psychiatry* (1985), Cambridge: Cambridge University Press.

—— 'Causation and the Excuses' (1985) 73 Cal LR 1091.

—— 'Intention and Mens Rea', in R. Gavison (ed), *Issues in Contemporary Legal Philosophy* (1987), Oxford: Oxford University Press.

Morgan, J., and Zedner, L., *Child Victims* (1992), Oxford: Oxford University Press.

Morris, N., *Madness and the Criminal Law* (1982), Chicago: University of Chicago Press.

Morris, A., 'Sex and Sentencing' [1988] Crim LR 163.

Morse, S., 'Culpability and Control' (1994) 142 U Pa Lr 1587.

—— 'Diminished Capacity', in S. Shute, J. Gardner and J. Horder (eds) *Action and Value in Criminal Law* (1993), Oxford: Oxford University Press.

Moston, S. and Stephenson, G., *The questioning and interviewing of suspects outside the police station*, RCCJ Research Study No. 22 (1993), London: HMSO.

National Audit Office, *Enforcing Health and Safety Legislation in the Workplace* (1994), London: HMSO.

Nelken, D., 'White Collar Crime', in M. Maguire, R. Morgan and R. Reiner (eds), *Oxford Handbook of Criminology* (1994), Oxford: Oxford University Press.

Nicholson D., and Sanghvi, R., 'Battered Women and Provocation: the Implications of *Ahluwalia*' [1993] Crim LR 728.

Norrie, A., *Crime, Reason and History* (1993), London: Weidenfeld & Nicolson.

Nozick, R., *Anarchy, State and Utopia* (1974), Oxford: Oxford University Press.

Oliphant, K., 'Mind the Gap' (1993) 4 KCLJ 69.

Olsen, F., 'Statutory Rape: A Feminist Critique of Rights Analysis' (1984) 63 Texas LR 387.

Orchard, G., ' "Agreement" in Criminal Conspiracy [1974] Crim LR 297.

—— 'Surviving without *Majewski* — a view from down under' [1993] Crim LR 26.

O'Regan, R. S., 'Indirect Provocation and Misdirected Retaliation [1968] Crim LR 319.

Pace, P. J., 'Delegation: A Doctrine in Search of a Definition [1982] Crim LR 627.

Pease, K., 'Crime Prevention', in M. Maguire, R. Morgan and R. Reiner (eds), *The Oxford Handbook of Criminology* (1994), ch 14, Oxford: Oxford University Press.

Pickard, T. 'Culpable Mistakes' (1980) 30 U Toronto LR 75.

Potas, I., *Just Deserts for the Mad* (1985), Canberra: Australia Institute of Criminology.

Rachels, J., 'Active and Passive Euthanasia' (1975) 292 New England Journal of Medicine 78.

Raz, J., *The Authority of Law* (1979), Oxford: Oxford University Press.

—— *The Morality of Freedom* (1986), Oxford: Oxford University Press.

Reiner, R., 'Investigative Powers and Safeguards for Suspects' [1993] Crim LR 808.

Reiss, A., 'Selecting Strategies of Social Control over Organizational Life', in K. Hawkins and J. M. Thomas (eds), *Enforcing Regulation* (1984), Oxford: Oxford University Press.

Report of the Committee on Mentally Abnormal Offenders (1975, Cmnd 6244), London: HMSO.

Report of the Interdepartmental Committee on the Distribution of Criminal Business between the Crown Court and the Magistrates' Courts (1975, Cmnd 6323), London: HMSO.

Report of the Road Traffic Law Review (1988), London: HMSO.

Report of the Royal Commission on Capital Punishment (1953, Cmd 8932), London: HMSO.

Report of the Royal Commission on the Law Relating to Indictable Offences (1879, 2345), London: HMSO.

Richards, D. A. J., 'Rights, Utility and Crime' (1981) 3 *Crime and Justice: An Annual Review* (1981), 274.

Richardson, G., 'Strict Liability for Regulatory Crime: The Empirical Research' [1987] Crim LR 295.

Richardson, G., Ogus, A., and Burrows, P., *Policing Pollution* (1982), Oxford: Oxford University Press.

Riley, D., and Vennard, J., *Triable Either Way Cases: Crown Court or Magistrates' Court?*, HORS 98 (1988), London: HMSO.

Roberts, J. V., and Mohr, R., (eds), *Confronting Sexual Assault: a Decade of Legal and Social Change* (1994), Toronto.

Robertson, G., *Whose Conspiracy?* (1974), London: National Council for Civil Liberties.

—— 'Entrapment Evidence: Manna from Heaven or Fruit of the Poisoned Tree?' [1994] Crim LR 805.

Robinson, P. H., *Criminal Law Defences* (1984), St. Paul: West Publishing.

—— *Fundamentals of Criminal Law* (1989), St. Paul: West Publishing.

—— 'Causing the Conditions of One's Own Defence: A Study in the Limits of Theory in Criminal Law Doctrine' (1985) 71 Virginia LR 1.

—— 'Criminal Law Defenses: A Systematic Analysis' (1982) 82 Columbia LR 199.

—— 'A Functional Analysis of Criminal Law' (1994) 88 Northwestern ULR 857.

—— 'Legality and Discretion in the Distribution of Criminal Sanctions' (1988) 25 Harvard Journal on Legislation 393.

—— 'Rules of Conduct and Principles of Adjudication' (1990) 57 U Chic LR 729.

—— 'Should the Criminal Law abandon the Actus Reus/Mens Rea Distinction?', in S. Shute, J. Gardner and J. Horder (eds), *Action and Value in Criminal Law* (1993), Oxford: Oxford University Press.

Robinson, P. H., and Darley, J. M., *Justice, Liability and Blame* (1994).

Robinson, P. H., and Grall, J., 'Element Analysis in Defining Criminal Liability: The Model Penal Code and Beyond' (1983) Stanford LR 681.

Rock, P., *The Social World of an English Crown Court* (1993), Oxford: Oxford University Press.

—— 'The Sociology of Deviancy and Conceptions of Moral Order' (1974) 14 BJ Criminology 139.

Rossi, P., *et al.*, 'Beyond Crime Seriousness: Fitting the Punishment to the Crime' (1985) *Journal of Quantitative Criminology* 29.

Rowan-Robinson, J., and Watchman, P. Q., *Crime and Regulation* (1990).

Royal Commission on Criminal Justice, *Report* (1993, Cmnd 2263), London: HMSO.

Sanders, A., 'Class Bias in Prosecutions' (1985) 24 Howard JCJ 176.

Sanders, A. and Young, R., *Criminal Justice* (1994), London: Butterworths.

Schonsheck, J., *On Criminalization* (1994), Dordrecht: Kluwer.

Schopp, R. F., *Automatism, Insanity, and the Psychology of Criminal Responsibility* (1991), Cambridge: Cambridge University Press.

Schulhofer, S. J., 'Taking Sexual Autonomy Seriously: Rape Law and Beyond' (1992) 11 *Law and Philosophy* 35.

Scottish Law Commission, No. 135, *Report on Family Law* (1992), Edinburgh: HMSO.

Sellin, T., and Wolfgang, M., *The Measurement of Delinquency* (1978).

Serious Fraud Office, *Annual Report 1993–94* (1994), London: HMSO.

Shapland, J., Willmore J., and Duff, P., *Victims in the Criminal Justice System* (1985), London: Heinemann.

Sharpe, S., 'Covert Police Operations and Discretionary Exclusion of Evidence' [1994] Crim LR 793.

Shiner, R., 'Intoxication and Responsibility' (1990) 13 Int J Law & Psychiatry 9.

Shute, S., and Horder, J., 'Thieving and Deceiving: What is the Difference?' (1993) 56 MLR 548.

Simester, A. P., 'Mistakes in Defence' (1992) 12 Oxford JLS 295.

—— 'Paradigm Intention' (1992) 11 Law and Philosophy 235.

Simpson, A. W.B. *Cannibalism and the Common Law* (1984), Chicago: University of Chicago Press.

Smith, A. T.H., *Offences against Public Order* (1987), London: Sweet & Maxwell.

—— *Property Offences* (1994), London: Sweet & Maxwell.

—— 'The Case for a Code' [1986] Crim LR 285.

—— 'Conspiracy to Defraud' [1988] Crim LR 508.

—— 'Error and Mistake of Law in Anglo-American Criminal Law' (1984) 14 Anglo-American LR 3.

—— 'The Idea of Criminal Deception' [1982] Crim LR 721.

—— 'Judicial Lawmaking in the Criminal Law' (1984) 100 LQR 46.

—— 'On Actus Reus and Mens Rea', in P. R. Glazebrook (ed), *Reshaping the Criminal Law* (1978), 95.

—— 'The Public Order Offences' [1995] Crim LR 19.

Smith, J. C., *Justification and Excuse in the Criminal Law* (1989), London: Sweet & Maxwell.

—— *The Law of Theft* (7th edn, 1993), London: Butterworths.

—— 'Aid, Abet, Counsel and Procure', in P. R. Glazebrook (ed), *Reshaping the Criminal Law* (1978), London: Sweet & Maxwell.

—— 'Intoxication and the Mental Element in Crime' in P. Wallington and R. Merkin (eds), *Essays in Honour of F. H. Lawson* (1987).

—— 'A Note on Intention' [1990] Crim LR 85.

—— 'The Presumption of Innocence' (1987) 38 NILQ 223.

—— 'Secondary Participation and Inchoate Offences', in C. Tapper (ed), *Crime, Proof and Punishment* (1981), London: Butterworths.

—— 'Using Force in Self-Defence and the Prevention of Crime' (1994) 47 CLP 101.

Smith, J. C., and Hogan, B., *Criminal Law* (5th edn, 1983), London: Butterworths.

Smith, K. J. M., *A Modern Treatise on the Law of Criminal Complicity* (1991), Oxford: Oxford University Press.

—— 'A Blueprint for Rationalism' [1994] Crim LR 239.

—— 'Liability for Endangerment: English *Ad Hoc* Pragmatism and American Innovation' [1983] Crim LR 127.

—— 'Must Heroes Behave Heroically?' [1989] Crim LR 22.

—— 'Proximity in Attempt: Lord Lane's Midway Course' [1991] Crim LR 576.

Smith, K. J. M., and Wilson, W., 'Impaired Voluntariness and Criminal Responsibility' (1993) 13 Oxford JLS 69.

Smith, L. J. F., *Domestic Violence*, Home Office Research Study No.107 (1989), London: HMSO.

——, *Concerns about Rape*, Home Office Research Study No. 106 (1989), London: HMSO.

Spencer, J. N., 'The Aggravated Vehicle-Taking Act 1992' [1992] Crim LR 699.

Spencer, J. R., 'Criminal Law and Criminal Appeals; the Tail that Wags the Dog' [1982] Crim LR 260.
—— 'Handling, Theft and the Purchaser who Takes a Chance' [1985] Crim LR 92 and 440.
—— 'Helping Others to Commit Crimes', in P. Smith (ed), *Criminal Law: Essays in Honour of J. C. Smith* (1987), London: Butterworths.
—— 'The Metamorphosis of Section 6 of the Theft Act' [1977] Crim LR 653.
—— 'The Mishandling of Handling' [1981] Crim LR 682.
—— 'Motor Vehicles as Weapons of Offence' [1985] Crim LR 29.
—— 'Road Traffic Law: a Review of the North Report' [1988] Crim LR 707.
Spicer, R., *Conspiracy Law, Class and Society* (1981), London: Lawrence & Wishart.
Staple, G., 'Serious and Complex Fraud: a New Perspective' (1993) 56 MLR 127.
Stephen, J. F., *A Digest of the Criminal Law* (1877).
——, *History of the Criminal Law* (1883).
Stevenson, R., *Winning the War on Drugs: to Legalise or Not?* (Institute of Economic Affairs, 1994).
Stone, C. D., 'The Place of Enterprise Liability in the Control of Corporate Conduct' (1980) 90 Yale LJ 1.
Sullivan, G. R., 'Fault Elements and Joint Enterprise' [1994] Crim LR 252.
—— 'Intent, Purpose and Complicity' [1988] Crim LR 641.
—— 'Intoxicants and Diminished Responsibility' [1994] Crim LR 156.
—— 'Involuntary Intoxication and Beyond' [1994] Crim LR 272.
—— 'The Law Commission Consultation Paper on Complicity: Fault Elements and Joint Enterprise' [1994] Crim LR 252.
Sutherland, E. H., *White Collar Crime* (1949), New Haven: Yale University Press.
Sutherland, P. and Gearty, D., 'Insanity and the European Court of Human Rights' [1992] Crim LR 418.
Syrota, G., 'A Radical Change in the Law of Recklessness?' [1982] Crim LR 97.
Taylor, R. D., 'Complicity and the Excuses' [1983] Crim LR 656.
Taylor, P. and Dalton, G. 'Pre-Menstrual Syndrome: A New Criminal Defense?' (1983) 19 Cal WLR 269.
Temkin, J., *Rape and the Legal Process* (1987), London: Sweet & Maxwell.
—— 'Do we need the Crime of Incest' (1991) 44 CLP 185.
—— 'Impossible Attempts: Another View' (1976) 39 MLR 55.
Thomas, D. A., 'Form and Function in Criminal Law', in P. R. Glazebrook (ed), *Reshaping the Criminal Law* (1978), London: Sweet & Maxwell.
Thomson, J. J. 'Self-Defense' (1990) 20 *Philosophy and Public Affairs* 283.
Tonry, M., 'Racial Disproportion in US Prisons' (1994) 34 Brit J Criminology 97.
Trivizas, E., 'Sentencing the "Football Hooligan" ' (1981) BJ Criminology 342.
Tuck, M., *Drinking and Disorder: A Study of Non-Metropolitan Violence*, Home Office Research Study No. 180 (1989), London: HMSO.
Tur, R., 'Dishonesty and Jury Questions', in A. Phillips Griffiths (ed), *Philosophy and Practice* (1985), Oxford: Oxford University Press.
—— 'Subjectivism and Objectivism: Towards Synthesis', in S. Shute, J. Gardner and J. Hoder (eds), *Action and Value in Criminal Law* (1993), Oxford: Oxford University Press.

Uniacke, S., *Permissible Killing: the Self-Defence Justification of Homicide* (1994), Cambridge: Cambridge University Press.

van Dijk, P., and van Hoof, G. J. H., *Theory and Practice of the European Convention on Human Rights* (2nd edn, 1990), Deventer: Kluwer.

Vennard, J., 'The Outcome of Contested Trials', in D. Moxon (ed), *Managing Criminal Justice* (1985), London: HMSO.

von Hirsch, A., *Censure and Sanctions* (1993), Oxford: Oxford University Press.

—— 'Desert and White Collar Criminality: A Reply to Dr Braithwaite' (1982), J Crim Law & Criminology 1164.

—— 'Injury and Exasperation' (1986) 84 Michigan LR 700.

von Hirsch, A., and Ashworth, A., *Principled Sentencing* (1993), Edinburgh: Edinburgh University Press.

——, —— 'Remote Harms' in A. Simester and A. T. H. Smith (eds), *Harm and Culpability* (Oxford University Press, forthcoming, 1995).

von Hirsch, A., and Jareborg, N., 'Gauging Criminal Harms: a Living Standard Analysis' (1991) 11 Oxford JLS 1.

——, —— 'Provocation and Culpability', in F. Schoemann (ed), *Responsibility, Character an the Emotions* (1988), Cambridge: Cambridge University Press.

von Hirsch, A., Knapp, K. A., and Tonry, M., *The Sentencing Commission and its Guidelines* (1987), Boston: Northeastern University Press.

Waddington, P. A. J., ' "Overkill" or "Minimum Force"?' [1990] Crim LR 695.

Waldron, J., *The Right to Private Property* (1988).

Walmsley, R., *Personal Violence,* Home Office Research Study No. 89 (1986), London: HMSO.

Ward, A., 'Making Some Sense of Self-Induced Intoxication' [1986] CLJ 247.

Ward, P., and Dobinson, I., 'Heroin: a Considered Response?', in M. Findlay and R. Hogg (eds), *Understanding Crime and Criminal Justice* (1988), Sydney: Law Book Co.

Wasik, M., *Crime and the Computer* (1991), Oxford: Oxford University Press.

—— *Emmins on Sentencing* (2nd edn, 1993), London: Blackstone.

—— 'Cumulative Provocation and Domestic Killing' [1982] Crim LR 29.

—— 'Duress and Criminal Responsibility' [1977] Crim LR 453.

—— 'A Learner's Careless Driving' [1982] Crim LR 411.

—— 'Partial Excuses in the Criminal Law' (1982) 45 MLR 515.

Wasik, M., and Thompson, M. P., 'Turning a Blind Eye as Constituting Mens Rea' (1981) 32 NILQ 328.

Weinreb, L. L., 'Desert, Punishment and Criminal Responsibility' (1986) 49 *Law and Contemporary Problems* (No. 3).

Wells, C., *Corporations and Criminal Responsibility* (1993), Oxford: Oxford University Press.

—— 'Battered Woman Syndrome and Defences to Homicide: where now?' (1994) 14 Legal Studies 266.

—— 'Corporate Liability and Consumer Protection' (1994) 57 MLR 817.

—— 'Corporations: Culture, Risk and Criminal Liability' [1993] Crim LR 551.

—— 'The Dealth Penalty for Provocation?' [1978] Crim LR 662.

—— 'Restatement or Reform?' [1986] Crim LR 314.

—— 'Swatting the Subjectivist Bug' [1982] Crim LR 209.

—— 'Whither Insanity?' [1983] Crim LR 787.

White, S. 'The Criminal Procedure (Insanity and Unfitness to Plead) Act' [1992] Crim LR 4.

——, 'Offences of Basic and Specific Intent' (1989) Crim LR 271.

Wilczynski, A., and Morris, A., 'Parents who Kill their Children' 1993] Crim LR 31.

Williams, G. 'The Unresolved Problem of Recklessness' (1988) 8 Legal Studies 74.

Williams, G., *Criminal Law: the General Part* (2nd edn, 1961), London: Stevens.

—— 'What should the Code do about Omissions?' (1987) 7 Legal Studies 92.

Glanville Williams, *Textbook of Criminal Law* (2nd edn, 1983), London: Stevens.

—— 'Homicide and the Supernatural' (1949) 65 LQR 491.

——'The Lords and Impossible Attempts' [1986] Camb LJ 33.

Williams, G., 'Alternative Elements and Included Offences [1984] CLJ 290.

—— 'Complicity, Purpose and the Draft Code' [1990] Crim LR 4.

—— 'Convictions and Fair Labelling' [1983] Camb LJ 85.

—— 'Criminal Omissions—the Conventional View' (1991) 107, LQR 86.

—— *'Finis for Novus Actus'* [1989] Camb LJ 391.

—— 'Handling, Theft and the Purchaser who Takes a Chance' [1985] Crim LR 432.

—— 'Intents in the Alternative' (1991) 50 Camb LJ 120.

—— 'Obedience to Law as a Crime' (1990) 53 MLR 445.

—— 'Oblique Intent' [1988] CLJ 417.

—— 'Offences and Defence' (1982) 2 Legal Studies 233.

—— 'The Problem of Reckless Attempts' 1983] Crim LR 365.

—— 'Recklessness Redefined' [1981] CLJ 252.

—— 'Statute Interpretation, Prostitution and the Rule of Law' in C. Tapper (ed), *Crime, Proof and Punishment* (1981), London: Butterworths.

—— 'Temporary Appropriation Should Be Theft' [1981] Crim LR 129.

—— 'Theft, Consent and Illegality' [1977] Crim LR 127.

—— 'The Theory of Excuses' [1982] Crim LR 732.

—— 'Which of You Did It?' (1989) 52 MLR 179.

Wilson, J. Q., and Herrnstein, R., *Crime and Human Nature* (1983), New York: Simon & Schuster.

Windlesham, Lord, 'Life Sentences: law, practice and release decisions, 1989–93' [1993] Crim LR 644.

Wolfram, S., 'Eugenics and the Punishment of Incest Act 1908' [1983] Crim LR 308.

Wood, J., 'The Serious Fraud Office' [1989] Crim LR 175.

Woodcock, G., *Anarchism* (1962), London: Harmondsworth.

Wootton, B., *Crime and the Criminal Law* (2nd edn, 1981), London: Sweet & Maxwell.

Wright, R., 'A Note on the Attrition of Rape Cases' (1984) 24 BJ Criminology 399.

Yale, D. E. C., 'A Year and a Day in Homicide' [1989] Camb LJ 202.

Yeo, S., *Compulsion in the Criminal Law* (1991), Sydney: Law Book Co.

—— *Partial Excuses to Murder* (1990), Sydney: Federation Press.

Young, W., *Rape Study: A Discussion of Law and Practice* (1983).

Zander, M. and Henderson, P., *Crown Court Study*, RCCJ Research Study No. 19 (1993), London: HMSO.

Zedner, L., 'Family, Sex and the State: Regulating Sexual Offences Within the Home', in I. Loveland (ed), *The Frontiers of Criminality* (1995), London: Sweet & Maxwell.

Zuckerman, A. A. S., *The Principles of Criminal Evidence* (1989), Oxford: Oxford University Press.

—— 'The Third Exception to the *Woolmington* Rule' (1976) 92 LQR 402.

Index